Fifth
Edition

INTERNATIONAL
ACCOUNTING

Frederick D. S. Choi
New York University

Gary K. Meek
Oklahoma State University

PEARSON EDUCATION INTERNATIONAL

Acquisitions Editor: Wendy Craven
Editorial Director: Jeff Shelstad
Assistant Editor: Kerri Tomasso
Marketing Manager: Beth Toland
Marketing Assistant: Melissa Owens
Managing Editor: John Roberts
Production Editor: Renata Butera
Permissions Coordinator: Charles Morris
Manufacturing Buyer: Michelle Klein

Design Director: Maria Lange
Cover Design: Bruce Kenselaar
Cover Illustration: David Gould/Image Bank/
 Getty Images, Inc.
Composition/Full-Service Project Management: PineTree
 Composition, Inc.
Printer/Binder: Phoenix Book Tech
Typeface: 10/12 Times Ten

Credits and acknowledgments borrowed from other sources and reproduced, with permission, in this textbook appear on appropriate page within the text.

Microsoft® and Windows® are registered trademarks of the Microsoft Corporation in the U.S.A. and other countries. Screen shots and icons reprinted with permission from the Microsoft Corporation. This book is not sponsored or endorsed by or affiliated with the Microsoft Corporation.

10 9 8 7 6 5 4 3 2 1
ISBN 0-13-129357-5

To our families.

Contents

Handwritten margin annotations: "history", "organisations", "Directives"

Preface

This book is written with the express purpose of sensitizing students to the international dimensions of accounting, financial reporting, and financial control. The world in which they will pursue their professional careers is a world dominated by global business and investment decisions. As most of these decisions are premised on financial data, a knowledge of international accounting is crucial for achieving proper understanding in external and internal financial communications. While ideal for upper division undergraduate students and master's students, we are pleased that the contents of this award-winning effort have also benefited practicing accountants, financial executives, investment managers, university educators, and professional administrators around the world.

This revision of a work that has spanned three decades features a number of enhancements. These include:

- Capital market, managerial, taxation, and institutional updates reflective of current trends and issues
- Discussion of the newly restructured International Accounting Standards Board
- Revised discussion of reporting and disclosure practices with new examples from both developed and emerging market countries
- Better organization of managerial accounting topics
- Examination of recent rulings in accounting for financial derivatives
- Expanded listings of relevant international Web site addresses and data sources
- Updated discussion questions, exercises, and cases.

A growing number of academics are writing on the international dimensions of accounting and reporting and their contributions have benefited our work. We have also benefited from the professional literature and from many of our students and faculty colleagues whose thoughtful comments have triggered new ideas for us to consider.

In addition, we wish to acknowledge the following individuals for reviewing, providing data, or offering constructive suggestions for improving our work:

Wai Yee Canri Chan, Monterey Institute of International Studies
David T. Collins, Bellarmine University
Sally Gilfillan, Longwood University
John R. McGowan, St. Louis University
Jenice Prather-Kinsey, University of Missouri–Columbia
Juan M. Rivera, University of Notre Dame
Karen Grossman Tabak, Maryville University

Nils Crasselt, Ruhr-Universität Bochum
Thorsten Sellhorn, Ruhr-Universität Bochum
Tatsuo Inoue, Kwansei Gakuin University

Many individuals furnished able assistance in producing the manuscript. We especially thank Mattie Kennedy and Alice Charney at New York University for their assistance with Web searches and exhibits and Bill Larkin and Jane Avery at Prentice Hall and Wendy Craven at Pearson Education for their encouragement and editorial support.

However hard one tries to avoid them, errors are bound to occur in a work of this magnitude. As authors, we accept full responsibility for all errors and omissions in the manuscript. As always, we welcome constructive comments from all who use this book, as the students are the ultimate beneficiaries of your thoughtfulness.

F. D. S. Choi
New York, New York

G. K. Meek
Stillwater, Oklahoma

INTERNATIONAL ACCOUNTING

CHAPTER

1

INTRODUCTION

Accounting plays a vital role in society. As a branch of economics, it provides information about a firm and its transactions to facilitate resource allocation decisions by users of that information. If the information reported is reliable and useful, scarce resources are allocated in an optimal fashion, and conversely, resource allocations are less than optimal when information is less reliable and useful.

International accounting, the subject of this text, is no different in its intended role. What makes its study distinctive is that the entity being reported on is either a multi-national company (MNC) with operations and transactions that cross national boundaries, or an entity with reporting obligations to users who are located in a country other than that of the reporting entity.

Recall that accounting entails several broad processes: measurement, disclosure, and auditing. *Measurement* is the process of identifying, categorizing, and quantifying economic activities or transactions. These measurements provide insights into the profitability of a firm's operations and the strength of its financial position. *Disclosure* is the process by which accounting measurements are communicated to their intended users. This area focuses on issues such as what is to be reported, when, by what means, and to whom. *Auditing* is the process by which specialized accounting professionals (auditors) attest to the reliability of the measurement and communication process. Whereas internal auditors are company employees who answer to management, external auditors are nonemployees who are responsible for attesting that the company's financial statements are prepared in accordance with generally accepted standards.

An understanding of the international dimensions of the accounting processes that were just described is important to those seeking to manage a business, or obtain or supply financing across national borders. Accounting amounts may vary significantly according to the principles that govern them. Differences in culture, business practices, political and regulatory structures, legal systems, currency values, local inflation rates, business risks, and tax codes all affect how the MNC conducts its operations and financial reporting around the world. Financial statements and other disclosures are impossible to understand without an awareness of the underlying accounting principles and business culture.

The importance of studying international accounting has grown over the years. We begin with a brief history of this subject.

HISTORICAL PERSPECTIVE

The history of accounting is an international history. The following chronology demonstrates that accounting has been remarkably successful in its ability to be transplanted from one national setting to another while allowing for continued development in theory and practice worldwide.

To begin, double-entry bookkeeping, generally thought of as the genesis of accounting as we know it today, emanated from the Italian city states of the 14th and 15th centuries. Its development was spurred by the growth of international commerce in northern Italy during the late Middle Ages and the desire of government to find ways to tax commercial transactions. "Bookkeeping in the Italian fashion" then migrated to Germany to assist the merchants of the Fugger era and the Hanseatic league. At about the same time, business philosophers in the Netherlands sharpened ways of calculating periodic income, and government officials in France found it advantageous to apply the whole system to governmental planning and accountability.

In due course, double entry accounting ideas reached the British Isles. The development of the British Empire created unprecedented needs for British commercial interests to manage and control enterprises in the colonies, and for the records of their colonial enterprises to be reviewed and verified. These needs led to the emergence of accounting societies in the 1850s and an organized public accounting profession in Scotland and England during the 1870s. British accounting practices spread not only throughout North America but throughout the British Commonwealth as it then existed.

Parallel developments occurred elsewhere. The Dutch accounting model was exported to Indonesia, among other places. The French accounting system found a home in Polynesia and French-administered territories in Africa, while the reporting framework of the Germans proved influential in Japan, Sweden, and czarist Russia.

As the economic might of the United States grew during the first half of the 20th century, its sophistication in matters of accounting grew in tandem. Business schools assisted in this development by conceptualizing the subject matter and eventually having it recognized as an academic discipline in its own right on college and university campuses. After World War II, U.S. accounting influence made itself felt throughout the Western world, particularly in Germany and Japan. To a lesser extent similar factors are directly observable in countries like Brazil, Israel, Mexico, the Philippines, Sweden, and Taiwan.

The paradox of the international heritage of accounting is that in many countries, accounting remains a nationalistic affair, with national standards and practices deeply anchored into national laws and professional regulations. There is little understanding of parallel requirements in other countries. Yet, accounting serves people and organizations whose decisions are increasingly international in scope.

Resolving the historical paradox of accounting has long been a concern of both users and preparers of accounting information. In recent years, institutional efforts to narrow differences in measurement, disclosure, and auditing processes around the world have intensified. A description of this effort and the major players with an important stake in attaining convergence of global accounting systems is the focus of Chapter 8.

CONTEMPORARY PERSPECTIVE

While the effort to reduce international accounting diversity is important in its own right, there are today a number additional factors that are contributing to the growing importance of studying international accounting. These factors stem from significant and continuing reductions in national trade barriers and capital controls together with advances in information technology.

National controls on capital flows, foreign exchange, foreign direct investment, and related transactions have been dramatically liberalized in recent years, reducing the barriers to international business. Appendix 1-1 presents selected information on changes in financial sector policy in a sample of developed and developing countries during the last three decades, and illustrates efforts by national governments to open their economies to private enterprise and international investors and business. It shows that, with a few exceptions, there has been a strong trend worldwide during this period to privatize government-owned financial enterprises (especially banks) and to reduce or eliminate foreign exchange controls and limits on cross-border investment.

Advances in information technology are also causing a radical change in the economics of production and distribution. Vertically integrated production is no longer proving an efficient mode of operation. Real-time, global information linkages mean that production is increasingly being outsourced to whomever of whatever size wherever in the world can do the job, or portions of the job, best. Adversarial, arm's-length relationships that have characterized companies' relations with their suppliers, middle persons, and customers are being replaced by cooperative global linkages with suppliers, suppliers' suppliers, middle persons, customers, and customers' customers.

Exhibit 1-1 provides a contemporary illustration of this outsourcing process for Hewlett-Packard's (H-P) production of its new ProLiant ML150, a small box that helps

Exhibit 1-1 Outsourcing Process for Hewlett-Packard's ProLiant ML150

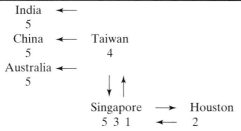

H-P's Path to Market

1. Idea for ML150 spawned in Singapore
2. Concept approved in Houston
3. Concept design performed in Singapore
4. Engineering design and initial manufacture in Taiwan
5. Final assembly in Australia, China, India, and Singapore. Machines produced in Australia, China, and India sold in local markets; machines assembled in Singapore marketed to Southeast Asia.

companies manage customer databases and run e-mail systems, among other things.[1] In producing the ML150, H-P turned to the usual sources of low-cost labor: China and India. However, it decided to also make some ML150s in higher-cost locations such as Singapore and Australia, which were closer to targeted customers. Initial design for the ML150 was done in Singapore and then handed off to an outside contractor in Taiwan. Although China possesses the lowest wage rates, it is but one part of a highly specialized manufacturing system. Considerations ranging from logistics to tariff policies reportedly kept H-P from putting all of its production lines in China. It would take too long for machines manufactured in China to reach customers in other Asian markets. Moreover, shipping goods to India triggered steep tariffs, so it made sense to produce some ML150s in India with imported parts for the local market.

Spurred by the twin developments we have just described, there are several factors that are contributing to the growing importance of the subject matter of this text. We describe each in turn.

GROWTH AND SPREAD OF MULTINATIONAL OPERATIONS

International business has traditionally been associated with foreign trade. This activity, rooted in antiquity, continues unabated. Current trends in exports and imports by region and selected economy are depicted in Exhibit 1-2.

What is not shown in Exhibit 1-2 is the composition of each region's exports and imports. To obtain a better picture of the pattern of global trade at the micro level, one need simply examine the foreign operations disclosures of any major MNC. Exhibit 1-3 contains the geographic distribution of sales of Solvay, the Belgian manufacturer of pharmaceuticals, chemicals, and plastics. As can be seen, the company's sales literally blanket every continent in the world. An aggregation of such disclosures for all MNCs in all countries would confirm that trade today is neither bilateral nor regional, but truly global.

A major accounting issue associated with export and import activities relates to accounting for foreign currency transactions. Assume, for example, that Solvay exports a certain quantity of pharmaceuticals to a Brazilian importer and invoices the sale in Brazilian reals. Should the real devalue relative to the euro prior to collection, Solvay will experience a foreign exchange loss as reals will yield less euros upon conversion after the devaluation than before. The measurement of this transaction loss is not straightforward and is a subject that is dealt with in Chapter 6.

Today, international business is increasingly associated with foreign direct investments, which include setting up manufacturing or distribution systems abroad by way of a wholly-owned affiliate, a joint venture, or a strategic alliance.

While there is clearly a developed country bias of foreign direct investors, the boom of foreign direct investment flows to developing countries since the early 1990s indicates that MNCs are increasingly finding these host countries to be attractive investment locations.[2]

At the level of the firm, foreign direct investment activities are captured by a company's segmental disclosures and its roster of shareholdings in affiliated compa-

---

[1]Rebecca Buckman, "H-P Outsourcing: Beyond China," *Wall Street Journal,* February 23, 2004, p. A14.
[2]For a recent account of determinants of foreign direct investment activities in developing countries, see Peter Nunnenkamp and Julius Spatz, "Determinants of FDI in Developing Countries: Has Globalization Changed the Rules of the Game?" *Transnational Corporations,* Vol. 11, No. 2, August 2002, pp. 1–34.

Exhibit 1-2	World Merchandise Trade by Region and Selected Economy (Billion Dollars and Percentage)						
	1948	1953	1963	1973	1983	1993	2002
	Exports						
World (value)	58.0	84.0	157.0	579.0	1835.0	3671.0	6272.0
World (share)	100.0	100.0	100.0	100.0	100.0	100.0	100.0
North America	27.3	24.2	19.3	16.9	15.4	16.6	15.1
Latin America	12.3	10.5	7.0	4.7	0.0	4.4	5.6
Mexico	1.0	0.7	0.6	0.4	5.8	1.4	2.6
Brazil	2.0	1.8	0.9	1.1	1.4	1.1	1.0
Argentina	2.8	1.3	0.9	0.6	1.2	0.4	0.4
Western Europe	31.5	34.9	41.4	45.4	38.9	44.0	42.4
C./E. Europe/Baltic States	6.0	8.1	11.0	9.1	9.5	2.9	5.0
Africa	7.3	6.5	5.7	4.8	4.4	2.5	2.2
South Africa	2.0	1.7	1.5	1.0	1.0	0.7	0.5
Middle East	2.0	2.7	3.2	4.1	6.8	3.4	3.9
Asia	13.6	13.1	12.4	14.9	19.1	26.1	25.8
Japan	0.4	1.5	3.5	6.4	8.0	9.9	6.6
China	0.9	1.2	1.3	1.0	1.2	2.5	5.2
India	2.2	1.3	1.0	0.5	0.5	0.6	0.8
Australia/New Zealand	3.7	3.2	2.4	2.1	1.4	1.5	1.3
Six E. Asian Traders	3.0	2.7	2.4	3.4	5.8	9.7	9.6
	Imports						
World (value)	66.0	84.0	163.0	589.0	1881.0	3768.0	6510.0
World (share)	100.0	100.0	100.0	100.0	100.0	100.0	100.0
North America	19.8	19.7	15.5	16.7	17.8	19.7	22.0
Latin America	10.6	9.3	6.8	5.1	4.5	5.1	5.4
Mexico	0.8	1.0	0.8	0.6	0.7	1.8	2.7
Brazil	1.7	1.6	0.9	1.2	0.9	0.7	0.8
Argentina	2.4	0.9	0.6	0.4	0.2	0.4	0.1
Western Europe	40.4	39.4	45.4	47.4	40.0	43.0	40.8
C./E. Europe/Baltic States	5.8	7.6	10.3	8.9	8.4	2.9	4.6
Africa	7.6	7.0	5.5	4.0	4.6	2.6	2.1
South Africa	2.2	1.5	1.1	0.9	0.8	0.5	0.4
Middle East	1.7	2.0	2.3	2.8	6.3	3.3	2.7
Asia	14.2	15.1	14.2	15.1	18.5	23.3	22.4
Japan	1.0	2.9	4.1	6.5	6.7	6.4	5.2
China	1.1	1.7	0.9	0.9	1.1	2.8	4.5
India	3.1	1.4	1.5	0.5	0.7	0.6	0.9
Australia/New Zealand	2.6	2.4	2.3	1.6	1.4	1.5	1.3
Six E. Asian Traders	3.0	3.4	3.1	3.7	6.1	9.9	8.4

Source: World Trade Organization, www.wto.org

Exhibit 1-3 Solvay's Geographic Distribution of Sales			
Net Sales %	2000	2001	2002
Europe	58.8	59.5	61.6
Belgium and Luxemburg	4.2	4.3	4.4
Netherlands	2.2	2.4	2.4
France	12.5	12.5	12.6
Italy	7.1	7.4	9.8
Germany	11.3	10.4	10.3
Spain	6.5	6.8	6.3
United Kingdom	3.8	4.0	3.8
Austria	1.3	1.3	1.3
Switzerland	1.3	1.3	1.2
Portugal	1.2	1.3	1.3
Central Europe + Scandinavia	7.4	7.8	8.2
Americas	35.2	34.0	30.4
United States	25.0	24.9	22.5
Brazil	4.7	3.6	3.0
Other American countries	5.5	5.5	4.9
Asia-Pacific	4.4	4.5	6.5
Africa + Middle East	1.6	2.0	1.5
Total	**100**	**100**	**100**

nies. Exhibit 1-4 provides regional statistics for AKZO Nobel, a multinational company headquartered in the Netherlands concentrating in healthcare products, coatings, and chemicals.

Exhibit 1-5 illustrates the extensive holdings in operating group companies of Sandvik AB. Sandvik is a high-technology engineering group, headquartered in Sweden, with over 37,000 employees and operations in 130 countries. While both AKZO and Sandvik's foreign operations are extensive, the numbers relating to capital

Exhibit 1-4 Foreign Operations Disclosures of AKZO Nobel					
	Net Sales by Destination	Net Sales by Origin	Operating Income	Capital Expenditures	Invested Capital	Number of Employees
Netherlands	825	2,546	212	173	2,354	12,700
Germany	1,147	1,088	89	27	619	4,100
Sweden	510	1,102	80	55	555	4,300
U.K.	840	798	(78)	26	760	4,600
Other-Europe	3,963	3,100	562	110	1,152	13,500
U.S./Canada	2,944	2,604	190	81	1,627	9,500
Latin America	704	470	60	18	259	4,600
Asia	1,413	1,022	173	81	567	9,000
Other regions	665	321	59	10	224	2,300

Exhibit 1-5   Sandvik AB's Shareholdings in Subsidiaries Outside of Sweden

Direct Shareholdings

	Company/Location	*Holding %*
Brazil	Dormer Tools S.A.	100
	Sandvik do Brazil S.A.	100
Bulgaria	Sandvik Bulgaria Ltd.	100
China	Sandvik China Ltd.	100
	Sandvik International Trading (Shanghai) Co., Ltd.	100
	Sandvik Process Systems (Shanghai) Ltd.	100
Czech Republic	Sandvik CZ s.r.o.	100
Germany	Sandvik GmbH	1
	Sandvik Holding GmbH	1
Greece	Sandvik A.E. Tools and Materials	100
Hungary	Sandvik KFT	100
India	Sandvik Asia Ltd.	89
	Sandvik Steel Asia Pvt Ltd.	100
Ireland	Sandvik SMC Distribution Ltd.	100
Italy	Sandvik Sorting Systems S.p.A.	100
Japan	Sandvik K.K.	100
Kenya	Sandvik Kenya Ltd.	96
Korea	Sandvik Korea Ltd.	100
Mexico	Sandvik Mexicana S.A. de C.V.	90
Morocco	Sandvik Maroc SARL	94
Netherlands	Sandvik Benelux B.V.	100
	Sandvik Finance B.V.	100
Peru	Sandvik del Peru S.A.	100
Poland	Sandvik Baildonit S.A.	100
	Sandvik Polska Sp.z o.o.	100
Slovakia	Sandvik Slovakia s.r.o.	100
Spain	Minas y Metalurgica Espanola S.A.	50
Turkey	Sandvik Endustriyel Mamuller Sanayi ve Ticaret A.s.	100
Zimbabwe	Sandvik(Private) Ltd.	100

Indirect Shareholdings in Significant Group Companies

	Company/Location	*Holding %*
Argentina	Sandvik Argentina S.A.	100
Australia	Sandvik Australia Pty. Ltd.	100
	Sandvik Materials Handling Pty. Ltd.	100
	Sandvik Tamrock Pty. Ltd.	100
	VA Eimco Australia Pty. Ltd.	100
	Walter Speedmax Pty. Ltd.	57
Austria	Gunther & Co. GmbH	100
	Montanwerke Walter GmbH	94
	Sandvik BPI Bohrtechnik GmbH & Co. KG	100
	Sandvik I n Austria GmbH	100
	Voest-Alpine Bergtechnik GmbH	100

(*continued*)

Indirect Shareholdings in Significant Group Companies

Company/Location		Holding %
	Voest-Alpine Materials Handling GmbH & Co. KG	100
Belgium	Walter Benelux N.V./S.A.	94
Bolivia	Tamrock Bolivia S.R.L.	100
Brazil	Kanthal Brazil Ltda.	100
	Sandvik Hurth-Infer S.A.	80
	Walter do Brazil Ltda.	94
Canada	Dormer Tools Inc.	100
	Prok Int. Canada Inc.	100
	Sanvik Canada Inc.	100
	Sandvik Tamrock Canada Ltd.	100
	Tamrock Loaders Inc. Canada	100
	Valenite-Modco Ltd.	100
Chile	Sandvik Bafco Servicios S.A.	100
	Sandvik Chile S.A.	100
China	Qingdao Sandvik Die Cutting Systems Co. Ltd.	100
	Walter Wuxi Co. Ltd.	94
Czech Republic	Sandvik Chomutov Precision Tubes s.r.o.	100
	Walter C.Z. s.r.o.	94
	Walter s.r.o. Kurim	94
Denmark	Sandvik A/S	100
Finland	Roxon Oy	100
	Sandvik Tamrock Oy	100
	Suomen Sandvik Oy	100
France	Cermep S.A.	51
	Gunther Tools S.A.S.	100
	Safety S.A.	100
	Sandvik CFBK S.A.S.	100
	Sandvik Hard Materials S.A.	100
	Sandvik Precitube S.A.	100
	Sandvik Process Systems S.A.	100
	Sandvik S.A.S.	100
	Sandvik Tamrock France S.A.S.	100
	Sandvik Tamrock Secoma S.A.S.	100
	Sandvik Tobler S.A.	100
	SCI La Balmette	94
	Walter France SARL	94
Germany	Alpine Westfalia GmbH	100
	Edmeston GmbH	100
	Global Tool Management	94
	Gurtec GmbH	100
	Gunther & Co. GmbH	100
	Prototyp-Werke GmbH	100
	Sandvik GmbH	100
	Sandvik Tamrock GmbH	100
	Walter A.G.	94

Indirect Shareholdings in Significant Group Companies

	Company/Location	Holding %
	Walter Hartmetall GmbH	94
	Walter Informationssysteme GmbH	47
Ghana	Sandvik Tamrock Ghana Ltd.	100
Hong Kong	Kanthal Electroheat Hk Ltd.	100
	Sandvik Hong Kong Ltd.	100
	Sandvik Tamrock (Far East) Ltd.	100
Hungary	Walter Hungaria Kft.	94
Indonesia	PT Sandvik Indonesia	80
	PT Sandvik SMC	100
Ireland	Sandvik Ireland Ltd.	100
Italy	Dormer Italia S.p.A.	100
	Impero S.p.A.	100
	Sandvik Italia S.p.A.	100
	Societa Italiana Kanthal S.p.A.	100
	Walter USAP S.R.L.	94
Japan	Kanthal K.K.	100
	Sandvik Sorting Sysdtems K.K.	100
	Sandvik Toyo Co. Ltd.	100
	Valenite Japan Inc.	100
Kazakhstan	Tamservice Ltd.	100
Korea	Suh Jun Trading Co.	70
	Walter Korea Ltd.	90
Malaysia	Sandvik Malaysia Sdn. Bhd.	100
	Sandvik Rock Processing (Malaysia) Sdn. Bhd.	100
Mexico	Sandvik de Mexico S.A. de C.V.	100
	Tamrock de Mexico S.A. de C.V.	100
	Valenite de Mexico S.A. de C.V.	100
Netherlands	Dormer Tools B.V.	100
	Sandvik Process Systems B.V.	100
New Zealand	Sandvik New Zealand Ltd.	100
Norway	Sandvik Norge A/S	100
	Sandvik Tamrock A/S	100
Philippines	Sandvik Philippines Inc.	100
	Sandvik Tamrock Philippines Inc.	100
Poland	Walter Polska Sp. z.o.o.	94
	Voest-Alpine Technika Tunelowa i Gornicza Sp. z.o.o.	100
Romania	Sandvik SRL	100
Russia	Sandvik-MKTC OAO	98
Singapore	Kanthal Electgroheat Pte. Ltd.	100
	Sandvik South East Asia Pte. Ltd.	100
	Sandvik Tamrock South East Asia Pte. Ltd.	100
	Sandvik Treasury (Far East) Pte. Ltd.	100
	Walter Singapore Pte. Ltd.	94
Slovenia	Sandvik d.o.o.	100

(continued)

9

Indirect Shareholdings in Significant Group Companies

	Company/Location	Holding %
South Africa	Sandvik (Pty) Ltd.	100
	Sandvik Tamrock South Africa (Pty) Ltd.	100
	Voest Alpine Mining & Tunneling Pty. Ltd.	100
Spain	Safety Iberica Metal Duro S.A.	100
	Sandvik Espanola S.A.	100
	Walter Tecno UTIL S.A.	57
Switzerland	Sandvik Handel (Schweitz) AG	100
	Sansafe AG	100
	Santrade Ltd.	100
	Walter (Schweiz) AG	94
Taiwan	Sandvik Hard Materials Taiwan Pty. Ltd.	100
	Sandvik Taiwan Ltd.	100
Tanzania	Sabdvik Tamrock Tanzania Ltd.	100
Thailand	Sandvik Thailand Ltd.	100
United Kingdom	Dormer Tools Ltd.	100
	Dormer Tools (Sheffield) Ltd.	100
	Eimco Great Britain Ltd.	100
	Kanthal Ltd.	100
	Osprey Metals Ltd.	100
	Protoyp UK Ltd.	100
	RGB Stainless Ltd.	100
	Safety Cutting Tools UK Ltd.	100
	Sandvik Ltd.	100
	Sandvik Process Systems Ltd.	100
	Sandvik Steel Ltd.	100
	Titex Tools Ltd.	100
	Walter GB Ltd.	94
Ukraine	Sandvik Ukraine	100
United States	Dormer Tools Inc.	100
	Driltech Mission LLC	100
	Eimco LLC	100
	The Kanthal Corporation	100
	MRL Industries Inc.	100
	Pennsylvania Extruded Tube Co.	70
	Precision Twist Drill Co.	100
	Sandvik Inc.	100
	Sandvik MGT LLC	100
	Sandvik Process Systems Inc.	100
	Sandvik Sorting Systems Inc.	100
	Sandvik Special Metals Corp.	100
	Sandvik Tamrock LLC	100
	Titex Tools Inc.	100
	Valenite Inc.	100
	Walter Grinders Inc.	94
	Walter Waukesha Inc.	94
Zambia	Sandvik Tamrock Zambia Ltd.	60

expenditures, invested capital, production sold locally, and number of foreign employees understate the extent of their foreign operations. They do not reflect the extent of either company's joint venture, strategic alliance, or other cooperative arrangements.

Operations conducted in foreign countries are exposing both financial managers and accountants alike to all kinds of problems they did not encounter when operating within the confines of a single country. As one example, how should an MNC like Sandvik report the results of its operations, both domestic and international, to its Swedish investors? Each affiliate listed in Exhibit 1-5 must prepare its accounts according to the generally accepted accounting principles of the country in which it is domiciled for statutory and tax purposes. As Chapters 3 and 4 will attest, national financial reporting principles can vary significantly from country to country as they are shaped by different socioeconomic environments. Environmental influences that impinge on accounting development are examined in Chapter 2. But Sandvik's Swedish shareholders are used to seeing reports on the basis of Swedish GAAP. Examination of Sandvik's accounting policies on consolidation suggests that the company first restates all of its foreign accounts to Swedish GAAP prior to consolidation. In the company's words:

> The consolidated accounts are prepared in accordance with the principles set out in the Swedish Financial Accounting Standards Council's standard.

But in restating from one set of principles to another, does something get lost in the translation?[3] To illustrate, Mexican companies adjust their financial statements for changing prices (a subject that we cover in Chapter 7), owing to serious bouts of inflation in the past. Sandvik's consolidation methodology would require adjusting these inflation accounting statements back to historical cost prior to consolidation. Does this methodology reduce the information content of the Mexican subsidiary's inflation-adjusted accounts? Might this explain why Japanese multinational company Yamaha, producer of world-reknown musical instruments and other lifestyle products, follows a different tack? The first footnote to Yamaha's consolidated financial accounts reads:

> Yamaha Corporation (the Company) and its domestic subsidiaries maintain their accounting records and prepare their financial statements in accordance with accounting principles and practices generally accepted in Japan, and its foreign subsidiaries maintain their books of account in conformity with those of their countries of domicile. The Company and all consolidated subsidiaries are referred to as the "Group." The accompanying consolidated financial statements have been prepared from the financial statements filed with the Ministry of Finance as required by the Securities and Exchange Law of Japan. Accordingly, the accompanying consolidated financial statements may differ in certain significant respects from accounting principles and practices generally accepted in countries and jurisdictions other than Japan.

Then there is the choice of exchange rate to use in converting foreign accounts to a single reporting currency. As Chapter 6 explains, there are a variety of rates that an

---

[3]Sandvik's shares are also traded in London, Helsinki, and the United States, so the financial reporting issue is even more complex. How should Solvay report to shareholders in these locations?

MNC like Sandvik can use. As foreign exchange rates are seldom constant, restating accounts using exchange rates that gyrate almost daily produces gains and losses that can have a significant effect on the reported profitability and perceived riskiness of multinational operations. As you might suspect, accounting treatments for these gains and losses are far from uniform internationally.

Financial managers and accountants must also understand the effects of environmental complexities of an MNE's accounting measurements. For example, understanding the effects of changes in foreign exchange and inflation rates is critical in areas such as the preparation of short- and long-term budgets for parent companies and their subsidiaries (or branches), measuring and evaluating the performance of local business units and managers, and making corporate-wide decisions on the allocation of investment capital and retained earnings, among others. To make matters more complex, foreign exchange and inflation rates do not work in tandem. The effect on accounting measurements of changes in foreign exchange rates and foreign inflation is so pervasive that domestic financial control systems cannot serve managers well in the absence of appropriate environmental adaptation. Managerial accounting from an international perspective includes possibly the most complex and detailed material in this book. Discussion of these topics begins in Chapter 10.

Chapter 12 addresses the important issues of international taxation and transfer pricing. Businesses that operate in more than one country need to carefully examine and manage their tax exposure. Knowledge of tax codes and currency values is only the beginning. It is very possible that steps taken to lower taxes in one place will raise taxes elsewhere, possibly by an amount greater than the original reduction. The effects of tax strategies on corporate budgeting and control procedures must be considered carefully. For example, a good strategy to reduce taxes might have unintended effects on the performance evaluation system. Transfer prices—the prices charged to business units for internal transactions that cross national borders—frequently are set with tax minimization in mind. The basic idea is to concentrate expenses (as far as possible) in high-tax countries and to concentrate revenues in low-tax countries, thus maximizing overall profit. Governments are well aware of this strategy and have adopted complex rules to prevent abusive use of this strategy. While the notion of the "arm's-length" price is widespread, its definition and the methods for calculating it have many variations. On top of all this, unexpected changes in exchange rates or inflation rates can wreak havoc on tax planning strategy. Generally, it is necessary to use complex computer modeling to calculate the overall expected impact of a company's tax strategy.

GLOBAL COMPETITION

Another factor contributing to the growing importance of international accounting is the phenomenon of global competition. Benchmarking, the act of comparing one's performance against an appropriate standard, is not new. What is new is that standards of comparison now transcend national boundaries. The relevant question today is not "How am I doing relative to my competitor who may be right across the street?", but "Am I adding more value to my customer base than my counterpart who may be located in another country?"

In benchmarking against international competitors, one must be careful to ensure that comparisons are indeed comparable. For example, one frequently used perfor-

Exhibit 1-6 Adjusting Electrolux's Earnings and Equity to U.S. GAAP	
As reported consolidated income (SEKm)	5,095
Adjustments before taxes:	
Acquisitions	53
Goodwill and other intangible assets	233
Development costs	−156
Restructuring and other provisions	−545
Pensions	74
Derivatives and hedging	579
Capitalization of computer software	−24
Securities	−5
Stock-based compensation	−69
Taxes on these adjustments	73
Net income per U.S. GAAP	5,308
As reported consolidated equity (SEKm)	27,629
Adjustment before taxes:	
Acquisitions	−594
Goodwill and other intangible assets	233
Development costs	−156
Restructuring and other provisions	—
Pensions	461
Derivatives and hedging	257
Capitalization of computer software	44
Securities	−5
Revaluation of assets	−147
Stock-based compensation	−35
Taxes on these adjustments	−107
Equity per U.S. GAAP	27,580

mance metric is return on equity (ROE). In comparing the ROE of an American consumer durables manufacturer with Sweden's Electrolux, are you really comparing *apples to apples* or are you comparing *apples to oranges*?

Exhibit 1-6 suggests that comparing a U.S. ROE against the Swedish ROE would be comparing apples to oranges. Exhibit 1-6 begins with the net income of Electrolux as reported in its recent consolidated financial statements. This figure is followed by a series of adjustments that would be required to restate those numbers to a basis consistent with U.S. GAAP. A comparable series of adjustments is provided for stockholders' equity. A comparison of the unadjusted ROE with the adjusted ROE yields return statistics of 18.4% and 19.2%, respectively. Statement readers who are not aware of national measurement differences and required adjustment algorithms are obviously at a disadvantage.

CROSS-BORDER MERGERS AND ACQUISITIONS

As the global trend toward industrial consolidation continues, news about international mergers and acquisitions is practically a daily occurrence. While mergers are normally rationalized in terms of operating synergies or economies of scale, accounting plays a crucial role in these mega-consolidations as accounting numbers are funda-mental in the corporate valuation process. Differences in national measurement rules can complicate the corporate valuation process (see Chapter 9).

For example, corporate valuations are often based on price-based multiples, such as the price-to-earnings (P/E) ratio. The approach here is to derive an average P/E multiple for comparable firms in the industry and apply this multiple to the reported earnings of the firm being valued to arrive at a reasonable offering price. A major con-cern of the acquiring firm when bidding for a foreign acquisition target is to what extent the E in the P/E metric is a true reflection of the attribute being measured, as opposed to the result of an accounting measurement difference!

Differences in accounting measurement rules could also create an unlevel playing field in the market for corporate control. Thus, if Company A in Country A is allowed to take purchased goodwill directly to reserves, while Company B in Country B must amortize purchased goodwill to earnings, Company A may very well enjoy a bidding advantage over B when seeking to acquire a common target company.

FINANCIAL INNOVATION

Risk management has become a hot buzzword in corporate and financial circles. The reason is not hard to find. With continued deregulation of financial markets and capital controls, volatility in the price of commodities, foreign exchange, credit, and equities has become the order of the day. Given this state of the world, financial managers need to identify their exposure to this volatility, decide which risks to hedge against, and to evaluate the results of their risk management strategy. At the same time, advances in financial technology have made it possible to shift market risks to someone else's shoulders. The burden of assessing counterparty risk, however, cannot be transferred and is now placed on the shoulders of a larger pool of market participants, many of whom may be located thousands of miles away. The dependence this creates on inter-national reporting practices and the resulting confusion caused by diversity in account-ing for financial risk products is obvious. Those with risk management skills are highly valued by the market. Hence we devote an entire chapter, Chapter 11, to the topic of financial risk management.

INTERNATIONALIZATION OF CAPITAL MARKETS

The factor that has perhaps contributed most to the growing interest in international accounting among corporate executives, investors, market regulators, accounting stan-dard setters and business educators alike is the internationalization of the world's cap-ital markets. PricewaterhouseCoopers reports that the dollar volume of cross-border equity offerings almost tripled between 1995 and 1999, with over US$500 billion raised during the 5-year period (These offerings only include the sales of securities outside the domestic market.). International offerings in bonds, syndicated loans, and other debt instruments also grew dramatically during the 1990s. These trends were damp-ened during the early years of the current decade, owing to the slowdown in world economic activity. However, business activity is now on the upswing and we expect these trends to continue during the balance of this decade.

The World Federation of Exchanges reports that the number of domestic companies with shares listed increased in some markets and decreased in others during the early part of this decade. However, the average sizes and annual trading volumes of listed companies have grown substantially, in part due to mergers and acquisitions, which also result in delistings of some of the entities involved.

Hundreds of foreign issuers[4] have had their equity listed on European, North American, and Japanese stock exchanges for years. However, the numbers of foreign companies listed in most markets other than the New York Stock Exchange (NYSE) and Nasdaq have been declining. This suggests that many issuers question the benefits of such listings, and that the benefits of a foreign listing generally are greater in the United States than elsewhere.

The three largest equity market regions[5] are North America, Asia-Pacific, and Europe.

North America

The U.S. economy and its stock markets had unprecedented growth during the 1990s. By 2000 both the NYSE and Nasdaq dominated other stock exchanges worldwide in terms of market capitalization, value of trading in domestic shares, value of trading in foreign shares (except for the London Stock Exchange [LSE]), capital raised by newly admitted companies, numbers of domestic listed companies, and numbers of foreign listed companies. Also, the *relative* importance of North America in the global equity market has increased: Market capitalization in North America as a percentage of the global total stood at 57.2 percent at the start of 2000.

Asia

Until recently, many experts predicted that Asia would become the second most important equity market region. The People's Republic of China (China) emerged as a major global economy, and the "Asian Tiger" nations experienced phenomenal growth and development. However, several Asian financial crises in the 1990s highlighted the fragility and immaturity of these economies, and slowed the growth of capital markets in the region.

Critics argue that Asian accounting measurement, disclosure, and auditing standards and the monitoring and enforcement of those standards are weak.[6] A number of Asian listed companies and market participants have been involved in organized

[4]An *issuer* is an entity that raises capital or has shares listed (with no capital raised) on a stock exchange. A *foreign issuer* is an issuer whose home country is different than the country of the capital market.
[5]Each equity market region is comprised of equity markets in multiple countries, and some of these national equity markets are comprised of several stock exchanges (as well as off-exchange trading systems). (For example, four stock exchanges operate in Spain, and eight stock exchanges operate in the United States.) A *stock exchange* is an entity that plays a central role in the regulation of trading markets and develops, operates, and manages those markets.
[6]These attributes are neither good nor bad. Each market develops in response to economic conditions, the nature of its investors, sources of financing, and other factors. In Japan, for example, banks have long been the primary sources of finance. These banks have had full access to inside information about Japanese companies, and so there has been less demand in Japan for credible external financial reporting.

crime, insider dealings, and other activities that deter potential investors.[7] Also, some Asian governments periodically announce that they will intervene in equity markets to boost share prices, and market manipulation is not uncommon.[8]

However, the prospects for future growth in Asian equity markets are strong. Market capitalization as a percentage of gross domestic product (GDP) in Asia is low compared with that in the United States and several major European markets, suggesting that equity markets can play a much larger role in many Asian economies. Also, Asian governments and stock exchanges are under pressure to improve market quality and credibility to attract investors.[9] Several Asian markets (e.g., China, India, Korea, Taiwan, and Hong Kong) have grown rapidly, and are experiencing heavy trading volume relative to market capitalization.

Western Europe

Europe is the second largest equity market region in the world in terms of market capitalization and trading volume.[10] Economic expansion significantly contributed to the rapid growth in European equity markets during the second half of the 1990s. A related factor in Continental Europe has been a gradual shift to an *equity orientation* that long has characterized the London and North American equity markets.[11] Privatizations of large government entities have made European equity markets more prominent and have attracted noninstitutional investors, who until recently were not active in Continental Europe. Finally, confidence in European markets has grown with the success of the European Monetary Union (EMU).

European equity markets will continue to grow. Pension reforms, for one, are creating new demand for investment opportunities.[12] Also, more and more foreign investors are entering European equity markets. Cross-border equity flows are increasing as a percentage of cross-border bond flows, in part because equity has been a prof-

---

[7]For example, in an "unusually aggressive" move, the Osaka Securities Exchange launched a campaign to bar companies linked to organized crime from Nasdaq Japan in November 2000. Harney Alexandra, "Osaka Market Targets Crime," *Financial Times* (November 16, 2000), p. 18.

[8]For example, Taiwan announced in November 2000 that it would institute emergency action to support share prices after a recent, dramatic fall. Mure Dickie, "Taiwan Offers Support as Share Prices Fall Sharply," *Financial Times* (November 21, 2000), p. 16.

[9]The Singapore Exchange, for example, has moved aggressively to position itself as the premier financial exchange in Asia outside of Japan. The exchange recently implemented new listing rules and more stringent disclosure requirements to attract new domestic and foreign listings. See PricewaterhouseCoopers' *International Briefings* (May, June, and September 2000). As a second example, see "An End to Make-Believe Accounting (in Japan)," *Financial Times* (April 5, 2000).

[10]International Federation of Stock Exchanges (FIBV) 1999 Annual Report (Paris: FIBV, 2000).

[11]Developed countries around the world can be divided roughly into those having a common law (English) orientation and those having a code law (Continental Europe) orientation (see Chapter 2). Common law countries include the United Kingdom, Canada, the United States, and Australia. In these countries, equity investors are widely dispersed and are the most important suppliers of capital. As a result, capital markets in many common law countries have evolved credible and open disclosure and accounting systems, and relatively stringent market regulation. In code law countries such as France, Germany, and Japan, banks provide most of the financing, and ownership tends to be concentrated among small groups of insiders. Demand for detailed public disclosure is generally lower in these countries than in common law countries, but is increasing.

[12]With aging populations causing the numbers of pensioners to increase, a major initiative across much of Europe has been to move toward the private funding of pensions. The goal is to relieve the strain on "pay-as-you-go" state pension schemes. The growing numbers of private pension funds are allocating more of their assets to equities to increase returns. Also, some countries are liberalizing restrictions on pension fund investment.

itable investment since the market crash of October 1987. In addition, the advent of the euro has prompted a rush of cross-border mergers, which are expected to continue.

EUROPEAN EQUITY MARKETS—A CLOSER LOOK

There are several good reasons to take a closer look at European equity markets. European capital markets are undergoing major, rapid changes, in part due to the globalization of the world economy and the increasing economic integration of the European Union. These changes reflect and exemplify changes taking place in capital markets around the world. Thus, a closer look at European equity markets will help lay the foundation for a better understanding of equity markets in general.

Continental Europe's New Equity Culture

A further basis for predicting continued growth in European equity markets is the growing equity culture in Europe. The successful but hostile takeover in 1999 of Mannesmann, the third largest German company in market capitalization, by Vodafone, a British company, at a value estimated at US$175 billion, was a watershed example of the growth in shareholder power. At first most observers expected Mannesmann to mount a successful traditional defense, but pressure from large shareholders forced management to accept the deal. "The shareholder is king," said Mannesmann's chairman, Klaus Esser, when he finally conceded.[13]

Intense rivalry among European stock exchanges has contributed to the development of an equity culture. During the 1990s Continental European markets became more investor oriented to increase their credibility and attract new listings. External investors, in particular foreign investors and institutional investors, are demanding expanded disclosure and improved corporate governance. In addition, equity market development has become increasingly important to national governments and regulators, who also compete for recognition and prestige. Many European securities regulators and stock exchanges have implemented more stringent market rules and are strengthening their enforcement efforts.

However, intense rivalry has also led stock exchanges and national regulators to ease listing rules and grant special exemptions to issuers. For example, the Paris Bourse exempted LibertySurf, a French company, from key requirements for admission to its main market after LibertySurf threatened to seek a listing on the Deutsche Börse if its demands were not met.[14]

Continental European companies have started to increase their disclosure levels, improve their financial reporting, and strengthen their corporate governance during the 1990s to attract new capital and investor interest. However, many of these companies, including some of the world's largest, still fall short of British and North American disclosure and listing standards.[15]

---

[13]See "Bidding for the Future," *The Economist* (February 12, 2000), p. 71.
[14]See S. Iskandar and B. Benoit, "Growing Competition Threatens Confidence," *Financial Times* (May 1, 2000).
[15]For example, *The Economist* (October 7, 2000), pp. 73–74, discusses the ambivalence of French companies toward outside scrutiny and investor-oriented corporate governance.

Cross-Border Equity Listing and Issuance

The current wave of interest in cross-border listings on the European new markets follows a period during the 1980s when hundreds of foreign companies listed on European stock exchanges. Listing costs were relatively low, and "everyone was doing it."

Evidence suggests that issuers seek cross-border listings in Europe to broaden their shareholder base, promote awareness in their products, and/or build public awareness of the company, particularly in countries where the company has significant operations and/or major customers. (European stock exchanges long have promoted these potential benefits.) However, there is little evidence that such benefits are realized in European markets. Most foreign equities in Continental Europe are thinly traded or are not traded at all, and have few local shareholders. As noted earlier, during the 1990s many foreign companies delisted from European stock exchanges after realizing minimal benefits from those listings.

National regulators and stock exchanges compete fiercely for foreign listings and trade volume, considered necessary for any stock exchange that seeks to become or remain a global leader. In response, European exchanges and market regulators have worked to make access faster and less costly for foreign issuers and at the same time increase their markets' credibility. As European markets become more specialized, each can offer unique benefits to foreign issuers.

Many European companies have difficulty deciding where to raise capital or list their shares. Knowledge of many equity markets with different laws, regulations, and institutional features is now required. Also required is an understanding of how issuer and stock exchange characteristics interact. The issuer's home country, industry, and offering size are just some of the factors that need to be considered.[16] In addition, the costs and benefits of different market combinations need to be understood. One entrepreneur planning to raise capital said, "I spoke to three investment banks about it, and I had three different answers about which would be the right market for me." A London broker who advises companies on where to raise capital states that "The landscape is moving so fast that no one knows what it's going to be like in 6 months' time."[17] Exhibit 1-7 presents a more detailed list of factors companies consider in choosing a foreign capital market.[18]

The rapid pace of change in European capital markets, including the growing importance of stock exchange alliances, the emergence of Europe's new markets, and alternative trading systems, presents a highly complex setting. However, although

---

[16]*Home country* is relevant because companies can raise capital more easily in foreign countries that have legal and regulatory environments similar to their own. For example, an Australian company can probably access the U.K. equity market more easily than the French equity market. *Industry* is important because, other things equal, issuers seek to raise capital in markets where other companies in the same industry are listed in order to improve the chances for adequate attention by financial analysts. For example, the SWX Swiss Exchange's New Market is attractive to biotechnology companies in part because Novartis and Roche (two of the world's largest pharmaceutical companies) are listed on the SWX Swiss Exchange and have attracted many pharmaceutical/biotech analysts to Zurich. Offering size is important because only relatively large offerings attract sufficient attention in the United States. Much smaller IPOs are common in Europe's new markets.

[17]Charles Fleming, "Europe's IPOs: Tough Choices on Just Where to Go Public," *The Wall Street Journal* (July 11, 2000), p. C1.

[18]Appendix 1-3 presents Web site addresses for stock exchanges in more than 50 countries. Many stock exchange Web sites include information on unique stock exchange features that may attract foreign companies considering listing or raising capital in those markets.

Exhibit 1-7   Factors Relevant in Choosing an Overseas Market

1. What is the extent of interest in a company shown by financial analysts and investors who normally participate in a market?
2. What is the level of trading activity on the exchange? Higher trading volume means more potential buyers of a company's securities.
3. How easy is it to raise capital? Some jurisdictions have complex listing or ongoing reporting requirements that may be difficult or impossible for a smaller company to meet.
4. What is the availability of capital in a market?
5. What is the reputation of the exchange? A growing international company may want the increased credibility and recognition that come with listing on a preeminent market such as the New York Stock Exchange.
6. To what extent does the company desire to raise its profile and establish its brand identity in a particular market? A stock exchange listing can benefit companies that operate or plan to operate in an overseas country.
7. To what extent are the market's regulatory environment and language similar to those in the company's home market? For example, a company from an English-speaking country with a common law (British-American) legal and regulatory system, such as Australia, might find it easier to list in the United Kingdom than in Continental Europe.
8. To what extent do institutional investors face statutory or self-imposed restrictions on the proportion of their investment portfolio that they can hold in securities of foreign companies? Sometimes these restrictions force a large international company to list on many stock exchanges to have access to sufficient institutional capital. These restrictions are difficult to overcome in some jurisdictions.
9. What are the nature and activities of investors in the market? For example, large pension funds in the Netherlands, Switzerland, and the United Kingdom invest heavily in equities of both domestic and foreign companies.
10. What is the likelihood that the company will be required to have locally listed shares to carry out a merger or acquisition in a particular country?
11. Will there be a need for locally listed shares to be used in employee stock option plans?

financial reporting regulation will remain complex, the differences in rules will continue to lessen from one country to the next.

WHERE ARE WE?

The rapid growth in global capital markets and cross-border investment activity means that the international dimensions of accounting are more important than ever for professionals who have to deal in one way or another with these areas. Accounting plays a critical role in the efficient functioning of capital markets. Lenders, investors, financial analysts, regulators, and stock exchanges require information about the financial performance, position, and the future prospects of companies seeking financing. In turn, the needs of capital market participants have strongly shaped the development of accounting practice, as discussed in Chapter 2. Demands of market participants strongly influence companies' accounting and disclosure choices and national and international efforts to harmonize accounting measurement, disclosure, and auditing practices around the world.

How does, for example, a British or American investor make sense of Japanese accounts or Swiss accounts where measurement and transparency rules are very different from what they are typically accustomed to? Should they attempt to restate all foreign accounts to a more familiar set of reporting norms prior to analysis? Or should they put themselves in the shoes of the foreign company's domestic shareholders and conduct their analysis from a local perspective? These and other related issues are covered in Chapter 9.

On the other side of the coin, a major factor motivating many corporations to raise monies abroad is to increase their access to funds and lower their capital costs. From a corporate issuer's point of view, how does one communicate with an investor base that is accustomed to providing capital on the basis of a different set of accounting norms, let alone a different language and currency? Should a corporate issuer restate its accounts to the reporting framework of the capital supplier's national domicile? Should it increase the quantity of information it provides to foreign readers, knowing full well that there may be competitive costs associated with doing so? The challenge here is trying to ensure that the *foreign* reader receives the same intended message as the *domestic* reader. This challenge is significant in a world where firms *compete* for funds, an issue explored in Chapter 5.

LEARNING OBJECTIVES

Having set the stage for your study of international accounting, we identify below the essential ideas that you should get out of each chapter. We invite you to revisit this section before you begin reading each chapter and upon completion of each chapter to be sure that you understand the essential ideas that are being conveyed. This text will not make you an expert in international accounting. Instead, it will sensitize you to the important concepts and issues in the field, and in so doing, enable you to ask the "right questions" as a reader of international financial statements, whether you opt for a career in the corporate, legal, financial services, or not-for-profit world.

After studying Chapter 1, you should be able to:

1. Explain how international accounting is distinct from other areas of accounting.
2. Identify and explain the three broad areas into which accounting can be divided.
3. Understand, in general terms, the historic development of international accounting and trends in national financial sector policy.
4. Understand the role accounting plays in business and global capital markets.
5. Be familiar with the three major equity market regions, as well as the important developments in each region since 1995.
6. Understand, in particular, recent developments in European equity markets.

After studying Chapter 2, you should be able to:

1. Identify and understand the importance of the eight factors that have a significant influence on accounting development.

2. Identify and explain four accounting value dimensions, and how each is likely to affect a nation's financial reporting practices.
3. Understand the four approaches to accounting development found in market-oriented Western economies and identify countries in which each is prevalent.
4. Have a basic working knowledge of accounting classifications and how they compare with one another.
5. Explain the difference between the "fair presentation" and "legal compliance" orientations and identify nations in which each is prevalent.
6. Identify important accounting issues in which the difference between "fair presentation" and "legal compliance" orientations has a significant impact.

After studying Chapter 3, you should be able to:

1. Define the terms "accounting standards" and "standard setting."
2. Understand how and why accounting practice may deviate from what standards require.
3. Understand, in general terms, the financial accounting systems of six highly developed countries (France, Germany, Japan, the Netherlands, the United Kingdom, and the United States).
4. Be able to identify the key similarities and differences among the accounting systems of these six countries.

After studying Chapter 4, you should be able to:

1. Understand in general terms the financial accounting systems of four emerging countries (Czech Republic, People's Republic of China, Taiwan, and Mexico).
2. Appreciate important similarities and differences among the accounting systems of these four emerging markets.
3. Contrast the accounting systems of the Czech Republic, PRC, Taiwan, and Mexico with the systems of the six developed countries studied in Chapter 3.

After studying Chapter 5, you should be able to:

1. Explain how national differences in accounting disclosure practices are influenced by national practices in corporate governance and finance.
2. Understand the important (and sometimes conflicting) incentives that affect managers' decisions to make (or not make) voluntary accounting disclosures.
3. Identify the broad objectives for accounting disclosure systems in investor-oriented equity markets.
4. Gain a basic understanding of national differences in the following selected corporate financial disclosure practices: (a) disclosures of forward-looking information, (b) segment disclosures, (c) cash and funds flow, (d) social responsibility disclosures, (e) special disclosures for nondomestic financial statement users, (f) corporate governance disclosures, and (g) Internet business reporting.

After studying Chapter 6, you should be able to:

1. Distinguish between foreign currency translation and foreign currency conversion.
2. Understand the nature of foreign currency transactions done in the spot, forward, and swap markets.
3. Understand the foreign currency translation terms set forth in Exhibit 6-1.

4. Be able to distinguish between translation gains and losses and transaction gains and losses.

5. Be able to account properly for translation gains and losses.

6. Use and understand the financial statement effects alternative foreign currency translation methods.

7. Be able to evaluate which of the available foreign currency translation methods are best under which specific business and currency market conditions.

8. Learn the history and content of FAS No. 52 and its application.

9. Understand the relationship between foreign currency translation and inflation.

10. Gain an overview of how foreign currency translation is handled outside the United States.

After studying Chapter 7, you should be able to:

1. Understand why and how financial statements potentially are misleading during periods of changing prices.

2. Define the inflation accounting terms listed in Exhibit 7-1.

3. Understand the effect of general price-level adjustments on financial statement amounts.

4. State two major ways in which the current cost accounting model differs from conventional accounting.

5. Explain the different approaches to inflation accounting taken by the United States, the United Kingdom, and Brazil.

6. Have a basic understanding of IAS 20 ("Financial Reporting in Hyperinflationary Economies").

7. Discuss whether constant dollars or current costs better measure the effects of inflation.

8. Define the "double dip" and explain why it must be dealt with in adjusting accounting amounts for changing prices.

After studying Chapter 8, you should be able to:

1. Define and understand the distinction between the terms "harmonization" and "standardization" as they apply to accounting standards.

2. Briefly state the pros and cons that have been mentioned with regard to international accounting standards harmonization.

3. Understand what is meant by "reconciliation" and "mutual recognition" (or "reciprocity") of different sets of accounting standards.

4. Identify the six organizations (in particular, the International Accounting Standards Board) that have leading roles in setting international accounting standards and in promoting international accounting harmonization, as well as understand their basic structure and functions.

5. Describe the European Union's "New Approach" and how it relates to the integration of European financial markets.

After studying Chapter 9, you should be able to:

1. Understand the special difficulties involved in doing international business strategy analysis and basic strategies for information gathering.

2. Describe the six steps involved in conducting an accounting analysis.

3. Understand the impact on accounting analysis of (a) cross-country variation in accounting measurement, disclosure, and auditing quality and (b) the difficulty in obtaining necessary information.
4. Have a working acquaintance with several coping mechanisms available to deal with cross-country accounting principle differences.
5. Understand (in a general way) the particular difficulties and pitfalls involved in doing an international prospective analysis.
6. Learn how to use the World Wide Web to obtain information for company research.

After studying Chapter 10, you should be able to:

1. State the four critical dimensions of business modeling.
2. Understand the distinction between standard and Kaizen costing concepts.
3. Measure expected returns of a foreign investment.
4. Understand (in general terms) the computation of cost of capital in a multinational framework.
5. Understand the basic issues and complexities involved in designing multinational information and financial control systems.
6. Be able to conduct an exchange rate variance analysis.
7. State the unique difficulties involved in designing and implementing performance evaluation systems in multinational companies.
8. Understand and be able to deal with the effects of inflation and exchange rate fluctuation on performance measurement of multinational companies.

After studying Chapter 11, you should be able to:

1. Identify the major components of international financial risk management.
2. State the four tasks involved in managing foreign exchange risk.
3. Define and calculate translation exposure.
4. Define and calculate transaction exposure.
5. Understand the distinction between accounting exposure and economic exposure.
6. Have a working knowledge of available exchange rate hedging (protection) strategies and their accounting treatments.
7. Understand accounting and control issues associated with foreign exchange risk management.

After studying Chapter 12, you should be able to:

1. Define basic international taxation concepts.
2. Understand concepts relating to the taxation of foreign source income.
3. Appreciate the rationale of the foreign tax credit.
4. Be sensitive to international tax planning dimensions that multinational enterprises must consider.
5. Have a working knowledge of variables that complicate international transfer pricing.
6. Understand basic issues involved in transfer pricing methodology.

Appendix 1-1

Exhibit 1-8 Changes in Financial Sector Policy in 34 Nations, 1973–1996		
Country	Privatization	International Capital Flows
Industrialized Countries		
United States	None	Limited controls imposed in the 1960s, abolished in 1974
Canada	None	None
Japan	Government controls roughly 15% of financial assets through the postal savings system.	Controls on capital inflows eased after 1979. Controls on capital outflows eased in the mid-1980s. Foreign exchange restrictions eased in 1980. Remaining restrictions on cross-border transactions removed in 1995.
United Kingdom	None	All remaining controls on foreign exchange purchase eliminated in 1979.
France	Some banks nationalized since 1945. All larger banks nationalized in 1982. Several French banks privatized in 1987 and 1993, including Banque Nationale de Paris.	Capital flows in and out of the country largely liberalized during 1986–1988. Liberalization was completed in 1990.
Germany	None	Most capital controls dismantled in 1973.
Italy	Credito Italiano and some other public banks privatized in 1993–1994.	Foreign exchange and capital controls eliminated by May 1990.
Australia	Some state-owned banks privatized in the 1990s. Commonwealth Bank of Australia privatized in 1997.	Capital and exchange controls tightened in late 1970s after the move to indirect monetary policy increased capital inflows. Capital account liberalized in 1984.
New Zealand	Bank of New Zealand (one of the four largest banks) privatized in the early 1990s. Development Finance Corporation closed. Government sold all remaining shares in state-owned banks by 1992.	All controls on inward and outward foreign exchange transactions removed in 1984. Controls on outward investment lifted in 1985. Restrictions on foreign-owned companies' access to domestic financial markets removed in late 1984. Controls on foreign direct and portfolio investment and repatriation of profits eased in 1985.
East Asia		
Hong Kong	None	None
Indonesia	Stock exchange privatized in 1990.	Most transactions on the capital account liberalized in 1971. Some restrictions on inflows remain. The regulation requiring exporters to sell their foreign-exchange holdings to banks abolished in 1982. Foreign direct investment regulations eased further in 1992.

Exhibit 1-8 Changes in Financial Sector Policy in 34 Nations, 1973–1996 (*Continued*)		
Country	Privatization	International Capital Flows
Korea	Government divested its shares in commercial banks in the early 1980s. State-owned banks' share of total assets 13% in 1994.	Controls on foreign borrowing under US$200,000 with maturities of less than 3 years eased in 1979. Restriction on foreign borrowing under US$1 million eased in 1982. Controls on outward and inward foreign investment gradually eased since 1985. Significant restrictions on inward investment in place until 1998.
Malaysia	Share of state-owned banks in total assets of the financial sector 8% in 1994 (BIS estimate). Government is the majority shareholder in the country's largest bank and wholly owns the second largest bank.	Capital account mostly liberalized in the 1970s. Inward foreign direct and portfolio investment deregulated further in the mid-1980s. Controls on short-term and portfolio inflows temporarily reimposed in 1994.
Philippines	Government took over some failed financial institutions during the early 1980s. Government's share of total bank assets was lowered to 22% by 1996. Government reduced its stake in PNB to 47% in December 1995.	Foreign exchange and investment channeled through government in the 1970s. Interbank foreign exchange trading limited to 30 minutes per day after 1983. Off-floor trading introduced in 1992. Restrictions on all current and most capital transactions eliminated over 1992–1995.
Singapore	None	Government freed exchange and capital controls by 1978. (Exception: Offshore banks may not transact in Singapore dollars.)
Taiwan	Privatization effort blocked by controlling interests in 1989.	Foreign-exchange controls removed in 1987. Inward and outward capital flows limited to US$5 million per person per year.
Thailand	Share of state-owned banks in total assets 8% in 1994 (BIS estimate).	Restrictions on inward long-term investment eased in the mid-1980s. Controls on short-term flows and outward investment eased in the 1990s. The reserve requirement on short-term foreign borrowing is 7%. Currency controls introduced in May and June 1997 to deter currency speculators. Limits on foreign ownership of domestic financial institutions relaxed in October 1997.
Latin America		
Argentina	Fifteen percent of the loan market privatized since 1992. Government still owns the largest commercial bank, Banco de la Nación Argentina.	Multiple exchange rate system unified between 1976 and 1978. Foreign loans at market exchange rates permitted in 1978. Controls on inward and outward capital flows loosened in 1977. Liberalization measures reversed in 1982. Capital and exchange controls eliminated in 1991.

(*continued*)

Exhibit 1-8 Changes in Financial Sector Policy in 34 Nations, 1973–1996 *(Continued)*		
Country	Privatization	International Capital Flows
Brazil	None	System of comprehensive foreign exchange controls abolished in 1984. Most capital outflows restricted in the 1980s. Controls on capital inflows strengthened and controls on outflows loosened in the 1990s.
Chile	Nineteen domestic commercial banks privatized in 1974. Banks nationalized during the 1982 crisis were reprivatized in the mid-1980s.	Capital controls gradually eased since 1979. Controls reimposed in 1982 and eased again in mid-1980s. Foreign direct and portfolio investment subject to a 1-year minimum holding period. Foreign loans subject to a 30% reserve requirement.
Colombia	Two large banks and a large finance company nationalized in 1982. Government intervened in over 20 financial institutions between 1982 and 1986. 30% of loan market privatized by 1995.	Controls on capital inflows relaxed in 1991. Exchange controls also reduced. Large capital inflows in the early 1990s led to the reimposition of reserve requirements on foreign loans in 1993.
Mexico	Authorities nationalized 18 commercial banks in 1982. Nationalized banks privatized in 1991.	Government given discretion over foreign direct investment in 1972. Ambiguous restrictions on foreign direct investment rationalized in 1989. Portfolio flows decontrolled further in 1989.
Peru	All five public development banks closed in early 1990s. All seven public commercial banks liquidated or divested over 1991–1995.	Capital controls removed in December 1990.
Venezuela	Four small public commercial banks liquidated or privatized in 1989. Public sector banks' share of total deposits 9% in 1993. Share increased to 29% after the nationalization of several banks during 1994–1996.	Foreign direct investment regime largely liberalized over 1989–1990. Exchange controls on all current and capital transactions imposed in 1994. System of comprehensive foreign exchange controls abandoned in April 1996.
Middle East and Africa		
Egypt	Some privatization of smaller state banks. The four largest public banks not slated for privatization as of 2004.	Foreign exchange system decontrolled and unified in 1991. Some controls on inward portfolio and direct investment lifted in 1990s.
Israel	Government nationalized leading banks in 1983. Union Bank (part of Bank Leumi) privatized in 1990s. 43% of Bank Hapoalim sold to Israeli-American consortium in 1997.	Capital controls eliminated in 1977 and reimposed in 1979. After 1987, restrictions on capital inflows gradually eliminated and restrictions on capital outflows gradually eased.

Exhibit 1-8   Changes in Financial Sector Policy in 34 Nations, 1973–1996 (*Continued*)

Country	Privatization	International Capital Flows
Morocco	The Casablanca stock market is state owned. One state-owned bank was privatized in 1995.	Current account convertibility achieved in the 1990s. Surrender requirements or export revenue and outward investment restrictions relaxed in the early 1990s. Restrictions on inward foreign direct and portfolio investment and external borrowing by residents eased after 1993.
South Africa	None	Capital controls tightened in 1985. Exchange controls on nonresidents eliminated in 1995. Controls on residents relaxed in 1995.
Turkey	State-owned banks' share in total assets of the bank system remained constant over 1980–1990, at approximately 52%.	Capital flows liberalized in 1989.
South Asia		
Bangladesh	Commercial banks nationalized in the 1970s. Two state-owned banks sold back to original owners in early 1980s. (These banks remain uncompetitive.)	Foreign exchange markets unified in 1991–1992. Restrictions on current transactions eliminated in 1994. Controls on capital inflows eased after 1991.
India	All large banks nationalized in 1969. Government divested part of its equity position in some public banks in the 1990s.	Regulations on portfolio and direct investment eased since 1991. The exchange rate was unified in 1993–1994. Current account convertibility achieved in 1994.
Nepal	Two large public-sector banks hold over half of total bank deposits. Government share of Nepal Bank Limited reduced to 41%.	Dual exchange rate system introduced in 1992. Current account became fully convertible in 1994. Some capital transactions liberalized in the 1990s, but restrictions remain.
Pakistan	Muslim Commercial Bank privatized in 1991. Allied Bank privatized in stages between 1991 and 1993. First Women Bank privatized in 1997.	Rupee convertible for current transactions since July 1994. Capital controls eased in the 1990s.
Sri Lanka	Two development finance banks privatized in 1990s.	Exchange rate unified in 1978. Rupee made convertible for current transactions in 1994. Capital controls on inflows eased in 1978. Foreign portfolio investment restrictions eased further in 1991. Restrictions on capital outflows remain.

Source: John Williamson and Molly Mahar, *A Survey of Financial Liberalization* (Princeton, NJ: Princeton University International Finance Section, Essays in International Finance #211).

Appendix 1-2

FINANCIAL STATEMENT AND AUDITOR'S REPORT FROM NIKKEN CHEMICAL CO. LTD.'S 2000 ANNUAL REPORT

CONSOLIDATED BALANCE SHEETS
Nikken Chemicals Co., Ltd. and Consolidated Subsidiary
As of March 31, 2000

Assets	2000 Millions of Yen	2000 Thousands of U.S. Dollars (Note 3)
Current assets:		
Cash and cash equivalents (Note 4)	¥ 2,139	$ 20,151
Time deposits	200	1,884
Marketable securities	1,162	10,947
Notes receivable, trade	4,865	45,831
Accounts receivable, trade	21,479	202,345
Allowances for sales rebates and loss on sales returns (Note 9)	(813)	(7,659)
Inventories (Note 6)	8,651	81,498
Deferred tax assets (Note 11)	1,080	10,174
Other current assets	320	3,015
Allowance for doubtful receivables	(103)	(970)
Total current assets	38,980	367,216
Investments:		
Marketable securities (Note 5)	1,900	17,899
Capital investments in and advances to unconsolidated subsidiaries	169	1,592
Investment securities	363	3,420
Total investments	2,432	22,911
Property, plant and equipment:		
Land	2,242	21,121
Buildings	12,798	120,565
Machinery and equipment	21,024	198,060
Construction in progress	91	857
	36,155	340,603
Accumulated depreciation (Note 7)	(21,348)	(201,112)
Total fixed assets	14,807	139,491
Other assets:		
Deferred tax assets (Note 11)	2,832	26,679
Lease guarantee deposits	814	7,669
Intangible and other assets	302	2,845
Total other assets	3,948	37,193
Total assets	¥60,167	$566,811

The accompanying notes are an integral part of these statements   (*continued*)

CONSOLIDATED BALANCE SHEETS (*continued*)
Nikken Chemicals Co., Ltd. and Consolidated Subsidiary
As of March 31, 2000

Liabilities and Shareholders' Equity	2000 Millions of Yen	2000 Thousands of U.S. Dollars (Note 3)
Current liabilities:		
Bank loans (Note 8)	¥ 6,060	$ 57,089
Current portion of long-term debt (Note 8)	40	377
Notes payable, trade	755	7,113
Accounts payable, trade	11,464	107,998
Accrued taxes on income	510	4,805
Consumption tax payable	322	3,033
Other accrued expenses	262	2,468
Other current liabilities	2,194	20,669
Total current liabilities	21,607	203,552
Long-term liabilities:		
Long-term borrowings (Note 8)	140	1,319
Accrued severance indemnities (Note 10)	9,480	89,307
Total long-term liabilities	9,620	90,626
Minority shareholders' equity in consolidated subsidiary	1,270	11,964
Commitments and contingent liabilities (Note 14)		
Shareholders' equity:		
Common stock, ¥50 par value—		
Authorized—160,000,000 shares		
Issued—71,979,164 shares	6,775	63,825
Additional paid-in capital	9,061	85,360
Legal reserve (Note 12)	881	8,300
General reserves	9,708	91,455
Unappropriated retained earnings (Note 17)	1,245	11,729
Total shareholders' equity	27,670	260,669
Liabilities and shareholders' equity	¥60,167	$566,811

The accompanying notes are an integral part of these statements.

CONSOLIDATED STATEMENTS OF INCOME
Nikken Chemicals Co., Ltd. and Consolidated Subsidiary
As of March 31, 2000

	2000 Millions of Yen	2000 Thousands of U.S. Dollars (Note 3)
Net sales	¥59,793	$563,288
Cost of sale	37,063	349,157
Gross profit	22,730	214,131
Selling, general and administrative expenses (Note 13)	20,584	193,914
Operating income	2,146	20,217
Other income (expenses):		
Interest and dividend income	132	1,244
Interest expenses	(48)	(452)
Provisions for severance indemnities for prior years	(4,358)	(41,055)
Amortization of prior service costs of pensions for prior years.	(724)	(6,821)
Reversal of money received attributable to warrants.	1,281	12,068
Loss on disposal of fixed assets	(57)	(537)
Other, net	367	3,457
	(3,407)	(32,096)
Income before income taxes	(1,261)	(11,879)
Income taxes (Note 11):		
Current provision	1,651	15,553
Deferred benefits	(2,083)	(19,623)
	(432)	(4,070)
Loss before minority interest	(829)	(7,809)
Minority interest in income in consolidated subsidiary	116	1,093
Net loss	¥ (945)	$ (8,902)

	Yen	U.S. dollars (Note 3)
Per share of common stock:		
Net income:		
Basic	¥(12.79)	$(0.120)
Fully-diluted.	(12.79)	(0.120)
Cash dividends	5.50	0.052

Pro forma amounts assuming the methods of (1) providing the methods of accruing severance indemnities and (2) amortization of prior service costs of pension are applied retroactively:

	2000 Millions of Yen	2000 Thousands of U.S. Dollars (Note 3)
Net income	¥1,799	$16,948

	Yen	U.S. Dollars (Note 3)
Net income per share	¥24.30	$0.229

The accompanying notes are an integral part of these statements.

CONSOLIDATED STATEMENTS OF SHAREHOLDERS' EQUITY
Nikken Chemicals Co., Ltd. and Consolidated Subsidiary
As of March 31, 2000

	Number of Shares Issued	Common Stock	Additional Paid-in Capital	Legal Reserve	General Reserves	Unappropriated Retained Earnings
			Millions of Yen			
Balance, April 1, 1999	74,259,164	¥6,775	¥10,029	¥835	¥8,981	¥1,658
2000 net income						(945)
Cash dividends						(433)
Transfer to legal reserve				46		(46)
Transfer to general reserves					727	(727)
Bonuses to directors						(38)
Retirement of treasury shares	(2,280,000)		(968)			
Deferred tax assets, prior years						1,776
Balance, March 31, 2000	71,979,164	¥6,775	¥ 9,061	¥881	¥9,708	¥1,245
			Thousands of U.S. Dollars (Note 3)			
Balance, April 1, 1999		$63,825	$94,479	$7,867	$84,606	$15,619
2000 net income						(8,902)
Cash dividends						(4,079)
Transfer to legal reserve				433		(433)
Transfer to general reserves					6,849	(6,849)
Bonuses to directors						(358)
Retirement of treasury shares			(9,119)			
Deferred tax assets, prior years						16,731
Balance, March 31, 2000		$63,825	$85,360	$8,300	$91,455	$11,729

The accompanying notes are an integral part of these statements.

CONSOLIDATED STATEMENTS OF CASH FLOWS
Nikken Chemicals Co., Ltd. and Consolidated Subsidiary
For the year ended March 31, 2000

	2000 Millions of Yen	2000 Thousands of U.S. Dollars (Note 3)
Cash flows from operating activities:		
Net loss ...	¥ (945)	$(8,902)
Adjustments to reconcile net income to net cash provided by operating activities—		
Depreciation and amortization	2,418	22,779
Loss on disposal of fixed assets.	58	546
Provision for severance indemnities	4,452	41,941
Deferred tax assets	(2,083)	(19,623)
Realized exchange gain on bonds with warrants	1,199	11,295
Reversal of money received attributable to warrants.	(1,281)	(12,068)
Write-down of securities	1	9
Dividend on company-owned group life insurance policy	(43)	(405)
Bonuses to directors	(38)	(358)
Minority interest in consolidated subsidiary	116	1,093
Changes in operating assets and liabilities—		
Trade receivables	806	7,593
Inventories	(413)	(3,891)
Other current assets	193	1,818
Trade payables	(1,154)	(10,871)
Accrued expenses and other current liabilities	(797)	(7,508)
Net cash provided by operating activities	2,489	23,448
Cash flows from investing activities:		
Acquisition of fixed assets	(4,725)	(44,512)
Disposal of fixed assets	(20)	(188)
Decrease in marketable securities	421	3,966
Refund of company-owned group life insurance policy	3,268	30,786
Other decrease in investments and other	403	3,796
Net cash used for investing activities	(653)	(6,152)
Cash flows from financing activities:		
Increase in bank loans	5,000	47,103
Borrowing of long-term bank loans	200	1,884
Repayment of long-term bank loans	(320)	(3,015)
Redemption of guaranteed bonds with warrants	(10,564)	(99,520)
Cash	(433)	(4,079)
Retirement of shares acquired.	(968)	(9,118)
Net cash used for financing activities	(7,085)	(66,745)
Net decrease in cash and cash equivalents	(5,249)	(49,449)
Cash and cash equivalents at:		
Beginning of period	7,388	69,600
End of period	¥ 2,139	$20,151
Supplemental information on cash flows:		
Cash paid during the period for—		
Interest	¥76	$716
Income taxes	2,821	26,576

The accompanying notes are an integral part of these statements.

NOTES TO CONSOLIDATED FINANCIAL STATEMENTS
Nikken Chemicals Co., Ltd. and Consolidated Subsidiary

1. Basis of presenting consolidated financial statements:
The Company and its subsidiaries maintain record[s] and prepare their financial statements in accordance with accounting principles generally accepted in Japan. The accompanying consolidated financial statements, which are also prepared in accordance with accounting principles generally accepted in Japan, incorporate certain modifications in format to the statutory financial statements and include statements of shareholders' equity and certain additional notes which were not contained in the statutory financial statements, so as to make the financial statements more meaningful to readers outside Japan. These modifications have no effect on net income or shareholders' equity. Up to the year ended March 31, 1999 the Company did not prepare the consolidated financial statements as there had been no significant subsidiary. During the current year the Japanese consolidation principles was revised with respect to the definition of a subsidiary being an enterprise which is controlled by another enterprise. As a result an affiliate owned 50-percent or less voting rights may be a subsidiary if a shareholder has control (the power to govern the financial and operating policies of such affiliate so as to obtain benefits from its activities). Based on the new definition of a subsidiary Nikken Fine Chemicals Co., Ltd. mentioned below is now classified as a subsidiary, and the Company prepares the consolidated financial statements for the year ended March 31, 2000.

---

2. Significant accounting policies Basis of consolidation and investments in unconsolidated subsidiaries—
The consolidated financial statements include the accounts of Nikken Chemicals Co., Ltd. and those of its 48-percent owned affiliate named Nikken Fine Chemicals Co., Ltd. (deemed subsidiary) over which the Company does have control. All significant intercompany transactions and accounts are eliminated. The other two subsidiaries are insignificant and investments therein are stated at costs.

Foreign currency securities, receivables, payables and bonds with warrants—
Marketable securities (bonds) denominated in foreign currencies are substantially covered by forward exchange contracts and are translated into yen at the forward contracted rates. Short-term receivables and payables denominated in foreign currencies are translated into yen at the exchange rate current at the end of each fiscal period. The resulting translation gains or losses are included in the determination of net income for the fiscal period. Bonds with warrants denominated in foreign currencies are also covered by forward exchange contract and are translated into yen at the forward contracted rate. The resulting translation gain is being deducted from interest expenses on such bonds or credited to interest income over the period through each maturity date for the bonds.

Accounting for sales rebates and loss on sales returns—
Sales rebates are subsequently paid to dealers against collections of sales proceeds, and are based on various factors, including each dealer's performance against its target. The allowance for rebates is provided based on outstanding receivables at year-end applying the actual sales rebates ratio for each year. The allowance for sales rebates is not deductible for tax purposes until the rebates actually take place. Sales returns are permitted within a specified period after delivery. An allowance for loss on sales returns is provided for gross profit and disposal of goods for potential sales returns. The potential loss arising from disposal of the goods accrued is not deductible for tax purposes until the return actually incurred and the loss realized.

Cash equivalents—
The Company considers all highly liquid investments with a remaining maturity of three months or less at the time of purchase to be cash equivalents.

Marketable securities—
Marketable securities (current and non-current), including equity securities, are stated at the amount of (i) the lower of the moving average cost or market for those having a ready market and (ii) the moving average cost for other securities.

Inventories—
Inventories are stated at the gross average cost.

Property, plant and equipment—
Property, plant and equipment is stated at cost. Depreciation is computed principally on the declining balance method at rates based on the estimated useful lives of the assets. Maintenance and repairs, including minor renewals and betterment, are charged to income as incurred.

Investment in company-owned group life insurance policy—
In 1997, the Company purchased a company owned group life insurance policy insuring employees' severance indemnities at their age limits. Premiums are accumulated in the policy and are accounted for as investment in company-owned group life insurance policy in the accompanying balance sheet. The invest-

ment is partially financing such severance indemnities for age limit separation. During the current year the Company surrendered such group life insurance policy.

Money received attributable to warrants—

In February 1994 the Accounting Committee of the Japanese Institute of Certified Public Accountants issued the guidance on accounting treatment on bonds with warrants effective from the fiscal period beginning on or after April 1, 1994. Such guidance is recognized as authoritative pronouncements on the generally accepted accounting principles in Japan. The guidance requires that bonds and warrants be separately accounted for to reflect the privilege of the lower rate of interest on such bonds with warrants than that on straight bonds. The face value (or issue value) of such bonds is recorded as long-term debt and the hypothetical proceeds only attributable to the assumed straight bonds under the same level of contractual debt servicing cost are presumed to be received by an issuing corporation, and the difference between the face value and such attributable proceeds is accounted for as "bond discount." The "bond discount" is being amortized over a period to the maturity of the bonds. The appraised value of the warrants, which is equivalent to the amount of "bond discount," is accounted for as "Money received attributable to warrants" in the current liabilities, and the proceeds thereof are included in cash together with a portion for the proceeds attributable to the assumed straight bonds as mentioned above. The balance of the "Money received attributable to warrants" is transferred to additional paid-in capital when warrant holders exercise their subscription rights and the remainder, if any, at the time of expiration of warrants is reversed to income. During the current year the balance of the money received attributable to warrants was reversed to income as expired.

Accrued severance indemnities—

Employees whose service with the Company and its consolidated subsidiary is terminated are, under most circumstances, entitled to lump-sum severance indemnities, determined by reference to current basic rate of pay, length of service and the conditions under which the termination occurs. The recorded liability for employees' severance indemnities at March 31, 1999 represents the present value of the amount (vested benefit) which would be required to be paid if all the eligible employees voluntarily retire at that date. During the year ended March 31, 2000 the Company and its consolidated subsidiary changed their policy to accrue severance indemnities at the full amount of the vested benefits not taking into consideration of the discount factor. Management believes that the new method of accruing severance indemnities is better measure in respect of recent employees' turnover. The resultant effect of this change was to increase accrued severance indemnities at March 31, 1999 by ¥4,358 million ($41,055 thousand) and was charged to other expenses. The Company and its consolidated subsidiary have adopted funded pension plans, covering 30 percent of the retirement benefits for employees of the Company and 70 percent of its consolidated subsidiary. The benefits are payable either as a monthly pension or, under certain circumstances at the option of retiring employees, in a lump-sum amount. The Company and its consolidated subsidiary's contributions to the plan include amortization of prior service costs. The amortization of prior service costs of the Company is amortized over 10 years up to the years ended March 31, 1999, and amortized in fiscal 2000 over two years. Management of the Company also considers that this shortening of the year of the amortization is sound policy based on various factors including lower actuarial gains due to market and increasing ratio of involuntary separation, or age limit retirement. The effect of the additional charge as of March 31, 1999 of ¥724 million ($6,821 thousand) for two-year amortization was included in other expenses. The amortization of prior service costs of the consolidated subsidiary is made over three years. Retirement benefits to directors and statutory auditors are also accrued at the amount of the estimated future liability in relation to service to the balance sheet date.

Income taxes—

Up to the year ended March 31, 1999 income taxes are provided based on amounts reflected in the tax returns and deferred income taxes relating to temporary differences was not recognized as interperiod income tax allocation was not practiced in Japan. Following to the dissemination of the authoritative pronouncements on interperiod tax allocation applicable to the year ended March 31, 2000 the Company and its consolidated subsidiary recorded deferred tax assets during the current year. The resultant effect for prior years at March 31, 1999 of ¥1,776 million ($16,731 thousand) was credited to unappropriated retained earnings at March 31, 1999.

Additional paid-in capital and stock splits—

Under the Japanese Commercial Code ("the Code"), the entire amount of the issue price (or conversion price) is required to be accounted for in the common stock account although a company may, by a resolution of its board of directors, account for an amount not exceeding one-half of the issue price of the shares as additional paid-in capital. The Code provides that a "Transfer of distributable profit to the common stock account" must be approved at the general meeting of shareholders as an appropriation of unappropriated retained earnings. The Code also permits the board of directors to make a "stock split" provided (i) the aggregate par value of all issued shares after the stock split does not exceed the common stock account and (ii) the amount of aggregate net worth in the latest balance sheet divided by all issued shares after the stock split is not less than the amount of ¥50.

Dividends—

Dividends charged to unappropriated retained earnings in the accompanying statements of shareholders' equity represent (i) dividends approved at the general meeting of shareholders held during the fiscal period and paid during such period plus (ii) interim dividends paid.

Net income and dividends per share—

Basic net income per share of common stock is based on the average number of shares of common stock outstanding during each period, appropriately adjusted for stock splits. Common stock equivalents on warrants and convertible notes are not taken into consideration for the above computation. Fully-diluted net income per share of common stock is computed assuming (i) outstanding warrants at the beginning of period are all exercised at that date reflecting average market price of the common shares and (ii) outstanding convertible notes at that date are all converted to common shares after adjustment of after-tax debt servicing costs, unless antidilutive effect results. The aforementioned basic and fully-diluted net income per share computation is based on the revision of the Ruling applicable to the financial statements for public corporations, effective from the fiscal year commencing April 1, 1995 and there-after. For fiscal 2000, fully-diluted net income per common stock is considered to be the same as basic net income per common stock, since the effect of potentially dilutive securities would be antidilutive. Cash dividends per share for each period in the accompanying statements of income represent dividends declared as applicable to the respective period, after appropriated adjustment for stock splits.

Stock and bond issue costs—

Stock and bond issue costs are charged to income as incurred.

3. U.S. dollar amounts:

The U.S. dollar amounts are included solely for convenience and have been translated as a matter of arithmetical computation only at the rate of ¥106.15 = $1, the current rate on March 31, 2000. This translation should not be construed as a representation that the Yen amounts actually represent, or could be converted into, U.S. dollars.

4. Cash and cash equivalents:

Cash and cash equivalents consist of the following:

	March 31, 2000	
	Millions of Yen	Thousands of U.S. Dollars (Note 3)
Demand deposits with banks and minor cash on hand	¥ 625	$ 5,888
Money market funds.	1,514	14,263
	¥2,139	$20,151

5. Marketable securities:

The aggregate cost and market value of marketable equity securities (non-current) of the Company are shown below:

	March 31, 2000	
At fiscal period end:	Millions of Yen	Thousands of U.S. Dollars (Note 3)
Aggregate cost	¥1,900	$17,899
Marketable value	2,944	27,734

6. Inventories:

Inventories comprise the following:

	March 31, 2000	
At fiscal period end:	Millions of Yen	Thousands of U.S. Dollars (Note 3)
Merchandise	¥2,875	$27,084
Finished products	3,954	37,249
Raw materials	701	6,604
Work in process	1,109	10,448
Supplies	12	113
	¥8,651	$81,498

7. Depreciation:

The estimated useful lives of fixed assets for computing depreciation, which are identical with the useful lives stipulated under the Japanese income tax regulations, are shown below:

	Years
Building, currently effective	3 to 50
Machinery and equipment	3 to 15

8. Bank loans:

Bank loans of ¥6,060 million ($57,089 thousand) at March 31, 2000 represent unsecured ninety-day notes payable bearing average annual interest of 1.375 percent, renewable at maturity. The unsecured long term bank loans of ¥180 million ($1,696 thousand), including current portion of ¥40 million ($377 thousand), at March 31, 2000 bears average annual interest of 2.210 percent.

9. Allowances for sales rebates and loss on sales returns:

Allowances for sales rebates and loss on sales returns consist of the following:

	March 31, 2000	
At fiscal period end:	Millions of Yen	Thousands of U.S. Dollars (Note 3)
Sales rebates	¥640	$6,029
Loss on sales returns	173	1,630
	¥813	$7,659

10. Severance indemnities:

The charges to income for severance indemnities and pension benefits to employees were as follows:

	Millions of Yen	Thousands of U.S. Dollars (Note 3)
Year ended March 31, 2000 (including amounts applicable to prior years of ¥5,082 million – $47,876 thousand, See Note 2)	¥5,999	$56,514
The charges to income for retirement benefits to directors and statutory auditors were as follows:	Millions of Yen	Thousands of U.S. Dollars (Note 3)
Year ended march 31, 2000	¥116	$1,093

Unfunded prior service cost in respect of pension benefits as of March 31, 2000 (the last valuation date of the pension fund) was ¥878 million ($8,271 thousand).

11. Income taxes:

The Company and its subsidiary are subject to a number of different income taxes which, in the aggregate, indicate a normal statutory tax rate of approximately 42 percent for the year ended March 31, 2000. The ordinary relationship between income tax expenses and pretax accounting income is distorted by a number of items, including temporary differences, various tax credits and the non-deductibility of certain expenses.

During the year ended March 31, 2000 the Company newly adopted interperiod tax allocation method and recorded deferred tax assets at March 31, 2000. The significant components of deferred tax assets and liabilities at March 31, 2000 are as shown below:

	March 31, 2000	
	Millions of Yen	Thousands of U.S. Dollars (Note 3)
Deferred tax assets—		
Deferred tax assets, current—		
Allowance for sales rebates	¥ 269	$ 2,534
Write-down of inventories	289	2,722
Other	522	4,918
	¥1,080	$10,174

(*continued*)

(*Continued*)

	March 31, 2000	
	Millions of Yen	Thousands of U.S. Dollars (Note 3)
Deferred tax assets, noncurrent—		
Accrued severance indemnities	¥2,728	$25,699
Other	176	1,658
	¥2,904	$27,357
Deferred tax liability—		
Deferred capital gain on sale of land	(72)	(678)
Deferred tax assets, noncurrent, net	¥2,832	$26,679

A reconciliation between the normal statutory tax (benefit) rate and the reported actual tax (benefit) rate is as shown below:

Reconciliation of tax rate	
"Expected" income tax (benefit) rate (normal statutory tax rate)	(42)%
Entertainment expense and other expense not deductible	19
Dividend income and other income not	(1)
Other	(10)
Actual income tax (benefit) rate (reported tax rate)	(34)%

12. Legal reserve:

The Code provides that an amount equal to at least 10 percent of cash outlays including each dividends and bonuses to directors be appropriated as a legal reserve. No further appropriation is required when the legal reserve equals 25 percent of the common stock account.

13. Research and development expenses:

Research and development expenses which were included in selling, general and administrative expenses were as follows:

	Millions of Yen	Thousands of U.S. Dollars (Note 3)
Year ended March 31, 2000	¥3,678	$34,649

14. Commitments and contingent liabilities:

Commitments outstanding as of March 31, 2000 for the purchase of property, plant and equipment were approximately ¥1,512 million ($14,244 thousand).

Rental expenses are shown below:

	Millions of Yen	Thousands of U.S. Dollars (Note 3)
Year ended March 31, 2000	¥1,817	$17,112

A significant portion of such rentals relates to cancelable short-term leases, many of which are renewed upon expiration.

Contingent liabilities for notes discounted at March 31, 2000 amounted to ¥900 million ($8,479 thousand).

15. Derivative instrument:

Derivative instruments as of March 31, 2000 comprise mainly currency swap agreements on marketable securities denominated in U.S. dollars into Yen. As described in Note 2 such marketable securities are recorded at the yen amounts receivable under such swap agreements.

16. Segment information:

Operating segment information for the year ended March 31, 2000 is shown below:

	Pharma-ceuticals	Fine Chemicals	Eliminations Corporate	Consolidated total	Pharma-ceuticals	Fine Chemicals	Elimination, Corporate	Consolidated total
	Millions of Yen				Thousands of U.S. Dollars (Note 3)			
Sales								
External customers	¥47,976	¥11,817	¥ —	¥59,793	$451,964	$111,324	$ —	$563,288
Intersegments	—	325	(325)	—	—	3,062	(3,062)	—
Total	47,976	12,142	(325)	59,793	451,964	114,386	(3,062)	563,288
Operating expenses	42,566	13,877	1,204	57,647	400,999	130,730	11,342	543,071
Operating income (loss)	¥ 5,410	¥(1,735)	¥(1,529)	¥2,146	$ 50,965	$(16,344)	$(14,404)	$ 20,217
Total assets	¥44,279	¥10,051	¥ 5,837	¥60,167	$417,136	$ 94,687	$ 54,988	$566,811
Depreciation	1,809	593	6	2,408	17,042	5,586	57	22,685
Capital expenditures	783	167	2	952	7,376	1,573	19	8,968

The Company and its subsidiary have no subsidiary or branch abroad nor overseas sales.

17. Subsequent events:

The following appropriations of unappropriated retained earnings of the Company for the year ended March 31, 2000 were approved at the general meeting of the shareholders held in June, 2000.

	Millions of Yen	Thousands of U.S. Dollars (Note 3)
Appropriations for—	¥ 198	$1,865
Transfer to legal reserve	20	188
Unappropriated balance carried forward	831	7,829
	¥1,049	$9,882

The above appropriations are not reflected in the accompanying financial statements (See "Dividends" in Note 2 above). The cash dividends were paid and recorded in June, 2000.

In May 2000 the Company acquired its 2,280,000 shares from the market and retired such treasury shares with a reversal of additional paid-in capital by the amount of ¥968 million ($9,119 thousand) which is equivalent to the aggregate cost of such treasury shares.

REPORT OF INDEPENDENT CERTIFIED PUBLIC ACCOUNTANTS

To the Board of Directors
of Nikken Chemicals Co., Ltd.

We have audited the accompanying consolidated balance sheet of Nikken Chemicals Co., Ltd., and its consolidated subsidiary as of March 31, 2000, and the related consolidated statement of income, shareholders' equity, and cash flows for the year then ended, stated in yen. These financial statements are the responsibility of the Company's management. Our responsibility is to express an opinion on these financial statements based on our audit.

We conducted our audit in accordance with auditing standards generally accepted in Japan. Those standards require that we plan and perform the audit to obtain reasonable assurance about whether the financial statements are free of material misstatement. An audit includes examining, on a test basis, evidence supporting the amounts and disclosures in the financial statements. An audit also includes assessing the accounting principles used and significant estimates made by management, as well as evaluating the overall financial statement presentation. We believe that our audit provides a reasonable basis for our opinion.

In our opinion, the consolidated financial statements audited by us present fairly, in all material respects, the financial position of Nikken Chemicals Co., Ltd., and its consolidated subsidiary as of March 31, 2000, and the results of their operations and their cash flows for the year then ended in conformity with accounting principles generally accepted in Japan.

As discussed in Note 2, the Company and its consolidated subsidiary changed their methods of accounting for accrued severance indemnities and amortization of prior service costs of pensions during the year ended March 31, 2000.

The United States dollar amounts in the consolidated financial statements have been translated for convenience only on the basis described in Note 3.

Tokyo, Japan
June 29, 2000

Toyo & Co.
TOYO & CO

Appendix 1-3

STOCK EXCHANGE WEB SITES

Country	Stock Exchange	Web Site
Argentina	Buenos Aires	www.bcba.sba.com.ar
Australia	Australia	www.asx.com.au
Austria	Vienna	www.wbag.at
Azerbaijan	Baku	www.az/bicex
Belgium	Euronext—Belgium	www.euronext.com
		www.stockexchange.be/enindex.htm
Bermuda	Bermuda	www.bsx.com
Brazil	Rio de Janeiro	www.bvrj.com.br (Portuguese only)
Brazil	Sao Paulo	www.bovespa.com.br (Portuguese only)
Canada	Montréal	www.me.org
Canada	Toronto	www.tse.com
Canada	Canadian Venture	www.cdnx.ca
Chile	Santiago	www.bolsadesantiago.com
China	Schenzhen	222.sse.org.cn
Colombia	Bogotá	www.bolsabogata.com.co/ (Spanish only)
Colombia	Medellín	www.bolsamed.com.co (Spanish only)
Croatia	Zagreb	www.zse.hr
Czech Republic	Prague	www.pse.cz
Denmark	Copenhagen	www.xcse.dk
Finland	Helsinki	www.hex.fi
France	Paris	www.euronext.com
		www.bourse-de-paris.fr/defaultgb.htm
Germany	Deutsche Börse	deutsche-boerse.com/
Greece	Athens	www.ase.gr
Hong Kong	Hong Kong	www.hkex.com.hk
India	National Stock Exchange	www.nseindia.com
India	Surabaya	www.bes.co.id
Indonesia	Jakarta	www.jsx.co.id
Iran	Tehran	www.tse.or.ir
Israel	Tel-Aviv	hebrew.tase.co.il/www/intro.asp
Italy	Italy	www.borsaitalia.it
Japan	Osaka	www.ose.or.jp
Japan	Tokyo	www.tse.or.jp
Jordan	Amman	www.access2arabia.com/AFM/
Luxembourg	Luxembourg	www.bourse.lu
Macedonia	Macedonian	www.mse.org.mk
Malaysia	Kuala Lumpur	www.klse.com.my
Mexico	Mexico	www.bmv.com.mx
Netherlands	Euronext—Netherlands	www.euronext.com
		www.aex.nl/aex.asp?taal=en
New Zealand	New Zealand	www.nzse.co.nz
Norway	Oslo	www.ose.no

Pakistan	Lahore	www.lse.brain.net.pk
Peru	Lima	www.bvl.com.pe
Philippines	Philippines	www.pse.org.ph
Poland	Warsaw	www.gpw.com.pl
Portugal	Lisbon	www.bvl.pt
Russia	Siberian	www.sse.nsk.su (Russian only)
Singapore	Singapore	www.ses.com.sg
Slovakia	Bratislava	www.bsse.sk
Slovenia	Ljubljana	www.ljse.si
South Africa	Johannesburg	www.jse.co.za
South Korea	Korea	www.kse.or.kr
Spain	Barcelona	www.borsabcn.es
Spain	Bilbao	www.bolsabilbao.es
Spain	Madrid	www.bolsamadrid.es
Sweden	Stockholm	www.xsse.se
Switzerland	Swiss	www.swx.ch
Taiwan	Taiwan	www.tse.com.tw
Thailand	Thailand	www.set.or.th
Turkey	Istanbul	www.ise.org
United Kingdom	London	www.londonstockexchange.com
United States	American (Amex)	www.amex.com
United States	Chicago	www.chicagostockex.com
United States	Nasdaq	www.nasdaq.com
		www.nasdaqnews.com
		www.nasdr.com
		www.nasdaqtrader.com
United States	New York	www.nyse.com

Note: All Web site addresses here begin with the prefix http://

Selected References

Agmon, T., Who Gets What: The MNE, the National State and the Distributional Effects of Globalization, *Journal of International Business Studies,* 34, No. 5 (2003): 416–427.

Beim, David O., and Charles W. Calomiris, *Emerging Financial Markets,* Boston: McGraw-Hill Irwin, 2001.

Bloomenthal, Harold S., and Samuel Wolff, eds., *International Capital Markets and Securities Regulation—Securities Law Series,* New York: West Group, December 2000.

Buckley, Peter J., and M. Casson, "The Future of the Multinational Enterprise in Retrospect and in Prospect," *Journal of International Business Studies,* 34, No.2 (2003): 219–222.

Eiteman, David K., Arthur I. Stonehill, and Michael H. Moffett, *Multinational Business Finance, 9th ed.,* New York: Addison-Wesley, 2001.

Federation of European Stock Exchanges (FESE), *Annual Report 2000,* Brussels: Federation of European Stock Exchanges, June 2001.

Gros, Daniel, and Karel Lannoo, *The Euro Capital Market,* West Sussex, England: John Wiley & Sons, 2000.

Hodgetts, Sally, ed., *2000 International Investment Review,* London: Euromoney Institutional Investor PLC, 2000.

Levinson, Marc, *Guide to Financial Markets, 2nd ed.,* London: The Economist Newspaper Ltd., 2000.

Makhija, Mona V., and Alice C. Stewart, "The Effect of National Context on Perceptions of Risk: A Comparison of Planned Versus Free-Market Managers," *Journal of International Business Studies,* 33, No. 4 (2002): 737–756.

Nachum, Lilach, "International Business in a World of Increasing Returns," *Management International Review,* 43, No. 2 (2003): 219–245.

Nobes, Christopher W., *GAAP 2000: A Survey of National Accounting Rules in 53 Countries,* London: Arthur Andersen, BDO, Deloitte Touche Tohmatsu, Ernst & Young International, Grant Thornton, KPMG, PricewaterhouseCoopers, 2000.

Nunnenkamp, Peter, and Julius Spatz, "Determinants of FDI in Developing Countries: Has Globalization Changed the Rules of the Game?" *Transnational Corporations,* 11, No. 2 (August 2002): 1–34.

PricewaterhouseCoopers LLC, *Doing Business In Series,* New York: PricewaterhouseCoopers, periodic updates.

Rathborne, David, and Deborah Ritchie, eds., *The Salomon Smith Barney Guide to World Equity Markets 2000,* London: Euromoney Books and Salomon Smith Barney, 2000.

Rosen, Robert C., ed., *International Securities Regulation: Stock Exchanges of the World: Selected Rules and Regulations,* Dobbs Ferry, N.Y.: Oceana Publications, 2000.

Standard & Poor's, *Emerging Markets Factbook 2000,* New York: May 2000.

Uhlfelder, Eric, *Investing in the New Europe,* Princeton, N.J.: Bloomberg Press, 2001.

Valdez, Stephen, *An Introduction to Global Financial Markets,* 3rd ed., London: Macmillan, 2000.

Discussion Questions

1. Some observers suggest that multinational enterprises are tightly controlled by many (and often conflicting) national laws. Others contend that no effective international law governs multinationals, and that this allows them too many freedoms and privileges. What do these two positions imply for future developments in international accounting? Answer in the form of two concise paragraphs.

2. Some have advocated that a single, widely spoken language be designated as the formal international accounting language. Write a two-paragraph statement in favor of choosing English as the designated language.

3. Explain the term *global capital markets.* This chapter primarily discusses global equity markets. What other types of financial instruments are traded in these markets? How important are global capital markets in the world economy?

4. Discuss at least three trends that clearly indicate the growing internationalization of financial markets.

5. Why have international accounting issues grown in importance and complexity in recent years?

6. Accounting may be viewed as having three components: measurement, disclosure, and auditing. What are the advantages and disadvantages of this classification? Can you suggest alternative classifications that might be useful?

7. Examine Exhibit 1-5. Why do you think Sandvik has chosen to own 100%, or close to 100%, of most of its foreign operations?

8. Capital markets often are grouped into two categories: those in developed countries and those in emerging market countries. Give your own definitions of

developed and emerging market countries. Which stock exchanges shown in Appendix 1-3 are in emerging market countries? What characteristics do they share?

9. Apendix 1-1 shows that between 1973 and 1996, national governments in many countries sold shares in state-owned financial institutions to nongovernmental entities. Discuss how these privatizations might affect the capital markets as well as the accounting systems of these companies.

10. Provide possible explanations for the low numbers of foreign listed companies that one observes in the Czech Republic, Mexico, Taiwan, and China.

11. Given the international heritage of accounting, do you feel that efforts to harmonize global accounting standards is a good thing? Why or why not?

12. Outsourcing, especially from vendors located abroad, has become a politically sensitive issue, especially in the United States of late. Do you think this argument has merit? What are the consequences of this debate for international accounting?

Exercises

1. In the second edition of this textbook (Prentice Hall, 1992) F.D.S. Choi and G. G. Mueller define international accounting as follows:

     International accounting extends general purpose, nationally oriented accounting in its broadest sense to: (1) international comparative analysis, (2) accounting measurement and reporting issues unique to multinational business transactions and the business form of the multinational enterprise, (3) accounting needs of international financial markets, and (4) harmonization of worldwide accounting and financial reporting diversity via political, organizational, professional, and standard-setting activities.

     Required: Critically evaluate the listed definition of international accounting. Propose changes to improve the definition, providing justification for any proposed changes. Alternatively, present your own definition of international accounting, and compare and contrast it with the Choi and Mueller definition.

2. The International Accounting Standards Committee (now the International Accounting Standards Board [IASB]) was founded in 1973 to promote worldwide accounting harmonization and to develop and encourage the use of International Accounting Standards.

     Required: Use your library or the World Wide Web to learn more about the IASB. (The IASB's Web site is http://www.iasb.org.) What are International Accounting Standards? How do individual companies and countries around the world use them?

3. The International Federation of Accountants (IFAC) is an organization of more than 100 professional accountancy bodies that promotes international auditing harmonization.

     Required: Use your library or the World Wide Web to learn more about IFAC's history and activities. (IFAC's Web site is http://www.ifac.org.) What are

International Standards on Auditing? Why have they been developed? How are they being used around the world?

4. Examine the Web sites of five exchanges listed in Appendix 1-3 that you feel would be most attractive to foreign listers. Which exchange in your chosen set proved most popular during the last two years? Provide possible explanations for your observation.

   Required: Rank the five exchanges with the highest number of foreign listings as of December 31, 2002, and note the trend in foreign listings on these exchanges between 2001 and 2002. Provide possible explanations for the popularity of these exchanges for foreign listers and reasons for the trends you observe.

5. Examine Exhibit 1-4. What international reporting issues are triggered by AKZO Nobel's foreign operations disclosures for investors? For managerial accountants?

6. Revisit Exhibit 1-6 and show how the ROE statistics of 18.4% and 19.2% were derived. Which of the two is the better performance measure to use when comparing Electrolux's performance with that of Maytag, the parent company of Hoover, which makes vacuum cleaners and other household products?

7. Exhibit 1-5 lists all of Sandvik's major foreign operating subsidiaries. In preparing consolidated accounts for its major shareholders, Sandvik must restate the financial accounts of its subsidiaries, which are kept in the currencies of each host country, to Swedish krone. What relation, if any, does this translation process have with the translation process described in Note 3 to Nikken Chemicals' financial statements contained in Appendix 1-2?

8. Revisit Appendix 1-3 and examine the listing statistics, both domestic and foreign, for the following exchanges: Deutsche Borse, London, Mexico, NYSE, Prague, Shenzhen, Taiwan, and Tokyo. Partition this group evenly into two categories that make sense to you. Examine the comparative listing statistics for both groups and then formulate your own hypotheses as to differences in disclosure, auditing, accounting measurement, and other institutional arrangements that might explain the disparities that you observe.

9. The World Wide Web provides low-cost access to a vast amount of information about financial reporting requirements and practices worldwide.

   Required: Refer to Appendix 1-3, which provides Web site addresses for stock exchanges in more than 50 countries. Select a stock exchange and do a Web search for information about financial reporting requirements for listed companies in that market. (Many stock exchange Web sites provide information on their own financial reporting requirements, such as those related to annual and interim reporting, and links to national securities regulatory bodies.) Present a brief overview of financial reporting regulation of the stock exchange you select. (Note: The IASB Web site, at www.iasb.org, also presents information about accounting principle requirements at stock exchanges around the world.)

10. Stock exchange Web sites vary considerably in the information they provide and their ease of use.

Required: Select any two of the stock exchanges presented in Appendix 1-3. Explore the Web sites of each of these stock exchanges. Prepare a table that compares and contrasts the sites for types and quality of information presented and the ease of using the Web site. Are English-language press releases of listed companies available? Links to listed companies' Web sites? Listing requirements? Price and volume data for listed securities? Helpful information for investors?

11. Refer to Appendix 1-2, which presents the income tax footnote (Note 11) from Nikken Chemical Co. Ltd.'s 2000 annual report.

    Required: What information about income taxes is not disclosed by Nikken that would be disclosed by a publicly traded company in your home country?

12. Refer to Nikken Chemical Co. Ltd.'s 2000 financial statements (including notes and auditor's report) in Appendix 1-2. Also consider an annual report for a publicly traded manufacturing company in your country.

    Required: Discuss five important differences between Nikken's financial statements and those of the company in your country.

CASE 1-1   E-CENTIVES, INC.—RAISING CAPITAL IN SWITZERLAND

On October 3, 2000, E-centives, incorporated in the United States, made an initial public offering on the Swiss Stock Exchange's New Market. The company raised approximately US$40 million. E-centive's offering circular stated that no offers or sales of the company's common stock would be made in the United States, and that there would be no public market for the common stock in the United States after the offering.

THE SWISS EXCHANGE'S NEW MARKET

The Swiss Exchange launched the New Market in 1999. The New Market is designed to meet the financing needs of rapidly growing companies from Switzerland and abroad. It provides firms with a simplified means of entry to the Swiss capital markets. Listing requirements for the New Market are simple. For example, companies must have an operating track record of 12 months, the initial public listing must involve a capital increase, and to ensure market liquidity, a bank must agree to make a market in the securities.

E-centives

E-centives, Inc., is a leading online direct marketing infrastructure company. The company offers systems and technologies that enable businesses to build large, rich databases of consumer profiles and interests. In return, consumers receive a free personalized service that provides them with promotional offers based on their interests. At the time of the public offering, E-centives maintained over 4.4 million e-centives online accounts for members. The company does not charge members a fee for its service. Instead, the company generates revenue primarily from marketers whose marketing matter is delivered to targeted groups of E-centives members. E-centives currently employs more than 100 people in its Bethesda, Maryland headquarters, and its offices in Redwood City, New York, and Los Angeles.

As of the offering date, the company had little revenue and had not been profitable. Revenue for the year-ended December 31, 1999, was US$740,000, with a net loss of about US$16 million. As of June 30, 2000, the company had an accumulated deficit of about US$39 million. E-centives' growth strategy is to expand internationally. To date, the company has focused on pursuing opportunities in the United States. E-centives intends to expand into Europe and other countries. The company is currently considering expanding into Switzerland, the United Kingdom, and Germany.[19]

REQUIRED

1. Refer to Exhibit 1-7, which lists factors relevant for choosing an overseas market for listing or raising capital. Which factors might have been relevant in E-centives' decision to raise capital and list on the Swiss Exchange's New Market?
2. Why do you believe E-centives chose not to raise public equity in the United States? What are the potential drawbacks related to E-centives' decision *not* to raise capital in the U.S. public markets?

---

[19]From E-centives' offering circular dated October 2, 2000.

3. What are the advantages and disadvantages to E-centives of using U.S. GAAP?
4. Should the SWX Swiss Exchange require E-centives to prepare its financial statements using Swiss accounting standards?
5. Learn more about the New Market at the SWX Swiss Exchange's Web site (http://www.swx.com). What are the listing requirements for the New Market? What are the financial reporting requirements? Does E-centives appear to fit the profile of the typical New Market company?

CASE 1-2   NIKKEN CHEMICALS CO., LTD.

Appendix 1-2 contains the financial statements (including notes) and auditor's report (Report of Independent Certified Public Accountants) from Nikken Chemicals Co., Ltd.'s 2000 Annual Report. Nikken Chemicals, founded in 1947, develops, manufactures, and markets pharmaceuticals. Nikken Chemicals' common stock is listed on the Tokyo Stock Exchange but not on any overseas markets. The company reported 2000 net sales of more than US$550 million.

A potential investor or business partner from outside Japan would need to consider many international accounting issues to effectively use the information in Nikken's Annual Report. What accounting principles are used? Should the financial statements be restated to a different set of accounting principles to be more useful? What types of information does Nikken *not* disclose that one would expect to find in financial statements of companies from the United States, the United Kingdom, or Canada? How does one compensate for Nikken's limited disclosure? What does the auditor's report reveal about the level of audit quality? What auditing standards were used? Are they acceptable? Does the auditor's opinion mean the same thing in Japan as it does in the reader's home country? How does Nikken account for marketable securities (refer to Notes 2 and 5 in its financial statements)? Is this approach different from or similar to the accounting approach used in financial statements from the reader's home country?

Nikken's financial statements also raise many managerial and tax issues with international dimensions. How are transactions in foreign currencies and financial instruments accounted for? What are the related financial statement disclosures? Does the financial reporting of these items provide useful information to managers for managing transactions in these areas? Does Nikken's tax expense reflect domestic taxes only? What are the tax consequences to Nikken of doing business abroad?

CHAPTER

2

DEVELOPMENT AND CLASSIFICATION

Accounting must respond to the ever-changing information needs of society and reflect the cultural, economic, legal, social, and political conditions within which it operates. The history of accounting and accountants reveals continuing change. At first, accounting was little more than a recording system for certain banking services and tax collection schemes. Double-entry bookkeeping systems were later developed to meet the needs of trading ventures. Industrialization and division of labor made cost behavior analysis and managerial accounting possible. The rise of the modern corporation stimulated periodic financial reporting and auditing. In keeping with society's increased environmental concerns and concerns over corporate integrity, accountants have found ways to measure and report environmental remediation liabilities and uncover money laundering and similar related white-collar crimes. It provides decision information for huge domestic and international public securities markets. It has extended into management consulting and incorporates ever-increasing information technology within its systems and procedures.

Why should we know how and why accounting develops? The answer is the same as it is for developmental studies in other fields. We can better understand a nation's accounting system by knowing the underlying factors that influence its development. Accounting clearly differs around the world, and knowledge of the developmental factors helps us see why. In other words, observable differences—as well as similarities—can be explained by these factors. Because accounting responds to its environment, different cultural, economic, legal, and political environments produce different accounting systems, and similar environments produce similar systems.

This leads us to classification. Why should we classify (compare) national or regional financial accounting systems? Classification is fundamental to understanding and analyzing why and how national accounting systems differ. We can also analyze whether these systems are converging or diverging. The goal of classification is to group financial accounting systems according to their distinctive characteristics. Classifications reveal fundamental structures that group members have in common and that distinguish the various groups from each other. By identifying similarities and differences, our understanding of accounting systems is improved. Classifications are a way of viewing the world.

DEVELOPMENT

Every nation's accounting standards and practices result from a complex interaction of economic, historical, institutional, and cultural factors. Diversity among nations is to be expected. The factors that influence national accounting development also help explain accounting diversity among nations.

We believe the following eight factors have a significant influence on accounting development. The first seven are economic, sociohistorical, and/or institutional in nature, and they have occupied most of the attention of accounting writers. More recently, the relationship between culture (the eighth item below) and accounting development has begun to be explored.

1. ***Sources of Finance.***   In countries with strong equity markets, such as the United States and United Kingdom, accounting focuses on how well management runs the company (profitability), and is designed to help investors assess future cash flows and the associated risks. Disclosures are extensive to meet the requirements of widespread public ownership. By contrast, in credit-based systems where banks are the dominant source of finance, accounting focuses on creditor protection through conservative accounting measurements. Because financial institutions have direct access to any information they want, extensive public disclosures are not considered necessary. Japan and Switzerland are examples.[1]

2. ***Legal System.***   The legal system determines how individuals and institutions interact. The Western world has two basic orientations: code (or civil) law and common (or case) law. Code law derives mainly from Roman law and the Code Napoléon.[2] In code law countries, laws are an all-embracing set of requirements and procedures. Codification of accounting standards and procedures is natural and appropriate there. Thus, in code law countries, accounting rules are incorporated into national laws and tend to be highly prescriptive and procedural.[3] By contrast, common law develops on a case-by-case basis with no attempt to cover all cases in an all-encompassing code. Of course, statute law does exist, but it tends to be less detailed and more flexible than in a code law system. This encourages experimentation and permits the exercise of judgment.[4] Common law derives from English case law. In most common law countries, accounting rules are established by private-sector professional organizations. This allows

---

[1]For further discussion of this point, see C. Nobes, "Towards a General Model of the Reasons for International Differences in Financial Reporting," *Abacus* (September 1998): 162–187. He points out that *outsiders* (such as individual and institutional shareholders) normally dominate ownership in strong equity countries, causing a demand for high levels of disclosure. *Insiders* (families, other companies, government, and banks) usually dominate ownership in credit-based countries, which is why low levels of disclosure are usually found there. Germany is an exception. Even though Germany is a credit-based country, German listed companies have high disclosures because of Germany's unusually large market in listed debt (p. 169).

[2]There are three major families within the code law tradition: French, German, and Scandinavian. French and German code law, as well as the common law, spread around the world through conquest, imperialism, or copying.

[3]There are exceptions to this generalization, for example, the Netherlands (Chapter 3) and Mexico (Chapter 4), where accounting is like that in common law countries.

[4]Irving Fantl, "The Case Against International Uniformity," *Management Accounting* (May 1971): 13–16.

them to be more adaptive and innovative. Except for broad statutory requirements, most accounting rules are not incorporated directly into statute law.[5] Exhibit 2-1 lists code and common law countries.

3. ***Taxation.*** In many countries, tax legislation effectively determines accounting standards because companies must record revenues and expenses in their accounts to claim them for tax purposes. This is the case, for example, in Germany and Sweden. In other countries, such as the Netherlands, financial and tax accounting are separate: taxable profits are essentially financial accounting profits adjusted for differences with the tax laws. Of course, even where financial and tax accounting are separate, tax legislation may occasionally require the application of certain accounting principles. Last in, first out (LIFO) inventory valuation in the United States is an example.

4. ***Political and Economic Ties.*** Accounting ideas and technologies are transferred through conquest, commerce, and similar forces. Double-entry bookkeeping, which originated in Italy in the 1400s, gradually spread across Europe along with other ideas of the Renaissance. British colonialism exported accountants and accounting concepts throughout the empire. German occupation during World War II led France to adopt its Plan Compatable (see Chapter 3). The United States forced U.S.-style accounting regulatory regimes on Japan after World War II. Many developing economies use an accounting system that was developed elsewhere, either because it was imposed on them (e.g., India) or by their own choice (e.g., countries of Eastern Europe now modeling their accounting systems after European Union [EU] regulations). As discussed more generally in Chapter 8, economic integration through the growth of international trade and capital flows is a powerful motivator for the convergence of accounting standards.

5. ***Inflation.*** Inflation distorts historical cost accounting and affects the tendency of a country to incorporate price changes into the accounts. Israel, Mexico, and certain countries of South America use general price-level accounting because of their experiences with hyperinflation.[6] In the late 1970s, in response to unusually high rates of inflation, both the United States and United Kingdom experimented with reporting the effects of changing prices. Accounting responses to inflation are explored in Chapter 7.

6. ***Level of Economic Development.*** This factor affects the types of business transactions conducted in an economy and determines which ones are most prevalent. The type of transactions, in turn, determines the accounting issues that are faced. For example, stock-based executive compensation or asset securitization makes little sense in economies with underdeveloped capital markets. Today, many industrial economies are becoming service economies. Accounting

---

[5]Under martial law or other national emergency situations, all aspects of the accounting function may be regulated by some central governmental court or agency. This was the case, for instance, in Nazi Germany when intensive war preparations and World War II itself required a highly uniform national accounting system for total control of all national economic activities.

[6]*Israel Accounting Standard No. 17* requires Israeli companies to discontinue inflation-adjusted accounting effective January 1, 2004.

Exhibit 2-1 Code and Common Law Countries

Code law—French origin		Common law
Africa	The Netherlands	**Africa**
Egypt	Portugal	Kenya
	Spain	Nigeria
Americas		South Africa
Argentina	**Code law—German origin**	Zimbabwe
Brazil	**Asia**	
Chile	Japan	**Americas**
Colombia	South Korea	Canada
Ecuador	Taiwan	United States
Mexico		
Peru	**Europe**	**Asia**
Uruguay	Austria	Hong Kong
Venezuela	Czech Republic	India
	Germany	Israel
Asia	Hungary	Malaysia
Indonesia	Slovak Republic	Pakistan
Jordan	Switzerland	Singapore
Philippines		Sri Lanka
Turkey	**Code law—Scandinavian origin**	Thailand
		Australasia
Europe	**Europe**	Australia
Belgium	Denmark	New Zealand
France	Finland	
Greece	Iceland	**Europe**
Italy	Norway	Ireland
Luxembourg	Sweden	United Kingdom

Source: Adapted from Rafael La Porta, Florencio Lopez-de-Salines, Andrei Shleifer, and Robert W. Vishny, "Law and Finance," *Journal of Political Economy* 106, no. 6 (1998): 1142–1143; and David Alexander and Simon Archer, *European Accounting Guide, 5th ed.*, New York: Aspen, 2003.

issues such as valuing fixed assets and recording depreciation, relevant in manufacturing, are becoming less important. New accounting challenges, such as valuing intangibles and human resources, are emerging.

7. *Education Level.* Highly sophisticated accounting standards and practices are useless if they are misunderstood and misused. For example, a complex technical report on cost behavior variances is meaningless unless the reader understands cost accounting. Disclosures about the risks of derivative securities are not informative unless they can be read competently.

Several of these first seven variables are closely associated. For example, the common law legal system originated in Britain and was exported to such countries as Australia, Canada, and the United States. These four countries all have highly developed capital markets, which dominate the orientation of their financial reporting. Financial and tax accounting are separate. By contrast, most of Continental Europe and Japan have code law legal systems and rely on banks or the government for most of their finance. Accounting rules there generally conform to tax laws.

Establishing cause and effect is difficult. The type of legal system may predispose a country toward its system of finance. A common law legal system emphasizes shareholder rights and offers stronger investor protection than a code law system. The outcome is that strong equity markets develop in common law countries and weak ones develop in code law countries.[7] Taxation is an important function of accounting in any country with a corporate income tax. Whether it dominates the orientation of accounting may depend on whether accounting has a major competing purpose, namely, informing outside shareholders. (Tax accounting is not suitable for this purpose.) Thus, if common law results in strong equity markets, taxation will not dominate. There will be two sets of accounting rules: one for taxation and another for financial reporting. Tax rules will dominate in code law/credit-based countries, and accounting for taxation and financial reporting will be the same.[8]

Two basic orientations of accounting have evolved out of these circumstances. One is oriented toward a fair presentation of financial position and results of operations, while the other is designed to comply with legal requirements and tax law. The *fair presentation* versus *legal compliance* distinction is further discussed at the end of this chapter.

   8. *Culture.* Here, culture means the values and attitudes shared by a society. Cultural variables underlie nations' institutional arrangements (such as legal systems). Hofstede enunciated four national cultural dimensions (or societal values): (1) individualism, (2) power distance, (3) uncertainty avoidance, and (4) masculinity. His analysis is based on data from employees of a large U.S. multinational corporation operating in 40 different countries.[9]

Briefly, *individualism* (versus *collectivism*) is a preference for a loosely knit social fabric over an interdependent, tightly knit fabric (*I* vs. *we*). *Power distance* is the extent to which hierarchy and an unequal distribution of power in institutions and organizations are accepted. *Uncertainty avoidance* is the degree to which society is uncomfortable with ambiguity and an uncertain future. *Masculinity* (vs. *femininity*) is the extent to which gender roles are differentiated and performance and visible achievement (traditional masculine values) are emphasized over relationships and caring (traditional feminine values). Some scholars now call this *achievement orientation.*[10]

---

[7]R. La Porta, F. Lopez-de-Silanes, A. Shleifer, and R.W. Vishny, "Legal Determinants of External Finance," *Journal of Finance* (July 1997): 1131–1150.

[8]C. Nobes, "Towards a General Model of the Reasons for International Differences in Financial Reporting," *Abacus* (September 1998): 162–187.

[9]G. Hofstede, *Culture's Consequences: International Differences in Work-Related Values,* Beverly Hills, CA: Sage, 1980.

[10]Later work documents a fifth cultural dimension, called *Confucian dynamism* (or *long-term orientation*). This later work contends that only individualism, power distance, and masculinity are universal across all cultures. Uncertainty avoidance is a unique characteristic of Western societies, whereas Confucian dynamism is unique to Eastern societies. [See G. Hofstede and M. H. Bond, "The Confucian Connection: From Cultural Roots to Economic Growth," *Organizational Dynamics* 16, no. 1 (1988): 4–21; and G. Hofstede, *Cultures and Organizations: Softwares of the Mind,* London: McGraw-Hill, 1991.] The existence of this fifth dimension has been contested. See R. Yeh and J. J. Lawrence, "Individualism and Confucian

Drawing on Hofstede's analysis, Gray proposed a framework linking culture and accounting.[11] He suggests four *accounting value dimensions* that affect a nation's financial reporting practices. They are:

1. Professionalism versus statutory control: a preference for the exercise of individual professional judgment and professional self-regulation as opposed to compliance with prescriptive legal requirements.

   A preference for independent professional judgment is consistent with a preference for a loosely knit social framework where there is more emphasis on independence, a belief in fair play and as few rules as possible, and where a variety of professional judgments will tend to be more easily tolerated. . . . [P]rofessionalism is more likely to be accepted in a small power-distance society where there is more concern for equal rights, where people at various power levels feel less threatened and more prepared to trust people, and where there is a belief in the need to justify the imposition of laws and codes.[12]

2. Uniformity versus flexibility: a preference for uniformity and consistency over flexibility in reacting to circumstances.

   A preference for uniformity is consistent with a preference for strong uncertainty avoidance leading to a concern for law and order and rigid codes of behaviour, a need for written rules and regulations, a respect for conformity and the search for ultimate, absolute truths and values. [Uniformity] is also consistent with a preference for collectivism . . . with its tightly knit social framework, a belief in organization and order, and respect for group norms. . . . [U]niformity is more easily facilitated in a large power-distance society in that the imposition of laws and codes of a uniform character are more likely to be accepted.[13]

3. Conservatism versus optimism: a preference for a cautious approach to measurement to cope with the uncertainty of future events instead of a more optimistic, risk-taking approach.

   A preference for more conservative measures of profits is consistent with strong uncertainty avoidance following from a concern with security and a perceived need to adopt a cautious approach to cope with uncertainty of future events. . . . [A]n emphasis on individual achievement and performance is likely to foster a less conservative approach to measurement.[14]

Dynamism: A Note on Hofstede's Cultural Root to Economic Growth," *Journal of International Business Studies* (Third Quarter 1995): 655–669. These authors note a data problem in Hofstede's subsequent work. Once an outlier is removed, Confucian dynamism no longer emerges as an independent construct; it reflects the same cultural dimension as individualism. It should also be pointed out that there are other cultural dimensions that are not considered by Hofstede. For example, religion, which extends beyond national boundaries, underlies business practices, institutional arrangements, and by extension, accounting. Language is another cultural input.
[11]S. J. Gray, "Towards a Theory of Cultural Influence on the Development of Accounting Systems Internationally ," *Abacus* (March 1988): 1–15.
[12]Ibid., 9.
[13]Ibid., 9–10.
[14]Ibid., 10.

4. Secrecy versus transparency: a preference for confidentiality and the restriction of business information on a need-to-know basis versus a willingness to disclose information to the public.

> A preference for secrecy is consistent with strong uncertainty avoidance following from a need to restrict information disclosures so as to avoid conflict and competition and to preserve security.... [H]igh power-distance societies are likely to be characterized by the restriction of information to preserve power inequalities. Secrecy is also consistent with a preference for collectivism ... with its concern for those closely involved with the firm rather than external parties.... [S]ocieties where more emphasis is given to the quality of life, people, and the environment, will tend to be more open especially as regards socially related information.[15]

Exhibit 2-2 shows how Gray's accounting values relate to Hofstede's cultural dimensions.[16]

Exhibit 2-2 Relationships between Gray's Accounting Values and Hofstede's Cultural Dimensions

Cultural Dimension (Hofstede)	Accounting Values (Gray)			
	Professionalism	*Uniformity*	*Conservatism*	*Secrecy*
Individualism	+	−	−	−
Power Distance	−	+	?	+
Uncertainty Avoidance	−	+	+	+
Masculinity	?	?	−	−

Note: "+" indicates a direct relationship between the variables; "−" indicates an inverse relationship. Question marks indicate that the nature of the relationship is indeterminate. Gray hypothesizes that individualism and uncertainty avoidance will influence accounting the most, followed by power distance, then masculinity.

Source: Adapted from Nabil Baydoun and Roger Willett, "Cultural Relevance of Western Accounting Systems to Developing Countries," *Abacus* (March 1995): 67–92. Used with permission of Blackwell Publishing.

---

[15]Ibid., 11.

[16]An empirical test of Gray's framework may be found in S. B. Salter and F. N. Niswander, "Cultural Influence on the Development of Accounting Systems Internationally: A Test of Gray's [1988] Theory," *Journal of International Business Studies* (Second Quarter 1995): 379–397. Using data from 29 countries, the authors find that, while the framework has statistical support overall, specific support is rather mild. Their evidence indicates that the framework is best at explaining actual financial reporting practices and relatively weak in explaining professional and regulatory structures. Furthermore, uncertainty avoidance is most strongly associated with Gray's accounting values. Individualism, which Gray thought would be relatively important overall, is only related to secrecy. Power distance is unrelated and masculinity is more strongly associated than Gray hypothesized. We caution that, while the study by Salter and Niswander is an important first one, single empirical studies are rarely the final word. Different data (and different countries) might produce different results.

CLASSIFICATION

International accounting classifications have been done two ways: judgmentally and empirically. Judgmental classifications rely on knowledge, intuition, and experience.[17] Empirically derived classifications apply statistical methods to databases of accounting principles and practices around the world.[18]

Four Approaches to Accounting Development[19]

The pioneering classification is the one proposed by Mueller in the mid-1960s. He identified four approaches to accounting development in Western nations with market-oriented economics systems. (1) Under the *macroeconomic* approach, accounting practices are derived from and designed to enhance national macroeconomic goals. Firm goals normally follow rather than lead national economic policies as business firms coordinate their activities with national policies. Thus, for example, a national policy of stable employment by avoiding big swings in business cycles would result in accounting practices that smooth income. Or, to promote the development of certain industries, a nation could permit rapid write-offs of capital expenditures in these industries. Accounting in Sweden developed from the macroeconomic approach. (2) Under the *microeconomic* approach, accounting develops from the principles of microeconomics. The focus is on individual firms whose main goal is to survive. To accomplish this goal, firms must maintain their physical capital. It is also critical that they clearly separate capital from income to evaluate and control their business activities. Accounting measurements based on replacement cost are advocated as fitting this approach the best. Accounting developed from microeconomics in the Netherlands. (3) Under the *independent discipline* approach, accounting derives from business practices and develops on an ad hoc, piecemeal basis from judgment and trial and error. Accounting is viewed as a service function that derives its concepts and principles from the business process it serves, not from a discipline such as economics. Businesses cope with real-world complexities and ever-present uncertainties through experience, practice, and intuition. Accounting develops the same way. For example, income is simply what seems to be the most useful in practice and disclosures respond pragmatically to user needs. Accounting developed as an independent discipline in the United Kingdom and the United States. (4) Under the *uniform* approach, accounting is standardized and employed as a tool for administrative control by central government. Uniformity in measurement, disclosure, and presentation makes it easier to use accounting information to control all types of businesses by government planners, tax authorities, and even

---

[17]Examples are C. W. Nobes, "A Judgmental International Classification of Financial Reporting Practices," *Journal of Business Finance and Accounting* (Spring 1983): 1–19; and C. Nobes, "Towards a General Model of the Reasons for International Differences in Financial Reporting," *Abacus* (September 1998): 162–187.

[18]Examples are R. D. Nair and W. G. Frank, "The Impact of Disclosure and Measurement Practices on International Accounting Classifications," *Accounting Review* (July 1980): 426–450; and T. S. Doupnik and S. B. Salter, "External Environment, Culture, and Accounting Practice: A Preliminary Test of a General Model of International Accounting Development," *International Journal of Accounting* 30, No. 3 (1995): 189–207.

[19]The concepts underlying these developmental patterns were first proposed in G. Mueller, *International Accounting,* New York: MacMillan, 1967. This work is the basis for most of the classifications of accounting systems worldwide.

managers. In general, the uniform approach is used in countries with strong governmental involvement in economic planning where accounting is used to measure performance, allocate resources, collect taxes, and control prices, among other things. France, with its national uniform chart of accounts, is the leading exponent of the uniform approach.[20]

Legal Systems: Common Law versus Code Law Accounting

Accounting may also be classified by a nation's legal system.[21] This view has dominated accounting thinking for the last 20 years or so. (1) Accounting in *common law* countries is characterized as oriented toward "fair presentation," transparency and full disclosure, and a separation between financial and tax accounting. Stock markets dominate as a source of finance and financial reporting is aimed at the information needs of outside investors. Accounting standard setting tends to be a private-sector activity with an important role played by the accounting profession. Common law accounting is often called "Anglo-Saxon," "British-American," or "micro based." Common law accounting originated in Britain and was exported to such countries as Australia, Canada, Hong Kong, India, Malaysia, Pakistan, and the United States. (2) Accounting in *code law* countries is characterized as legalistic in its orientation, opaque with low disclosure, and an alignment between financial and tax accounting. Banks or governments ("insiders") dominate as a source of finance and financial reporting is aimed at creditor protection. Accounting standard setting tends to be a public-sector activity with relatively less influence by the accounting profession. Code law accounting is often called "continental," "legalistic," or "macro-uniform." It is found in most Continental European countries and their former colonies in Africa, Asia, and the Americas.

This characterization of accounting parallels the so-called "stockholder" and "stakeholder" models of corporate governance in common and code law countries, respectively. As noted earlier in this chapter, a nation's legal system and its system of finance may be linked in a cause-and-effect way.[22] A common law legal system emphasizes shareholder rights and offers stronger investor protection than a code law system. Laws protect outside investors and are generally well enforced. The outcome is that strong capital markets develop in common law countries and weak ones develop in code law countries. Relative to code law countries, firms in common law countries raise

---

[20]European academics, such as K. Käfer (Switzerland), L.L. Illetschko (Austria), E. Schmalenbach (Germany), and A. ter Vehn (Sweden), are largely identified with generalizing accounting processes from comprehensive flow charts of accounts.

[21]See, for example, C. W. Nobes, "A Judgmental International Classification of Financial Reporting Practices," *Journal of Business Finance and Accounting* (Spring 1983): 1–19; I. Berry, "The Need to Classify Worldwide Accountancy Practices," *Accountancy* (October 1987): 90–91; T. S. Doupnik and S. B. Salter, "An Empirical Test of a Judgmental International Classification of Financial Reporting Practices," *Journal of International Business Studies* 24, No. 1 (1993): 41–60; and R. Ball, S. P. Kothari, and A. Robin, "The Effect of International Institutional Factors on Properties of Accounting Earnings," *Journal of Accounting and Economics* 29, No. 1 (2000): 1–51.

[22]R. La Porta, F. Lopez-de-Salines, A. Shleifer, and R. W. Vishny, "Legal Determinants of External Finance," *Journal of Finance* (July 1997): 1131–1150; R. La Porta, F. Lopez-de-Salines, A. Shleifer, and R. W. Vishny, "Law and Finance," *Journal of Political Economy* (December 1998): 1113–1155; and R. La Porta, F. Lopez-de-Salines, A. Shleifer, and R. W. Vishny, "Investor Protection and Corporate Governance," *Journal of Financial Economics* 58, Issues 1–2 (2000): 3–27.

substantial amounts of capital through public offerings to numerous investors. Because investors are at arm's length to the firm, there is a demand for accounting information that accurately reflects a firm's operating performance and financial position. Public disclosure resolves information asymmetry between the firm and investors.

By contrast, ownership of firms in code law countries tends to be concentrated in the hands of families, other corporations, and large commercial banks. Firms satisfy substantial fractions of their capital needs from the government or through bank borrowing. Debt as a source of finance is relatively more important in code law countries than in common law countries. Conservative accounting measurements provide a cushion to lenders in the event of default. Major lenders and significant equity investors may occupy seats on boards of directors, along with other stakeholders such as labor and important suppliers and customers. Because information demands are satisfied by private communication, there is less demand for public disclosure. Accounting income is the basis for income taxes owed and often the basis for dividends and employee bonuses, resulting in pressures for smooth income amounts from year to year.

Practice Systems: Fair Presentation versus Legal Compliance Accounting

Many accounting distinctions at the national level are becoming blurred. There are several reasons for this. (1) Hundreds of companies are now listing their shares on stock exchanges outside their home countries. As discussed in Chapter 5, many internationally listed companies prepare dual financial reports. One set complies with local, domestic financial reporting requirements while the other uses accounting principles and contains disclosures aimed at international investors. The two sets of financial statements are clearly distinguishable. Moreover, this duality is now sanctioned in some code law countries, including France, Germany, and Italy. In these countries, individual company financial statements comply with national legal standards while consolidated financial statements may comply with other standards, such as International Financial Reporting Standards (IFRS) or U.S. generally accepted accounting principles (GAAP). By 2005, all European listed companies must adopt IFRS for their consolidated financial statements (Chapter 8), further accelerating the trend toward dual statements.[23] In other words, it is necessary to distinguish accounting practice at the *national* level from that at the *transnational* level. (2) Some code law countries, in particular Germany and Japan (Chapter 3), are shifting responsibility for accounting standard setting from the government to independent professional, private-sector groups. This change makes the standard-setting process more like that in common law countries such as Australia, Canada, the United Kingdom, and the United States. (3) The importance of stock markets as a source of finance is growing around the world. Stock market development is a top priority in many countries, especially those emerging from centrally planned to market-oriented economies. Two such countries are China and the Czech Republic, discussed in Chapter 4. Capital is increasingly global, creating pressure for a world standard of corporate reporting. Global convergence of financial reporting standards (Chapter 8) will reduce companies' cost of complying with different accounting rules and is expected to reduce their cost of capital. These points indi-

---

[23]Approximately 7,000 listed companies in Europe are affected by this requirement.

cate that another framework besides legal systems is needed to classify accounting worldwide.[24]

We believe that a classification based on *fair presentation* versus *legal compliance* describes accounting in the world today.[25] The distinction between fair presentation and legal compliance has pervasive effects on many accounting issues such as: (1) depreciation, where the expense is determined based on the decline in an asset's usefulness over its economic useful life (fair presentation) or the amount allowed for tax purposes (legal compliance); (2) leases that are in substance a purchase of property are treated as such (fair presentation) or are treated like regular operating leases (legal compliance); and (3) pensions with costs accrued as earned by employees (fair presentation) or expensed on a pay-as-you-go basis (legal compliance). Furthermore, the issue of deferred income taxes never arises when tax and financial accounting are the same.

Another issue is the use of discretionary reserves to smooth income from one period to the next. Generally, these reserves work the following way. In good years extra expenses are provided for, with the corresponding credit going to a reserve account in shareholders' equity. In lean years reserves are dissolved to boost income. This process smooths out year-to-year fluctuations in income. Because this practice jeopardizes a fair presentation, it is less common in fair presentation countries than in legal compliance countries. Of course, if such manipulations are fully disclosed, investors can undo the effects on income. This may not be the case; reserves often are secret.

Fair presentation and *substance over form* characterize common law accounting described above. It is oriented toward the decision needs of external investors. Financial statements are designed to help investors judge managerial performance and predict future cash flows and profitability. Extensive disclosures provide additional information relevant for these purposes. IFRS are also aimed at fair presentation.

---

[24]The common law versus code law distinction may be criticized on other grounds. For example, there are exceptions: the Netherlands (Chapter 3) and Mexico (Chapter 4) are code law countries with "fair presentation" accounting. Some observers doubt that legal systems are the cause of differences in accounting systems worldwide, but one of several contributing factors, including sources of finance and colonial or cultural influence. They say that there are too many exceptions for causality to run from legal system to accounting system. [See in particular, C. Nobes and A. Roberts, "Towards a Unifying Model of Systems of Law, Corporate Financing, Accounting and Corporate Governance," *Australian Accounting Review* 10, No. 1 (2000): 26–34.] Enforcement is another significant point. If laws and accounting standards are not enforced, they exist on paper only. Distinctions based on legal systems are less clear in countries where standards are not enforced. [See C. Leuz, D. Nanda, and P. Wysocki, "Investor Protection and Earnings Management: An International Comparison," *Journal of Financial Economics* (September 2003): 505–527.]

[25]For completeness, *inflation-adjusted* accounting should also be considered. Accounting in Israel and Mexico is fair presentation/full disclosure with general price-level accounting added on. (Chapter 4 discusses accounting in Mexico.) Certain countries in South America have legal compliance accounting, but with inflation adjustments. Countries also abandon inflation adjustments once inflation is tamed, as happened a few years ago in Brazil. Israel also plans to abandon inflation adjustments.

Islamic accounting, which has a theological base, is also omitted from this framework. It prohibits recognizing interest on money and current market values are favored as measures of assets and liabilities. Islamic accounting has not yet evolved to the point where it represents a comprehensive pattern of accounting. (See www.islamic-accounting.com.)

IFRS are particularly relevant for companies relying on international capital markets for finance. Fair presentation accounting is found in the United Kingdom, the United States, the Netherlands, and other countries influenced by political and economic ties to them (such as British influence throughout the former British Empire and U.S. influence on Canada, Mexico, and the Philippines). Many companies from code law countries (e.g., German and Swiss companies) now adopt IFRS in preparing their consolidated financial statements. Some Japanese companies use U.S. GAAP in their consolidated financial statements. Thus, fair presentation is also the basis of reporting for these companies. After 2005, all listed European companies will follow fair presentation accounting in their consolidated statements since they will use IFRS. Furthermore, IFRS are the benchmark standards now being developed in Japan (Chapter 3) and China (Chapter 4).

Legal compliance accounting is designed to satisfy government-imposed requirements such as calculating taxable income or complying with the national government's macroeconomic plan. The income amount may also be the basis for dividends paid to shareholders and bonuses paid to managers and employees. Conservative measurements ensure that prudent amounts are distributed. Smooth patterns in income from year to year mean that tax, dividend, and bonus payouts are more stable. Legal compliance accounting will continue to be used in individual-company financial statements in those code law countries where consolidated statements adopt fair presentation reporting. In this way, consolidated statements can inform investors while individual company accounts satisfy legal requirements.

We believe that the integration of the world's capital markets will be the most significant influence shaping accounting development in the future. This development is the reason behind the trend is toward fair presentation accounting, at least for consolidated financial statements. It is also the key driver behind the activities of the International Accounting Standards Board and the European Union's "IFRS 2005" decision, and it is why financial statement analysis is increasingly global in nature.

Selected References

Ball, R., S. P. Kothari, and A. Robin, "The Effect of International Institutional Factors on Properties of Accounting Earnings," *Journal of Accounting and Economics* 29, no. 1 (2000): 1–51.

Bartov, E., S. R. Goldberg, and M.-S. Kim, "The Valuation-Relevance of Earnings and Cash Flows: An International Perspective," *Journal of International Financial Management and Accounting* 12, no. 2 (Summer 2001): 103–132.

Baydoun, N., and R. Willett, "Cultural Relevance of Western Accounting Systems to Developing Countries," *Abacus* (March 1995): 67–92.

Chanchani, S., and A. MacGregor, "A Synthesis of Cultural Studies in Accounting," *Journal of Accounting Literature* 18 (1999): 1–30.

Doupnik, T. S., and S. B. Salter, "External Environment, Culture, and Accounting Practice: A Preliminary Test of a General Model of International Accounting Development," *The International Journal of Accounting* 30, no. 3 (1995): 189–207.

Gray, S. J., "Towards a Theory of Cultural Influence on the Development of Accounting Systems Internationally," *Abacus* (March 1988): 1–15.

Guenter, D. A., and D. Young, "The Association between Financial Accounting Measures and Real Economic Activity: A Multinational Study," *Journal of Accounting and Economics* 29, no. 1 (2000): 53–72.

La Porta, R., F. Lopez-de-Silanes, A. Shleifer, and R. W. Vishny, "Law and Finance," *Journal of Political Economy* 106, no. 6 (1998): 1113–1155.

Meek, G. K., and S. M. Saudagaran, "A Survey of Research on Financial Reporting in a Trans-national Context," *Journal of Accounting Literature* 9 (1990): 145–182.

Nobes, C. W., *Developments in International Accounting—General Issues and Classification,* Cheltenham, U.K.: Edward Elgar, 2004.

Nobes, C. W., *International Accounting—General Issues and Classification,* Cheltenham, U.K.: Edward Elgar, 1996.

Nobes, C., "Towards a General Model of Reasons for International Differences in Financial Reporting," *Abacus* (September 1998): 162–187.

Nobes, C., and A. Roberts, "Towards a Unifying Model of Systems of Law, Corporate Financing, Accounting and Corporate Governance," *Australian Accounting Review* 10, no. 1 (2000): 26–34.

Parker, R. H., "European Languages of Account," *The European Accounting Review* 10, no. 1 (2001): 133–147.

Parker, R. H., "Importing and Exporting Accounting: The British Experience," in A. G. Hopwood (ed.), *International Pressures for Accounting Change,* Hemel Hempstead, U.K.: Prentice Hall International (U.K.), 1989, 7–29.

Perera, H., "Culture and International Accounting: Some Thoughts on Research Issues and Prospects," *Advances in International Accounting* 7 (1994): 267–285.

Porcano, T. M., and A. V. Tran, "Relationship of Tax and Financial Accounting Rules in Anglo-Saxon Countries, *The International Journal of Accounting* 33, no. 4 (1998): 433–454.

Roberts, A., "The Very Idea of Classification in International Accounting," *Accounting, Organizations and Society* 20, no. 7/8 (1995): 639–664.

Saudagaran, S. M., and J. G. Diga, "Evaluation of the Contingency-Based Approach in Comparative International Accounting: A Case for Alternative Research Paradigms," *Journal of Accounting Literature* 18 (1999): 57–95.

Zarzeski, M. T., "Spontaneous Harmonization Effects of Culture and Market Forces on Accounting Disclosure Practices," *Accounting Horizons* (March 1996): 18–37.

Discussion Questions

1. The chapter identifies seven economic, sociohistorical, and institutional factors believed to influence accounting development. Explain how each one affects accounting practice.

2. Referring to the seven factors in Question 1, rank them from most to least important as far as accounting development is concerned, then justify both the top and bottom items in your ranking.

3. How do cultural values influence accounting? Are there parallel influences between the factors identified in Question 1 and the cultural factors identified here?

4. Are national differences in accounting practice better explained by culture or by economic and legal factors? Why?

5. The four approaches to accounting development discussed in the chapter were originally outlined in 1967. Are these four patterns still valid today? Why or why not?

6. Countries that tend to have relatively conservative measurement practices also tend to be secretive in disclosure, while countries that tend to have less conservative measurement practices tend to be transparent in disclosure. Why is this so?

7. What is the purpose of classifying systems of accounting?

8. What is the difference between a judgmental and an empirical classification of accounting?

9. What are the major accounting models in the world? What are the distinguishing features of each model?

10. Why does the chapter contend that many distinctions of accounting at the national level are becoming blurred? Do you agree? Why or why not?

11. Your authors contend that a classification based on fair presentation versus legal compliance describes accounting in the world today better than one based on common law and code law legal systems. Do you agree? Why or why not?

12. What are the prospects of a convergence or harmonization of national systems of accounting and financial reporting? What factors might be influential in promoting or inhibiting change?

Exercises

1. Accounting in common law countries differs markedly from accounting in code law countries.

   Required: Choose one country from each of these two categories. Compare and contrast accounting in these two countries. (Hint: Refer to the References in Chapters 3 and 4.)

2. The chapter identifies seven economic, historical, and/or institutional variables that influence accounting development: sources of finance, legal system, taxation, political and economic ties, inflation, level of economic development, and education level.

   Required:

   a. Choose a country of the world other than your own and describe it on the basis of these seven dimensions. Web sites include the Encyclopaedia Britannica Online (www.eb.com) and The World Factbook (www.odci.gov/cia/publications/factbook/).
   b. Using this description, predict a general profile of financial accounting in that country.
   c. Go to the library and find a reference that describes accounting in the country that you chose. Is your prediction accurate? Why or why not?

3. Consider the following countries: (1) Belgium, (2) China, (3) Czech Republic, (4) Gambia, (5) India, (6) Mexico, (7) Senegal, and (8) Taiwan.

   Required: Where would they be classified based on legal systems? Where would they be classified based on accounting practice systems? Justify your answers. (Hint: Web sites with information on countries of the world include the

Encyclopaedia Britannica Online (www.eb.com) and The World Factbook (www.odci.gov/cia/publications/factbook/).)

4. The text distinguishes four approaches to accounting development. Naturally, these four approaches overlap and hence are not found in completely pure forms. Within generally accepted accounting principles in the United States, LIFO inventory-pricing methods are available for financial purposes only if they are also applied in parallel fashion for tax accounting purposes. This scenario is a good example of the uniform approach to accounting development.

   Required: For each of the other three approaches to accounting development, identify two specific financial accounting standards, principles, or practices in your home country that illustrates the respective pattern.

5. Consider the following countries classified according to legal systems:

Common law	**Code law**
Australia	France
Canada	Germany
Ireland	Italy
New Zealand	Japan
United Kingdom	The Netherlands
United States	Sweden

   Required:

   a. Obtain an annual report from a company headquartered in one of the six common law countries above and another one from one of the six code law countries. Two sources are www.carolworld.com and www.corporateinformation.com.
   b. Compare and contrast the two annual reports along measurement and disclosure dimensions.
   c. Do the similarities and differences conform to your expectations?

6. Go to the World Federation of Exchanges Web site (www.world-exchanges.com) and obtain the latest annual report. Part 1 of the Statistics section has information on the numbers of domestic and foreign companies listed on member stock exchanges.

   Required: Which five stock exchanges have the most foreign listed companies? Which five stock exchanges have the highest proportion of foreign to total listed companies? Discuss possible reasons for this.

7. One alleged benefit of classifying accounting systems is that developing countries can save the resources that would be used to create national accounting standards by choosing a model of accounting and then emulating that type of accounting.

   Required: Choose some country with an emerging market economy and find a recent article or report describing accounting there. Which type of accounting

does this country seem to be following? Why is it doing so? (Hint: You may
to choose a country for which annual reports are available. Exhibit 9-4 lists We
sites for obtaining annual reports online.)

8. The European Union (EU)—formerly known as the European Community and
at its start, the European Common Market—was formed in 1957 and had 15
members at the end of 2003: Austria, Belgium, Denmark, Finland, France,
Germany, Greece, Ireland, Italy, Luxembourg, the Netherlands, the United
Kingdom, Spain, Sweden, and Portugal. To encourage capital movement and capital formation, the EU has issued various *Directives* designed to harmonize the
generally accepted accounting principles of its member countries.

Required: Which of the factors affecting accounting development are likely to be
the most serious obstacles to the EU harmonization effort? What factors indicate
the EU harmonization effort can succeed?

9. Refer to Exercise 8. In May 2004 the EU expanded to incorporate 10 Central and
Eastern European nations—Cyprus, Czech Republic, Estonia, Hungary, Latvia,
Lithuania, Malta, Poland, Slovakia, and Slovenia.

Required: Which factors affecting accounting development are likely to be the
most serious obstacles to achieving accounting harmonization with the other 15
member nations?

10. Many companies refer to International Financial Reporting Standards (IFRS) in
their annual reports.

Required: Go to the Web site of the International Accounting Standards Board
(www.iasb.com) and find the list of companies referring to IFRS. Which five countries have the most companies referring to IFRS? Are they common law or code
law countries? Discuss a possible reason for this pattern.

11. A U.S. accounting professor insists that U.S. accounting is the best in the world. To
bolster his point, he notes what he sees as weaknesses of accounting in other
countries:
   • The Netherlands: Too much wiggle room
   • Germany: Too conservative and too much income smoothing
   • France: They can pick French GAAP, U.S. GAAP, or international stan-
     dards—so which one's right?
   • Switzerland: Full of holes—just like Swiss cheese
   • United Kingdom: They don't even have to follow their own rules

Required: Which countries' comments are consistent with the development/clas-
sification scheme described in this chapter and which countries' comments are
inconsistent? What might explain these (in)consistencies?

12. Think ahead 10 years from now. Prepare a classification of accounting systems
that you think will exist then. What factors motivate your particular classification?

ARE CLASSIFICATIONS OF ACCOUNTING OUTMODED?

Consider the following statements by David Cairns, former Secretary-General of the International Accounting Standards Committee.[26]

> Simplistic classifications of accounting are . . . of little relevance in the complex world of the 1990s; when we look at the way that countries or companies account for particular transactions and events, it is increasingly difficult to distinguish in a systematic way so-called Anglo-American accounting from Continental European accounting or American accounting from, say, German accounting.[27]

> I am increasingly persuaded . . . that the distinction between Anglo-American accounting and Continental European accounting is becoming less and less relevant and more and more confused. In reaching this conclusion, I do not dispute that different economic, social and legal considerations have influenced the development of accounting in different countries. I also do not dispute the fact that there have been, and still are, differences in the means by which different countries determine accounting requirements and the form of the resulting requirements. I do believe, however, that those who continue to favour these classifications are ignoring what is happening in the world and how companies actually account for transactions and events.

> It is increasingly apparent that the different economic, social and legal considerations which have influenced national accounting do not necessarily result in different accounting and that countries are reaching the same answers irrespective of their different cultural backgrounds (or reaching different answers in spite of the similar cultural backgrounds). In fact, there are now probably far more similarities between American and German accounting than there are between American and British accounting. There are many reasons for this not least the increasing practice of standard setting bodies and other regulators to share ideas and learn from one another. They do this in the IASC, the UN, the OECD, the EU, and such groupings as G4. This cross-fertilization of ideas is not surprising because standard setting bodies in all countries are having to address the same accounting problems.[28]

REQUIRED

1. Do you agree with Mr. Cairns's assertion that classifications of accounting are simplistic and of little relevance in today's world? Are attempts to classify accounting futile and outmoded? Why or why not?

---

[26]D. Cairns, "The Future Shape of Harmonization: A Reply," *European Accounting Review* 6, no. 2 (1997): 305–348.

[27]Ibid., 306.

[28]Ibid., 316.

2. Some observers contend that financial reporting is becoming more and more alike among "world-class" companies—the world's largest multinational corporations—and particularly those listed on the major stock exchanges such as London, New York, and Tokyo. What is the relevance of this contention for classifications of accounting and what are the factors that would cause this to happen?

CASE 2-2   VOLKSWAGEN GROUP

The Volkswagen Group adopted International Accounting Standards (IAS, now International Financial Reporting, or IFRS) for its 2001 fiscal year. The following is taken from Volkswagen's 2001 annual report. It discusses major differences between the German Commercial Code (HGB) and IAS, as they apply to Volkswagen.

GENERAL

In 2001 VOLKSWAGEN AG has for the first time published its consolidated financial statements in accordance with International Accounting Standards (IAS) and the interpretations of the Standing Interpretations Committee (SIC). All mandatory International Accounting Standards applicable to the financial year 2001 were complied with. The previous year's figures are also based on those standards. IAS 12 (revised 2000) and IAS 39, in particular, were already complied with in the year 2000 consolidated financial statements. The financial statements thus give a true and fair view of the net assets, financial position, and earning performance of the Volkswagen Group.

The consolidated financial statements were drawn up in Euros. Unless otherwise stated, all amounts are quoted in millions of Euros (million €).

The income statement was produced in accordance with the internationally accepted cost of sales method.

Preparation of the consolidated financial statements in accordance with IAS requires assumptions regarding a number of line items that affect the amounts entered in the consolidated balance sheet and income statement as well as the disclosure of contingent assets and liabilities.

The conditions laid down in Section 292a of the German Commercial Code (HGB) for exemption from the obligation to draw up consolidated financial statements in accordance with German commercial law are met. Assessment of the said conditions is based on German Accounting Standard No. 1 (DSR 1) published by the German Accounting Standards Committee. In order to ensure equivalence with consolidated financial statements produced in accordance with German commercial law, all disclosures and explanatory notes required by German commercial law beyond the scope of those required by IAS are published.

TRANSITION TO INTERNATIONAL ACCOUNTING STANDARDS

The accounting valuation and consolidation methods previously applied in the financial statements of VOLKSWAGEN AG as produced in accordance with the German Commercial Code have been amended in certain cases by the application of IAS.

Amended accounting, valuation, and consolidation methods in accordance with the German Commercial Code

- Tangible assets leased under finance leases are capitalized, and the corresponding liability is recognized under liabilities in the balance sheet, provided the risks and rewards of ownership are substantially attributable to the companies of the Volkswagen Group in accordance with IAS 17.
- As a finance lease lessor, leased assets are not capitalized, but the discounted leasing installments are shown as receivables.
- Movable tangible assets are depreciated using the straight line method instead of the declining balance method; no half-year or multishift depreciation is used. Furthermore, useful lives are now based on commercial substance and no longer on tax law. Special depreciation for tax reasons is not permitted with IAS.
- Goodwill from capital consolidation resulting from acquisition of companies since 1995 is capitalized in accordance with IAS 22 and amortized over its respective useful life.
- In accordance with IAS 2, inventories must be valued at full cost. They were formerly capitalized only at direct cost within the Volkswagen Group.
- Provisions are only created where obligations to third parties exist.
- Differences from the translation of financial statements produced in foreign currencies are not recorded in the income statement.
- Medium- and long-term liabilities are entered in the balance sheet including capital take-up costs, applying the effective interest method.

Amended accounting, valuation, and consolidation methods that differ from the German Commercial Code

- In accordance with IAS 38, development costs are capitalized as intangible assets provided it is likely that the manufacture of the developed products will be of future economic benefit to the Volkswagen Group.
- Pension provisions are determined according to the Projected Unit Credit Method as set out in IAS 19, taking account of future salary and pension increases.
- Provisions for deferred maintenance may not be created.
- Medium- and long-term provisions are shown at their present value.
- Securities are recorded at their fair value, even if this exceeds cost, with the corresponding effect in the income statement.
- Deferred taxes are determined according to the balance sheet liability method. For losses carried forward deferred tax assets are recognized, provided it is likely that they will be usable.
- Derivative financial instruments are recognized at their fair value, even if it exceeds cost. Gains and losses arising from the valuation of financial instruments serving to hedge future cash flows are recognized by way of a special reserve in equity. The profit or loss from such contracts is not recorded in the income statement until the corresponding due date. In contrast, gains and losses arising from the valuation of derivative financial instruments used to hedge balance sheet items are recorded in the income statement immediately.
- Treasury shares are offset against capital and reserves.
- Receivables and payables denominated in foreign currencies are valued at the

middle rate on the balance sheet, and not according to the imparity principle.
• Minority interests of shareholders from outside the Group are shown separately from capital and reserves.

The adjustment of the accounting and valuation policies to International Accounting Standards with effect from January 1, 2000, was undertaken in accor-dance with SIC 8, with no entry in the income statement, as an allocation to or withdrawal from revenue reserves, as if the accounts had always been produced in accordance with IAS.

The reconciliation of the capital and reserves to IAS is shown in the following table:

	million €
Capital and reserves according to the German Commercial Code as at January 1, 2000	**9,811**
Capitalization of development costs	3,982
Amended useful lives and depreciation methods in respect of tangible and intangible assets	3,483
Capitalization of overheads in inventories	653
Different treatments of leasing contracts as lessor	1,962
Differing valuation of financial instruments	897
Effect of deferred taxes	−1,345
Elimination of special items	262
Amended valuation of pension and similar obligations	−633
Amended accounting treatment of provisions	2,022
Classification of minority interests not as part of equity	−197
Other changes	21
Capital and reserves according to IAS as at January 1, 2000	**20,918**

Source: Volkswagen AG Annual Report 2001, pp. 84–86.

REQUIRED

1. Based on the information provided in the chapter, describe the basic features of German accounting. What developmental factors cause these features?
2. What differences between the accounting requirements in the HGB and IAS are highlighted in Volkswagen's disclosure? Are the German requirements consistent with your characterizations in requirement 1?
3. What is the relevance of Volkswagen's adoption of IAS to the classifications studied in this chapter?

CHAPTER

3 | COMPARATIVE ACCOUNTING I

In Chapter 2 we learned about the factors that affect the development of a nation's accounting system, including its sources of finance, legal system, taxation, political and economic ties, and inflation. Chapter 2 went on to classify accounting systems according to their common elements and distinctive features.

Chapters 3 and 4 more closely examine accounting in a few selected countries. Specific knowledge of accounting in a country is needed to analyze financial statements from that country. Chapter 3 deals with six highly developed countries: France, Germany, Japan, the Netherlands, the United Kingdom, and the United States. Chapter 4 deals with four "emerging market" countries: China, the Czech Republic, Mexico, and Taiwan.

Exhibit 3-1 contains some comparative economic data about the six countries chosen for Chapter 3. Together they are home to the vast majority of the world's multi-

Exhibit 3-1 Economic Data

	France	Germany	Japan	Netherlands	United Kingdom	United States
Area: sq. km (in thousands)	547	357	378	42	245	9,631
Population (in millions)	59.5	82.0	127.3	15.9	58.7	285.9
Gross Domestic Product (in billions)	$1,310	$1,846	$4,141	$380	$1,424	$10,065
GDP Per Capita	$22,030	$22,510	$32,520	$23,860	$23,920	$35,200
GDP by Sector						
Agriculture	3%	1%	1%	3%	1%	2%
Industry	26%	31%	31%	25%	25%	18%
Services	71%	68%	68%	72%	74%	80%
Imports (in billions)	$299.3	$486.0	$349.1	$194.4	$321.0	$1,141
Exports Market (in billions)	$294.8	$571.4	$403.5	$216.1	$267.3	$729.1
Capitalization, (in billions) end 2001	$1,174	$1,072	$2,252	$458	$2,217	$13,810
Major Trading Partners	Germany, Italy, U.K., U.S.	France, U.S., U.K., Netherlands	U.S., China, So. Korea, Taiwan	Germany, Belgium, U.K., France	U.S., Germany, France, Netherlands	Canada, Mexico, Japan, China

Source: Compiled from *Pocket World in Figures 2004 Edition,* London: *The Economist,* 2003; and *The World Factbook,* www.cia.gov/cia/publications/factbook/, January 2004.

national corporations. As such, their companies are likely to be the subjects of analysis. These six countries dominate the development of international accounting today. All six were among the founders of the International Accounting Standards Committee (now, International Accounting Standards Board, or IASB), and they have a major role in directing the IASB's agenda.

Accounting standards are the regulations or rules (often including laws and statutes) that govern the preparation of financial statements. *Standard setting* is the process by which accounting standards are formulated. Thus, accounting standards are the products of standard setting. However, actual practice may deviate from what the standards require. There are at least four reasons for this. First, in many countries the penalties for noncompliance with official accounting pronouncements are weak or ineffective. Second, companies may voluntarily report more information than required. Third, some countries allow companies to depart from accounting standards if doing so will better represent a company's results of operations and financial position. Finally, in some countries accounting standards apply only to individual company financial statements, not to consolidated statements. In those countries, companies are free to choose different accounting standards for their consolidated financial statements. To gain a complete picture of how accounting works in a country, we must pay attention to the accounting standard-setting process, the resulting accounting standards, and actual practice. *Auditing* adds credibility to financial reports. Thus, we also discuss the role and purpose of auditing in the countries we examine.

Accounting standard setting normally involves a combination of private- and public-sector groups. The private sector includes the accounting profession and other groups affected by the financial reporting process such as users and preparers of financial statements and employees. The public sector includes such agencies as tax authorities, ministries responsible for commercial law, and securities commissions. Stock exchanges may influence the process and may be in either the private or public sector, depending on the country in question. The roles and influence of these groups in setting accounting standards differ from country to country. These differences help explain why standards vary around the world.

The relationship between accounting standards and accounting practice is complex and does not always move in a one-way direction. In some cases, practice derives from standards; in others, standards are derived from practice. Practice can be influenced by market forces such as those related to the competition for funds in capital markets. Companies competing for funds may voluntarily provide information beyond what is required in response to the demand for information by investors and others. If the demand for such information is strong enough, standards may be changed to mandate disclosures that had been voluntary.

Chapter 2 distinguished the fair presentation and legal compliance orientations of accounting. Fair presentation accounting is usually associated with common law countries, while legal compliance accounting is typically found in code law countries. This distinction applies in standard setting, in that the private sector is relatively more influential in fair presentation, common law countries, while the public sector is relatively more influential in legal compliance, code law countries. Auditing parallels the type of legal system and the role and purpose of financial reporting. The auditing profession tends to be more self-regulated in fair presentation countries, especially those influenced by the United Kingdom. Auditors also exercise more judgment when the purpose of an audit is to attest to the fair presentation of financial reports. By contrast, in code law countries the accounting profession tends to be more state regulated. In those countries, the main purpose of an audit is to ensure that the company's records and financial statements conform to legal requirements.

The trend in financial reporting is toward fair presentation, at least for consolidated financial statements. Code law countries such as France, Germany, and Japan are adapting their traditional legal compliance approach to accounting to reflect the reality of global capital markets. Chapter 8 discusses the role played by the IASB and other organizations in promoting this movement toward fair presentation consolidated financial statements.

SIX NATIONAL FINANCIAL ACCOUNTING SYSTEMS[1]

France

France is the world's leading advocate of national uniform accounting. The Ministry of National Economy approved the first formal Plan Comptable Général (national accounting code) in September 1947. A revised plan came into effect in 1957. A further revision of the plan was enacted in 1982 under the influence of the Fourth Directive of the European Union (EU). In 1986 the plan was extended to implement the requirements of the EU Seventh Directive on consolidated financial statements, and it was further revised in 1999.

The Plan Comptable Général provides

- objectives and principles of financial accounting and reporting
- definitions of assets, liabilities, shareholders' equity, revenues, and expenses
- recognition and valuation rules
- a standardized chart of accounts, requirements for its use, and other bookkeeping requirements
- model financial statements and rules for their presentation[2]

The mandatory use of the national uniform chart of accounts does not burden French businesses because the plan is widely accepted in practice. Moreover, various schedules required for income tax returns are based on the standardized models of the income statement and balance sheet and the state statistical office produces macroeconomic information by aggregating the financial statements of enterprises.

French accounting is so closely linked to the plan that it is possible to overlook the fact that commercial legislation (i.e., the Code de Commerce) and tax laws dictate many of France's actual financial accounting and reporting practices. Both of these predate the plan. The Code de Commerce has its roots in the 1673 and 1681 ordinances of Colbert (finance minister to Louis XIV) and was enacted by Napoleon in 1807 as a part of the legal system he created, based on written law. The first income tax law was passed in 1914, thereby linking taxation and the need to keep accounting records.

The main bases for accounting regulation in France are the 1983 Accounting Law and 1983 Accounting Decree, which made the Plan Comptable Général compulsory for all

---

[1]The discussion in this section draws on the references cited at the end of the chapter.
[2]The Plan Comptable Général is available in French and English at www.finances.gouv.fr/CNCompta/.

companies. Both texts are inserted in the Code de Commerce.[3] Commercial legislation in the Code de Commerce has extensive accounting and reporting provisions. Annual inventories of assets and liabilities are required. The true and fair view for financial reporting must be evidenced, and certain accounting records are granted a privileged role in specified judicial proceedings. Accounting records, which legally serve purposes of proof and verification, increasingly are considered sources of information for decision making.

Each enterprise must establish an accounting manual if it believes that this is necessary to understand and control the accounting process. At a minimum, this manual includes a detailed flow chart and explanations of the entire accounting system, descriptions of all data-processing procedures and controls, a comprehensive statement of the accounting principles underlying annual financial statements, and the procedures used in the mandatory annual counting of inventory.

Tax laws also significantly influence accounting in France. Business expenses are deductible for tax purposes only if they are fully booked and reflected in annual financial statements.

A feature of French accounting is the dichotomy between individual company financial statements and those for the consolidated group. Even though individual company accounts must follow statutory reporting requirements, the law allows French companies to follow International Financial Reporting Standards (IFRS) or even U.S. generally accepted accounting principles (GAAP) in their consolidated financial statements. The main reason for this flexibility is that when the EU Seventh Directive was implemented in 1986, many French multinationals were already preparing consolidated statements based on Anglo-Saxon principles for purposes of stock exchange listings abroad. French companies referring to IFRS or U.S. GAAP often declare that their financial statements comply both with French standards and with international or U.S. standards. As European Union accounting initiatives converge with IFRS (see Chapter 8), the U.S. GAAP option will be eliminated.

Accounting Regulation and Enforcement

Five major organizations are involved in setting standards in France[4]:

1. Counseil National de la Comptabilité or CNC (National Accounting Board)
2. Comité de la Réglementation Comptable or CRC (Accounting Regulation Committee)
3. Autorité des Marches Financiers or AMF (Financial Markets Authority)[5]
4. Ordre des Experts-Comptables or OEC (Institute of Public Accountants)
5. Compagnie Nationale des Commissaires aux Comptes or CNCC (National Institute of Statutory Auditors)

The CNC consists of 58 members representing the accounting profession, civil servants, and employer, trade union, and other private-sector groups. Attached to the Ministry of Economy and Finance, the CNC issues rulings and recommendations on

---

[3]The legal framework for accounting includes laws passed by Parliament, government decrees dealing with the application of these laws, and ministerial orders by the Ministry of Economy and Finance.

[4]The Web site addresses are: CNC and CRC, www.finances.gouv.fr/CNCompta; AMF, www.amf-france.org; OEC, www.experts-comptables.com; CNCC, www.cncc.fr.

[5]The AMF was established in 2003 from the merger of the Commission des Operations de Bourse (COB), Conseil des Marchés Financiers, and the Conseil de Discipline de la Gestion Financière. The COB was the previous organization with authority over the stock exchanges.

accounting issues and has major responsibility for keeping the plan current. It is consulted on accounting matters requiring regulation, but has no regulatory or enforcement powers itself. Most of the CNC's technical work is done by committees of CNC members and staff. An Urgent Issues Committee is attached to the CNC to address accounting issues needing quick resolution. Appointments to the CNC are highly prestigious and its recommendations carry much weight.

Due to a need for a flexible and expeditious means of providing regulatory authority for accounting standards, the CRC was established in 1998. The CRC converts CNC rulings and recommendations into binding regulations. Under the jurisdiction of the Ministry of Economy and Finance, it has 15 members that include representatives of different ministries, the CNC, AMF, OEC, and CNCC, and judges from the two highest courts in France. CRC regulations are published in the Official Journal of the French Republic after ministerial approval. Thus, the CRC has real regulatory power.

French companies traditionally have relied less on capital markets than on other sources of finance.[6] The French equivalent of the U.S. Securities and Exchange Commission—the AMF—has important but limited influence. The AMF supervises the new issues market and the operations of regional and national stock exchanges. It has authority to issue additional reporting and disclosure rules for listed companies. The president of France appoints the chairman of the AMF, and the commission reports annually to the president. This arrangement provides independence from other government departments. A predecessor body to the AMF, the Commission des Opérations de Bourse (COB), was an early advocate of consolidation requirements for French companies and, in general, sought French acceptance of world-class accounting and reporting standards—at least for larger publicly listed French companies. The COB pressed for better accounting and disclosure, and successfully improved the quality of information in French consolidated financial statements.

In France the accounting and auditing professions have historically been separate. French accountants and auditors are represented by two bodies, the OEC and the CNCC, despite substantial overlap in their memberships. Indeed, 80 percent of qualified accountants hold both qualifications in France. The two professional bodies maintain close links and cooperate on issues of common interest. Both participate in the development of accounting standards through the CNC and CRC and they represent France on the IASB.

The practice of public accounting and the right to the title *expert-comptable* is restricted to OEC members, who contract with clients to maintain and review accounting records and prepare financial statements. They may also provide tax, information systems, and management advisory services. The OEC is under the jurisdiction of the Ministry of Economy and Finance. Most of its effort is devoted to professional practice issues, though before the CRC was established it issued interpretations and recommendations on the application of accounting legislation and regulations.

By contrast, the CNCC (professional association of statutory auditors *commissaires aux comptes*), is under the jurisdiction of the Ministry of Justice.[7] By law,

---

[6]France has a tradition of family businesses and nationalized industries, both of which rely on debt financing.

[7]A major change to the French auditing system occurred in 2003 with the establishment of the Haut Conseil du Commissariat aux Comptes (High Council of External Auditors). Under the Ministry of Justice,

only statutory auditors may audit and give an opinion on financial statements.[8] The CNCC publishes a member handbook that contains extensive professional standards. It also publishes information bulletins that provide technical assistance. Audits in France are generally similar to their counterparts elsewhere. However, French auditors must report to the state prosecutor all criminal acts that they become aware of during the audit.

Financial Reporting
French companies must report the following:

1. Balance sheet
2. Income statement
3. Notes to financial statements
4. Directors' report
5. Auditor's report

Financial statements of all corporations and other limited liability companies above a certain size must be audited. Large companies also must prepare documents relating to the prevention of business bankruptcies and a social report, both of which are unique to France. There are no requirements for a statement of changes in financial position or cash flow statement. However, the CNC recommends a cash flow statement and nearly all large French companies publish one. Individual company and consolidated statements are both required, though small groups are exempt from the consolidation requirement. The Code de Commerce allows simplified financial statements for small and medium-sized companies.

To give a true and fair view (*image fidèle*), financial statements must be prepared in compliance with legislation (*régularité*) and in good faith (*sincérité*). A significant feature of French reporting is the requirement for extensive and detailed footnote disclosures, including the following items:

- Explanation of measurement rules employed (i.e., accounting policies)
- Accounting treatment of foreign currency items
- Statement of changes in fixed assets and depreciation
- Details of provisions
- Details of any revaluations
- Breakdown of receivables and liabilities by maturity
- List of subsidiaries and share holdings
- Amount of commitments for pensions and other retirement benefits
- Details of the impact of taxes on the financial statements
- Average number of employees listed by category
- Analysis of turnover by activity and geographically

it will be in charge of monitoring the auditing profession as well as overseeing its independence and professional code of ethics.

[8]The same person can practice both accounting and auditing. However, independence rules prohibit the statutory auditor from also providing accounting services to the same client firm.

The directors' report includes a review of the company's activities during the year, the company's future prospects, important post–balance sheet events, research and development activities, and a summary of the company's results for the past 5 years. The financial statements of commercial companies must be audited, except for small, limited liability companies and partnerships.

Listed companies must provide half-yearly interim reports and, starting in 2003, the results of their environmental activities. Among other items, information must be given on:

- Water, raw material, and energy consumption, and actions taken to improve energy efficiency;
- Activities to reduce pollution in the air, water, or ground, including noise pollution, and their costs; and
- Amount of provisions for environmental risks.

French law also contains provisions aimed at preventing bankruptcies (or mitigating their consequences). The idea is that companies with a good understanding of their internal financial affairs and that prepare sound projections can better avoid financial difficulties. Accordingly, larger companies (those with net sales in excess of €18 million or more than 300 employees) prepare four documents: a statement of cash position, a statement of changes in financial position or cash flow statement, a forecast income statement, and a business plan. These documents are not audited, but are given a limited examination by the auditors. They are submitted only to the board of directors and employee representatives; they are not made available to the shareholders or the general public unless provided voluntarily (such as the cash flow statement). Thus, this information is designed as an internal early warning signal for management and workers.

A social report also is required for all companies with 300 or more employees. This report describes, analyzes, and reports on matters of training, industrial relations, health and safety conditions, wage levels and other employment benefits, and many additional relevant work environment conditions. The report is required for individual companies, not consolidated groups.

Accounting Measurements

As noted earlier, French accounting is characterized by a duality: individual companies must follow fixed regulations, while consolidated groups have more flexibility. Accounting for individual companies is the legal basis for distributing dividends and for calculating taxable income.

Tangible assets are normally valued at historical cost. Although revaluations are allowed, they are taxable and, therefore, are seldom found in practice. Fixed assets are depreciated according to tax provisions, normally on a straight-line or declining balance basis. Extra tax depreciation is sometimes available, in which case the additional amount taken is shown as an exceptional charge on the income statement and the corresponding credit as a tax-related provision in equity. Inventory must be valued at the lower of cost or realizable value using either first in, first out (FIFO) or weighted-average methods.

Research and development costs are expensed as incurred, but may be capitalized in restricted circumstances. If capitalized, research and development costs must be amortized over no more than 5 years. Leased assets are not capitalized, and the rent paid is expensed. Pension and other retirement benefits are normally expensed when paid and future commitments are seldom recognized as liabilities. Probable losses whose amounts can be determined with reasonable accuracy are accrued. Many other risks and uncertainties may be provided for, such as those relating to litigation, restructurings, and self-insurance; these allow income-smoothing opportunities. Given the link between book and tax income, companies do not account for deferred taxes in individual company financial statements. Legal reserves must be created by appropriating 5 percent of income each year until the reserve equals 10 percent of legal capital.

With a few exceptions, French consolidated financial statements follow the fair presentation approach of reporting substance over form. Two exceptions are that liabilities for post-employment benefits do not have to be recognized and finance leases do not have to be capitalized. Deferred taxes are accounted for using the liability method, and are discounted when the reversal of timing differences can be reliably estimated. The purchase method is normally used to account for business combinations, but the pooling method is allowed in some circumstances. Goodwill normally is capitalized and amortized to income, but no maximum amortization period is specified. Goodwill is not required to be impairments tested. Proportional consolidation is used for joint ventures and the equity method is used to account for investments in nonconsolidated entities over which significant influence is exercised. Foreign currency translation practice is consistent with IAS 21. The assets and liabilities of an autonomous subsidiary are translated at the closing (year-end) exchange rate and the translation difference is included in equity. The financial statements of a nonautonomous subsidiary are translated using the historical rate (temporal) method, with the translation difference included in income (see Chapter 6). International Financial Reporting Standards will be the basis for French consolidated statements after 2005.

Germany

The German accounting environment has changed continuously and remarkably since the end of World War II. At that time, business accounting emphasized national and sectional charts of account (as in France). The Commercial Code stipulated various principles of "orderly bookkeeping," and independent auditing barely survived the war.

In a major turn of events, the 1965 Corporation Law moved the German financial reporting system toward British-American ideas (but only for larger corporations). More disclosure, limited consolidation, and a corporate management report were required. The management report and additional audit requirements became legal requirements through the 1969 Corporate Publicity Law.

In the early 1970s the European Union (EU) began issuing its harmonization directives, which member countries were required to incorporate into their national laws. The Fourth, Seventh, and Eighth EU Directives all entered German law through the Comprehensive Accounting Act of December 19, 1985. This legislation is remarkable because (1) it integrates all existing German accounting, financial reporting, disclosure, and auditing requirements into a single law; (2) this single law is specified as the *third book* of the German Commercial Code (HGB), thus becoming applicable to all business entities, from limited partnerships to private and publicly held corporations; and (3) the legislation is based predominantly on European concepts and practices.

Two new laws were passed in 1998. The first added a new paragraph in the third book of the German Commercial Code allowing companies that issue equity or debt on organized capital markets to use internationally accepted accounting principles in their consolidated financial statements. The second allowed the establishment of a private-sector organization to set accounting standards for consolidated financial statements.

Creditor protection is a fundamental concern of German accounting as embodied in the Commercial Code. Conservative balance sheet valuations are central to creditor protection. This creates a tendency to undervalue assets and overvalue liabilities. Reserves are seen as protection against unforeseen risks and possible insolvency. These practices also result in a conservative income amount, which is the basis for dividends to owners. Thus, German accounting is designed to compute a prudent income amount that leaves creditors unharmed after distributions are made to owners.

Tax law also largely determines commercial accounting. The *determination principle (Massgeblichkeitsprinzip)* states that taxable income is determined by whatever is booked in a firm's financial records. Available tax provisions can be used only if they are fully booked. This means, among other things, that any special or highly accelerated depreciation used for tax purposes must also be booked for financial reporting purposes. The dominance of tax accounting means that no distinction is made between financial statements prepared for tax purposes and those published in financial reports.

The third fundamental characteristic of German accounting is its reliance on statutes and court decisions. Nothing else has any binding or authoritative status. To understand German accounting, one must look to both HGB and a considerable body of case law.

Accounting Regulation and Enforcement

Before 1998, Germany had no financial accounting standard-setting function, as it is understood in English-speaking countries. The German Institute provided consultation in various processes of lawmaking that affected accounting and financial reporting, but legal requirements were absolutely supreme. Similar consultation was given by the Frankfurt Stock Exchange, German trade unions, and accounting academics. The 1998 law on control and transparency (abbreviated KonTraG) introduced the requirements for the Ministry of Justice to recognize a private national standard-setting body to serve the following objectives:

- Develop recommendations for the application of accounting standards for consolidated financial statements.
- Advise the Ministry of Justice on new accounting legislation.
- Represent Germany in international accounting organizations such as the IASB.

The German Accounting Standards Committee (GASC), or in German, the *Deutsches Rechnungslegungs* Standards Committee (DRSC), was founded shortly thereafter, and duly recognized by the Ministry of Justice as the German standard-setting authority.[9]

---

[9]The GASC Web site is www.drsc.de.

The GASC oversees the German Accounting Standards Board (GASB), which does the technical work and issues the accounting standards. The GASB is made up of seven independent experts with a background in auditing, financial analysis, academia, and industry. Working groups are established to examine and make recommendations on the issues before the board. As a rule, these working groups have representatives from trade and industry and the auditing profession, a university professor, and a financial analyst. GASB deliberations follow a due process and meetings are open. Once issued, the standards must be approved and published by the Ministry of Justice.

The new German accounting standard-setting system is broadly similar to that in the United Kingdom and the United States, as discussed later in this chapter, and to the IASB (see Chapter 8). It is important to emphasize, however, that GASB standards are authoritative recommendations that only apply to consolidated financial statements. They do not restrict or alter HGB requirements. The GASB was created to develop a set of German standards compatible with international accounting standards. Since its founding, the GASB has issued German Accounting Standards (GAS) on issues such as the cash flow statement, segment reporting, deferred taxes, and foreign currency translation. However, in 2003, the GASB adopted a new strategy and aligned its work program with the IASB's efforts to achieve a convergence of global accounting standards. These changes recognize the EU requirement for IFRS for listed companies in 2005.

Certified public accountants in Germany are called *Wirtschaftsprüfer* (WPs), or enterprise examiners.[10] WPs are legally required to join the official Chamber of Accountants (*Wirtschaftsprüferkammer*), which was established in 1971 as the regulatory agency for WPs. By international standards, the German auditing (accounting) profession is small. The 1985 Accounting Act extended the audit requirement to many more companies. As a result, a second-tier body of auditors was created in the late 1980s. These individuals are Sworn Book Examiners (*Vereidigte Buchprüfer*) who are only allowed to audit small and medium-sized companies, as defined in the act. Thus, two classes of auditors are legally sanctioned to conduct independent audit examinations of companies.

Financial Reporting

The 1985 Accounting Act specifies different accounting, auditing, and financial reporting requirements according to company size, not according to the form of business organization.[11] There are three size classes—small, medium, and large—defined in terms of balance sheet totals, annual sales totals, and numbers of employees. Companies with publicly traded securities are always classified as large. The 1985 Accounting Act specifies the content and format of financial statements, which include the following:

---

[10]The Institute der Wirtschaftsprüfer's Web site is www.wpk.de.

[11]The three major forms of business organizations in Germany are (1) *Aktiengesellschaft* (AG), (2) *Kommanditgesellschaft auf Aktien* (KGaA), and (3) *Gesellschaft mit beschränkter Haftung* (GmbH).

AGs are typically large corporations with two senior boards: a management board and a supervisory board. The supervisory board appoints and dismisses members of the management board, supervises the management board, and reviews and approves annual financial statements. The KGaA is a mixture of the limited partnership and the corporate form of business organization. It must have at least one shareholder who is personally liable for the company's indebtedness (the remaining shareholders are liable only to the extent of their investments in the company). KGaAs are unknown in English-speaking countries. GmbHs are privately held companies. Most medium and small businesses operate in this form.

1. Balance sheet
2. Income statement
3. Notes
4. Management report
5. Auditor's report

Small companies are exempt from the audit requirement and may prepare an abbreviated balance sheet. Small and medium-sized companies may prepare abbreviated income statements. Small and medium-sized companies also have fewer disclosure requirements for their notes. Publicly traded companies must provide a consolidated statement of cash flows, but it is not required for other companies.

The 1985 act expanded required note disclosure. The notes section of the financial statements is usually extensive, especially for large companies. Footnote disclosures are seen as a way to achieve a true and fair view while still preparing tax-based financial statements. Disclosures include the accounting principles used, the extent to which results are affected by claiming tax benefits, unaccrued pension obligations, sales by product line and geographic markets, unaccrued contingent liabilities, and average number of employees. The management report describes the financial position and business developments during the year, important post–balance sheet events, anticipated future developments, and research and development activities. The 1998 act required publicly traded companies to provide additional segment disclosures and a statement of changes in equity in their consolidated reports.

A feature of the German financial reporting system is a private report by the auditors to a company's managing board of directors and supervisory board. This report comments on the company's future prospects and, especially, factors that may threaten its survival. The auditor must describe and analyze items on the balance sheet that have a material impact on the company's financial position. The auditor also has to evaluate the consequences of and pass judgment on all significant accounting choices. This report can run several hundred pages for large German companies. As noted, it is private information, not available to shareholders.

Consolidated financial statements are required for enterprises under unified management and with a majority of voting rights, dominant influence by virtue of control contracts, or the right to appoint or remove a majority of the board of directors. For purposes of consolidation, all companies in the group must use identical accounting and valuation principles. However, they need not be the same as those used in individual company statements. In this way, tax-driven accounting methods in individual accounts can be eliminated in the group accounts. Consolidated accounts are not the basis for either taxation or profit distributions.

Legislation enacted in 1998 allows companies issuing debt or equity on organized capital markets to use internationally accepted standards (such as IFRS or U.S. GAAP) in consolidated financial statements in lieu of the German Commercial Code.[12] The law (abbreviated KapAEG) was a concession made for the growing number of German companies forced to prepare a second set of consolidated financial

---

[12]Of the top 100 listed German companies as of January 1, 2002, approximately 40 percent used German standards, 40 percent used IFRS, and 20 percent used U.S. GAAP. See Christian Leuz and Jens Wüsterman, "The Role of Accounting in the German Financial System, in *The German Financial System,* Jan P. Krahnen and Reinhard H. Schmidt, eds., Oxford: Oxford University Press, 2004.

statements in order to raise capital on international markets. This concession is valid until 2004, after which the European Union's initiative on the use of IFRS will be effective. In 2003, other companies were also given the option to prepare consolidated financial statements under IFRS.

Accounting Measurements

Under the Commercial Code (HGB), the purchase (acquisition) method is the primary consolidation method, though pooling of interests is acceptable in limited circumstances. Two forms of the purchase method are permitted: the book value method and the revaluation method. (They essentially differ in the treatment of minority interests.[13]) Assets and liabilities of acquired enterprises are brought up to current value and any amount left over is goodwill. Goodwill can either be offset against reserves in equity or amortized systematically over its economic life. The law mentions a 4-year period as the regular amortization period, but ranges up to 20 years are acceptable. The equity method must be used for nonconsolidated entities that are owned 20 percent or more. Joint ventures may be accounted for using either proportional consolidation or the equity method. The HGB has no requirements for foreign currency translation and German companies use a number of methods. Translation differences are dealt with in many ways. As a result, special attention should be paid to the notes, where the foreign currency translation method must be described.

GAS are more restrictive than the HGB regarding consolidated financial statements. Under GAS 4, the revaluation method must be used, whereby assets and liabilities acquired in a business combination are revalued to fair value, and any excess allocated to goodwill. Goodwill is amortized over no more than 20 years and is tested annually for impairment. GAS 14 adopts the functional currency approach to foreign currency translation, in line with IAS 21 (see Chapter 6).

Historical cost is the basis for valuing tangible assets. (Germany is among the world's staunchest adherents to the historical cost principle. Strong anti-inflation attitudes have resulted from the ravages of two debilitating inflationary periods in Germany in the 20th century.) Inventory is stated at the lower of cost or market; FIFO and average are acceptable methods of determining cost. Depreciable fixed assets are subject to tax depreciation rates.

Research and development costs are expensed when incurred. Financial leases typically are not capitalized, but pension obligations are accrued based on their actuarially determined present value consistent with tax laws. Deferred taxes do not normally arise in individual company accounts, because these are tax determined. However, they may arise in consolidated statements if accounting methods used for consolidations are different from those used for the individual accounts. In this case deferred taxes must be set up using the liability method.

Provisions as estimates of future expenses or losses are used heavily. Provisions must be set up for deferred maintenance expenses, product guarantees, potential losses from pending transactions, and other uncertain liabilities. Optional provisions, such as those for future major repairs, are also allowed. Most companies make provisions as large as possible because legally booked expenses directly affect the determination of

---

[13]Dieter Ordelheide, "Germany: Group Accounts," in *Transnational Accounting,* Dieter Ordelheide, ed., London: Macmillan, 1995, pp. 1599–1602.

taxable income. Provisions give German companies many opportunities to smooth income. Portions of retained earnings often are allocated to specific reserves, including a mandated legal reserve and those resulting from the provisions just described.

As noted earlier, German companies now can choose to prepare their consolidated financial statements according to German rules described above, International Accounting Standards, or U.S. GAAP. All three choices are found in practice, and the reader of German financial statements must be careful to know which accounting standards are being followed.

Japan

Japanese accounting and financial reporting reflect a mixture of a number of domestic and international influences. Two separate government agencies have responsibility for accounting regulations, and there is the further influence of Japanese corporate income tax law. In the first half of the 20th century, accounting thinking reflected German influences; in the second half, U.S. ideas were pervasive. More recently, the effects of the International Accounting Standards Board have been felt, and in 2001 a profound change occurred with the establishment of a private-sector accounting standard-setting organization.[14]

To understand Japanese accounting, one must understand Japanese culture, business practices, and history. Japan is a traditional society with strong cultural and religious roots. Group consciousness and interdependence in personal and corporate relationships in Japan contrast with independent, arm's-length relationships among individuals and groups in Western nations. Japanese companies hold equity interests in each other, and often jointly own other firms. These interlocking investments yield giant industrial conglomerates—notably the *keiretsu*. Banks are often a part of these industrial groups. The widespread use of bank credit and debt capital to finance large enterprises is unusually great from a Western perspective, and corporate managements must primarily answer to banks and other financial institutions rather than shareholders. Central government also exerts tight control on many activities in Japan, which means a strong bureaucratic control over business affairs, including accounting. Knowledge of corporate activities is primarily limited to the corporation and other insiders such as the banks and the government.

This *keiretsu* business model is being transformed as the Japanese undertake structural reforms to counteract the economic stagnation that began in the 1990s. The financial crisis that followed the bursting of Japan's *bubble economy* also prompted a review of Japanese financial reporting standards. It became clear that many accounting practices hid how badly many Japanese companies were doing. For example:

1. Loose consolidation standards allowed Japanese companies to bury loss-making operations in affiliates. Investors could not see how profitable a company's entire operations really were.
2. Pension and severance obligations were only accrued to 40 percent of the amount owed because that was the limit of their tax deductibility. This practice led to substantial underfunding of pension obligations.

---

[14]Until the late 1990s, external influences came to bear only gradually. In terms of what we would consider world-class reporting, accounting was slow to develop in Japan. For example, consolidated financial statements date from 1976 and requirements for segment reporting began in 1990.

3. Securities holdings were valued at cost, not market prices. Designed to reinforce the cohesion of the *keiretsu*, these cross-holdings are vast. Companies held on to the ones with losses, but sold those with gains to prop up sagging profits.

An accounting "Big Bang" was announced in the late 1990s to make the economic health of Japanese companies more transparent and to bring Japan more in line with international standards. These accounting reforms are described later.[15]

Accounting Regulation and Enforcement

The national government still has the most significant influence on accounting in Japan. Accounting regulation is based on three laws: the Commercial Code, the Securities and Exchange Law, and the Corporate Income Tax Law. These three laws are linked and interact with each other. A leading Japanese scholar refers to the situation as a "triangular legal system."[16]

The Commercial Code is administered by the Ministry of Justice (MOJ). It is at the center of accounting regulation in Japan and has had the most pervasive influence. Developed from German commercial law, the original code was enacted in 1890, but not implemented until 1899. Creditor and shareholder protection is its fundamental principle with an unequivocal reliance on historical cost measurements. Disclosures on credit worthiness and the availability of earnings for dividend distribution are of primary importance. All companies incorporated under the Commercial Code are required to meet its accounting provisions, which are contained in the "regulations concerning the balance sheet, income statement, business report, and supporting schedules of limited liability companies."

Publicly owned companies must meet the further requirements of the Securities and Exchange Law (SEL), administered by the Ministry of Finance.[17] The SEL is modeled after the U.S. Securities Acts and was imposed on Japan by the United States during the U.S. occupation following World War II. The main objective of the SEL is to provide information for investment decision making. Although the SEL requires the same basic financial statements as the Commercial Code, the terminology, form, and content of financial statements are more precisely defined under the SEL; certain financial statement items are reclassified for presentation and additional detail is provided. Net income and shareholders' equity are, however, the same under the code and the SEL.

The Business Accounting Deliberation Council (BADC) is a special advisory body to the Ministry of Finance responsible for developing accounting standards under the SEL. The BADC is, arguably, the major source of generally accepted accounting principles in Japan today. However, the BADC cannot issue a standard at variance with commercial law (or the tax law, as discussed next). Members of the BADC are appointed by the Ministry of Finance and serve on a part-time basis. They are drawn from academic, government, and business circles as well as members of the Japanese

---

[15]"Japan on the Brink," *The Economist* (April 11, 1999): 15–17; "Japan Restructures, Grudgingly," *The Economist* (February 6, 1999): 63–65; "The Secrets Pour Out," *Business Week* (August 2, 1999): 50–51; "Reshaping Standards," *Accountancy* (June 2000): 110; "Japan: Restoring Investor Confidence," *IASC Insight* (September 2000): 8; and "Going International," *Accountancy* (March 2002): 102–103.
[16]Kiyomitsu Arai, *Accounting in Japan*, Tokyo: Institute for Research in Business Administration, Waseda University, 1994, p. 5.
[17]The Ministry of Finance Web site is www.mof.go.jp.

Institute of Certified Public Accountants (JICPA). (BADC members have an accounting background, in contrast to the legal backgrounds of individuals working on Commercial Code matters at the Ministry of Justice.) The BADC is supported by a research organization known as the Corporation Finance Research Institute.

Finally, the influence of the tax code is significant. Similar to France, Germany, and elsewhere, expenses can be claimed for tax purposes only if they are fully booked. Taxable income is based on the amount calculated under the Commercial Code, but if the code does not prescribe an accounting treatment, the one in the tax law is often followed.

Under the Commercial Code, the financial statements and supporting schedules of small and medium-sized companies are subject to audit only by statutory auditors. Both statutory and independent auditors must audit large corporations. Independent auditors must audit financial statements of publicly held companies in accordance with the Securities and Exchange Law. Statutory auditors do not need any particular professional qualifications and are employed by the company on a full-time basis. Statutory audits focus mainly on the managerial actions of the directors and whether they perform their duties in compliance with legal statutes. Independent audits involve examining the financial statements and records and must be performed by certified public accountants (CPAs).

The JICPA is the professional organization of CPAs in Japan. All CPAs must belong to the JICPA.[18] In addition to providing guidance on the conduct of an audit, the JICPA publishes implementation guidelines on accounting matters and consults with the BADC in developing accounting standards. Generally accepted auditing standards (similar to those in the United States), are promulgated by the BADC rather than the JICPA. The Certified Public Accountant and Auditing Oversight Board was established in 2003. A government agency, it is designed to monitor and oversee the auditing profession and improve the quality of Japanese audits.

A major change in accounting standard setting in Japan occurred in 2001 with the establishment of the Accounting Standards Board of Japan (ASBJ) and its related oversight foundation known as the Financial Accounting Standards Foundation (FASF). They were established by 10 private-sector organizations, including the JICPA, the Japan Federation of Economic Organizations (Keidanren), the Tokyo Stock Exchange, and the Japanese Bankers Association. The ASBJ is to have sole responsibility for developing accounting standards and implementation guidance in the future.[19] It has 13 members, three of whom are full time. It also has a full-time technical staff to support its activities. The FASF is responsible for funding and naming its members. Funding comes from companies and the accounting profession, not the government. As an independent private-sector organization, the ASBJ is expected to be stronger and more transparent, and subject to fewer political and special-interest pressures, than the BADC. The ASBJ also collaborates with the IASB in developing IFRS.[20]

Financial Reporting

Companies incorporated under the Commercial Code are required to prepare a statutory report for approval at the annual shareholders' meeting, consisting of the following:

---

[18]The JICPA's Web site is www.jicpa.or.jp.
[19]The BADC continues to issue standards that were in progress when the ASBJ was established.
[20]The FASF and ASBJ Web site is www.asb.or.jp.

1. Balance sheet
2. Income statement
3. Business report
4. Proposal for appropriation of retained earnings
5. Supporting schedules

Notes accompanying the balance sheet and income statement describe the accounting policies and provide supporting details, as is typical in other countries. The business report contains an outline of the business and information about its operations, financial position, and operating results. A number of supporting schedules are also required, separate from the notes, including:

- Changes in capital stock and the statutory reserve
- Changes in bonds and other short- and long-term debt
- Changes in fixed assets and accumulated depreciation
- Collateralized assets
- Debt guarantees
- Changes in provisions
- Amounts due to and from the controlling shareholders
- Equity ownership in subsidiaries and the number of shares of the company's stock held by those subsidiaries
- Receivables due from subsidiaries
- Transactions with directors, statutory auditors, controlling shareholders, and third parties that create a conflict of interest
- Remuneration paid to directors and statutory auditors

This information is prepared for a single year on a parent company basis and is audited by the statutory auditor. The Commercial Code does not require a statement of cash or funds flow.

Listed companies also must prepare financial statements under the Securities and Exchange Law (SEL), which generally requires the same basic statements as the Commercial Code plus a statement of cash flows. However, under the SEL, consolidated financial statements, not the parent company statements, are the main focus. Additional footnotes and schedules are also required.[21] Financial statements and schedules submitted under the SEL must be audited by independent auditors.

A cash flow forecast for the next 6 months is included as supplemental information in filings with the Ministry of Finance. Other forecast information is also reported such as forecasts of new capital investments and production levels and activities. Overall, the amount of corporate forecast reporting is extensive in Japan. However, this information is reported in statutory filings and rarely appears in the annual report to shareholders.

---

[21]Additional footnotes include information about such things as subsequent events and liabilities for employee retirement and severance benefits. Additional schedules detail items on the financial statements such as marketable securities, tangible and intangible assets, investments in and loans to or from affiliated companies, bonds payable and other long-term borrowings, and reserves and allowances.

Accounting Measurements

The Commercial Code requires large companies to prepare consolidated financial statements.[22] In addition, listed companies must prepare consolidated financial statements under the SEL. Individual company accounts are the basis for the consolidated statements, and normally the same accounting principles are used at both levels. Subsidiaries are consolidated if a parent directly or indirectly controls their financial and operational policies. Though pooling is allowed, the purchase method of accounting for business combinations is normally used. Goodwill is measured on the basis of the fair value of the net assets acquired and is amortized over a maximum of 20 years.[23] The equity method is used for investments in affiliated companies when the parent and subsidiaries exert significant influence over their financial and operational policies. The equity method is also used to account for joint ventures; proportional consolidation is not allowed. Under the foreign currency translation standard revised in 1999, assets and liabilities of foreign subsidiaries are translated at the current (year-end) exchange rate, revenues and expenses at the average rate, and translation adjustments are in stockholders' equity.

Inventory may be valued at cost or the lower of cost or market; cost is most often used. However, inventory must be written down to market if there is a significant and permanent decline in value. FIFO, LIFO, and average are all acceptable cost flow methods, with average the most popular. Investments in securities are valued at market. Fixed assets are valued at cost and depreciated in accordance with the tax laws. The declining-balance method is the most common depreciation method.

Research and development costs are expensed when incurred. Leases that transfer ownership to the lessee are capitalized. Other finance leases may be either capitalized or treated as operating leases. Deferred taxes are provided for all timing differences using the liability method. Contingent losses are provided for when they are probable and can be reasonably estimated. Pension and other employee retirement benefits are fully accrued as employees earn them and unfunded obligations are shown as a liability. Legal reserves are required: Each year a company must allocate an amount equal to at least 10 percent of cash dividends and bonuses paid to directors and statutory auditors until the legal reserve reaches 25 percent of capital stock.

Many of the accounting practices previously described were implemented in the last several years as a result of the accounting "Big Bang" referred to earlier. These recent changes include: (1) requiring listed companies to report a statement of cash flows; (2) extending the number of subsidiaries that are consolidated based on control rather than ownership percentage; (3) extending the number of affiliates accounted for using the equity method based on significant influence rather than ownership percentage; (4) valuing investments in securities at market rather than cost; (5) full provisioning of deferred taxes; and (6) full accrual of pension and other retirement obligations. Accounting in Japan is being reshaped to bring it in line with IFRS.

---

[22] This requirement is effective for fiscal years beginning in 2004.

[23] Effective 2006, the pooling of interests method will be required if certain criteria are met. Otherwise, a business combination will be accounted for as a purchase. Goodwill is to be amortized over 20 years or less and is subject to an impairments test.

The Netherlands

Dutch accounting presents several interesting paradoxes. The Dutch have relatively permissive statutory accounting and financial reporting requirements but very high professional practice standards. The Netherlands is a code law country, yet accounting is oriented toward fair presentation. Financial reporting and tax accounting are two separate activities. Furthermore, the fairness orientation developed without a strong stock market influence. The United Kingdom and the United States have influenced Dutch accounting as much (or more) than other continental European countries, and, unlike the rest of continental Europe, the accounting profession has had a significant influence on accounting standards and regulations.[24]

Accounting in the Netherlands is considered a branch of business economics. As a result, much economic thought has been devoted to accounting topics and especially to accounting measurements. Highly respected professional accountants are often part-time professors. Thus, academic thought has a major influence upon ongoing practice.

Dutch accountants are also willing to consider foreign ideas. The Dutch were among the earliest proponents of international standards for financial accounting and reporting, and the statements of the IASB receive substantial attention in determining acceptable practice. The Netherlands is also home to several of the largest multinational enterprises in the world, including Philips, Royal Dutch/Shell, and Unilever.[25] These enterprises have been internationally listed since the 1950s and have been influenced by foreign (particularly U.K. and U.S.) accounting. Through example, these large multinationals have influenced financial reporting of other Dutch companies. The influence of the Amsterdam Stock Exchange, however, has been minimal because it does not provide much new business capital.

Accounting Regulation and Enforcement

Accounting regulations in the Netherlands remained liberal until 1970, when the Act on Annual Financial Statements was enacted. The act was a part of an extensive program of changes in company legislation and was introduced partly to reflect the coming harmonization of company law within the EU. Among the major provisions of the 1970 act are the following:

- Annual financial statements shall show a fair picture of the financial position and results of the year, and all items therein must be appropriately grouped and described.
- Financial statements must be drawn up in accordance with sound business practice (i.e., accounting principles acceptable to the business community).

---

[24]The idea that the business community is capable of adequate financial reporting is well entrenched in Dutch thinking. The first limited liability companies were formed in the 17th century without a clear legal framework on the matter. The first commercial code, introduced in the 19th century, viewed shareholders as responsible for management, which prompted little need for extensive accounting requirements in the law. Similar to the United Kingdom, the Dutch accounting profession emerged in the 19th century and has had a substantial influence on accounting. By the time an income tax on corporations was introduced (in 1940), financial reporting was already too well developed to be dominated by tax accounting. See Kees Canfferman, "The History of Financial Reporting in the Netherlands," in *European Financial Reporting: A History,* Peter Walton, ed., London: Academic Press, 1995.

[25]Royal Dutch/Shell and Unilever are binational (British and Dutch) concerns.

- The bases of stating assets and liabilities and determining results of operations must be disclosed.
- Financial statements shall be prepared on a consistent basis and material effects of changes in accounting principles properly disclosed.
- Comparative financial information for the preceding period shall be disclosed in the financial statements and accompanying footnotes.

The 1970 act introduced the mandatory audit. It also set into motion the formation of the Tripartite Accounting Study Group (replaced in 1981 by the Council on Annual Reporting), and it gave birth to the Enterprise Chamber. The act, incorporated into the civil code in 1975, was amended by legislation in 1983 to incorporate the EU Fourth Directive, and further amended in 1988 to incorporate the EU Seventh Directive.

The Council for Annual Reporting issues guidelines on generally acceptable (not accepted) accounting principles. The council is composed of members from three different groups:

1. Preparers of financial statements (employers)
2. Users of financial statements (representatives of trade unions and financial analysts)
3. Auditors of financial statements (the Netherlands Institute of Registeraccountants, or NIvRA)[26]

The council is a private organization and is financed by grants from the business community and NIvRA. Even though the council's guidelines do not have the force of law, they are followed by most large companies and auditors.[27] The guidelines are comprehensive in scope and incorporate as far as possible the standards of the IASB. Nevertheless, the only legally enforceable accounting rules are those specified in the accounting and financial reporting provisions of the Dutch civil code.

The Enterprise Chamber, a specialist court connected with the High Court of Amsterdam, is a unique feature of the Dutch system of enforcing compliance with accounting requirements. Any interested party may complain to this chamber if it believes that a company's financial statements do not conform to applicable law. Shareholders, employees, trade unions, and even the public prosecutor (but not independent auditors) may bring proceedings to the chamber. The chamber is composed of three judges and two expert accountants, and there is no jury. Chamber decisions may lead to modifications of financial statements or various penalties. Even though the rulings apply only to defendant companies, they sometimes state general rules that may influence the reporting practices of other companies.

Auditing in the Netherlands is a self-regulated profession. Its governing body is the Netherlands Institute of Registeraccountants (NIvRA), which has approximately 13,000 members.[28] It is fully autonomous in setting auditing standards and its strong professional code of conduct has statutory status.

---

[26]Neither the Amsterdam Stock Exchange nor shareholder representatives participate in the council.
[27]However, auditors can issue an unqualified opinion when there is noncompliance with a guideline, as long as the financial statements still convey a true and fair view.
[28]The NIvRA Web site is www.nivra.nl.

Until 1993, only members of NIvRA could certify financial statements, but changes were made that year to incorporate the EU Eighth Directive. In the Netherlands there are two kinds of auditors: registeraccountants (RAs, or chartered accountants) and administrative accountants (AAs).[29] The 1993 changes allowed AAs to also certify financial statements, if they undergo additional training. Over time, educational and training qualifications for RAs and AAs will be standardized and the code of conduct will be the same in relation to audit work, the auditor's responsibilities, and independence. One set of disciplinary rules also will apply. However, NIvRA is likely to continue to dominate auditing and accounting in the Netherlands.

NIvRA is involved in everything that is accounting related in the Netherlands. It participates in the Council for Annual Reporting and in commissions charged with revising the accounting statutes of the civil code. NIvRA members serve on the Enterprise Chamber, as accounting faculty at leading Dutch universities, on the IASB, and on committees of the EU, the Organization of Economic Cooperation and Development (OECD), the United Nations, and the International Federation of Accountants.

Financial Reporting

The quality of Dutch financial reporting is uniformly high. Statutory financial statements should be filed in Dutch, but English, French, and German are also acceptable. The financial statements must include the following:

1. Balance sheet
2. Income statement
3. Notes
4. Directors' report
5. Other prescribed information

A cash flow statement is not required, but is recommended by a council guideline, and most Dutch companies provide one. The notes must describe the accounting principles used in valuation and the determination of results, and the reasoning behind any accounting changes made. The directors' report reviews the financial position at the balance sheet date and performance during the financial year. It also provides information about the expected performance during the new financial year and comments on any significant post–balance sheet events. "Other prescribed information" must include the auditor's report and profit appropriations for the year.

Annual financial reports must be presented on both a parent-company-only and a consolidated basis. The same accounting principles are used in both. Group companies for the purpose of consolidation consist of those companies that form an economic unit under common control. Consistent with EU directives, reporting requirements vary by company size. Small companies are exempt from the requirements for an audit and for consolidated financial statements, and they may file an abbreviated income statement and balance sheet. Medium-sized companies must be audited, but may publish a condensed income statement. Small, medium-sized, and large companies are defined in the civil code. Dutch companies are permitted to prepare financial statements using IFRS or U.S. GAAP instead of Dutch accounting standards.

---

[29]The Nederlandse Orde van Accountants-Administratieconsultenen (NovAA) Web site is www.novaa.nl.

Accounting Measurements

Even though the pooling-of-interests method of accounting for business combinations is allowed in limited circumstances, it is rarely used in the Netherlands. The purchase method is the normal practice. Goodwill is the difference between the acquisition cost and the fair value of the assets and liabilities acquired. It is capitalized and amortized over its estimated useful life, up to a maximum of 20 years. The equity method is required when the investor exercises significant influence on business and financial policy. Joint ventures may be accounted for using either the equity method or proportional consolidation. The council recommendation on foreign currency translation is consistent with International Accounting Standard 21. The balance sheet of a foreign entity that is independent of the parent is translated at the closing (year-end) rate, while the income statement is translated at the closing or average rate. Translation adjustments are charged to shareholders' equity. The temporal method is used for foreign entities that are not independent of the parent, with the translation adjustment charged to income.

The Dutch flexibility toward accounting measurements may be most evident in permitting the use of current values for tangible assets such as inventory and depreciable assets. When current values are used for these assets, their corresponding income statement amounts, cost of goods sold, and depreciation are also stated at current values. Current value can be replacement value, recoverable amount, or net realizable value. Current value accounting is expected to be consistently applied; piecemeal revaluations normally are not allowed. Revaluations are offset by a revaluation reserve in shareholders' equity. Companies using current values should provide additional historical cost information in the notes. Historical cost is also acceptable. While much has been made of current value accounting in the Netherlands, few companies actually use it. Philips, arguably the most conspicuous example, started using current value accounting in 1951, but abandoned it in 1992 in the interests of international comparability. Nevertheless, current values have a place in Dutch accounting because companies that use historical cost for the balance sheet and income statement are expected to disclose supplemental current cost information in their notes.

When historical cost is used for inventory, generally it is stated at the lower of cost or market, with cost determined by FIFO, LIFO, or average methods. Research and development costs are capitalized only when the amounts are recoverable and sufficiently certain. Leases, contingencies, and pension costs are generally measured as they are in the United Kingdom and United States, although applicable rules are more general. Deferred income taxes are recognized on the basis of the comprehensive allocation concept (full provision) and measured according to the liability method. Current value accounting is not acceptable for tax purposes, so when current values are used for financial reporting, permanent rather than timing differences arise.

Because Dutch companies have flexibility in applying measurement rules, one would suspect that there are opportunities for income smoothing. In addition, certain items can bypass the income statement through direct adjustment to reserves in shareholders' equity. These include:

- Losses due to a disaster that would have been impossible or unusual to insure against

- Losses from a nationalization or similar expropriation
- The consequences of a financial restructuring

United Kingdom

Accounting in the United Kingdom developed as an independent discipline, pragmatically responding to the needs and practices of business.[30] Over time, successive companies legislation added structure and other requirements, but still allowed accountants considerable flexibility in the application of professional judgment. Since the 1970s, the most important source of development in company law has been the EU directives, most notably the Fourth and Seventh Directives. At the same time, accounting standards and the standard-setting process have become more authoritative.

The legacy of British accounting to the rest of the world is substantial. The United Kingdom was the first country in the world to develop an accountancy profession as we know it today.[31] The concept of a fair presentation of financial results and position (the true and fair view) is also of British origin. Professional accounting thinking and practice was exported to Australia, Canada, the United States, and other former British possessions including Hong Kong, India, Kenya, New Zealand, Nigeria, Singapore, and South Africa.

Accounting Regulation and Enforcement

The two major sources of financial accounting standards in the United Kingdom are companies law and the accounting profession. Activities of companies incorporated in the United Kingdom are broadly governed by statutes called companies acts. Companies acts have been updated, extended, and consolidated through the years. For example, in 1981 the EU Fourth Directive was implemented, adding statutory rules regarding formats, accounting principles, and basic accounting conventions. This introduced standardized formats for financial statements into Britain for the first time. Companies may choose from alternative balance sheet formats and four profit and loss account formats. The 1981 act also sets out five basic accounting principles:

1. Revenues and expenses are matched on an accrual basis.
2. Individual asset and liability items within each class of assets and liabilities are valued separately.
3. The principle of conservatism (prudence) is applied, especially in the recognition of realized income and all known liabilities and losses.
4. Consistent application of accounting policies from year to year is required.
5. The going concern principle is applicable to the entity being accounted for.

---

[30]The United Kingdom of Great Britain and Northern Ireland is a union of England, Scotland, Wales, and Northern Ireland. Even though the United Kingdom has an integrated system of laws, monetary and fiscal policies, and social rules and regulations, important individual differences remain among these four countries. The term Britain is often used for the United Kingdom. "British, " "Anglo," and "Anglo-Saxon" are often used interchangeably to describe accounting in the United Kingdom.

[31]The first recognized accounting society was the Society of Accountants in Edinburgh, which was granted a royal charter in 1854. Similar societies were officially recognized in Glasgow in 1855 and in Aberdeen in 1867. Professional accounting began with these early professional societies. The United Kingdom has less than 1 percent of the world's population, yet has more than 13 percent of its accountants. See Bob Parker, "Accountants Galore," *Accountancy* (November 2001): 130–131.

The act contains broad valuation rules in that the accounts may be based on either historical or current cost.

The Companies Act 1985 consolidated and extended earlier legislation and was amended in 1989 to recognize the EU Seventh Directive. This act requires the consolidation of financial statements, although consolidation was already standard practice and consolidation techniques are left to private-sector accounting standards.[32] The legal stipulations are general and allow considerable flexibility in case-by-case applications. Additional accounting recommendations are made through private-sector, self-regulated professional bodies.

The following six accountancy bodies in the United Kingdom are linked through the Consultative Committee of Accountancy Bodies (CCAB), formed in 1970.[33]

1. The Institute of Chartered Accountants in England and Wales
2. The Institute of Chartered Accountants in Ireland
3. The Institute of Chartered Accountants of Scotland
4. The Association of Chartered Certified Accountants
5. The Chartered Institute of Management Accountants
6. The Chartered Institute of Public Finance and Accountancy

British standard setting evolved from recommendations on accounting principles (issued by the Institute of Chartered Accountants in England and Wales) to the 1970 formation of the Accounting Standards Steering Committee, later renamed the Accounting Standards Committee (ASC). The ASC promulgated Statements on Standard Accounting Practice (SSAPs). SSAPs were issued and enforced by the six accounting bodies, any one of which could effectively veto the standard. The veto power of these organizations often led to excessive delays and compromises in developing SSAPs. In addition, SSAPs were more in the nature of recommendations than compulsory requirements, and had little authority.

The Dearing Report, issued in 1988, expressed dissatisfaction with the existing standard-setting arrangement.[34] It recommended a new structure for setting accounting standards and enhanced authoritative support for them. The Companies Act 1989 was important not only for incorporating the EU Seventh Directive but also for enacting the recommendations of the Dearing Report. The 1989 act created a new Financial Reporting Council (FRC) with the duty of overseeing its three offshoots: the Accounting Standards Board (ASB), which replaced the ASC in 1990, an Urgent Issues Task Force (UITF), and a Financial Reporting Review Panel.[35]

The FRC sets general policy. It is an independent body whose members are drawn from the accounting profession, industry, and financial institutions. The ASB has a full-time chair, a technical director, and seven paid part-time members, and is empowered to issue accounting standards. The ASB issues Financial Reporting Standards (FRSs)

---

[32]The Companies Act 1985 (as amended by the Companies Act 1989) applies to England, Scotland, and Wales. Similar legislation for Northern Ireland is embodied in the Companies (Northern Ireland) Order 1986.

[33]The Web site addresses are as follows: ICAEW, www.icaew.co.uk; ICAI, www.icai.ie; ICAS, www.icas.org.uk; ACCA, www.acca.co.uk; CIMA, www.cimaglobal.com; and CIPFA, www.cipfa.org.uk.

[34]Sir Ron Dearing (The Dearing Report), "The Making of Accounting Standards, Report of the Review Committee," presented to the Consultative Committee of Accountancy Bodies, 1988.

[35]The Web site of these organizations is www.frc.org.uk.

after considering comments on Discussion Papers and Financial Reporting Exposure Drafts (FREDs). The ASB is guided by a Statement of Principles for Financial Reporting, a conceptual framework for setting accounting standards.[36] The ASB also established the UITF to respond quickly to new problems and to issue clarifications of the accounting standards and other regulations (called UITF Abstracts). Because of the EU 2005 initiative, the ASB has adopted a policy of convergence of U.K. GAAP and IFRS.

The 1989 act established legal sanctions for companies that do not comply with accounting standards. Both the Financial Reporting Review Panel and the Department of Trade and Industry can investigate complaints about departures from accounting standards. They can go to court to force a company to revise its financial statements. Companies must adopt accounting policies most appropriate to their particular circumstances in order to give a true and fair view, and they must regularly review their policies to ensure that they remain appropriate.

All but very small limited liability companies must be audited. Of the six accountancy bodies listed earlier, only members of the first four are allowed to sign audit reports. The audit report affirms that their financial statements present a true and fair view and comply with the Companies Act 1985. Until 2000, auditing standards were the responsibility of the Auditing Practices Board, controlled by the CCAB. In that year the Accountancy Foundation was set up to regulate and oversee the auditing profession.[37] It has four subsidiary organizations: the Review Board, the (reformed) Auditing Practices Board (APB), the Ethics Standards Board (ESB), and the Investigation and Discipline Board (IDB). The Review Board acts as a watchdog over the work of the accountancy bodies in the CCAB and the APB, ESB, and IDB. The APB prescribes the basic principles and practices that an auditor is expected to follow when conducting an audit. The ESB sets ethical standards for the profession and the IDB investigates the role of accountants and auditors in major cases of public interest. The Accountancy Foundation is responsible for funding and for appointing members of each of the boards. This regulatory framework is in the private sector. However, it is independent of the accounting profession.

Financial Reporting

British financial reporting is among the most comprehensive in the world. Financial statements generally include:

1. Directors' report
2. Profit and loss account and balance sheet
3. Cash flow statement
4. Statement of total recognized gains and losses
5. Statement of accounting policies
6. Notes that are referenced in the financial statements
7. Auditor's report

The directors' report addresses principal business activities, review of operations and likely developments, important post–balance sheet events, recommended dividends,

---

[36]Work on the Statement of Principles began soon after the ASB was formed and was completed in 1999.
[37]The foundation's Web site is www.accountancyfoundation.com.

names of the directors and their shareholdings, and political and charitable contributions. Listed companies must include a statement on corporate governance with disclosures on directors' remuneration, audit committees and internal controls, and a declaration that the company is a going concern. Financial statements must present a "true and fair view" of a company's state of affairs and profits. To achieve this, additional information may be necessary and, in exceptional circumstances, requirements may be overridden. The latter is known as the "true and fair override."

Group (consolidated) financial statements are required in addition to a parent-only balance sheet. Control of subsidiary "undertakings" occurs with ownership of more than 50 percent of another company's equity capital or control of the board of directors without regard to percentage ownership. The London Stock Exchange requires that listed companies provide half-year interim reports. Listed companies must also report basic and diluted earnings per share.

Another feature of U.K. financial reporting is that small and medium-sized companies are exempt from many financial reporting obligations. The Companies Act sets out size criteria. In general, small and medium-sized companies are permitted to prepare abbreviated accounts with certain minimum prescribed information. Small and medium-sized groups are exempt from preparing consolidated statements.

Accounting Measurements

The United Kingdom allows both the acquisition and merger methods of accounting for business combinations. However, the conditions for the use of the merger method (*pooling-of-interests* in the United States) are so narrow that it is almost never used.

Under the acquisition method, goodwill is calculated as the difference between the fair value of the consideration paid and the fair value of the net assets acquired. FRS 7 specifies that fair values are assigned to identifiable assets and liabilities that exist at the date of acquisition, reflecting the conditions at that time. Future operating losses and reorganization costs cannot be considered in the calculation of goodwill, but must be reflected in post-acquisition income. Goodwill is capitalized and amortized over 20 years or less; however, a longer period or an indefinite period (resulting in no amortization) is possible if goodwill is subject to an annual impairment review. Proportional consolidation is only permitted for unincorporated joint ventures. The equity method is used for *associated* undertakings (in which a company owns 20 percent or more of the voting rights and is not consolidated) and for joint ventures that are companies. SSAP 20 deals with foreign currency translation and requires the closing rate (current rate) method for independent subsidiaries and the temporal method for integrated subsidiaries. Under the former, translation differences are included in shareholders' equity reserves; under the latter, they are included in the profit and loss account. Both the closing and the average exchange rates may be used to translate the profit and loss account. The financial statements of subsidiaries operating in hyperinflationary countries must be adjusted to reflect current price levels before translation.[38]

Assets may be valued at historical cost, current cost, or (as most companies do) using a mixture of the two. Thus, revaluations of land and buildings are permissible. Depreciation and amortization must correspond to the measurement basis used for the

---

[38]FRED 24, published May 2002, would supercede SSAP 20. It retains the basic provisions of SSAP 20 reviewed here, but would no longer allow the closing exchange rate to translate the profit and loss account.

underlying asset. Research expenditures are written off in the year of the expenditure, and development costs may be deferred under specific circumstances. However, in practice, few British companies capitalize any development costs. Inventory (referred to as "stocks") is valued at the lower of cost or net realizable value on a FIFO or average cost basis; LIFO is not acceptable.

Leases that transfer the risks and rewards of ownership to the lessee are capitalized and the lease obligation is shown as a liability. The costs of providing pensions and other retirement benefits must be recognized systematically and rationally over the period during which the employees' services are performed.[39] Contingent losses are accrued when they are probable and can be estimated with reasonable accuracy. Deferred taxes are calculated under the liability method on a full provision basis for most timing differences. Long-term deferred tax balances may be valued at discounted present value. Income smoothing opportunities exist given the flexibility that exists in asset valuation and other measurement areas. Concern has been expressed in the United Kingdom over "creative accounting," and whether its use to mislead rather than inform has increased in recent years.[40] Indeed, the ASB focused much of its early attention on remedying abuses in U.K. accounting.

In 2003, the Department of Trade and Industry announced that, starting January 2005, all U.K. companies will be permitted to use IFRS instead of U.K. GAAP just described. Thus, the EU 2005 initiative for listed companies is extended to nonlisted U.K. companies as well.

United States

Accounting in the United States is regulated by a private-sector body (the Financial Accounting Standards Board, or FASB), but a governmental agency (the Securities and Exchange Commission, or SEC) underpins the authority of its standards. The key link allowing this shared power system to work effectively is the 1973 SEC Accounting Series Release (ASR) No. 150. This release states:

> The Commission intends to continue its policy of looking to the private sector for leadership in establishing and improving accounting principles. For purposes of this policy, principles, standards, and practices promulgated by the FASB in its statements and interpretations, will be considered by the Commission as having substantial authoritative support, and those contrary to such FASB promulgations will be considered to have no such support.[41]

---

[39]FRS 17, published November 2000, introduces a new approach to account for defined benefit schemes. It would require that pension assets be measured at market value and pension liabilities be measured at their present value based on a corporate bond rate. The resulting surplus or deficit, shown on the balance sheet, would be more volatile than under current practices. It is effective for fiscal years starting on or after January 1, 2005.

[40]Christopher Nobes and Robert Parker, *Comparative International Accounting*, 7th ed., Harlow, UK: Pearson Education, 2002, p. 151. For an interesting case history, see A. K. Shah, "Exploring the Influences and Constraints on Creative Accounting in the United Kingdom," *European Accounting Review* 7, no. 1 (1998): 83–104.

[41]Securities and Exchange Commission, *Statement of Policy on the Establishment and Improvement of Accounting Principles and Standards*, Accounting Series Release No. 150. Reprinted in *The Development of SEC Accounting*, G. J. Previts, ed., Reading, MA: Addison-Wesley, 1981, p. 228. The SEC reaffirmed the FASB as the designated accounting standard-setting body in April 2003. This reaffirmation followed an SEC study of the U.S. accounting standards-setting process, as mandated by the 2002 Sarbanes-Oxley Act (discussed later).

Until 2002, the American Institute of Certified Public Accountants (AICPA), another private-sector body, set auditing standards. In that year, the Public Company Accounting Oversight Board (PCAOB) was established with broad powers to regulate audits and auditors of public companies. The PCAOB, discussed later, is a private organization overseen by the SEC.[42]

Accounting Regulation and Enforcement

The U.S. system has no general legal requirements for publication of periodic audited financial statements. Corporations in the United States are formed under state law, not federal law. Each state has its own corporate statutes; in general, these contain minimal requirements for keeping accounting records and publishing periodic financial statements. Many of these statutes are not rigorously enforced, and reports rendered to local agencies are often unavailable to the public. Thus, annual audit and financial reporting requirements realistically exist only at the federal level as specified by the SEC. The SEC has jurisdiction over companies listed on U.S. stock exchanges and companies traded over-the-counter.[43] Other limited-liability companies have no such compulsory requirements for financial reporting, making the United States unusual by international norms.

Even though the SEC has the legal authority to prescribe accounting and reporting standards for public companies, it relies on the private sector to set them. The SEC works with the FASB and exerts pressure when it believes the FASB is moving too slowly or in the wrong direction. At times, the SEC has delayed or overruled pronouncements or has imposed its own requirements.

The SEC is an independent regulatory agency, which means that Congress and the president have no direct influence over its policies. However, the five full-time SEC commissioners are appointed by the president and confirmed by the Senate, and the SEC has only those powers that Congress has granted it by statute. As part of the regulatory process, the SEC issues Accounting Series Releases, Financial Reporting Releases, and Staff Accounting Bulletins. Regulations SX and SK contain the rules for preparing financial reports that must be filed with the SEC. Annual filings by U.S. and Canadian companies are on Form 10K, while those from non-Canadian foreign companies are on Form 20F.

The FASB was established in 1973[44] and has issued 150 Statements of Financial Accounting Standards (SFASs) as of December 2003. The objective of SFASs is to provide information that is useful to present and potential investors, creditors, and others who make investment, credit, and similar decisions. The FASB has seven full-time members: three from professional accounting (CPA) practice, two from industry, and

---

[42]The Web sites of these organizations are: Securities and Exchange Commission, www.sec.gov; Financial Accounting Standards Board, www.fasb.org; American Institute of Certified Public Accountants, www.aicpa.org; and Public Company Accounting Oversight Board, www.pcaobus.org.

[43]Companies traded on the "pink sheets" over-the-counter market are exempt from the SEC's periodic filing requirements if they meet a minimum size test and certain other requirements.

[44]Two other private-sector bodies established U.S. GAAP before the FASB. These were the Committee on Accounting Procedure (1938 to 1959) and the Accounting Principles Board (1959 to 1973).

one each from academia and government. Board members must sever all economic and organizational ties to prior places of employment or ownership in order to serve. The FASB's use of a conceptual framework is a significant feature of accounting standard setting in the United States. Statements of Financial Accounting Concepts set forth fundamentals on which financial accounting and reporting standards are based.

The FASB goes through lengthy due process procedures before issuing an SFAS. In developing its work agenda, it listens to individuals, professional firms, courts of law, companies, and government agencies. It also relies on an emerging issues task force and an advisory council to help identify accounting issues that need attention. Once a topic is added to the agenda, the FASB technical staff does research and analysis and an advisory task force is appointed. A Discussion Memorandum or other discussion document is disseminated for comment, and public hearings are held. The FASB considers oral and written comments in meetings open to the public. Next, an Exposure Draft is issued and further public comments are considered. An SFAS must be approved by four of the seven members. It normally takes at least 2 years to develop and finalize a new standard. The process ensures that standard setting in the United States is both political and technical.   *US GAAP*

Generally accepted accounting principles (GAAP) are comprised of all financial accounting standards, rules, and regulations that must be observed in the preparation of financial reports. The SFASs are the major component of GAAP. Accounting and auditing regulations in the United States are probably more voluminous than in the rest of the world combined and substantially more detailed than in any other country. For this reason, the FASB and SEC are considering moving U.S. GAAP away from rules-based standards toward principles-based standards.

The FASB did not seriously engage itself internationally until the 1990s. In 1991, the FASB developed its first strategic plan for international activities. In 1994, the FASB added the promotion of international comparability to its mission statement. The FASB is now a major cooperative international player, committed to converging U.S. GAAP and IFRS. In 2002, the FASB and IASB formalized their commitment to convergence by signing the so-called Norwalk Agreement. Under this agreement, the two boards pledge to remove existing differences between their standards and coordinate future standard-setting agendas so that major issues are worked on together.

The Sarbanes-Oxley Act was signed into law in 2002, significantly expanding U.S. requirements on corporate governance, disclosure and reporting, and the regulation of the audit profession. Among its more important provisions is the creation of the PCAOB, a new nonprofit organization overseen by the SEC. The PCAOB is responsible for:

- Setting auditing, quality control, ethics, independence, and other standards relating to the preparation of audit reports on companies issuing securities to the public;
- Overseeing the audit of public companies that are subject to the securities laws;
- Inspecting registered public accounting firms;
- Conducting investigations and disciplinary proceedings; and
- Sanctioning registered public accounting firms and referring cases to the SEC or other enforcement bodies for further investigation.

Previously, the AICPA issued auditing standards, was responsible for the Code of Professional Ethics, and disciplined auditors. The PCAOB effectively assumed these responsibilities from the AICPA.[45]

Financial statements are supposed to "present fairly" the financial position of the company and the results of its operations "in conformity with generally accepted accounting principles." Compliance with GAAP is the test for fair presentation. There is no subjective override, such as the "true and fair" override in the United Kingdom. The SEC also expects compliance with GAAP and will not accept an auditor's report with an "adverse" opinion.

Financial Reporting

A typical annual financial report of a large U.S. corporation includes the following components:

1. Report of management
2. Report of independent auditors
3. Primary financial statements (income statement, balance sheet, statement of cash flows, statement of comprehensive income, and statement of stockholders' equity)
4. Management discussion and analysis of results of operations and financial condition
5. Disclosure of accounting policies with the most critical impact on financial statements[46]
6. Notes to financial statements
7. Five- or ten-year comparison of selected financial data
8. Selected quarterly data

Consolidated financial statements are required and published U.S. financial reports typically do not contain parent-company-only statements. Consolidation rules require that all controlled subsidiaries (i.e., ownership of more than 50 percent of the voting shares) be fully consolidated, including those with nonhomogeneous operations.[47] Interim (quarterly) financial reports are required for companies listed on

---

[45]The Sarbanes-Oxley Act was passed in the wake of numerous corporate and accounting scandals, such as Enron and WorldCom. It is the most substantial piece of U.S. business legislation since the 1934 Securities Exchange Act established the SEC. The act limits the services that audit firms can offer clients and prohibits auditors from offering certain nonaudit services (including types of consulting services) to audit clients.

The PCAOB has five board members, two CPAs and three non-CPAs. Board members are appointed by the SEC after consultation with the Chairman of the Federal Reserve Board and the Secretary of the Treasury. They serve 5-year terms. The PCAOB is funded by fees assessed against SEC-registered public companies and registered accounting firms. The PCAOB has adopted on an interim basis the auditing, attestation, quality control, ethics, and independence standards previously issued by the AICPA and its Auditing Standards Board. However, it has made clear that it will not delegate audit standard setting to other organizations, such as the AICPA.

The PCAOB has proposed a standard requiring management and auditors to disclose material weaknesses in a company's internal controls. At the time of writing, the PCAOB is still filling its staff, which is eventually expected to be about 300 people.

[46]A study of 65 of the Fortune 100 companies revealed that these were policies affecting contingencies, goodwill and intangibles, revenue recognition, pension benefits, and derivative securities. See Shearman and Sterling, "Survey: Fortune 100 Critical Accounting Policies Disclosure" (www.realcorporatelawyer .com).

[47]The FASB has proposed extending the consolidation requirement to other entities that a company controls based on its ability to direct the entity's policies and management.

major stock exchanges. These reports typically contain only abbreviated, unaudited financial statements and a concise management commentary.

Accounting Measurements

Accounting measurement rules in the United States assume that a business entity will continue as a going concern. Accrual basis measurements are pervasive, and transactions and events recognition rules rely heavily on the matching concept. A consistency requirement insists on uniformity of accounting treatment of like items within each accounting period and from one period to the next. If changes in practices or procedures occur, the changes and their effects must be disclosed.

Business combinations must be accounted for as a purchase. Goodwill is capitalized as the difference between the fair value of the consideration given in the exchange and the fair value of the underlying net assets acquired (including other intangibles). It is reviewed for impairment annually and written off and expensed to earnings when its book value exceeds its fair value.[48] Proportional consolidation is not practiced. Joint ventures are accounted for using the equity method as are investments nonconsolidated, 20 percent- to 50 percent-owned affiliated companies. Foreign currency translation follows the requirements of SFAS No. 52, which relies on the foreign subsidiary's functional currency to determine translation methodology.

The United States relies on historical cost to value tangible and intangible assets. Revaluations are permitted only after a business combination accounted for as a purchase. Both accelerated and straight-line depreciation methods are permissible. Estimated economic usefulness determines depreciation and amortization periods. All research and development costs are typically expensed as incurred, though there are special capitalization rules for computer software costs.

LIFO, FIFO, and average cost methods are permissible and widely used for inventory pricing. LIFO is popular because it can be used for federal income tax purposes. However, if LIFO is used for tax purposes, it must also be used for financial reporting purposes.

When financial leases are in substance the purchase of property, the value of the property is capitalized and a corresponding liability is booked. The costs of pensions and other post-retirement benefits are accrued over the periods in which employees earn their benefits and unfunded obligations are reported as a liability. Contingent losses/liabilities are accrued when they are probable and the amount can be reasonably estimated. Income smoothing techniques are not allowed.

Finally, there is the issue of deferred taxes because (except for LIFO) financial and tax reporting are distinct. Income taxes are accounted for using the liability method. Deferred taxes are accrued for the tax effects of temporary differences between financial and tax accounting methods, and are measured based on the future tax rates that will apply when these items reverse. Comprehensive income tax allocation is required.

Exhibit 3-2 summarizes the significant accounting practices in the six countries surveyed in this chapter.

---

[48]Both the purchase and pooling-of-interests (merger) methods were previously used to account for business combinations. They were not alternatives: pooling-of-interests was used when the combination met specified criteria. Under the purchase method, goodwill was capitalized and amortized on a straight-line basis over a maximum of 40 years and the amortization amount was included in current period income. SFAS 141 and 142, issued in 2001, changed how business combinations were accounting for, as described above.

Exhibit 3-2 Summary of Significant Accounting Practices

	France	Germany	Japan	The Netherlands	United Kingdom	United States
1. Business combinations: purchase or pooling	Purchase[a]	Purchase[a]	Purchase[a]	Purchase[a]	Purchase[a]	Purchase
2. Goodwill	Capitalize & amortize	Capitalize & amortize	Capitalize & amortize[b]	Capitalize & amortize	Capitalize & amortize[c]	Capitalize & impairment tested
3. Affiliated companies	Equity method	Equity method	Equity method	Equity method	Equity method	Equity method
4. Foreign currency translation: current rate method	Autonomous subsidiaries	Autonomous subsidiaries[d]	All subsidiaries	Autonomous subsidiaries	Autonomous subsidiaries	Autonomous subsidiaries
Temporal method	Integrated subsidiaries	Integrated subsidiaries[d]	Not used	Integrated subsidiaries	Integrated subsidiaries	Integrated subsidiaries
5. Asset valuation	Historical cost	Historical cost	Historical cost	Historical & current cost	Historical & current cost	Historical cost
6. Depreciation charges	Economic based[e]	Tax based	Tax based	Economic based	Economic based	Economic based
7. LIFO inventory valuation	Not used	Not used	Not used	Not used	Not acceptable	Used
8. Finance leases	Not capitalized	Not capitalized	Capitalized[f]	Capitalized	Capitalized	Capitalized
9. Deferred taxes	Accrued[g]	Accrued[g]	Accrued	Accrued	Accrued	Accrued
10. Reserves for income smoothing	Used	Used	No	Some	Some	No

[a]Pooling also allowed in narrow circumstances, but not widely used.
[b]Under HGB, may also be written off to reserves.
[c]Nonamortization permitted if subject to annual impairment review.
[d]Under HGB, no requirements.
[e]In consolidated statements; tax based in individual company statements.
[f]When ownership is transferred; other finance leases do not have to be capitalized.
[g]In consolidated statements only; not accrued in individual company statements.

Selected References

Alexander, D., and S. Archer, eds., *European Accounting Guide,* 5th ed., New York: Aspen, 2003.

Arai, K., *Accounting in Japan,* Tokyo: Waseda University Institute for Research in Business Administration, 1994.

Baker, C.R., A. Mikol, and R. Quick, "Regulation of the Statutory Auditor in the European Union: A Comparative Survey of the United Kingdom, France and Germany," *The European Accounting Review* 10, no. 4 (2001): 763–786.

Deloitte, "Country Accounting Standards Update," IAS Plus Web site (www.iasplus.com).

Ding, Y., H. Stolowy, and M. Tenenhaus, "Shopping Around for Accounting Practices: The Financial Statement Presentation of French Groups," *Abacus* 39, no. 1 (February 2003): 42–65.

Eberhartinger, E. L. E., "The Impact of Tax Rules on Financial Reporting in Germany, France, and the U.K.," *The International Journal of Accounting* 34, no. 1 (1999): 93–119.

Glaum, M., "Bridging the GAAP: The Changing Attitude of German Managers Towards Anglo-American Accounting and Accounting Harmonization," *Journal of International Financial Management and Accounting* (Spring 2000): 23–47.

KPMG, *IFRS Compared with U.S. GAAP and French GAAP* (www.kpmg.fi/attachment.asp?Section=181&Item=1058), 2003.

KPMG, *Sarbanes-Oxley: A Closer Look,* Montvale: KPMG, January 2003.

McLeay, S., ed. *Accounting Regulation in Europe,* London: Macmillan, 1999.

Meek, G. K., ed., *Country Studies in International Accounting—Americas and the Far East,* Cheltenham, UK: Edward Elger, 1996.

Nobes, C., and R. Parker, *Comparative International Accounting,* 7th ed., Harlow, U.K.: Pearson Education, 2002.

Ordelheide, D., and KPMG, eds., *Transnational Accounting,* 2nd ed., Hampshire & New York: Palgrave, 2001.

Ordre des Experts-Comptables and Compagnie Nationale des Commissaires aux Comptes, *Developments in French Accounting and Auditing 1998,* Paris: Expert Comptable Média, 1999.

Parker, R. H., and C. Nobes, *An International View of True and Fair Accounting,* London: Routledge, 1994.

Singleton, W.R., and S. Globerman, "The Changing Nature of Financial Disclosure in Japan," *The International Journal of Accounting* 37, no. 1 (2002): 95–111.

Walton, P., ed., *European Financial Reporting: A History,* London: Academic Press, 1995.

Walton, P., ed., *Country Studies in International Accounting—Europe.* Cheltenham, UK: Edward Elgar, 1996.

Zeff, S. A., "How the U.S. Accounting Profession Got Where It Is Today: Part I," *Accounting Horizons* 17, no. 3 (September 2003): 189–205.

Zeff, S.A., "How the U.S. Accounting Profession Got Where It Is Today: Part II," *Accounting Horizons* 17, no. 4 (December 2003): 267–286.

Discussion Questions

1. Auditor oversight bodies have recently been established in most countries discussed in this chapter. Identify the auditor oversight bodies discussed in this chapter and when they were formed. What is the reason for this recent trend?

2. In most countries, published financial accounting standards differ from those actually used in practice. What causes such differences and who should be concerned about them?

3. Code law countries typically have portions of their financial accounting and reporting requirements anchored in the law itself and other portions derived from professional standards or recommendations. Explain whether extensive formal legal requirements lead to high-quality levels of financial reporting.

4. Large companies often list their equity shares on different stock exchanges around the world. What accounting issues does this practice raise?

5. Consider the following statement: "Experience shows that the needs of national and international markets, for international harmonization in particular, are better served by self-regulation and development than by governmental regulation." Do you agree? Why or why not?

6. In France, financial accounting standards and practices originate primarily from three authoritative sources: (a) companies legislation (Plan Comptable Général and Code de Commerce), (b) professional opinions and recommendations (CNC, CRC, OEC, and CNCC), and (c) stock exchange regulations (AMF). Which of these three has the greatest influence on day-to-day French accounting practice?

7. Consider the following statement: "The German Accounting Standards Committee has been modeled on Anglo-American and international practice." Do you agree? Why or why not?

8. What is the reason for the Japanese "Big Bang" and what changes in accounting practice have resulted from it?

9. The most novel feature of the Dutch accounting scene is the Enterprise Chamber of the Court of Justice of Amsterdam. What is the mission of the Enterprise Chamber? How is this mission carried out?

10. Cite three examples of Dutch flexibility in financial reporting requirements.

11. U.K. financial statements are "true and fair" while U.S. financial statements "present fairly." What is the difference between these two concepts?

12. What is the difference between principles-based and rules-based accounting standards? What evidence exists that U.S. GAAP is rules-based?

Exercises

1. This chapter provides synopses of national accounting practice systems in six developed countries.

   Required: For each country, list:

   a. the name of the national financial accounting standard-setting board or agency
   b. the name of the agency, institute, or other organization charged with supervising and enforcing financial accounting standards

2. Refer to your answer to Exercise 1.

   Required: Other than the United States, which country appears to have the most effective accounting and financial reporting supervision mechanism for companies whose securities are traded in public financial markets? Should each country that has a stock exchange (and therefore a public financial market) also have a regulatory agency that enforces accounting and financial reporting rules? Write a concise paragraph to support your answer.

3. Empirical research supports the idea that accounting diversity complicates business decision making. These complications seem particularly pronounced in multinational business operations.

   Required:

   a. From the perspective of multinational business decision making, list five distinct advantages and five distinct disadvantages of existing worldwide accounting diversity.
   b. As far as you can judge, which of the six countries has the most benign financial accounting environment in terms of multinational business operations and from the perspective of corporate management?

4. French and German companies are allowed to use International Financial Reporting Standards or U.S. GAAP in their consolidated financial statements. Many internationally listed French and German companies take advantage of this flexibility.

   Required: Go to the Web site of the New York Stock Exchange (www.nyse.com), Nasdaq (www.nasdaq.com), or the London Stock Exchange (www.londonstock exchange.com) and identify three listed companies from either France or Germany. Refer to these companies' annual reports to document the accounting principles used. (Hint: You may link to corporate Web sites through www.corporate information.com and www.carolworld.com. The NYSE and Nasdaq Web sites also have links to their listed companies.)

5. The United Kingdom and United States have a common accounting heritage and are linked by history and language. *Anglo-American* accounting is a term sometimes used to denote their accounting styles, which are similar in orientation, purpose, and approach. Yet accounting differences still exist between these two countries.

   Required:

   a. Identify the major differences between U.K. and U.S. accounting that are discussed in this chapter.
   b. Which country is likely to be systematically more conservative in measuring reported earnings? Why do you think so?

6. The International Federation of Accountants (IFAC) is a worldwide organization of professional accounting bodies. IFAC's Web site (www.ifac.org) has links to a number of accounting bodies around the world.

   Required: Visit IFAC's Web site. List the accounting organizations discussed in this chapter that are linked to IFAC's Web site.

7. Analysts often try to restate financial statement amounts from one GAAP to another. For example, the financial statements of companies from legal compliance countries are often restated to a fair presentation basis.

Required: List the major financial statement items that you think would need to be adjusted to convert from a legal compliance to a fair presentation basis.

8. Reread Chapter 3 and its discussion questions.

Required:

a. As you go through this material, prepare a list of 10 expressions, terms, or short phrases that are unfamiliar or unusual in your home country.
b. Write a concise definition or explanation of each item.

9. The following describes Japanese accounting before the "Big Bang":

The preparation of consolidated financial statements is based on the Securities and Exchange Law. Individual company accounts are the basis for the consolidated statements, and normally the same principles are used at both levels. Subsidiaries are consolidated if a parent directly or indirectly owns more than 50 percent of the shares. (However, Japanese regulations have materiality tests that can lead to the exclusion of significant subsidiaries in consolidation.) The purchase method of accounting for business combinations is normally used for business combinations. Goodwill is measured on the basis of the book value of the net assets acquired, not the fair market value as is common in most other countries. Goodwill is amortized over 5 years. The equity method is used in consolidated statements for investments in nonconsolidated subsidiaries and 20 percent- to 50 percent-owned affiliated companies, but the cost method is used in individual company statements. The equity method is also used to account for joint ventures; proportional consolidation is not allowed. Under the foreign currency translation standard, assets and liabilities of foreign subsidiaries are translated at the current (year-end) exchange rate, revenues and expenses at either the year-end or average rate, and translation adjustments are carried as an asset or liability on the balance sheet.

Accounting measurements based on historical cost are pervasive. Inventory may be valued at cost of the lower of cost or market; cost is most often used. However, in the event of a significant and permanent decline in value, inventory must be written down to market. FIFO, LIFO, and average are all acceptable cost flow methods, with average the most popular. Fixed assets are valued at cost and depreciated in accordance with the tax laws.

Research and development costs may be capitalized if they relate to new products or techniques, the exploitation of resources, or the development of markets. When capitalized, research and development is amortized over 5 years. Finance leases, those transferring the risks and rewards of ownership to the lessee, are capitalized whereas lease payments on operating leases are charged to income when incurred.

Deferred taxes are not provided for (or needed) in individual company accounts. They are permitted in consolidated financial statements, but normally not provided there, either. Contingent losses are provided for when they are probable and can be reasonably estimated. Tax regulations limit the deductibility of employee retirement and severance benefits to 40 percent of the amount and so are normally only accrued up to this amount. Pension costs are expensed as paid and unfunded obligations are not accrued. Legal reserves are required: each year a company must allocate an amount equal to at least 10 percent of cash dividends and bonuses paid to directors and statutory auditors until the legal reserve reaches 25 percent of capital stock.

Required: Identify the major changes in Japanese accounting since the Big Bang occurred.

10. Analyze the six national accounting practice systems summarized in this chapter.

Required:

a. For each of the six countries treated in this chapter, select the most important financial accounting practice or principle at variance with international norms.
b. For each selection you make, state briefly your reasons for its inclusion on your list.

11. Accounting standard setting in most countries involves a combination of private- and public-sector groups. The private sector includes the accounting profession and other groups affected by the financial reporting process, such as users and preparers of financial statements, and organized labor. The public sector includes government agencies such as tax authorities, ministries responsible for commercial law, and securities commissions. The stock market is another potential influence.

Required: Complete a matrix indicating whether each of the above groups significantly influences accounting standard setting in the six countries discussed in this chapter. List the groups across the top and the countries down the side; indicate the influence of each group with a yes or a no.

12. Listed below are certain financial ratios used by analysts:
   - *Liquidity:* current ratio; cash flow from operations to current liabilities
   - *Solvency:* debt to equity; debt to assets
   - *Profitability:* return on assets; return on equity

Required: Assume that you are comparing the financial ratios of companies from two countries discussed in this chapter. Discuss how the accounting practices identified in Exhibit 3-2 would affect your comparison for each of the six ratios in the list.

CASE 3-1   STANDING ON PRINCIPLES

Recent U.S. accounting scandals, such as Enron and WorldCom, have caused some to question whether current U.S. generally accepted accounting principles (GAAP) are really protecting investors. Critics, including the U.S. Securities and Exchange Commission (SEC), charge that the rules-based approach to U.S. GAAP encourages a check-the-box mentality that inhibits transparency in financial reporting. Some observers express a preference for principles-based standards such as International Financial Reporting Standards or those found in the United Kingdom. Both the Financial Accounting Standards Board (FASB) and the SEC have released reports on the feasibility of principles-based accounting standards in the United States.[49]

The following appeared in a leading British professional accounting journal:

Ever since the Enron debacle first hit the news, smug U.K. accountants have found a new excuse for feeling superior to their transatlantic cousins. The U.S. Financial Accounting Standards Board's massive *oeuvre* have been scoffed at as being merely a whole bunch of rules that don't hang together. Both British and International standards, by way of contrast, are asserted to be based on principles. This essential difference, it is argued, helps to explain why the U.S. profession has got itself into such deep trouble.

Perhaps. But probably not. It certainly seems true that the highly detailed American standards have tended to invite legalistic interpretations and loopholing, whereas the U.K.'s paramount requirement to present a true and fair view has helped to remind us that accounting is more than a compliance activity. However, it is much too glib to characterise their accounting standards as lacking in principle compared to ours; in terms of their intellectual rigour, American accounting standards compare favourably with any others in the world....

How is it that the U.K. and International Accounting Standards Boards appear to have found reliable principles on which to base their own standards, principles that have eluded FASB? After all, both bodies have themselves adopted conceptual frameworks that are largely copies of the FASB's version, and claim to follow them. The answer is that they haven't. Our standards aren't really more principled than the American ones, they are simply less detailed. And even that is changing—both the U.K. and IASB rulebooks have swollen very considerably in recent years, often inspired (if that is the word) by the content of the equivalent American standards....[50]

---

[49]Financial Accounting Standards Board, "Proposal: Principles-Based Approach to U.S. Standard Setting," www.fasb.org/proposals/principles-based_approach.pdf (October 21, 2002); and Securities and Exchange Commission, "Study Pursuant to Section 108(d) of the Sarbanes-Oxley Act of 2002 on the Adoption by the United States Financial Reporting System of a Principles-Based Accounting System," www.sec.gov/news/studies/principlesbasedstand.htm#1f (July 25, 2003).

[50]Ron Paterson, "A Matter of Principle," *Accountancy* (February 2003): 98.

REQUIRED

1. What is the difference between rules-based and principles-based accounting standards and what are the advantages and disadvantages of each?
2. Why has U.S. GAAP evolved into a rules-based approach? Would principles-based standards be effective in the United States? Why or why not?
3. What needs to change in the United States to make principles-based standards effective?
4. Are investors and analysts better served by rules-based or principles-based accounting standards? Why do you say so?

CASE 3-2   WHAT DIFFERENCE DOES IT REALLY MAKE?

As an analyst for a securities firm, you are aware that accounting practices differ around the world. Yet you wonder whether these differences really have any material effect on companies' financial statements. You also know that the SEC in the United States requires non-U.S. registrants to reconcile key financial data from their home country GAAP to U.S. GAAP. You obtain two such reconciliations for the 2002 reporting year. The sources are the 2002 Form 20F SEC filings for Groupe Danone (a French food products company) and BASF (a German chemicals company).

GROUPE DANONE

CONSOLIDATED FINANCIAL STATEMENTS

NOTES TO THE CONSOLIDATED FINANCIAL STATEMENTS

Summary of differences between accounting principles followed by the Company and United States generally accepted accounting principles

The accompanying financial statements have been prepared in accordance with French GAAP, which differ in certain significant respects from U.S. GAAP.

Description of differences

These differences have been reflected in the financial information given in the paragraphs below and mainly relate to the following items:

1. Brand names and goodwill amortization.
Under French GAAP, the brand names that have been separately identified on the acquisition of subsidiaries are not systematically amortized but can be exceptionally impaired. Goodwill is systematically amortized over a period that reflects, as fairly as possible, the assumptions, objectives, and prospects existing at the acquisition time. Management periodically evaluates whether changes occurred that would require revision of the estimated useful life of the goodwill or would result in an impairment.

Under U.S. GAAP, in accordance with SFAS 142, goodwill and indefinite-lived intangible assets are not amortized but are tested for impairment annually. On January 1, 2002, for the purpose of this reconciling statement, the Company adopted SFAS 142, which is to be applied on a prospective basis. Therefore, amortization charges of goodwill recorded in the Group's financial statements (€122 million in 2002) are reversed in this reconciling statement.

Under U.S. GAAP, prior to SFAS 142, in accordance with APB 17, intangible assets such as brand names and goodwill had to be amortized over their useful life, which could not exceed 40 years. Prior to SFAS 142, for the purpose of reconciling to U.S. GAAP, brand names were amortized over a 40 year period (which represented amortization charges of €42 million and €43 million for 2001 and 2000, respectively).

Consequently, the net book value of goodwill and brand names under French GAAP differ from their net book value under U.S. GAAP and impairment charges and capital gains or losses resulting from disposals may be different under French GAAP and under U.S. GAAP.

2. Goodwill relating to the acquisition of foreign subsidiaries.

Goodwill relating to the acquisition of subsidiaries in the euro zone (relating to the acquisition of most foreign subsidiaries until 2000) are translated in the Group's accounts using a historical exchange rate when U.S. GAAP require the use of the closing exchange rate. Under U.S. GAAP, the difference is part of the "Translation adjustments" component of stockholders' equity.

Amortization of goodwill relating to the acquisition of subsidiaries in the euro zone (amortization of most goodwill relating to the acquisition of foreign subsidiaries until 2000) is computed on the basis of gross values translated at the historical exchange rate. Under U.S. GAAP, prior to SFAS 142, the annual amortization charge

was translated at the average exchange rate during the year.

3. Stock options.

Until January 1999, the Company granted stock options to eligible employees under fixed plans with a discount, at a price lower than the prevailing market price; since that date, all grants are made at fair value at the date of grant. Accounting for this discount is not addressed by French GAAP and these transactions have no effect on the statement of income. Under U.S. GAAP, the discount, measured at the date of grant, is considered as compensation to employees. The effect of the decrease to net income and increase to stockholders' equity (in other comprehensive income) for the amount of compensation expense is reflected as a U.S. GAAP adjustment and shown below.

4. Available-for-sale securities.

Under French GAAP, available-for-sale securities are recorded at the lower of their acquisition cost and their fair value; in case of a decline in fair value, an impairment loss is recognized in earnings. Under U.S. GAAP, available-for-sale securities are carried at market value, with the unrealized gains and losses recorded directly in other comprehensive income, a component of stockholders' equity.

5. Deferred income taxes on brand names.

Deferred income taxes on brand names resulting from purchase price allocation are not recorded. Consequently, the goodwill arising on the acquisition of the related subsidiaries is not increased by the amount of such deferred tax liability. Under U.S. GAAP, a deferred tax liability computed at the local tax rate applicable to long-term capital gains is recorded, and goodwill is increased by the same amount. Prior to SFAS 142, the deferred tax liability was reversed to profit as the related intangible asset was amortized, whereas the amortization charge of the additional goodwill matched this profit.

Had U.S. GAAP been applied, deferred income taxes (long-term liabilities) and goodwill would be increased by €252 million as of December 31, 2002 (€326 million as of December 31, 2001).

Goodwill amortization, offset by an equal amount of deferred tax benefit of €10 million and €11 million for 2000 and 2001, respectively, would have been recorded under U.S. GAAP.

6. Purchase accounting—Fair value.
Purchase accounting applied to a less than wholly-owned subsidiary results in all of the assets and liabilities of the purchased subsidiary being recorded at fair values when the parent purchases its majority interest, and the minority interest in the subsidiary net assets is adjusted to reflect its share of the revalued net assets (excluding goodwill).

Under U.S. GAAP, no write-up in fair value of the net assets of the subsidiary related to the minority interest should occur. Accordingly, the write-up to fair values in brand names related to the minority interest should be reversed, thus decreasing brand names and minority interest by €133 million as of December 31, 2002 (€134 million as of December 31, 2001). The remainder of the write-ups to fair value in other net assets related to the minority interest is not considered material.

7. Derivative instruments.
Under French GAAP, the interest rates and currency derivatives, that are hedging instruments, are not reported on the balance sheet, except for related cash out- or in-flows. Any gain or loss on those derivatives are deferred until the period in which earnings are affected by the underlying hedged items.

Under U.S. GAAP, all derivative instruments are reported on the balance sheet at fair value. If the derivative is designated as a fair value hedge, the changes in the fair value

of the derivative and of the hedged item are recognized in earnings. If the derivative is designated as a cash flow hedge, the effective portions of changes in the fair value of the derivative are recorded in other comprehensive income and are recognized in the income statement when the hedged item affects earnings. Ineffective portions of changes in the fair value of cash flow hedges are recognized in earnings.

8. Restructuring costs.
Under French GAAP, restructuring costs are recorded as soon as a detailed restructuring plan has been decided by the management and communicated to third parties. These restructuring costs include costs related to employee benefits, costs associated with the elimination and reduction of production lines, and losses on assets impairments and disposals of assets.

Under U.S. GAAP, certain employee benefits, such as relocation costs or transfer benefits, do not qualify as exit costs and are expensed as incurred.

9. Pension liability.
Under U.S. GAAP, if the fair value of plan assets for pension plans is lower than the Accumulated Benefit Obligation, the liability has to be adjusted to reflect the difference. An equal amount has to be recorded as an intangible asset or as a reduction of equity for the portion that exceeds the amount of unrecognized prior service cost.

10. Comprehensive income.
Comprehensive income is the term used to define all nonowner changes in shareholders' equity. Comprehensive income is a concept not addressed by French GAAP. Under U.S. GAAP, comprehensive income includes, in addition to net income:

- additional paid-in capital related to compensation cost on shares issued to employees

- net unrealized holding gains/losses arising during the period on available-for-sale securities
- movements in cumulative translation adjustments
- negative equity adjustments as an additional pension liability not yet recognized as net periodic pension cost
- effective portion of changes in the fair value of the derivative instruments designated as cash flow hedges.

Reconciling Statements

Reconciliation of Net Income— Determination of Comprehensive Income and Reconciliation of Stockholders' Equity. The reconciliation of net income from French GAAP to U.S. GAAP, together with the reporting of U.S. GAAP comprehensive income, and a reconciliation of stockholders' equity from French GAAP to U.S. GAAP is as follows:

	Year ended December 31,		
(All amounts in millions of euros except per share data)	*2000*	*2001*	*2002*
Net income under French GAAP	**721**	**132**	**1,283**
US GAAP adjustments:			
1. Brand names and goodwill amortization	(43)	(42)	122
2. Brand names and goodwill impairment losses	69	20	(2)
3. Additional capital gain (or loss) on disposal under US GAAP	79	—	(7)
4. Amortization of goodwill of foreign subsidiaries	(3)	3	—
5. Compensation costs under stock option plans	(1)	(1)	—
6. Derivative instruments	—	9	36
7. Available-for-sale securities	—	—	9
8. Restructuring costs	—	13	(13)
Net income with US GAAP adjustments before tax effect and minority interests	822	134	1,428
Tax effect of the above adjustments	(19)	67	(8)
Minority interests effect of above adjustments	4	4	—
Net income under US GAAP	**807**	**205**	**1,420**
Basic earnings per share under US GAAP	5.74	1.47	10.77
Diluted earnings per share under US GAAP	5.71	1.48	10.43
Net income under US GAAP, a component of comprehensive income	**807**	**205**	**1,420**
Other comprehensive income, net of tax:			
• Additional paid-in capital related to compensation costs on shares issued to employees	1	1	—
• Change in net unrealized gains/losses on available-for-sale securities	6	(24)	(38)
less: Reclassification adjustment for net gains/losses included in net income	—	—	—
• Change in cumulative translation adjustments	209	(508)	(1,221)
less: Reclassification adjustment for net gains/losses included in net income	18	—	141
• Minimum pension liability	—	(25)	(17)

	Year ended December 31,		
(All amounts in millions of euros except per share data)	*2000*	*2001*	*2002*
Other comprehensive income (loss) under US GAAP	**234**	**(556)**	**(1,135)**
Comprehensive income (loss) under US GAAP	**1,041**	**(351)**	**285**
Stockholders' equity under French GAAP	7,189	5,947	5,087
US GAAP adjustments:			
1. Brand names and goodwill amortization	(353)	(455)	(260)
2. Goodwill relating to the acquisition of foreign subsidiaries	125	51	(45)
3. Unrealized gains on available-for-sale securities	128	99	65
4. Derivative instruments	—	9	20
5. Restructuring costs	—	13	—
6. Minimum pension liability	—	(36)	(60)
7. Other	—	(25)	—
Tax effect of the above adjustments	(84)	(82)	(4)
Minority interests effect of above adjustments	36	33	33
Stockholders' equity under US GAAP	**7,041**	**5,554**	**4,836**

BASF GROUP

NOTES TO THE CONSOLIDATED FINANCIAL STATEMENTS

Reconciliation to U.S. GAAP

The Consolidated Financial Statements comply with U.S. GAAP as far as permissible under German GAAP. The remaining differences between German and U.S. GAAP relate to valuation methods that are required under U.S. GAAP but which are not permissible under German GAAP.

The following is a summary of the significant adjustments to net income and stockholders' equity that would be required if U.S. GAAP had been fully applied rather than German GAAP.

Reconciliation of Net Income to U.S. GAAP

	Note		Year ended December 31,		
		2002	*2002*	*2001*	*2000*
			(euros and dollars in millions except per share amounts)		
Net income as reported in the Consolidated Financial Statements of income under German GAAP		$1,577.3	€1,504.4	€5,858.2	€1,239.8
Adjustments required to conform with U.S. GAAP:					
Capitalization of interest	(a)	(6.7)	(6.4)	50.7	53.7
Capitalization of software developed for internal use	(b)	32.0	30.5	64.1	51.0
Valuation of pension funds	(c)	74.7	71.2	81.7	118.9
					(continued)

	Note	2002	2002	2001	2000
		(euros and dollars in millions except per share amounts)			
Accounting for derivatives at fair value and valuation of long-term foreign currency items at year end rates	(d)	(150.9)	(143.9)	(74.3)	69.4
Valuation of securities at market values	(e)	—	—	(4.5)	—
Valuation adjustments relating to companies accounted for under the equity method	(f)	13.5	12.9	(30.3)	8.3
Reversal of goodwill amortization and write-offs due to permanent impairment	(g)	221.2	211.0	—	—
Other adjustments	(h)	(0.5)	(0.5)	(6.8)	(9.0)
Deferred taxes and recognition of tax credit for dividend payments	(i)	50.4	48.1	(252.0)	(73.7)
Minority interests	(j)	(10.9)	(10.4)	5.6	(4.8)
Net income in accordance with U.S. GAAP		**$1,800.1**	**€1,716.9**	**€5,692.4**	**€1,453.6**

Reconciliation of Stockholders' Equity to U.S. GAAP

	Note	2002	2002	2001
		(euros and dollars in millions)		
Stockholders' equity as reported in the Consolidated Balance Sheets under German GAAP		$17,763.9	€16,942.2	€17,521.8
Minority interests		(415.5)	(396.3)	(359.7)
Stockholders' equity excluding minority interests		17,348.4	16,545.9	17,162.1
Adjustments required to conform with U.S. GAAP:				
Capitalization of interest	(a)	569.1	542.8	566.5
Capitalization of software developed for internal use	(b)	202.2	192.8	165.2
Valuation of pension funds	(c)	958.3	914.0	860.9
Accounting for derivatives at fair value and valuation of long-term foreign currency items at year end rates	(d)	(120.7)	(115.1)	37.6
Valuation of securities at market values	(e)	105.5	100.6	363.3
Valuation adjustments relating to companies accounted for under the equity method	(f)	145.0	138.3	126.0
Reversal of goodwill amortization and write-offs due to permanent impairment	(g)	217.5	207.4	—
Other adjustments	(h)	113.1	107.9	116.5
Deferred taxes and recognition of tax credit for dividend payments	(i)	(722.2)	(688.8)	(841.3)
Minority interests	(j)	(27.3)	(26.0)	(18.6)
Stockholders' equity in accordance with U.S. GAAP		**$18,788.9**	**€17,919.8**	**€18,538.2**

(a) Capitalization of interest: For U.S. GAAP purposes, the Company capitalizes interest on borrowings during the active construction period of major capital projects. Capitalized interest is added to the cost of the underlying assets and is amortized over the useful lives of the assets. The capitalization of interest relating to capital projects is not permissible under German GAAP.

In calculating capitalized interest, the Company has made assumptions with respect to the capitalization rate and the average amount of accumulated expenditures. The Company's subsidiaries generally use the entity-specific weighted-average borrowing rate as the capitalization rate.

(b) Capitalization of software developed for internal use: Certain costs incurred for computer software developed or obtained for the Company's internal use are to be capitalized beginning in 1999 and amortized over the expected useful life of the software. Such costs have been expensed in these financial statements because the capitalization of self-developed intangible assets is not permissible under German GAAP.

(c) Valuation of pension funds: Pension benefits under Company pension schemes are partly funded in a legally independent fund "BASF Pensionskasse VVaG" ("BASF Pensionskasse"). Pension liabilities and plan assets of BASF Pensionskasse are not included in BASF Group's balance sheet. However, contributions to the BASF Pensionskasse are included in expenses for pensions and assistance.

BASF guarantees the commitments of the BASF Pensionskasse. For U.S. GAAP purposes, BASF Pensionskasse would be classified as a defined benefit plan and therefore included in the calculation of net periodic pension cost as well as the projected benefit obligation and plan assets. The valuation of the pension obligations under the projected unit credit method and of the fund assets of BASF Pensionskasse at market values would result in a prepaid pension asset according to U.S. GAAP that is not recorded in the Consolidated Financial Statements under German GAAP.

Net periodic pension cost according to U.S. GAAP would be lower than showing the Company's contribution to the BASF Pensionskasse as expense. Information about the funded status of the BASF Pensionskasse is provided in the following table:

	2002	2001
	(euros in millions)	
Plan assets as of December 31,	€3,527.9	€3,886.4
Projected benefit obligation as of December 31,	3,413.1	3,294.3
Funded status	114.8	592.1
Unrecognized actuarial losses	593.3	59.8
Prepaid pension asset	€ 708.1	€ 651.9

The valuation of certain pension plans of foreign subsidiaries, according to SFAS 87, also resulted in prepaid pension assets (Note 23), included in the reconciliation to U.S. GAAP. After consideration of unrecognized actuarial gains and losses, €205.9 million in 2002 and €209.0 million in 2001 were included in the reconciliation to U.S. GAAP.

(d) Accounting for derivatives at fair value and valuation of long-term foreign currency items: Beginning in 2001, derivative contracts are to be accounted for at fair values as required by SFAS 133 and 138.

Where hedge accounting is not applicable, changes in the fair values of derivative contracts are to be included in net income, together with foreign exchange gains and losses of the underlying transactions.

Under German GAAP, long-term receivables and liabilities denominated in a foreign currency are converted into euros at the exchange rates of the date when the transactions took place or the lower exchange rates at the end of the year for receivables and the higher exchange rates for liabilities. U.S. GAAP requires conversion at the exchange rate at the end of the year.

Under German GAAP, unrealized gains on swaps and other forward contracts are deferred until settlement or termination while unrealized expected losses from firm commitments are recognized as of each period end. Under U.S. GAAP, these contracts are marked to market.

Furthermore, hedge accounting by a combined valuation of underlying transaction and derivatives is allowed by SFAS 133 to a lower extent than applied in these financial statements.

(e) Valuation of securities: Under U.S. GAAP, available-for-sale securities are recorded at market values on the balance sheet date. If the effect comes from unrealized profits or nonpermanent impairments, the change in valuation is immediately recognized in a separate component of stockholders' equity. Realized profits and losses are credited or charged to income, as are other than temporary impairments of value. The major part of securities and other investments are considered to be available-for-sale. Under German GAAP, such securities and other investments are valued at the lower of acquisition cost or market value at the balance sheet date.

(f) Valuation adjustments relating to companies accounted for under the equity method: For purposes of the reconciliation to U.S. GAAP, the earnings of companies accounted for using the equity method have been determined using valuation principles prescribed by U.S. GAAP.

(g) Reversal of goodwill amortization and write-offs due to permanent impairment: Goodwill is amortized over its useful life in accordance with German GAAP. The new U.S. GAAP standard SFAS 142 "Goodwill and Other Intangible Assets," which was enacted in June 2001 and has to be applied for the first time in 2002, only requires write-offs in case of expected permanent impairment of value. The goodwill amortizations included in these financial statements have to be reversed and added back to net income. Write-offs due to impairment were not necessary.

In 2001 the retroactive application of SFAS 142 would have resulted in an increase of earnings in accordance with U.S. GAAP of €243.3 million after deduction of €75.0 million income taxes. Earnings per share would have increased by €0.40 in 2001. The increase in 2000 would have been €290.9; accounting for deferred taxes of €88.4 million, earnings per share would have increased by €0.47.

(h) Other adjustments: This item primarily includes the reversal of maintenance provisions and reclassification of provisions for stock compensation. German GAAP requires companies to accrue provisions as of the end of the year for the expected costs of omitted maintenance procedures expected to take place in the first 3 months of the following year. Such costs would be expensed as incurred under U.S. GAAP. The amounts included in the reconciliation of net income related to maintenance provisions were €6.4 million in 2002, €(5.6) million in 2001, and €(1.4) in 2000; the amounts in the reconciliation of stockholders' equity were €33.7 million in 2002 and €27.3 million in 2001.

Following a resolution by the Board of Executive Directors in 2002, stock options are to be settled in cash. Under U.S. GAAP, such obligations are to be accounted for as stock appreciation rights based on the intrinsic value of the options on the balance sheet date. Under U.S. GAAP, options granted in prior years, for which cash settlement was not foreseen, are to be accounted for in accordance with SFAS 123 as equity instruments based upon the fair value on the grant date.

In the present Financial Statements, all obligations resulting from stock options are accounted for based upon the fair value on the balance sheet date. A provision is accrued over the vesting period of the options. The different accounting methods led to a reduction in net income in accordance with U.S. GAAP of €10.7 million in 2002 and €8.3 million in 2001.

In the present Financial Statements, obligations resulting from stock options are shown as provisions. In accordance with U.S. GAAP, options for which cash settlement was not originally foreseen are still recorded as additions to stockholders' equity.

Overall, the issuance of option rights resulted in an increase in stockholders' equity of €11.2 million in 2002 and €30.2 million in 2001.

(i) Deferred taxes: The adjustments required to conform with U.S. GAAP would result in taxable temporary differences between the valuation of assets and liabilities in the Consolidated Financial Statements and the carrying amount for tax purposes. Resulting adjustments for deferred taxes primarily relate to the following:

		Stockholders' equity		Net income		
		2002	*2001*	*2002*	*2001*	*2000*
				(euros in millions)		
Capitalization of interest	(a)	€(196.6)	€(209.3)	€ 7.3	€ (17.4)	€ 4.9
Capitalization of software developed for internal use	(b)	(73.0)	(62.3)	(10.4)	(23.1)	(16.5)
Valuation of pension funds	(c)	(333.0)	(316.4)	(22.2)	(30.2)	26.7
Accounting for derivatives at fair value and valuation of long-term foreign currency items at year end rates	(d)	30.1	(24.3)	35.3	28.1	(24.3)
Valuation of securities at market values	(e)	—	(134.0)	62.2	0.7	—
Valuation adjustments relating to companies accounted for under the equity method	(f)	—	(45.7)	45.7	(0.5)	12.9
Reversal of goodwill amortization and write-offs due to permanent impairment	(g)	(59.7)	—	(60.7)	—	—
Other adjustments	(h)	67.6	77.1	(11.3)	(83.2)	(77.4)
Recognition of tax credit for dividend payments	(i)	(124.2)	(126.4)	2.2	(126.4)	—
		€(688.8)	€(841.3)	€48.1	€(252.0)	€(73.7)

Other adjustments include in 2001 expenses from the elimination of deferred taxes on tax loss carryforwards, which are recorded in the financial statement since 2001.

The change of the deferred taxes for foreign currency translation adjustments is recognized in other comprehensive income.

In accordance with German GAAP, the tax credit related to the distribution of retained earnings previously taxed at higher rates is accounted for as a reduction of income tax expense in the financial year for which the distribution has been recommended. The revised corporation tax system in Germany starting in 2001 recognizes such credits as a reduction of income taxes payable in the year the dividend is paid.

According to U.S. GAAP, such tax credits are to be recognized as a reduction of income tax expenses in the period in which the tax credits will be recognized for tax purposes. In 2001, this led to a deferral of the recognition of the reduction of taxes of €126.4 million to the dividend payment in 2002. In 2002, the impact on net income of €2.2 million includes the realization of the tax credits for 2001 and the deferral of the reduction of taxes for the proposed dividend for the year 2002 to 2003.

(j) Minority interests: The share of minority shareholders in the aforementioned reconciliation items to U.S. GAAP of net income and stockholders' equity are reported separately.

Consolidation of Majority-Owned Subsidiaries

U.S. GAAP requires the consolidation of all controlled subsidiaries. Under German GAAP, the Company does not consolidate certain subsidiaries if their individual or their combined effect on financial position, results of operations, and cash flows is not material. The effect of nonconsolidated subsidiaries for 2002, 2001, and 2000, on total assets, total liabilities, stockholders' equity, net sales, and net income was less than 2%.

Additionally, under German GAAP, the Company accounts on a prospective basis for previous unconsolidated subsidiaries that are added to the scope of consolidation. U.S. GAAP requires consolidation for all periods that a subsidiary is controlled. The effects of unconsolidated companies on net sales, net income, assets, and liabilities would have been immaterial.

New U.S. GAAP Accounting Standards Not Yet Adopted

In June 2001, the Financial Accounting Standards Board (FASB) issued SFAS 143, "Accounting for Asset Retirement Obligations." SFAS 143 addresses financial accounting and reporting for obligations and costs associated with the retirement of tangible long-lived assets and has to be adopted in the fiscal year 2003 for the first time. The expected obligations and costs associated with the demolition of plants and removal of potential damage to the environment have to be accrued as of the start of production as additional costs for the related plants and are depreciated over the useful life. This also includes the change of these potential liabilities due to adjustments to the conditions as of the balance sheet date.

In June 2002 the FASB issued SFAS 146, "Accounting for Costs Associated with Exit and Disposal Activities," which was adopted for the first time in the fiscal year 2003. The expected costs associated with the exit or disposal of business activities can only be accrued when a liability against a third party exists. This includes severance payments for employees, the cancellation of contracts, the shutdown of production facilities, and the relocation of employees.

BASF is verifying the effects of the adoption of SFAS 143 and SFAS 146 on the net sales, net income, assets, and liabilities of the BASF Group.

Reporting of Comprehensive Income

Comprehensive income in accordance with SFAS 130, "Reporting Comprehensive Income," includes the impact of expenses and earnings that are not included in net income under U.S. GAAP.

	Year ended December 31,		
	2002	*2001*	*2000*
	(euros in millions)		
Net income in accordance with U.S. GAAP (before other comprehensive income)	€1,716.9	€5,692.4	€1,453.6
Change of foreign currency translation adjustments			
Gross	(908.6)	(116.0)	113.2
Deferred taxes	24.3	0.7	138.2
Changes in unrealized holding gains on securities			
Gross	(262.8)	113.5	158.3
Deferred taxes	71.8	(38.2)	(48.4)
Changes in unrealized losses from cash flow hedges			
Gross	(4.6)	—	—
Deferred taxes	1.6	—	—
Additional minimum liability for pensions			
Gross	(17.8)	—	(0.2)
Deferred taxes	5.4	—	0.1
Other comprehensive income (loss), net of tax	(1,090.7)	(40.0)	361.3
Comprehensive income, net of tax	€ 626.2	€5,652.4	€1,814.9

Statement of stockholders' equity

	Year ended December 31,	
	2002	*2001*
	(euros in millions)	
Stockholders' equity according to U.S. GAAP before accumulated other comprehensive income	€18,226.7	€17,754.4
Accumulated other comprehensive income:		
Translation adjustments		
Gross	(348.4)	560.2
Deferred taxes	14.0	(10.3)
Unrealized holding gains on securities		
Gross	105.8	368.6
Deferred taxes	(62.9)	(134.7)
Unrealized losses from cash flow hedges		
Gross	(4.6)	—
Deferred taxes	1.6	—
Additional minimum liability for pension		
Gross	(17.8)	—
Deferred taxes	5.4	—
Accumulated other comprehensive income:	(306.9)	783.8
Total stockholders' equity according to U.S. GAAP including comprehensive income	€17,919.8	€18,538.2

REQUIRED

1. Document the effects of the GAAP differences in the two 20Fs by doing the following:

    a. For the current year and for each company, calculate the percentage change for net income and for total shareholders' equity indicated by the reconciliation and using the respective non-U.S. GAAP numbers as a base.

    b. Repeat the same calculations for the preceding year. Are the percentage changes approximately the same? What is significant about your findings?

    c. For each company and for the current year, identify the two income statement items and the two balance sheet items that exhibit the relatively largest differences. Would you expect other multinational companies in the two countries analyzed to be subject to similar item-by-item differences?

2. Should a U.S. reader of non-U.S. financial statements find these SEC-mandated reconciliations useful?

3. Various corporate management and financing decisions are made with consequences on corporate financial statements in mind. If a given management would have had to report under a different set of GAAP, different business decisions might have been made. If we accept this assertion, then GAAP reconciliations have only limited informational value. Suggest a procedure that would represent a better solution to international financial reporting difficulties.

CHAPTER

4

COMPARATIVE ACCOUNTING II

Chapter 3 looked at accounting in six economically developed countries. All six have well-established mechanisms for developing accounting and auditing standards that provide comprehensive guidance for financial reporting and auditing. The four countries examined in this chapter are commonly referred to as emerging economies.[1] They are the Czech Republic, People's Republic of China (China), Republic of China (Taiwan), and Mexico.

The Czech Republic and China are converting from centrally planned economies to ones that are more market oriented. However, the extent to which they are embracing market reforms is different. The Czech Republic is moving toward a complete market economy, while China is taking a middle course in moving to a *socialist market economy,* that is, a planned economy with market adaptations. Both countries are finding it necessary to completely overhaul their accounting systems. Since the Czech Republic and China are taking different approaches to restructuring their respective economies, they are also taking different approaches to restructuring their accounting systems. Both efforts began in the 1990s and are constantly changing.

Taiwan and Mexico are capitalist countries but with traditionally heavy central government intervention and government ownership of key industries. Historically, their economies have been somewhat closed to foreign investment and international competition. This relative isolation is now changing, as both governments are privatizing their industry holdings and opening up to the global economy. Their financial accounting systems are more developed in terms of standard setting, requirements, and practices than the Czech Republic and China. Naturally, evolution in accounting is occurring in these two countries as well, but not as rapidly as in the Czech Republic and China.

REASONS FOR CHOOSING THESE FOUR COUNTRIES

Why did we choose these four countries to survey? China may be obvious: It is the most populous country in the world. Companies from all around the world are eager to do business with China, and its accounting developments are an important part of the structural changes in its economy.

---

[1]The term "emerging economies" refers loosely to newly industrialized countries (NICs) and those countries in transition from planned to free-market economies. NICs have experienced rapid industrial growth, but their economies are not yet rich in terms of per capita gross domestic product. Mexico and Taiwan are NICs and China and the Czech Republic have economies in transition.

We wanted to include a former member of the Soviet bloc. We chose the Czech Republic because accounting developments there are representative of those in other former Soviet bloc countries.

Taiwan is a so-called "Asian Tiger," one of several Asian countries experiencing rapid growth in gross domestic product in recent years, led by growth of industrial exports. Other such countries include Hong Kong (returned to China by Great Britain in 1997), South Korea, and Singapore. We think that Taiwan's historical and cultural connection to (mainland) China adds interest because of the very different directions that accounting has taken in these two economies.

Finally, we wanted to include a Latin American country. Free-market reforms accelerated in the 1990s throughout most of Latin America. These reforms involved removing protectionist barriers to imports, welcoming foreign investment, and privatizing state-owned companies. These reforms have gone furthest in Argentina, Chile, Mexico, and Peru.[2] We chose Mexico because the 1994 North American Free Trade Agreement (NAFTA) created much new interest in Mexican accounting in Canada, the United States, and elsewhere. Accounting in Mexico shares many features of accounting with other Latin American countries.

SOME OBSERVATIONS ABOUT THE FOUR COUNTRIES AND THEIR ACCOUNTING

Exhibit 4-1 contains some comparative economic data about the four countries that are the focus of this chapter. China's area, population, and resulting gross domestic product (GDP) obviously dwarf the other three. However, China's imports and exports relative to GDP show how insular the Chinese economy is now. Taiwan stands in stark contrast: Trading with the rest of the world is significant to its economy. Another contrast is GDP per capita and by sector. Overall, China is significantly poorer than the other three nations and its economy is much more agricultural. Both of these are signs of significant development potential. Per capita GDP shows that Taiwan has a relatively high standard of living. The Czech Republic and Mexico are comparable, but lower. "Services" is the most important part of the economies of the Czech Republic, Taiwan, and Mexico.

The information on major trading partners reveals a pattern that is true in general, namely, that most international trade is regional in nature. This is most obvious with Mexico, where the United States accounts for more than three-fourths of Mexico's imports and exports. Most of the Czech Republic's trading is with neighboring countries, as is much of China's. This pattern is less true with Taiwan, since the United States is Taiwan's largest trading partner.[3]

---

[2]*The Economist,* "Back on the Pitch: A Survey of Business in Latin America" (December 6, 1997): 3–4.
[3]The anomaly has a historical explanation, as discussed later in this chapter in the section on Taiwan. When the Nationalists on mainland China fled to Taiwan in 1949 following the Communist victory on the mainland, the United States soon began providing substantial amounts of economic development aid to Taiwan. Trade with mainland China was out of the question, and the other countries in the region, including Japan (still recovering from World War II), were too poor and underdeveloped. The link to the United States remains to this day.

Exhibit 4-1 Economic Data				
	Czech Republic	China	Taiwan	Mexico
Area: sq. km	79 thousand	9.60 million	36 thousand	1.97 million
Population	10.3 million	1.29 billion	22.3 million	100.4 million
Gross Domestic Product	$57 billion	$1,159 billion	$282 billion	$618 billion
GDP Per Capita	$5,530	$900	$12,660	$6,150
GDP by Sector				
Agriculture	4%	15%	2%	4%
Industry	41%	52%	31%	26%
Services	55%	33%	67%	70%
Imports	$38.3 billion	$243.6 billion	$107.3 billion	$168.4 billion
Exports	$33.4 billion	$266.1 billion	$122.7 billion	$158.4 billion
Stock Market				
Capitalization, end 2001	$9 billion	$524 billion	$293 billion	$126 billion
Major Trading Partners	Germany, Slovakia	Japan, U.S., Hong Kong, S. Korea	U.S., Japan	U.S., Japan, Canada

Source: Compiled from *Pocket World in Figures 2004 Edition,* London: *The Economist,* 2003; and *The World Factbook,* www.cia.gov/cia/publications/factbook/, January 2004.

Exhibit 4-2 has other data concerning the number of Top 200 emerging market companies[4] and use of the London and New York Stock Exchanges and Nasdaq for raising capital. The number of Top 200 companies indicates that Taiwan's economy and stock market outpaces those of the other three countries. The listing patterns show that Chinese and Mexican companies prefer the New York over the London Stock Exchange, while the reverse is true for companies from the Czech Republic and Taiwan. Overall, almost no companies from the four countries discussed in this chapter have listed on Nasdaq.

Exhibit 4-2 Other Data				
	Czech Republic	China	Taiwan	Mexico
No. of Top 200 emerging market companies[a]	3	18	27	13
No. of companies listed on London Stock Exchange[b]	3	5	12	0
No. of companies listed on New York Stock Exchange[c]	0	15	5	23
No. of companies listed on Nasdaq[d]	0	0	2	0

[a] *Source: BusinessWeek* (July 14, 2003): 67–69.
[b] *Source:* London Stock Exchange Web site (www.londonstockexchange.com), January 5, 2004.
[c] *Source:* New York Stock Exchange Web site (www.nyse.com), December 31, 2003.
[d] *Source:* Nasdaq Web site (www.nasdaq.com), January 5, 2004.

---

[4]Based on market capitalization expressed in U.S. dollars.

As you read about accounting in the four countries in this chapter, keep in mind the factors affecting accounting development that were discussed in Chapter 2: (1) sources of finance, (2) legal system, (3) taxation, (4) political and economic ties, (5) inflation, (6) level of economic development, (7) education level, and (8) culture. Their influence on accounting in nations with developed economies should be clear from reading Chapter 3. Do they also explain accounting in developing countries? We think so. However, the relative importance of certain factors may be quite different in developing economies than in developed ones, and the influences may appear in different ways.

To illustrate, the effect of the type of legal system is less important in the countries discussed in this chapter than the ones in Chapter 3. For example, Mexico has a civil law legal system similar to that in France and other Continental European countries, yet accounting in Mexico is oriented toward fairness, not legal compliance. Political and economic ties are arguably more important for the countries in this chapter. Mexico's substantial economic contact with the United States, which extends to accounting, explains why Mexico has fairness-oriented accounting. The United States has similar influence in Taiwan. In the Czech Republic, the effect of political and economic ties is more anticipatory than historical. European Union Directives originally provided the framework for the development of accounting principles when the Czech Republic applied for EU membership. That target changed after the EU decided to require International Accounting Standards (IAS, now International Financial Reporting Standards, or IFRS) for listed EU companies by 2005 (see Chapter 8). Now, the Czech Republic is shaping its accounting around IAS/IFRS. China is basing its new accounting standards on IAS/IFRS because it hopes to better communicate with foreign investors who are vital to its economic development plans.

FOUR NATIONAL FINANCIAL ACCOUNTING SYSTEMS[5]

Czech Republic

The Czech Republic (CR) is located in Central Europe with Germany to the west and northwest, Austria to the south, the Slovak Republic to the east, and Poland to the north. Its territory was a part of the Austro-Hungarian Empire for nearly 300 years (from 1620 to 1918), ruled by the Austrian monarchy, the Hapsburgs. The empire collapsed at the end of World War I, and the independent nation of Czechoslovakia was formed in 1918. Between the two world wars, Czechoslovakia was a prosperous parliamentary democracy with universal voting rights. This ended in 1938 when Britain and France allowed Nazi Germany to annex Czechoslovakia's ethnically German border territories. Within a year, Adolf Hitler controlled the rest of the nation and the Nazi occupation began. The 1946 elections and subsequent political maneuvering brought the Communist Party to power. This began the Soviet Union's domination over Czechoslovakia, which lasted until 1989. The internal disintegration of the Soviet regime and the collapse of the Czechoslovak Communist government in that year led to the so-called "Velvet Revolution" and the formation of a new government. In 1993

---

[5]The discussion in this section draws on the references cited at the end of the chapter.

Czechoslovakia peacefully split into two nations, the Czech Republic and the Republic of Slovakia.

Accounting in the Czech Republic has changed direction several times in the 20th century, reflecting its political history. Accounting practice and principles reflected those of the German-speaking countries of Europe until the end of World War II. Then, as a centrally planned economy was being constructed, accounting practice was based on the Soviet model. The administrative needs of various central government institutions were satisfied through such features as a uniform chart of accounts, detailed accounting methods, and uniform financial statements, obligatory for all enterprises. The focus on production and costing, based on historical costs, was emphasized over external reporting. A unified system of financial and cost accounting used the same pricing and other principles.

Of course, prices did not reflect the market forces of supply and demand. They were centrally determined and controlled, primarily on the *cost plus* basis. Losses were normally subsidized. Accounting was of limited importance in managing an enterprise. Furthermore, accounting information was considered to be secret and financial statements were not published. While accounting information was inspected, it was not independently audited.[6]

After 1989 Czechoslovakia moved quickly toward a market-oriented economy. The government revamped its legal and administrative structure to stimulate the economy and attract foreign investments. Commercial laws and practices were adjusted to fit Western standards. Price controls were lifted. Accounting again turned westward, this time reflecting the principles embodied in the European Union Directives.

The division of Czechoslovakia did not appreciably affect this process. In 1993 the Prague Stock Exchange began regular operations. Considering the high level of economic and political development achieved in pre-1938 Czechoslovakia, these events were more a matter of returning to previously held norms than discovering new ones.[7]

Privatization of the economy involved the return of property to former owners, small privatizations in which more than 20,000 shops, restaurants, and other small businesses were sold to Czech citizens by public auction, and a series of large privatizations. A key element of the latter was a coupon voucher system allowing adult Czech citizens to buy investment vouchers for a nominal price. These vouchers were used to acquire shares of newly privatized large industrial concerns. However, many Czechs, with no experience as shareholders, sold their shares to investment funds owned by state-controlled Czech banks. One result was a conflict of interest for the banks, which ended up owning the same companies to whom they were lending money. A second round of privatizations involved auctions or direct sales, often to the companies' own managers. Many of these newly privatized businesses subsequently failed, leaving little or no collateral and overloading the court system with business cases. Both waves of privatizations are now viewed as a mistake of trying to do too much at once. The economic reforms are ongoing. The last of the state-owned enterprises are to be privatized by 2005. Among the more pressing issues are strengthening the bankruptcy laws, improv-

---

[6]Rudolf Schroll, "The New Accounting System in the Czech Republic," *European Accounting Review* 4, no. 4 (1995): 827–832; and Jan Dolezal, "The Czech Republic," in *European Accounting Guide*, 2nd ed., David Alexander and Simon Archer, eds., San Diego, Calif.: Harcourt Brace Jovanovich, 1995.
[7]Willie Seal, Pat Sucher, and Ivan Zelenka, "The Changing Organization of Czech Accounting," *European Accounting Review* 4, no. 4 (1995): 667.

ing the openness and transparency of stock market operations through tighter regulations, and restructuring enterprises.[8]

In 1995 the Czech Republic became the first post-Communist member of the OECD. The Czech Republic joined NATO in 1999 and joined the European Union in May 2004.[9]

Accounting Regulation and Enforcement

The new Commercial Code was enacted by Parliament in 1991 and became effective on January 1, 1992.[10] Influenced by the Austrian roots of the old commercial code and modeled on German commercial law, it introduced a substantial amount of legislation relating to businesses. (Czech law is based on the civil code law system of Continental Europe.) This legislation includes requirements for annual financial statements, income taxes, audits, and shareholders' meetings.

The Accountancy Act that sets out the requirements for accounting was passed in 1991 and became effective on January 1, 1993. Based on the EU Fourth and Seventh Directives, the act specifies the use of a chart of accounts for record keeping and the preparation of financial statements.[11] It was significantly amended with effect from January 1, 2002, primarily to bring Czech accounting closer to IAS/IFRS. The Ministry of Finance is responsible for accounting principles. Ministry of Finance decrees set out acceptable measurement and disclosure practices that companies must follow. Thus, accounting in the CR is influenced by the Commercial Code, the Accountancy Act, and Ministry of Finance decrees. The Stock Exchange has so far had little influence and, despite the German origins of the Commercial Code, tax legislation is not directly influential. As discussed in the following section, the *true and fair view* embodied in the Accountancy Act and taken from EU Directives is interpreted to mean that tax and financial accounts are treated differently.[12] Nevertheless, legal form takes precedence over economic substance in some cases. The Ministry of Finance also oversees the Czech Securities Commission, responsible for supervising and monitoring the capital market and enforcing the Securities Act.

---

[8]U.S. Department of State, "Background Notes: Czech Republic" (March 1999): 10; U.S. Central Intelligence Agency, "The World Factbook 2000—Czech Republic" (2000), 6; Daniel Michaels and John Reed, "Halfway There," *Wall Street Journal Interactive Edition* (September 18, 1997): 1–6; Mark Andress, "Czech, Please!," *Accountancy* (September 2000): 60–61; and Zuzana Kawaciukova, "Privatization Theft," *The Prague Post Online* (July 24, 2003).

Czech capital markets are largely illiquid. In 1995 and 1996, after the initial large privatizations, there were over 1,600 Czech companies listed on the Prague Stock Exchange. However, in 1997 the exchange started delisting securities that were rarely traded. By the end of 1999, the Prague Stock Exchange had approximately 200 listed companies and there were less than 100 at the end of 2002. The Czech stock market is not seen as a place to raise new capital. For example, there has not been an initial public offering of shares since the 1930s. Transparent reporting, tight regulations, investor protection, and judicial enforcement are still lacking. See Pat Sucher, Peter Moizer, and Marcela Zarova, "The Images of the Big Six Audit Firms in the Czech Republic," *European Accounting Review* 8, no. 3 (1999): 503, 519; and "After the Chaos: A Survey of Finance in Central Europe," *The Economist* (September 14, 2002): 5–7, 10–11.

[9]The Czech Republic will not adopt the euro until 2010.

[10]In 1991 legislation was passed by the then-Czechoslovak Parliament. The Czech Republic carried forward its provisions after the division.

[11]Charts of accounts are not new to the Czech Republic because their use was required under Communism. The Czechs based their new system on the French Plan Comptable and received substantial help from the French Ministry of Finance and the French accounting profession in developing their new charts of accounts.

[12]Pat Sucher, Willie Seal, and Ivan Zelenka, "True and Fair View in the Czech Republic: A Note on Local Perceptions," *European Accounting Review* 5, no. 3 (1996): 551.

Auditing is regulated by the Act on Auditors, passed in 1992. This act established the Chamber of Auditors, a self-regulated professional body that oversees the registration, education, examination, and disciplining of auditors, the setting of auditing standards, and the regulation of audit practice, such as the format of the audit report. An audit of financial statements is required for all corporations (joint stock companies) and for large limited-liability companies (those with prior year turnover exceeding CzK80 million or net assets exceeding CzK40 million).[13] The audit is designed to ensure that the accounts have been kept according to applicable legislation and decrees and that the financial statements present a true and fair view of the company's financial position and results.

Financial Reporting

Financial statements must be comparative, consisting of:

1. Balance sheet
2. Profit and loss account (income statement)
3. Notes

Consistent with the requirements of EU Directives, the notes include a description of the accounting policies and other relevant information for assessing the financial statements. Examples of the latter include employee information, revenues by segment, and contingencies. The notes must also include a cash flow statement. Consolidated financial statements are required for groups meeting at least two of the following criteria: (1) assets of CzK350 million, (2) revenues of CzK700 million, or (3) 500 employees. Controlling interest in a subsidiary is based on either owning a majority of shares or having a direct or indirect dominant influence. In general the requirements for consolidated financial statements are the same whether or not a company is listed on the Prague Stock Exchange. However, small and other companies not subject to audit have abbreviated disclosure requirements. Financial statements are approved at the annual meeting of shareholders. Listed companies are also required to present quarterly income statements. Czech companies have the option of using IAS/IFRS or Czech accounting standards in preparing their consolidated financial statements. However, companies listed on the PSE Main Market are required to prepare audited financial statements according to IAS/IFRS.

Accounting Measurements

The acquisition (purchase) method is used to account for business combinations. Goodwill arising from a business combination is written off in the first year of consolidation or capitalized and amortized over no more than 15 years. The equity method is used for associated companies (those over which the company exercises significant influence but which are not consolidated) and proportional consolidation is used for joint ventures. The year-end (closing) exchange rate is used to translate both the income statement and balance sheet of foreign subsidiaries. There are no guidelines for reporting foreign currency translation adjustments.

Tangible and intangible assets are valued at cost and written off over their expected economic lives. Inventory is valued at the lower of cost or market, and FIFO

---

[13]Corporations issue shares whereas limited-liability companies do not. The latter are similar to limited partnerships.

and weighted average are allowable cost flow assumptions (LIFO is not). Research and development costs may be capitalized if they relate to projects completed successfully and capable of generating future income. Leased assets are typically not capitalized, an example of form over substance. Deferred income taxes are provided in full for all temporary differences. Contingent losses are recorded when they are probable and can be reliably measured. Legal reserves are also required: Profits are appropriated annually until they reach 20 percent of equity for corporations and 10 percent for limited-liability companies.

China[14]

China has a quarter of the world's population, and market-oriented reforms have helped generate rapid economic growth.[15] In the late 1970s, Chinese leaders began to move the economy from Soviet-style central planning to one that is more market oriented but still under Communist Party control. To achieve this, authorities switched to a system of household responsibility in agriculture instead of the old collectivization, increased the authority of local officials and plant managers in industry, permitted a wide variety of small-scale enterprises in services and light manufacturing, and opened the economy to increased foreign trade and investment. In 1993 China's leadership approved additional long-term reforms aimed at giving more flexibility for market-oriented institutions. Central features include the share system of ownership, privatizations, the development of organized stock exchanges, and the listing of shares in Chinese companies on Western exchanges. Nevertheless, state enterprises still continue to dominate many key industries in what the Chinese call a "socialist market economy," that is, a planned economy with market adaptations.[16]

Accounting in China has a long history. Its functioning in a stewardship role can be detected as far back as 2200 B.C. during the Hsiu Dynasty, and documents show that it was used to measure wealth and compare achievements among dukes and princes in the Xia Dynasty (2000 to 1500 B.C.). The young Confucius (551 to 479 B.C.) was a manager of warehouses and his writings mention that the job included proper accounting—keeping the records of receipts and disbursements up-to-date. Among the teachings of Confucius is the imperative to keep history, and accounting records are viewed as part of that history.

The principal characteristics of accounting in China today date from the founding of the People's Republic of China in 1949. China installed a highly centralized planned economy, reflecting Marxist principles and patterned after that of the Soviet Union. The state controlled the ownership, the right to use, and the distribution of all means of

[14]In 1997, Great Britain ceded control of Hong Kong to China. Under the agreement between China and Britain, China has guaranteed to operate a "one country, two systems" arrangement in which Hong Kong's lifestyle will be unchanged for 50 years and basic freedoms and rights will be guaranteed by law. Accounting in Hong Kong is similar to that of the United Kingdom, described in Chapter 3. The discussion of China in this chapter refers to mainland China and excludes Hong Kong.
[15]China's real gross domestic product grew at an average annual rate of 9.8 percent between 1991 and 2001, the second highest growth rate of any nation. See *The Economist Pocket World in Figures 2004 Edition,* London: *The Economist* (2003): 30.
[16]The Chinese economy is now the sixth largest in the world. A central feature of China's reforms is a gradualist approach to economic liberalization. See Robert J. Barro, "China's Slow Yet Steady March to Reform, *BusinessWeek* (September 30, 2002): 28; and Fareed Zakaria, "The Big Story Everyone Missed," *Newsweek* (January 6, 2003): 52.

production, and enacted rigid planning and control over the economy. Production was the top priority of state-owned enterprises. Their sales and pricing were dictated by the state's planning authorities, and their financing and product costing were administered by the state's finance departments. Under this system, the purpose of accounting was to serve the needs of the state for economic planning and control. A uniform set of standardized accounts was developed to integrate information into the national economic plan. The uniform accounting system contained all-inclusive accounting rules that were mandatory for state-owned enterprises across the country.

Financial reporting was frequent and detailed. The main feature was a fund management orientation where *funds* meant the property, goods, and materials used in the production process. Financial reporting emphasized the balance sheet, which reflected the source and application of funds. It focused on stewardship and accountability, or the fulfilling of production and other goals, as well as compliance with governmental policies and regulations. Accounting emphasized counting quantities and the comparison of costs and quantities. Although accounting focused more on managerial than financial objectives, its role in decision making by the managers of individual enterprises was nevertheless subordinated to the central authorities.

China's economy today is best described as a hybrid economy in which the state controls strategic commodities and industries, while other industries, as well as the commercial and private sectors, are governed by a market-oriented system. The recent economic reforms involve privatizations, including the conversion of state-owned enterprises into share-issuing corporations. New accounting rules have had to be developed for newly privatized companies and other independent limited-liability companies, as well as for foreign business entities such as joint ventures. The role of the government has been changing from managing both the macro- and microeconomy to one managing at the macro level only.[17] Accounting standards were needed to reflect this new reality.

Accounting Regulation and Enforcement

The Accounting Law, last amended in 2000, covers all enterprises and organizations including those not owned or controlled by the state. It outlines the general principles of accounting and defines the role of the government and the matters that require accounting procedures. The State Council (an executive body corresponding to a cabinet) has also issued Financial Accounting and Reporting Rules for Enterprises (FARR). These focus on bookkeeping, the preparation of financial statements, reporting practices, and other financial accounting and reporting matters. FARR apply to all enterprises other than very small ones that do not raise funds externally. The Ministry of Finance, supervised by the State Council, formulates accounting and auditing standards. Besides accounting and auditing matters, the ministry is responsible for a wide range of activities affecting the economy. Generally, these activities include formulat-

---

[17]The ownership relationship between the government and state-owned enterprises has been redefined. Regulations issued by the Ministry of Finance in 1994 announced for the first time that the state is an investor in the enterprise and is responsible for the enterprise's debts limited to the amount of its capital; the enterprise has its own legal status, enjoying its own property rights and bearing independent civil responsibilities. See Zezhong Xiao and Aixiang Pan, "Developing Accounting Standards on the Basis of a Conceptual Framework by the Chinese Government," *The International Journal of Accounting* 32, no. 3 (1997): 282. For further discussion of China's reforms of state-owned enterprises, see "The Longer March," *The Economist* (September 30, 2000): 71–73.

ing long-term economic strategies and setting the priorities for the allocation of government funds. More specifically, the ministry's responsibilities include:

- formulating and enforcing economic, tax, and other finance-related policies
- preparing the annual state budget and fiscal report
- managing state revenue and expenditure
- developing the financial management and tax system[18]

Accounting and auditing matters fall into the last category.

In 1992 the Ministry of Finance issued Accounting Standards for Business Enterprises (ASBE), a conceptual framework designed to guide the development of new accounting standards. These standards will eventually harmonize domestic practices and harmonize Chinese practices with international practices. Effective on July 1, 1993, the ASBE was a landmark event in China's move to a market economy. Before the ASBE, more than 40 different uniform accounting systems were in use, varying across industries and types of ownership. Even though each one of these may individually be labeled as *uniform,* they resulted in inconsistent practices overall. Thus, one motive for issuing the ASBE was to harmonize domestic accounting practices. Moreover, existing practices were incompatible with international practices and unsuited for a market-oriented economy. Harmonizing Chinese accounting to international practices serves to remove barriers of communication with foreign investors and helps meet the needs of the economic reforms already under way.

After the issuance of the ASBE, the Ministry of Finance replaced the more than 40 uniform accounting systems mentioned previously with 13 industry-based and two ownership-based accounting systems. These systems were viewed as transitional until specific accounting standards could be promulgated that would apply to all enterprises operating in China. These systems are now being phased out.

A new ASBE was issued in 2001. It applies to nearly 500,000 enterprises, including joint stock limited companies, foreign investment enterprises, and most new companies established after January 1, 2003.[19] By 2005, all state-owned enterprises will be required to adopt the ASBE and it will eventually extend to all medium-sized and large enterprises. The ASBE consists of chapters covering fundamental principles, financial statement elements, recognition principles, and financial reporting and disclosure requirements. Exhibit 4-3 summarizes the contents of the ASBE.[20]

The China Accounting Standards Committee (CASC) was established in 1998 as the authoritative body within the Ministry of Finance responsible for developing accounting standards. The standard-setting process includes assigning necessary research to task forces, the issuance of exposure drafts, and public hearings. CASC members are experts drawn from academia, accounting firms, government, professional accounting associations, and other key groups concerned with the development of accounting in China. The CASC has issued accounting standards on issues such as cash flow statements, debt restructuring, revenue, nonmonetary transactions, contingencies, and leases.

---

[18]"Role of the Ministry of Finance," Ministry of Finance Web site (www.mof.gov.cn), December 16, 2000.
[19]An English translation is available at www.iasplus.com/country/chinasystem.pdf.
[20]There are two specialized industry accounting systems for financial institutions (such as banks, insurance companies, brokerages, and leasing companies)—one for listed and another for unlisted financial institutions.

Exhibit 4-3   China's Accounting System for Business Enterprises

- **Fundamental principles:** going concern, substance over form, consistency, timeliness, understandability, accrual basis, matching, prudence, materiality, impairment.
- Definitions of **elements:** assets, liabilities, owners' equity, revenues, expenses, profits.
- Classifications and principles for **recognition and measurement:** assets, liabilities, equity.
- Principles for revenue and expense **recognition,** and their classification.
- Contents of **financial and accounting reports.**

The China Securities Regulatory Commission (CSRC) regulates China's two stock exchanges: Shanghai, which opened in 1990, and Shenzhen, which opened in 1991. It sets regulatory guidelines, formulates and enforces market rules, and authorizes initial public offers and new shares. The CSRC also issues additional disclosure requirements for listed companies. Thus, disclosure requirements for listed companies are established by two government bodies, the Ministry of Finance and the CSRC.[21]

Until 1995 China had two professional accounting organizations. The Chinese Institute of Certified Public Accountants (CICPA), established in 1988 under the jurisdiction of the Ministry of Finance, regulated the audit of private-sector enterprises. The Chinese Association of Certified Public Auditors (CACPA) was responsible for auditing state-owned enterprises and was under the authority of a separate organization, the State Audit Administration. In 1995 CICPA and CACPA merged, keeping the name of the CICPA.

The CICPA sets the requirements for becoming a CPA, administers the CPA examination, develops auditing standards, and is responsible for the code of professional ethics. With the exception that the CICPA reports to a government agency, the regulation of public accounting practice in China may be compared to the system in the United States.

Financial Reporting

The accounting period is required to be the calendar year. Financial statements consist of:

1. Balance sheet
2. Income statement
3. Cash flow statement
4. Notes
5. Explanation of financial condition

---

[21]China's stock markets rank eighth in the world (and second in Asia behind Japan) in terms of market capitalization; 1,200 companies are listed and there are officially 66 million individual investors. Nevertheless, the state holds roughly two-thirds of the shares of listed companies, meaning that two-thirds of the market capitalization is not traded. Most companies are listed for political rather than economic reasons and almost all of them benefit from government favoritism. Disclosures are still poor and enforcement of market rules is weak. Much of the individual trading is based on rumor rather than reliable information. The stock markets are not yet effective as a way to allocate capital. See "Fools in Need of Institutions," *The Economist* (June 30, 2001): 65–66; "Banking on Growth," *The Economist* (January 18, 2003): 67–68; and "A Survey of Asian Finance: Casino Capital," *The Economist* (February 8, 2003): 10–12.

Additional statements are required disclosing asset impairments, changes in capital structure, and appropriations of profits. Listed companies must disclose segment information, consistent with international standards. The notes include a statement of accounting policies. As applicable, they discuss such matters as contingencies, important post–balance sheet events, and related party transactions. A memorandum is required discussing the enterprise's operations, financial position, results, cash flows, and items affecting them. Financial statements must be consolidated, comparative, in Chinese, and expressed in the Chinese currency, the renminbi. The annual financial statements must be audited by a Chinese CPA. A quarterly balance sheet, income statement, and notes are required for listed companies. Listed companies issuing shares to foreign investors (so-called B-shares) must put English and Chinese language versions of their annual reports on the CSRC Web site.[22]

Accounting Measurements

The purchase method must be used to account for business combinations, and goodwill is written off over no more than 10 years. The equity method is used when the ownership of another enterprise exceeds 20 percent. Proportional consolidation is used for joint ventures. The accounts of a subsidiary are consolidated when ownership exceeds 50 percent and/or there is power to control. For overseas subsidiaries, the balance sheet is translated at the year-end exchange rate, the income statement is translated at the average-for-the-year exchange rate, and any translation difference is shown as a reserve in equity.

Historical cost is the basis for valuing tangible assets; revaluations are not allowed. They are depreciated over their expected useful lives, normally on a straight-line basis. Accelerated and units-of-production depreciation are also acceptable. FIFO, average, and LIFO are acceptable costing methods, and inventory is written down for price declines and obsolescence. Acquired intangibles are also recorded at cost and amortized over the periods benefited. Intangible assets with no contractual or legal life must be amortized over no more than 10 years. Because land and much of the industrial property in China is owned by the state, companies that acquire the right to use land and industrial property rights show them as intangibles. Assets are revalued when a change in ownership takes place, such as when a state-owned enterprise is privatized. Certified asset assessment firms or CPA firms determine these valuations.

Research and development costs are expensed. Finance leases are capitalized. Three methods of accounting for deferred taxes are allowed: (1) the flow-through method, in which deferred taxes are not provided, (2) the deferral method, in which deferred taxes are not adjusted for subsequent changes in tax rates, and (3) the liability method, in which deferred taxes are adjusted for subsequent changes in tax rates. Contingent obligations are provided for when they are both probable and a reliable estimate can be made of their amount.

Taiwan

Taiwan was originally known in the West as Formosa, a name meaning "beautiful island," given to it by Portuguese sailors in the 15th century. Taiwan has been predominantly Chinese since becoming a protectorate of the Chinese Empire in 1206. In 1887

---

[22]www.csrc.gov.cn.

Taiwan became a province of China, but from 1895 until 1945 it was a Japanese colony. At the end of World War II, Taiwan reverted to China.

The constitution of the Republic of China was written in 1946. In 1949, defeated by the Communists, the remnants of the Republic of China, led by Chiang Kai-shek, fled to Taiwan and established a provisional government there. Today, Taiwan is officially known as the Republic of China, while mainland China is known as the People's Republic of China. Each maintains claims over the other, which fosters a delicate and complex relationship between them.

Over four decades, Taiwan transformed itself from an underdeveloped, agricultural island to an economic power that is a leading producer of high-technology goods. This outstanding growth has been based on the success of its manufactured products in export markets. Taiwan's economy has developed in three distinct phases since 1949. During the 1950s, agriculture and import-substituting industries dominated economic growth. The second phase began in the 1960s and focused on export expansion, propelled by the assembly of imported component parts for consumer goods and low technology, light industry. The most recent phase involves high technology and capital-intensive industries. Early growth was fueled by substantial economic aid from the United States. Today Taiwan is an aid donor and major investor, especially in Asia. (In fact, Taiwan has significant investments in mainland China.)

Taiwan has a dynamic capitalist economy with gradually decreasing government guidance of investment and foreign trade. Small, family-owned businesses are the basis of the economy.[23] Certain strategic industries, such as military goods, petroleum refining, and public utilities, are owned by the state, but the government is now gradually privatizing its ownership in these firms.

Taiwan can be said to have a credit-based financial system along the lines of Germany and Japan (described in Chapter 3) rather than a capital market-based system. The Taiwan Stock Exchange opened in 1962 and has grown steadily since the second half of the 1980s. Improving the capital market is an important priority of the Taiwanese government. Although most Taiwanese companies are small and closely held by controlling families, the Taiwan Stock Exchange has the second largest market capitalization of any emerging stock market (behind China). Taiwan is the 17th largest economy in the world. The United States is Taiwan's largest trading partner, taking 23 percent of its exports and supplying 17 percent of its imports.[24]

The influence of the United States on accounting in Taiwan is also strong. Financial reporting, auditing, and other aspects of accounting are similar to those found in the United States. However, Taiwan has now started working toward convergence with IAS/IFRS.

Accounting Regulation and Enforcement

The Commercial Accounting Law, as amended in 1987, regulates accounting records and financial statements in Taiwan. It applies to enterprises established under the Business Regulation and Company Laws, except for small partnerships or sole proprietors. The law sets forth the accounting records that must be kept and lays out broad provisions for the financial statements, notes, and other disclosures. Requirements

---

[23]Ninety-eight percent of Taiwan's companies are small to medium-sized.
[24]*The Economist, Pocket World in Figures 2004 Edition,* London: *The Economist,* 2003, 24, 64–65.

include accrual accounting and a calendar year fiscal period. The law also emphasizes that financial accounting is distinct from tax accounting.[25]

Accounting standards are set by the Financial Accounting Standards Committee (FASC) of the Accounting Research and Development Foundation (ARDF). The ARDF, modeled on the Financial Accounting Foundation in the United States, was established in 1984 to upgrade the level of accounting study, advance the development of accounting and auditing standards, and help industrial and commercial enterprises improve their accounting systems. It is an endowed private institution, but is supervised by the Ministry of Finance. Its board of directors includes government officials, practicing CPAs, academics, representatives of business, and officials of the Taiwan Securities and Futures Commission. The FASC, also established in 1984, follows a due process procedure much like the U.S. Financial Accounting Standards Board. Before it issues a standard, the FASC prepares an exposure draft, solicits opinions from parties concerned, holds public hearings if necessary, and sometimes prepares revised exposure drafts. Another committee of the ARDF, the Auditing Standards Committee, issues auditing standards, following a process much like the FASC. Accounting and auditing standards are based on national requirements, with reference to both U.S. GAAP and IAS/IFRS. Companies listed on the Taiwan Stock Exchange face additional disclosure requirements of the Securities and Futures Commission (SFC), an agency within the Ministry of Finance.[26]

The ARDF has now committed Taiwan to convergence with IAS/IFRS. The Framework of Financial Accounting Concepts and Financial Report Preparation (a conceptual framework) was revised in 2002 based on the IASC framework. All new and existing projects undertaken by the FASC will be aligned with IAS/IFRS. Existing differences between Taiwanese accounting principles and IAS/IFRS will also be identified so that Taiwanese principles can be revised to conform to IAS/IFRS. The SFC also encourages listed companies to adopt IAS/IFRS on topics where there are no Taiwanese accounting standards.

The National Federation of CPA Associations (NFCPAA), an organization mandated by the CPA Law of Taiwan, represents the accounting profession. Practicing CPAs in Taiwan belong to one of the provincial or municipal CPA associations, which in turn make up the NFCPAA. The NFCPAA coordinates with government regulatory authorities on matters of concern to the profession, issues statements on professional ethics, and provides continuing professional education. Before the establishment of the ARDF, the NFCPAA also issued accounting and auditing standards.[27] The examination and licensing of CPAs is a government responsibility: The exam is administered by

---

[25]S. T. Chiang, "Taiwan," chap. 4 in *Financial Reporting in the West Pacific Rim,* T. E. Cooke and R. H. Parker, eds., New York: Routledge, 1994, p 138.

[26]Young H. Chang, "Taiwan's Accounting Profession: A Response to National Economic Growth," *The International Journal of Accounting* 27, no. 1 (1992): 63–67.

[27]The NFCPAA was founded in 1946 on mainland China in the city of Nanking, and moved with the Nationalist government when it moved to Taiwan in 1949. In the 1950s, a number of American CPAs, working with the U.S. Agency for International Development, assisted in training Taiwanese government accounting personnel. American accounting textbooks are used most often for accounting education in Taiwan, so most CPAs are oriented toward U.S. standards . See S. T. Chiang, "Taiwan," chap. 4 in *Financial Reporting in the West Pacific Rim,* T. E. Cooke and R. H. Parker, eds., New York: Routledge, 1994, pp. 140–141.

the Ministry of Examinations and CPA certificates are issued by the Ministry of Finance.[28]

Financial Reporting

The Commercial Accounting Law requires the following financial statements:

1. Balance sheet
2. Income statement
3. Statement of changes in owners' equity
4. Statement of cash flows
5. Notes

The notes must disclose the following information:

- Summary of significant accounting policies
- Reasons for changes in accounting policies and their effect on the financial statements
- Creditors' rights to specific assets
- Material commitments and contingent liabilities
- Limitations on the distribution of profits
- Significant events relating to owners' equity
- Significant subsequent events
- Other items that require explanation to avoid misleading impressions or that require clarification to assist in presenting the financial statements fairly.

Financial statements must be comparative and the fiscal period must be the calendar year. Financial statements audited by CPAs are required for publicly held companies and for larger nonpublic companies. Banks, insurance companies, and securities firms must have their financial statements audited by CPAs. State-run government enterprises are audited by government auditors. Companies listed on the stock exchange must also provide audited semiannual financial statements, quarterly financial statements reviewed by a CPA, and a monthly sales report.

Accounting Measurements

Consolidated financial statements are required when a company controls another entity, normally more than 50 percent of ownership. The purchase method is required for business combinations; the pooling of interests method is not used. Under the purchase method, assets are transferred on the basis of book values, though adjustments can be made for higher market values. Goodwill is normally capitalized and amortized over 20 years or less. The equity method is used when there is 20 percent or more ownership in another company. Foreign currency translation is consistent with International Accounting Standard 21 and the U.S. SFAS No. 52. The balance sheets of foreign entities that are independent of the parent are translated at the year-end rate and the income statement is translated at the average rate. Translation adjustments are charged to shareholders' equity. The temporal method is used for nonautonomous subsidiaries and the translation adjustment is charged to income.

[28]Young H. Chang, "Taiwan's Accounting Profession: A Response to National Economic Growth," *The International Journal of Accounting* 27, no. 1 (1992): 66.

Fixed assets, including land and natural resources, and intangible assets may be revalued. The government announces values for land each year, and enterprises are allowed to restate land values (annually) in accordance with the government-announced value. Other assets may be revalued in accordance with a government price index when prices rise by more than 25 percent since purchase or previous revaluation. Capital reserve accounts are credited when assets are revalued. Depreciation and amortization are calculated on the basis of estimated useful lives. The method used does not have to conform to the tax law. Intangible assets are amortized over a maximum period of 20 years. Depreciation and amortization of revalued assets are based on their carrying values after revaluation.

Inventory is stated at the lower of cost or market; FIFO, LIFO, and average are all acceptable cost flow assumptions. As with depreciation, books need not conform to tax law. Research and development costs are charged to expense when incurred. Accounting for leases, contingencies, and deferred taxes are consistent with U.S. and international approaches. Thus, finance (called *capital*) leases are capitalized and contingent losses are accrued when they are both probable and subject to a reasonable estimate. Interperiod tax allocation is required if timing differences exist; thus, deferred taxes are accrued. Taiwanese companies must also set up a legal reserve in shareholders' equity: Ten percent of net income is appropriated each year until the reserve equals the total authorized capital stock of the company.[29]

Mexico

Before the Spanish conquest in the 1500s, Mexico was home to several highly advanced cultures, including the Olmecs, Mayas, Toltecs, and Aztecs. Hernando Cortés conquered Mexico in 1521 and founded a Spanish colony that lasted for nearly 300 years. Mexico declared independence in 1810 and an 1821 treaty recognized Mexican independence from Spain. Except for 30 years of internal peace under General Porfírio Díaz (1877 to 1880 and 1884 to 1911), Mexico experienced political and military strife until 1929, when what is now known as the Institutional Revolutionary Party (PRI) was formed. The PRI controlled Mexico's government continuously for 70 years. The 2000 presidential election was won by the National Action Party (PAN), a center-right opposition party, thus ending the supremacy of the PRI in Mexican politics.

Mexico is the most populous Spanish-speaking country in the world and the second most populous country in Latin America (after Portuguese-speaking Brazil).[30] Mexico has a largely free market economy: government-owned or controlled companies dominate petroleum and public utilities, but private enterprise dominates manufacturing, construction, mining, entertainment, and the service industries. In recent years, the government has also been privatizing its holdings in nonstrategic industries. Free-market economic reforms during the 1990s helped reduce inflation, increase the rate of economic growth, and deliver healthier economic fundamentals. Reforms include dismantling protectionist trade barriers, opening up to foreign investment, and signing regional trade agreements. The most important agreement for Mexico is the

---

[29]Taiwan law requires that year-end bonuses to employees be accounted for as a distribution of retained earnings instead of an expense on the income statement. This practice is the major departure with international norms.
[30]The capital, Mexico City, is the second most populous city in the world.

North American Free Trade Agreement (NAFTA), signed with Canada and the United States in 1994. The United States accounts for two-thirds of Mexico's imports and nearly 90 percent of Mexico's exports. Mexico has the ninth largest economy (in terms of gross domestic product) in the world.[31]

Family-controlled conglomerates dominate Mexico's private sector and, by world standards, are relatively small.[32] Although Mexico's stock market is the third largest in Latin America, it is still relatively small by international standards, as firms prefer to raise capital through debt rather than equity. This is changing, however, and more and more Mexican firms are entering U.S. capital markets.

Given the dominance of family-controlled enterprises, Mexican companies traditionally guarded their information and were secretive in their financial reporting. This too is changing. Disclosure practices of Mexican companies are increasingly influenced by the expectations of the U.S. market. Another significant feature of Mexican accounting is the use of comprehensive general price-level accounting as a measurement basis.

The U.S. influence on Mexico's economy extends to accounting. "[M]any of the early leaders of the Mexican profession grew up on 'American accounting'"[33] and U.S. textbooks and professional literature (either in the original English or translated into Spanish) are used extensively in the education of accountants and as guidance on accounting issues. NAFTA accelerated a trend toward closer cooperation between professional accounting organizations in Mexico, Canada, and the United States. Today, the accounting standard-setting bodies in these three countries[34] are committed to a program of harmonization and are attempting to work in concert wherever possible. As a founding member of the International Accounting Standards Committee (now International Accounting Standards Board), Mexico is also committed to harmonization with IAS/IFRS. Mexico increasingly looks to the IASB for guidance on accounting issues, especially in cases where there is no corresponding Mexican standard.

Accounting Regulation and Enforcement

The Mexican Commercial Code and income tax laws contain requirements for keeping certain summary accounting records and preparing financial statements, but their influence on financial reporting is generally minimal. The Mexican Institute of Public Accountants (*Instituto Mexicano de Contadores Públicos*) issues accounting and auditing standards in Mexico. Accounting standards are developed by the Institute's Accounting Principles Commission; auditing standards are the responsibility of its Auditing Standards and Procedures Commission. The institute, a federation of state and other local associations of registered public accountants, is an independent, nongovernmental, professional association representing the overwhelming majority of

---

[31]*The Economist, Pocket World in Figures 2004 Edition,* London: *The Economist,* 2003, 166.

[32]*The Economist* notes an interesting paradox. "Capitalism has a much longer history in Latin America than in many parts of Asia. Yet whereas the largest Asian firms have grown swiftly to become household names across the world, their Latin American counterparts have remained almost unknown outside their own region, or even their own country" (p. 7). See *The Economist,* "Back on the Pitch: A Survey of Business in Latin America" (December 6, 1997): 1–27.

[33]Stephen A. Zeff, *Forging Accounting Principles in Five Countries: A History and an Analysis of Trends,* Champaign, IL: Stipes Publishing, 1971, pp. 96–97.

[34]The Instituto Mexicano de Contadores Públicos, Canadian Institute of Chartered Accountants, and the Financial Accounting Standards Board, respectively.

public accountants. The Mexican accounting profession is mature, well organized, and highly regarded by the business community.

Despite a legal system based on civil law, accounting standard setting in Mexico takes a British-American, or Anglo-Saxon, approach rather than a Continental European one. The standard-setting process is well developed. Before standards are finalized, exposure drafts of proposed standards are issued for review and public comment. Accounting standards are recognized as authoritative by the government, in particular, by the National Banking and Securities Commission, which regulates the Mexican Stock Exchange. Mexican accounting principles do not distinguish between large and small companies, and so are applicable to all business entities. In some cases the National Banking and Securities Commission issues rules for listed companies, which generally limit certain options in generally accepted accounting principles.

Requirements for preparing financial statements and having them audited vary by type and size of company. All companies incorporated under Mexican law (*sociedades anónimas*) must appoint at least one statutory auditor to report to the shareholders on the annual financial statements. Statutory auditors do not have to be public accountants, but when a firm uses independent auditors, a member of the auditing firm frequently acts as statutory auditor. Companies or consolidated groups that meet certain size criteria must file a tax-compliance audit report every year with the Federal Tax Audit Department of the Ministry of Finance. The report consists of audited financial statements, additional schedules, and a statement by the auditor that no irregularities were observed regarding compliance with tax laws. This audit must be done by a Mexican public accountant. Finally, companies listed on the Mexican Stock Exchange must submit annual consolidated financial statements, audited by a Mexican public accountant, to the exchange and to the National Banking and Securities Commission.

Financial Reporting

The fiscal year of Mexican companies must coincide with the calendar year. Comparative consolidated financial statements must be prepared, consisting of:

1. Balance sheet
2. Income statement
3. Statement of changes in stockholders' equity
4. Statement of changes in financial position
5. Notes

Financial statements must be adjusted for inflation. The effects of the adjustment are shown in the statement of changes in stockholders' equity. The format of the statement of changes in financial position is similar to the statement of cash flows and is divided into operating, investing, and financing activities. However, because it is also prepared in constant pesos, the resulting "cash flows" do not represent cash flows as understood under historical cost accounting.

Notes are an integral part of the financial statements (covered by the auditor's report) and include the following:

- Accounting policies of the company
- Material contingencies
- Commitments for substantial purchases of assets or under lease contracts
- Details of long-term debt and foreign currency exposure

- Limitations on dividends
- Guarantees
- Employees' pension plans
- Transactions with related parties
- Income taxes

Accounting Measurements[35]

Consolidated financial statements are prepared when a parent company controls another company. Control is indicated by the ability to determine operating and financial policies of a company. Control normally exists when more than 50 percent of a company's common stock is owned, but it can be obtained in other ways, including the ability to appoint management or a majority of the board of directors. The equity method is used when there is influence but not control, normally meaning an ownership level between 10 and 50 percent. Joint ventures may be proportionally consolidated or accounted for using the equity method. Mexico has adopted International Accounting Standard No. 21 on foreign currency translation.[36]

Both the purchase and the pooling of interests methods of accounting for business combinations may be used, depending on the circumstances. If a majority of the shareholders of the acquired company do not retain an interest in the continuing business, the purchase method is used; if they do, pooling is used. Goodwill is the excess of purchase price over the current value of the net assets acquired. It is amortized to income over the expected benefit period, which is limited to 20 years.

General price-level accounting is used in Mexico. The historical costs of nonmonetary assets are restated in pesos of current purchasing power by applying factors derived from the National Consumer Price Index (NCPI). The components of stockholders' equity are also restated using the NCPI. The gain or loss from holding monetary assets and liabilities is included in current period income, but the effects of other restatements are in stockholders' equity. Cost of sales and depreciation expense are expressed in constant pesos on the income statement, consistent with the treatment of inventory and fixed assets. A tangible fixed asset is depreciated over its useful life. An intangible asset is amortized over its useful life (normally no more than 20 years) unless the life is indefinite, in which case it is not amortized but subject to an annual impairment test.

Research costs are expensed as incurred, while development costs are capitalized and amortized once technological feasibility has been established. Leases are classified as financing or operating. Financing leases—those transferring substantially all the benefits and risks of ownership of the asset—are capitalized, while rents from operating leases are expensed on the income statement. Contingent losses are accrued when they are likely and measurable. General contingency reserves are not acceptable under

---

[35]As noted earlier, the Mexican Institute of Public Accountants looks to the United States as well as the International Accounting Standards Board in developing generally accepted accounting principles. While the standards do not cover all areas, overall practice is fairness oriented.

[36]General price-level accounting (described later) is integrated with foreign currency translation: (1) The financial statements of integrated operations are adjusted by the National Consumer Price Index after translation into pesos; (2) financial statements of "foreign entities" (i.e., subsidiaries that are not integrated operations) are first adjusted to reflect the purchasing power of the home currency, then translated into pesos using the closing exchange rate.

Exhibit 4-4   Summary of Significant Accounting Practices

	Czech Republic	China	Taiwan	Mexico
1. Consolidated financial statements	Required	Required	Required	Required
2. Statement of cash flows	In notes	Required	Required	Required
3. Business combinations: purchase or pooling	Purchase	Purchase	Purchase	Both
4. Goodwill	Immediate write-off or capitalize & amortize; 15-year maximum	Capitalize & amortize; 10-year maximum	Capitalize & amortize; 20-year maximum	Capitalize & amortize; 20-year maximum
5. 20% to 50% owned affiliates	Equity method	Equity method	Equity method	Equity method[a]
6. Asset valuation	Historical cost	Historical cost	Revaluation allowed	Constant purchasing power
7. Depreciation	Economic based	Economic based	Economic based	Economic based
8. LIFO inventory valuation	Not used	Acceptable	Acceptable	Acceptable[b]
9. Finance leases	Not capitalized	Capitalized	Capitalized	Capitalized
10. Deferred taxes	Accrued	Optional accrual[c]	Accrued	Accrued

[a]When ownership exceeds 10%.
[b]But with inflation accounting, not used.
[c]Three methods are allowed, including nonaccrual.

Mexican GAAP. Deferred taxes are provided for in full, using the liability method. The costs of employee pensions, seniority premiums,[37] and termination pay are accrued currently when they can be reasonably estimated based on actuarial calculations. Statutory (legal) reserves are created by allocating 5 percent of income each year until the reserve equals 20 percent of the value of the outstanding capital stock.

Exhibit 4-4 summarizes the significant accounting practices in the four countries surveyed in this chapter.

Selected References

Canadian Institute of Chartered Accountants, *Significant Differences in GAAP in Canada, Chile, Mexico, and the United States: An Analysis of Accounting Pronouncements as of October 2002,* Toronto: CICA, 2002.

Chen, C. J. P., F. A. Gu, and X. Su, "A Comparison of Reported Earnings under Chinese GAAP vs. IAS: Evidence from the Shanghai Stock Exchange," *Accounting Horizons* (June 1999): 91–111.

Chen, Y., P. Jubb, and A. Tran, "Problems of Accounting Reform in the People's Republic of China," *The International Journal of Accounting* 32, no. 2 (1997): 139–153.

Davis-Friday, P. Y., and J. M. Rivera, "Inflation Accounting and 20-F Disclosures: Evidence

[37]Seniority premiums are compensation amounts paid at the termination of employment based on how long the employee has worked. Generally, employees who voluntarily retire must work at least 15 years, but there is no minimum number of years for other types of termination, such as redundancy layoffs, or if an employee dies.

from Mexico," *Accounting Horizons* (June 2000): 113–135.

Doležal, J., "The Czech Republic," in *European Accounting Guide*, 5th ed., D. Alexander and S. Archer, eds., New York: Aspen, 2003.

Gordon, E. A., "Accounting for Changing Prices: The Value Relevance of Historical Cost, Price Level, and Replacement Cost Accounting in Mexico," *Journal of Accounting Research* 39, no. 1 (June 2001): 177–200.

Graham, R. C., and C. C. Wang, "Taiwan and International Accounting Standards: A Comparison," *The International Journal of Accounting* 30, no. 2 (1995): 149–167.

Hilmy, J., "Communists Among Us in a Market Economy: Accountancy in the People's Republic of China," *The International Journal of Accounting* 34, no. 4 (1999): 491–515.

Hussey, R., "The IASB and the White Rabbit," *Accountancy* (March 2003): 98–99.

Jeffrey, G., "Down Mexico Way," *Accountancy International* (March 1999): 90–102.

Jindrichovska, I., "The Relationship between Accounting Numbers and Returns: Some Empirical Evidence from the Emerging Market of the Czech Republic," *The European Accounting Review* 10, no. 1 (2001): 107–131.

Lin, Z. J., F. Chen, and Z. Tang, "The Perceptions of Chinese Financial Reporting Regulations by Various Stakeholders," *Journal of International Accounting Auditing and Taxation* 10, no. 1 (2001): 23–49.

Ma, R., ed., *Financial Reporting in the Pacific Asia Region*, Singapore: World Scientific Publishing, 1997.

PricewaterhouseCoopers, *IAS, US GAAP and CZ GAAP: Similarities and Differences*, Prague: PWC, April 2002 (available at www.pwcglobal.com/cz).

Schroll, R., "The New Accounting System in the Czech Republic," *The European Accounting Review* 4, no. 4 (1995): 827–832.

Sucher, P., P. Moizer, and M. Zarova, "The Images of the Big Six Audit Firms in the Czech Republic," *The European Accounting Review* 8, no. 3 (1999): 499–521.

"Survey: Asian Business," *The Economist* (April 7, 2001): 1–18.

"A Survey of Finance in Central Europe," *The Economist* (September 14, 2002): 1–16.

Xiang, B., "Institutional Factors Influencing China's Accounting Reforms and Standards," *Accounting Horizons* (June 1998): 105–119.

Xiao, Z., "Corporate Disclosures Made by Chinese Listed Companies," *The International Journal of Accounting* 34, no. 3 (1999): 349–373.

Discussion Questions

1. Level of education affects a nation's accounting development (see Chapter 2). One measure of education level is the literacy rate. *Pocket World in Figures 2004 Edition* (London: *The Economist,* 2003) gives the following literacy rates: China, 85 percent; Czech Republic, 99 percent; Mexico, 92 percent; and Taiwan, 96 percent. What do these literacy rates suggest about accounting in these four countries?

2. Exhibit 4.2 shows that 23 Mexican companies are listed on the New York Stock Exchange (as of December 31, 2003). The 23 listings occurred as follows: 1991, 2; 1992, 2; 1993, 4; 1994, 6; 1995, 0; 1996, 2; 1997, 2; 1998, 2; 1999, 1; 2000, 1; 2001, 1; 2002, 0; 2003, 0. What does the pattern of listings between 1991 and 2003 suggest?

3. The chapter states that accounting and auditing standard setting in Taiwan is patterned after that in the United States. What are the similarities and differences in standard setting in the two nations?

4. Does the development of accounting lead or lag behind the development of a nation's economy? Cite evidence from this chapter to support your answer.

5. Both China and the Czech Republic are restructuring their economies from central planning to more of a market orientation. What are the similarities and differences in the approaches each country is taking in embracing market reforms?

6. Even before Hong Kong reverted to China in 1997, China was well on the way toward developing accounting standards compatible with those of the International Accounting Standards Board. How will the return of Hong Kong likely affect China's accounting standards?

7. What are the important features of accounting and financial reporting that are necessary to develop an efficient stock market with fair trading? How likely is it that the countries in this chapter will develop such a stock market? Why do you think so?

8. What is the role of tax legislation on financial accounting practices in each of the four countries treated in this chapter?

9. The Czech Republic is developing a body of accounting requirements consistent with European Union requirements. What evidence is there that Czech accounting requirements comply with these requirements? (Hint: You may want to refer to the discussion of the European Union in Chapter 8.)

10. China's aim is to develop accounting standards that are harmonized with international practices. What examples are there that Chinese accounting standards are consistent with "world-class" practices?

11. What evidence is there that accounting practices in Taiwan are similar to those found in the United States?

12. Mexican companies that list their shares on the New York Stock Exchange are required by the U.S. Securities and Exchange Commission to reconcile net income and stockholders' equity from Mexican to U.S. GAAP. What are likely to be the most significant reconciliation items?

Exercises

1. This chapter provides synopses of national accounting practice systems in four emerging economies.

   Required: For each country, list:

   a. The name of the national financial accounting standard-setting board or agency.
   b. The name of the agency, institute, or other organization charged with supervising and enforcing financial accounting standards.

2. The International Federation of Accountants (IFAC) is a worldwide organization of professional accounting bodies. IFAC's Web site (www.ifac.org) has links to accounting bodies around the world.

   Required: Visit IFAC's Web site. List the accounting organizations discussed in this chapter that are linked to IFAC's Web site.

3. Reread Chapter 4 and its discussion questions.

Required:

   a. As you go through this material, prepare a list of eight expressions, terms, or short phrases unfamiliar or unusual in your home country.

   b. Write a concise definition or explanation of each item.

4. Analyze the four national accounting practice systems summarized in the chapter.

Required:

   a. For each of the four countries treated in the chapter, select the most important financial accounting practice or principle at variance with international norms.

   b. For each selection you make, briefly state your reasons for including it on your list.

5. Refer to Exhibit 4-2.

Required: Discuss the factors that might explain the listing patterns observed in the table.

6. Several companies from the four countries treated in this chapter are listed on the New York Stock Exchange (NYSE), Nasdaq, and the London Stock Exchange.

Required: Go to the NYSE Web site (www.nyse.com). Identify the companies listed on the NYSE from each of the four countries treated in this chapter and indicate the year that each company became listed. Do the same for the Nasdaq (www.nasdaq.com) and the London Stock Exchange (www.londonstockexchange.com).

7. Chapter 2 discussed certain socioeconomic and institutional factors that affect accounting development. These were: (1) sources of finance, (2) legal system, (3) taxation, (4) political and economic ties, (5) inflation, (6) level of economic development, and (7) education level.

Required:

   a. Identify the factor that you think is the most important influence on accounting in each of the four countries treated in this chapter.

   b. Explain the significance of this factor and why you think it is the most important one.

8. Refer to Exercise 7.

Required:

   a. Identify the factor that you think is the least important influence on accounting in each of the four countries treated in this chapter.

   b. Explain why you think it is the least important one.

9. Several companies from the four countries treated in this chapter refer to International Financial Reporting Standards (IFRS) in their annual reports.

Required: Go to the Web site of the International Accounting Standards Board (www.iasb.org). Identify the companies from China, the Czech Republic, Mexico, and Taiwan that refer to IFRS.

10. The role of government in developing accounting and auditing standards varies in the four countries treated in this chapter.

    Required: Compare the role of government in developing accounting and auditing standards in China, the Czech Republic, Mexico, and Taiwan.

11. Accounting standard setting in most countries involves a combination of private- and public-sector groups. The private sector includes the accounting profession and other groups affected by the financial reporting process, such as users and preparers of financial statements and organized labor. The public sector includes government agencies such as tax authorities, ministries responsible for commercial law, and securities commissions. The stock market is another potential influence.

    Required: Complete a matrix indicating whether each of these groups significantly influences accounting standard setting in the four countries discussed in this chapter. List the groups across the top and the countries down the side; indicate the influence of each group with a yes or no.

12. The following are certain financial ratios used by analysts:
    • *Liquidity:* current ratio; cash flow from operations to current liabilities
    • *Solvency:* debt to equity; debt to assets
    • *Profitability:* return on assets; return on equity

    Required: Assume that you are comparing the financial ratios of companies from two countries discussed in this chapter. Discuss how the accounting practices identified in Exhibit 4-4 would affect your comparisons for each of the six ratios listed.

CASE 4-1   DOES SECRECY PAY?

SIGN OF THE TIMES: TRANSPARENCY AWARDS

Prague: Czech Republic[38]
By Robert Patton

If the "ABN AMRO Signum Temporis Awards for disclosure" had been held in 1994, Seliko probably would not have walked off with a prize.

Back then, an analyst for Atlantik Financial Markets brokerage asked the managers of this Czech food producer to discuss their business plans. Sure, they said—for $200 an hour.

Several weeks of the analyst's phone calls finally wore down Seliko's top brass, which eventually met with him free of charge.

Still, the episode is a particularly appalling example of an all-too-common problem: Czech managers are notoriously tight-fisted with company information.

Through events such as the bank's Signum Temporis ("sign of the time") awards for best corporate disclosure, planned for Feb. 27 at the Prague Stock Exchange (PSE) Ball, brokers are trying to persuade executives to be more open. Award officials say some Czech companies are finally realizing that to attract more investment, they must let investors know what they're getting into.

But analysts say many Czech companies continue to frustrate investors' attempts to obtain such information. Despite the progress made so far, regional rivals Poland and Hungary have left the Czechs in the dust.

Some Czech firms simply give out as little information as possible, analysts say, and others take months to release basic financial data. Still others fail to publicize results.

A company might release new financial data, "but unless you call them, you don't know about it," said ING Barings analyst Vojtech Kraus. "They'll just tell investors who happened to come see them that week."

Some Czech companies, particularly large conglomerates, may have good intentions but simply aren't experienced at quickly compiling and disseminating their financial data. Financial-industrial giant Skoda Plzen is a good example of this, said Patria Finance analyst Ondrej Datka.

Leaving aside the shady managers with something to hide, many others simply don't believe it's important to keep investors informed.

Secretive companies often have managers with attitudes forged during the '70s and '80s, said Pavel Kohout, a portfolio manager at ING Investment Management. Under communism, secrecy—not transparency—was the watchword.

The conglomerate Chemapol is the quintessential example of a company run by old dogs who can't or simply won't learn new capitalist tricks. They've been "used to being opaque since communism," Kohout said.

Coupon privatization did little to change such attitudes. Many managers find themselves in publicly traded companies against their will.

Many Czech companies "didn't come to the stock market," said Datka. "They found themselves on the stock market as a result of privatization."

By contrast, many Polish and Hungarian firms have issued initial public offerings (IPOs) of stock and so are more concerned with investor satisfaction.

---

[38]*The Prague Post* (February 25, 1998), www.praguepost.cz

Analysts typically want a balance sheet, profit/loss statement, a cash-flow statement, and basic information about corporate outlook and goals. Legislation and PSE regulations help investors by forcing companies to divulge key financial data.

Every company with tradable securities must publish annual and semiannual reports and send them to the Finance Ministry and Czech Statistical Office. And companies whose stock is traded on the PSE's primary and secondary markets must also release quarterly financial reports.

But the PSE doesn't enforce its deadlines strictly enough, said Datka. And some companies submit financial data to the PSE that is timely but "unconsolidated"—that is, it does not incorporate data for subsidiaries.

That's not very useful, because in many cases "unconsolidated data don't mean anything," Datka said, and consolidated figures often don't appear until months later.

The semiannual reports to the Ministry of Finance, too, often linger "somewhere on the table of some clerk in the Finance Ministry" for as long as two months before becoming available to the public, complained Milon Miller, project manager for the Prague branch of Consultants PlanEcon.

Investors hope capital-markets reform will stimulate foreign strategic investment into Czech companies and help make them more transparent. Strategic investors are more likely to discipline managers, said Central Europe Privatization Fund President Howard Golden.

Under such owners, secretive executives "would be more transparent or they would be out," Golden said.

The trend may have already begun. Komercni Banka, SPT Telecom and trammaker CKD have become more generous, analysts say. In many cases, such firms are providing more information partly to attract investors.

Several analysts said the improvement is steady but incremental. Golden went so far as to say that Czech firms are "light-years ahead of where they were two to three years ago."

Is Seliko riding this wave of increasing transparency? Well, sort of.

Now that it's partly owned by the Olpran Group, Seliko wouldn't try to charge for information, Olpran spokeswoman Marie Logrova insisted.

"We wouldn't go that far, but the information we'd give out probably wouldn't be that precise," she said. "We'd have to check with the other shareholders of Seliko before providing more specific information."

And who are Seliko's other shareholders? "I'm not authorized to answer that."

REQUIRED

1. Describe the financial reporting practices of Czech companies, as characterized in the newspaper article.
2. What are the likely causes of these practices?
3. How do these practices compare to the reporting requirements identified in the chapter?
4. What are the consequences of these practices for investors, the reporting companies, and the Prague Stock Exchange?

CASE 4-2   CASINO CAPITAL

What conditions are necessary to develop an efficient stock market with fair trading? What role does accounting and financial reporting play in stock market development? Consider the case of China:

Those Chinese who think of themselves as street-smart tell a joke about three fools. The first is the boss who plays around with his secretary and ends up her husband. The second is the investor who plays the property market and ends up a homeowner. And the third is the punter who plays the stock market and finds himself a shareholder. This sums up the culture of China's fledgling capital markets. "Trading, not ownership," is the approach of China's investors, says Anthony Neoh, a former head of Hong Kong's Securities and Futures Commission who is now the chief outside adviser to China's regulatory body. "That's what we need to change."

This marks a shift in China's capital market reforms. So far, Beijing has focused almost entirely on the "supply side" of the securities market. This has included listing more, and better, companies, and forcing them to adopt better standards of corporate governance and disclosure. Such efforts have a long way to go.

However, the government now realizes that is also need to work on the "demand side." At present, China's stock market, Asia's second largest by capitalization, consists of 60m mainly clueless retail investors, driven to trade almost entirely on rumor.[39]

[T]he balance sheets of Chinese companies are, by common consent, a joke. In January [2001] the government's official auditing body admitted that more than two-thirds of the 1,300 biggest state-owned enterprises cook their books. Johnny Chen, the Beijing head of Pricewaterhouse-Coopers, says that even this is an understatement. Quite simply, the SOEs' numbers are whatever the key man wants them to be. And without genuinely independent directors to chair an audit committee, that will not change.[40]

Even China's mostly hapless stock market investor (66m of them, officially) had something to cheer about this month, after the country's highest court said that shareholders could file individual or class action lawsuits against companies that lie about their accounts. There appear to be a lot of liars about. Around 900 shareholder suits are pending, in a country with 1,200 listed companies.

It remains to be seen whether these steps amount to mere tinkering, or herald the new and bolder approach to financial reform that China badly needs. Its markets for labor, goods, and services are nowadays more liberal than those in some capitalist economies. Its capital markets, by contrast, have changed only cosmetically since the days of central planning. In effect, all capital in China is allocated, one way or the other, by the government, which wastes much of it.

The decade-old stock market is dominated by state-owned enterprises that were listed for political rather than economic reasons. Some two-thirds of the market's capitalization is not traded, so the state retains total control. There is no corporate bond market to speak of.[41]

---

[39]"Fools in Need of Institutions," *The Economist* (June 30, 2001): 65.

[40]"Survey: Asian Business," *The Economist* (April 7, 2001): 13.

[41]"Banking on Growth," *The Economist* (January 18, 2003): 67.

[A]ll is not what it seems in China's capital markets. For a start, growth in the domestic stock market has outstripped the efforts—game as they are—of the regulators and the legal system to police it. The authorities say that computer matching of share transactions has allowed them pretty much to stop powerful syndicates ramping up share prices. They have even sent the biggest manipulators to jail, yet insider trading is still rife on a heroic scale. Stock exchange executives reckon that the real number of investors is around half the official number: investors use multiple accounts for dodgy share dealings.

The real issue is the quality of the listed companies themselves, says one financial official. Even some of the better regarded ones indulge in all sorts of market abuses, such as lending money raised on the stock market to the parent company rather than investing it, or speculating in the stock market on their own account. Almost all companies allowed a listing are the beneficiaries of government favoritism. Their profitability is usually abysmal, their levels of disclosure poor, and—with the state holding roughly two-thirds of the shares of companies listed in Shanghai and Shenzhen—their treatment of minority shareholders appalling.[42]

REQUIRED

1. Describe the conditions necessary to develop a stock market in an emerging economy.
2. How do these conditions compare to the situation in China?
3. How likely is China to develop a stock market with fair trading? Why do you say so?
4. Outline a plan of reforms necessary to achieve stock market development in China.

---

[42]"A Survey of Asian Finance," *The Economist* (February 8, 2003): 10–11.

CHAPTER

5 | REPORTING AND DISCLOSURE

In this chapter we examine the communication of financial and nonfinancial information in an international setting. Much of our discussion addresses disclosure related to financial reporting for external users. We focus on selected topics and do not attempt to discuss every disclosure issue that applies to financial statement users, preparers, and financial professionals.

The relative importance of equity markets in national economies is growing and individual investors are becoming more active in those markets. As a result, public disclosure, investor protection, shareholder value, and stock market–driven forms of corporate governance are becoming increasingly important. Thus, although disclosure practices vary substantially from country to country, they are converging. Hundreds of companies have increased their disclosures by (1) voluntarily adopting International Financial Reporting Standards (IFRS) or U.S. GAAP; (2) complying with domestic and overseas stock exchange and regulatory requirements; or (3) responding to various demands for information from investors and analysts.[1] However, important differences among countries will continue to affect all but the largest firms, particularly those that are not active in international capital or product markets.

Government regulators who seek to maintain or increase the credibility of their national capital markets also influence disclosure practices around the world. Stock exchanges have concluded that their continued growth and success depends on offering a high-quality market with effective investor protection. As a result, oversight by regulators and stock exchanges is increasing and disclosure requirements are becoming more stringent. The trend toward greater investor protection and enhanced disclosure will continue as stock exchanges face growing competition from each other and from less-regulated trading systems.

---

[1]For example, Schering AG, a German company, states the following in its *Annual Report 2002:* "We aim to strengthen investor confidence in our Company continuously by providing transparent, timely and fair reporting. Schering AG has always complied with all legal provisions and supplementary regulations on corporate governance." The Schering AG Web site further states, "Our open communication creates transparency and trust in our company. It is our policy to show you the growth-oriented development of our company and our ambitious targets. Together with our shareholders, we profit from the long-term improvement of our market capitalization."

DEVELOPMENT OF DISCLOSURE

The development of disclosure systems closely parallels the development of accounting systems discussed in Chapter 2.[2] Disclosure standards and practices are influenced by sources of finance, legal systems, political and economic ties, level of economic development, education level, culture, and other influences.

National differences in disclosure are driven largely by differences in corporate governance and finance. In the United States, the United Kingdom, and other Anglo-American countries, equity markets have provided most corporate financing and have become highly developed. In these markets, ownership tends to be spread among many shareholders, and investor protection is emphasized. Institutional investors play a growing role in these countries, demanding financial returns and increased shareholder value. Public disclosure is highly developed in response to companies' accountability to the public.

In many other countries (such as France, Germany, Japan, and numerous emerging market countries), shareholdings remain highly concentrated and banks (and/or family owners) traditionally have been the primary source of corporate financing. Structures are in place to protect incumbent management. Banks (which sometimes are both creditors and owners) and other insiders (such as corporate members of interlocking shareholder groups) provide discipline. These banks, insiders, and others are closely informed about the company's financial position and its activities. Public disclosure is less developed in these markets and large differences in the amount of information given to large shareholders and creditors vis-à-vis the public may be permitted.

Voluntary Disclosure

Managers have better information about their firm's current and future performance than do external parties. Several studies show that managers have incentives to disclose such information voluntarily. Benefits of enhanced disclosure may include lower transaction costs in the trading of the firm's securities, greater interest in the company by financial analysts and investors, increased share liquidity, and lower cost of capital. In one recent report,[3] the Financial Accounting Standards Board (FASB) describes a FASB business reporting project that supports the view that companies can achieve capital markets benefits by enhancing their voluntary disclosure. The report includes guidance on how companies can describe and explain their investment potential to investors.

As investors around the world demand more detailed and timely information, voluntary disclosure levels are increasing in both highly developed and emerging market countries. It is widely recognized, however, that financial reporting can be an imperfect mechanism for communicating with outside investors when managers' incentives are not perfectly aligned with the interests of all shareholders. In one classic paper, the

---

[2]The terms "disclosure systems" and "accounting systems" overlap considerably. Often, as in Chapter 2 of this text, "accounting development" refers to the development of accounting standards and practices. "Disclosure development" as discussed in this chapter refers to the development of financial and nonfinancial disclosures presented in financial reports. We do not discuss disclosures made in press releases, although much of the discussion in this chapter applies to this area.

[3]Financial Accounting Standards Board, *Improving Business Reporting: Insights into Enhancing Voluntary Disclosures,* www.fasb.org/brrp/BRRP2.PDF, 2001.

authors argue that managers' communication with outside investors is imperfect when: (1) managers have superior information about their firm; (2) managers' incentives are not perfectly aligned with all shareholders' interests; and (3) accounting rules and auditing are imperfect.[4] The authors state that contracting mechanisms (such as compensation linking managers' rewards to long-term share values) can reduce this conflict.

Evidence strongly indicates that corporate managers often have strong incentives to delay the disclosure of adverse news, "manage" their financial reports to convey a more positive image of the firm, and overstate their firms' financial performance and prospects. For example, executives face significant risks of being dismissed in firms whose financial or stock market performance is relatively weak. Seriously stressed firms may have a higher risk of bankruptcy, acquisition, or hostile takeover, leading to a management change. Also, the possible competitive disadvantage created when proprietary information is made public may offset the benefits of full disclosure.

Regulation (such as accounting and disclosure regulation) and third-party certification (such as auditing) can improve the functioning of markets. Accounting regulation attempts to reduce managers' ability to record economic transactions in ways that are not in shareholders' best interests. Disclosure regulation sets forth requirements to ensure that shareholders receive timely, complete, and accurate information. External auditors try to ensure that managers apply appropriate accounting policies, make reasonable accounting estimates, maintain adequate accounting records and control systems, and provide the required disclosures in a timely manner.

Although these mechanisms can strongly influence practice, managers occasionally conclude that the benefits of noncompliance with reporting requirements (e.g., a higher stock price due to inflated earnings) outweigh the costs (e.g., the risk of job loss and litigation resulting in criminal or civil penalties if the noncompliance is detected and reported). Thus, managers' disclosure choices reflect the combined effects of disclosure requirements and their incentives to disclose information voluntarily.

Regulatory Disclosure Requirements

To protect investors, most securities exchanges (together with professional or government regulatory bodies such as the U.S. Securities and Exchange Commission and the Ministry of Finance in Japan) impose reporting and disclosure requirements on domestic and foreign companies that seek access to their markets. These exchanges want to make sure that investors have enough information to allow them to evaluate a company's performance and prospects. Nowhere is this concern more evident than in the United States, whose disclosure standards generally are considered to be the most stringent in the world.

Stock exchanges and government regulators generally require foreign listed firms to furnish almost the same financial and nonfinancial information as that required of domestic companies. Foreign listed firms generally have some flexibility in the accounting principles used and the extent of disclosure. In many countries, foreign listed firms must file with the stock exchange any information made public, distributed to shareholders, or filed with regulators in the domestic market. However, many coun-

---

[4]See P. M. Healy and K. G. Palepu, "The Effect of Firms' Financial Disclosure Strategies on Stock Prices," *Accounting Horizons* 7 (March 1993): 1–11.

tries do not monitor or enforce this "cross-jurisdictional conformity of disclosure" requirement.

Shareholder protection varies substantially among countries. Anglo-American countries such as Canada, the United Kingdom, and the United States provide extensive and strictly enforced shareholder protection. In contrast, shareholder protection receives less emphasis in other parts of the world. For example, while China prohibits insider trading, a weak judiciary makes enforcement almost nonexistent. Shareholder protection codes in the Czech Republic, Mexico, and many other emerging market countries also are rudimentary.[5] Even in many developed countries, the concept of investor protection is of recent origin, and many commentators argue that it still is inadequate. For example, insider trading was not a criminal offense in Germany until the enactment of the Securities Trading Act 1994.

Exhibit 5-1 presents the broad objectives of investor-oriented equity markets. As noted earlier, investor protection is a primary goal of these markets. As Exhibit 5-1

Exhibit 5-1 Broad Objectives for Investor-Oriented Equity Markets	
Objectives: Investor Protection	Market Quality
Investors are provided with material information and are protected through monitoring and enforcement.	Markets are fair, orderly, efficient, and free from abuse and misconduct.

Specifically:

1. Provide investors with material information.	1. Promote equitable access to information and trading opportunities (market fairness).
2. Monitor and enforce market rules.	2. Enhance liquidity and reduce transaction costs (market efficiency).
3. Inhibit fraud in the public offering, trading, voting, and tendering of securities.	3. Contribute to freedom from abuse through monitoring and enforcement.
4. Seek comparability of financial and non-financial information (allow investors to compare companies across industries and domiciles).	4. Foster investor confidence.
	5. Facilitate capital formation.
	6. Seek conditions in which prices reflect investor perceptions of value without being arbitrary or capricious (market orderliness).

Principles:

1. *Cost Effectiveness.* The cost of market regulation should be proportionate to the benefits it secures.
2. *Market Freedom and Flexibility.* Regulation should not impede competition and market evolution.
3. *Transparent Financial Reporting and Full and Complete Disclosure.*
4. *Equal Treatment of Foreign and Domestic Firms.*

Source: Carol A. Frost and Mark Lang, "Foreign Companies and U.S. Securities Markets: Financial Reporting Policy Issues and Suggestions for Research," *Accounting Horizons* 10 (March 1996): 95–109. Used with permission of American Accounting Association.

---

[5]Refer to Case 4-1, "Does Secrecy Pay?," in Chapter 4 and Case 8-2, "Accounting Quality in East Asia" in Chapter 8.

shows, this requires that investors receive timely material information and are protected through effective monitoring and enforcement. Disclosure should be sufficient to allow investors to compare companies across industries and domiciles. Implicit in Exhibit 5-1 is the idea that full and credible disclosure will enhance investor confidence, which will increase liquidity, reduce transaction costs, and improve overall market quality.

The U.S. SEC Financial Reporting Debate

The SEC generally requires foreign registrants to furnish financial information substantially similar to that required of domestic companies. However, foreign registrants' financial statements need not be prepared in accordance with U.S. GAAP if they are presented in accordance with another comprehensive body of accounting principles and are accompanied by a quantitative reconciliation to U.S. GAAP of net income, shareholders' equity, and earnings per share, if materially different.

Whether the reconciliation requirement helps or hinders the SEC in meeting its regulatory objectives is widely debated. The SEC's reporting requirements are generally consistent with the objectives of investor protection and market quality. However, stringent reporting requirements may achieve the goal of investor protection at the cost of reducing investment opportunities or imposing high transaction costs on investing.

Some commentators argue that the SEC's financial reporting requirements for foreign companies deter these companies from making their securities available in the United States.[6,7] As a result, it is claimed that U.S. investors are more likely to trade in markets such as the U.S. Over-the-Counter (OTC) market or overseas markets where liquidity may be relatively low, transaction costs relatively high, and investor protection less important than on the national exchanges in the United States. It then is argued that the SEC could provide U.S. investors with more investment opportunities within the regulated U.S. markets by relaxing its financial reporting requirements; this, in turn, would better balance the SEC's objectives of investor protection and market quality. It also is argued that the SEC's registration requirements actually may mislead U.S. investors by giving a false appearance of comparability to foreign financial statements that may require a significantly different interpretation than U.S. statements. Others counter that the current accounting and disclosure system both protects investors and ensures the quality of U.S. capital markets.[8] Underlying this argument are the principles of full disclosure and equal treatment of foreign and domestic issuers. If investors in domestic securities require financial information based on U.S. GAAP to make informed decisions, then such information is just as necessary for

---

[6]See J. L. Cochrane, "Are U.S. Regulatory Requirements for Foreign Firms Appropriate?" *Fordham International Law Journal* 17 (Symposium, 1994), S58–S67; J. L. Cochrane, J. E. Shapiro, and J. E. Tobin, "Foreign Equities and U.S. Investors: Breaking Down the Barriers Separating Supply and Demand," *Stanford Journal of Law, Business and Finance,* 1997.

[7]New regulations enacted by the 2002 Sarbanes-Oxley Act are also said to deter foreign companies from a U.S. listing. See John Rossant, "Who Needs U.S. Markets?" *BusinessWeek* (February 16, 2004): 13.

[8]See Richard C. Breeden, "Foreign Companies and U.S. Securities Markets in a Time of Economic Transformation," *Fordham International Law Journal* 17 (Symposium, 1994), S77–S96; and Pat McConnell, "Practical Company Experience in Entering U.S. Markets: Significant Issues and Hurdles from the Advisor's Perspective," *Fordham International Law Journal* 17 (Symposium, 1994), S120–S128; and remarks by SEC Commissioner Isaac C. Hunt, Jr., at the Second European FASB-SEC Financial Reporting Conference, Frankfurt, Germany (March 23, 2000), available at www.sec.gov/news/speech/spch363.htm.

making informed decisions about non-U.S. securities. Indeed, the competitive strength of U.S. capital markets, including their substantial liquidity and high level of investor confidence, often is attributed (at least in part) to the SEC's existing disclosure system and vigorous enforcement. It also has been argued that the SEC's reporting requirements are not the primary obstacles to foreign companies desiring to list securities in the United States.

REPORTING AND DISCLOSURE PRACTICES

What do companies around the world actually disclose in their annual reports? Annual report disclosure practices reflect managers' responses to regulatory disclosure requirements and their incentives to provide information to financial statement users voluntarily. In many parts of the world, disclosure rules mean little and monitoring and enforcement are largely absent. Insofar as disclosure rules are not enforced, the required disclosures are (in practice) voluntary, because corporate managers will not comply with disclosure rules if compliance is more costly than the expected costs of noncompliance. Therefore, it is important to clearly distinguish between disclosures that are "required" and disclosures that actually are made. It is misleading to focus on disclosure rules without also looking at actual disclosure practices.

For some types of disclosure (such as disclosures about material developments) managerial discretion plays such an important role that monitoring (and hence enforcement) is difficult. Therefore, these types of disclosure are more or less voluntary. Finally, disclosure rules vary dramatically worldwide in areas such as cash flow and changes in equity statements, related party transactions, segment reporting, fair value of financial assets and liabilities, and earnings per share.

In this section we focus on (1) disclosures of forward-looking information, (2) segment disclosures, (3) cash and funds flow statements, (4) social responsibility disclosures, (5) special disclosures for nondomestic financial statement users, (6) corporate governance disclosures, and (7) Internet business reporting and disclosure. These disclosure and reporting items are selected because of their importance to financial statement users. For example, financial analysts and regulators have emphasized the importance of corporate disclosures of forward-looking information, such as that related to corporate goals and planned expenditures, and business segment information. Cash and funds (working capital) flow information is also considered highly relevant for financial statement users. For instance, the AICPA Special Committee on Financial Reporting has recommended that cash flow statistics be reported for business segments, and accounting standards in many countries now require the presentation of cash flow statements.

Disclosures of Forward-Looking Information

Disclosures of forward-looking information are considered highly relevant in equity markets worldwide. For example, the EU's Fourth Directive states that the annual report should include an indication of the company's likely future development. The SEC's Regulation S-K requires companies to disclose presently known information that will materially impact future liquidity, capital resources, and operating results. As a third example, the Tokyo Stock Exchange TSE "requests" management of listed firms to provide forecasts of sales, earnings, and dividends in their annual and semiannual press releases.

Here we use the term "forward-looking information" to include: (1) forecasts of revenues, income (loss), earnings (loss) per share (eps), capital expenditures, and other financial items; (2) prospective information about future economic performance or position that is less definite than forecasts in terms of projected item, fiscal period, and projected amount[9]; and (3) statements of management's plans and objectives for future operations.

Exhibit 5-2 presents evidence on forward-looking disclosures made in the annual reports distributed by 200 large public companies, 40 each from France, Germany, Japan, the United Kingdom, and the United States. Panel A shows that most of the firms in each country subsample disclosed information about management's plans and objectives. In contrast, fewer firms disclosed forecasts, ranging from a low of two firms in Japan to a high of 31 firms in the United States. Most of the U.S. forecasts involved capital expenditures, not earnings and sales, as in Germany. Finally, panel C shows that most of the firms in France, Germany, the United Kingdom, and the United States (but not Japan) also disclosed "softer" prospective information.

Exhibit 5-3 illustrates the types of forward-looking disclosures made by the 200 firms. Exhibit 5-3 presents the forecast disclosure from the Schering AG (a German

Exhibit 5-2 Number of Firms Disclosing Forward-looking Information in 1993/94 Annual Reports

	France	Germany	Japan	United Kingdom	United States
Number of sample firms	40	40	40	40	40
Firms making no forward-looking disclosures	3	0	5	3	0
Firms making one or more forward-looking disclosures	37	40	35	37	40
A. Firms disclosing management's plans or objectives	29	28	33	25	39
B. Firms disclosing forecasts:					
Earnings	4	11	2	2	3
Sales	7	11	1	1	2
Capital expenditures	2	6	0	4	22
Other	2	13	0	9	18
At least one forecast	11	22	2	11	31
C. Firms disclosing "softer" prospective information	29	36	10	31	36

Source: Carol A. Frost and Kurt P. Ramin, "Corporate Financial Disclosure: A Global Assessment," in Frederick D. S. Choi, ed., *International Finance and Accounting Handbook 3e.* Copyright © 2003 John Wiley & Sons. This material is used by permission of John Wiley & Sons, Inc.

[9]For convenience we use the term "prospective" disclosure to refer to "softer" nonforecast disclosures.

Exhibit 5-3   Forecast Disclosure by Schering AG

Forecast 2003

We expect the Schering AG Group to record high single-digit growth in net sales after adjustment for exchange rate effects. We are forecasting increases in net sales in local currencies for all Regions, with growth in the U.S. being particularly pronounced.

The key drivers for this increase in net sales include our successful products Yasmin® and Mirena®, as well as the anticipated continued positive development of our leading product Betaferon®.

We expect an increase in net profit in the high single-digit range in comparison to the net profit of 2002 excluding the positive one-time effects.

However, this increase will not yet be apparent in the first two quarters of 2003. Since the exchange rates for the US dollar, yen, and important Latin American currencies weakened over the course of 2002, the forecasted increase will first materialize in the second half of 2003.

As a consequence of our high rate of production-capacity utilization, we have allocated approximately €300m in capital expenditure to expand our production facilities.

We will continue to implement our growth strategy in 2003:

- In the Gynecology & Andrology business area, we will further expand our leading role in female fertility control and extend this expertise to the field of male fertility control. In addition, we will increase our market presence with our innovative products for the treatment of climacteric complaints.
- In the case of Specialized Therapeutics, we aim to increase acceptance of high-dose MS therapy with Betaferon® through a range of activities and increased communication with physicians and patients. In the field of hematological oncology, our goal is to ensure a strong market position with our homogeneous product portfolio.
- In the Diagnostics & Radiopharmaceuticals business area, we are focusing on consolidating our global leading position in the markets for MRI contrast agents.
- With regard to Dermatology, we will focus on the indications of eczema, acne and psoriasis and promote our business in our key markets.

We intend to realize the opportunities open to us to consolidate and expand our leading positions in specialized markets.

firm) Annual Report 2002. Schering forecasts "high single-digit growth" in net sales and net profit in 2003. A forecast such as this is reasonably precise, but still open to interpretation. For example, a financial statement reader might reasonably expect an increase in sales and profits between 7 and 9 percent. Schering also discloses the amount of planned capital expenditures and its product development emphasis in the coming year.

Segment Disclosures

Investor and analyst demand for information about firms' industry and geographic segment operations and financial results is significant and growing. For example, financial analysts in the United States consistently have requested financial statement data disaggregated in much greater detail than it is now. International Financial Reporting Standards (IFRS) include highly detailed segment reporting, as do accounting standards in many countries.[10] Segment disclosures help financial statement users better understand how the parts of a company make up the whole. After all, product lines and areas of the world vary in terms of risks, returns, and opportunities. A disaggregation by lines of business and geographic area should make for more informed judgments about the overall company.

Exhibit 5-4 presents the business segment and geographic area disclosure made in the 2002 Annual Report of Lafarge (a French firm). The business segment disclosure reveals the most recent 3 years' sales, operating income, investments in equity affiliates, capital employed, total assets and capital expenditures for Lafarge's four main product lines, or divisions.[11] The geographic area disclosure shows sales, property, plant and equipment, and capital employed by regions of the world and selected countries. Lafarge also discusses its product and geographic markets in significant detail elsewhere in the annual report.

Exhibit 5-4 Segment Disclosures by Lafarge

Business Segment and Geographic Area Information

Operating segments are defined as components of an enterprise for which separate financial information is available that is evaluated regularly by the Company's chief operating decision makers in order to allocate resources and assess performance. Since January 1, 2001, the Company has operated in the following four business segments: Cement, Aggregates and Concrete, Roofing, and Gypsum which represent separately managed strategic business units that have different capital requirements and marketing strategies. Until December 31, 2000, the Company also operated in the Specialty Products segment which produced and sold a variety of component products used in the construction industry. The Company's retained minority interest in this business is now included in the segment described as "Other". Each of the business segments are managed separately because each business segment develops, manufactures and sells distinct products.

Company management evaluates internally its performance on operating income on ordinary activities (defined as operating income before net gains on disposals and other expenses, net) and capital employed (defined as the total of goodwill, intangible and tangible assets, investments in equity affiliates and working capital) as disclosed in its business segment and geographic area information.

The Cement segment produces and sells a wide range of cement and hydraulic binders adapted to the needs of the construction industry. The Aggregates and Concrete segment produces and sells construction aggregates, ready mix concrete and other concrete products. The Roofing segment produces and sells roof tiles, roofing accessories and chimney systems. The Gypsum segment mainly produces and sells drywall for the commercial and residential construction sectors.

The accounting policies applied to the segment earnings are in agreement with those described in Note 2.

(continued)

---

[10]Refer to Lee H. Radebaugh and Donna L. Street, "Segmental and Foreign Operations Disclosure," in *International Finance and Accounting Handbook,* 3rd ed., F. D. S. Choi, ed., New York: John Wiley & Sons, 2003, for a detailed discussion of segment and foreign operations disclosure.
[11]Note that a fifth product line, specialty products, was sold in 2000.

Exhibit 5-4 Segment Disclosures by Lafarge

A | Business segment information

(in million euros)	Cement	Aggregates and Concrete	Roofing	Gypsum	Specialty Products	Other	Total
2002							
Gross sales	7,520	4,787	1,538	1,155	—	210	15,210
Less: intersegment	(572)	(19)	—	(9)	—	—	(600)
Sales	**6,948**	**4,768**	**1,538**	**1,146**	**—**	**210**	**14,610**
Depreciation	(545)	(216)	(116)	(69)	—	(23)	(969)
Operating income on ordinary activities	1,606	336	132	51	—	7	2,132
Operating income	1,694	349	72	8	—	(300)	1,823
Investments in equity affiliates	248	15	72	33	—	284	652
Capital employed	13,584	3,220	2,415	1,177	—	610	21,006
Total assets	15,417	4,835	2,856	1,423	—	2,108	26,639
Capital expenditures	707	212	90	83	—	57	1,149
2001							
Gross sales	6,476	4,824	1,585	1,064	—	243	14,192
Less: intersegment	(481)	(18)	—	8	—	(3)	(494)
Sales	**5,995**	**4,806**	**1,585**	**1,072**	**—**	**240**	**13,698**
Depreciation	(511)	(214)	(118)	(66)		(19)	(928)
Operating income on ordinary activities (a)	1,434	378	128	3	—	(9)	1,934
Operating income (a)	1,397	415	75	(7)	—	176	2,056
Investments in equity affiliates	250	20	51	50	—	68	439
Capital employed	14,825	4,058	2,677	1,279	—	514	23,353
Total assets	17,416	5,798	3,182	1,554	—	1,952	29,902
Capital expenditures	894	288	131	117	—	25	1,455
2000							
Gross sales	4,798	3,741	1,685	1,006	1,408	8	12,646
Less: intersegment	(378)	(16)	(1)	(6)	(21)	(8)	(430)
Sales	**4,420**	**3,725**	**1,684**	**1,000**	**1,387**	**—**	**12,216**
Depreciation	(385)	(181)	(116)	(55)	(44)	(7)	(788)
Operating income on ordinary activities (a)	1,104	304	205	52	139	—	1,804
Operating income (a)	1,090	308	148	46	128	113	1,833
Investments in equity affiliates	211	17	46	40	107	(1)	420
Capital employed	6,789	3,235	2,848	1,166	*294	50	14,382
Total assets	9,242	4,767	3,325	1,426	*722	1,415	20,897
Capital expenditures	559	265	145	229	81	28	1,307

*These amounts exclude the part of the Specialty Products segment that was considered sold on December 28, 2000.
(a) Revised for the change in presentation of equity affiliates (Note 4).

Exhibit 5-4 Segment Disclosures by Lafarge

B | Geographic area information

(in million euros)	2002			2001			2000		
	Sales	Property, plant and equipment	Capital employed	Sales	Property, plant and equipment	Capital employed	Sales	Property, plant and equipment	Capital employed
Western Europe	6,005	4,455	9,113	5,490	4,814	9,945	5,717	3,510	6,159
Of which:									
France	2,007	1,052	1,587	1,945	1,113	1,399	2,367	1,130	1,479
Germany	642	846	1,529	747	944	1,770	962	974	2,046
Spain	616	271	1,074	592	355	833	599	342	959
United Kingdom	1,483	1,166	2,513	1,140	1,229	3,265	852	562	604
North America	4,405	3,077	4,955	4,431	3,598	5,241	3,292	2,356	3,349
Of which:									
United States	3,071	2,373	3,883	2,898	2,785	3,926	2,307	1,533	2,030
Canada	1,334	704	1,072	1,533	813	1,315	985	823	1,319
Mediterranean Basin	562	628	1,031	637	850	1,310	666	746	1,211
Central and Eastern Europe	661	713	1,124	514	623	1,016	501	522	868
Latin America	720	416	892	760	650	1,292	761	450	829
Africa	869	580	969	765	716	1,084	525	239	406
Asia/Pacific	1,388	1,798	2,922	1,101	2,102	3,465	754	1,059	1,560
Total	**14,610**	**11,667**	**21,006**	**13,698**	**13,353**	**23,353**	**12,216**	***8,882**	***14,382**

*These amounts exclude the part of the Specialty Products segment that was considered sold on December 28, 2000.

Cash Flow and Funds Flow Statements

IFRS and accounting standards in the United States, the United Kingdom, and a growing number of other countries require the presentation of cash flow statements. The recent adoption of cash flow statement requirements in nations such as Japan and China reflects the growing emphasis on cash flow information by analysts and other financial statement users.

Exhibits 5-5 and 5-6 illustrate the variation in content and presentation format found in cash and funds flow statements around the world. Exhibit 5-5 presents the cash flow statement and supporting note from the annual report of the British company, Fuller Smith & Turner. Exhibit 5-6 is the capital flow statement of Bosch Group (Germany). The cash flow statement is an area where substantial worldwide convergence can be expected. Differences such as those seen in these two exhibits should soon disappear due to capital market pressures and the acceptance of IFRS.

Social Responsibility Disclosures

Increasingly, companies are being called upon to answer to a wide range of "stakeholders"—employees, customers, suppliers, governments, activist groups, and the general public—who have areas of concern other than a company's ability to create economic value. Social responsibility reporting refers to the measurement and communication of

Exhibit 5-5   Cash Flow Statement and Supporting Note of Fuller Smith & Turner

Group Cash Flow Statement for the 52 Weeks Ended 29 March 2003

	Note	52 Weeks to 29 March 2003	52 Weeks to 30 March 2002
		£000	£000
Net Cash Inflow From Operating Activities	25	28,597	24,642
Returns on Investments and Servicing of Finance			
Preference dividends paid		(120)	(120)
Interest received		216	501
Interest paid		(2,091)	(2,234)
		(1,995)	(1,853)
Taxation			
Corporation tax paid		(4,354)	(4,942)
Capital Expenditure and Financial Investment			
Payments to acquire tangible fixed assets		(11,973)	(26,980)
Payments to acquire fixed asset investments		–	(328)
Receipts from sales of tangible fixed assets		1,595	3,684
		(10,378)	(23,624)
Equity dividends paid		(3,801)	(3,631)
Total net cash inflow/(outflow) before the use of liquid resources and financing		8,069	(9,408)
Management of liquid resources[†]		1,415	11,391
Financing			
Issue of equity shares		278	719
Repurchase of equity shares		(10,634)	(498)
		(10,356)	221
Movement in cash in the year	25	(872)	2,204

[†]Management of liquid resources is the movement in current asset investments, namely cash on short term deposit at financial institutions.

25 Cash Flow Statement	2003	2002
	£000	£000
Reconciliation of Operating Profit to Net Inflow from Operating Activities		
Operating profit	18,379	15,426
Depreciation	8,521	8,287
Loss on disposal of tangible fixed assets	50	78
Impairment of fixed assets	–	1,350
Earnings before interest, tax, depreciation and amortisation	26,950	25,141
(Increase)/Decrease in Working Capital		
Stocks	(2)	191
Debtors	890	(941)
Creditors	759	251
Net cash inflow from operating activities	28,597	24,642

Exhibit 5-5   Cash Flow Statement and Supporting Note of Fuller Smith & Turner *(Continued)*

	2003	2002
	£000	£000
Reconciliation of Net Cash Flow to Movement in Net Debt		
Movement in cash in the year	(872)	2,204
Cash inflow from the movement in liquid resources	(1,415)	(11,391)
Amortisation of issue costs	(11)	(11)
Movement in net debt in the year	(2,298)	(9,198)
Net debt at beginning of the year	(19,649)	(10,451)
Net debt at end of the year	(21,947)	(19,649)

	March 2002	Cash flow	Other Non-cash Movements	March 2003
	£000	£000	£000	£000
Analysis of Net Debt				
Cash, at bank and in hand	5,275	(872)	—	4,403
Debenture stock	(26,974)	—	(11)	(26,985)
Current asset investments	2,050	(1,415)	—	635
Total	(19,649)	(2,287)	(11)	(21,947)

information about a company's effects on employee welfare, the local community, and the environment. It reflects a belief that companies owe stakeholders an annual accounting of their social and environmental performance, just like the financial information they provide shareholders. More importantly, as suggested by the saying, "What gets measured, gets managed," social responsibility reporting is a way to demonstrate corporate citizenship. "Sustainability" reports that integrate economic, social, and environmental performance are referred to as "triple bottom-line reporting." Moreover, to avoid criticism that the reporting is "green-wash" (a public relations ploy without substance), such information is increasingly being verified by independent third parties.[12]

Information on employee welfare has long been of interest to labor groups.[13] Particular areas of concern relate to working conditions, job security, equal opportunity, workforce diversity, and child labor. Employee disclosures also are of interest to investors in that they provide useful insights about a firm's labor relations, costs, and productivity.

Information disclosure regarding number of employees has been of great interest to national governments. Number-of-employees disclosure by geographic area gives host governments information on the employment effect of multinational companies. Employee disclosure by line of business, in turn, helps identify those industries and activities that foreign direct investors find economically attractive. If there is a conflict between the behavior of the investors and the goals of the host government—for

[12]Mel Wilson and Rosie Lombardi, "Globalization and its Discontent: The Arrival of Triple-Bottom-Line Reporting, *Ivey Business Journal* 66, 1 (September/October 2001): 69–72.
[13]For many years, workers have been considered business partners in Continental Europe, with worker participation in works councils mandatory in the large companies of many countries.

Exhibit 5-6   Capital Flow Statement of Bosch Group

Financial Statements of the Bosch Group Worldwide Capital Flow Statement[a]

(million euro)	2002	2001
Net income for the year	650	650
Depreciation of fixed assets	2,509	2,551
Increase in long-term accruals and accruals with valuation reserve portion	193	480
Cash flow	3,352	3,681
Decrease in inventories and leased products	162	278
Decrease in receivables	1,081	513
Increase in short-term accruals	83	188
Change in liabilities	20	−857
Additions to funds from business activities (1)	4,698	3,803
Additions to fixed assets	−4,386	−2,860
Retirements of fixed assets	254	432
Changes in the consolidated group		−430
Application of funds to investment activities (2)	−4,132	−2,858
Dividends 2001/2000	−50	−2,603
Capital increase Robert Bosch GmbH		2,470
Change in liabilities from financing	−475	587
Other changes in balance-sheet items	−444	92
Decreases in/additions to funds from financial activities (3)	−969	546
Change in liquidity (1) + (2) + (3)	−403	1,491
Liquidity at the beginning of the year	6,868	5,084
Changes in the consolidated group	19	293
Liquidity at the end of the year	6,484	6,868

[a]not published in the Federal Gazette

example, if investors invest in operations that employ low-skill workers while the government seeks to expand high-skill employment—an alert government could take steps to encourage foreign investment in the desired direction. When combined with geographical and/or line-of-business reporting, employee disclosure by function enables governments and labor groups to examine whether employment practices of multinational companies are consistent with local laws and norms.

Environmental issues include the impact of production processes, products, and services on air, water, land, biodiversity, and human health. As an example, starting in 2003 French listed companies are required to publish the results of their environmental activities. Among other items, information must be given on:

- Water, raw material, and energy consumption, and actions taken to improve energy efficiency;
- Activities to reduce pollution in the air, water, or ground, including noise pollution, and their costs;
- Amount of provisions for environmental risks.

Social responsibility reporting is becoming mainstream among large multinational companies. A recent survey found the number of companies issuing environmental, social, or sustainability reports, in addition to their annual financial reports, is growing. Nearly half of the largest 250 companies in the world have such reports. Reporting rates are highest in countries with large corporations, such as France, Germany, Japan, the United Kingdom, and the United States. Reporting rates are also highest in certain industries, notably chemicals and synthetics, pharmaceuticals, electronics and computers, automotive, and oil and gas.[14]

Exhibits 5-7, 5-8, and 5-9 present examples of social responsibility disclosures. They are taken from the 2003 Sustainability Report of the Swiss company Roche. Exhibit 5-7 shows employment levels and personnel costs by division and region of the world. The disclosure also discusses the reasons for employee reductions and the effect of the sale of one of its divisions on the company's employment levels. Exhibit 5-8 discusses Roche's safety and environmental record. Finally, Exhibit 5-9 is the auditor's report on the company's Sustainability Report.[15]

Exhibit 5-7   Employment Disclosure by Roche

The fine performance of the core businesses Pharmaceuticals and Diagnostics is also reflected in our personnel figures: In 2003, 2,000 new jobs were created in the non-divested businesses.

Business and Personnel Development—Growth Leads to Increased Staffing Levels

In 2003, Roche showed, as projected, above-average market growth. Double-digit growth in sales and profits has led to the creation of 2,000 new jobs. The acquisition of Disetronic resulted in 900 new employees for the Group so that, including further acquisitions, a total of 2,959 jobs were created. This organic growth is contrasted by the loss of 7,200 employees with the sale of the Vitamins and Fine Chemicals Division in October 2003.

Headcount and personnel costs by division:

	2002	2003	Change	Personnel costs 2003 in CHF million
Roche Group	69,659	65,357	−4,302	8,254
Pharmaceuticals	44,901	46,625	+1,724	5,435
Diagnostics	17,068	18,302	+1,234	2,133
Vitamins and Fine Chemicals	7,261	0	7,261	532
Others	429	430	+1	154
Continuing Group businesses	62,398	65,357	+2,959	

(continued)

---

[14]KPMG, *KPMG International Survey of Corporate Sustainability Reporting 2002,* www.kpmg.com, June 2002.

[15]Refer to Helen Gernon and Gary K. Meek, *Accounting: An International Perspective,* 5th ed., Boston: Irwin McGraw-Hill, 2001, and Carol Adams, Geoffrey Frost, and Sidney J. Gray, "Corporate Social and Environmental Disclosures," in *International Finance and Accounting Handbook,* 3rd ed., F. D. S. Choi, ed., New York: John Wiley & Sons, 2003, for further discussion and illustrations. Also see Jee Hong Kim, in Ki Joo and Frederick D. S. Choi, "The Information Content of Productivity Measures: An International Comparison," *Journal of International Financial Management and Accounting* 7 (1996): 167–190.

Exhibit 5-7   Employment Disclosure by Roche (*Continued*)

Headcount by region (2003 without Vitamins and Fine Chemicals Division):

	2002	2003	Change
Europe (all)	32,551	29,416	−3,135
Switzerland	8,569	7,358	−1,211
North America	17,988	18,439	451
Latin America	5,816	5,443	−373
Asia (all)	11,550	10,482	−1,068
Japan	6,361	6,226	−135
Africa, Australia, Oceania	1,754	1,577	−177

Personnel costs (salaries, pensions and benefits) in 2003 amounted to 8,254 million Swiss francs representing 28% of revenues. Total fluctuation in personnel came to 3,507 employees (~ 5.4% staff). In 2003, Roche employed a total of 5,366 new staff (8.2%) and through acquisitions took on almost 1,100 employees. 53% of the new staff is female.

Headcount by Region
As the majority of employees in the Vitamins and Fine Chemicals Division worked in Europe, Roche has recorded a reduction of 3,135 jobs in Europe. The most important locations for the Vitamins and Fine Chemicals Division were in Kaiseraugst and Sisseln, explaining why almost half of the reduction in headcount took place in Switzerland. In North America, there was growth in staffing levels in the Pharmaceuticals business, which corresponds to the current trend in this market. In Latin America and Asia the drop in head-count caused by the sales of Vitamins and Fine Chemicals Division was made up for in part by the integration of Disetronic as well as by business and job growth in these regions.

Sale of Vitamins and Fine Chemicals Division
On 1 October 2003, the Roche Vitamins and Fine Chemicals Division became the property of DSM. All the employees were also transferred to DSM on the same day. All retired employees of the Vitamins and Fine Chemicals Division will be treated in the same way as their colleagues who also worked for Roche. All employees who take retirement by the end of 2004 are treated as Roche retirees.

DSM and Roche have agreed that the separation from the Roche retirement plan should take place on 31 December 2004 so that DSM has time to extend its own pension and benefits system. In the meantime, Roche is continuing to carry out certain personnel services (salary book-keeping, executive management system) for the former Vitamins and Fine Chemicals Division. DSM, however, has full responsibility for personnel decisions and conditions of employment.

Exhibit 5-8 Safety and Environmental Disclosure by Roche

In brief

Incidents and accidents	In 2003, there were no significant incidents. The level of accidents has also improved. Both the frequency and severity of accidents went down.
Energy	Higher production volumes and the extreme climatic conditions of summer 2003 resulted in an increase in energy consumption.
Greenhouse effect	Roche's contribution to the anthropogenic greenhouse effect decreased further in 2003.
Emissions	Nitrogen oxide and sulphur dioxide emissions responsible for acid rain as well as that of volatile organic compounds (VOCs) were reduced in 2003 as a result of technical improvements to installations.
Waste	The volume of chemical waste products increased in 2003.

Development of Safety and Environmental Protection

Roche made further improvements in many areas that are relevant to safety and environmental protection.

Scope of Reporting

This year safety and environmental reporting covers the Roche Group with the Pharmaceuticals and Diagnostics Divisions: the key figures that refer to the Vitamins and Fine Chemicals Division that was divested in October 2003 are not included. Data for our joint-venture companies Chugai and Genentech is being submitted for the first time. This data will be integrated in future reporting when congruency with existing S&E data submitted by Roche can be ensured and as soon as trends can be developed.

In absolute terms the key figures show impressive changes in comparison with those of the previous year. The withdrawal of the significant contributions from the chemical plants of the Vitamins and Fine Chemicals Division has led to considerable reductions in particular in raw materials and energy consumption as well as in emission and waste products. A new basis was established in order to provide an accurate comparison with figures from the previous year.

Results

Improvements in the safety and environmental protection (S&E) area came from training and further education for employees as well as from ongoing upgrading of production plant to take advantage of the newest technology. In contrast, the increase in production volumes led to higher volumes of waste. For the first time since 1992, S&E performance is presented as part of sustainability reporting in an abbreviated form in comparison with previous years.

Performance evaluation that takes the new Group structure with the Pharmaceuticals and Diagnostics Divisions into consideration shows that sites whose S&E parameters did not previously stand out among the high figures from Vitamins and Fine Chemicals Division have recently moved into the spotlight. In this way it was possible to tell, for example, that no longer are subsidiaries with chemical plants the greatest consumers of energy but the large administrative centres that are recorded as part of reporting.

It further became clear that batch production, that is typical for the chemical industry, results in strong fluctuations in terms of time for individual key figures. Consumption of certain raw materials, such as chlorinated solvents, as well as the amount of waste material that is formed are defined by a plant's production schedule. In this way the figures submitted are subject to fluctuations caused by deliveries that come in batches.

(continued)

Exhibit 5-8   Safety and Environmental Disclosure by Roche (*Continued*)

The S&E record of achievement at Roche in 2003 compared with the previous year

↑ **Production**

The total volume of chemical, pharmaceutical and diagnostic production increased by 3.5%, and the total volume of energy and waste-intensive chemical production increased by 6%.

↑ **Energy**

Total energy consumption in the Roche Group increased by some 5%.

→ **Carbon dioxide**

Emissions of the most important greenhouse gas increased slightly by 2.3%. Roche's contribution to the global greenhouse effect, expressed in metric tons of CO_2 equivalent per 1 million CHF in sales declined, however, by 4.9%.

↓ **Acid rain**

Total emissions of nitrogen oxides (NO_x) and sulphur dioxide (SO_2), which are the compounds responsible for acidification of soil and water and are produced by combustion of fossil fuels and wastes, were reduced by 26.9%. Individually NO_x emissions went down 25.1% and SO_2 emissions were reduced by 30.3%.

↓ **Summer smog**

Emissions of volatile organic compounds (VOCs), which contribute significantly to ozone formation in the lower atmosphere, decreased by 39.7%.

↓ **Water consumption**

Total water consumption by the Roche Group was down 9.9%. The amount of water that goes into wastewater treatment increased by 7.4%.

↓ **Wastewater**

The amount of total organic carbon (TOC) discharged into surface waters after wastewater treatment declined by 0.1%. Heavy metal releases decreased by 36.7%.

↑ **Waste**

Chemical wastes from production, research and development, power generation, wastewater treatment and waste incineration increased by 8.7%. At the same time, the volume of valorised by-products was down 12.8%. The volume of general wastes decreased by 4.2%.

↑ **Chlorinated solvents**

The consumption of chlorinated solvents increased by 19.1%.

→ **Halogenated hydrocarbons**

The consumption of halogenated hydrocarbons, which play a major role in the depletion of the ozone layer and in the greenhouse effect, decreased by 22.2% to a total of 7.6 metric tons. The inventory of these compounds in refrigeration and fire extinguishing systems rose by 9.7% to 128.6 metric tons.

↑ **S&E expenditures**

Capital expenditure for S&E increased by 37.8% and operating expenses by 4.7% so that total costs for S&E went up by 14.7%.

Exhibit 5-8 Safety and Environmental Disclosure by Roche (*Continued*)

↓ **Incidents and accidents**

The number of reported incidents remained at a low level. The frequency of work-related accidents decreased by 2.4% while the severity declined by 19.7%. The number of lost workdays recorded due to work-related illnesses increased but was significantly lower than the number of absences due to work-related accidents.

Key Figures and Goals on Safety and Environmental Protection

Safety and environmental protection are part of a long tradition at Roche and are well integrated in all our activities as a matter of course. Roche complies with the principles for sustainable development and strives continuously for improvements.

Outlook and Goals

Improvements in S&E are achieved by changing behaviour and by applying technical measures such as adapting equipment to the new standards or aiming for the development of new innovative processes. A sustainable effect can only be achieved within a longer time frame. We want to continue this trend of continuous improvement of our performance in the various areas of S&E and achieve progress everywhere where it is possible and economically viable. This is why the following goals have been decided on for the next five years:

- Savings in energy consumption of 10%.
- Reduction of greenhouse emissions of 10%: reducing CO_2 by making savings in energy consumption and by phasing out halogenated hydrocarbons used in refrigeration and air conditioning installations.
- Reduction of VOC emissions by a further 10%.

Indicator[a]	2002 Roche	2003 Roche	Pharma	Diagnostics
Investments in S&E (in millions of CHF)	98	135	93	42
Operating costs for S&E (in millions of CHF)	225	236	163	73
Work-related accidents	462	503	359	144
Work-related fatalities	0	0	0	0
Work-related accidents per million working hours	6.65	6.54	7.01	5.59
Workdays lost due to work-related accidents	4,959	4,368	3,027	1,331
Total days worked	8,680,054	9,617,473	6,397,747	3,219,726
Occupational illnesses	184	152	129	23
Occupational illnesses per million working hours	2.65	1.97	2.52	0.93
Workdays lost due to occupational illnesses	193	669	542	127
Number of transport accidents				0
Road	1			
Air		1	1	
Transport accidents per ton transported				0
Road	1×10^{-6}			
Air		3×10^{-6}	$3 \times 10 \times^6$	

(continued)

Exhibit 5-8 Safety and Environmental Disclosure by Roche (*Continued*)				
Indicator[a]	2002 Roche	2003 Roche	Pharma	Diagnostics
Total energy consumption (t/year)	7,697	8,102	6,104	1,998
CO_2 (t/year)	326,362	333,879	237,941	95,938
NO_x (t/year)	423	317	215	102
SO_2 (t/year)	228	159	47	112
VOCs (t/year)	744	449	379	70
Particulate matter (t/year)	42	44	33	11
Water consumption (in million cubic meters per year)	21.6	19.4	17.4	2.0
TOC (t/year)	683	682	212	470
Heavy metals (t/year)	0.654	0.414	0.359	0.055
Total hazardous waste (t/year)	39,060	49,947	42,030	7,917
Full-time S&E personnel	457	476	341	135
Total number of employees (430 employees not assigned to a division)	62,398	65,357	46,625	18,305

[a] Based on the CEFIC Health, Safety and Environment Reporting Guidelines (November 1998)

Exhibit 5-9 Auditor's Report on Sustainability Report of Roche

ASSURANCE

Auditing of reporting for sustainable development by an external body not only increases credibility with external partners, but also serves to protect standards of quality internally.

Assurance Report on the Roche Sustainability Report 2003

We have been engaged to provide assurance on the Roche Sustainability Report 2003 ('Report'). We have performed review procedures on the sustainability management and reporting processes as well as on the 2003 data of the table entitled 'key figures' on page 48 of the Report ('S&E data'). We have also performed review procedures on some of the social dimension data ('social data').

The scope of our review procedures was to:

- Review the Roche Group internal S&E reporting guidelines with respect to the Responsible Care Health. Safety and Environmental reporting guidelines published by the European Chemical Industry Council CEFIC;
- Review the procedures by which the S&E data and the social data are prepared, collated and aggregated internally and the control environment over the accuracy and completeness of the S&E data and the social data;
- Review how Roche staff apply the Group internal sustainability reporting guidelines at the site level using a sample of six production sites covering the Pharmaceutical and Diagnostics divisions;
- Test the effectiveness of the internal sustainability reporting system used to collect S&E data and the social data from Group sites;
- Observe compliance with the Group internal sustainability reporting guidelines at selected sites; and
- Perform specific procedures to check, on a sample basis, the S&E data and the social data.

Exhibit 5-9   Auditor's Report on Sustainability Report of Roche (*Continued*)

We conducted our review procedures based on the underlying principles within the Proposed International Standards on Assurance Engagements (ISAE) 2000 issued in March 2003. The standards require that we plan and perform our procedures to obtain a reasonable basis for our conclusions. We have not performed an audit in accordance with International Standards on Auditing and, accordingly, do not express an audit opinion.

Our review procedures included:

- Visiting selected sites in Switzerland, Germany, Spain, United Kingdom and the United States;
- Interviewing the responsible staff for data collection and sustainability reporting on the sites we visited;
- Reading and performing tests of the relevant documentation on a sample basis, including Group policies, management and reporting structures, documentation and systems used to collect, analyze and aggregate reported S&E data and social data; and
- Performing tests on a sample basis on evidence supporting selected S&E data and social data with regard to the reported data aggregation from the selected sites to Group level.

Based on these review procedures, we conclude that:

- The Roche Group internal S&E reporting guidelines are–with the qualifications and explanations mentioned on page 16, 46 and 74–in line with the Responsible Care Health, Safety and Environmental reporting guidelines published by the European Chemical Industry Council CEFIC;
- The procedures by which the S&E data was prepared, collated and aggregated and the control environment at the selected sites are based on established and accepted measurement and analytical methods;
- The Roche Group internal S&E reporting guidelines are applied properly at the selected sites. The Roche Group internal S&E reporting system to collect the S&E data is functioning as designed;
- The social dimension reporting provides an appropriate basis for the disclosure of social dimension information;
- Nothing has come to our attention that cause us to believe that the reported S&E data and social data from the sites do not give a fair picture of the S&E and social dimension performance.

This statement should be read in conjunction with the inherent limitations of accuracy and completeness for sustainability data, as well as in connection with the Roche Group internal reporting guidelines explained on page 74 and the 'scope of reporting' on page 16.

PricewaterhouseCoopers AG
Basel, 27 January 2004

Dr. Thomas Scheiwiller   Clive Bellingham

Special Disclosures for Nondomestic Financial Statement Users and Accounting Principles Used

Annual reports can include special disclosures to accommodate nondomestic financial statement users. Such disclosures include: (1) "convenience restatements" of financial information to a nondomestic currency; (2) limited restatements of financial results and position to a second set of accounting standards; (3) a complete set of financial statements prepared in conformance with a second set of accounting principles; and

(4) discussion of differences between accounting principles used in the primary financial statements and some other set of accounting principles. Many firms in countries where English is not the primary language also translate entire annual reports from the home country language to English. Also, some firms prepare financial statements that conform to accounting standards more widely accepted than domestic standards (primarily IFRS or U.S. GAAP), or that conform both to domestic standards and a second set of accounting principles.

Exhibit 5-10 presents reconciliation disclosures and discussion of differences between U.S. and Swedish GAAP presented in the financial statements of Tele2 AB, a Swedish company listed on the Nasdaq Stock Market. Tele2's disclosures are highly detailed, as are financial statement disclosures made by many non-U.S. companies that have listed equity in the United States and must comply with SEC financial reporting requirements. Chapter 9 presents further discussion and evidence on special disclosures made for nondomestic financial statement users.

Corporate Governance Disclosures

Corporate governance relates to the internal means by which a corporation is operated and controlled—the responsibilities, accountability, and relationships among shareholders, board members, and managers designed to meet corporate objectives. Among corporate governance issues are the rights and treatment of shareholders, the responsibilities of the board, disclosure and transparency, and the role of stakeholders. Companies' corporate governance practices are receiving increasing attention from regulators, investors, and analysts. The United States, United Kingdom, and Australia are among the growing number of countries that require listed companies to make specific corporate governance disclosures in their annual reports. Exhibit 5-11 presents an example of a corporate governance disclosure from the annual report of Southern Pacific Petroleum, an Australian company.

Internet Business Reporting and Disclosure

The World Wide Web is increasingly being used as an information dissemination channel, with print media often playing a secondary role. Electronic information dissemination offers the advantage of often being less expensive than use of print media, and offers instantaneous communication. The Web also allows interactive information dissemination in a manner not possible in print form.[16] Securities trading using the Internet has increased the demand for Web-based business and financial reporting. Individual investors are increasingly using the Web to trade and make investment decisions, and use the Web as an important information source.

One important development that will facilitate Web-based business reporting is eXtensible Business Reporting Language (XBRL). XBRL is on the verge of revolutionizing financial reporting. This language will be built into nearly all future releases of accounting and financial reporting software, and most users will not need to learn how to manipulate it directly in order to enjoy its benefits.[17]

---

[16]See International Accounting Standards Committee, Business Reporting on the Internet, A Discussion Paper Issued by the IASC Staff, London: November 1999, 103 pages.
[17]See Kurt Ramin, "Fair Values," *Business Excellence for the Intellectual Capital Investor* 1 (Summer 2000): 13–16; and Stanley Zarowin and Wayne E. Harding, "Finally, Business Talks the Same Language," *Journal of Accountancy* (August 2000): 24–30.

Exhibit 5-10   Discussion of U.S. GAAP by Tele2 AB

THE UNITED STATES GENERALLY ACCEPTED ACCOUNTING PRINCIPLES (US GAAP)

The consolidated balance sheets and income statements are drawn up in accordance with Swedish accounting principles. These differ in certain respects from generally accepted accounting principles in the United States (US GAAP).

The following adjustments are required for reporting profit/loss for the year and shareholders' equity in line with US GAAP.

	Group		
	2002	2001	2000
Profit/loss for the year:			
Profit/loss for the year according to Swedish accounting principles:	223	392	−396
Adjustments required for compliance with US GAAP.			
a) Transactions between companies under common control	9	21	24
b) Amortization of goodwill	1,512	—	—
c) Lease agreements	1	2	3
d) Tangible fixed assets	−81	9	31
e) Stock options	9	5	−196
f) Software development cost	—	—	80
g) Accounting for step acquisitions	—	−8	−317
h) Accounting for acquisitions	25	−367	−104
i) Deferred tax liability	—	828	—
j) Alecta refund	—	—	−8
k) Changes in accounting principles	—	−156	21
l) Hedge accounting	1	−2	—
Net adjustment	1,476	332	−466
Deferred tax effect on above, US GAAP adjustments	−7	39	−38
Profit/loss for the year according to US GAAP	**1,692**	**763**	**−900**
Earnings per share:			
Profit/loss or the year according to US GAAP	1,692	763	−900
Number of shares weighted average	147,360,175	145,003,847	114,087,366
Earnings per share	**SEK 11.48**	**SEK 5.26**	**SEK −7.89**
Profit/loss of the year according to US GAAP	1,692	763	−900
Reversal: Interest after tax on convertibles during the year	—	—	—
Adjusted earnings for the year after full dilution	1,692	763	−900
Number of outstanding shares after full dilution, weighted average[a]	147,596,866	145,215,999	114,087,366
Earnings per share after full dilution	**SEK 11.46**	**SEK 5.25**	**SEK −7.89**

[a]In contrast to Swedish accounting principles, US GAAP does not calculate earnings per share after dilution at the present value of the exercise price for the options.

(continued)

Exhibit 5-10   Discussion of U.S. GAAP by Tele2 AB (*Continued*)

	Group		
	2002	2001	2000
Adjusted profit/loss for the year:			
Profit/loss for the year according to US GAAP	1,692	763	−900
Reversal: amortization of goodwill	—	1,845	610
Adjusted profit/loss for the year according to US GAAP	**1,692**	**2,608**	**−290**
Adjusted earnings per share:			
Profit/loss or the year according to US GAAP	1,692	763	−900
Reversal: amortization of goodwill	–	1,845	610
Adjusted earnings for the year	1,692	2,608	−290
Number of shares, weighted average	147,360.175	145,003.847	114,087.366
Adjusted earnings per share	**SEK 11.48**	**SEK 17.99**	**SEK −2.54**
Profit/loss or the year according to US GAAP	1,692	763	−900
Reversal: interest after tax on convertibles during the year	–	–	
Reversal: amortization of goodwill	–	1,845	610
Adjusted earnings for the year after full dilution	1,692	2,608	−290
Number of outstanding shares after full dilution, weighted average*	147,596,866	145,215,999	114,087,366
Adjusted earnings per share after full dilution	**SEK 11.46**	**SEK 17.96**	**SEK −2.54**

*In contrast to Swedish accounting principles, US GAAP does not calculate earnings per share after dilution at the present value of the exercise price for the options.

	Group		
	Dec. 31, 2002	Dec. 31, 2001	Dec. 31, 2000
Shareholders' equity:			
Shareholders' equity according to Swedish accounting principles	28,728	29,517	26,539
Adjustments required for compliance with US GAAP			
a) Transactions between companies under common control	−18	−27	−47
b) Amortization of goodwill	1,512	—	—
c) Lease agreements	14	13	11
d) Tangible fixed assets	−21	60	51
e) Stock options	−4	−25	−30
g) Accounting for step acquisitions	−103	−102	−94
h) Accounting for acquisitions	6,500	6,630	6,592
i) Deferred tax liability	—	—	−828
j) Alecta refund	2	−7	−7
k) Changes in accounting principles	—	—	156
l) Hedge accounting	—	−2	—
Net adjustment	7,882	6,540	5,804
Deferred tax effect on above US GAAP adjustments	−32	−16	−54
Shareholders' equity according to US GAAP	**36,578**	**36,041**	**32,289**

Exhibit 5-10   Discussion of U.S. GAAP by Tele2 AB (*Continued*)

	Group		
	Dec. 31, 2002	Dec. 31, 2001	Dec. 31, 2000
Change in shareholders' equity:			
Opening shareholders' equity, Jan. 1, according to US GAAP	36,041	32,289	5,772
Items reported directly against shareholders' equity			
Gradual acquisitions	—	−8	−33
Exchange-rate difference, according to US GAAP	−1,181	2,144	785
Total items reported directly against shareholders' equity	−1,181	2,136	752
Other changes in shareholders' equity			
New share issue, acquisition of SEC according to US GAAP	—	—	26,628
New share issue, acquisition of Tele2 Russia, according to US GAAP	—	838	—
New share issue, convertibles, according to US GAAP	26	15	37
Profit/loss for the year, according to US GAAP	1,692	763	−900
Closing shareholders' equity, Dec. 31, according to US GAAP	**36,578**	**36,041**	**32,289**

	Group	
	2002	2001
Deferred tax liability/asset:		
Deferred tax liability/asset. according to Swedish acc, principles	1,246	1,764
Deferred tax, adjustment according to US GAAP	−32	−16
Total deferred tax liability (−)/asset (+) according to US GAAP	**1,214**	**1,748**

	Group					
	Swedish Accounting Principles		Adjustment Items		US GAAP	
	Dec. 31, 2002	Dec. 31, 2001	Dec. 31, 2002	Dec. 31, 2001	Dec. 31, 2002	Dec. 31, 2001
Extract from consolidated balance sheet:						
Fixed assets	36,373	39,692	7,952	6,612	44,325	46,304
Current assets	10,499	9,566	—	—	10,499	9,566
Total assets	**46,872**	**49,258**	**7,952**	**6,612**	**54,824**	**55,870**
Shareholders' equity	28,728	29,517	7,850	6,524	36,578	36,041
Minority interest	22	28	—	—	22	28
Long-term liabilities	7,927	11,082	97	80	8,024	11,162
Current liabilities	10,195	8,631	5	8	10,200	8,639
Total shareholders' equity and liabilities	**46,872**	**49,258**	**7,952**	**6,612**	**54,824**	**55,870**

(*continued*)

Exhibit 5-10   Discussion of U.S. GAAP by Tele2 AB (*Continued*)

Explanation of current differences between Swedish accounting principles and US GAAP:

The account below presents a description of the adjustments that must be made to report Tele2 Group's profit/loss for 2000, 2001 and 2002 and shareholders' equity as of December 31, 2000, 2001 and 2002 in accordance with US GAAP.

a) *Transactions between companies under common control*

In 1993 and 1994, the company acquired Tele2 and Comviq from the Industriförvaltnings AB Kinnevik Group. The acquisition method was used to report the transactions. Accordingly, the difference between the acquisition value and market value of net assets was reported as goodwill. According to US GAAP, acquisitions of operations from "jointly owned companies" should be conducted at historical values. Thus, as a US GAAP adjustment, all re-evaluations of plants, materials and supplies, goodwill etc. that arise on the transaction date are eliminated and the resulting depreciation/amortization is reversed.

b) *Amortization of goodwill*

According to Swedish accounting principles, all intangible fixed assets, including goodwill, must be amortized. Amortization rates are based on the acquisition value of the fixed assets and the estimated utilization period. According to US GAAP, effective 2002, goodwill and certain other intangible assets need not be amortized but may instead be tested, at least annually, to identify any impairment loss. Accordingly, this year's amortization of these assets under Swedish GAAP is reversed and instead a potential write-down based on the completed impairment test is recognized.

c) *Lease agreements*

The Group has certain leasing transactions which, according to generally accepted accounting principles in Sweden, have been treated as operating leases, but which, according to US GAAP, are viewed as finance leases.

d) *Tangible fixed assets*

Certain costs have been capitalized in accordance with Swedish accounting principles should be expensed according to US GAAP. According to US GAAP, certain costs attributable to installations of networks are capitalized and not expensed.

e) *Stock options*

According to US GAAP, as a result of the terms and conditions of the options programs in 1997, a liability is calculated based on the market value of the underlying shares. According to US GAAP, the commitments to employees should not be dissolved. Commitments to others should be valued at the value of the option on the date on which the decision was made to settle it through a new share issue and report it directly against shareholders' equity.

f) *Software development cost*

Through 1999, Tele2 has capitalized development costs for software for external sales. According to US GAAP, this should be expensed and depreciation attributable to capitalization be reversed until the product is technically finalized. As a result of the sale of 4T Solutions AB in 2000, there is currently no difference vis-a-vis US GAAP.

g) *Accounting for step acquisitions*

The gradual acquisitions of OU Levicom and Société Européene de Communications S.A. during 1999–2001 has, according to Swedish accounting principles, resulted in a restatement of adjustment of shareholders' equity corresponding to shares in profit of the holdings from the original acquisition date based on the equity method rather than historical acquisition values. According to US GAAP, not only should shareholders' equity be adjusted against the share in profit/loss but also goodwill and depreciation should be taken into account from the original acquisition date.

Exhibit 5-10   Discussion of U.S. GAAP by Tele2 AB (*Continued*)

h) *Accounting for acquisitions*
    The acquisition of Société Européene de Communications S.A. in 2000 was conducted via a non-cash share issue, in which newly issued shares in Tele2 were offered in exchange for the outstanding shares in Sociéte Européene de Communications S.A. According to Swedish accounting principles, the acquisition price is calculated at a value corresponding to the share price of Tele2 on the transaction date. According to US GAAP, the acquisition price should be set at the share price on the date at which the offer was announced. There are also certain differences between acquired net assets according to US GAAP and Swedish accounting principles.

i) *Deferred tax liability*
    According to US GAAP, deferred taxes should be reported for all temporary differences apart from certain exceptions. The reversal of deferred tax liabilities as a result of changes in circumstances is done restrictively. According to Swedish accounting principles, changes in circumstances can be taken into account in the assessment. In conjunction with the liquidation of Société Européene de Communications S.A. in 2001, there was no longer any differences vis-a-vis US GAAP.

j) *Alecta refund*
    According to Swedish accounting principles, the value of the refund received by Tele2 from Alecta should be reported via the income statement in 2000. According to US GAAP, only the cash portion received should be reported as income.

k) *Changes in accounting principles*
    According to Swedish accounting principles, changes in accounting principles are reported through a recalculation of the opening shareholders' equity as if the new principles had been applied already when the transaction arose. According to US GAAP, the change is reported across the income statement when changes in principles are made.

l) *Hedge accounting*
    According to US GAAP, to qualify a hedge for accounting purposes, the hedge has to comply with very strict criteria in terms of the documentation of hedge relationship with hedged item and proof of its effectiveness. Swedish accounting principles does not require compliance with this strict criteria. Effective 2002, these requirements are fulfilled and thus there is no difference via-à-vis US GAAP.

Stock options:

In accordance with Swedish accounting principles, the option liability for the 1997 incentive program was dissolved in its entirety in 2000 as a result of the decision to settle the option through an issue of convertibles. According to US GAAP, depending on the conditions of the option program, a liability should be calculated based on the difference between the market value of the underlying shares and the exercise price. During 2002, stock options were issued as part of a new incentive program. This program is not reported as an expense in the income statement. A valuation in accordance with the Black-Scholes option model would have the following effect on profit/loss according to US GAAP. The calculation is based on a risk-free rate of interest of 4.7% (2001: 5.0%), no dividend (due to the uncertainty as to whether or not the Board will propose a dividend), volatility of 57.9% (2001: 45.5%) and the fact that the options expire on April 20, 2003 and September 1, 2005.

	Group		
	2002	*2001*	*2000*
Profit/loss for the year, reported as above	1,692	763	−900
Adjusted earnings per share after full dilution	SEK 11.46	SEK 5.25	SEK −7.89
Profit/loss for the year, pro forma	1,687	760	−904
Adjusted earnings per share after full dilution	SEK 11.43	SEK 5.23	SEK −7.92

(*continued*)

Exhibit 5-10   Discussion of U.S. GAAP by Tele2 AB (*Continued*)

Advertising expenses:

Total advertising expenses for the year amount to SEK 979 million (2001: 1,031 million and 2000: 630 million).

Critical accounting principles according to US GAAP:

The presentation below shows the accounting principles that are based on the most critical assessments and estimates used in drawing up the accounts in line with US GAAP, and which differ from the preparation of financial reports in accordance with Swedish accounting principles:

- When assessing the need for future write-down requirements for intangible and tangible fixed assets, Swedish accounting principles indicate that a future discounted cash flow be calculated and compared with the book value. Swedish accounting principles stipulate the application of schedule amortization of goodwill. In contrast, according to US GAAP, a non-discounted cash flow is to be calculated. No further amortization of goodwill should be applied according to US GAAP as of 2002.

Effects of new US GAAP accounting pronouncements:

In June 2001, the Financial Accounting Standards Board (FASB) issued a Statement of Financial Accounting Standards No. 143 (SFAS 143), entitled "Accounting for Asset Retirement Obligations". SFAS 143 states when and how accounting for liabilities and expenses attributable to the retirement of fixed assets should be done. Tele2 will apply SFAS 143 as of January 1 2003. The application of this statement is not expected to have any significant effect on Tele2's earnings and financial position.

In November 2002 FASB issued FASB interpretation No. 45 (FIN 45), "Guarantor's Accounting and Disclosure Requirements for Guarantees, Including Indirect Guarantees of Indebtedness of Others." FIN 45 requires that a liability should be reported at the fair value of assumed commitments in accordance with certain guarantee agreements on the date on which a company issued a guarantee. The provisions shall be applied with effect for guarantees that were issued or changed after December 31, 2002.

Exhibit 5-11   Corporate Governance Disclosure by Southern Pacific Petroleum

CORPORATE GOVERNANCE

The Directors and management are committed to high standards of corporate governance for which the Board is ultimately responsible. The corporate governance practices set out below have operated for the whole of the year except as indicated.

Board Composition and Membership

As at the date of the Directors' Report the Board is comprised of the Chairman, three executive Directors and five non-executive Directors. The Board believes that this provides an appropriate mix of qualifications, skills and experience for this stage of the company's development. The Constitution requires that one third of Directors retire each year by rotation and that no Director shall remain in office for more than three years without re-election. Directors have the ability to seek professional advice at the company's expense.

Conduct of Directors

Directors are required to conduct themselves to the highest ethical standards. Statutory requirements are regarded as the minimum standard to be attained. Directors must avoid any matter that may result in an actual or perceived conflict of interest and must avoid acting in a manner that is in contradiction to the interests of shareholders.

Exhibit 5-11 Corporate Governance Disclosure by Southern Pacific Petroleum
(Continued)

Board Committees

Audit and Corporate Governance Committee

The Audit and Corporate Governance Committee operated for the whole of the year. Members of the Audit and Corporate Governance Committee are B.H. Davidson (Committee Chairman and non-executive Director), C.M. Anderson (Chairman of the Board and non-executive Director) and V.H. Kuss (executive Director). Financial officers of the company and auditors attend by invitation. The responsibilities of the Committee are to:

- assist the Board of Directors in fulfilling its responsibilities relating to accounting and reporting practices of the company and each of its subsidiaries;
- oversee, co-ordinate and appraise the quality of the audits conducted by the company's external auditors;
- maintain, by regular meetings, lines of communications among the Board, the Company's accounting staff and external auditors to exchange views and information, as well as confirm their respective authority and responsibilities;
- serve as an independent and objective party to review the financial information submitted by management to the Board for issue to shareholders, regulatory authorities and the general public; and
- review the corporate governance aspects of the business and ensure that appropriate policies and procedures are established to meet corporate governance guidelines.

Environment, Health and Safety Committee

Members of the Committee are N.W. Stump (Committee Chairman and non-executive Director), B.C. Wright (non-executive Director), E.A. Parkinson-Marcoux (non-executive Director) and J.D. McFarland (Managing Director). The responsibilities of the Committee are to:

- receive reports from and consult with management and monitor the due compliance by the company and each of its subsidiary companies, with those EH&S matters which may impact on the position of the company's employees, contractors, and the community;
- review and make recommendations to the Board with respect to the adoption of and changes to Group policies in respect of EH&S; and
- supervise the implementation and maintenance of and adherence to appropriate systems to monitor compliance on EH&S matters.

Compensation Committee

Members of the Committee are C.M. Anderson (Committee Chairman and Chairman of the Board) and J.D. McFarland (Managing Director). R. Bryan was a member of the Committee from the beginning of the year until his resignation as non-executive Director on 30 June 2002. Since Mr Bryan's resignation, all Australian-based non-executive Directors have been invited to attend meetings of the Committee. This arrangements was formalised in January 2003 when B.H. Davidson (non-executive Director), N.W. Stump (non-executive Director), and B.C. Wright (non-executive Director) were appointed as members of the Committee. The responsibilities of the Committee are to:

- provide guidelines on how remuneration for executive and non-executive Directors is set;
- make recommendations to the Board on remuneration of the Managing Director;
- make recommendations to the Board on remuneration for other Board members;
- provide guidelines on how the Equity Participation Share (EPS) scheme will be administered and recommend changes as required for Board and shareholder approval; and
- make recommendations to the Board on overall remuneration policies in respect of employees of the group. *(continued)*

Exhibit 5-11   Corporate Governance Disclosure by Southern Pacific Petroleum (*Continued*)

Risk Assessment

The Board monitors operational and financial risk through a combination of departmental reporting and purpose-specific risk management committees including the Titles Committee, Calls Paid Committee, Audit and Corporate Governance Committee, Compensation Committee and Environment, Health and Safety Committee. In addition, during the 2002 financial year, significant work was undertaken through the Due Diligence Committee which met on 11 occasions during the year to facilitate the company's fundraising activities. B.H. Davidson (non-executive Director) and V.H. Kuss (executive Director) participated in these meetings as representatives of the Board.

Code of Conduct

Employees are required to observe high ethical standards. The purpose of the company's written Code of Conduct is to encourage an awareness of these obligations and to provide guidance on their observance. The Code of Conduct covers compliance with the law, protection of company material, dealing in the company's securities, conflict of interest, occupational health and safety, record keeping, discrimination and the promotion of a positive work environment. The company has adopted Corporate Values which further develop the principles espoused in the Code of Conduct and ensure that the business of the company is conducted in an honest, open and ethical manner.

The concept of a universal financial reporting computer language emerged in 1999. Soon after, Microsoft and IBM recognized both its potential and the need to develop a single standard cooperatively rather than have each software company develop its own standard, which would undermine the very idea of making the language universal. Because it has been developed cooperatively, XBRL is free to software companies that wish to use it in their software, and extensions of XBRL developed for specific industries are free for downloading from the Internet.

Once implemented, XBRL will automatically translate any desired item of business information—words or numbers—so that the information need be entered only once. Once entered, this information then can be used and worked with in many ways without being reformatted.[18]

Stock exchanges, regulators, and public companies are increasingly using the Internet to provide financial statement users with immediate and low-cost access to company information. For example, more and more stock exchanges now use electronic news services to provide immediate access to all listed company announcements. These services offer an important benefit to listed companies and investors: All listed company announcements, not just those deemed "newsworthy" by the financial press, are made publicly available on a single Web site. Appendix 1–3 lists Web site addresses for selected stock exchanges around the world. Many stock exchange Web sites provide links to corporate Web addresses where examples of disclosures discussed in this chapter can be found.

---

[18]Further information is available at www.xbrl.org.

ANNUAL REPORT DISCLOSURES IN EMERGING MARKET COUNTRIES

Disclosures in annual reports of companies in emerging market countries are generally less extensive and less credible than those of companies in developed countries. For example, insufficient and misleading disclosure and lax investor protection have been cited as reasons contributing to the East Asia financial crisis of 1997.

Low disclosure levels in emerging market countries are consistent with systems of corporate governance and finance in those countries. Equity markets are not well developed, banks and insiders such as family groups supply most of the financing, and so in general there has been less demand for credible, timely public disclosure than in more developed economies.

However, investor demand for timely and credible information about companies in emerging market countries has been growing, and regulators have responded to this demand by making disclosure requirements more stringent, and by stepping up their monitoring and enforcement efforts.

One study from the 1990s presents several types of evidence supporting the view that disclosure levels and quality are lower in emerging market countries than in developed countries.[19] For example, Exhibit 5-12 shows that 12 of the 20 countries with

Exhibit 5-12   Disclosure Levels of Industrial Companies in Selected Emerging Market and Developed Countries

Rank	Country	Average Score	Rank	Country	Average Score
1	United Kingdom	85	11	Spain, Zimbabwe[a]	72
2	Finland, Sweden	83	12	Japan, Mexico[a]	71
3	Ireland	81	13	Nigeria[a]	70
4	Australia, New Zealand, Switzerland	80	14	Argentina[a], Belgium, South Korea[a]	68
5	Malaysia[a]	79	15	Germany	67
6	Chile[a]	78	16	Italy, Thailand	66
7	United States	76	17	Philippines[a]	64
8	Canada, Denmark, Norway	75	18	Austria	62
9	Israel, Netherlands, Sri Lanka[a]	74	19	Greece[a], India[a]	61
10	Hong Kong, Pakistan[a]	73	20	Colombia[a], Taiwan[a], Turkey[a]	58

[a]Emerging market country

Source: Shahrokh M. Saudagaran and Joselito G. Diga, "Financial Reporting in Emerging Capital Markets: Characteristics and Policy Issues," *Accounting Horizons* 11 (June 1997): 41–64. Used with permission of American Accounting Association.

---

[19]See S. M. Saudagaran and G. D. Joselito, "Financial Reporting in Emerging Capital Markets: Characteristics and Policy Issues," *Accounting Horizons* 11 (June 1997): 41–64.

Exhibit 5-13 Earnings Opacity Ranking of Countries from Least to Most

1. United States	13. Switzerland	24. Turkey[a]
2. Norway	14. Sweden	25. South Africa[a]
3. Portugal	15. Germany	26. Malaysia[a]
4. Brazil[a]	16. The Netherlands	27. Italy
5. Belgium	17. Finland	28. Pakistan[a]
6. Mexico[a]	18. Austria	29. Japan
7. Canada	19. Thailand[a]	30. Chile[a]
8. France	20. Ireland	31. India[a]
9. Australia	21. Hong Kong[a]	32. Indonesia[a]
10. Spain	22. Singapore[a]	33. South Korea[a]
11. United Kingdom	23. Taiwan[a]	34. Greece[a]
12. Denmark		

[a]Emerging market country

Source: Utpal Bhattacharya, Hazem Daouk, and Michael Welker, "The World Price of Earnings Opacity," *The Accounting Review* 78, 3 (July 2003): 641–678. Used by permission of American Accounting Association.

relatively low disclosure levels are emerging market countries. In contrast, only three of the countries with relatively high disclosure levels are emerging market countries. A more recent study presents a similar conclusion.[20] Here, the authors are concerned with the "opacity" of earnings in 34 countries around the world. Opacity, the opposite of transparency, may be thought of as the extent to which an earnings amount obscures real economic performance. Exhibit 5-13 ranks countries in terms of their overall earnings opacity from least to most opaque. Emerging market countries tend to have the most opaque earnings.

Exhibit 5-14 presents information on the relative numbers of auditors in emerging markets and in developed markets. Exhibit 5-14 shows that, in general, there are more auditors per 100,000 population in developed markets than in emerging markets. Because monitoring and enforcement of sound financial reporting are enhanced by the presence of adequate numbers of accountants and auditors, Exhibit 5-14 suggests potential enforcement difficulties in the emerging markets shown there.

Empirical evidence on disclosure practices in emerging market countries has been limited until recently. However, as these countries' stock markets and listed companies seek to increase their presence, researchers are developing more evidence on what these practices are and how they differ from those in developed countries.

[20]See Utpal Bhattacharya, Hazem Daouk, and Michael Welker, "The World Price of Earnings Opacity," *The Accounting Review* 78, 3 (July 2003): 641–678.

Exhibit 5-14 Accountants and Auditors in Emerging Market and Developed Countries

Emerging Markets	Number of Auditors Per 100,000 Population	Developed Markets	Number of Auditors Per 100,000 Population
Chile	87	New Zealand	550
Argentina	71	Australia	539
Malaysia	48	United Kingdom	352
South Africa	35	Canada	350
Philippines	31	Singapore	273
Taiwan	17	Ireland	262
Mexico	15	United States	168
Poland	14	Hong Kong	110
Greece	12	Italy	110
Zimbabwe	11	Denmark	106
India	9	Switzerland	53
Sri Lanka	9	Netherlands	52
Nigeria	8	France	45
South Korea	7	Sweden	41
Thailand	5	Belgium	38
Colombia	2	Germany	26
Indonesia	2	Spain	18
Pakistan	2	Finland	10
Brazil	1	Japan	10

Source: Shahrokh M. Saudagaran and Joselito G. Diga, "Financial Reporting in Emerging Capital Markets: Characteristics and Policy Issues," *Accounting Horizons* 11 (June 1997): 41–64. Used by permission of American Accounting Association.

IMPLICATIONS FOR FINANCIAL STATEMENT USERS AND MANAGERS

Financial statement users should expect wide variation in disclosure levels and financial reporting practices. Although managers in many firms continue to be strongly influenced by the costs of disclosing proprietary information, the levels of both mandatory and voluntary disclosure are increasing worldwide. Managers in traditionally low-disclosure countries should consider whether adopting a policy of enhanced disclosure might provide significant benefits for their firms. (The requirement to adopt IFRS no later than 2005 will require many European companies outside the United Kingdom to increase their disclosures substantially.) In addition, managers who decide to provide enhanced disclosures in areas investors and analysts consider important, such as segment and reconciliation disclosures, might obtain a competitive advantage over firms with restrictive disclosure policies. Further study of the costs and benefits of enhanced disclosure in international settings should provide important evidence in this area.

Selected References

Adams, C., G. Frost, and S. J. Gray, "Corporate Environmental and Social Reporting," in *International Finance and Accounting Handbook,* 3rd ed., F.D.S. Choi, ed., New York: John Wiley & Sons, 2003.

Bhattacharya, U., H. Daouk, and M. Welker, "The World Price of Earnings Opacity, *The Accounting Review* 78, 3 (July 2003): 641–678.

Choi, F. D. S., "Financial Reporting Requirements for Non-U.S. Registrants: International Market Perspectives," *Financial Markets, Institutions & Instruments* 6, no. 5 (December 1997): 23–44.

Choi, F. D. S., and R. M. Levich, "Accounting Diversity," in *The European Equity Markets: The State of the Union and an Agenda for the Millennium,* B. Steil, ed., London: European Capital Markets Institute, 1996, 259–320.

Frost, C. A., and M. Lang, "Foreign Companies and U.S. Securities Markets: Financial Reporting Policy Issues and Suggestions for Research," *Accounting Horizons* 10 (March 1996): 95–109.

Frost, C. A., and K. P. Ramin, "Corporate Financial Disclosure: A Global Assessment," in *International Finance and Accounting Handbook,* 3rd ed., F. D. S. Choi, ed., New York: John Wiley & Sons, 2003.

Gernon, H., and G. K. Meek, *Accounting, An International Perspective,* 5th ed., Boston: Irwin McGraw-Hill, 2001.

Gilmour, G., and A. Caplan, "Who Cares?", *Accountancy* (September 2001): 44–45.

KPMG, *KPMG International Survey of Corporate Sustainability Reporting 2002* (www.kpmg.com), June 2002.

LaPorta, R., F. Lopez-de-Silanes, A. Shleifer, and R. Vishny, "Legal Determinants of External Finance," *The Journal of Finance* 52 (July 1997): 1131–1150.

Leuz, C., D. Nanda, and P.D. Wysocki, "Earnings Management and Investor Protection," *Journal of Financial Economics* 69, 3 (September 2003): 505–527.

Meek, G. K., C. B. Roberts, and S. J. Gray, "Factors Influencing Voluntary Annual Report Disclosures by U.S., U.K. and Continental European Multinational Corporations," *Journal of International Business Studies* (Third Quarter 1995): 555–572.

Organisation for Economic Cooperation and Development, "OECD Principles of Corporate Governance, Draft Revised Text," (www.oecd.com), June 2004.

Radebaugh, L. H., and D. L. Street, "Segmental and Foreign Operations Disclosure," in *International Finance and Accounting Handbook,* 3rd ed., F. D. S. Choi, ed., New York: John Wiley & Sons, 2003.

Ramin, K., "Fair Values," *Business Excellence for the Intellectual Capital Investor* 1 (Summer 2000): 13–16.

Robb, S. W. G., L. E. Single, and M. T. Zarzeski, "Non-financial Disclosures across Anglo-American Countries," *Journal of International Accounting Auditing and Taxation* 10, 1 (2001): 71–83.

Saudagaran, S. M., and J. G. Diga, "Financial Reporting in Emerging Capital Markets: Characteristics and Policy Issues," *Accounting Horizons* 11 (June 1997): 41–64.

Saudagaran, S. M., and G. K. Meek, "A Review of Research on Financial Reporting in International Capital Markets," *Journal of Accounting Literature,* 16 (1997): 127–159.

Stulz, R. M., and R. Williamson, "Culture, Openness, and Finance," *Journal of Financial Economics* 70, 3 (December 2003): 313–349.

"True and Fair is Not Hard and Fast," *The Economist* (April 26, 2003): 61–63.

Discussion Questions

1. Briefly explain the distinction between accounting measurement and accounting disclosure. Which of the two reporting processes do you think promises substantial innovative advances during the next 10 years? Why?

2. Why are multinational corporations increasingly being held accountable to constituencies other than traditional investor groups?

3. Should foreign companies seeking to issue securities in the United States be required to disclose as much as U.S. companies issuing securities in the United States? Critically evaluate the arguments presented in this chapter.

4. Accounting rules in Japan, France, and Germany now require disclosure of business segment financial results. However, managers in these countries traditionally have been opposed to disclosing detailed segment information. Why have managers chosen to disclose relatively little information about the business segments of their companies, and why have accounting rules become more stringent despite their opposition?

5. What is the distinction between voluntary disclosure and mandatory disclosure? Provide at least two explanations for differences in managers' voluntary disclosure practices. Provide at least two explanations for differences in managers' mandatory disclosure practices.

6. What is triple bottom-line reporting and why is it a growing trend among large multinational corporations? There are now few requirements for this type of reporting. Is more regulation necessary? Why or why not?

7. Do you expect to observe more or less voluntary disclosure by companies in emerging market countries than in developed countries? Why?

8. Do you expect to observe more or less regulatory disclosure requirements in emerging market countries than in developed countries? Why?

9. What are the two broad objectives for investor-oriented markets? Which of these do you think is the most important? Present reasons for your response.

10. From the perspective of a securities market regulator, is more required disclosure always better than less? Why or why not?

11. Why do you think that French and German annual reports contain earnings and sales forecasts more frequently than U.K. and U.S. annual reports? (Refer to Exhibit 5-2 for comparative evidence.)

12. What is corporate governance? Listed companies in some countries are required to disclose information about their corporate governance practices. Why might investors and analysts find such information useful?

Exercises

1. Exhibit 5-1 presents objectives for investor-oriented equity markets. Appendix 1-3 presents selected stock exchange Web site addresses.

   Required: Use the World Wide Web or other information sources to learn about the equity market in your home country.

   a. What types of information would help you assess whether it has the desired characteristics presented in the exhibit?
   b. Do the stock exchanges in your country provide such information?
   c. Present your best evaluation of whether your equity market has achieved the goals of investor protection and market quality.

2. Exhibit 5-2 presents information on disclosures of forward-looking information made by firms in France, Germany, Japan, the United Kingdom, and the United States. Panel B of the exhibit shows the frequency with which sample firms made earnings forecasts, sales forecasts, and capital expenditure forecasts in each country.

Required: Using evidence in the table, prepare a discussion in reasonable detail of the similarities and differences in annual report forecasting among companies in the five countries.

3. Exhibit 5-3 presents forecast disclosures appearing in the annual report of Schering AG.

Required: Provide (1) a list of items forecasted (e.g., sales, profits, economic growth), (2) the forecast horizon (e.g., 1 year ahead, 6 months ahead, not stated), and (3) the amount forecasted (e.g., 10 percent growth). How might an investor or analyst use such forecast information? Overall, how useful is Schering AG's forecast disclosure? Why do you say so?

4. Exhibits 5-5 and 5-6 present cash flow and capital flow information disclosed by companies from two different countries.

Required:

a. Compare and contrast the information content of the two statements.
b. Which statement is more useful to investors and analysts, and why?

5. Excerpts from Roche's Sustainability Report 2003 are presented in Exhibits 5-7, 5-8, and 5-9.

Required: Examine the complete report on Roche's Web site (www.roche.com) and outline its contents. Is this an example of triple bottom-line reporting? Why or why not?

6. Exhibit 5-8 presents the safety and environmental disclosure of Roche.

Required: Comparing the 2 years: (1) Which measures show an improved record of safety and environmental protection? (2) Which measures show a worse record of safety and environmental protection? What is your overall conclusion about Roche's safety and environmental record for the 2 years presented?

7. Exhibit 5-10 presents the reconciliation disclosures made by the Swedish company Tele2 AB. As discussed in the chapter, the U.S. SEC requires foreign listed firms to present reconciliation information for material differences in net income (loss), earnings per share, and/or shareholders' equity.

Required:

a. Discuss why the SEC requires such reconciliation disclosures.
b. Specifically, how would U.S. investors use information presented in such disclosures?
c. Identify the three Swedish GAAP/U.S. GAAP accounting principle differences that have the largest impact on financial measures of Tele2 AB for each of the periods shown.

8. The Organization for Economic Cooperation and Development (OECD) published its Principles of Corporate Governance in 1999 and issued draft revised principles in 2004.

   Required: Obtain both documents from the OECD Web site (www.oecd.org) and compare the Disclosure and Transparency recommendations in the two documents. What new issues are covered in the latest document? Why do you think that the OECD added these issues?

9. Exhibit 5-13 ranks 34 countries on earnings opacity. Which five countries have the most surprising placement? Why do you say so?

10. Exhibit 5-14 presents information on accountants and auditors in emerging market and developed countries.

    Required: Use the World Wide Web or other information sources to compare and contrast the auditing profession in an emerging market country with that in a developed country. Discuss the expected effect of any observed differences on disclosure quality in companies in the two countries.

11. Exhibit 5-12 ranks countries in terms of their disclosure levels. Exhibit 5–13 ranks countries in terms of earnings opacity.

    Required: Compare and contrast these two rankings. What are possible reasons for any differences noted?

12. Exhibits 2-1 and 3-1 show the stock market capitalization for six developed and four developing economies, respectively. Exhibit 5-14 lists the number of auditors per 100,000 in certain developed and developing economies.

    Required: Is there a correlation between economic development and the accounting profession?

CASE 5-1   INFORMATION ACCESS
IN MEXICO

The following Wall Street Journal *article discusses the limited access to information in Mexico:*

"MEXICO ISN'T FREE WITH INFORMATION"

In Mexico, information is power. And just try to get your hands on any, be it mundane or profound. Everything from the number of billboards in Mexico City to the details of past presidential lives is closely guarded by government and business. The first line of defense of a Mexican secretary is the phrase *"No sabría decirle,"*—"I wouldn't know what to tell you."

This frustrates everyone from bankers to travel agents. John Donnelly, head of Chase Manhattan Bank here, says the lack of credible credit information has stymied renewed lending growth since the 1994 peso collapse. Iris de Buendía, an agent at the Viajes Wilfer travel agency, says it is nearly impossible to get a straight answer from Mexican airlines on the timing of price promotions. "Everything is always top secret here," she says, sighing.

This vagueness has deep roots in Mexican history. The Aztecs, who commanded the central valleys of this land from the twelfth century to the fifteenth, kept their vassals in awe with a changing cast of hard-to-understand and unpredictable, but powerful, deities. The Spanish who followed were big on bureaucratic minutiae but rarely shared the details with the people they ruled. For the

Source: The Wall Street Journal, September 10, 1998, p. 1a. Used by permission of *Wall Street Journal* and Dow Jones.

past 70 years, the reigning Institutional Revolutionary Party, or PRI, has worked hard to make sure inconvenient information doesn't end up in the wrong hands.

"In Mexico, powerful people have traditionally kidnapped information," says historian and novelist Hector Aguilar Camin. "Part of the process of democratization is freeing it." But, he adds, "there is still a tendency to want to hold it hostage for some kind of benefit."

History, particularly when it damages the reputations of the living, is closely guarded. When researchers sought to confirm the details of a childhood shooting incident involving former president Carlos Salinas de Gortari, they found newspaper morgues purged of any reference to the event. Nor did they have better luck at the National Archives. The head of security there says a squad of government functionaries arrived to mop up Mr. Salinas's personal files when he took office in 1988.

The debate over access to information has become more explosive with the growth of a free press, the rise of opposition political parties and a big jump in the number of foreign investors doing business here who are demanding more transparency . . .

Lawmakers haven't had much better luck, so far, clarifying exactly what happened during the post-1994 bailout of the banking system orchestrated by President Ernesto Zedillo and his team. Finance Ministry officials say they are reluctant to give sensitive information to Congress, citing the country's bank-secrecy laws which, uniquely, protect not just data on deposits but also on loans. Lawmakers suspect the ministry is trying to protect hundreds of well-connected businessmen whose bum debts ended up being bought by Mexico's deposit insurance fund and which will, in the end, be borne by taxpayers.

REQUIRED

1. Discuss at least five characteristics that predict relatively low disclosure levels in Mexico. Your response should be based on a review of material presented in Chapters 2 and 4 and this chapter, in addition to the previous article.

2. Discuss characteristics or features that predict relatively *high* disclosure levels in Mexico. Again, refer to Chapters 2, 4, and 5 for relevant information.

3. Accounting measurement and disclosure practices are improving (from an investor protection viewpoint) in many emerging market economies. What are some of the recent improvements in these areas in Mexico? Discuss the underlying factors that help explain why the improvements are occurring.

CASE 5-2   TELE2 AB

Exhibit 5-10 presents Note 40 from Tele2 AB's annual financial statements filed with the U.S. Securities and Exchange Commission, which includes the following information: (1) reconciliations of net income and shareholders' equity from a Swedish accounting principles basis to a U.S. GAAP basis; (2) explanations of current differences between Swedish accounting principles and U.S. GAAP; and (3) additional U.S. GAAP information.

REQUIRED

1. Identify the four Swedish–U.S. GAAP accounting principles differences that cause the largest differences in Tele2's 2002 net income prepared in conformance with the two sets of accounting principles.

2. Prepare a table showing for each of the four accounting principles differences:
   a. treatment under Swedish GAAP
   b. treatment under U.S. GAAP

   c. effect of the accounting principle difference on Tele2's net income in 2002, 2001, and 2000
   d. effect of the accounting principle difference on NetCom's shareholders' equity for 2002, 2001, and 2000
   e. evaluation of the two treatments (Swedish GAAP vs. U.S. GAAP). Which treatment do you believe provides more useful information?

3. Does Tele2's discussion of differences between Swedish accounting principles and U.S. GAAP provide enough information for the financial statement reader to critically compare the two sets of accounting principles? Present an explanation for your response.

4. Assume that Tele2 forecasts (Swedish GAAP-based) net income of 450 million SEK for the next year. Develop a forecast of Tele2's U.S. GAAP-based net income using information provided in Note 40. How reliable is your U.S. GAAP-based forecast, and how might you use the forecast?

CHAPTER

6

FOREIGN CURRENCY TRANSLATION

E xamine the following performance data and related commentary. They are extracted from a press release issued by Alcan Aluminum, a Canadian-based multinational company and global leader in aluminum and specialty packaging.

US$ millions, unless otherwise noted	Third Quarter		Nine Months		Second Quarter
	20X3	*20X2*	*20X3*	*20X2*	*20X3*
Sales and operating revenues	**3,480**	3,170	**10,161**	9,204	3,468
Total aluminum volume	**1,146**	1,131	**3,402**	3,278	1,155
Ingot product realizations (US$ per tonne)	**1,552**	1,495	**1,566**	1,510	1,570
Average London Metal Exchange 3-month price (US$ per tonne)	**1,420**	1,329	**1,397**	1,367	1,379
Operating earnings–excluding foreign currency balance sheet translation and Other Specified Items	**151**	153	**417**	411	144
Foreign currency balance sheet translation	**(8)**	55	**(250)**	(29)	(146)
Other Specified Items	**(25)**	(16)	**(12)**	(31)	26
Net Income from continuing operations	**118**	192	**155**	351	24
Loss from discontinued operations	**18**	(1)	**(131)**	(3)	(113)
Net Income (loss)	**100**	191	**24**	348	(89)

Continuing Operations
Sales and operating revenues of US$3.5 billion in the third quarter benefited from the acquisitions of packaging (VAW FlexPac) and composite (Baltek) businesses, higher metal prices, and the strengthening of the Euro. Increased third-party shipments of alumina and aluminum, together with better pricing, also contributed to the improvement over the year-ago quarter. . . .

Third quarter operating earnings from continuing operations, at least US$151 million, were little changed from the comparable quarter of last year. Benefits from cost reduction initiatives and improved prices offset higher pension, fuel and recycled metal costs, higher depreciation expense and the negative impact of foreign currency movements. . . .

Net income from continuing operations was US$118 million, down US$74 million from the year-ago quarter mainly due to the unfavorable impact of foreign currency balance sheet translation, which represented a loss of US$8 million in this year's third quarter versus a gain of US$55 million a year earlier. Net income from continuing operations rose by US$94 million compared to this year's second quarter, which was negatively impacted by foreign currency balance sheet translation losses of US$146 million.

Each paragraph of the commentary above suggests a different way in which Alcan's reported performance, which the company chooses to report in U.S. dollars, is impacted by foreign currencies. The first paragraph suggests that a reduction in the value of the U.S. dollar relative to the euro, the new official currency of countries belonging to the European Union,[1] had a positive impact on sales and operating revenues. To understand why, assume Alcan is selling aluminum ingots, priced in U.S. dollars, to an importer in Italy. As Italy is a member of the European Union, the Italian importer must exchange euros for dollars to effect payment. Assume further that the value of the U.S. dollar unexpectedly falls in relation to the euro. The Italian buyer benefits from having to exchange less euros for dollars than would otherwise be the case, effectively lowering the price of Alcan's ingots. If the euro does not change in value relative to other national currencies, this would make Alcan's products cheaper relative to similar aluminum products supplied from other countries. The result would be increased demand for Alcan's products in Italy, and hence, larger sales volume than originally anticipated. Similarly, an unexpected fall in the value of the dollar relative to the euro would have an adverse impact on Alcan's future expenses, such as planned advertising expenditures in Italy. The effect of changes in foreign currency values on a firm's future sales and future costs is referred to as *economic exposure* and is a major concern of business entities engaged in global commerce and investment. Strategies to minimize the risk of loss arising from unexpected changes in the prices of foreign currencies is the subject of Chapter 11.

The currency effects reported in the remaining two paragraphs of Alcan's commentary are less future oriented and are the principle subject of this chapter. Both relate to a process in which accounts denominated in foreign currency are translated to Alcan's reporting currency, U.S. dollars. The currency effects in the second paragraph relate to foreign currency transactions, that is, sales, purchase, borrowing, or lending transactions that are denominated in foreign currency. The currency effects reported in the third paragraph occur because Alcan prepares a single set of financial statements that consolidates the results of all of its subsidiaries to afford its readers a more holistic view of Alcan's total operations, both foreign and domestic. Consolidated statements, in turn, require that financial statements expressed in foreign currency be translated to the reporting currency of the parent company.

Do reported currency effects resulting from the translation process matter? Some studies suggest that they do not.[2] Others suggest that they do. Bartov and Bodner provide evidence of a lagged relation between changes in currency values and stock

---

[1]At the time of this writing, members of the European Union include Austria, Belgium, Finland, France, Germany, Greece, Ireland, Italy, Luxembourg, the Netherlands, Portugal, and Spain.
[2]Dhaliwal et al. find no evidence that adding foreign currency translation gains and losses to reported earnings affects the association between earnings and security returns. D. Dhaliwal, K. Subra, and R. Trezevant, "Is Comprehensive Income Superior to Net Income as a Measure of Firm Performance?" *Journal of Accounting and Economics* (1999): 43–67. Cahan et al. find no evidence that separate disclosure of comprehensive income components, most notably the foreign currency translation adjustment, provides any value-relevant information over and above the aggregate comprehensive income figure. Steven F. Cahan, Stephen M. Courtenay, Paul L. Gronewoller, and David Upton, "Value Relevance of Mandated Comprehensive Income Disclosures," *Journal of Business Finance and Accounting* 27, Nos. 9 & 10 (November/December 2000): 1273–1301.

returns but not for all translation methods employed by reporting entities.[3] Pinto finds that lagged values of per share foreign currency translation adjustments are useful in predicting year to year changes in earnings per share.[4] On the other hand, while balance sheet translation gains and losses are associated with firm value, they often produce results that are not in keeping with the economic effects of exchange rate changes.[5]

Financial executives also attach mixed importance to gains and losses associated with foreign currency translation. While some assert that accounting gains and losses generated by accounting measurements have no impact on their operational decisions,[6] others express great concern over the distortions they cause in reported corporate earnings. History is replete with instances of management expending resources to minimize the effects of balance sheet translation gains and losses on reported performance.[7] That concern among executives over foreign currency translation effects continues to the present time is evident in the following disclosure norm adopted by Alcan:

> "Alcan presents operating earnings from continuing operations in addition to net income from continuing operations and reported net income, as it is consistent with the basis on which the Company manages and evaluates the performance of business groups. The company believes that operating earnings from continuing operations provides investors with a meaningful basis for evaluating underlying earnings trends by excluding items that are not indicative of on-going operating results, such as Other Specified Items. Also excluded is the impact of foreign currency balance sheet translation. This non-cash impact results from movements in exchange rates that can be pronounced from quarter to quarter, but which may average out over time."

What are the implications of the foregoing discussion? To properly interpret the reported performance of multinational companies, statement readers must understand the nature of foreign exchange gains and losses, how these numbers are derived, and what they mean. To facilitate this understanding, we begin with an examination of why foreign currency translation is necessary.

---

[3]See E. Bartov, "Foreign Currency Exposure of Multinatioinal Firms: Accounting Measures and Market Valuation," *Contemporary Accounting Research,* 14 (1997): 623–652.

[4]Jo Ann M. Pinto, "Foreign Currency Translation Adjustments as Predictors of Earnings Changes," *Journal of International Accounting, Auditing and Taxes* (2001): 51–69.

[5]Henock Lewis, "The Value Relevance of the Foreign Translation Adjustment," *Accounting Review* 78, No. 4 (2003): 1027–1047.

[6]Richard K. Goeltz, "International Accounting Harmonization: The Impossible (And Necessary?) Dream," *Accounting Horizons* (March 1991): 86.

[7]For example, see T. G. Evans, W. R. Folks, and M. Jilling, *The Impact of Financial Accounting Standards No. 8 on the Foreign Exchange Risk Management Practices of American Multinationals: An Economic Impact Study,* Stamford, CT: FASB, 1978; J. K. Shank, J. F. Dillard, and R. J. Murdock, *Assessing the Economic Impact of FASB 8,* New York: Financial Executives Research Foundation, 1979; and F. D. S. Choi, H. D. Lowe, and R. G. Worthley, "Accountors, Accountants, and Standard No. 8," *Journal of International Business Studies,* Fall 1978, and Carol O. Houston, "Translation Exposure Hedging Post SFAS No. 52," *Journal of International Financial Management and Accounting* (Summer & Autumn 1990): 145–169.

REASONS FOR TRANSLATION

Companies with significant overseas operations prepare consolidated financial statements that afford their statement readers a holistic view of the firm's operations, both domestic and foreign. To accomplish this, financial statements of foreign subsidiaries that are denominated in foreign currencies are restated to the reporting currency of the parent company. This process of restating financial information from one currency to another is called *translation*.

Many of the problems associated with currency translation stem from the fact that the relative value of foreign currencies are seldom fixed. Variable rates of exchange, combined with a variety of translation methods that can be used and different treatments of translation *gains* and *losses*, make it difficult to compare financial results from one company to another, or in the same company from one period to the next. In these circumstances, it becomes a challenge for multinational enterprises to make informative disclosures of operating results and financial position as per Alcan's example. Financial analysts find that interpreting such information can also be quite challenging and these troubles extend to evaluating managerial performance.

Additional reasons for foreign currency translation are recording foreign currency transactions, measuring a firm's exposure to the effects of currency gyrations, and communicating with foreign audiences-of-interest. Like consolidation, foreign currency transactions, such as the purchase of merchandise from China by a Canadian importer, must be translated because financial statements cannot be prepared from accounts that are expressed in more than one currency. How, for example, is one to prepare cost of goods sold when purchases are denominated in Chinese renminbi, Russian rubles, and Argentine pesos?

For accounting purposes, a foreign currency asset or liability is said to be exposed to currency risk if a change in the rate at which currencies are exchanged causes the parent (reporting) currency equivalent to change. The measurement of this exposure will vary depending on the translation method a firm chooses to employ.

Finally, the expanded scale of international investment increases the need to convey accounting information about companies domiciled in one country to users in others. This need occurs when a company wishes to list its shares on a foreign stock exchange, contemplates a foreign acquisition or joint venture, or wants to communicate its operating results and financial position to its foreign stockholders. Many Japanese companies translate their entire financial statements from Japanese yen to U.S. dollars when reporting to interested American audiences. This practice is often called a *convenience translation* and is described more fully in Chapter 9.

BACKGROUND AND TERMINOLOGY

Translation is not the same as *conversion*, which is the physical exchange of one currency for another. Translation is simply a change in monetary expression, as when a balance sheet expressed in British pounds is restated in U.S. dollar equivalents. No physical exchange occurs, and no accountable transaction takes place as it does in conversion.

Foreign currency balances are translated to domestic currency equivalents by the foreign exchange rate: the price of a unit of one currency expressed in terms of another. The currencies of major trading nations are bought and sold in global markets. Linked by sophisticated telecommunications networks, market participants include banks and other currency dealers, business enterprises, individuals, and professional traders. By providing a venue for buyers and sellers of currencies, the foreign exchange market facilitates the transfer of international payments (e.g., from importers to exporters), allows international purchases or sales to be made on credit (e.g., bank letters of credit that permit goods to be shipped in advance of payment to an unfamiliar buyer), and provides a means for individuals or businesses to protect themselves from the risks of unstable currency values. (Chapter 11 gives a fuller discussion of exchange risk management.)

Foreign currency transactions take place in the spot, forward, or swap markets. Currency bought or sold *spot* normally must be delivered immediately, that is, within 2 business days. Thus, an American tourist departing for Geneva can purchase and immediately receive Swiss francs by paying the spot rate in dollars. Spot market rates are influenced by many factors, including different inflation rates among countries, differences in national interest rates, and expectations about the direction of future rates. Spot market exchange rates may be direct or indirect.[8] In a direct quote, the exchange rate specifies the number of domestic currency units needed to acquire a unit of foreign currency. For example, on a given day, the U.S. dollar price of an Indian rupee might be $0.022737. An indirect quote is the reciprocal of the direct quote: the price of a unit of the domestic currency in terms of the foreign currency. In this example, it would take approximately 43.98 rupees to acquire 1 U.S. dollar.

Translation of foreign currency balances is straightforward with either direct or indirect quotes. Domestic currency equivalents are obtained by multiplying foreign currency balances by direct exchange rate quotations or dividing foreign currency balances by indirect quotations. To illustrate, suppose that the cash balance of a U.S. subsidiary located in Bombay, India, on January 31 is Rpe1,000,000. The direct (spot) exchange rate on that date is $0.0218. The U.S. dollar equivalent of the rupee cash balance on January 31 is $21,800, calculated by translating Rpe1,000,000 in either of the following ways:

$$\text{Rpe}1,000,000 \times \$0.0218 = \$21,800 \text{ or}$$
$$\text{Rpe}1,000,000 \div \text{Rpe}43.98 \cong \$21,800$$

Transactions in the forward market are agreements to exchange a specified amount of one currency for another at a future date. Quotations in the forward market are expressed at either a *discount* or a *premium* from the spot rate. If spot Swiss francs are offered at $0.7573, while the 6-month forward franc is offered at $0.7589, 6-month forward Swiss francs are selling at a premium of .42 percent in the United States, calculated as follows: forward premium (discount) − (forward rate spot rate)/spot rate × 12/n, where n is the number of months in the forward contract. Thus, ($0.7578 − $0.7573)/$0.7573 × 12/6 = 0.42. Had the Swiss franc been quoted indirectly, the premium would have been determined as: forward premium (discount) = (spot rate − forward rate)/forward rate × 12/n, or (Swfr.3204 − Swfr.3177)/1.3177 12/6 ≅ 0.42.

Spot and forward quotes for major foreign currencies on any business day can be found in the business section of many major newspapers. Exhibit 6-1 contains spot and

---

[8]For a daily listing of foreign exchange rates, visit www.wallstreetjournal.com.

Exhibit 6-1 Sample of Spot and Forward Foreign Exchange Quotes				
	Foreign Currency in Dollars		Dollars in Foreign Currency	
Currency	*Mon.*	*Fri.*	*Mon.*	*Fri.*
British pound	1.694	1.703	.5895	.5870
30-day fwd	1.6916	1.700	.5912	.5882
60-day fwd	1.6879	1.6962	.5925	.5896
90-day fwd	1.6837	1.6921	.5939	.5910
EU euro	1.1770	1.1915	.8496	.8393
30-day fwd	1.1757	1.1904	.8506	.8401
60-day fwd	1.1747	1.1894	.8513	.8408
90-day fwd	1.1737	1.1884	.8520	.8415
Japanese yen	.009138	.009191	109.43	108.80
30-day fwd	.009149	.009199	109.30	108.71
60-day fwd	.009158	.009208	109.20	108.60
90-day fwd	.009168	.009218	109.08	108.48
Swiss franc	.7573	.7706	1.3204	1.2977
30-day fwd	.7583	.7718	1.3187	1.2957
60-day fwd	.7589	.7724	1.3177	1.2947
90-day fwd	.7596	.7730	1.3165	1.2936

forward quotes for selected currencies. A more comprehensive listing can be found by clicking on www.federalreserve.gov.

A swap transaction involves the simultaneous spot purchase and forward sale, or spot sale and forward purchase, of a currency. Investors often use swap transactions to take advantage of higher interest rates in a foreign country while simultaneously protecting themselves against unfavorable movements in the foreign exchange rate. As an example, should interest rates in the United States exceed those in Switzerland, Swiss investors could purchase dollars in the spot market and invest them in higher-yielding U.S. dollar debt instruments, say 6-month U.S. Treasury notes. In doing so, however, Swiss investors would lose this yield advantage if the U.S. dollar loses value relative to the Swiss franc in the 6-month period. To protect against this possibility, Swiss investors could simultaneously sell the dollars they expect to receive in 6 months at the guaranteed forward rate. Such swap transactions work well when the U.S./Swiss interest rate differential is greater than the discount on forward dollars (i.e., the difference between spot and 6-month forward dollars). Over time, foreign currency traders will eliminate this difference, thereby creating *interest rate parity*.

Exhibit 6-2 defines the foreign currency translation terms used in this chapter.

THE PROBLEM

If foreign exchange rates were relatively stable, currency translation would be no more difficult than translating inches or feet to their metric equivalents. However, exchange rates are seldom stable. The currencies of most industrialized countries are free to find their own values in the currency market. For an illustration of the volatility of

Exhibit 6-2   Glossary of Foreign Currency Translation Terms

attribute.   The quantifiable characteristic of an item that is measured for accounting purposes. For example, historical cost and replacement cost are attributes of an asset.

conversion.   The exchange of one currency for another.

current rate.   The exchange rate in effect at the relevant financial statement date.

discount.   When the forward exchange rate is below the current spot rate.

exposed net asset position.   The excess of assets that are measured or denominated in foreign currency and translated at the current rate over liabilities that are measured or denominated in foreign currency and translated at the current rate.

foreign currency.   A currency other than the currency of the country being referred to; a currency other than the reporting currency of the enterprise being referred to.

foreign currency financial statements.   Financial statements that employ foreign currency as the unit of measure.

foreign currency transactions.   Transactions (e.g., sales or purchases of goods or services or loans payable or receivable) whose terms are stated in a currency other than the entity's functional currency.

foreign currency translation.   The process of expressing amounts denominated or measured in one currency in terms of another currency by use of the exchange rate between the two currencies.

foreign operation.   An operation whose financial statements are (1) combined or consolidated with or accounted for on an equity basis in the financial statements of the reporting enterprise and (2) prepared in a currency other than the reporting currency of the reporting enterprise.

forward exchange contract.   An agreement to exchange currencies of different countries at a specified rate (forward rate) at a specified future date.

functional currency.   The primary currency in which an entity does business and generates and spends cash. It is usually the currency of the country where the entity is located and the currency in which the books of record are maintained.

historical rate.   The foreign exchange rate that prevailed when a foreign currency asset or liability was first acquired or incurred.

local currency.   Currency of a particular country being referred to; the reporting currency of a domestic or foreign operation being referred to.

monetary items.   Obligations to pay or rights to receive a fixed number of currency units in the future.

reporting currency.   The currency in which an enterprise prepares its financial statements.

settlement date.   The date on which a payable is paid or a receivable is collected.

spot rate.   The exchange rate for immediate exchange of currencies.

transaction date.   The date at which a transaction (e.g., a sale or purchase of merchandise or services) is recorded in a reporting entity's accounting records.

translation adjustments.   Translation adjustments result from the process of translating financial statements from the entity's functional currency into the reporting currency.

unit of measure.   The currency in which assets, liabilities, revenue, and expense are measured.

Source: Adapted from Statement of Financial Accounting Standard No. 52, 1981.

Exhibit 6-3 Fixed Euro Conversion Rates	
Country	Rate
EU euro	1.0
Austrian schilling	13.7603
Belgian franc	40.3399
Finnish markka	5.94573
French franc	6.55957
German mark	1.95583
Irish punt	.787564
Italian lira	1936.27
Luxemburg franc	40.3399
Dutch guilder	2.20371
Portuguese escudo	200.482
Spanish peseta	166.386

exchange rates of selected countries, examine the data compiled by the Federal Reserve Bank at www.federalreserve.gov/releases/H10/hist/.

Fluctuating exchange values are particularly evident in Eastern Europe, Latin America, and certain parts of Asia. Currency fluctuations increase the number of translation rates that can be used in the translation process and create foreign exchange gains and losses. Currency movements are also closely tied to local rates of inflation, the subject of Chapter 7.

Alcan Aluminum's press release at the beginning of this chapter mentions a recent addition to the foreign currency scene, the *euro*. On January 1, 2002, the euro became the official currency of the 12 EU nations that fixed their national currencies to the euro and include Austria, Belgium, Finland, France, Germany, Greece, Ireland, Italy, Luxemburg, the Netherlands, Portugal, and Spain. EU members that may yet do so are Britain, Denmark, and Sweden as well as all of the 10 countries joining the EU in May 2004.[9]

As illustrated in Exhibit 6-3, euro quotes are expressed in six digits. The European Commission requires that all conversions between Euroland currencies must be made through the euro. Thus, the lira equivalent of 100 Austrian schillings is determined by first converting schillings to euros and then from euros to lira; that is, 100 schillings = 7.26728 euros = 14,071.4 lira. Additional information on the European Economic and Monetary Union and the euro can be obtained by clicking on europa.eu.int/euro.

FINANCIAL STATEMENT EFFECTS OF ALTERNATIVE TRANSLATION RATES

The following three exchange rates can be used to translate foreign currency balances to domestic currency. First, the *current* rate is the exchange rate prevailing as of the financial statement date. Second, the *historical* rate is the prevailing exchange rate

---

[9]Benjamin J. Cohen, "Global Currency Rivalry: Can the Euro Ever Challenge the Dollar?" *Journal of Common Market Studies* 41, No. 4 (2003): 575–595.

when a foreign currency asset is first acquired or a foreign currency liability first incurred. Finally, the *average* rate is a simple or weighted average of either current or historical exchange rates. As average rates are simply variations of current or historical rates, the following discussion focuses on the latter two.

What then are the financial statement effects of using historical as opposed to current rates of exchange as foreign currency translation coefficients? Historical exchange rates generally preserve the original cost equivalent of a foreign currency item in the domestic currency statements. Suppose that a foreign subsidiary of a U.S. parent company acquires an item of inventory for 1,000 foreign currency (FC) units when the exchange rate (indirect quote) is FC2 = $1. This asset would appear in the U.S. consolidated statements at $500. Now assume that the exchange rate changes from FC2 = $1 to FC4 = $1 by the next financial statement date and that the inventory item is still on hand. Will the U.S. dollar equivalent of the inventory now change to $250? It would not. As long as we translate the original FC1,000 cost at the rate that prevailed when the asset was acquired (historical rate), it will appear in the U.S. financial statements at $500, its historical cost expressed in U.S. dollars. *Use of historical exchange rates shields financial statements from foreign currency translation gains or losses*, that is, from increases or decreases in the dollar equivalents of foreign currency balances due to fluctuations in the translation rate between reporting periods. *The use of current rates causes translation gains or losses.* Thus, in the previous example, translating the FC1,000 piece of inventory at the current rate (FC4 $1) would yield a translation loss of $250 (FC1,000 ÷ 2 − FC1,000 ÷ 4).

Here we must distinguish between *translation* gains and losses and *transaction* gains and losses, both of which fall under the label *exchange gains and losses*. Foreign currency transactions occur whenever an enterprise purchases or sells goods for which payment is made in a foreign currency or when it borrows or lends foreign currency. Translation is necessary to maintain the accounting records in the currency of the reporting enterprise.

Of the two types of transaction adjustments, the first, *gains and losses on settled transaction*s, arises whenever the exchange rate used to book the original transaction differs from the rate used at settlement. Thus, if a U.S. parent company borrows FC1,000 when the exchange rate is FC = 2 $1 and then converts the proceeds to dollars, it will receive $500 and record a $500 liability on its books. If the foreign exchange rate rises to FC1 $1 when the loan is repaid, the U.S. company will have to pay out $1,000 to discharge its FC1,000 debt. The company has suffered a $500 conversion loss.

The second type of transaction adjustment, *gains or losses on unsettled transaction*s, arises whenever financial statements are prepared before a transaction is settled. In the preceding example, assume that the FC1,000 is borrowed during year 1 and repaid during year 2. If the exchange rate prevailing at the financial statement date is FC1.5 = $1, the dollar equivalent of the FC1,000 loan will be $667, creating an exchange loss of $167. Until the foreign currency debt is actually repaid, however, this *unrealized* exchange loss is similar in nature to a translation loss as it results from a restatement process.

Exhibit 6-4 lays out the distinction between transaction and translation gains and losses. Differences in exchange rates in effect at the various dates shown cause the various types of exchange adjustments.

Exhibit 6-4   Types of Exchange Adjustments

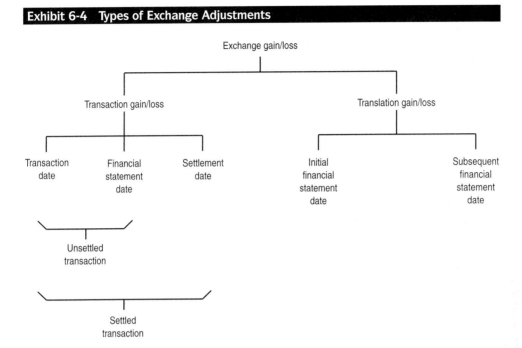

When considering exchange gains and losses, it is critical to distinguish between transaction gains and losses and translation gains and losses. A realized (or settled) transaction creates a real gain or loss. Accountants generally agree that such a gain or loss should be reflected immediately in income. In contrast, translation adjustments (including gains or losses on unsettled transactions) are *unrealized* or *paper* items. The appropriate accounting treatment of these gains or losses is less obvious.

Fluctuating exchange rates cause several major issues in accounting for foreign currency translation:

1. Which exchange rate should be used to translate foreign currency balances to domestic currency?
2. Which foreign currency assets and liabilities are exposed to exchange rate changes?
3. How should translation gains and losses be accounted for?

These issues are treated in the balance of this chapter.

FOREIGN CURRENCY TRANSACTIONS

The distinguishing feature of a foreign currency transaction is that settlement is effected in a foreign currency. Thus, foreign currency transactions occur whenever an enterprise purchases or sells goods for which payment is made in a foreign currency or when it borrows or lends foreign currency. As an example, a company purchasing inventories denominated in Saudi Arabian riyals suffers an exchange loss should the riyal gain in value before settlement.

A foreign currency transaction may be *denominated* in one currency but *measured* or recorded in another. To understand why, consider first the notion of the *functional currency*. The functional currency of an entity is defined as the currency of the primary economic environment in which it operates and generates cash flows. If a foreign subsidiary's operation is relatively self-contained and integrated within the foreign country (i.e., one that manufactures a product for local distribution), it will normally generate and spend its local (country-of-domicile's) currency. Hence, the local currency (e.g., euros for the Belgian subsidiary of a U.S. parent) is its functional currency. If a foreign entity keeps its accounts in a currency other than the functional currency (e.g., the Indian accounts of a U.S. subsidiary whose functional currency is really British pounds, rather than Indian rupees), its functional currency is the third-country currency (pounds). If a foreign entity is merely an extension of a U.S. parent company (e.g., a Mexican assembly operation that receives components from its U.S. parent and ships the assembled product back to the United States), its functional currency is the U.S. dollar. Exhibit 6-5 identifies circumstances justifying use of either the local or parent currency as the functional currency.

To illustrate the difference between a transaction being denominated in one currency but measured in another, assume that a U.S. subsidiary in Hong Kong purchases merchandise inventory from the People's Republic of China payable in renminbi. The subsidiary's functional currency is the U.S. dollar. In this instance, the subsidiary would measure the foreign currency transaction—denominated in renminbi—in U.S. dollars, the currency in which its books are kept. From the parent's point of view, the subsidiary's liability is denominated in renminbi but measured in U.S. dollars, its functional currency, for purposes of consolidation.

Exhibit 6-5 Functional Currency Criteria		
Economic Factors	Circumstances Favoring Local Currency as Functional Currency	Circumstances Favoring Parent Currency as Functional Currency
Cash flows	Primarily in the local currency and do not impact parent's cash flows	Directly impact parent's cash flows and are currently remittable to the parent
Sales price	Largely irresponsive to exchange rate changes and governed primarily by local competition	Responsive to changes in exchange rates and determined by worldwide competition
Sales market	Largely in the host country and denominated in local currency	Largely in the parent country and denominated in parent currency
Expenses	Incurred primarily in the local environment	Primarily related to productive factors imported from the parent company
Financing	Primarily denominated in local currency and serviced by local operations	Primarily from the parent or reliance on parent company to meet debt obligations
Intercompany transactions	Infrequent, not extensive	Frequent and extensive

Adapted from: Financial Accounting Standards Board, *Statement of Financial Accounting Standards No. 52,* Stamford, CT: FASB, 1981, Appendix A.

FAS No. 52, the U.S. authoritative pronouncement on accounting for foreign currency, mandates the following treatment for foreign currency transactions[10]:

1. At the date the transaction is *recognized,* each asset, liability, revenue, expense, gain, or loss arising from the transaction shall be measured and recorded in the functional currency of the recording entity by use of the exchange rate in effect at that date.
2. At each *balance sheet date,* recorded balances that are denominated in a currency other than the functional currency of the recording entity shall be adjusted to reflect the current exchange rate.

On this basis, a foreign exchange adjustment (i.e., gain or loss on a settled transaction) is necessary whenever the exchange rate changes between the transaction date and the settlement date. Should financial statements be prepared before settlement, the accounting adjustment (i.e., gain or loss on an unsettled transaction) will equal the difference between the amount originally recorded and the amount presented in the financial statements.

The FASB rejected the view that a distinction should be drawn between gains and losses on settled and unsettled transactions, because such distinctions cannot be applied in practice. Two accounting treatments for transactions gains and losses are possible.

Single-Transaction Perspective

Under a single-transaction perspective, exchange adjustments (both settled and unsettled) are treated as an adjustment to the original transaction accounts on the premise that a transaction and its settlement are a single event. The following example illustrates this treatment.

On September 1, 20X5, a U.S. manufacturer sells, on account, goods to a Swedish importer for 1 million Swedish krona (SEK). The dollar/krona exchange rate is $0.14 = SEK 1, the krona receivable are due in 90 days, and the U.S. company operates on a calendar-year basis. The krona begins to depreciate before the receivable is collected. By the end of the month, the dollar/krona exchange rate is $0.13 = SEK 1; on December 1, 20X5, it is $0.11 = SEK 1. (These transactions are posted in Exhibit 6-6.)

In this illustration, until the account is collected, the initial dollar amount recorded for both accounts receivable and sales is considered an estimate to be subsequently adjusted for changes in the dollar/krona exchange rate. Further depreciation of the krona between the financial statement date (September 1) and the settlement date (December 1) would require additional adjustments.

Two-Transaction Perspective

Under a two-transaction perspective, collection of the krona receivable is considered a separate event from the sale that gave rise to it. In the previous illustration, the export sale and related receivable would be recorded at the exchange rate in effect at that date. Depreciation of the krona between September 1 and December 1 would result in

---

[10]Financial Accounting Standards Board, *FASB Statement No. 52,* Stamford, CT: FASB, par. 15. This pronouncement has proven influential and has become the basis for similar standards elsewhere.

Exhibit 6-6   U.S. Company's Record: Single-Transaction Perspective

		Foreign Currency	U.S. Dollar Equivalent
Sept. 1, 20X5	Accounts receivable	SEK 1,000,000	140,000
	Sales	SEK 1,000,000	140,000
	(To record credit sale)		
Sept. 30, 20X5	Sales		10,000
	Accounts receivable (To adjust existing accounts for initial exchange rate change: SEK 1,000,000 $0.14 minus SEK 1,000,000 $0.13)		10,000
Dec. 1, 20X5	Retained earnings		20,000
	Accounts receivable (To adjust accounts for additional rate change: SEK 1,000,000 × $0.13 minus SEK 1,000,000 x $0.11)		20,000
Dec. 1, 20X5	Foreign currency	SEK 1,000,000	110,000
	Accounts receivable (To record - settlement of outstanding foreign currency receivables)	SEK 1,000,000	110,000

---

an exchange loss (i.e., loss on an unsettled transaction) and currency receivable on December 1, 20X5, at the even lower exchange rate would result in a further exchange loss (i.e., loss on a settled transaction). See Exhibit 6-7.

In the interest of uniformity, FAS No. 52 requires the two-transaction method of accounting for foreign currency transactions. Gains and losses on settled and unsettled transactions are included in the determination of income. Major exceptions to this requirement occur whenever (1) exchange adjustments relate to certain long-term intercompany transactions and (2) transactions are intended and effective as hedges of net investments (i.e., hedges of foreign operations' exposed net asset/liability posi-

---

Exhibit 6-7   U.S. Company's Record: Two-Transaction Perspective

		Foreign Currency	U.S. Dollar Equivalent
Sept. 1, 20X5	Accounts receivable	SEK 1,000,000	$140,000
	Sales	SEK 1,000,000	$140,000
	(To record credit sale at Sept. 1, 20X5 exchange rate)		
Sept. 30, 20X5	Foreign exchange loss		10,000
	Accounts receivable		10,000
	(To record effect of initial rate change)		
Dec. 1, 20X5	Foreign currency	SEK 1,000,000	110,000
	Foreign exchange loss		20,000
	Accounts receivable	SEK 1,000,000	130,000
	(To record settlement of foreign currency receivable)		

tions) and foreign currency commitments. (The notion of an exposed asset or liability position is described shortly.)

FOREIGN CURRENCY TRANSLATION

Companies operating internationally use a variety of methods to express, in terms of their domestic currency, the assets, liabilities, revenues, and expenses that are stated in a foreign currency. These translation methods can be classified into two types: those that use a *single* translation rate to restate foreign balances to their domestic currency equivalents and those that use *multiple* rates. Exhibit 6-8 summarizes the treatment of specific balance sheet items under these translation methods.

Single Rate Method

The single rate method, long popular in Europe, applies a single exchange rate, the current or closing rate, to all foreign currency assets and liabilities. Foreign currency revenues and expenses are generally translated at exchange rates prevailing when these items are recognized.

For convenience, however, these items are typically translated by an appropriately weighted average of current exchange rates for the period. Under this method, the financial statements of a foreign operation (viewed by the parent as an autonomous entity) have their own reporting domicile: the local currency environment in which the foreign affiliate does business.

Under the current rate method, the consolidated statements preserve the original financial statement relationships (such as financial ratios) of the individual entities as all foreign currency financial statement items are translated by a single rate. That is,

Exhibit 6-8   Exchange Rates Employed in Different Translation Methods for Specific Balance Sheet Items

	Current	Current Noncurrent	Monetary Nonmonetary	Temporal
Cash	C	C	C	C
Accounts receivable	C	C	C	C
Inventories				
Cost	C	C	H	H
Market	C	C	H	C
Investments				
Cost	C	H	H	H
Market	C	H	H	C
Fixed assets	C	H	H	H
Other assets	C	H	H	H
Accounts payable	C	C	C	C
Long-term debt	C	H	C	C
Common stock	H	H	H	H
Retained earnings	*	*	*	*

Note: C, current rate; H, historical rate; and *, residual, balancing figure representing a composite of successive current rates.

consolidated results reflect the currency perspectives of each entity whose results go into the consolidated totals, not the single-currency perspective of the parent company. Some people fault this method on the grounds that using multiple currency perspectives violates the basic purpose of consolidated financial statements.

For accounting purposes, a foreign currency asset or liability is said to be *exposed* to exchange rate risk if its parent currency equivalent changes owing to a change in the exchange rate used to translate that asset or liability. Given this definition, the current rate method presumes that all local currency assets are exposed to exchange risk as the current (vs. the historical) rate changes the parent currency equivalent of all foreign currency assets every time exchange rates change. This seldom accords with economic reality as inventory and fixed asset values are generally supported by local inflation.

Consider the following example. Suppose that a foreign affiliate of a U.S. multinational corporation (MNC) buys a tract of land at the beginning of the period for FC1,000,000. The exchange rate (historical rate) was FC1 = $1. Thus, the historical cost of the investment in dollars is $1,000,000 (FC1,000,000 × FC1). Due to changing prices, the land rises in value to FC1,500,000 (unrecognized under U.S. GAAP) while the exchange rate declines to FC1.4 = $1 by period's end. If this foreign currency asset were translated to U.S. dollars using the current rate, its original dollar value of $1,000,000 would now be recorded at $714,286 (FC1,000,000 = FC1.4) implying an exchange loss of $285,714. Yet the increase in the fair market value of the land indicates that its current value in U.S. dollars is really $1,071,285 (FC1,500,000 = FC1.4) This suggests that translated asset values make little sense without making local price-level adjustments first. Also, translation of a historical cost number by a current market-determined exchange rate (e.g., FC1,000,000 = FC1.4 = $714,286) produces a result that resembles neither historical cost ($1,000,000) nor current market value ($1,071,285).

Finally, translating all foreign currency balances by the current rate creates translation gains and losses every time exchange rates change. Reflecting such exchange adjustments in current income could significantly distort reported measures of performance. Many of these gains and losses may never be fully realized, as changes in exchange rates often reverse direction.

Multiple Rate Methods

Multiple rate methods combine current and historical exchange rates in the translation process.

Current–Noncurrent Method

Under the current–noncurrent method, a foreign subsidiary's current assets and current liabilities are translated into their parent company's reporting currency at the current rate. Noncurrent assets and liabilities are translated at historical rates. Income statement items (except for depreciation and amortization charges) are translated at average rates applicable to each month of operation or on the basis of weighted averages covering the whole period being reported. Depreciation and amortization charges are translated at the historical rates in effect when the related assets were acquired.

Unfortunately, this method makes little economic sense. Using the year-end rate to translate current assets implies that foreign currency cash, receivables, and inventories are equally exposed to exchange risk. This is simply not true. For example, if the local price of inventory can be increased after a devaluation, its value is protected from currency exchange risk. On the other hand, translation of long-term debt at the historical rate shifts the impact of fluctuating currencies to the year of settlement. Many consider this to be at odds with reality. Moreover, current and noncurrent definitions are merely a classification scheme, not a conceptual justification, of which rates to use in translation.

Monetary–Nonmonetary Method[11]

The monetary–nonmonetary method also uses a balance sheet classification scheme to determine appropriate translation rates. *Monetary* assets and liabilities are translated at the current rate. *Nonmonetary* items—fixed assets, long-term investments, and inventories—are translated at historical rates. Income statement items are translated under procedures similar to those described for the current–noncurrent framework.

Unlike the current–noncurrent method, this method views monetary assets and liabilities as exposed to exchange rate risk. Since monetary items are settled in cash, use of the current rate to translate these items produces domestic currency equivalents that reflect their realizable or settlement values. It also reflects changes in the domestic currency equivalent of long-term debt in the period in which they occur, producing a more timely indicator of exchange rate effects.

Note, however, that the monetary–nonmonetary method relies on a classification scheme to determine appropriate translation rates. This may lead to inappropriate results. For example, this method translates all nonmonetary assets at historical rates, which is not reasonable for assets stated at current market values (such as investment securities and inventory and fixed assets written down to market). Multiplying the current market value of a nonmonetary asset by a historical exchange rate yields an amount in the domestic currency that is neither the item's current equivalent nor its historical cost. This method also distorts profit margins by matching sales at current prices and translation rates against cost of sales measured at historical costs and translation rates.

Temporal Method[12]

With the temporal method, currency translation is a measurement conversion process or a restatement of a given value. It does not change the *attribute* of an item being measured; it only changes the unit of measure. Translation of foreign balances restates the currency denomination of these items, but not their actual valuation. Under U.S. GAAP, cash is measured in terms of the amount owned at the balance sheet date. Receivables and payables are stated at amounts expected to be received or paid when due. Other assets and liabilities are measured at money prices that prevailed when the items were acquired or incurred (historical prices). Some, however, are measured at prices prevailing as of the financial statement date (current prices), such as inventories under the lower of cost or market rule. In short, a time dimension is associated with these money values.

[11]This method was originally proposed in Samuel R. Hepworth, *Reporting Foreign Operations,* Ann Arbor: University of Michigan, 1956.
[12]This method was originally proposed in Leonard Lorensen, "Reporting Foreign Operations of U.S. Companies in U.S. Dollars," *Accounting Research Study No. 12,* New York: American Institute of Certified Public Accountants, 1972.

In the temporal method, monetary items such as cash, receivables, and payables are translated at the current rate. Nonmonetary items are translated at rates that preserve their original measurement bases. Specifically, assets carried on the foreign currency statements at historical cost are translated at the historical rate. Why? Because *historical* cost in foreign currency translated by a *historical* exchange rate yields *historical* cost in domestic currency. Similarly, nonmonetary items carried abroad at current values are translated at the current rate because *current* value in foreign currency translated by a *current* exchange rate produces *current* value in domestic currency. Revenue and expense items are translated at rates that prevailed when the underlying transactions took place, although average rates are suggested when revenue or expense transactions are voluminous.

When nonmonetary items abroad are valued at historical cost, the translation procedures resulting from the temporal method are virtually identical to those produced by the monetary–nonmonetary method. The two translation methods differ only if other asset valuation bases are employed, such as replacement cost, market values, or discounted cash flows.

Because it is similar to the monetary–nonmonetary method, the temporal method shares most of its advantages and disadvantages. In deliberately ignoring local inflation, this method shares a limitation with the other translation methods discussed. (Of course, historical cost accounting ignores inflation as well!).

All four methods just described have been used in the United States at one time or another and can be found today in various countries. In general, they produce noticeably different foreign currency translation results. The first three methods (i.e., the current rate, current–noncurrent, and monetary–nonmonetary) are predicated on identifying which assets and liabilities are exposed to, or sheltered from, currency exchange risk. The translation methodology is then applied consistent with this distinction. The current rate method presumes that the entire foreign operation is exposed to exchange rate risk since all assets and liabilities are translated at the year-end exchange rate. The current–noncurrent rate method presumes that only the current assets and liabilities are so exposed, while the monetary–nonmonetary method presumes that monetary assets and liabilities are exposed. In contrast, the temporal method is designed to preserve the underlying theoretical basis of accounting measurement used in preparing the financial statements being translated.

Financial Statement Effects

Exhibits 6-9 and 6-10 highlight the financial statement effects of the major translation methods described. The balance sheet of a hypothetical Mexican subsidiary of a U.S.-based multinational enterprise appears in pesos in the first column of Exhibit 6-9. The second column depicts the U.S. dollar equivalents of the Mexican peso (P) balances when the exchange rate was P1 $0.13. Should the peso depreciate to P1 $0.10, several different accounting results are possible.

Under the current rate method, exchange rate changes affect the dollar equivalents of the Mexican subsidiary's *total* foreign currency assets (TA) and liabilities (TL) in the current period. Since their dollar values are affected by changes in the current rate, they are said to be *exposed* (in an *accounting* sense) to foreign exchange risk. Accordingly, under the current rate method, an exposed net asset position (TA > TL) results in a translation loss if the Mexican peso loses value, and an exchange gain if the peso gains

Exhibit 6-9 Mexican Subsidiary Balance Sheet

	Pesos	($ 0.13 P1)	U.S. Dollars before Peso Devaluation		U.S. Dollars after Peso Depreciation ($ 0.10 P1)	
			Current Rate	Current–Noncurrent	Monetary–Nonmonetary	Temporal
Assets						
Cash	P 3,000	$ 390	$ 300	$ 300	$ 300	$ 300
A/R	6,000	780	600	600	600	600
Inventories	9,000	1,170	900	900	1,170	900[a]
F/A (net)	18,000	2,340	1,800	2,340	2,340	2,340
Total	P 36,000	$4,680	$3,600	$4,140	$4,410	$4,140
Liabilities and Owners' Equity						
S-T payables	P 9,000	$1,170	$ 900	$ 900	$ 900	$ 900
L-T debt	12,000	1,560	1,200	1,560	1,200	1,200
O/E	15,000	1,950	1,500	1,680	2,310	2,040
Total	P 36,000	$4,680	$3,600	$4,140	$4,410	$4,140
Accounting exposure (P)			15,000	9,000	(12,000)	(3,000)
Translation gain (loss) ($)			(450)	(270)	360	90

Note: If the exchange rate remained unchanged over time, the translated statements would be the same under all translation methods.
[a] Assume inventories are carried at lower of cost or market. If they were carried at historical cost, the temporal balance sheet would be identical to the monetary–nonmonetary method.

Exhibit 6-10 Mexican Subsidiary Income Statement

	Pesos	($ 0.10 P1)	U.S. Dollars before Peso Devaluation		U.S. Dollars after Peso Depreciation ($ 0.13 P1)	
			Current Rate	Current–Noncurrent	Monetary–Nonmonetary	Temporal
Sales	P 40,000	$5,200	$4,000	$4,000	$4,000	$4,000
Cost of sales	20,000	2,600	2,000	2,000	2,600	2,600[a]
Depreciation[b]	1,800	234	180	234	234	234
Other expenses	8,000	1,040	800	800	800	800
Pre-tax income	10,200	1,326	1,020	966	366	366
Income tax (30%)	3,060	(398)	(306)	(306)	(306)	(306)
Translation g/l[c]	—	—	(450)	(270)	360	(90)
Net income/(loss)	P 7,140	$ 928	$ 264	$ 390	$ 420	$ (30)

Note: This example assumes that the income statement is prepared the day after devaluation.
[a]Assumes that inventories were written down to market at period's end.
[b]Estimated life of fixed assets is assumed to be 10 years.
[c]This example reflects what reported earnings would look like if all translation gains or losses were immediately reflected in current income.

value. An exposed peso net liability position (TA < TL) produces a translation gain if the Mexican peso loses value and a loss if the peso gains value. In our example, current rate translation yields a $450 translation loss, since the dollar equivalent of the Mexican subsidiary's net asset position *after* the peso depreciation is $1,500 (P15,000 × $0.10), whereas the dollar equivalent *before* the depreciation was $1,950 (P15,000 × $0.13).

Under the current–noncurrent method, the U.S. company's accounting exposure is measured by its peso net current asset or liability position (a positive P9,000 in our example). Under the monetary–nonmonetary method, exposure is measured by its net peso monetary asset or liability position (a negative P12,000). Accounting *exposure* under the temporal principle depends on whether the Mexican subsidiary's inventories or other nonmonetary assets are valued at historical cost (and therefore not exposed) or some other valuation basis (a negative P3,000 in our example).

To summarize, the different translation methods in our example give a wide array of accounting results, ranging from a $450 loss under the current rate method to a $360 gain under the monetary–nonmonetary method. This difference is large given that all the results are based on the same facts. What is more, operations reporting respectable profits before currency translation may well report losses or much lower earnings after translation (the converse is also true). To protect themselves against the financial statement effects of currency swings, financial managers may execute protective maneuvers known as *hedging strategies*. Chapter 11 covers hedging options and foreign exchange risk management in greater detail.

Which Is Best?

We reject the traditional assumption that a single translation method can be appropriate for all circumstances in which translations occur and for all purposes that translation serves. Circumstances underlying foreign exchange translation differ widely. Translating accounts from a stable to an unstable currency is not the same as translating accounts from an unstable currency to a stable one. Likewise, there is little similarity between translations involving import- or export-type transactions and those involving a permanently established affiliate or subsidiary company in another country that reinvests its local earnings and does not intend to repatriate any funds to the parent company in the near future.

Second, translations are made for different purposes. Translating the accounts of a foreign subsidiary to consolidate those accounts with those of the parent company has very little in common with translating the accounts of an independent company mainly for the convenience of various foreign audiences-of-interest.

We pose three questions:

1. Is it reasonable to use more than one translation method?
2. If so, what should be the acceptable methods and under what conditions should they be applied?
3. Are there situations in which translations should not be done at all?

As to the first question, it is clear that a single translation method cannot equally serve translations occurring under different conditions and for different purposes. More than one translation method is needed.

Regarding the second question, we think that three different translation approaches can be accepted: (1) the historical method, (2) the current method, and (3) no translation at all. Financial accounts of foreign entities can be translated either from a parent company perspective or from a local perspective. Under the parent company perspective, foreign operations are extensions of parent company operations and are, in large measure, sources of domestic currency cash flows. Accordingly, the object of translation is to change the unit of measure for financial statements of foreign subsidiaries to the domestic currency, and to make the foreign statements conform to accounting principles generally accepted in the country of the parent company. We think these objectives are best achieved by translation methods that use historical rates of exchange. We prefer the temporal principle, as it generally maintains the accounting principles used to measure assets and liabilities originally expressed in foreign currency units.[13] Because foreign statements under a parent company perspective are first adjusted to reflect parent company accounting principles (*before* translation), the temporal principle is appropriate, as it changes a measurement in foreign currency into a measurement in domestic currency without changing the basis of measurement. The temporal translation method is easily adapted to processes that make accounting adjustments during the translation. When this is so, adjustments for differences between two or more sets of accounting concepts and practices are made along with the translation of currency amounts. For example, inventories or certain liabilities may be restated according to accounting practices different from those originally used. The temporal principle can accommodate any asset valuation framework, be it historical cost, current replacement price, or net realizable values.

The current rate method of translation is a straightforward translation (restatement) from one *currency language* to another. There is no change in the nature of the accounts; only their particular form of expression is changed. The current rate method is appropriate when the translated accounts of foreign subsidiaries keep the local currency as the unit of measure; that is, when foreign entities are viewed from a local (as opposed to a parent) company perspective. Translation at the current rate does not change any of the initial relationships (e.g., financial ratios) in the foreign currency statements, as all account balances are simply multiplied by a constant. This approach is also useful when the accounts of an independent company are translated for the convenience of foreign stockholders or other external user groups.

A second use of the current rate method happens when price-level-adjusted accounts are to be translated to another currency. If reliable price-level adjustments are made in a given set of accounts and if domestic price-level changes for the currency are reflected closely in related foreign exchange rate movements, the current rate translation of price-level-adjusted data yields results that are comparable to translating historical cost accounts under the historical rate translation method.[14] This topic is covered in Chapter 7.

---

[13]See Frederick D. S. Choi and Gerhard G. Mueller, *An Introduction to Multinational Accounting*, Upper Saddle River, NJ: Prentice Hall, 1978.

[14]Alas, empirical evidence suggests that exchange rate changes and differential inflation are seldom perfectly negatively correlated. For recent evidence on the distortions caused by this market anomaly, see David A. Ziebart and Jong-Hag Choi, "The Difficulty of Achieving Economic Reality Through Foreign Currency Translation," *International Journal of Accounting* 33, no. 4 (1998): 403–414.

Are there situations in which translations should not be done at all? We think so. No translation is appropriate between highly unstable and highly stable currencies. Translation of one into the other will not produce meaningful information using any translation method. No translation also means nonconsolidation of financial statements. We think this is reasonable. If a currency is unstable enough to put account translations out of the question, financial statement consolidation should also be out of the question. No translation is necessary when financial statements of independent companies are issued for purely informational purposes to residents in another country that is in a comparable stage of economic development and has a comparable national currency situation. Finally, certain special management reports should not be translated. Effective international managers should be able to evaluate situations and reach decisions in terms of more than one currency unit. Some internal company reports may have several different columns of monetary amounts, each in a different currency unit. Translation may be impossible for certain other reports (such as those on a possible international acquisition) because historical foreign exchange rate information may not be available. Still other types of reports may translate current or monetary items only and leave other items untranslated.

Appropriate Current Rate

Thus far we have referred to rates of exchange used in translation methods as either *historical* or *current.* Average rates are often used in income statements for expediency. The choice of an appropriate exchange rate is not clear-cut because several exchange rates are in effect for any currency at any time. There are buying rates and selling rates, spot rates and forward rates, official rates and free-market rates, and many rate differentials in between. We believe that an appropriate translation rate should reflect economic and business reality as closely as possible. The free-market rate quoted for spot transactions in the country where the accounts to be translated originate is the only rate that appropriately measures current transaction values.

Sometimes a country applies different exchange rates to different transactions. In these situations, one must choose among several existing rates. Several possibilities have been suggested: (1) dividend remittance rates, (2) free-market rates, and (3) any applicable penalty or preference rates, such as those associated with imports or exports. Your authors believe that free-market rates are preferable, with one exception: Where specific exchange controls are in effect (i.e., when certain funds are definitely ear-marked for specific transactions to which specific foreign exchange rates apply), the applicable rates should be used. For instance, if a Latin American subsidiary of a U.S. parent has received permission to import certain goods from the United States at a favorable rate and has set aside certain funds to do so, the ear-marked funds should be translated to dollars at the special preference rate. The current year-end free-market rate should then be applied to the balance of the foreign cash account. This procedure translates portions of a foreign currency cash account at two or more different translation rates. That is fine as long as it properly and fully reflects economic reality.

Translation Gains and Losses

Exhibit 6-9 illustrated four translation adjustments resulting from applying various translation methods to foreign currency financial statements. Internationally, accounting treatments of these adjustments are as diverse as the translation procedures.

Approaches to accounting for translation adjustments range from *deferral* to *no deferral* with hybrid approaches in between.[15]

Deferral

Exclusion of translation adjustments in current income is generally advocated because these adjustments merely result from a restatement process. Changes in the domestic currency equivalents of a foreign subsidiary's net assets are unrealized and have no effect on the local currency cash flows generated by the foreign entity. Therefore, it would be misleading to include such adjustments in current income. Under these circumstances, translation adjustments should be accumulated separately as a part of consolidated equity. Parkinson offers additional reasons to support deferral:

> It can be argued that the gain or loss relates to a very long-term investment—perhaps even a permanent investment—of a . . . parent in a foreign subsidiary; that the gain or loss will not become realized until the foreign operation is closed down and all the net assets are distributed to the parent; that at or before such time the change in the exchange rate may have reversed— i.e., that no gain or loss will ever be realized. It can also be argued that operating results recorded in the periods following the currency revaluation (and translated at the then current exchange rate) will indicate the increased or decreased worth of the foreign operation and that in these circumstances there is no need to record a one-time translation gain or loss in the income statement—that in fact the recording of such a gain or loss might be misleading.[16]

Deferral may be opposed on the grounds that exchange rates may not reverse themselves. Even if they do, deferral of exchange adjustments is premised on predicting exchange rates, a most difficult task. Some argue that deferring translation gains or losses masks the behavior of exchange rate changes; that is, rate changes are historical facts and financial statement users are best served if the effects of exchange rate fluctuations are accounted for when they occur. According to FAS No. 8 (par. 199), "Exchange rates fluctuate; accounting should not give the impression that rates are stable."

Deferral and Amortization

Some favor deferring translation gains or losses and amortizing these adjustments over the life of related balance sheet items. As an example, assume that the acquisition of a fixed asset is financed by issuing debt. It can be argued that principal and interest payments on the debt are *covered* by cash flows generated from using the fixed asset. Here,

---

[15]For additional treatment of the issues discussed here, see Financial Accounting Standards Board, "An Analysis of Issues Related to Accounting for Foreign Currency Translation," *FASB Discussion Memorandum,* Stamford, CT: FASB, February 21, 1974, 79–102.

[16]MacDonald R. Parkinson, *Translation of Foreign Currencies,* Toronto: Canadian Institute of Chartered Accountants, 1972, 101–102.

the translation gain or loss associated with the debt would be deferred and amortized over the life of the related fixed asset, that is, released to income in a manner compatible with depreciation expense. Alternatively, the translation gain or loss arising from the debt could be deferred and amortized over the remaining life of the debt as an adjustment to interest expense.

Such approaches can be criticized on theoretical and practical grounds. For example, finance theory tells us that capital budgeting decisions about fixed asset investments are independent of decisions about how to finance them. Linking the two looks more like a device to smooth income. Adjusting interest expense is also suspect. Domestic borrowing costs are not adjusted to reflect changes in market interest rates or the fair value of the debt. Why should fluctuations in currency values have such an effect?

Partial Deferral

A third option in accounting for translation gains and losses is to recognize losses as soon as they occur, but to recognize gains only as they are realized. Although conservative, deferring a translation gain solely because it is a gain denies that a rate change has occurred. Moreover, deferral of translation gains while recognizing translation losses is logically inconsistent. This approach also lacks any explicit criteria to determine when to realize a translation gain. Also, those who favor deferral of translation gains are at a loss to determine how much to defer. In the past, companies have netted current gains against prior losses and deferred the difference. This implies that translation gains or losses are not period items and will "wash out" in the long run. If this were so, deferrals would be a questionable practice.

No Deferral

A final option is to recognize translation gains and losses in the income statement immediately. This option views deferral of any type as artificial and misleading. Deferral criteria are often attacked as internally inconsistent and impossible to implement. However, including translation gains and losses in current income introduces a random element to earnings that could result in significant earning fluctuations whenever exchange rates change. Moreover, including such paper gains and losses in reported earnings can mislead statement readers, because these adjustments do not always provide information compatible with the expected economic effects of rate changes on an enterprise's cash flows.

Where Are We?

The objectives of translation have an important bearing on the nature of any potential translation adjustment. If a local currency perspective is maintained (local company perspective), reflecting a translation adjustment in current income is unwarranted. Recall that a local company perspective requires the current rate translation method in order to preserve relationships existing in the foreign currency statements. In our opinion, including translation gains or losses in income distorts original financial relationships and may mislead users of the information. Translation gains or losses should be treated from a local currency perspective as adjustments to the owners' equity.

If the reporting currency of the parent company is the unit of measure for the translated financial statements (parent company perspective), it is advisable to recognize translation gains or losses in income immediately. The parent company perspective views a foreign subsidiary as an extension of the parent. Translation gains and losses reflect increases or decreases in the domestic currency equity of the foreign investment and should be recognized.

TRANSLATION ACCOUNTING DEVELOPMENT

Translation accounting practices have evolved over time in response to the increasing complexity of multinational operations and changes in the international monetary system. To provide some historical perspective on the current state of translation accounting, we briefly chronicle financial reporting initiatives in the United States as they are representative of experiences elsewhere.

Pre-1965

Before 1965 the translation practices of many U.S. companies were guided by *Accounting Research Bulletin No. 4* (ARB No. 4),[17] later reissued as Chapter 12 of ARB No. 43.[18] This statement advocated the current–noncurrent method. Transaction gains or losses were taken directly to income. Translation gains or losses were netted during the period. Net translation losses were recognized in current income, while net translation gains were deferred in a balance sheet suspense account and used to offset translation losses in future periods.

1965–1975

Chapter 12 of ARB No. 43 allowed certain exceptions to the current–noncurrent method. Under special circumstances, inventory could be translated at historical rates. Long-term debt incurred to acquire long-term assets could be restated at the current rate when there was a large (presumably permanent) change in the exchange rate. Any accounting difference caused by debt restatement was treated as part of the asset's cost. Translating *all* foreign currency payables and receivables at the current rate was allowed after *Accounting Principles Board Opinion No. 6* was issued in 1965.[19] This change to ARB No. 43 gave companies another translation option.

1975–1981

To end the variety of treatments allowed under previous translation standards, the FASB issued the controversial FAS No. 8 in 1975.[20] This statement significantly changed U.S. practice and that of foreign companies subscribing to U.S. GAAP by

---

[17]American Institute of Certified Public Accountants, Committee on Accounting Procedure, "Foreign Operations and Foreign Exchange," *Accounting Research Bulletin No. 4,* New York: AICPA, 1953.

[18]American Institute of Certified Public Accountants, Committee on Accounting Procedure, "Restatement and Revision of Accounting Research Bulletins," *Accounting Research Bulletin No. 43,* New York: AICPA, 1953.

[19]American Institute of Certified Public Accountants, "Status of Accounting Research Bulletins," *Accounting Principles Board Opinion No. 6,* New York: AICPA, 1965.

[20]Financial Accounting Standards Board, "Accounting for the Translation of Foreign Currency Transactions and Foreign Currency Financial Statements," *Statement of Financial Accounting Standards No. 8,* Stamford, CT: FASB, 1975.

requiring the temporal method of translation. Equally important, deferral of translation gains and losses was no longer permitted. Translation and transaction exchange gains and losses had to be recognized in income during the period of the rate change.

Corporate reaction to FAS No. 8 was mixed. While some applauded it for its theoretical merits, many condemned it for the distortions it caused in reported corporate earnings. FAS No. 8 was criticized for producing accounting results not in accord with economic reality. The yo-yo effect of FAS No. 8 on corporate earnings also caused concern among executives of multinational companies. They worried that their companies' reported earnings would appear more volatile than those of domestic companies, and thereby depress their stock prices.

1981–Present

In May 1978, the FASB invited public comment on its first 12 pronouncements. Most of the 200 letters received related to FAS No. 8, urging that it be changed. Responding to the dissatisfaction, the FASB reconsidered FAS No. 8 and, after many public meetings and two exposure drafts, issued *Statement of Financial Accounting Standards No. 52* in 1981.[21]

FEATURES OF STANDARD NO. 52

The objectives of translation under FAS No. 52 differ substantially from those of FAS No. 8. FAS No. 8 adopted a parent company perspective by requiring that foreign currency financial statements be presented as if all transactions had taken place in U.S. dollars. Standard No. 52 recognizes that both the parent company and the local company perspectives are valid reporting frameworks. Its translation rules are thus designed to

1. Reflect, in consolidated statements, the financial results and relationships measured in the primary currency in which each consolidated entity does business (its *functional currency*).
2. Provide information that is generally compatible with the expected economic effects of an exchange rate change on an enterprise's cash flows and equity.

These objectives are based on the concept of a *functional currency*. Recall that the functional currency of an entity is the currency of the primary economic environment in which it operates and generates cash flows. Moreover, the functional currency designation determines the choice of translation method employed for consolidation purposes and the disposition of exchange gains and losses.

---

[21]Financial Accounting Standards Board, "Foreign Currency Translation," *Statement of Financial Accounting Standards No. 52,* Stamford, CT: FASB, 1981.

Translation When Local Currency Is the Functional Currency

If the functional currency is the foreign currency in which the foreign entity's records are kept, its financial statements are *translated* to dollars using the current rate method. Resulting translation gains or losses are disclosed in a separate component of consolidated equity. This preserves the financial statement ratios as calculated from the local currency statements. The following current rate procedures are used:

1. All foreign currency assets and liabilities are translated to dollars using the exchange rate prevailing as of the balance sheet date; capital accounts are translated at historical rates.
2. Revenues and expenses are translated using the exchange rate prevailing on the transaction date, although weighted average rates can be used for expediency.
3. Translation gains and losses are reported in a separate component of consolidated stockholders' equity. These exchange adjustments do not go into the income statement until the foreign operation is sold or the investment is judged to have permanently lost value.

Translation When the U.S. Dollar Is the Functional Currency

When the U.S. dollar is a foreign entity's functional currency, its foreign currency financial statements are remeasured to dollars using the temporal method. All translation gains and losses resulting from the translation process are included in determining current period income. Specifically:

1. Monetary assets and liabilities and nonmonetary assets valued at current market prices are translated using the rate prevailing as of the financial statement date; other nonmonetary items and capital accounts are translated at historical rates.
2. Revenues and expenses are translated using average exchange rates for the period except those items related to nonmonetary items (e.g., cost of sales and depreciation expense), which are translated using historical rates.
3. Translation gains and losses are reflected in current income.

Translation When Foreign Currency Is the Functional Currency

A foreign entity may keep its records in one foreign currency when its functional currency is another foreign currency. In this situation, the financial statements are first remeasured from the local currency into the functional currency (temporal method) and then translated into U.S. dollars using the current rate method.

Exhibit 6-11 charts the translation procedures described here, and the appendix to this chapter demonstrates the mechanics of foreign currency translation.

An exception to the current rate method is required for subsidiaries located in places where the cumulative rate of inflation during the preceding 3 years exceeds 100 percent. In such hyperinflationary conditions, the dollar (the stronger currency) is considered the functional currency, requiring use of the temporal translation method.

Where an entity has more than one distinct and separable operation (e.g., a branch or division), each operation may be considered as a separate entity with its own func-

Exhibit 6-11   Translation Procedure Flowchart

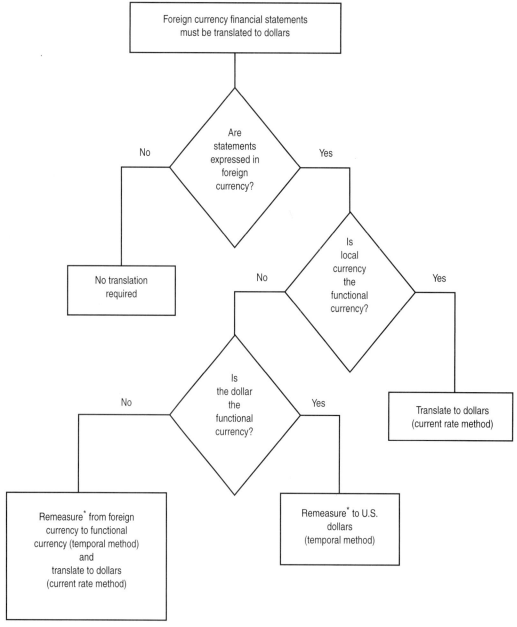

*The term *remeasure* means to translate so as to change the unit of measure from a foreign currency to the functional currency.

tional currency. Thus, a U.S. parent might have a self-contained manufacturing opera-tion in Mexico designed to serve the Latin American market and a separate sales out-let for the parent company's exported products. Under these circumstances, financial statements of the manufacturing operation would be translated to dollars using the current rate method. The peso statements of the Mexican sales outlet would be remea-sured in dollars using the temporal method.

Once the functional currency for a foreign entity is determined, FAS No. 52 requires that it be used consistently unless changes in economic circumstances clearly indicate that the functional currency has changed. If a reporting enterprise can justify the change in conformity with Accounting Principles Board Opinion No. 20, "Accounting Changes," the accounting change need not be accounted for retroactively.

Alcan Inc., introduced at the beginning of this chapter, is a Canadian-based multi-national company. It has chosen, however, to report the results of its consolidated oper-ations in U.S. dollars. Foreign accounts denominated in foreign currency that are inte-gral to Alcan's operations are thus translated (remeasured) to its functional currency, Canadian dollars, using the temporal method. The results of this remeasurement process are then translated to U.S. dollars using the current rate method. The transla-tion gains or losses generated by the remeasurement process appear in Alcan Inc.'s consolidated earnings numbers as *foreign currency balance sheet translation gains and losses* (see its earlier press release on page 184). The translation adjustment following restatement from Canadian to U.S. dollars appears in consolidated equity, as illustrated below.

Alcan Inc.
Interim Consolidated Balance Sheet
September 30
(unaudited for 20X3)

(in millions of US$)	
Shareholders' equity:	
Redeemable nonretractable preference shares	160
Common shareholders' equity:	
Common shares	4,720
Retained earnings	3,329
Deferred translation adjustments[22]	507
	8,556

---

[22]Multinational companies adhering to the tenets of FAS Statement 130 would include these translation gains or losses as part of a figure labeled *comprehensive income,* which would include such items as mini-mum pension liability adjustments and unrealized gains and losses on certain investments in debt and equity securities. The purpose of this reporting requirement is to report all changes in the equity of an enterprise that occurred during the period whether realized or not. Financial Accounting Standards Board, "Reporting Comprehensive Income," *Statement of Financial Accounting Standards No. 130,* Stamford, CT: FASB, 1997.

THE DEBATE

FAS No. 52 was designed to quiet many of the criticisms leveled at FAS No. 8.[23] Recent empirical evidence also lends support to FAS No. 52.[24] New issues stir new controversies,[25] and the following sections discuss several of them.

Reporting Perspective

In adopting the notion of functional currency, FAS No. 52 accommodates both local and parent company reporting perspectives in the consolidated financial statements. Several questions may be posed. First, are financial statement readers better served by incorporating two different reporting perspectives and, therefore, two different currency frameworks in a single set of consolidated financial statements? Is a translation adjustment produced under the temporal method any different in substance from that produced under the current rate method? If not, is any useful purpose served by disclosing some translation adjustments in income and others in stockholders' equity? Is FAS No. 8's concept of a single unit of measure (the parent company's reporting currency) the lesser of two evils? Should we stop translating foreign currency financial statements altogether? Doing so would avoid many of the pitfalls associated with current translation methods, including the problem of incorporating more than one perspective in the translated results.[26]

It has also been suggested that FAS No. 52 is inconsistent with the theory of consolidation, which is to show the statements of a parent company and its subsidiaries as if the group were operating as a single company. Yet subsidiaries whose functional currency is the local currency operate relatively independently of the parent. If the multinational doesn't operate as a single company, then why consolidate those parts that are independent?[27]

---

[23]For evidence of market reactions to FAS No. 52 versus FAS No. 8, see David A. Ziebart and David H. Kim, "An Examination of the Market Reactions Associated with SFAS No. 8 and SFAS No. 52," *Accounting Review* (April 1987): 343–357; Zabihollah Rezaee, "Capital Market Reactions to Accounting Policy Deliberations: An Empirical Study of Accounting for Foreign Currency Translation 1974–1982," *Journal of Business Finance and Accounting* (Winter 1990): 635–648; and Zabihollah Rezaee, R. Phillip Malone, and Russell Briner, "Capital Market Response to SFAS No. 8 and 52: Professional Adaptation," *Journal of Accounting, Auditing, and Finance* (Summer 1993): 313–332.

[24]As examples, Ziebart and Kim found significant share price and volume reactions upon the release of FAS 52, David H. Kim and David A. Ziebart, "An Investigation of the Price and Trading Reactions to the Issuance of SFAS No. 52," *Journal of Accounting, Auditing and Finance* (Winter 1991): 35–47. Bartov finds that FAS 52 produces a better accounting measure for economic exposure than FAS No. 8, Eli Bartov "Foreign Currency Exposure of Multinational Firms: Accounting Measures and Market Valuation," *Contemporary Accounting Research* (Winter 1997): 623–652. Ayres and Rodgers show that reliance on FAS 52 improves analysts' earnings forecasts, Frances L. Ayres and Jacci L. Rodgers, "Further Evidence on the Impact of SFAS 52 on Analysts' Earnings Forecasts," *Journal of International Financial Management and Accounting* (June 1994): 120–141.

[25]One opinion survey rated FAS No. 52 as one of the best and worst American accounting standards issued to date. Cheri L. Reither, " What Are the Best and the Worst Accounting Standards?" *Accounting Horizon* 12, no. 3 (1998): 283–292.

[26]Paul Rosenfield, "Accounting for Foreign Operations," *Journal of Accountancy* (August 1987): 112.

[27]C. W. Nobes, "An Analysis of the Use of 'Theory' in the UK and US Currency Translation Standards," reprinted in C. W. Nobes, *Issues in International Accounting,* New York: Garland, 1986, pp. 129–130.

What Happened to Historical Cost?

As noted earlier in the chapter, translating a balance measured under historical cost at the current exchange rate produces an amount in U.S. dollars that is neither the item's historical cost nor its current value equivalent. Such a translated amount defies theoretical description. Historical cost is the basis of U.S. GAAP and most overseas assets of most multinationals will have historical cost measurements. Yet the current rate method is used for translation whenever a local currency is deemed to be the functional currency. Even if financial statement users can still make sense of the consolidated amounts, the theoretical incoherence remains.

Concept of Income

Under FAS No. 52, adjustments arising from the translation of foreign currency financial statements and certain transactions are made directly to shareholders' equity, thus bypassing the income statement. The apparent intention of this was to give statement readers more accurate and less confusing income numbers. Some, however, dislike the idea of burying translation adjustments that were previously disclosed. They fear readers may be confused as to the effects of fluctuating exchange rates on a company's worth.[28]

Managed Earnings

FAS No. 52 provides opportunities to manage earnings. Consider the choice of functional currencies. An examination of the functional currency criteria shown in Exhibit 6-5 suggests that the choice of a functional currency is not straightforward. A foreign subsidiary's operations could satisfy opposing criteria. For example, a foreign subsidiary may incur its expenses primarily in the local country and make its sales primarily in the local environment and denominated in local currency. These circumstances would favor selection of the local currency as the functional currency. Yet the same operation may be financed entirely by the parent company with cash flows remitted to the parent. Therefore, the parent currency could be selected as the functional currency. The different possible outcomes involved in selecting functional currencies may be one reason why Exxon-Mobil Oil chooses the local currency as the functional currency for most of its foreign operations, while Chevron-Texaco and Unocal choose the dollar. When choice criteria conflict and the choice can significantly affect reporting outcomes, there are opportunities for earnings management.

Research to date is inconclusive as to whether managers manipulate income (and other financial statement amounts) by the choice of functional currency.[29] Some evidence of earnings management appears when one looks at when companies chose to

---

[28]Of course there are other equity adjustments, namely unrealized gains and losses on certain debt and equity securities and minimum pension liability adjustments. Under FAS No. 130 (effective for fiscal years beginning after December 15, 1997), U.S. companies must report these amounts in *comprehensive income* as an adjustment to net income.

[29]For example, see J. H. Amernic and B. J. B. Galvin, "Implementing the New Foreign Currency Rules in Canada and the United States: A Challenge to Professional Judgement," *International Journal of Accounting* (Spring 1984): 165–180; Thomas G. Evans and Timothy S. Doupnik, *Determining the Functional Currency Under Statement 52,* Stamford, CT: FASB, 1986, 11–12; Dileep R. Mehta and Samanta B. Thapa, "FAS 52, Functional Currency, and the Non-comparability of Financial Reports," *International Journal of Accounting* 26, no. 2 (1991): 71–84; Robert J. Kirsch and Thomas G. Evans, "The Implementation of FAS 52: Did the Foreign Currency Approach Prevail?" *International Journal of Accounting* 29, No. 1 (1994): 20–33; and M. Aiken and D. Ardern, "Choice of Translation Methods in Financial Disclosure: A Test of Compliance With Environmental Hypotheses," *British Accounting Review,* 35 (2003): 327–348.

adopt FAS No. 52 (they had three choices: 1981, 1982, or 1983). Evidence shows that companies chose the adoption date, in part, based on when the effects on income were the most favorable.[30] Such motives as these reduce the credibility of multinationals' consolidated financial statements.

FOREIGN CURRENCY TRANSLATION AND INFLATION

An inverse relationship between a country's rate of inflation and its currency's external value has been empirically demonstrated.[31] Consequently, use of the current rate to translate the cost of nonmonetary assets located in inflationary environments will eventually produce domestic currency equivalents far below their original measurement bases. At the same time, translated earnings would be greater because of correspondingly lower depreciation charges. Such translated results could easily mislead rather than inform. Lower dollar valuations would usually understate the actual earning power of foreign assets supported by local inflation, and inflated return on investment ratios of foreign operations could create false expectations of future profitability.

The FASB decided against inflation adjustments before translation, believing such adjustments to be inconsistent with the historical cost valuation framework used in basic U.S. statements. As a solution, FAS No. 52 requires use of the U.S. dollar as the functional currency for foreign operations domiciled in hyperinflationary environments (those countries where the cumulative rate of inflation exceeds 100 percent over a 3-year period). This procedure would hold constant the dollar equivalents of foreign currency assets, as they would be translated at the historical rate (by the temporal method). This method has its limitations. First, translation at the historical rate is meaningful only if differential rates of inflation between the subsidiary's host country and parent country are perfectly negatively correlated with exchange rates. If not, the dollar equivalents of foreign currency assets in inflationary environments will be misleading. Should inflation rates in the hyperinflationary economy fall below 100 percent in a future 3-year period, switching to the current rate method (because local currency would become the functional currency) could produce a significant translation adjustment to consolidated equity, as exchange rates may change significantly during the interim. Under these circumstances, charging stockholders' equity with translation losses on foreign currency fixed assets could have a significant effect on financial ratios with stockholders' equity in the denominator. The issue of foreign currency translation cannot be separated from the issue of accounting for foreign inflation, which is treated at greater length in the next chapter.

---

[30]For evidence of earnings motivation for switching currency translation methods, see Dahli Gray, "Corporate Preferences for Foreign Currency Accounting Standards," *Journal of Accounting Research* (Autumn 1984): 760–764; James J. Benjamin, Steven Grossman, and Casper Wiggins, "The Impact of Foreign Currency Translation on Reporting During the Phase-in of SFAS No. 52," *Journal of Accounting, Auditing, and Finance* 1, No. 3 (1996): 174–184; Frances L. Ayres, "Characteristics of Firms Electing Early Adoption of SFAS 52," *Journal of Accounting and Economics* (June 1986): 143–158; and Robert W. Rutledge, "Does Management Engage in the Manipulation of Earnings?" *Journal of International Accounting, Auditing, and Taxation* 4, No. 1 (1995): 69–86.

[31]B. Balassa, "The Purchasing Power Parity Doctrine: A Reappraisal," *Journal of Political Economy* (1964): 145–154; R. Z. Aliber and C. P. Stickney, "Accounting Measures of Foreign Exchange Exposure: The Long and Short of It," *Accounting Review* (January 1975): 44–57; and W. Beaver and M. Wolfson, "Foreign Currency Translation in Perfect and Complete Markets," *Journal of Accounting Research* (Autumn 1982): 528–560.

FOREIGN CURRENCY TRANSLATION ELSEWHERE

We now look briefly at foreign currency translation in other parts of the world. FAS No. 52 has become the basis for similar standards elsewhere. The Canadian Institute of Chartered Accountants (CICA), the U.K.'s Accounting Standards Board, and the International Accounting Standards Board all participated in the deliberations that led to FAS No. 52. It is not surprising to find that their corresponding standards are largely compatible with it.[32]

The main difference between the Canadian standard (CICA 1650) and FAS No. 52 concerns foreign long-term debt. In Canada, gains and losses from translation are deferred and amortized; in the United States, they are recognized in income immediately. Canada has issued a second exposure draft proposing to eliminate its defer and amortize approach.[33]

The major difference between the U.K. and U.S. standard relates to self-contained subsidiaries in hyperinflationary countries. In the United Kingdom, financial statements must first be adjusted to current price levels and then translated using the current rate; in the United States, the temporal method is used.

Finally, there is an important distinction between IAS 21 (as revised) and FAS No. 52. Under IAS 21, the financial statements of subsidiaries in highly inflationary environments must be adjusted to reflect changes in the general price level before translation, a treatment like that in the U.K. standard.

Australia and New Zealand issued standards in 1988. Compared to FAS No. 52, the Australian standard calls for revaluing noncurrent, nonmonetary assets for subsidiaries in high inflation countries prior to translation. The New Zealand standard is silent on the issue. The New Zealand standard also calls for the monetary–nonmonetary method of translation for subsidiaries with operations integrated with the parent. Since this produces results very similar to the temporal method, this difference with FAS No. 52 has little practical effect.

The foreign currency translation standards discussed here are broadly comparable with FAS No. 52. Nevertheless, multinationals following these standards could still produce differing consolidated financial statements, depending on their circumstances. This inconsistency would, in turn, inhibit comparison and complicate decision making.[34]

Practice elsewhere is more diverse. Japan recently changed its standard to require the current rate method in all circumstances, with translation adjustments shown on the balance sheet in stockholders' equity. The EU Fourth and Seventh Directives (see Chapter 8) have no provisions on foreign currency translation. Most Continental EU

---

[32]All three standards were issued in 1983, roughly 18 months after FAS No. 52. The Canadian standard is Accounting Recommendation 1650 and the British standard is Statement of Standard Accounting Practice 20; both are titled "Foreign Currency Translation." The original International Accounting Standard 21 was modified in 1993 and is now called, "The Effects of Changes in Foreign Exchange Rates."

[33]Rotenberg provides evidence suggesting that the impact of the proposed changes on reported leverage and profitability of Canadian companies would be significant. W. Rotenberg, "Harmonization of Foreign Currency Translation Practices: Canadian Treatment of Long Term Monetary Items," *International Journal of Accounting* 33, no. 4 (1998): 415–431.

[34]Robert J. Kirsch and Dawn Becker-Dermer, "Proposed Revisions of International Accounting Standard No. 21 and Their Implications for Translation Accounting in Selected English-Speaking Countries," *International Journal of Accounting* 30, no. 1 (1995): 1–24.

no.

no.

countries, including France and Germany, have no standards. As a result, practice is up to the companies. A survey of six German chemical companies found that two used the temporal method, two based their approach on the principle of functional currency, and two used the closing rate method.[35] However, in 2005, foreign currency translation practices in Europe will narrow considerably as International Financial Reporting Standards become the reporting norm for listed EU companies.

CURRENT TRENDS

Foreign currency translation remains a vexing and controversial technical issue. Where are we headed internationally? Will we ever reach closure? We think that the answer depends on how the harmonization activities of the IASB unfold. Chapter 8 discusses this effort, and its likelihood for success. An increasing number of internationally listed companies are following IAS, now referred to as IFRS (International Financial Reporting Standards) and (as discussed in Chapter 8) the world's stock exchanges are under increasing pressure to allow IFRS in lieu of domestic standards for foreign company listings. (Many stock exchanges already do this.) In the United States, foreign companies are allowed to follow the international standard (IAS 21) instead of the U.S. standard (FAS No. 52) in foreign currency translation. In time, the FASB may resolve the differences between FAS No. 52 and IAS 21 in favor of the international standard. We think this would encourage other standards setters to do likewise in resolving their differences with IAS 21.

APPENDIX: TRANSLATION AND REMEASUREMENT UNDER FAS NO. 52

Exhibit 6-12 presents comparative foreign currency balance sheets at December 31, 20X5 and 20X6, and a statement of income for the year ended December 31, 20X6, for CMP Corporation, a wholly-owned foreign subsidiary of a U.S. company. The statements conform with U.S. generally accepted accounting principles before translation to U.S. dollars.

Capital stock was issued and fixed assets acquired when the exchange rate was FC1 $.17. Inventories at January 1, 20X6, were acquired during the fourth quarter of 20X5. Purchases (FC6, 250), sales, other expenses, and dividends (FC690) occurred evenly during 20X6. Retained earnings in U.S. dollars at December 31, 20X5, under the temporal method were $316. Exchange rates for calendar 20X6 were as follows:

January 1, 20X6	FC1 $.23
December 31, 20X6	FC1 $.18
Average during 20X6	FC1 $.22
Average during fourth quarter, 20X5	FC1 $.23
Average during fourth quarter, 20X6	FC1 $.19

[35]Peter Fiege, "How 'Uniform' Is Financial Reporting in Germany?—The Example of Foreign Currency Translation," *European Accounting Review* 6, no. 1 (1997): 109–122.

Exhibit 6-12 **Financial Statements of CMP Corporation**		
Balance Sheet	12/31/X5	12/31/X6
Cash	FC 300	FC 500
Accounts receivable (net)	1,300	1,000
Inventories (lower of FIFO cost or market)	1,200	1,500
Fixed assets (net)	9,000	8,000
Total assets	FC 11,800	FC 11,000
Accounts payable	FC 2,200	FC 2,400
Long-term debt	4,400	3,000
Capital stock	2,000	2,000
Retained earnings	3,200	3,600
Total liabilities and owners' equity	FC 11,800	FC 11,000

Income Statement		Year ended 12/31/X6
Sales		FC 10,000
Expenses		
Cost of sales	5,950	
Depreciation (straight-line)	1,000	
Other	1,493	8,443
Operating income		FC 1,557
Income taxes		467
Net income		FC 1,090

Current Rate Method

Translation adjustments under the current rate method arise whenever (1) year-end foreign currency balances are translated at a current rate that differs from that used to translate ending balances of the previous period, and (2) foreign currency financial statements are translated at a current rate that differs from exchange rates used during the period. The translation adjustment is calculated by (1) multiplying the beginning foreign currency net asset balance by the change in the current rate during the period. and (2) multiplying the increase or decrease in net assets during the period by the difference between the average exchange rate and the end-of-period exchange rate. Exhibit 6-13 depicts how the FAS No. 52 translation process applies to these figures.

As can be seen, translation procedures under the current rate method are straightforward. However, the derivation of the beginning cumulative translation adjustment merits some explanation. Assume that calendar 20X6 is the first year in which the current rate method is adopted (e.g., the previous translation method was the temporal method, as the U.S. dollar was considered functional before 20X6). Under this scenario, a one-time translation adjustment would be calculated as of January 1, 20X6. This figure approximates the amount by which beginning stockholders' equity would differ in light of the switch from the temporal to the current rate method. It is calculated by translating CMP Corporation's January 1, 20X6, foreign currency net asset position at the current rate prevailing on that date. (This result simulates what CMP's beginning net asset position would be had it used the current rate method all along.) The difference between this amount and the amount of net assets under the temporal

Exhibit 6-13 Current Rate Method of Translation (Local Currency is Functional Currency)

	Foreign Currency	Exchange Rate	Dollar Equivalents
Balance Sheet Accounts			
Assets			
Cash	FC 500	$.18	$ 90
Accounts receivable	1,000	.18	180
Inventories	1,500	.18	270
Fixed assets	8,000	.18	1,440
Total	FC 11,000		$1,980
Liabilities and Stockholders' Equity			
Accounts payable	FC 2,400	.18	$ 432
Long-term debt	3,000	.18	540
Capital stock	2,000	.17	340
Retained earnings	3,600	a	404
Translation adjustment (cumulative)		b	264
Total	FC 11,000		$1,980
Income Statement Accounts			
Sales	FC 10,000	.22	$2,200
Cost of sales	(5,950)	.22	(1,309)
Depreciation	(1,000)	.22	(220)
Other expenses	(1,493)	.22	(328)
Income before income taxes	FC 1,557		$ 343
Income taxes	(467)	.22	(103)
Net income	FC 1,090		$ 240
Retained earnings, 12/31/X5	3,200		316
Less: dividends	(690)	.22	(152)
Retained earnings, 12/31/X6	FC 3,600		$ 404

a See statement of income and retained earnings.
b The cumulative translation adjustment of $264 is comprised of two parts: (1) the cumulative translation adjustment at the beginning of the year and (2) the translation adjustment for the current year.

method constitutes CMP Corporation's beginning-of-period cumulative translation adjustment, as illustrated here.

Net assets, 12/31/X5 (1/1/X6)		FC 5,200
Multiplied by exchange rate as of 1/1/X6 (FC1 × $.23)		× $.23
Less: As reported stockholders' equity, 12/31/X5:		1,196
Capital stock	$340	
Retained earnings (per temporal method)	316	656
Cumulative translation adjustment, 1/1/X5		$ 540

Given this information, the following steps yield a translation adjustment of $(276) for calendar 20X6.

1. Net assets, 12/31/X5 (1/1/X6)		FC 5,200	
Multiplied by change in current rate:			
Rate, 12/31/X5 (1/1/X6)	FC1 $.23		
Rate, 12/31/X6	FC1 $.18	×$(.05)	$(260)
2. Change in net assets during year		FC 400	
(net income less dividends)			
Multiplied by difference between average			
and year-end rate:			
Average rate	FC1 $.22		
Year-end rate	FC1 $.18	×$(.04)	$ (16)
Total			$(276)

The final cumulative translation adjustment for 20X6 of $264 is reached by adding the $(276) translation adjustment for 20X6 to the beginning balance of $540.

Temporal Method

Exhibit 6-14 illustrates the FAS No. 52 remeasurement process when the dollar is the functional currency.

In contrast to the current rate method, the temporal method translates foreign currency balances using historical as well as current exchange rates. Calculation of the exchange adjustment, which aggregates both transaction and translation gains and losses, also differs. In this example, the first component of the translation adjustment is found by multiplying the beginning net monetary asset position by the change in the current rate during the year. Thus:

$$(12/31/X1 \text{ Monetary assets} - \text{monetary liabilities}) \times \text{change in current rate}$$
$$= (FC1,600 - FC6,600) \times (\$.18 - \$.23)$$
$$= \$250$$

The second component is found by first identifying the variables (i.e., sources and uses of monetary items) that caused the foreign subsidiary's net monetary asset position (exposure) to change, and then multiplying these items by the difference between the year-end exchange rate and the rates that pertain to them. This is illustrated here.

Change in net monetary asset position:

12/31//X5	FC (5,000)
12/31/X6	FC (3,900)
	FC 1,100

Exhibit 6-14   Temporal Method of Translation (U.S. Dollar is Functional Currency)

Currency Rate Equivalents	Foreign	Exchange	Dollar
Balance Sheet Accounts			
Assets			
Cash	FC 500	$.18	$ 90
Accounts receivable	1,000	.18	180
Inventories	1,500	.19	285
Fixed assets	8,000	.17	1,360
Total	FC 11,000		$1,915
Liabilities and Stockholders' Equity			
Accounts payable	FC 2,400	.18	$ 432
Long-term debt	3,000	.18	540
Capital stock	2,000	.17	340
Retained earnings	3,600	a	603
Translation adjustment	—	b	—
Total	FC 11,000		$1,915
Income Statement Accounts			
Sales	FC 10,000	.22	$2,200
Cost of sales	(5,950)	c	(1,366)
Depreciation	(1,000)	.17	(170)
Other expenses	(1,493)	.22	(328)
Aggregate exchange gain (loss)	—	d	206
Income taxes	467	.22	(103)
Net income	FC 1,090		$ 439
Retained earnings, 12/31/X5	3,200		316
Dividends	(690)	.22	(152)
Retained earnings, 12/31/X6	FC 3,600		$ 603

[a] See statement of income and retained earnings.
[b] Under the temporal method, translation adjustments ("gains and losses") appear directly in consolidated income as opposed to stockholders' equity.
[c] The dollar equivalent of cost of sales is derived by translating the components of cost of sales—namely, purchases or cost of production plus beginning and ending inventories by appropriate exchange rates as follows:

Beginning inventories	FC 1,200 at $.23 = $ 276
Purchases	FC 6,250 at $.22 = $1,375
Cost of goods available for sale	$1,651
Ending inventories	FC 1,500 at $.19 = $ 285
Cost of sales	$1,366

[d] The aggregate exchange gain or loss figure combines both transaction and translation gains and losses.

Composition of change:

Sources of monetary items multiplied by difference between year-end and average rate:

Net income	FC 1,090
Depreciation	FC 1,000
	$2,090 \times (.18 - .22) = \$ (84)$

Uses of monetary items multiplied by the difference between the year-end and average rate:

Increase in inventories	FC 300
Dividends	FC <u>690</u>

$$900 \times (.18 - .22) = \$40$$

The aggregate exchange adjustment is the sum of any transaction gain or loss together with the individual translation components derived, that is, $250 + ($84) + $40 = $206.

Selected References

Aiken, M. and D. Ardern, "Choice of Translation Methods in Financial Disclosure: A Test of Compliance With Environmental Hypotheses," *British Accounting Review,* 35 (2003): 327–348.

Ayres, Frances L., and Jacci L. Rodgers, "Further Evidence on the Impact of SFAS 52 on Analysts' Earnings Forecasts," *Journal of International Financial Management and Accounting* (June 1994): 120–141.

Bartov, Eli, "Foreign Currency Exposure of Multinational Firms: Accounting Measures and Market Valuation," *Contemporary Accounting Research* (Winter 1997): 623–652.

Cahan, Steven F., Stephen M. Courtenay, Paul L. Gronewoller, and David Upton, "Value Relevance of Mandated Comprehensive Income," *Journal of Business Finance and Accounting* 27, Nos. 9 & 10 (November/December, 2000): 1273–1301.

Cohen, Benjamin J. "Global Currency Rivalry: Can the Euro Ever Challenge the Dollar?" *Journal of Common Market Studies* 41, No. 4 (2003): 575–595.

Collins, Daniel W., and William K. Salatka, "Noisy Accounting Earnings Signals and Earnings Response Coefficients: The Case of Foreign Currency Accounting," *Contemporary Accounting Research* (Fall 1993): 119–159.

Dhaliwal, D., K. Subra, and R. Trezevant, "Is Comprehensive Income Superior to Net Income as a Measure of Firm Performance?" *Journal of Accounting and Economics* (1999): 43–67.

Estrada, Anette W., and Sander S. Wechsler, "Are You Euro-Fluent?" *Journal of Accountancy* (June 1999): 22–27.

Financial Accounting Standards Board, "Foreign Currency Translation," *Statement of Financial Accounting Standards No. 52*, Stamford, CT: FASB, December 1981.

Goldberg, Stephen R., and Joseph H. Godwin, "Foreign Currency Translation Under Two Cases—Integrated and Isolated Economies," *Journal of International Financial Management and Accounting* (June 1994): 97–119.

Granger, C. J., "Accounting for Foreign Operations—19th Century Contributions to the Accounting Literature," *British Accounting Review* (June 1993): 151–176.

Harris, Trevor S., "Foreign Currency Translation: A Primer," in *Apples to Apples*, New York: Morgan Stanley Dean Witter, March 18, 1999, 28–45.

Houston, Carol Olson, "Foreign Currency Translation Research: A Review and Synthesis," *Journal of Accounting Literature* (1989): 25–48.

International Accounting Standards Committee, "The Effects of Changes in Foreign Exchange Rates," *International Accounting Standard 21* (revised), London: IASC, 1993.

Kirsch, Robert J., and Dawn Becker-Dermer, "Proposed Revisions of International Accounting Standard No. 21 and their Implications for Translation Accounting in Selected English-Speaking Countries," *International Journal of Accounting* 30, no. 1 (1995): 1–24.

Lewis, Henock. "The Value Relevance of the Foreign Translation Adjustment," *Accounting Review* 78, No. 4 (2003): 1027–1047.

Pinto, Jo Ann M. "Foreign Currency Translation Adjustments as Predictors of Earnings

Changes," *Journal of International Accounting, Auditing and Taxes* (2001): 51–69.

Rotenberg, W., "Harmonization of Foreign Currency Translation Practices: Canadian Treatment of Long Term Monetary Items," *International Journal of Accounting* 33, no. 4 (1998): 415–431.

Soo, Billy S., and Lisa Gilbert Soo, "Accounting for the Multinational Firm: Is the Translation Process Valued by the Stock Market?" *Accounting Review* (October 1994): 617–637.

Ziebart, David A., and Jong-Hag Choi, "The Difficulty of Achieving Economic Reality Through Foreign Currency Translation," *International Journal of Accounting* 33, no. 4 (1998): 403–414.

Discussion Questions

1. What is the difference between the *spot, forward,* and *swap* markets? Illustrate each description with an example.

2. What do *current, historical,* and *average* exchange rates mean in the context of foreign currency translation? Which of these rates give rise to translation gains and losses? Which do not?

3. A foreign currency transaction can be *denominated* in one currency, yet *measured* in another. Explain the difference between these two terms using the case of a Canadian dollar borrowing on the part of a Mexican affiliate of a U.S. parent company that designates the U.S. dollar as the functional currency.

4. What is the difference between a *transaction* gain or loss and a *translation* gain or loss?

5. Briefly explain the nature of foreign currency translation as (a) a *restatement process* and (b) a *remeasurement process*.

6. Compare and contrast features of the major foreign currency translation methods introduced in this chapter. Which method do you think is best? Why?

7. Why is the current rate method of translation inconsistent with historical cost? Give an example.

8. Do you agree with the definition of foreign exchange exposure presented in this chapter? Why or why not?

9. Describe the conceptual underpinnings of "functional currency," a key concept in FAS No. 52.

10. How does the treatment of translation gains and losses differ between the current and temporal translation methods under FAS No. 52, and what is the rationale for the differing accounting treatments?

11. What lessons, if any, can be learned from examining the history of foreign currency translation in the United States?

12. FAS No. 52 can be viewed as a practical compromise to the foreign currency translation problem. Do you think FAS No. 52 will end the foreign currency translation debate?

Exercises

1. Assume that your Japanese affiliate reports sales revenue of 250,000 yen. Referring to Exhibit 6-1, translate this revenue figure to U.S. dollars using Friday's spot indirect quote for yen. Do the same using a direct quote.

2. Refer to Exhibit 6-3 in this chapter. Using the information provided, determine the *cross rate* (i.e., a rate computed from two other exchange rates) between the Luxemburg franc and the Dutch guilder, using the methodology required by the European Commission.

3. Company X is headquartered in Country A and reports in the currency unit of Country A, the A$. Company Y is headquartered in Country B and reports in the currency unit of Country B, the Bkr. Company X and Company Y hold identical assets, A$100 and Bkr100, at the beginning and at the end of the year. At the beginning of the year, the exchange rate is A$1 Bkr1.25. At the end of the year, the exchange rate is A$1 Bkr2. No transactions occur during the year.

   Required:
   a. Calculate total assets reported by Company X and Company Y at the beginning and at the end of the year. Which company has a gain and which has a loss for the year?
   b. Does your answer to Question 3 make sense? Would it matter if Companies X and Y intended to repatriate their respective foreign assets rather than keep them invested permanently?
   c. What is the lesson from all of this? Is it all a shell game?

4. On April 1, A. C. Corporation, a calendar-year U.S. electronics manufacturer, buys 32.5 million yen worth of computer chips from the Sando Company paying 10 percent down, the balance to be paid in 3 months. Interest at 8 percent per annum is payable on the unpaid foreign currency balance. The U.S. dollar/Japanese yen exchange rate on April 1 was $1.00 ¥120; on July 1 it was $1.00 ¥110.

   Required: Prepare dated journal entries in U.S. dollars to record the incurrence and settlement of this foreign currency transaction assuming:

   a. A. C. Corporation adopts a single-transaction perspective, and
   b. it employs a two-transactions perspective.

5. On January 20X5, the wholly-owned Mexican affiliate of a Canadian parent company acquired an inventory of computer hard drives for its assembly operation. The cost incurred was 15,000,000 pesos when the exchange rate was 15 pesos = C$1. By year-end, the Mexican affiliate had used three-fourths of the acquired hard drives. Due to advances in hardware technology, the remaining inventory was marked down to its net realizable value of 1,750,000 pesos. The year-end exchange rate was 17 pesos = C$1. The average rate during the year was 16 pesos = C$1.

   Required:
   a. Translate the ending inventory to Canadian dollars assuming the Mexican affiliate's functional currency is the Mexican peso.

b. Would your answer change if the functional currency were the Canadian dollar? Please explain.

6. Dragon Corporation, the Taiwanese affiliate of a U.S. manufacturer, has the balance sheet shown in Exhibit 6-15. The current exchange rate is $.035 = NT $1 (29 Taiwanese dollars to the U.S. dollar).

Required:
a. Translate the Taiwanese dollar balance sheet of Dragon Corporation into U.S. dollars at the current exchange rate of $.035 = NT $1. All monetary accounts in Dragon's balance sheet are denominated in Taiwanese dollars.
b. Assume the Taiwan dollar revalues from $.035 = NT $1 to $.045 = NT $1. What would be the translation effect if Dragon's balance sheet is translated by the current–noncurrent method? By the monetary–nonmonetary method?
c. Assume instead that the Taiwan dollar weakens from $.035 = NT $1 to $.027 = NT $1. What would be the translation effect under each of the two translation methods?

7. Use the information provided in Exercise 6.

Required:
a. What would be the translation effect if Dragon Corporation's balance sheet were translated by the temporal method assuming the Taiwanese dollar appreciates by 25 percent? By the current rate method?
b. If the Taiwanese dollar depreciates by 25 percent, what would be the translation effects under each of the two methods in requirement a?
c. Based on your previous calculations and in Exercise 6, which translation method—current–noncurrent, monetary–nonmonetary, temporal, or current—gives statement readers the most meaningful information?

8. A 100 percent–owned foreign subsidiary's trial balance consists of the accounts listed as follows. Which exchange rate—current, historical, or average—would be used to translate these accounts to dollars assuming that the foreign currency is the functional currency? Which rates would be used if the U.S. dollar were the functional currency?

Exhibit 6-15   Balance Sheet of Dragon Corporation (000,000's)

Assets		Liabilities	
Cash	NT $ 5,000	Accounts payable	NT $21,000
Accounts receivable	14,000	Long-term debt	27,000
Inventories[a] (cost = 24,000)	22,000		
Fixed assets, net	39,000	Stockholders' equity	32,000
Total assets	NT $80,000	Total liab & SE	NT $80,000

[a]Inventories are carried at the lower of cost or market.

Trial Balance Accounts	
Cash	Common stock
Marketable securities (cost)	Premium on common stock
Accounts receivable	Retained earnings
Inventory (market)	Sales
Equipment	Purchases
Accumulated depreciation	Cost of sales
Prepaid expenses	General and administrative expenses
Goodwill	Selling expenses
Accounts payable	Depreciation
Due to parent (denominated in dollars)	Amortization of goodwill
Bonds payable	Income tax expense
Income taxes payable	Intercompany interest expense
Deferred income taxes	

9. U.S. Multinational Corporation's subsidiary in Bangkok has on its books fixed assets valued at 7,500,000 baht. One-third of the assets were acquired 2 years ago when the exchange rate was B40 = $1. The other fixed assets were acquired last year when the exchange rate was B38 = $1. Each layer of fixed assets is being depreciated straight-line with an estimated useful life of 20 years. Relevant exchange rates for the current year are:
    Year-end rate: B36 = $1
    Average rate: B37 = $1

    Required:
    a. Calculate the Thai subsidiary's depreciation expense for the current year, assuming the baht is the functional currency.
    b. Repeat requirement a, assuming instead that the U.S. dollar is the functional currency.

10. Trojan Corporation USA borrowed 1,000,000 Australian dollars at the beginning of the calendar year when the exchange rate was $.54 = A$1. Before repaying this 1-year loan, Trojan Corporation learns that the Australian dollar has depreciated to $.46 = A$1. It also discovers that its Australian subsidiary has an exposed net asset position of A$3,000,000, which will produce a translation loss upon consolidation. What is the exchange gain or loss that will be reported in consolidated income if
    a. The U.S. dollar is the foreign operation's functional currency?
    b. The Australian dollar is the foreign operation's functional currency?

11. On December 15, A.C. Corporation acquires 100 percent of the net assets of the Sando Company based in Tokyo, Japan, for ¥60,000,000. At the time, the exchange rate was $1.00 = ¥105. The acquisition price is traceable to the following identifiable assets:

Cash	¥6,450,000
Inventory	16,000,000
Fixed assets	37,550,000

As a calendar-year company, A.C. Corporation prepares consolidated financial statements every December 31. However, by the consolidation date, the Japanese yen depreciates such that the new spot rate is $1.00 = ¥115.

Required:
a. Assuming no transactions took place before consolidation, what would be the translation gain or loss if Sando's balance sheet were translated to dollars by the temporal rate method?
b. How does the translation adjustment affect A.C. Corporation's cash flows?

12. Reproduced below is the interim consolidated income statement for Alcan Inc.

Required: Using the information provided in Alcan's press release, disclosed at the beginning of this chapter, determine where Alcan is disclosing its foreign currency translation gains or losses during the period. Would you take into account these gains and losses in evaluating Alcan's operating performance? Do you think an average investor, who has not had any exposure to foreign exchange accounting, would agree with you?

Alcan Inc.
Interim Consolidated Statement of Income
Periods ended September 30
(in millions of US$)
(unaudited)

	Third Quarter	
	20X3	*20X2*
Sales and operating revenues	**3,480**	3,170
Costs and expenses		
Cost of sales and operating expenses	2,741	2,499
Depreciation and amortization	237	207
Selling, administrative, and general expenses	186	136
Research and development expenses	34	28
Interest (note 3)	52	52
Restructuring, impairment, and other special charges	5	6
Other expenses (income) – net	33	(12)
Income from continuing operations before taxes and other items	192	254
Income taxes	77	64
Income from continuing operations before other items	115	190
Equity income (loss)	2	(1)
Minority interests	1	3
Income from continuing operations	**118**	192
Loss from discontinued operations (note 2)	(18)	(1)
Net income	**100**	191

CASE 6-1   REGENTS CORPORATION

Regents Corporation is a recently acquired U.S. manufacturing subsidiary located on the outskirts of London. Its products are marketed principally in the United Kingdom with sales invoiced in pounds and prices determined by local competitive conditions. Expenses (labor, materials, and other production costs) are mostly local, although a significant quantity of components is now imported from the U.S. parent. Financing is primarily in U.S. dollars provided by the parent.

Headquarters management must decide on the functional currency for its London operation: Should it be the U.S. dollar or the British pound? You are asked to advise management on the appropriate currency designation and its relative financial statement effects. Prepare a report that supports your recommendations and identify any policy issues your analysis uncovers.

Exhibit 6-16 on page 228 presents comparative balance sheets for Regents Corporation at December 31, 20X5 and 20X6, and a statement of income for the year ended December 31, 20X6. The statements conform with U.S. generally accepted accounting principles prior to translation to dollars.

CASE 6-2   MANAGING OFFSHORE INVESTMENTS: WHOSE CURRENCY?

The Offshore Investment Fund (OIF) was incorporated in Fairfield, Connecticut, for the sole purpose of allowing U.S. shareholders to invest in Spanish securities. The fund is listed on the New York Stock Exchange. The fund custodian is the Shady Rest Bank and Trust Company of Connecticut ("Shady Rest"), which keeps the fund's accounts. The question of which currency to use in keeping the fund's books arose at once. Shady Rest prepared the fund's books in euros, since the fund was a country fund that invested solely in securities listed on the Madrid Stock Exchange. Subsequently, the fund's auditors stated that, in their opinion, the functional currency should be the U.S. dollar. This case is based on an actual occurrence. Names and country of origin have been changed to ensure anonymity.

EFFECTS OF THE DECISION

The decision to possibly adopt the U.S. dollar as the functional currency for the fund created considerable managerial headaches. For one thing, the work of rewriting and reworking the accounting transactions was a monumental task that delayed the publication of the annual accounts. The concept of the functional currency was a foreign concept in Spain, and the effects of the functional currency choice were not made clear

Exhibit 6-16 Regents Corporation Financial Statements

Balance Sheet	12/31/X5	12/31/X6
Assets		
Cash	£ 1,060	£ 1,150
Accounts receivable	2,890	3,100
Inventory (FIFO)	3,040	3,430
Fixed assets	4,400	4,900
-Accumulated depreciation	(420)	(720)
Intangible asset (patent)		70
Total	£10,970	£11,930
Liabilities and Stockholders' Equity		
Accounts payable	£ 1,610	£ 1,385
Due to parent	1,800	1,310
Long-term debt	4,500	4,000
Deferred taxes	80	120
Common stock	1,500	1,500
Retained earnings	1,480	3,615
Total	£10,970	£11,930

Income Statement Year Ended 12/31/X6		
Sales		£16,700
Expenses		
Cost of sales	£11,300	
General and administrative	1,600	
Depreciation	300	
Interest	480	13,680
Operating income		£ 3,020
Transaction gain (loss)		125
Income before taxes		£ 3,145
Income taxes Current	£ 670	
Deferred	40	710
Net income		£ 2,435
Retained earnings at 12/31/X5		1,480
		3,915
Dividends		300
Retained earnings at 12/31/X6		£ 3,615

EXH Exchange rate information and additional data:
1. Exchange rates:

December 31, 20X5	$1.50 = £1
December 31, 20X6	$1.60 = £1
Average during 20X6	$1.56 = £1
Average during fourth quarter 20X5	$1.48 = £1
Average during fourth quarter 20X6	$1.58 = £1

2. Common stock was acquired, long-term debt issued, and original fixed assets purchased when the exchange rate was $1.40 = £1.
3. **Due to parent** account is denominated in U.S. dollars.
4. Exchange rate prevailing when the intangible asset (patent) was acquired and additional fixed assets purchased was $1.52 = £1.
5. Purchases and dividends occurred evenly during 20X6.
6. Of the £300 depreciation expense for 20X6, £20 relates to fixed assets purchased during 20X6.
7. Deferred taxes are translated at the current rate.
8. Inventory represents approximately 3 months of production.

to the managers. Consequently, they continued to manage the fund until late in November without appreciating the impact the currency choice had on the fund's results.

Additional difficulties caused by the functional currency choice were:

a. Shady Rest, with some $300 billion in various funds under management, still had not developed an adequate multi-currency accounting system. Whereas accounting for a security acquisition would normally be recorded in a simple bookkeeping entry, three entries were now required. In addition, payment for the purchase itself could impact the income statement in the current period.

b. More serious problems related to day-to-day operations. When a transaction was initiated, the fund manager had no idea of its ultimate financial effect. As an example, during the first year of operations, the Fund manager was certain that his portfolio sales had generated a profit of more than $1 million. When the sales finally showed up in the accounts, the transaction gain was offset by currency losses of some $7 million!

REASONS GIVEN FOR CHOOSING THE DOLLAR AS FUNCTIONAL

The auditors gave the following reasons for choosing the dollar as the fund's functional currency:

a. Incorporation in the United States
b. Funded with U.S. shareholder capital
c. Dividends determined and paid in U.S. dollars
d. Financial reporting under U.S. GAAP and in U.S. dollars
e. Administration and advisory fees calculated on U.S. net assets and paid in U.S. dollars

f. Most expenses incurred and paid in U.S. dollars
g. Accounting records kept in U.S. dollars
h. Subject to U.S. tax, SEC, and 1940 Exchange Act regulations

Since the fund was set up to invest in Spain, it is assumed that U.S. shareholders are interested in the impact of an exchange rate change on the fund's cash flows and equity; that is, the shareholders do not invest in Spanish securities only because of attractive yields, but also are making a currency play that directly affects the measurement of cash flow and equity.

MANAGEMENT'S VIEWPOINT

Management disagreed with the auditors. Following is its rebuttal:

a. *Incorporation in the United States with U.S. shareholders.* FAS 52 clearly states that the functional currency should be determined by "the primary economic environment in which that entity operates rather than by the technical detail of incorporation." Similarly, nowhere does FAS 52 state that the facts that the company has U.S. shareholders and pays dividends in U.S. dollars are relevant. In fact, FAS 52 concerns itself throughout with the firm and its management rather than its shareholders.

b. *Financial reporting in U.S. dollars under U.S. GAAP.* The auditors fail to differentiate between reporting currency and functional currency. It is clear that the U.S. dollar should be the reporting currency, but that alone does not mean that the U.S. dollar is the functional currency.

c. *Payment of certain expenses in dollars.* The payment of expenses in U.S. dollars is no reason to make the dollar the functional currency. While expenses of some $8 million for calendar year 20X5 were incurred in U.S. dollars, income of over $100 million was earned in euros.

d. *U.S. tax and SEC regulations.* These considerations are relevant for the reporting currency, not the functional currency.

The decisive argument against identifying the dollar as the functional currency is that doing so does not provide information that is, in the words of FAS 52, "generally compatible with the expected economic effect of a rate change on an enterprise's cash flow and equity." Specifically, the operating cash flow of the Fund is located entirely in Spain once the initial transfer of funds raised by the issue of capital is made. The Fund buys and sells investments in Spain, and receives all its income from Spain. If the functional currency is euros, then realized currency fluctuations are recognized only when money is repatriated to the United States. The present practice of "realizing" an exchange profit or loss when, for example, cash in Spain is exchanged for an investment purchased in Spain is wrong and misleading.

Consider an example. Suppose that the fund deposits €100,000,000 in a Spanish bank when the exchange rate is €1 = $0.8496. One week later, when the exchange rate is €1 = $0.8393, the fund purchases and pays for an investment of €100,000,000, which it sells for cash on the same day, having decided the investment was unwise. Ignoring transaction costs, the fund has €100,000,000 in cash in Madrid at both the beginning and the end of the week. If the functional currency is euros, there is no realized gain or loss. However, translation to dollars generates an unrealized currency loss of $1,030,000, which would be realized only when the amount in question is repatriated to the United States. This is analogous to the purchase of a stock whose price later falls. If the U.S. dollar is the functional currency, the transaction in question would result in a realized loss on exchange of $1,030,000. This

result is absurd in terms of any common-sense view of cash flow; indeed, it highlights that, given the fund's purpose, the effect on the reporting of income of adopting the U.S. dollar as the functional currency is equally absurd.

The net asset value of the fund is determined each week in U.S. dollars, and reported to stockholders in U.S. dollars. This is entirely consistent with having the U.S. dollar as the appropriate reporting currency. Using the dollar as the functional currency implies that there is a realistic and practical option on each transaction of moving between the dollar and the euro. This assumption is patently wrong; the fund will only repatriate its base capital under two circumstances: (1) liquidation or (2) as a temporary expedient if Spanish yields fall below U.S. yields.

GENERAL THRUST OF FAS 52

The language of FAS 52 indicates that its authors did not write it with direct reference to a situation such as that of the Offshore Investment Fund, that is, a company that raises money for the single purpose of investing it in a foreign country. FAS 52 seems rather to be written from the viewpoint of an operating holding company owning a separate, distinct foreign operating subsidiary.

FAS 52 defines the functional currency of an entity as the currency of the primary economic environment in which that entity operates. Had the fund been incorporated in Malta and, as a separate entity, borrowed the funds from its U.S. parent, use of the local currency would have been automatic. If substance is to prevail over form, one must conclude that the euro should still be used.

Paragraph 6 of FAS 52 states, "for an entity with operations that are relatively self-contained and integrated within a particular country, the functional currency generally would be the currency of that country." This statement reinforces the operational aspect that governs the choice of the functional currency; it is surely wrong to argue that the operations of the fund are conducted anywhere but in Spain.

Paragraph 8 reinforces the contention that "management's judgment will be required to determine the functional currency in which financial results and relationships are measured with the greatest degree of relevance and reliability."

Finally, paragraphs 80 and 81 draw a very clear distinction that reinforces our (management's) contention. Paragraph 80 reads:

> In the first class are foreign operations that are relatively self-contained and integrated within a particular country or economic environment. The day-to-day operations are not dependent upon the economic environment of the parent's functional currency; the foreign operation primarily generates and expends foreign currency. The foreign currency net cash flows that it generates may be reinvested and converted and

distributed to the parent. For this class, the foreign currency is the functional currency.

This definition should be contrasted with paragraph 81, which states:

> In the second class . . . the day-to-day operations are dependent on the economic environment of the parent's currency, and the changes in the foreign entity's individual assets and liabilities impact directly on the cash flows of the parent company in the parent's currency. For this class, the U.S. dollar is the functional currency.

Since the purpose of single-country funds is to create entities of the first rather than the second class, paragraph 80 precisely describes the operations of the Overseas Investment Fund.

REQUIRED

Based on the arguments presented, what do you think should be the functional currency in this case?

CHAPTER

7

FINANCIAL REPORTING AND CHANGING PRICES

Fluctuating currencies and changes in money prices of goods and services are integral features of international business. Chapter 6 focused on the former. This chapter dwells on the financial statement effects of changing prices.

Grupo Modello S.A., the largest beer manufacturer in Mexico, operates in an environment where changing prices have been nontrivial. To see if these price changes are reflected in the company's published accounts, examine Exhibit 7-1, which contains selected excerpts from Grupo Modello S.A.'s financial statements and related notes.

A quick scan of Modelo's income statement reveals an account, labeled *Integral results from financing.* Two of its components should be familiar to you. The first relates to interest on the firm's receivables and payables. The second, discussed in Chapter 6, is the translation gains or losses resulting from the currency translation process [examine footnote 2. d) in Exhibit 7-1]. The third component, *Loss from monetary position,* is probably new to you and stems from Modelo's attempts to reflect the effects of changing prices on its financial accounts. But what does this figure mean and how is it derived?

Grupo Modelo's balance sheet also introduces financial statement items that are unfamiliar to most statement readers. The first relates to its fixed assets. Footnote 6 suggests that the 2002 balance of P35,680,073 for Property, Plant, and Equipment, net of accumulated depreciation, consists of two components: one labeled *Net historical cost,* the other, *Net restatement.* While the former may be a familiar term, the latter probably is not. Another novel balance sheet account appears in stockholders' equity, labeled *Insufficiency in Restatement of Stockholders' Equity.*

Finally, footnote 2. c) states that all figures disclosed in Model's comparative statements, and notes thereto, are expressed in December 2002 purchasing power. What does the term "December 2002 purchasing power" mean and what is its rationale? And, more importantly, do statement readers actually impound the foregoing information in their security pricing and managerial decisions?

Subsequent sections of this chapter are devoted to answering these and related questions. The managerial implications of changing prices are covered in Chapter 10. To make informed decisions, financial analysts must understand the contents of financial accounts that have been adjusted for changing prices. Moreover, they must have some facility for adjusting accounts for changing prices in those instances where companies choose not to account for price changes so as to facilitate apple-to-apple comparisons over time and/or with companies that do.

Exhibit 7-1   Selected Excerpts from Grupo Modelo's Financial Accounts

GRUPO MODELO S.A. DE C.V. AND SUBSIDIARIES

Consolidated Income Statements

For the years ended December 31, 2002 and 2001

(Amounts in thousands of constant Mexican pesos as of December 2002)

	2002	2001
Operating profit	P 9,425,260	P 8,301,265
Other (expenses) and income, net	(276,756)	388,019
Integral results from financing:		
Interest earned and paid, net	623,517	752,600
Foreign exchange profit(loss), net	48,562	(25,257)
Loss from monetary position	(556,924)	(326,215)
	115,155	401,128
Profit before provisions	9,263,659	9,090,412
Provisions for (Note 10)		
Income and asset tax	2,796,437	3,063,702
Employees' profit sharing	820,234	727,757
	3,616,671	3,791,459
Consolidated net income for the year	P 5,646,988	P 5,298,953

CONSOLIDATED BALANCE SHEETS

As of December 31, 2002 and 2001 (Notes 1, 2, and 13)

(Amounts in thousands of constant Mexican pesos as of December 31, 2002)

Assets	2002	2001
Current		
Cash and marketable securities	P 10,221,902	8,775,867
Accounts and notes receivable (Note 3)	1,098,013	1,099,054
Inventories (Note 4)	4,871,564	4,764,754
Prepaid expenses and other current items	2,125,205	2,060,270
Total current assets	P 18,316,684	16,699,945
Property, Plant, and Equipment (Note 6)	52,123,316	50,684,422
Accumulated depreciation	(16,443,243)	(15,939,462)
	35,680,073	34,744,960
Stockholders' Equity		
Common Stock (Note 8)	13,421,848	13,421,848
Premium on Share Subscription	893,865	893,865
Accumulated income (Note 10):		
Legal reserve	1,234,596	1,046,890
Reserve for acquisition of own shares	564,596	564,596
Retained earnings	20,772,655	18,249,244
Profit for the year	4,255,750	3,829,312
	26,797,597	23,690,042

(*continued*)

Exhibit 7-1   Selected Excerpts from Grupo Modelo's Financial Accounts (*Continued*)

Assets	2002	2001
Initial effect of deferred tax	(4,485,183)	(4,485,183)
Adjustment to capital for labor obligations upon retirement (Note 7)	(504,164)	(545,124)
Insufficiency in Restatement of Stockholders' Equity	(521,459)	(414,903)
Total majority stockholders' equity	35,602,504	32,560,545

NOTES TO THE CONSOLIDATED FINANCIAL STATEMENTS

As of December 31, 2002 and 2001

(Amounts in thousands of constant Mexican pesos as of December 31, 2002)

2. *Accounting policies*

The main accounting policies applied by the Group in the preparation of the consolidated financial statements are in line with generally accepted accounting principles in Mexico. These accounting principles require that Group Management makes estimates based on circumstances and apply certain assumptions in determining valuation of some items included in the consolidated financial statements.

c) **Comparability**—The figures shown in the consolidated financial statements and the notes thereto are stated consistently in Mexican pesos at the purchasing power of December 31, 2002, by applying factors derived from the National Consumer Price Index (NCPI).

d) **Translation of the financial information of subsidiaries located abroad**—Translation of the financial information of the subsidiaries abroad to Mexican pesos, required for consolidation, was conducted in accordance with the guidelines of Bulletin B-15 "Transactions in Foreign Currency and Translation of the Financial Statements of Operations Abroad," issued by MIPA, through the method of integrated foreign operations. The free-purchase exchange rate of P10.25 per U.S. dollar (P9.11 in 2001) was used in translating monetary items; nonmonetary items and the income statement were translated into Mexican pesos at the exchange rates prevailing on the dates on which the transactions that originated them were carried out. The effects derived from this translation are shown in the integral result from financing.

1. Property, Plant, and Equipment—Net

a) The balance of this account is made up as follows:

	2002			2001
Item	*Net historical cost*	*Net restatement*	*Net total value*	*Net total value*
Land	P 1,083,022	P 2,699,656	P 3,782,678	P 3,585,016
Machinery and equipment	7,640,449	6,670,296	14,310,745	13,861,805
Transportation equipment	3,886,936	5,554,278	9,441,214	8,711,321
Computer equipment	218,625	23,319	241,944	225,251
Furniture and other equip.	226,313	141,895	368,208	210,959
Antipollution equipment	453,797	224,506	678,303	617,585
Construction in progress	4,084,605	308,133	4,392,738	5,040,120
	P 19,318,956	P 16,361,117	P 35,680,073	P 34,744,960

Depreciation for the period amounted to P1,736,614 (P1,677,868 in 2001).

CHANGING PRICES DEFINED

To understand what the term *changing prices* means, we must distinguish between general and specific price movements, both of which are embraced by the term. A *general price level change* occurs when, on average, the prices of *all* goods and services in an economy change. The monetary unit gains or loses purchasing power. An overall increase in prices is called *inflation;* a decrease, *deflation.* What causes inflation? Evidence suggests that aggressive monetary and fiscal policies designed to achieve high economic growth targets, excessive spending associated with national elections, and the international transmission of inflation are causal explanations.[1] The issue, however, is complex.

A *specific price change,* on the other hand, refers to a change in the price of a specific good or service caused by changes in demand and supply. Thus, the annual rate of inflation in a country may average 5 percent while the specific price of one-bedroom apartments may rise by 50 percent during the same period. Exhibit 7-2 defines additional terminology used in this chapter.

Exhibit 7-2   Glossary of Inflation Accounting Terms

attribute.   The quantifiable characteristic of an item that is measured for accounting purposes. For example, historical cost and replacement cost are attributes of an asset.

current cost adjustments.   Adjusting asset values for changes in specific prices.

disposable wealth.   The amount of a firm's net assets that could be withdrawn without reducing its beginning level of net assets.

gearing adjustment.   The benefit to shareholders' purchasing power gain from debt financing and signals that the firm need not recognize the additional replacement cost of operating assets to the extent they are financed by debt. The U.S. expression for gearing is leverage.

general purchasing power equivalents.   Currency amounts that have been adjusted for changes in the general level of prices.

general purchasing gains and losses.   *See* **monetary gains and losses.**

historical cost-constant currency.   *See* **general purchasing power equivalents.**

holding gain.   Increase in the current cost of a nonmonetary asset.

hyperinflation.   An excessive rate of inflation as when the general level of prices in an economy increases by more than 25 percent per annum.

inflation.   Increase in the general level of prices of all goods and services in an economy.

monetary asset.   A claim to a fixed amount of currency in the future, like cash or accounts receivable.

monetary gains.   Increases in general purchasing power that occur when monetary liabilities are held during a period of inflation.

monetary liability.   An obligation to pay a fixed amount of currency in the future such as an account payable or debt that bears a fixed rate of interest.

monetary losses.   Decreases in general purchasing power that occur when monetary assets are held during a period of inflation.

(continued)

---

[1] John F. Boschen and Charles L. Weise, "What Starts Inflation: Evidence from the OECD Countries," *Journal of Money, Credit and Banking* (June 2003): 323.

Exhibit 7-2 Glossary of Inflation Accounting Terms (*Continued*)

monetary working capital adjustment. The effect of specific price changes on the total amount of working capital used by the business in its operations.

nominal amounts. Currency amounts that have not been adjusted for changing prices.

nonmonetary asset. An asset that does not represent a fixed claim to cash, such as inventory or plant and equipment.

nonmonetary liability. A debt that does not require the payment of a fixed sum of cash in the future such as a customer advance. Here the obligation is to provide the customer a good or service whose value may change because of inflation.

parity adjustment. An adjustment that reflects the difference in inflation between the parent and host countries.

permanent assets. A Brazilian term for fixed assets, buildings, investments, deferred charges and their respective depreciation, and depletion or amortization amounts.

price index. A cost ratio where the numerator is the cost of a representative "basket" of goods and services in the current year and the denominator is the cost of the same basket of goods and services in a benchmark year.

purchasing power. The general ability of a monetary unit to command goods and services.

real profit. Net income that has been adjusted for changing prices.

replacement cost. The current cost of replacing the service potential of an asset in the normal course of business.

reporting currency. The currency in which an entity prepares its financial statements.

restate-translate method. Used when a parent company consolidates the accounts of a foreign subsidiary located in an inflationary environment. With this method, first the subsidiary's accounts are restated for local inflation, and then are translated to parent currency.

specific price change. The change in the price of a specific commodity, such as inventory or equipment.

translate-restate method. A consolidation method that first translates a foreign subsidiary's accounts to parent currency and then restates the translated amounts for parent country inflation.

As consumers, we are well aware of inflation's effects on our material standard of living. We immediately feel its impact on our pocketbooks when the price of oil (and hence, gasoline) or a Big Mac increases. The social and political devastation resulting from bouts of hyperinflation (i.e., when the inflation rate soars by more than 50% per month) are well documented[2] and explain why stable prices are a national priority for much of the world.[3] Businesses also feel inflation's effects when the prices of their factor inputs rise.

While changing prices occur worldwide, their business and financial reporting effects vary from country to country. Europe and North America, for instance, have enjoyed relatively modest general price-level increases, averaging less than 3 percent per year during the last decade. By contrast, Eastern Europe, Latin America, and Africa have experienced much higher inflation rates. Annual rates of inflation have been as high as 106 percent in Turkey, 2,076 percent in Brazil, and 540% in the Congo.[4]

---

[2]Peter Bernolz, *Monetary Regimes and Inflation,* Surrey, UK: Edward Elgar, 2003.
[3]Laurence H. Meyer, "Inflation Targets and Inflation Targeting," *North American Journal of Economics and Finance* 13 (2002): 147–162.
[4]For quotes on current inflation rates, click on www.nationamaster.com and www.worldfactsnow.com.

Local inflation affects exchange rates used to translate foreign currency balances to their domestic currency equivalents. As we shall see, it is hard to separate foreign currency translation from inflation when accounting for foreign operations.

WHY ARE FINANCIAL STATEMENTS POTENTIALLY MISLEADING DURING PERIODS OF CHANGING PRICES?

During a period of inflation, asset values recorded at their original acquisition costs seldom reflect their current (higher) value. Understated asset values result in understated expenses and overstated income. From a managerial perspective, these measurement inaccuracies distort (1) financial projections based on unadjusted historical time series data, (2) budgets against which results are measured, and (3) performance data that fail to isolate the uncontrollable effects of inflation. Overstated earnings may in turn lead to:

- Increases in proportionate taxation
- Requests by shareholders for more dividends
- Demands for higher wages by workers
- Disadvantageous actions by host governments (e.g., imposition of excess profit taxes)

Should a firm distribute all of its overstated earnings (in the form of higher taxes, dividends, wages, and the like), it may not keep enough resources to replace specific assets whose prices have risen, such as inventories and plant and equipment.

Failure to adjust corporate financial data for changes in the purchasing power of the monetary unit also makes it hard for financial statement readers to interpret and compare reported operating performances of companies. In an inflationary period, revenues are typically expressed in currency with a lower general purchasing power (i.e., purchasing power of the current period) than applies to the related expenses. Expenses are expressed in currency with a higher general purchasing power because typically they reflect the consumption of resources that were acquired when the monetary unit had more purchasing power. Subtracting expenses based on historical purchasing power from revenues based on current purchasing power results in an inaccurate measure of income. Conventional accounting procedures also ignore purchasing power gains and losses that arise from holding cash (or equivalents) during an inflationary period. If you held cash during a year in which the inflation rate was 100 percent, it would take twice as much cash at the end of the year to have the same purchasing power as your original cash balance. This further distorts business performance comparisons for financial statement readers.

Therefore, it is useful to recognize inflation's effects explicitly for several reasons:

1. The effects of changing prices depend partially on the transactions and circumstances of an enterprise. Users do not have detailed information about these factors.
2. Managing the problems caused by changing prices depends on an accurate understanding of the problems. An accurate understanding requires that business performance be reported in terms that allow for the effects of changing prices.

3. Statements by managers about the problems caused by changing prices are easier to believe when businesses publish financial information that addresses those problems.[5]

Even when inflation rates slow, accounting for changing prices is useful because the cumulative effect of low inflation over time can be significant. As examples, the cumulative inflation rate in the United States during the past decade was 28 percent; it was 17.5 percent for Singapore and 36.8 percent for Italy for the same time period. The distorting effects of prior inflation can also persist for many years, given the long lives of many assets. And, as mentioned earlier, specific price changes may be significant even when the general price level does not change much.

TYPES OF INFLATION ADJUSTMENTS

Statistical series that measure changes in both general and specific prices do not generally move in parallel.[6] Each type of price change has a different effect on measures of a firm's financial position and operating performance and is accounted for with different objectives in mind. Hereafter, accounting for the financial statement effects of general price-level changes is called the *historical cost-constant purchasing power* model. Accounting for specific price changes is referred to as the *current cost* model.

GENERAL PRICE-LEVEL ADJUSTMENTS

Currency amounts adjusted for general price-level (purchasing power) changes are called *historical cost-constant currency* or *general purchasing power equivalents*. Currency amounts that have not been so adjusted are called *nominal amounts*. For example, during a period of rising prices, a long-lived asset that is on the balance sheet at its original acquisition cost is expressed in *nominal* currency. When its historical cost is allocated to the current period's income (in the form of depreciation expense), revenues, which reflect current purchasing power, are matched with costs that reflect the (higher) purchasing power of the earlier period when the asset was bought. Therefore, nominal amounts must be adjusted for changes in the general purchasing power of money to match them appropriately with current transactions.

Price Indexes
General price-level changes are measured by a price level index of the form $\Sigma p_1 q_1 / \Sigma p_0 q_0$, where p = price of a given commodity and q = quantity consumed. A price index is a cost ratio. For example, if a family of four spends $20,000 to buy a representative basket of goods and services at the end of year 1 (the base year = start of year 2) and

[5]Financial Accounting Standards Board, "Financial Reporting and Changing Prices," *Statement of Financial Accounting Standards No. 33*, Stamford, CT: FASB, September 1979.
[6]Carlos Dabus, "Inflationary Regimes and Relative Price Variability: Evidence from Argentina," *Journal of Development Economics* 62 (2000): 535–547.

$22,000 to buy that same basket a year later (start of year 3), the year-end price index for year 2 is $22,000/$20,000, or 1.100. This figure implies a 10 percent rate of inflation during year 2. Similarly, if the basket in question costs our family of four $23,500 2 years later (end of year 3), the general price-level index would be $23,500/$20,000, or 1.175, implying 17.5 percent inflation since the base year. The index for the base year is $20,000/$20,000, or 1.000.

Use of Price Indexes.

Price index numbers are used to translate sums of money paid in past periods to their end-of-period purchasing power equivalents (i.e., historical cost-constant purchasing power).The method used is as follows:

$$GPL_c/GPL_{td} \times \text{Nominal amount}_{td} = PPE_c$$

where

GPL = general price index
c   = current period
td   = transaction date
PPE = general purchasing power equivalent

For example, suppose that $500 is spent at the end of the base year and $700 1 year later. To restate these expenditures at their year 3 purchasing power equivalents, using price index numbers from our example, we would do the following:

End of:	Nominal Expenditure	Adjustment Factor	Year 3 Purchasing Power Equivalent
Year 1	$500	1.175/1.000	$587.50
Year 2	$700	1.175/1.100	$747.73

It would take $587.50 at the end of year 2 to buy (in general) what $500 would have bought at the end of year 1. Similarly, it would take $747.73 at the end of year 3 to buy (in general) what $700 would have bought a year earlier. Alternatively, during a period of inflation, the nominal expenditures of $500 at the end of year 1, and $700 a year later, are not comparable unless they are expressed in terms of a common denominator, which is year 3 general purchasing power equivalents. This is why Grupo Modello, cited earlier in the chapter, restates all of its trend data to December 31, 20X6, purchasing power.

Price-level adjusted figures do not represent the current cost of the items in question; they are still historical cost numbers. The historical cost numbers are merely restated in a new unit of measure—general purchasing power at the end of the period. When transactions occur uniformly throughout a period (such as revenues from the sale of goods or services), a shortcut price-level adjustment can be used. In expressing revenues as end-of-period purchasing power equivalents, rather than price-level adjusting each day's revenues (365 calculations!), one could multiply total annual revenues by the ratio of the year-end index to the average general price-level index (such as a monthly weighted average) for the year. Thus:

$$GPL_c / GPL_{avg} \times \text{Total revenues} = PPE_c$$

Object of General Price-Level Adjustments

Let us briefly review the conventional notion of enterprise income. Traditionally, income (disposable wealth) is that portion of a firm's wealth (i.e., net assets) that the firm can withdraw during an accounting period without reducing its wealth beneath its original level. Assuming no additional owner investments or withdrawals during the period, if a firm's beginning net assets were £ 30,000 and its ending net assets increased to £ 45,000 due to profitable operations, its income would be £ 15,000. If it paid a dividend of £ 15,000, the firm's end-of-period wealth would be exactly what it was at the beginning. Hence, conventional accounting measures income as the maximum amount that can be withdrawn from the firm without reducing its original money capital.

If we cannot assume stable prices, the conventional measure of income may not accurately measure a firm's disposable wealth. Assume that the general price-level rises by 21 percent during a year. To keep up with inflation, a firm that begins the year with $100 would want its original investment to grow to at least $121, because it would take that much at year's-end to buy what $100 would have bought at the beginning. Suppose that, using conventional accounting, the firm earns $50 (after tax). Withdrawing $50 would reduce the firm's nominal end-of-period wealth to the original $100, less than it needs to keep up with inflation ($121). The historical cost-constant purchasing power model takes this discrepancy into account by measuring income so that the firm could pay out its entire income as dividends while having as much purchasing power at the end of the period as at the beginning.

To illustrate, suppose that an Argentine merchandiser begins the calendar year with AP 100,000 in cash (no debt), which is immediately converted into salable inventory (e.g., 10,000 compact discs of an Argentinian rock star at a unit cost of 10 pesos). The firm sells the entire inventory uniformly during the year at a 50 percent markup. Assuming no inflation, enterprise income would be AP 50,000, the difference between ending and beginning net assets ($150,000 − $100,000), or as revenue minus expenses (cost of CDs sold). Withdrawal of AP 50,000 would leave the firm with AP 100,000, as much money capital as at the start of the year, maintaining its original investment.

Suppose instead that the period had a 21 percent inflation rate with the general price level (1.21 at year-end) averaging 1.10 during the year. Inflation-adjusted income would be measured (in thousands) as follows:

	Nominal Pesos	Adjustment Factor	Constant Pesos
Revenues	AP 150	1.21/1.10	AP 165
− Expenses	100	1.21/1.00	121
Operating income	AP 50		AP 44
− Monetary loss	—		15
Net income	AP 50		AP 29

In these calculations, sales took place at the same rate throughout the year, so they are adjusted by the ratio of the end-of-year index to the year's average price index. Because the inventory sold during the year was bought at the beginning of the year, cost of sales is adjusted by the ratio of the year-end index to the beginning-of-year index.

Where did the monetary loss come from? During inflation, firms will have changes in wealth that are unrelated to operating activities. These arise from *monetary assets or liabilities,* claims to or obligations to pay a fixed amount of currency in the future. Monetary assets include cash and accounts receivable, which generally lose purchasing power during periods of inflation. Monetary liabilities include most payables, which generally create purchasing power gains during inflation. In our example, the firm received and held cash during a period when cash lost purchasing power. As inventory was sold for cash, cash was received uniformly throughout the year. The firm's cash balance at the end of the year is only AP 150,000, resulting in a AP 15,000 loss in general purchasing power (a monetary loss) despite AP 165,000 in revenue. This explains the *Loss from monetary position* figure appearing in Grupo Modelo's income statement cited earlier. During 20X5 and 20X6, Modelo had more monetary assets on its books than monetary liabilities, giving rise to a purchasing power loss each year.

In contrast to conventional accounting, income using the historical cost-constant purchasing power model is only $29,000. However, withdrawing AP 29,000 makes the firm's end-of-period wealth AP 121,000 (AP 150,000 − AP 29,000), giving it as much purchasing power at the end of the period as at the beginning.

Mexico's inflation accounting pronouncement B-10 is consistent with the historical cost-constant purchasing power model. Exhibit 7-3 contrasts Mexico's reporting requirements for the income statement with those for U.S. GAAP. Exhibit 7-4 summarizes inflation reporting requirements for Mexican balance sheets.

Exhibit 7-3   Comparison between Mexican B-10 and U.S. GAAP

B-10	FASB (U.S. GAAP)
Sales	Sales
-GPL cost of goods sold	-Historical Cost of goods sold
-Revalued depreciation	-Historical depreciation
Gross profit	Gross profit
-Selling, general, and administrative costs	-Selling, general, and administrative costs
Operating profit	Operating profit
-Net interest expense	-Net interest expense
-Net foreign exchange loss	-Net foreign exchange loss
+**Monetary gain or loss**	
Pretax income	Pretax income
-Taxes	-Translation gain or loss[a]
	-Taxes
Net income	Net income

[a] Assuming U.S. dollar is the functional currency.

Exhibit 7-4 B-10 Balance Sheet Requirements

Inventories	→	Must be restated using general price indexes
Fixed assets		Recognition of write-up on nonmonetary
Other nonmonetary assets		assets disclosed in shareholders' equity
Accumulated depreciation		
Depreciation expense		
Cost of goods sold		
Monetary gains/losses	→	Calculated by applying price index to net monetary position (i.e., monetary assets – monetary liabilities); recognized in the income statement
Components of shareholders' equity	→	Restated by applying price index
Foreign exchange gains/losses	→	All are assumed to be realized; must flow through the income statement
Constant currency restatement	→	Legislation B-12 requires that all financial statements presented must be restated in general purchasing power at the date of the balance sheet presented

CURRENT COST ADJUSTMENTS

The current cost model differs from conventional accounting in two major respects. First, assets are valued at their current cost rather than their historical cost. Second, income is the amount of resources that the firm can distribute during a period (not counting tax considerations) while maintaining its productive capacity or physical capital. One way to maintain capital is to adjust a firm's original net asset position (using appropriate specific price indexes or direct pricing) to reflect changes in the asset's current cost equivalent during the period. Continuing our previous example, the transactions of our hypothetical merchandiser under the current costing framework can be illustrated using the accounting equation as our analytical framework (figures given in thousands):

	Assets	=	Liabilities	+	Owners' Equity
	Cash		*Inventory*		*Capital*
1.	100				100
2.	(100)		100		
3.	150				150 rev.
4.			40		40 OE reval.
5.			(140)		(140) exp.

Line 1 depicts the financial statement effects of the initial 100,000 investment into the firm. Line 2 depicts the exchange of cash for inventory. Assuming a 50 percent mark-up, line 3 shows the sale of inventory for cash, which increases owners' equity by the same amount. To reflect the current cost of the sale, the merchandiser increases the carrying value of inventories by 40 percent, as depicted in line 4. The offset to the 40 percent write-up of inventory is an AP 40 increase in an owners' equity revaluation account. This adjustment does two things. The owners' equity revaluation amount tells statement readers that the firm must keep an additional AP 40 in the business to enable it to replace inventories whose replacement costs have risen. The inventory revaluation, in turn, increases the cost of resources consumed (cost of sales), line 5. Thus, current revenues are matched against the current economic cost (not the historical cost) incurred to generate those revenues. In our example, current cost-based net income is measured as AP150,000 − (AP100,000 × 140/100) = AP10,000. The current cost profit of AP 10,000 is the amount the firm could spend without reducing its business operations. Thus, the current cost model attempts to preserve a firm's physical capital or *productive capacity*. An instructive example of current cost reporting provided by a Swedish manufacturer appears in Exhibit 7-5 on page 244.

WHICH METHOD IS BEST?

Proponents of the historical cost-constant purchasing power model argue that the current cost model violates the historical cost measurement framework because it is not based on original acquisition costs. They also claim it is based on hypothetical expected costs and, therefore, is too subjective and too hard to implement in practice. Ignoring changes in the general purchasing power of money makes interperiod comparisons hard to interpret and also fails to consider gains and losses from holding monetary items such as debt. Those who favor current cost adjustments argue that businesses are not affected by general inflation, but rather by increases in specific operating costs and plant expenditures. Often, it could be misleading to record purchasing power gains from holding debt during inflation. Highly leveraged firms could show large monetary gains while on the brink of bankruptcy.[7] In some countries it is possible that general price indexes could be politicized.

The *current cost-constant purchasing power* model combines the features of both the historical cost-constant purchasing power and the current cost models. This hybrid framework recognizes increases in an asset's current value as a gain in wealth, and in so doing facilitates comparisons between current income and income in prior periods. The firm is considered to be better off only if the asset appreciates more than the general rate of inflation.[8] Thus, if a stock investment increases in value from $100 to $150 while the general price level increases from 100 to 130, the real gain from this investment is only $20 ($150 − $100 × 130/100). Monetary gains or losses, which the current cost model generally ignores, are part of the measurement. Designed to capture the benefits of the two other models we have considered, this hybrid reporting construct is the one employed by Grupo Modelo, introduced at the start of this chapter. The essence of

[7]R. Vancil, "Inflation Accounting—The Great Controversy," *Harvard Business Review* (March–April 1976): 58–67.
[8]Robert R. Sterling, "Relevant Financial Reporting in an Age of Price Changes," *Journal of Accountancy* (February 1975): 42–51.

Exhibit 7-5   Current Cost Accounting Example

Current Cost Income Statement

	20X2	20X1
Invoiced sales	25,121	24,454
Current cost of goods sold	−21,488	−21,126
Current cost depreciation	−982	−856
Operating profit after depreciation	2,651	2,472
Price changes, inventory	74	65
Price changes, fixed assets	−35	110
Operating profit before financial items	2,690	2,647
Financial items	139	175
Purchasing power adjustment, equity	0	−221
Real profit after financial items	2,829	2,601
Taxes	−1,107	−990
Minority interest	−25	−27
Net profit	1,697	1,584

Current Cost Balance Sheet

Assets	20X2	20X1
Cash, bank, and short-term investments	2,485	1,886
Receivables	6,031	6,021
Inventories	5,102	5,136
Fixed assets	10,474	10,221
Total assets	24,092	23,264

Liabilities and Shareholders' Equity		
Current liabilities	7,311	7,853
Long-term liabilities	4,086	3,852
Unrealized price changes	844	1,085
Shareholders' equity	11,851	10,474
Total liabilities and shareholders' equity	24,092	23,264

Reconciliation between Traditional and Current Cost Accounting

Profit after net financial items according to traditional accounting			3,070
Change, unrealized price changes:			
Price change, goods sold	−69		
Price change, depreciation	−211	−280	
Price change for the year:			
Inventory	74		
Fixed assets	−35	39	−241
Adjustment for inflation			0
Real profit after financial items			2,829

Grupo Modelo's approach is revealed in the notes to its financial statements, which we reproduce here:

- Inventories—These items are valued by the last-in, first-out method, and are restated using the replacement or manufacturing costs method. Such restatement does not exceed market value.
- Cost of sales—Restatement of this account was carried out based on the restated value of inventories.
- Property, plant, and equipment—These items are recorded at acquisition cost, and are restated by applying the inflation factors derived from the NCPI (National Consumer Price Index) to the net replacement value determined by independent expert appraisers through December 31, 20X2, and in accordance with their acquisition date, in the case of purchases subsequent to that date.
- Depreciation—This item was calculated based on the restated values of property, plant, and equipment, considered as a basis, the probable useful life as determined by independent appraisers.
- Restatement of stockholders' equity—This account is restated by applying inflation factors derived from the NCPI, according to their age or contribution date. The effects of that restatement are presented in the consolidated financial statements, in each of the accounts that gave rise to them.
- Insufficiency in the restatement of stockholders' equity—The balance of this account is represented by the algebraic sum of the items "Result from holding nonmonetary assets" and "Accumulated equity monetary result," which are described below.
- Result from holding nonmonetary assets—This item represents the change in the value of nonmonetary assets due to causes other than inflation. It is determined only when the specific cost method is used, since these costs are compared with restatements determined through the NCPI. If the specific costs are higher than the indexes, there will be a gain from said holding; otherwise, a loss will occur. The result from holding nonmonetary assets generated through 20X2, due to the restatement of fixed assets, is restated as the other stockholders' equity accounts are.
- Accumulated equity monetary result—This item is the result originated in the initial restatement of the financial statement figures.

INTERNATIONAL PERSPECTIVE ON INFLATION ACCOUNTING

Several countries have experimented with different inflation accounting methods. Actual practices have also reflected pragmatic considerations such as the severity of national inflation and the views of those directly affected by inflation accounting numbers. Examining several different inflation accounting methods is valuable in assessing the current state of the art.

United States

In 1979 the FASB issued *Statement of Financial Accounting Standards (SFAS) No. 33.* Entitled "Financial Reporting and Changing Prices," this statement required U.S. enterprises with inventories and property, plant, and equipment (before deducting accumulated depreciation) of more than $125 million, or total assets of more than $1 billion (after deducting accumulated depreciation), to experiment for 5 years with disclosing *both* historical cost-constant purchasing power and current cost-constant purchasing power. These disclosures were to supplement rather than replace historical cost as the basic measurement framework for primary financial statements.[9]

Many users and preparers of financial information that complied with SFAS No. 33 found that (1) the dual disclosures required by the FASB were confusing, (2) the cost of preparing the dual disclosures was excessive, and (3) historical cost-constant purchasing power disclosures were less useful than current cost data. Since then, the FASB has decided to encourage, but no longer require, U.S. reporting entities to disclose either historical cost-constant purchasing power or current cost-constant purchasing power information.[10] The FASB published guidelines (SFAS 89) to assist enterprises that report the statement effects of changing prices and to be a starting point for any future inflation accounting standard.[11]

Reporting enterprises are encouraged to disclose the following information for each of the 5 most recent years:

- Net sales and other operating revenues
- Income from continuing operations on a current cost basis[12]
- Purchasing power (monetary) gains or losses on net monetary items
- Increases or decreases in the current cost or lower recoverable amount (i.e., the net amount of cash expected to be recoverable from use or sale) of inventory or property, plant, and equipment, net of inflation (general price-level changes)
- Any aggregate foreign currency translation adjustment, on a current cost basis, that arises from the consolidation process
- Net assets at year-end on a current cost basis
- Earnings per share (from continuing operations) on a current cost basis
- Dividends per share of common stock
- Year-end market price per share of common stock
- Level of the Consumer Price Index (CPI) used to measure income from continuing operations

To increase the comparability of this data, information may be presented either in (1) average (or year-end) purchasing power equivalents, or (2) base period (1967) dollars used in calculating the CPI. Whenever income on a current cost-constant purchasing power basis differs significantly from historical cost income, firms are asked to provide more data.

SFAS No. 89 disclosure guidelines also cover foreign operations included in the consolidated statements of U.S. parent companies. Enterprises that adopt the dollar as the functional currency for measuring their foreign operations view these operations from a parent currency perspective. Accordingly, their accounts should be translated to dollars, then adjusted for U.S. inflation (the translate–restate method). Multinational

---

[9]Financial Accounting Standards Board, "Financial Reporting and Changing Prices," *Statement of Financial Accounting Standards No. 33,* Stamford, CT: FASB, 1979.

[10]Financial Accounting Standards Board, "Financial Reporting and Changing Prices," *Statement of Financial Accounting Standards No. 89,* Stamford, CT: FASB, December 1986.

[11]Ibid., pars. 7–62.

[12]After-tax income excluding the results of discontinued operations, extraordinary items, cumulative effects of accounting changes, translation adjustments, monetary gains and losses, and holding gains (i.e., increases or decreases in the current cost or lower recoverable amount of nonmonetary assets and liabilities).

enterprises adopting the local currency as functional for most of their foreign operations adopt a local currency perspective. The FASB allows companies to use either the translate–restate method or adjust for foreign inflation and then translate to U.S. dollars (the restate–translate method). (Appendix 7-1 illustrates this methodology.) Accordingly, adjustments to current cost data to reflect inflation may be based on either the U.S. *or* the foreign general price-level index. Exhibit 7-6 summarizes these provisions.

United Kingdom

The U.K. Accounting Standards Committee (ASC) issued *Statement of Standard Accounting Practice No. 16* (SSAP No. 16), "Current Cost Accounting," on a 3-year experimental basis in March 1980. Although SSAP No. 16 was withdrawn in 1988, its methodology is recommended for companies that voluntarily produce inflation adjusted accounts.[13]

SSAP No. 16 differs from SFAS No. 33 in two major respects. First, whereas the U.S. standard required both constant dollar and current cost accounting, SSAP No. 16 adopted only the current cost method for external reporting. Second, whereas the U.S. inflation adjustment focused on the income statement, the U.K. current cost statement

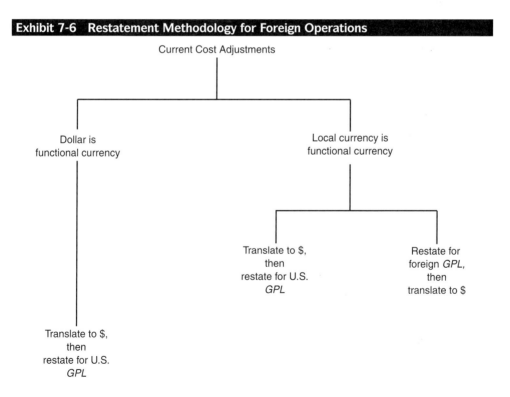

Exhibit 7-6   Restatement Methodology for Foreign Operations

Current Cost Adjustments

Dollar is functional currency

Local currency is functional currency

Translate to $, then restate for U.S. GPL

Restate for foreign *GPL*, then translate to $

Translate to $, then restate for U.S. GPL

---

[13]Accounting Standards Committee, *Handbook on Accounting for the Effects of Changing Prices*, London: Chartac Books, 1986.

required both a current cost income statement and a balance sheet, with explanatory notes. The U.K. standard allowed three reporting options:

1. Presenting current cost accounts as the basic statements with supplementary historical cost accounts.
2. Presenting historical cost accounts as the basic statements with supplementary current cost accounts.
3. Presenting current cost accounts as the only accounts accompanied by adequate historical cost information.

In its treatment of gains and losses related to monetary items, FAS No. 33 required separate disclosure of a single figure. SSAP No. 16 required two figures, both reflecting the effects of *specific* price changes. The first, called a *monetary working capital adjustment* (MWCA), recognized the effect of specific price changes on the total amount of working capital used by businesses in their operations. The second, called the *gearing adjustment,* allowed for the impact of specific price changes on a firm's nonmonetary assets (e.g., depreciation, cost of sales, and monetary working capital). As a formula, the gearing adjustment equals:

$$[(TL - CA) / (FA + I + MWC)] \ (CC \ Dep. \ Adj. + CC \ Sales \ Adj. + MWCA)$$

where

TL	=	total liabilities other than trade payables
CA	=	current assets other than trade receivables
FA	=	fixed assets including investments
I	=	inventory
MWC	=	monetary working capital
CC Dep. Adj.	=	current cost depreciation adjustment
CC Sales Adj.	=	current cost of sales adjustment
MWCA	=	monetary working capital adjustment

The gearing adjustment acknowledges that the income statement need not recognize the additional replacement cost of operating assets so far as they are financed by debt.

Brazil

Inflation is often an accepted part of the business scene in Latin America, Eastern Europe, and Southeast Asia. Brazil's past experience with hyperinflation makes its inflation accounting initiatives instructive.

Although no longer required,[14] recommended inflation accounting in Brazil today reflects two sets of reporting options—Brazilian Corporate Law and the Brazil Securities and Exchange Commission.[15] Inflation adjustments complying with corporate law restate permanent assets and stockholders' equity accounts using a price index

---

[14]Financial analysts and Brazilian financial executives we have interviewed continue to adjust Brazilian accounts for changing prices to facilitate their analyses. Should significant inflation recur in Brazil, the inflation adjustments we describe will likely be reinstated.

[15]Coopers & Lybrand, *1993 International Accounting Summaries,* New York: John Wiley & Sons, 1993, B-25.

recognized by the federal government for measuring devaluation of the local currency.[16] Permanent assets include fixed assets, buildings, investments, deferred charges and their respective depreciation, and amortization or depletion accounts (including any related provisions for losses).[17] Stockholders' equity accounts comprise capital, revenue reserves, revaluation reserves, retained earnings, and a capital reserves account used to record the price-level adjustment to capital. The latter results from revaluing fixed assets to their current replacement costs less a provision for technical and physical depreciation.

Inflation adjustments to permanent assets and stockholders' equity are netted with the excess being disclosed separately in current earnings as a monetary correction gain or loss. Exhibit 7-7 contains an illustration of this inflation accounting methodology.

The price-level adjustment to stockholders' equity (R$275) is the amount by which the shareholders' beginning-of-period investment must grow to keep up with inflation. A permanent asset adjustment that is less than the equity adjustment causes a purchasing power loss reflecting the firm's exposure on its net monetary assets (i.e., working capital). To illustrate, let:

M = monetary assets
N = nonmonetary assets
L = liabilities
E = equity
i = inflation rate

Then

$$M + N = L + E \tag{7.1}$$

Multiplying both sides of Equation (7.1) by $(1 + i)$ quantifies the impact of inflation on the firm's financial position. Thus

$$M(1 + i) + N(1 + i) = L(1 + i) + E(1 + i) \tag{7.2}$$

Equation (7.2) can be reexpressed as

$$M + Mi + N + Ni = L + Li + E + Ei \tag{7.3}$$

Regrouping Equation (7.3) as:

$$\underbrace{M + N + Ni}_{\substack{\text{permanent} \\ \text{asset} \\ \text{adjustment}}} = L + \underbrace{E + Ei}_{\substack{\text{owner's} \\ \text{equity} \\ \text{adjustment}}} + \underbrace{(L - M)\,i}_{\substack{\text{monetary} \\ \text{gain or loss}}} \tag{7.4}$$

---

[16]Ibid., B-27.
[17]Permanent assets do not include inventories, which is a conceptual shortcoming of this inflation accounting model.

Exhibit 7-7   Inflation Adjustments, Brazilian Style

Historical Amounts			Inflation-Corrected Amounts Assuming a 25% Rate of Inflation	
Balance Sheet	1/1/X5	12/31/X5		12/31/X5
Current assets	R $ 150	R $ 450	Current assets	R $ 450
Permanent assets	1,600	1,600	Permanent assets	1,000[a]
Provision for depreciation	(200)	(300)	Provision for Depreciation	(300)
			Monetary correction	(75)[b]
			Correction of historical charge to P&L	(25)[c] (400)
Total	R $1,550	R $1,750	Total	R $2,050
Current liabilities	R$ 50	R$ 50	Current liabilities	R$ 50
Long-term debt	400	400	Long-term debt	400
Equity:			Equity:	
Capital	800	800	Capital	800
			Capital reserve	200[d]
Reserves	300	300	Reserves	375[e]
Profit of period		200	Profit of period	225
Total	R $1,550	R $1,750	Total	R $2,050
Income Statement				
Year Ended 12/31/X5			Year Ended 12/31/X5	
Operating profit		R $ 500	Operating profit	R $ 500
Depreciation of period (historical)		100	Depreciation of period 100	
			Correction of depreciation 25 125	
Trading profit		400	Trading profit	375
			Inflationary loss:	
Exchange loss on foreign debt		(100)	Exchange loss on foreign debt (100)	
Monetary correction on local debt		(100)	Monetary correction on local debt (100)	
			Gain on correction of balance sheet 50[f] (150)	
Net profit		R $ 200	Net profit	R $ 225

[a]Represents the original R$1,600 plus a 25 percent (R$400) adjustment.
[b]25 percent of the original R$300.
[c]25 percent of the period's depreciation expense (typically based on the average value of fixed assets).
[d]25 percent of the original capital balance of R$800.
[e]Represents the original R$300 plus a 25 percent (R$75) adjustment.
[f]Gain on correction of the balance sheet:

Correction of permanent assets	R $400	
Correction of depreciation allowance	75	325
Correction of capital	200	
Correction of reserves	75	275
		50

Since M + N = L + E:

$$Ni = Ei + (L - M)\,i \qquad (7.5)$$

Or

Ni		Ei	=	(L − M)i	(7.6)
inflation		inflation		monetary	
adjustment		adjustment		gain or loss	
to nonmonetary		to owners'			
(permanent)		equity			
assets					

Conversely, a permanent asset adjustment greater than the equity adjustment produces a purchasing power gain, suggesting that some of the assets have been financed by borrowing. For example, suppose that a firm's financial position before monetary correction is

Permanent assets	1,000	Liabilities	500
		Owners' equity	500

With an annual inflation rate of 30 percent, a price-level adjusted balance sheet would show:

Permanent assets	1,300	Liabilities	500
		Capital	500
		Capital reserve	150
		Monetary gain	150[18]

The Brazilian Securities Exchange Commission requires another inflation accounting method for publicly traded companies.[19] Listed companies must remeasure all transactions during the period using their functional currency. At the end of the period, the prevailing general price-level index converts units of general purchasing power into units of nominal local currency. Also:

- Inventory is included as a nonmonetary asset and is remeasured with the functional currency.
- Noninterest-bearing monetary items with maturities exceeding 90 days are discounted to their present values to allocate resulting inflationary gains and losses to appropriate accounting periods (e.g., the discount on trade receivables is treated as a reduction of sales, the discount on accounts payable reduces purchases, and so forth).
- Balance sheet adjustments are similarly reclassified to appropriate line items in the income statement (e.g., the balance sheet adjustment to accounts receivable is reclassified as a reduction of sales).

---

[18]This analysis (monetary gain) assumes that liabilities are of the fixed rate variety or are floating rate obligations where the actual rate of inflation exceeds the expected rate that is incorporated into the terms of the original borrowing.

[19]Coopers & Lybrand, *1993 International Accounting Summaries,* New York: John Wiley & Sons, 1993, B32-B33

To relieve Brazilian firms from having to present two sets of financial statements in their annual reports, the Securities Exchange Commission blended features of the corporate law methodology into its price-level accounting methodology.

INTERNATIONAL ACCOUNTING STANDARDS BOARD

The IASB has concluded that reports of financial position and operating performance in local currency are not meaningful in a hyperinflationary environment. IAS 29, "Financial Reporting in Hyperinflationary Economies," requires (rather than recommends) the restatement of primary financial statement information. Specifically, financial statements of an enterprise that reports in a currency of a hyperinflationary economy, whether based on a historical or current cost valuation framework, should be reexpressed in terms of constant purchasing power as of the balance sheet date. This rule also applies to corresponding figures for the preceding period. Purchasing power gains or losses related to a net monetary liability or asset position are to be included in current income. Reporting enterprises should also disclose

1. The fact that restatement for changes in the general purchasing power of the measuring unit has been made
2. The asset valuation framework employed in the primary statements (i.e., historical or current cost valuation)
3. The identity and level of the price index at the balance sheet date, together with its movement during the reporting period
4. The net monetary gain or loss during the period[20]

INFLATION ISSUES

Four inflation accounting issues are especially troublesome. They are (1) whether constant dollars or current costs better measure the effects of inflation, (2) the accounting treatment of inflation gains and losses, (3) accounting for foreign inflation, and (4) avoiding the *double-dip* phenomenon. We discuss issue 1 together with issue 3.

Inflation Gains and Losses
Treatment of gains and losses on monetary items (i.e., cash, receivables, and payables) is controversial. Our survey of various country practices reveals important variations in this respect.

Gains or losses on monetary items in the United States are determined by restating, in constant dollars, the beginning and ending balance of, and transactions in, all monetary assets and liabilities (including long-term debt). The resulting figure is disclosed as a separate item. This treatment views gains and losses in monetary items as different in nature from other types of earnings.

---

[20]International Accounting Standards Committee, "Financial Reporting in Hyperinflationary Economies," *International Accounting Standard No. 29,* London: IASC, 1989.

In the United Kingdom, gains and losses on monetary items are partitioned into monetary working capital and a gearing adjustment. Both figures are determined in relation to specific (not general) price changes. The gearing adjustment indicates the benefit (or cost) to shareholders from debt financing during a period of changing prices. This figure is added (deducted) to (from) current cost operating profit to yield a disposable wealth measure called "Current Cost Profit Attributable to Shareholders."

The Brazilian approach, no longer required, does not adjust current assets and liabilities explicitly, as these amounts are expressed in terms of realizable values.[21] However, as Exhibit 7-7 shows, the adjustment from netting price-level adjusted permanent assets and owners' equity represents the general purchasing power gain or loss in financing working capital from debt or equity. A permanent asset adjustment that exceeds an equity adjustment represents that portion of permanent assets being financed by debt, creating a purchasing power gain. Conversely, an equity adjustment greater than the permanent asset adjustment denotes the portion of working capital financed by equity. A purchasing power loss is recognized for this portion during an inflationary period.

SSAP No. 16 has great merit in dealing with the effects of inflation. Along with inventories and plant and equipment, an enterprise needs to increase its net nominal monetary working capital to maintain its operating capability with increasing prices. It also benefits from using debt during inflation. However, the magnitude of these phenomena should not be measured in general purchasing power terms because a firm rarely, if ever, invests in an economy's market basket. We believe that the purpose of inflation accounting is to measure the performance of an enterprise and enable anyone interested to assess the amounts, timing, and likelihood of future cash flows.[22]

A firm can measure its command over specific goods and services by using an index to calculate its monetary gains and losses.[23] Because not all enterprises can construct firm-specific purchasing power indexes, the British approach is a good practical alternative. However, rather than disclose the gearing adjustment (or some equivalent), we prefer to treat it as a reduction of the current cost adjustments for depreciation, cost of sales, and monetary working capital. We think that current cost charges from restating historical cost income during inflation are offset by the reduced burden of servicing debt used to finance those operating items. (See Exhibit 7-8 on page 254 for an illustration.)

Holding Gains and Losses
Current value accounting divides total earnings into two parts: (1) operating income (the difference between current revenues and the current cost of resources consumed) and (2) unrealized gains that result from the possession of nonmonetary assets whose replacement value rises with inflation. Even though the measurement of holding gains is straightforward, their accounting treatment is not. Should portions of raw materials inventory gains be realized in periods when the respective inventories are turned into finished goods and sold? Are there ever unrealized adjustment gains or losses that

[21]Price Waterhouse, *Doing Business in Brazil,* New York: Price Waterhouse World Firm Limited, 1994.
[22]Financial Accounting Standards Board, "Objectives of Financial Reporting by Business Enterprises," *Statement of Financial Accounting Concepts No. 1,* Stamford, CT: FASB, November 1978, par. 37.
[23]Frederick D. S. Choi, "Foreign Inflation and Management Decisions," *Management Accounting* (June 1977): 21–27.

Exhibit 7-8   Alternative Current Cost Monetary Disclosures

SSAP No. 16 (Alt.1)			SSAP No. 16 (Alt. 2)			Suggested Method		
Historical cost-based operating income		2,900	Historical cost-based operating income		2,900	Historical cost-based operating income		2,900
Less: Current cost adjustments			Less: Current cost adjustments			Less: Current cost adjustments		
Cost of sales	(460)		Cost of sales	(460)		Cost of sales	(460)	
Monetary working capital	(100)		Monetary capital	(100)		Depreciation	(950)	
Working capital	(560)		Working capital	(560)		Monetary working capital	(100)	
Depreciation	(950)	(1,510)	Depreciation	(950)	(1,510)	Gearing adjustment	166	(1,344)
Current cost operating income		1,390	Current cost operating income		1,390	Current cost-based operating income		1,556
Gearing adjustment	166		Interest payable less receivable		(200)	Interest payable less receivable		(200)
Interest payable less receivable	(200)	(34)			1,190			
Current cost profit before taxation		1,356	Taxation		(730)	Current cost-based net income before taxes		1,356
Taxation		(730)	Current cost profit after interest and taxation		460	Taxes		(730)
Current cost profit attributable to shareholders		626	Gearing adjustment		166	Current cost-based net income		626
			Current cost profit attributable to shareholders		626			

should be deferred? Or should all such gains or losses be lumped together and disclosed in a special new section within stockholders' equity?

We think that increases in the replacement cost of operating assets (e.g., higher projected cash outflows to replace equipment) are not gains, realized or not. Whereas current cost-based income measures a firm's approximate disposable wealth, changes in the current cost of inventory, plant, equipment, and other operating assets are revaluations of owners' equity, which is the portion of earnings that the business must keep to preserve its physical capital (or productive capacity). Assets held for speculation, such as vacant land or marketable securities, do not need to be replaced to maintain productive capacity. Hence, if current cost adjustments include these items, increases or decreases in their current cost (value) equivalents (up to their realizable values) should be stated directly in income.

Accounting for Foreign Inflation

We have not yet decided which inflation accounting approach is best. In the United States, the FASB tried to cope with inflation by requiring large reporting entities to experiment with both historical cost-constant purchasing power and current cost disclosures. FAS No. 89, which encourages (but no longer requires) companies to account for changing prices, leaves the issue unresolved at two levels. First, companies may continue to maintain the value of their nonmonetary assets at historical cost (restated for general price-level changes) or restate them to their current cost equivalents. Second, companies that elect to provide supplementary current cost data for foreign operations have a choice of two methods for translating and restating foreign accounts in U.S. dollars. How do we choose between these two methods? We can choose with a decision-oriented framework.

Investors care about a firm's dividend-generating potential, since their investment's value ultimately depends on future dividends. A firm's dividend-generating potential is directly related to its capacity to produce goods and services. Only when a firm preserves its productive capacity (and thus its earning power) will there be future dividends to consider.

Therefore, investors need specific, not general price-level adjusted statements. Why? Because specific price-level adjustments (our current cost model) determine the maximum amount that the firm can pay as dividends (disposable wealth) without reducing its productive capacity.

This conclusion implies that the restate–translate versus translate–restate issue is trivial. Both methods are based on a valuation framework that has little to recommend it—historical cost. Neither method changes that framework. No matter how it's adjusted, the historical cost model is still the historical cost model!

We favor the following price-level adjustment procedure:

1. Restate the financial statements of all subsidiaries, both domestic and foreign, and the statements of the parent to reflect changes in specific prices (e.g., current costs).
2. Translate the accounts of all foreign subsidiaries into domestic currency equivalents using a constant (e.g., the current or a base-year foreign exchange rate).
3. Use specific price indexes that are relevant to what the firm consumes in calculating monetary gains or losses. A parent company perspective requires domestic price indexes; a local company perspective requires local price indexes.

Restating both foreign and domestic accounts to their specific current price equivalents produces decision-relevant information. This information provides investors the greatest possible amount of information concerning future dividends. It would be much easier to compare and evaluate the consolidated results of all firms than it is now. This reporting philosophy was stated by Dewey R. Borst, comptroller of Inland Steel Company:

> Management seeks the best current information to monitor how they have done in the past, and to guide them in their current decision making. Outsiders value financial statements for the same general purpose of determining how the firm has done in the past and how it is likely to perform in the future. Therefore, there is no legitimate need to have two distinct sets of data and methods of presentation of financial information. The same data now available through the development of managerial accounting is also suitable for outsiders.[24]

---

[24]"Accounting vs. Reality: How Wide Is the 'GAAP,'" *The Week in Review* (July 13, 1982): 1.

Avoiding the Double-Dip

When restating foreign accounts for foreign inflation, care must be taken to avoid the *double-dip*. This problem exists because local inflation directly affects the exchange rates used in translation. While economic theory assumes an inverse relationship between a country's internal rate of inflation and the external value of its currency, evidence suggests that this relationship seldom holds (at least in the short run).[25] Accordingly, the size of the resulting adjustment to eliminate the double-dip will vary depending on to what degree exchange rates and differential inflation are negatively correlated.

As noted before, inflation adjustments to cost of sale or depreciation expense are designed to reduce "as reported" earnings to avoid overstating income. However, due to the inverse relationship between local inflation and currency values, changes in the exchange rate between successive financial statements, generally caused by inflation (at least over a period of time), will make at least part of the impact of inflation (i.e., currency translation adjustments) affect a company's "as reported" results. Thus, to avoid adjusting for the effects of inflation twice, the inflation adjustment should take into account the translation loss already reflected in a firm's "as reported" results.

This adjustment is relevant to U.S.-based multinational corporations (MNCs) that have adopted the dollar as the functional currency for their foreign operations under FAS No. 52 and that translate inventories using the current exchange rate. It is also germane to non-U.S.-based MNCs that recognize translation gains and losses in current income. It is especially pertinent to European MNCs in view of currently used currency translation methods. A survey of foreign currency translation practices in Denmark, France, Germany, the Netherlands, Sweden, Switzerland, and the United Kingdom showed that companies there tend to use the current rate method of translation.[26] Even though many companies reported currency translation gains and losses in balance sheet reserves, a significant number—particularly in Germany, the Netherlands, and Sweden—reflected such gains and losses directly in current earnings. Absent any offsetting adjustments, such companies could reduce or increase earnings twice when accounting for foreign inflation.

The following inventory accounting example shows the relationship between inflation and foreign currency translation. The company in question uses the FIFO inventory costing method and translates inventory to dollars at the current exchange rate. We assume the following:

- Local country inflation was 20 percent in the year just ended. U.S. inflation was 6 percent during the year.
- The opening exchange rate on January 1 was LC1 = $1.00.
- The closing exchange rate on December 31 was LC1 = $0.88.

---

[25]Michael Adler and Bernard Dumans, "International Portfolio and Corporation Finance: A Synthesis," *Journal of Finance* (June 1983): 925–984.

[26]For example, see David Alexander and Simon Archer, eds., *European Accounting Guide,* 4th ed., New York: Aspen Law and Business, 2001.

- Currency devaluation during the year to maintain purchasing power parity was 12 percent.
- Local currency inventory was LC200 on January 1 and LC240 on December 31.
- No change occurred in the physical quantity of inventory during the year.

The dollar equivalent of beginning and ending inventory is calculated as follows:

	LC Amount	Exchange Rate	$ Amount
Jan. 1 FIFO inventory	200	LC = $1.00	$200
Dec. 31 FIFO inventory	240	LC = $0.88	$211

"As reported" income will reflect a translation loss of $29 (assuming that the currency was devalued at year-end), the difference between translating LC240 inventory on December 31 at $0.88 versus $1.00.

During the next inventory turnover period, "as reported" cost of sales will, therefore, be LC240 in local currency, $211 in dollars.

If cost of sales were adjusted for inflation by the restate–translate method, this company might do as follows:

- Remove the year's 20 percent inflation from December 31 local currency inventory (240/1.20), reducing it to LC 200—the same as it was on January 1 (before inflation).
- The local currency cost of sales adjustment would then be LC40, the amount required to change December 31 inventory from LC240 to LC200.
- Next, translate the local currency cost of sales adjustment (LC40) to dollars at $1.00, making a $40 cost of sales adjustment (LC40 × $1.00 = $40).

Note that on an inflation-adjusted basis, this company has reduced earnings by a $29 translation loss and a $40 cost of sales inflation adjustment—a total of $69, or 34 percent of what began as $200 of inventory on January 1. Yet inflation was only 20 percent! Double dipping caused this difference. The dollar calculations include a partial overlap between the currency devaluation loss, which *results* from inflation, and the cost of sales adjustment for inflation, which is *a root cause* of the currency devaluation. The restate–translate cost of sales inflation adjustment alone was enough. It would offset not only the U.S. inflation rate (6 percent in this example) but also the 12 percent inflation differential between this country's 20 percent rate and the U.S. 6 percent rate—which led to the 12 percent devaluation. We conclude that if cost of sales is adjusted to remove local country inflation, it is necessary to reverse any inventory translation loss that was reflected in "as reported" earnings. Appendix 7-2 provides a case analysis.

Appendix 7-1

SUPPLEMENTARY CURRENT COST DISCLOSURES

Here we illustrate how to prepare supplementary current cost information for a foreign subsidiary located in Italy whose functional currency is the euro. Exhibit 7-9 presents comparative financial statements for our hypothetical subsidiary, Bocconi Corporation. Exhibit 7-10 gives exchange rate and general price-level information. To simplify the illustration, we assume that

Bocconi Corporation has equipment but no inventory. The equipment was acquired at the beginning of 20X5 and is being depreciated in straight-line fashion with a useful life of 10 years and no salvage value. No equipment was acquired or disposed of during the year. The current cost of the equipment at year-end is as follows:

	20X5	20X6
Current cost (in thousands)	Euro 8,000	Euro 11,000
Accumulated depreciation	(800)	(2,200)
Net current cost	Euro 7,200	Euro 8,800

Exhibit 7-9	Historical Cost Financial Statements of Bocconi Corporation (in thousands)	
	20X5	20X6
Balance Sheet		
Cash	Euro 2,500	Euro 5,100
Equipment, net	4,000	3,500
Total assets	Euro 6,500	Euro 8,600
Current Liabilities		
	Euro 1,000	Euro 1,200
Long-term debt	3,000	4,000
Owner's equity	2,500	3,400
Total equities	Euro 6,500	Euro 8,600
Income Statement		
Revenue		Euro 10,000
Operating expenses	Euro 7,700	
Depreciation	500	
Other	900	9,100
Net income		900
Owners' equity: 20X5		2,500
Owners' equity: 20X6		Euro 3,400

Exhibit 7-10	Hypothetical Price Data

Exchange Rates:

12/31/X5	Euro 1.800 = $1
Average for 20X6	Euro 1.875 = $1
12/31/X6	Euro 1.950 = $1

General Price Level Indexes:

	Italy	United States
12/31/X5	200	130
Average for 20X6	215	134
12/31/X6	230	138

Management has determined that the equipment's recoverable amount exceeds its net current cost.

The Translate–Restate Method

First, we translate current cost accounts (denominated in euros) to dollars. Then we convert these amounts to current cost-constant dollar equivalents by restating them for changes in the U.S. general price level.

Current cost depreciation of the equipment is calculated as follows (in millions):

Current cost: 12/31/X5	Euro 8,000
Current cost: 12/31/X6	11,000
	19,000
	÷ 2
Average current cost	Euro 9,500
	× 10%
Current cost depreciation	Euro 950

Then, this current cost depreciation is translated to dollars and restated for U.S. inflation. Restatement is simplified if current cost (in euro) is translated to average-for-

the-year dollars. This is done by translating the current cost depreciation (in euro) to dollars using an average exchange rate. Here, current cost depreciation in average-for-the-year dollars (which simulates *average* rather than *year-end* purchasing power equivalents) is 506,667 (Euro 950,000 × 1/1.875).

Adding back historical cost depreciation (Euro 500,000) to reported earnings (Euro 900,000) and subtracting the current cost equivalent computed previously (Euro 950,000) yields current cost-based income from continuing operations of Euro 450,000. Current cost-based income in constant dollars is $240,000 (Euro 450,000 × 1/1.875).

Next we calculate increases in the current cost of equipment (net of general inflation). The effect of exchange rate changes during the period must be held constant. To handle rate changes, we translate beginning-of-period and end-of-period current cost balances to dollars at the average exchange rate, then restate these dollar equivalents to average purchasing power (i.e., constant dollar) equivalents. This procedure is illustrated below:

	Current Cost (in Thousands Euro)		Translate (Avg. Rate)		Current Cost ($1,000s)		Restate (U.S. GPL)		Current Cost/ Constant $ (in 1,000s)
Current cost, net									
12/31/X5	Euro 7,200	×	1/1.875	=	$3,840	×	134/130	=	$3,958
Depreciation	(800)	×	1/1.875	=	(533)			=	(533)
Current cost, net									
12/31/X6	8,800	×	1/1.875	=	4,693	×	134/138	=	4,557
	Euro 2,400				$1,386				$1,132

Because depreciation is measured in constant euros, we assume it is expressed in constant dollars upon translation at the average exchange rate. Here, the difference between the nominal dollar ($1,386) and constant dollar equivalent ($1,132), or $254, is the inflation component of the equipment's current cost increase.

As Bocconi Corporation maintained a net monetary liability position during the year (see Exhibit 7-9), it gained purchasing power. We calculate this monetary gain as follows:

	Euro (in Thousands)	Avg. Exchange Rate		Dollars (in Thousands)		Restate		Constant dollars (in Thousands)
Net monetary liabilities 12/31/X5	Euro (1,500)	× 1/1.875	=	$(800)	×	134/130	=	$(825)
Decrease during year	1,400	× 1/1.875	=	747				747
Net monetary liabilities 12/31/X6	Euro 100	× 1/1.875	=	$ (53)	×	134/138	=	52
Monetary gain								$ 26

Translation of euro balances to U.S. dollars when exchange rates have changed causes a translation adjustment. This translation adjustment is the amount necessary to reconcile beginning owners' equity on a current cost basis with current cost-based ending owners' equity in constant dollars. Current cost equity in nominal euros at the beginning and end of 20X5 is computed by adding net monetary items and equipment net of depreciation at current cost. Current cost equity in nominal dollars is determined by translating the nominal euro balances by the average exchange rate (see Exhibit 7-11). The translation adjustment is calculated as follows:

```
Owners' equity, 12/31/X5 (in avg. 20X6 constant dollars):
    $3,166 × 134/130 =                                         $3,263
+ Current cost-based income                                       240
+ Purchasing power gain                                                       26
+ Increase in current cost of equipment, net of inflation      1,132       1,398
                                                                           4,661
- Translation adjustment                                                    (328)
= Owners' equity = 12/31/X6 (in avg. 20X6 constant dollars):
    $4,462 × 134/138 =                                                      $4,333
```

The Restate–Translate Method

We follow procedures similar to the translate–restate method. The major difference is that we adjust for general inflation in Italy using an Italian general price-level index before translating to U.S. dollars.

Current cost depreciation in lira and operating income are determined as before.

Exhibit 7-11   Current Cost Equity in Nominal Euro (in thousands) and Dollars (in thousands)

	December 31					
	20X5			*20X6*		
	Euro	*Exchange Rate*	*$*	*Euro*	*Exchange Rate*	*$*
Cash	2,500	1/1.900	389	5,100	1/1.950	2,615
Current liability	(1,000)	1/1.800	(556)	(1,200)	1/1.950	(615)
Long-term debt	(3,000)	1/1.800	(1,667)	(4,000)	1/1.950	(2,051)
Net monetary liability	(1,500)		(834)	(100)		(51)
Equipment, net	7,200	1/1,200	4,000	8,800	1/1.950	4,513
Current cost-based equity	5,700		3,166	8,700		4,462

For Bocconi Corporation, these amounts are Euro 950,000 and Euro 450,000, respectively. The increase in the current cost of equipment, net of inflation, is determined by restating both the beginning-of-year and end-of-year equipment current cost balances using appropriate Italian general price-level indexes. Thus:

	Nominal Euro (in Thousands)		Restate for Italy's GPL		Constant Euro (in Thousands)
Current cost, net 12/31/X5	Euro 7,200	×	215/200	=	Euro 7,740
Depreciation	(800)				(800)
Current cost, net 12/31/X6	8,800	×	215/230	=	8,226
	Euro 2,400				Euro 1,286

Boconni Corporation's monetary gain, expressed in constant euros, is calculated as follows:

	Nominal Euro (in Thousands)		Restate for Italy's GPL		Constant Euro (in Thousands)
Net monetary liability 12/31/X5	Euro 1,500	×	215/200	=	Euro 1,612
Decrease during year	(1,400)				(1,400)
Net monetary liability	100	×	215/230	=	(93)
Purchasing power gain				Euro	119

Translation of current cost/constant euro balances to U.S. dollars using the restate–translate method causes the following translation adjustment:

	Constant Euro (in Thousands)		Translate		Constant Euro in Dollars (in Thousands)
Owners' equity, 12/31/X5 (in avg. 20X6 constant euro):					
Lit 5,700 × 215/200 =	Lit 6,251	×	1/1.800	=	$3,473
+ Current cost-based income	450	×	1/1.875	=	240
+ Monetary gain	119	×	1/1.875	=	64
+ Current cost increase, net of inflation	1,286	×	1/1.875	=	686
Subtotal					4,463
− Translation adjustment					(292)
Owners' equity-12/31/X6 (in avg. 20X6 constant lira):					
Euro 8,700 × 215/230 =	Euro 8,133	×	1/1.950	=	$4,171

Parity Adjustment

The restate–translate method requires a *parity adjustment* in addition to the translation adjustment. Why? The restate–translate method produces current cost/constant euro performance measures expressed in U.S. dollar equivalents. When these numbers are part of the 5-year supplementary current costs disclosures, they must be expressed in constant dollars to enable trend analysis. Thus, expressing current cost/constant euro balances in terms of constant dollars results in a restate–*translate–restate* procedure. The parity adjustment reflects the differences in inflation between the parent and host country in restating beginning and ending owners' equity to average currency units and reconciles the restate–translate disclosures (had the latter approach been employed instead).

In our example, the increase in owners' equity (per the translate–restate method) is $1,070 ($4,333 − $3,263). Under the restate–translate method, the increase in the *dollar equivalents* of owners' equity expressed in average *constant euros* is $698 ($4,171 − $3,473). The difference between these two amounts, $372 ($1,070 − $698), is the parity adjustment.

Appendix 7-2

ACCOUNTING FOR FOREIGN INFLATION: A CASE ANALYSIS

The following case study highlights how a leading U.S.-based MNE, the General Electric Company (GE), accounts for foreign inflation. Most of our discussion will be limited to inventory and cost of sales, as well as monetary gains and losses. The procedures for inventories and cost of sales also apply to fixed assets and their related cost expirations when these accounts are translated using the current rate.[27]

GE uses the temporal method of foreign currency translation because the U.S. dollar is its functional currency for most of its foreign operations. Inventories are generally translated at the current rate to signal that they are exposed to exchange-rate risk. GE management believes that it needs the restate–translate method of accounting for inflation, using specific local price indexes for fixed assets and inventory, to properly measure its foreign operations on an inflation-adjusted basis. Accordingly, GE adjusts the local currency cost of foreign fixed assets and inventory for local specific price changes and then translates at the current exchange rate. Restatement of fixed assets, from which restated depreciation expense is derived, uses generally understood practices (i.e., restate for current cost and then translate to dollars) and is not repeated here. For

inventory, however, the cost of sales inflation adjustment cannot be derived from the restated balance sheet inventory value. Therefore, we will explain these two inflation adjustments separately.

Current Cost Inventory Adjustment

For FIFO inventories that are not material in amount or that turn over very frequently, GE assumes that current cost and FIFO book cost are essentially equivalent. Accordingly, the historical book cost is reported as current cost.

With LIFO inventories, and FIFO inventories not excluded by the previous criteria, GE restates ending inventories to their current cost equivalents using local specific price indexes before translation to dollars at the current rate. If the inventory input rate is relatively constant, the current cost inventory adjustment is approximated by applying one-half of the local inflation rate during the inventory accumulation period. Thus, assuming a 4-month accumulation period, an annual inflation rate of 30 percent, an ending inventory balance of LC1,000,000, and an ending exchange rate of LC1 = $0.40, the dollar FIFO inventory value restated to a current cost basis would be:

$$[(2.5\% \text{ per mo.} \times 4 \text{ mos.})/2] \times LC1,000,000 = LC50,000$$
$$LC1,000,000 + LC50,000 = LC1,050,000 \times \$0.40 = \$420,000$$

---

[27]The following discussion is excerpted from Frederick D. S. Choi, "Resolving the Inflation/Currency Translation Dilemma," *Management International Review 27*, no. 2 (1987): 28–33.

If the foreign subsidiary carries its inventories on a LIFO basis, its restated FIFO value is calculated in the same manner, using its LIFO cost index as the inflation rate.

Current Cost of Sales Adjustment: Simulated LIFO

When a foreign operation uses LIFO accounting for its "as reported" results, the cost of sales is close to market. Therefore, no cost of sales inflation adjustment is made. For foreign operations that use FIFO accounting, GE's inflation adjustment simulates what would have been charged to cost of sales under LIFO accounting. However, to avoid the double-dip effect, the company also takes into account any inventory translation loss that is already reflected in "as

reported" results. To illustrate, suppose that the December 31 FIFO inventory balance is LC5,000, that the year's inflation rate was 30 percent (January 1 index 100, December 31 index 130), and that the currency devalued by 20 percent from LC1 = \$0.50 at January 1 to LC1 = \$0.40 at December 31.

The following sequential analysis shows how the double-counting phenomenon is minimized. Steps 1 through 3 illustrate how the current cost of sales adjustment is derived in local currency. Step 4 expresses this inflation adjustment in parent currency (i.e., U.S. dollars). Step 5 identifies the translation loss that has already been booked as a result of having translated inventories to dollars at a current rate that fell during the year. Finally, step 6 subtracts the translation loss already reflected in "as reported" results from the current cost of sales adjustment.

1. December 31 FIFO inventory subject to simulated LIFO charge LC5,000
2. Restate line 1 to January 1 cost level (LC5,000 × 100/130) LC3,846
3. Difference between line 1 and line 2 inventory values represents current year local currency FIFO inventory inflation LC1,154
4. Translate line 3 to dollars at the *January 1* exchange rate (LC1,154 = \$0.50). The result is simulated *dollar* LIFO expense for the current year .... \$ 577
5. Calculate the translation loss on FIFO inventory (line 1) that was already reflected in "as reported" results:
    a. Translate line 1 to January 1 exchange rate (LC5,000 3 \$0.50) \$2,500
    b. Translate line 1 at December 31 exchange rate (LC5,000 × \$0.40) \$2,000
    c. The difference is inventory translation loss already reflected in "as reported" results .... \$(500)
6. The net of line 4 and 5c is the cost of sales adjustment in dollars:
    a. Simulated dollar LIFO expense from line 4 .... \$ 577
    b. Less: Inventory translation loss already reflected in "as reported" results (from line 5c) .... \$(500)
    c. The difference is the net dollar current cost of sales adjustment .... \$ 77

Usually, when inflation outpaces devaluation, the dollar current cost of sales adjustment will be positive (i.e., a deduction from "as reported" earnings). However, if devaluation outpaces inflation, the adjustment will be negative (i.e., the dollar cost of sales adjust-

ment would be subtracted from, rather than added to, "as reported" dollar cost of sales).

Current Cost Monetary Adjustment

The final inflation adjustment described here relates to the fact that debtors typically gain during inflation because typically they repay fixed monetary obligations in currencies of reduced purchasing power. Accordingly, if a foreign affiliate has used debt to finance part of its fixed assets and inventory, its inflation-adjusted data include a monetary adjustment (i.e., a purchasing power gain). However, because GE limits its inflation adjustments to inventories, fixed assets, and their related cost expirations, it limits the monetary adjustment to that portion of liabilities used to finance fixed assets and inventories— hereafter known as *applied liabilities.* As a *debtor's gain,* the monetary adjustment recognizes that the interest expense being paid on applied liabilities includes compensation to the lender for the eroding purchasing power of the funds loaned. It also partly offsets income-reducing inflation adjustments for depreciation expense and cost of sales due to the impact of inflation on fixed assets and inventory replacement costs.

Calculation of the monetary adjustment involves two steps, because local inflation impacts exchange rates used to translate local currency liabilities to their dollar equivalents. Thus, the purchasing power gain on local currency liabilities used to finance fixed assets and inventories during an inflationary period is partly or fully offset by a reversal of any translation gains (or losses) on these liabilities already reflected in "as reported" results. These gains result from having translated monetary liabilities by an exchange rate that fell during the period.

In the following illustration, assume that a foreign subsidiary's local currency cost of fixed assets and FIFO inventory add up to LC10,600, that its net worth is LC7,500, that differential inflation between the parent and host country is 30 percent, and that the local currency devalued by 20 percent from LC1 = $0.50 at January 1 to LC1 = $0.40 at December 31. The current cost monetary adjustment is calculated as follows.

Steps 1 through 5 identify the portion of monetary liabilities employed to finance assets whose values have been adjusted for inflation. Steps 6 and 7 calculate the monetary gains on these applied liabilities in local currency. Step 8 reexpresses this gain in U.S. dollars. Step 9 identifies the translation gain resulting from having translated monetary liabilities to dollars by an exchange rate (the current rate) that depreciated during the year. Finally, step 10 subtracts the translation gain on the monetary liabilities from the purchasing power gain on the same accounts to yield (in this example) a net monetary gain from changing prices.

1. Local currency cost fixed assets at December 31	LC 5,600
2. FIFO inventory at December 31	LC 5,000
3. Total of lines 1 and 2	LC 10,600
4. Subtract net worth at December 31	LC (7,500)
5. The balance represents "applied liabilities"	LC 3,100
6. Restate December 31 applied liabilities to their January 1 purchasing power equivalent (i.e., multiply LC 3,100 by 100/130)	LC 2,385
7. The difference between lines 5 and 6 is the purchasing power gain on applied liabilities	LC 715
8. Translate line 7 to dollars at the *January 1* exchange rate. The result is the debtor's gain from inflation in *dollars* (LC 715 × $0.50)	$ 358
9. Calculate the year's translation gain (loss) on applied LC liabilities already reflected in "as reported" results:	
a. Line 5 times January 1 exchange rate (LC 3,100 × $0.50)	$1,550
b. Line 5 times December 31 exchange rate (LC 3,100) × $0.40)	$1,240
c. The difference is the translation gain	$ 310

10. The difference between line 8 and line 9c. is the dollar current cost
monetary adjustment:

    a. Line 8 (debtor's gain from inflation) $358 cr.

    b. If line 9c. is a translation gain, show it as a debit to reverse it
and vice versa $(310) dr.

    c. Add lines 10(a) and 10(b). If the sum is a credit, treat it as an addition
to "as reported" income and vice versa $ 48

Selected References

Aboody, D., M.E. Barth, and R. Kasnik, "Revaluation of Fixed Assets and Future Firm Performance: Evidence from the UK," *Journal of Accounting and Economics* 26 (1999): 149–78.

Accounting Standards Committee, *Handbook on Accounting for the Effects of Changing Prices,* London:ASC, 1986.

Archambault, Jeffrey J., and Marie E. Archambault, "A Cross-National Test of Determinants of Inflation Accounting Practices," *International Journal of Accounting* 34, no. 2 (1999): 189–207.

Barniv, Ran, "The Value Relevance of Inflation-Adjusted and Historical Cost Earnings During Hyperinflation," *Journal of International Accounting, Auditing and Taxation* 8, no. 2 (1999): 269–287.

Bernholz, Peter, *Monetary Regimes and Inflation,* Surrey, U.K.: Edward Surrey, 2003.

Boschen, John F., and Charles L. Weise, "What Starts Inflation: Evidence from the OECD Countries," *Journal of Money, Credit and Banking* 35 (June 2003): 323–337.

Choi, Frederick D. S., "Financial Reporting in Hyperinflationary Environments: A Transaction Analysis Framework for Management," in *International Finance Accounting and Finance Handbook, 3rd ed.,* F. D. S. Choi, ed., New York: John Wiley & Sons, 2003, p. 27.

Davis, Nicole, and Ali M. Kutan, " Inflation and Output as Predictors of Stock Returns and Volatility: International Evidence," *Applied Financial Economics* 13 (September 2003): 693.

Davis-Friday, Paquita, "Equity Valuation and Current Cost Disclosures: The Case of Mexico," *Journal of International Financial Management and Accounting* 12, No. 3 (Autumn 2001): 260–285.

Easton, P.D., "Discussion of Revalued Financial, Tangible and Intangible Assets: Associations with Share Prices and Non-Market-Based Value Estimates," *Journal of Accounting Research* (Supplement 1998): 235–247.

Epstein, Barry J., and Abbas Ali Mirza, *IAS 2000: Interpretation and Application of International Accounting Standards,* New York: John Wiley & Sons, 2000.

Financial Accounting Standards Board, "Financial Reporting and Changing Prices," *Statement of Financial Accounting Standards No. 33,* Stamford, CT: FASB, September 1979.

Financial Accounting Standards Board, "Financial Reporting and Changing Prices," *Statement of Financial Accounting Standards No. 89,* Stamford, CT: FASB, December 1986.

Gordon, Elizabeth A., "Accounting for Changing Prices: The Value Relevance of Historical Cost, Price Level, and Replacement Cost Accounting in Mexico," *Journal of Accounting Research* 39, No. 1 (June 2001): 177–200.

International Accounting Standards Committee, "Information Reflecting the Effects of Changing Prices," *International Accounting Standard 15,* London: IASC, November 1981.

International Accounting Standards Committee, "Financial Reporting in Hyperinflationary Economies," *International Accounting Standard 29,* London: IASC, 1989.

Lin, Y. C., and K. V. Peasnell, "Asset Revaluation and Current Cost Accounting: UK Corporate Disclosure Decisions in 1983," *British Accounting Review* (June 2000): 161–187.

Meyer, Laurence, "Inflation Targets and Inflation Targeting," *North American Journal of Economics and Finance* 13 (2002): 147–162.

Sharpe, Steven A., "Reexamining Stock Valuation and Inflation: The Implications of

Analysts' Earnings Forecasts," *Review of Economics and Statistics,* forthcoming.

Wyman, H. E. "Accounting for the Effects of Inflation," in *International Finance Accounting and Finance Handbook, 3rd ed.,* F. D. S. Choi, ed., New York: John Wiley & Sons, 2003, p. 20.

Discussion Questions

1. Consider the statement: "The object of accounting for changing prices is to ensure that a company is able to maintain its operating capability." How accurate is it?

2. From a user's perspective, what is the inherent problem in attempting to analyze historical cost-based financial statements of a company domiciled in an inflationary, devaluation-prone country?

3. What is a general price-level index and of what use is it for financial statement readers?

4. Following are the remarks of a prominent American congressman. Explain why you agree or disagree with them.

   The plain fact of the matter is that inflation accounting is a premature, imprecise, and underdeveloped method of recording basic business facts. To insist that any system of inflation accounting can afford the accuracy and fairness needed for the efficient operation of our tax system is simply foolish. My years on the Ways and Means Committee have exposed me to the many appeals of business—from corporate tax "reform" to the need for capital formation—which have served as a guise for reducing the tax contributions of American business. In this respect, I see inflation accounting as another in a long line of attempts to minimize corporate taxation through backdoor gimmickry.

5. Professional accountancy bodies the world over generally agree that inflation may become so great that conventional financial statements lose much of their significance and price-level adjusted statements become more meaningful. Since domestic rates of inflation vary significantly from country to country, at what point do price-level adjusted financial statements become more meaningful? How does one determine whether the benefits of price-level adjusted accounting information exceed its costs?

6. Briefly describe the nature of the historical cost-constant purchasing power and current cost models. How are they similar? How do they differ?

7. Refer to Exhibit 7-5, which contains the current costing disclosure format used by a Swedish manufacturer. Can you explain how the income statement items *Price changes, inventory* and *Price changes, fixed assets* were derived? What do these numbers mean? Do you agree that they should be included in reported earnings?

8. What might explain the reluctance of accounting standard setters (primarily those in the highly industrialized countries) to require the disclosure of changing prices information in general-purpose financial statements? Can you identify any problems associated with such a policy? Can you identify any advantages?

9. As a potential investor in the shares of multinational enterprises, which inflation method—restate–translate or translate–restate—would give you consolidated information most relevant to your decision needs? Which information set is best from the viewpoint of the foreign subsidiary's shareholders?

10. What is a *gearing adjustment* and on what ideas is it based?

11. How does accounting for foreign inflation differ from accounting for domestic inflation?

12. What does *double-dipping* mean in accounting for foreign inflation?

Exercises

1. Zonolia Enterprises has equipment on its books that it acquired 2 years ago. The equipment is being depreciated in straight-line fashion over a 10-year period and has no salvage value. The current cost of this equipment at the end of year 2 was 8,000,000,000 zonos (Z). During year 3, the specific price index for equipment increased from 100 to 137.5.

   Required: Based on this information, calculate the equipment's net current cost (i.e., current cost less accumulated depreciation) at the end of year 3.

2. General price-level index information for the country of Zonolia is as follows:

12/31/X5	30,000
Average	32,900
12/31/X6	36,000

   Required: Using this information and the information in exercise 1, calculate the increase in the current cost of Zonolia Enterprise's equipment, net of inflation?

3. Now assume that Zonolia Enterprises is a foreign subsidiary of a U.S.-based multinational corporation and that its financial statements are consolidated with those of its U.S. parent. Relevant exchange rate and general price-level information for the year are given here (general price-level information for Zonolia are provided in exercise 2):
   Exchange rate:

12/31/X5	Z 4,400 = $1
Average 20X6	Z 4,800 = $1
12/31/X6	Z 5,290 = $1

   Required: What would be the increase in the current cost of Zonolia Enterprise's equipment, net of inflation, when expressed in U.S. dollars under the restate–translate methodology? Under the translate–restate method?

4. Assume that Zonolia Enterprise's comparative balance sheets (at historical cost) for 20X5 and 20X6 are as follows:

Balance Sheet	20X5	20X6
Cash	Z 2,500	Z 5,100
Equipment, net	4,000	3,500
Total assets	Z 6,500	Z 8,600
Current liabilities	Z 1,000	Z 1,200
Long-term debt	3,000	4,000
Owners' equity	2,500	3,400
Total	Z 6,500	Z 8,600

Required: What was the change in Zonolia's net monetary asset or liability position?

5. Calculate Zonolia Enterprise's net monetary gain or loss in local currency for 20X6 based on the general price-level information provided in exercise 2.

6. Based on the price information provided in previous exercises, calculate Zonolia Enterprise's net monetary gain in dollars under the restate–translate method and under the translate–restate method.

7. Sobrero Corporation, a Mexican affiliate of a major U.S.-based hotel chain, starts the calendar year with 1 billion pesos (P) cash equity investment. It immediately acquires a refurbished hotel in Acapulco for P 900 million. Owing to a favorable tourist season, Sobrero Corporation's rental revenues were P 144 million for the year. Operating expenses of P 86,400,000 together with rental revenues were incurred uniformly throughout the year. The building, comprising 80 percent of the original purchase price (balance attributed to land), has an estimated useful life of 20 years and is being depreciated in straight-line fashion. By year-end, the Mexican consumer price index rose to 420 from an initial level of 263, averaging 340 during the year.

Required:
a. Prepare financial statements for Sobrero Corporation's first year of operations in terms of the historical cost model and the historical cost-constant dollar model.
b. Compare and evaluate the information content of rate-of-return statistics computed using each of these models.

8. Based on the operating information provided in exercise 7, now assume that Mexico's construction cost index increased by 80 percent during the year while the price of vacant properties adjacent to Sobrero Corporation's hotel increased in value by 90 percent.

Required: Using this information to restate the value of the company's nonmonetary assets, what would Sobrero Corporation's financial statements look like under the current cost model?

9. The balance sheet of Rackett & Ball plc., a U.K.-based sporting goods manufacturer, is presented here. Figures are stated in millions of pounds (£m). During the year, the producers' price index increased from 100 to 120, averaging 110.The

aggregate current cost of sales, depreciation, and monetary working capital adjustment is assumed to be £216m.

Required: Assuming that changes in the producers price index are a satisfactory measure of the change in R&B's purchasing power, calculate, as best as you can, R&B's monetary working capital adjustment and its gearing adjustment.

	20X5 £m	20X6 £m
Fixed Assets:		
Intangible assets	56	150
Tangible assets	260	318
Investments	4	5
	320	479
Current Assets:		
Inventory	175	220
Trade receivable	242	270
Marketable securities	30	50
Cash	25	25
	472	565
Current Liabilities:		
Trade payables	(170)	(160)
Net current assets	302	405
Total assets less current liabilities	622	884
Long-term liabilities	85	128
Total net assets	237	356
Owner's Equity:		
Common stock	42	42
Premium on common stock	87	87
Retained earnings	108	227
Total owner's equity	237	356

10. Aztec Corporation, a U.S. subsidiary in Mexico City, begins and ends its calendar year with an inventory balance of P 500 million. The dollar/peso exchange rate on January 1 was $0.02 = P 1. During the year, the U.S. general price level advances from 180 to 198 while the Mexican general price level doubles. The exchange rate on December 31 was $0.015 = P 1.

    Required:
    a. Using the temporal method of translation, calculate the dollar equivalent of the inventory balance by first restating for foreign inflation, then translating to U.S. dollars.
    b. Repeat part (a), but translate the nominal peso balances to dollars before restating for U.S. inflation.
    c. Which dollar figure do you think provides the more useful information?
    d. If you are dissatisfied with either result, suggest a method that would provide more useful information than those in parts (a) or (b).

11. Doosan Enterprises, a U.S. subsidiary domiciled in South Korea, accounts for its inventories on a FIFO basis. The company translates its inventories to dollars at the current rate. Year-end inventories are recorded at 10,920,000 won. During the year, the replacement cost of inventories increases by 20 percent. Inflation and exchange rate information are as follows:

| January 1: | Specific price index = 100; | $1 = won1,300 |
| December 31: | Specific price index = 120; | $1 = won1,690 |

Required: Based on this information, calculate the dollar current cost adjustment for cost of sales while avoiding a double charge for inflation.

12. The year-end balance sheet of Helsinki Corporation, a wholly owned British affiliate in Finland, is reproduced here. Relevant exchange rate and inflation information is also provided.

Balance Sheet Yr. Ended 20X6			
Cash	FIM 2,000	Short-term debt	FIM 8,000
Inventory	8,000	Long-term debt	25,000
Plant & equipment, net	20,000		
Other assets	5,000	Owners' equity	2,000
Total	FIM 35,000		FIM 35,000

Exchange rate and price information:

January 1:	General price index = 300
	FIM 7.2 = £1
December 31:	General price index = 390
	FIM 9.0 = £1

Required: Using this information, calculate the monetary adjustment without double counting for the effects of foreign inflation (assume that the U.K inflation rate is negligible).

CASE 7-1 KASHMIR ENTERPRISES

Kashmir Enterprises, an Indian carpet manufacturer, begins the calendar year with the
following Indian rupee (Rpe) balances:

Cash	920,000	Accounts payable	420,000
Inventory	640,000	Owners' equity	1,140,000
	$1,560,000		$1,560,000

During the first week in January, the company acquires additional manufacturing supplies costing Rpe 2,400,000 on account and a
warehouse for Rpe 3,200,000 paying Rpe
800,000 down and signing a 20-year, 10 percent note for the balance. The warehouse
(assume no salvage value) is depreciated
straight-line over the period of the note. Cash
sales were Rpe 6,000,000 for the year, selling
and administrative expenses, including office
rent, were Rpe 1,200,000. Payments on
account totaled Rpe 2,200,000 while inventory
on hand at year-end was Rpe 80,000. Except
for interest expense paid on December 31, all
other cash receipts and payments took place
uniformly throughout the year.

On January 1, the U.S. dollar/rupee
exchange rate was $.025 = Rpe 1; at year-end
it was $.02 = Rpe 1. The average exchange
rate during the year was $.022. The Indian
consumer price index rose from 128 to 160
by December 31, averaging 144 during the
year. At the new financial statement date,
the cost to replace supplies had increased by
30 percent; the cost to rebuild a comparable
warehouse (based on the construction cost
index) was approximately Rpe 480,000.

REQUIRED

1. Assuming beginning inventories were
   acquired when the general price index

level was 128, prepare Kashmir Enterprises' financial statements (i.e., income
statement and balance sheet) under the
(a) conventional original transactions
cost model, (b) historical cost-constant
rupee model, and (c) current cost model.

2. Comment on which financial statement
   set gives Indian readers the most useful
   performance and wealth measures.

3. Now assume that Kashmir Enterprises'
   U.S. headquarters management wants to
   see the Indian rupee statements in U.S.
   dollars. Two price-level foreign currency
   translation procedures are requested.
   The first is to translate Kashmir's unadjusted rupee statements to dollars (use
   the current rate method) and then
   restate the resulting dollar amounts
   accounting for U.S. inflation (the U.S.
   general price level at the financial statement date was 108, up 8 percent from
   the previous year). The second is to
   restate the Indian rupee statements
   accounting for inflation (using the historical cost-constant franc model), then
   translate the adjusted amounts to dollars using the current rate. Comment on
   which of the two resulting sets of dollar
   statements you prefer for use by
   American readers. (The U.S. general
   price level averaged 104 during the
   year.)

CASE 7-2   ICELANDIC ENTERPRISES, INC.

In 1993 Icelandic Enterprises was incorporated in Reykjavik to manufacture and distribute women's cosmetics in Iceland. All of its outstanding stock was acquired at the beginning of 2001 by International Cosmetics, Ltd. (IC), a U.S.-based MNE headquartered in Sandy Hook, Connecticut.

Competition with major cosmetics manufacturers both within and outside Iceland was very keen. As a result, Icelandic Enterprises (now a wholly-owned subsidiary of International Cosmetics), was under constant pressure to expand its product offerings. This required frequent investment in new equipment. Competition also affected the company's pricing flexibility. As the demand for cosmetics was price elastic, Icelandic lost market share every time it raised its prices. Accordingly, when Icelandic increased selling prices, it did so in small amounts while increasing its advertising and promotional efforts to minimize the adverse effects of the price increase on sales volume.

International Cosmetics' financial policies with respect to Icelandic were dictated by two major considerations: the continued inflation and devaluation of the Icelandic kronur (Ikr). To counter these, headquarters management was eager to recoup its dollar investment in Icelandic Enterprises through dollar dividends. If dividends were not possible, subsidiary managers were instructed to preserve IC's original equity investment in Icelandic kronur. Due to the unstable kronur, all financial management analyses were made in dollars. International Cosmetics designated the dollar as Icelandic Enterprise's functional currency. Accordingly, it adopted the temporal method when translating Icelandic's kronur accounts to their dollar equivalents. All monetary assets and liabilities were translated to dollars using the current exchange rate. All nonmonetary items, except those assets that were carried at current values, were translated using historical rates. Income and expense accounts were translated at average exchange rates prevailing during the year, except depreciation and amortization charges that were related to assets translated at historical exchange rates. Translation gains and losses were taken directly to consolidated earnings.

Adjusting Icelandic's accounts for inflation was not attempted. Management believed that such restatements were too costly and subjective. IC's management also claimed that translating Icelandic's accounts to dollars automatically approximated the impact of inflation. The following is a comparative balance sheet and income statement for Icelandic Enterprises, along with relevant foreign exchange and general price-level indexes.

REQUIRED

1. Comment on International Cosmetic's policies on the basis of "as reported" earnings.
2. Is management correct in stating that by translating their financial reports into dollars they "automatically approximate the impact of inflation"?
3. What revised actions/policies would you recommend based on inflation-adjusted figures?

Balance Sheet	2001		2002	
(000's)	Dollars	Kronur	Dollars	Kronur
Cash	7,715	221,176	9,086	368,414
Accts. receivable	18,000	516,078	21,202	859,633
Inventory	118,706	2,949,017	154,988	4,912,187
PP&E, net[a]	283,252	2,202,500	265,706	3,057,000
Other assets	22,022	719,250	28,838	1,024,950
Total	449,695	5,179,521	479,820	8,172,284
Current liab's	94,748	2,716,438	82,673	3,351,980
Due to parent	50,000	1,433,500	50,000	2,027,250
Capital stock[b]	98,758	713,430	98,758	713,430
Retained earnings	206,189	316,153	248,389	2,079,624
Total	449,695	5,179,521	479,820	8,172,284

Income Statement	2001		2002	
	Dollars	Kronur	Dollars	Kronur
Net sales	328,805	8,168,500	462,248	14,650,500
Cost of sales	150,012	3,726,750	199,874	6,334,800
Gross margin	178,793	4,341,750	262,354	8,315,700
Selling expenses	78,493	1,950,000	110,841	3,513,000
Gen. & adm. exp.	28,680	712,500	49,647	1,573,500
Depreciation	44,056	221,250	47,002	305,700
Operating income	27,564	1,458,000	54,864	2,923,500
Interest expense	7,064	175,500	11,453	363,000
Income before taxes[c]	20,500	1,282,500	43,411	2,560,500

	1997	1998	1999	2000	2001	2002
National Inflation and Exchange Rates[d]						
Consumer price index:						
Iceland	63.1	100.0	150.6	224.7	418.2	547.0
United States	88.1	100.0	110.4	117.1	120.9	126.1
Kronur per dollar:						
Year-end	3.949	6.239	8.173	16.625	28.670	40.545
Average	3.526	4.798	7.224	12.352	24.843	31.694

[a]Plant and equipment were acquired at the beginning of each period as follows: 1998, Ikr 1,250,000; 1999, Ikr 427,500; 2000, Ikr 375,000; 2001, Ikr 160,000; 2002, Ikr 844,500. Depreciation is calculated at 10 percent per annum. A full year's depreciation is charged in the year of acquisition. Assume there were no disposals during any of the years.

[b]Common stock was acquired when the exchange rate was Ikr 7.224 = $1.

[c]Inclusive of translation gains and losses.

[d]The inflation and exchange rate relationships used here are based on actual data for an earlier period.

8 | INTERNATIONAL ACCOUNTING HARMONIZATION

INTRODUCTION

"Harmonization" is a process of increasing the compatibility of accounting practices by setting limits on how much they can vary. Harmonized standards are free of logical conflicts, and should improve the comparability of financial information from different countries.

Efforts to harmonize accounting standards began even before the creation of the International Accounting Standards Committee (IASC) in 1973.[1] More recently, companies seeking capital outside of their home markets and investors attempting to diversify their investments internationally faced increasing problems resulting from national differences in accounting measurement, disclosure, and auditing. In response, harmonization efforts accelerated during the 1990s. International accounting harmonization now is one of the most important issues facing accounting standard setters, securities market regulators, stock exchanges, and those who prepare or use financial statements.

People occasionally use the terms *harmonization* and *standardization* interchangeably, but in contrast to harmonization, standardization generally means the imposition of a rigid and narrow set of rules, and may even apply a single standard or rule to all situations. Standardization does not accommodate national differences and, therefore, is more difficult to implement internationally. Harmonization is much more flexible and open; it does not take a one-size-fits-all approach, but accommodates some differences and has made a great deal of progress internationally in recent years.[2]

Comparability of financial information is a more clear-cut concept than is *harmonization*. Financial information produced under different accounting, disclosure, and/or auditing systems is comparable if it is similar in enough ways that financial statement users can compare it (at least along some dimensions) without needing to be intimately familiar with more than one system. The substantial differences in financial reporting requirements and practices around the world, and the increasing need of financial statement users to compare information from different countries, have been the driving forces behind the movement to harmonize accounting.

---

[1]The IASC is the predecessor body to the International Accounting Standards Board (IASB).

[2]*Convergence* of accounting standards entered the vernacular with the IASB (discussed later). Convergence of international and national accounting standards involves the gradual elimination of differences though the cooperative efforts of the IASB, national standard setters, and other groups seeking best solutions to accounting and reporting issues.

Accounting harmonization includes the harmonization of (1) accounting standards (which deal with measurement and disclosure); (2) disclosures made by publicly traded companies in connection with securities offerings and stock exchange listings; and (3) auditing standards.[3]

Efforts to achieve international accounting harmonization have been marked by sharp debates. Should accounting standards be harmonized, made uniform, or left alone? Should all enterprises, large and small, in all industries be subject to the same standards? Is it reasonable that less-developed countries adopt the same accounting standards as those used in highly developed countries?

A SURVEY OF INTERNATIONAL HARMONIZATION

Advantages of International Harmonization

Proponents of international harmonization claim that harmonisation (or even standardization) has many advantages. Sir Bryan Carsberg, former Secretary General of the IASC, wrote the following in September 2000:

A thoughtful approach to assessing the desirability of international harmonisation recognises that the costs and benefits vary from case to case. Those of us who have English as their mother tongue probably feel fortunate that English is becoming a widely used second language throughout the world. But, even if it were feasible, we would stop short of seeking agreement that English or some other common language should replace the 6,800 or so languages currently in use. We would recognise that language is an indispensable vehicle for culture and that the elimination of different languages would entail enormous losses in literature and other expressions of culture.

What about the harmonisation of taxation and social security systems? Businesses would experience considerable benefits in planning, systems costs, training and so on from harmonisation. But this case shows us another disadvantage of harmonisation. Taxation and social security systems have powerful influences on economic efficiency. Different systems have different effects. The ability to compare the working of different approaches in different countries enables countries to make improvements to their systems. Countries are in competition and the competition forces them to adopt efficient systems through the operation of a kind of market force. Agreement on a unified system of taxation would be like the establishment of a cartel and would deprive us of the benefits of competition among countries.

The case for harmonisation in accounting standards is a particularly strong one. Accounting has relatively low cultural value. Competition among different accounting approaches, while not without merit, probably is better

---

[3]This is just a partial listing. Harmonization also is concerned with such diverse areas as offering and listing requirements, auditor education, and immediate public disclosure of material information, to name a few. In this chapter, the term "accounting" often refers to accounting standards, which deal with both measurement and disclosure.

left to optional extras in reporting rather than the basic reporting systems; and the potential cost savings and other benefits are very great....

The accounting profession really is becoming global. But perhaps that term is better avoided. Perhaps we should raise our sights and look for universal accounting standards.[4]

A recent paper has also argued for harmonized, "global GAAP." Among the benefits cited are:

- Capital markets are global and investment capital can move seamlessly around the globe. High-quality financial reporting standards that are used consistently around the world would improve the efficiency with which capital is allocated.
- Investors can make better investment decisions; portfolios are more diverse and financial risk is reduced.
- Companies can improve their strategic decision making in the merger and acquisition area.
- The best ideas arising from national standard-setting activities can be leveraged in developing global standards of the highest quality.[5]

To summarize, most arguments for accounting harmonization relate in one way or another to increasing the operational and allocational efficiency of capital markets.

Criticisms of International Standards

The internationalization of accounting standards has also had critics. As early as 1971 (before the IASC was formed), some said that international standards setting was too simple a solution for a complex problem. It was claimed that accounting, as a social science, has built-in flexibility and that its ability to adapt to widely different situations is one of its most important values. It was doubted that international standards could be flexible enough to handle differences in national backgrounds, traditions, and economic environments, and some thought that it would be a politically unacceptable challenge to national sovereignty.

Other observers have argued that international accounting standard setting is essentially a tactic of the large international accounting service firms to expand their markets. Multinational accounting firms are indispensable, it is said, to apply international standards in national environments where those standards might seem distant and complex. Also, as international financial institutions and international markets insist on the use of international standards, only large international accounting firms can meet this demand.

Moreover, it has been feared that adoption of international standards may create "standards overload." Corporations must respond to an ever-growing array of national, social, political, and economic pressures and are hard-put to comply with additional complex and costly international requirements. A related argument is that national political concerns frequently intrude on accounting standards and that international political influences would compromise accounting standards unacceptably.

[4]Sir Bryan Carsberg, "Raising Our Sights," *Accountancy* (September 2000): 1.
[5]PricewaterhouseCoopers, *Global GAAP: The Future of Corporate Reporting* (www.pwcglobal.com), 2003.

Still others argue that there is now a well-developed international capital market that has grown rapidly in recent years without global GAAP. One commentator states:

> Harmonization of international accounting principles is unlikely to come about. Too many different national groups have vested interests in maintaining their own standards and practices which have developed from widely different perspectives and histories. There is not a single powerful champion of the proposal for harmonization. There is no authoritative body with the ability to mandate the adoption of Global GAAP. . . . I have argued that Global GAAP is unlikely to be achieved due to the institutional impediments in the standard setting process and because there is no demonstrated need in order to fuel the growth of robust international capital markets.[6]

Developments since the above article have not been in line with this statement. As discussed later in this chapter, international harmonization has moved forward with increasing speed, and many of the "different national groups" have been prominent in this convergence effort.

Reconciliation and Mutual Recognition

As international equity issuance and trading grow, problems related to distributing financial statements in nondomestic jurisdictions become more important. Some supporters argue that international harmonization will help resolve problems associated with filings of cross-border financial statements.

Two other approaches have been advanced as possible solutions to problems related to cross-border financial statement filings: (1) reconciliation and (2) mutual recognition (also known as "reciprocity").[7] With reconciliation, foreign firms can prepare financial statements using home country accounting standards, but also must provide a reconciliation between critical accounting measures (such as net income and shareholders' equity) of the home country and the country where the financial statements are being filed. For example, the U.S. Securities and Exchange Commission (SEC) permits foreign registrants to use accounting principles other than U.S. GAAP as the basis for financial statements they file. However, the SEC also requires reconciliation disclosures (see Chapter 5).

Reconciliations are less costly than preparing a full set of financial statements under a different set of accounting principles. However, they only provide a summary, not the full picture of the enterprise.

Mutual recognition exists when regulators outside the home country accept a foreign firm's financial statements based on home country principles. For example, the London Stock Exchange accepts U.S. GAAP-based financial statements in filings made by foreign companies. Reciprocity does not improve the cross-country comparability of financial statements, and can create an "unlevel playing field" in that it may

---

[6]Richard K. Goeltz, "International Accounting Harmonization: The Impossible (And Unnecessary?) Dream," *Accounting Horizons* (March 1991): 85–88.
[7]See Carrie Bloomer, ed., *The IASC-U.S. Comparison Project: A Report on the Similarities and Differences Between IASC Standards and U.S. GAAP*, 2nd ed., Norwalk, CT: Financial Accounting Standards Board, 1999.

allow foreign companies to apply less rigorous standards than apply to domestic companies.

Evaluation

The harmonization debate may never be completely settled. Some arguments against harmonization have merit. However, increasing evidence shows that the goal of international harmonization of accounting, disclosure, and auditing has been so widely accepted that the trend toward international harmonization will continue or accelerate. Harmonization debates aside, all dimensions of accounting *are* becoming harmonized worldwide. Growing numbers of companies are voluntarily adopting International Financial Reporting Standards (IFRS). Many countries have adopted IFRS in their entirety, base their national standards on IFRS, or allow the use of IFRS. Leading international organizations and standard-setting bodies throughout the world (European Commission, World Trade Organization, Organization for Economic Cooperation and Development, among others) endorse the goals of the International Accounting Standards Board (IASB). Progress in harmonizing disclosure and auditing has been impressive.

Finally, national differences in the underlying factors that lead to variation in accounting, disclosure, and auditing practice are narrowing as capital and product markets become more international. Many companies have voluntarily adopted IFRS. These companies see economic benefits in adopting accounting and disclosure standards that are credible internationally. Also, as discussed in Chapter 5, companies are voluntarily expanding their disclosures in line with IFRS in response to demand from institutional investors and other financial statement users. The success of recent harmonization efforts by international organizations may demonstrate that harmonization is happening as a natural response to economic forces.

Applicability of International Standards

International accounting standards are used as a result of (a) international or political agreement, (b) voluntary (or professionally encouraged) compliance, or (c) decisions by national accounting standard setters. The application of the EU accounting-related directives results from an international political agreement. Increasing numbers of companies are deciding that the use of IFRS is in their interest even if it is not required. Many countries now allow companies to base their financial statements on IFRS, and some require it.

When accounting standards are applied through political, legal, or regulatory procedures, statutory rules typically govern the process. Interested parties determine what the rules are and how they should be implemented. Legal and regulatory cases flesh out the details. The EU is the only instance to date where a form of internationalization of accounting standards is broadly applicable and legally enforceable.

Other international standards efforts in accounting are voluntary in nature. Their acceptance depends on those who use accounting standards. There is no problem when an international standard and a national standard are the same, but when national and international standards differ, national standards usually come first (take primacy). For example, multinational companies may use international accounting standards and also accept and use national standards. When companies adopt more than one set of accounting standards, the result is often that they must issue one set of reports for each set of accounting standards they adopt. The answer to multiple reporting is a convergence of national and international accounting standards.

SOME SIGNIFICANT EVENTS IN THE HISTORY OF INTERNATIONAL ACCOUNTING STANDARD SETTING

1959—Jacob Kraayenhof, founding partner of a major European firm of independent accountants, urges that work on international accounting standards begin.

1961—Groupe d'Etudes, consisting of practicing accounting professionals, is established in Europe to advise European Union authorities on matters concerning accounting.

1966—Accountants International Study Group is formed by professional institutes in Canada, the United Kingdom, and the United States.

1973—International Accounting Standards Committee (IASC) is created.

1976—Organization for Economic Cooperation and Development (OECD) issues its Declaration on Investment in Multinational Enterprises containing guidelines on "Disclosure of Information."

1977—International Federation of Accountants (IFAC) is founded.

1977—Group of Experts appointed by United Nations Economic and Social Council issues four-part report on *International Standards of Accounting and Reporting for Transnational Corporations.*

1978—Commission of the European Community issues Fourth Directive as first move toward European accounting harmonization.

1981—IASC establishes consultative group of nonmember organizations to widen the input to international standard setting.

1984—London Stock Exchange states that it expects listed companies not incorporated within the United Kingdom or Ireland to comply with international accounting standards.

1987—The International Organization of Securities Commissions (IOSCO) resolves at its annual conference to promote the use of common standards in accounting and auditing practices.

1989—IASC issues Exposure Draft 32 on comparability of financial statements. *Framework for the Preparation and Presentation of Financial Statements* is published by IASC.

1995—IASC Board and IOSCO Technical Committee agree on a work plan whose successful completion will result in IAS forming a comprehensive core set of standards. Successful completion of these standards will allow the IOSCO Technical Committee to recommend endorsement of IAS for cross-border capital raising and listing purposes in all global markets.

1995—European Commission adopts a new approach to accounting harmonization that would allow the use of IAS by companies listing on international capital markets.

1996—U.S. Securities and Exchange Commission (SEC) announces that it "... supports the IASC's objective to develop, as expeditiously as possible, accounting standards that could be used for preparing financial statements that could be used in cross-border offerings."

1998—IOSCO publishes the report "International Disclosure Standards for Cross-Border Offerings and Initial Listings by Foreign Issuers."

1999—International Forum on Accountancy Development (IFAD) meets for the first time in June.

2000—IOSCO accepts, in toto, all 40 core standards prepared by the IASC in response to IOSCO's 1993 wish list.

2001—The European Commission proposed a regulation that would require all EU companies listed on a regulated market to prepare consolidated accounts in accordance with IAS by 2005.

2001—International Accounting Standards Board (IASB) succeeded the IASC and assumed its responsibilities on April 1. IASB standards are designated International Financial Reporting Standards (IFRS), and include IAS issued by the IASC.

2002—European Parliament endorses the Commission proposal that virtually all EU listed companies must follow IASB standards starting no later than 2005 in their consolidated financial statements. Member states may extend the requirement to nonlisted companies and to individual company statements. The European Council later adopts enabling regulation.

2002—The IASB and FASB sign the so-called "Norwalk Agreement" committing them to the convergence of international and U.S. accounting standards.

2003—European Council approves amended EU Fourth and Seventh Directives removing inconsistencies between the old directives and IFRS.

2003—IASB publishes IFRS 1 and revisions to 15 IAS.

OVERVIEW OF MAJOR INTERNATIONAL ORGANIZATIONS PROMOTING ACCOUNTING HARMONIZATION

Six organizations have been key players in setting international accounting standards and in promoting international accounting harmonization:

1. International Accounting Standards Board (IASB)
2. Commission of the European Union (EU)
3. International Organization of Securities Commissions (IOSCO)
4. International Federation of Accountants (IFAC)
5. United Nations Intergovernmental Working Group of Experts on International Standards of Accounting and Reporting (ISAR), part of United Nations Conference on Trade and Development (UNCTAD)
6. Organization for Economic Cooperation and Development Working Group on Accounting Standards (OECD Working Group)

The IASB represents private-sector interests and organizations. The EU Commission, referred to as the European Commission (EC), the OECD Working Group, and the ISAR are political entities that derive their powers from international agreements. IFAC's main activities include issuing technical and professional guidance and promoting the adoption of IFAC and IASB pronouncements. IOSCO promotes high standards of regulation, including harmonized accounting and disclosure standards for cross-border capital raising and trading.

The International Forum on Accountancy Development (IFAD) had its first meeting in 1999. Its main objective is to build accounting and auditing capacity in developing countries. It provides a mechanism through which interested parties (such as the accounting profession, regulators, standard setters, and governments) can communicate and develop partnerships to promote effective and efficient change in such countries. IFAC, the World Bank, the seven largest accounting firms (at that time), and many other organizations were instrumental in organizing IFAD.

Also important is the International Federation of Stock Exchanges (FIBV), the trade organization for regulated securities and derivative markets worldwide. The FIBV promotes the professional business development of financial markets. One of the FIBV's goals is to establish harmonized standards for business processes (including financial reporting and disclosure) in cross-border trading in securities, including cross-border public offerings.

Many regional accounting organizations (such as the ASEAN Federation of Accountants and the Nordic Federation of Accountants) participate in some cross-country standard setting within their respective regions. The Fédération des Experts Comptables Européens (FEE) (Federation of European Accountants) represents national accounting bodies in Europe. Other regional organizations include the Fédération des Bourses Européennes (FESE), or Federation of European Stock Exchanges, and The Forum of European Securities Commissions (FESCO), created in December 1997 and consisting of 17 securities regulators from 17 European nations.

Refer to Exhibit 8-1 for Web sites offering information about major international organizations and accounting harmonization activities. Exhibit 8-2 (see pages 283–285) presents the Web site addresses of national regulatory and accountancy organizations, many of which are actively involved in accounting harmonization activities.

INTERNATIONAL ACCOUNTING STANDARDS BOARD

The International Accounting Standards Board (IASB), formerly the IASC, is an independent private-sector standards-setting body founded in 1973 by professional accounting organizations in nine countries and restructured in 2001. (The reorganization made IASC into an umbrella organization under which the IASB carries out its work.) Before the restructuring, the IASC issued 41 International Accounting Standards (IAS) and a Framework for the Preparation and Presentation of Financial Statements. The IASB's objectives are:

1. To develop, in the public interest, a single set of high-quality, understandable, and enforceable global accounting standards that require high-quality, transparent, and comparable information in financial statements and other financial reporting to help participants in the world's capital markets and other users make economic decisions.
2. To promote the use and rigorous application of those standards.
3. To bring about convergence of national accounting standards and International Accounting Standards and International Financial Reporting Standards to high-quality solutions.[8]

---

[8]See the IASB Web site (www.iasb.org).

Exhibit 8-1	Web Sites Offering Information about Major International Organizations and Accounting Harmonization Activities (Note: All Web Site Addresses Begin with "http://")
Organization	Web Site Address
Bank for International Settlements	www.bis.org
Confederation of Asian & Pacific Accountants (CAPA)	capa.com.my
Deloitte IAS Plus Web site	www.iasplus.com
European Union (EU)	europa.eu.int
European Commission—Internal Market and Financial Services	europa.eu.int/comm/internal_market/en/index.htm
Fédération des Experts Comptables Européens (FEE) a/k/a European Federation of Accountants	www.fee.be
FEE *Euro Information Service*	www.euro.fee.be
Federation of European Securities Exchanges a/k/a Fédération des Bourses Européennes (FESE)	www.fese.be
International Accounting Standards Board (IASB)	www.iasb.org.
International Association of Insurance Supervisors (IAIS)	www.iaisweb.org
International Federation of Accountants (IFAC)	www.ifac.org
International Federation of Stock Exchanges (FIBV)	www.fibv.com
International Finance & Commodities Institute (IFCI) a/k/a International Financial Risk Institute	risk.ifci.ch
International Forum on Accountancy Development (IFAD)	www.ifad.net
International Monetary Fund (IMF)	www.imf.org
International Organization of Securities Commissions (IOSCO)	www.iosco.org
Organization for Economic Co-operation and Development (OECD)	www.oecd.org
United Nations Conference on Trade and Development (UNCTAD)	www.unctad.org
World Bank	www.worldbank.org
World Trade Organization (WTO)	www.wto.org

Note: This listing was correct when this book went to press. Web site addresses often change, and occasionally are discontinued. Active Web sites are sometimes temporarily inaccessible due to technical problems.

The IASB represents accounting organizations from approximately 100 countries. With a remarkably broad base of support, IASB is the driving force in international accounting standard setting. Exhibit 8-3 (see pages 286–287) lists the current IASB Standards (as of February 2004).[9] IASB Standards are closely compatible with accounting standards promulgated in the United States, Canada, the United Kingdom, and other countries that use Anglo-Saxon accounting. Thus, IASB standards follow the principles of fair presentation and full disclosure (see Chapter 2). The IASB Web site (www.iasb.org) presents a summary of current IASB standards.

During the first decade of the IASC, international accounting standards were more descriptive than prescriptive. These early standards codified similar national

---

[9]Standards issued by the IASB are referred to as International Financial Reporting Standards (IFRS), while those issued by the IASC are called International Accounting Standards (IAS). The IASB has adopted all previously issued IAS. All references to IFRS include IAS.

Exhibit 8-2 Web Site Addresses of Selected Regulatory and Accountancy Organizations (All Addresses Begin with the Prefix http://www)	
Organization	Web Site Address

Government and Regulatory Organizations

U.K. Financial Services Authority (FSA)	fsa.gov.uk
U.S. Securities and Exchange Commission (SEC)	sec.gov
U.S. Securities and Exchange Commission (SEC) Edgar Database	sec.gov/edgar.shtml
Search Edgar Database via FreeEdgar	freeedgar.com
French Autorité des Marché Financiers (AMF)	amf-frances.org

National Professional Accountancy Organizations

Argentina—Federación Argentina de Consejos Profesionales de Ciencias Económicas	facpce.org.ar
Barbados—The Institute of Chartered Accountants of Barbados	icab.bb
Belgium—Institut des Experts Comptables	accountancy.be
Belgium—Institut des Réviseurs d'Entreprises	accountancy.be
Canada—CMA Canada	cma-canada.org
Canada—Canadian Institute of Chartered Accountants	cica.ca
Canada—Certified General Accountants' Association of Canada	cga-canada.org
China —Chinese Institute of Certified Public Accountants	cicpa.org.cn
Cyprus—The Institute of Certified Public Accountants of Cyprus	icpac.org.cy
Czech Republic—Union of Accountants of the Czech Republic	svaz-ucetnich.cz
France—Conseil Supérieur de l'Ordre des Experts Comptables	experts-comptables.com
Georgia—Georgian Federation of Professional Accountants and Auditors	itic.org.ge/gfpaaa/
Germany—Institut der Wirtschaftsprufer in Deutschland	idw.de
Hong Kong—Hong Kong Society of Accountants	hksa.org.hk
Hong Kong—Hong Kong Association of Accounting Technicians	hkaat.org.hk
India—Institute of Chartered Accountants of India	icai.org
Ireland—Institute of Chartered Accountants in Ireland	icai.ie
Japan—Japanese Institute of Certified Public Accountants	jicpa.or.jp
Jordan—Arab Society of Certified Accountants	ascasociety.org
Kenya—Institute of Certified Public Accountants of Kenya	icpak.com
Korea—Korean Institute of Certified Public Accountants	kicpa.or.kr
Malaysia—The Malaysian Institute of Accountants	mia.org.my
Malta—The Malta Institute of Accountants	miamalta.org
Mexico—Instituto Mexicano de Contadores Públicos	imcp.org.mx
Nepal—Institute of Chartered Accountants of Nepal	ican.org.np
Netherlands—Koninklijk Nederlands Instituut van Registeraccountants	nivra.nl
New Zealand—Institute of Chartered Accountants of New Zealand	icanz.co.nz
Nigeria—Institute of Chartered Accountants of Nigeria	ican-ngr.org
Norway—Den norske Revisorforening (DnR)	revisornett.no
Pakistan—Institute of Cost and Management Accountants of Pakistan	icmap.com.pk

Exhibit 8-2 Web Site Addresses of Selected Regulatory and Accountancy Organizations (All Addresses Begin with the Prefix http://www) (*Continued*)

Organization	Web Site Address
Pakistan—The Institute of Chartered Accountants of Pakistan	icap.org.pk
Philippines—Philippine Institute of Certified Public Accountants	picpa.com.ph
Romania—Corpul Expertilor Contabili si Contabililor Autorizati din Romania	ceccar.ro
Singapore—Institute of Certified Public Accountants of Singapore	accountants.org.sg
South Africa—The South African Institute of Chartered Accountants (SAICA)	saica.co.za
South Africa—Institute of Commercial and Financial Accountants of Southern Africa	cfa-sa.co.za
Sri Lanka—The Institute of Chartered Accountants of Sri Lanka	icasrilanka.com
Sweden—Föreningen Auktoriserade Revisorer	far.se
Taiwan—Federation of CPA Associations of Taiwan	nfcpaa.org.tw
Turkey—Union of Chambers of Certified Public Accountants of Turkey	turmob.org.tr
U.K.—The Institute of Chartered Accountants in England & Wales	icaew.co.uk
U.K.—Chartered Institute of Management Accountants	cimaglobal.com
U.K.—The Association of Chartered Certified Accountants	acca.org.uk
U.K.—The Chartered Institute of Public Finance and Accountancy	cipfa.org.uk
U.K.—The Institute of Chartered Accountants of Scotland	icas.org.uk
U.K.—Association of Accounting Technicians	aat.co.uk
U.S.—American Institute of CPAs	aicpa.org
U.S.—National Association of State Boards of Accountancy	nasba.org
U.S.—Public Oversight Board Panel on Audit Effectiveness	pobauditpanel.org
U.S.—Public Company Accounting Oversight Board	pcaobus.org
U.S.—Institute of Management Accountants	imanet.org
U.S.—The Institute of Internal Auditors	theiia.org
Zimbabwe—The Institute of Chartered Accountants of Zimbabwe	icaz.org.zw
Accounting Standard-Setting Bodies	
Australia—Accounting Standards Board (AASB)	aasb.com.au
Canada—Accounting Standards Board (ASB)	cica.ca/cica/cicawebsite.nsf/public/
France—Conseil National de la Comptabilité (CNC)	finances.gouv.fr
Germany—German Accounting Standards Committee (GASC)	drsc.de
Japan—Accounting Standards Board (ASBJ)	asb.org.jp
New Zealand—Accounting Standards Board	icanz.co.nz
United Kingdom—Accounting Standards Board (ASB)	asb.org.uk
United States—Financial Accounting Standards Board (FASB)	fasb.org

Note: This listing was correct when this book went to press. Web site addresses often change and occasionally are discontinued. Active Web sites are sometimes temporarily inaccessible due to technical problems

Exhibit 8-3   Current IASB Standards

Standard	Effective Date	Description
IAS 1	July 1, 1998	Presentation of Financial Statements (Revised December 2003)
IAS 2	January 1, 1995	Inventories (Revised December 2003.)
IAS 3		No longer effective. Replaced by IAS 27 and IAS 28.
IAS 4		No longer effective. Replaced by IAS 16, 22 and IAS 38.
IAS 5		No longer effective. Replaced by IAS 1.
IAS 6		No longer effective. Replaced by IAS 15.
IAS 7	January 1, 1979	Cash Flow Statements
IAS 8	January 1, 1979	Profit or Loss for the Period, Fundamental Errors and Changes in Accounting Policies (Revised December 2003)
IAS 9		No longer effective. Replaced by IAS 38.
IAS 10	January 1, 2000	Events Occurring after the Balance Sheet Date (Revised December 2003)
IAS 11	January 1, 1980	Construction Contracts
IAS 12	January 1, 1998	Income Taxes
IAS 13		No longer effective.
IAS 14	July 1, 1998	Segment Reporting
IAS 15	January 1, 1983	No longer effective. Withdrawn December 2003.
IAS 16	January 1, 1983	Property, Plant, and Equipment (Revised December 2003)
IAS 17	January 1, 1999	Leases (Revised December 2003)
IAS 18	January 1, 1984	Revenue
IAS 19	January 1, 1985	Employee Benefits
IAS 20	January 1, 1984	Accounting for Government Grants and Disclosure of Government Assistance
IAS 21	January 1, 1985	The Effects of Changes in Foreign Exchange Rates (Revised December 2003)
IAS 22	January 1, 1985	Business Combinations
IAS 23	January 1, 1986	Borrowing Costs

practices and excluded outlier practices. The IASC started to address more difficult issues during its second 10 years and responded to concerns that its standards included too many alternative accounting treatments and were not rigorous enough.

IASC's Core Standards and the IOSCO Agreement

The IASB (and the former IASC) has been striving to develop accounting standards that will be accepted by securities regulators around the world. As part of that effort, the IASC adopted a work plan to produce a comprehensive core set of high-quality standards. In July 1995 the IOSCO Technical Committee stated its agreement with the work plan as follows:

> The [IASC] Board has developed a work plan that the Technical Committee agrees will result, upon successful completion, in IAS comprising a comprehensive core set of standards. Completion of comprehensive core standards that are acceptable to the [IOSCO] Technical Committee will allow the

Exhibit 8-3   Current IASB Standards (*Continued*)

Standard	Effective Date	Description
IAS 24	January 1, 1986	Related Party Disclosures (Revised December 2003)
IAS 25		No longer effective. Replaced by IAS 39 and IAS 40.
IAS 26	January 1, 1988	Accounting and Reporting by Retirement Benefit Plans
IAS 27	January 1, 1990	Consolidated Financial Statements and Accounting for Investments in Subsidiaries (Revised December 2003)
IAS 28	January 1, 1990	Accounting for Investments in Associates (Revised December 2003)
IAS 29	January 1, 1990	Financial Reporting in Hyperinflationary Economies
IAS 30	January 1, 1991	Disclosures in the Financial Statements of Banks and Similar Financial Institutions
IAS 31	January 1, 1992	Financial Reporting of Interests in Joint Ventures (Revised December 2003)
IAS 32	January 1, 1996	Financial Instruments: Disclosures and Presentation (Revised December 2003)
IAS 33	January 1, 1998	Earnings Per Share (Revised December 2003)
IAS 34	January 1, 1999	Interim Financial Reporting
IAS 35	January 1, 1999	Discontinuing Operations
IAS 36	July 1, 1999	Impairment of Assets
IAS 37	July 1, 1999	Provisions, Contingent Liabilities, and Contingent Assets
IAS 38	July 1, 1999	Intangible Assets
IAS 39	January 1, 2001	Financial Instruments: Recognition and Measurement (Revised December 2003)
IAS 40	January 1, 2001	Investment Property (Revised December 2003)
IAS 41	January 1, 2003	Agriculture
IFRS 1	January 1, 2004	First-time Adoption of International Financial Reporting Standards
IFRS 2	January 1, 2005	Share-based Payment

Note: As of February 20, 2004. Consult IASB Web site, www.iasb.org, for current list.

Technical Committee to recommend endorsement of IAS for cross border capital raising and listing purposes in all global markets. IOSCO has already endorsed IAS 7, Cash Flow Statements, and has indicated to the IASC that 14 of the existing International Accounting Standards do not require additional improvement, providing that the other core standards are successfully completed.[10]

The Core Standards were completed with the approval of IAS 39 (Financial Instruments: Recognition and Measurement) in December 1998. IOSCO's review of the Core Standards began in 1999, and in 2000 it endorsed the use of IASB Standards for cross-border offerings and listings.

[10]In October 1993, Working Party I of IOSCO's Technical Committee agreed to a set of accounting issues that would have to be addressed in a core set of international accounting standards appropriate for use in cross-border offerings and multiple listings.

The New IASB Structure

The IASC board formed a Strategy Working Party (SWP) to consider what IASC's strategy and structure should be after completion of the core standards work program. In December 1998, the SWP approved a discussion paper, "Shaping IASC for the Future," to encourage and focus discussion. In November 1999 the IASC board unanimously approved a resolution supporting a proposed new structure with the following main features: (1) IASC would be established as an independent organization; (2) the organization would have two main bodies, the trustees and the board, as well as a Standing Interpretations Committee (now called International Financial Reporting Interpretations Committee) and Standards Advisory Council; and (3) the trustees would appoint the board members, exercise oversight, and raise the funds needed, whereas the board would have sole responsibility for setting accounting standards.

The restructured IASB met for the first time in April 2001. The IASB, as reorganized, includes the following bodies.[11]

1. **Trustees.**   The IASB has 19 trustees: six from North America, six from Europe, four from the Asia/Pacific region, and three from any area ("subject to establishing overall geographic balance").[12] The trustees appoint the members of the board, the International Financial Reporting Interpretations Committee, and the Standards Advisory Council. The trustees are responsible for raising funds, and supervise and review the priorities and operations of the IASB.

2. **IASB Board.**   The board establishes and improves standards of financial accounting and reporting for businesses. Its responsibilities include "complete responsibility for all IASB technical matters including the preparation and issuing of International Accounting Standards, International Financial Reporting Standards, and Exposure Drafts . . . and final approval of interpretations by the International Financial Reporting Interpretations Committee," and approving project proposals and methods and procedures for developing standards. The board consists of 14 members, appointed by the trustees to provide "the best available combination of technical skills and background experience of relevant international business and market conditions." All board members are paid IASB employees; 12 are to be full time and two may be part time. Seven of the full-time members have liaison responsibilities with national standard setters.[13] (The intention is to partner with these national bodies as they work together to achieve the convergence of accounting standards worldwide.) Members are appointed for a 5-year term, renewable once.

3. **Standards Advisory Council.**   The Standards Advisory Council, appointed by the trustees, is made up of "thirty or more members, having a diversity of geographic and professional backgrounds, appointed for renewable terms of three

---

[11]Much of this section is based on information published on the IASB Web site (www.iasb.org). The new IASB structure is modeled after the U.S. accounting standard-setting structure, as described in Chapter 3.
[12]All direct quotations in this section are from the IASB Constitution (revised July 2002), found on its Web site (www.iasb.org).
[13]These national standard-setting bodies are the Australian Accounting Standards Board and Financial Reporting Standards Board (Australia/New Zealand), Accounting Standards Board (Canada), Conseil Nationale de la Comptabilité (France), German Accounting Standards Committee (Germany), Accounting Standards Board (Japan), Accounting Standards Board (United Kingdom), and Financial Accounting Standards Board (United States).

years." The Standards Advisory Council normally meets three times each year. Its responsibilities are to give the board advice on its agenda and priorities, to inform the board of the views "of the organizations and individuals on the council on major standard-setting projects," and to give "other advice" to the board or the trustees.

4. **International Financial Reporting Interpretations Committee (IFRIC).** The IFRIC consists of 12 members appointed by the trustees. The IFRIC interprets "the application of International Accounting Standards and International Financial Reporting Standards, in the context of IASB's Framework," publishes draft interpretations and reviews public comments on them, and obtains board approval for final interpretations.

The IASB follows due process in setting accounting standards. For each standard, the board may publish a "Draft Statement of Principles" or other discussion document that sets out the various possible requirements for the standard and the arguments for and against each one. Subsequently, the board publishes an "Exposure Draft" for public comment, and it then examines the arguments put forward in the comment process before deciding on the final form of the standard. An Exposure Draft and final standard can be issued only when eight members of the board have voted in favor of doing so.[14]

Recognition and Support for the IASB

International Financial Reporting Standards are now widely accepted around the world. For example, they are (1) used by many countries as the basis for national accounting requirements; (2) used as an international benchmark in many major industrialized countries and emerging market countries that develop their own standards; (3) accepted by many stock exchanges and regulators that allow foreign or domestic companies to file financial statements prepared in conformance with IFRS; and (4) recognized by the EC and other supranational bodies. In 1995, the EC endorsed IFRS. Rather than amend existing directives, the EC determined that the EU should associate with IASC/IASB and IOSCO efforts toward a broader international harmonization of accounting standards. Nearly all EU companies listed on recognized stock exchanges must use IFRS in preparing consolidated financial statements no later than 2005.

Many large European companies (particularly German and Swiss) have already switched to IFRS in response to investor and analyst demand for enhanced disclosure and improved financial reporting quality.[15] For example, Bayer's chairman stated that use of IAS would "provide our stockholders, lenders, and the general public with more comprehensive information. It also improves the international comparability of our figures."[16]

Finally, the signing of the 2002 "Norwalk Agreement" by the IASB and U.S. Financial Accounting Standards Board symbolizes the commitment of national standard

---

[14]Source: IASB Web site (www.iasb.org), February 12, 2004.
[15]That many German and Swiss companies adopted IFRS suggests that they believed that financial statements based on IFRS would give them more credibility than financial statements based on national accounting requirements. This is not surprising, because low levels of disclosure and a great degree of accounting flexibility have characterized both German and Swiss accounting.
[16]Daren Nickel Anhalt, "Accounting Move Aids Growth," *Pensions & Investments* (June 12, 1995): 14, 17.

setters to converge toward a single set of international accounting standards world-wide. Standard setters from Australia/New Zealand, Canada, France, Germany, Japan, the United Kingdom, and the United States actively partner with the IASB in their standard-setting activities.

U.S. Securities and Exchange Commission Response to IFRS

The SEC does not accept IFRS as a basis for financial statements filed by companies listing on U.S. stock exchanges. However, the SEC is under increasing pressure to make U.S. capital markets more accessible to non-U.S. issuers. The SEC has expressed support for the IASB's objective to develop accounting standards for use in financial statements used in cross-border offerings. However, the SEC also stated that three conditions must be met for it to accept IASB standards. By stating these conditions (in the following list), the SEC has given itself great flexibility as to how far it will accept the use of IFRS by foreign registrants.[17]

1. The standards must include a core set of accounting pronouncements that constitutes a comprehensive, generally accepted basis of accounting.
2. The standards must be of high quality, they must result in comparability and transparency, and they must provide for full disclosure.
3. The standards must be rigorously interpreted and applied.

Recently, senior officials of the SEC have indicated that if the IASB and FASB make sufficient progress in converging their standards and if sufficient progress is made in creating an infrastructure for interpreting and enforcing accounting standards, the SEC will consider allowing foreign registrants to file in the United States using IFRS without reconciling to U.S. GAAP. For example, Scott Taub, SEC Deputy Chief Accountant, has stated:

> We are preparing for a time when IFRS financial statements can be accepted without reconciliation to U.S. GAAP. I absolutely believe that, if things continue as they have been going—if the IASB continues as a strong independent standard setter in the manner it has been, if the commitment to quality application of IFRS remains, etc.—we will at some point eliminate the reconciliation. The trickier bit is when. And I'll be honest—I don't know.[18]

Comparisons between IFRS and Other Comprehensive Bodies of Accounting Principles

Numerous analyses have compared IFRS to other bodies of accounting principles. There are several motivations for these analyses. Regulators and standard setters in many nations want to be aware of the degree of conformity between home principles and IFRS, the extent to which home principles have to be revised to be in conformance with IFRS, or the acceptability of IFRS using home country standards as a benchmark.

The U.S. Financial Accounting Standards Board (FASB) began a major project comparing (then) IAS and U.S. standards in 1995, and published detailed reports in

---

[17]U.S. Securities and Exchange Commission, "News Release—SEC Statement Regarding International Accounting Standards," Washington, D.C.: U.S. Securities and Exchange Commission, April 11, 1996.
[18]December 2003 speech to an AICPA conference on current SEC developments, quoted in *IAS Plus* (www.iasplus.com), January 2004, p. 19.

1996 and 1999.[19] The IASC-U.S. GAAP Comparison Project was part of FASB's plan for international activities, which includes promotion of international comparability of accounting standards. A key goal of the study was to provide information for assessing the acceptability of IAS for securities listings in the United States.

Similarly, the U.K. Accounting Standards Board (ASB) commissioned a study comparing IAS (IFRS) and U.K. GAAP. First published in 2000, *The Convergence Handbook* has been updated annually since.[20] It is designed to encourage convergence between U.K. GAAP and IFRS, and to assist U.K. companies adopting IFRS. As discussed later, EU listed companies must adopt IFRS by 2005. However, nonlisted British companies also have the option of IFRS as an alternative to U.K. GAAP from 2005 (see Chapter 3). By highlighting differences between IFRS and U.K. GAAP, it points to those areas where U.K. companies must change accounting and disclosure practices to conform to IFRS.

Other studies have been conducted with the aim of promoting convergence between national accounting standards and IFRS. IFAD sponsored *GAAP 2000,* a survey of differences between IFRS and national accounting rules in 53 countries. This was followed by *GAAP 2001,* a comparison of accounting rules in 62 countries, and *GAAP Convergence 2002,* an assessment of countries' plans to promote and achieve convergence with IFRS.[21] The Australian Accounting Standards Board published *The Australian Convergence Handbook* in 2002.[22] In addition, accounting firms have also compared various national accounting standards to IFRS.[23]

EUROPEAN UNION (EU)

The Treaty of Rome established the EU in 1957, with the goal of harmonizing the legal and economic systems of its member states. As of May 2004, the EU comprises 25 member countries (Austria, Belgium, Cyprus, Czech Republic, Denmark, Estonia, Finland, France, Germany, Greece, Hungary, Ireland, Italy, Latvia, Lithuania, Luxembourg, Malta, the Netherlands, Poland, Portugal, Slovakia, Slovenia, Spain, Sweden, and the United Kingdom). In contrast to the IASB, which has no authority to

---

[19]Bloomer, Carrie, ed., *The IASC-U.S. Comparison Project: A Report on the Similarities and Differences between IASC Standards and U.S. GAAP,* Norwalk, CT: Financial Accounting Standards Board, 1996; and Bloomer, Carrie, ed., *The IASC-U.S. Comparison Project: A Report on the Similarities and Differences between IASC Standards and U.S. GAAP,* 2nd ed., Norwalk, CT: Financial Accounting Standards Board, 1999.

[20]The fourth update, published September 2003, is the latest one at the time of this writing. *The Convergence Handbook* is published by the Institute of Chartered Accountants in England and Wales (ICAEW) and is available on the ICAEW Web site (www.icaew.co.uk).

[21]C. W. Nobes, ed., *GAAP Convergence 2000: A Survey of National Accounting Rules in 53 Countries* (December 2000); C. W. Nobes, ed., *GAAP 2001: A Survey of National Accounting Rules Benchmarked against International Accounting Standards* (October 2001); and D. L. Street, *GAAP Convergence 2002* (2002). These reports are available on the IFAD Web site (www.ifad.net).

[22]Available at www.asb.com.au.

[23]For example, PricewaterhouseCoopers, *Similarities and Differences: A Comparison of IFRS and U.S. GAAP* (February 2004), available at www.pwc.com/ifrs; and KPMG, *IFRS Compared with U.S. GAAP and French GAAP* (February 2003), available at www.kpmg.fi/attachment.asp?Section=181&Item=1058. Deloitte's IAS Plus Web site (www.iasplus.com) compares IFRS and the GAAP of Australia, Canada, Central Europe, China, Hong Kong, the Netherlands, Singapore, South Africa, the United Kingdom, and the United States.

require implementation of its accounting standards, the European Commission (EC, the governing body of the EU) has full enforcement powers for its accounting directives throughout the member states.

One of the EU's goals is to achieve integration of European financial markets. Toward this end, the EC has introduced directives and undertaken major new initiatives to achieve a single market for:

- raising capital on an EU-wide basis;
- establishing a common legal framework for integrated securities and derivatives markets; and
- achieving a single set of accounting standards for listed companies.

The EC embarked on a major program of company law harmonization soon after it was formed.[24] EC directives now cover all aspects of company law. Several have a direct bearing on accounting. Of these, many consider the Fourth, Seventh, and Eighth Directives to be historically and substantively the most important.

Fourth, Seventh, and Eighth Directives

The EU's Fourth Directive, issued in 1978, is the broadest and most comprehensive set of accounting rules within the EU framework. Both public and private companies above certain minimum size criteria must comply. Fourth Directive requirements apply to individual company accounts and include format rules for financial statements, disclosure requirements, and valuation rules. The true and fair view is the overriding requirement and holds for footnote disclosures, just as it does for financial statements. The Fourth Directive also requires that financial statements be audited. It aims to ensure that European companies disclose comparable and equivalent information in their financial statements.

The Seventh Directive, issued in 1983, addresses the issue of consolidated financial statements. At the time, consolidated financial statements were the exception rather than the rule. They were the norm in Ireland, the Netherlands, and the United Kingdom, and Germany required consolidation of German subsidiaries (only). However, they were rare elsewhere in Europe. The Seventh Directive requires consolidation for groups of companies above a certain size, specifies disclosures in notes and the directors' report, and requires an audit. Because of the newness of consolidations as a legal requirement, member states were given wide latitude and many options for incorporating the Seventh Directive into their individual national company law.

The Eighth Directive, issued in 1984, addresses various aspects of the qualifications of professionals authorized to carry out legally required (statutory) audits. Essentially, this directive lays down minimum qualifications of auditors. The Eighth Directive does not deal with mutual recognition of auditors from one EU country to another. It also does not encompass freedom of professional establishment among the

---

[24]EU directives become law of member states through a complex, lengthy process. Preliminary work leads to the issuance of a draft directive (i.e., exposure draft) by the EU. When a draft directive is broadly acceptable (after hearings and other evaluation procedures), it is submitted to the member states for ratification after approval from the European Council. After the EU adopts a directive, each member state adopts and implements it. Directives are binding on member states, but the method of implementation is left to the discretion of national authorities.

EU countries.[25] Required training must be completed under the supervision of an approved auditor. Independence is required, but the Eighth Directive gives discretionary power to EU countries to determine conditions of independence. (Thus, professional independence requirements for auditors still vary greatly among the EU member countries.)[26]

Have EU Harmonization Efforts Been Successful?

The Fourth and Seventh Directive had a dramatic impact on financial reporting throughout the EU, bringing accounting in all EU member states up to a good and reasonably uniform level. It harmonized the presentation of the profit and loss account (income statement) and balance sheet and added minimum supplementary information in the notes, in particular a disclosure of the impact of tax regulations on reported results. It accelerated accounting development in many EU countries and also influenced accounting in neighboring, non-EU countries.

However, the success of EU harmonization efforts at the end of the 20th century has been debated. For example, member states generally did not scrap their existing accounting rules when adopting EU directives. Instead, they adapted the new rules to their existing ones. Another issue has been the extent to which member states enforced compliance with the directives. Thus, some questioned whether the directives harmonized accounting as much as had been intended when the directives were issued.[27]

Karel van Hulle, head of the accounting and audit unit at the European Commission, described some of the difficulties in this manner:[28]

> It must be admitted that the comparability achieved through the harmonisation process is far from perfect. First of all, the Accounting Directives contain primarily minimum rules. They are *not* dealing with a number of important accounting issues. Secondly, the provisions of the Directives are not always interpreted in the same way by Member States. A number of questions relating to the interpretation of the Directives have been dealt with by the Contact Committee on the Accounting Directives.[29] Other questions have remained on the table. It has been difficult to arrive at an agreed position on these questions because the text of the Directives often leaves much scope for interpretation and Member States were not prepared to compromise on the interpretation. The general wording of some of the provisions in the Accounting Directives has been an important reason why the Commission

---

[25]However, Article II of this directive states that member states may approve professionals who have obtained all or part of their qualifications in another EU country on the condition that these qualifications can be considered equivalent and that the professionals concerned furnish proof of sufficient knowledge about local law.

[26]See Arnold Schilder, "Research Opportunities in Auditing in the European Union," *Accounting Horizons* 10 (December 1996): 98–108.

[27]Peter Walton, "European Harmonization," in *International Finance and Accounting Handbook*, 3rd ed., F.D.S. Choi, ed., New York: John Wiley & Sons, 2003.

[28]Karel van Hulle, "International Harmonisation of Accounting Principles: A European Perspective," *Wirtschaftsprüferkammer—Mitteilungen*, special edition (June 1997): 44–50.

[29]European Commission Contact Committee on the Accounting Directives, The Accounting Harmonisation in the European Community, *Problems of Applying the Fourth Directive on the Annual Accounts of Limited Companies,* Luxembourg: Office for Official Publications of the European Communities, 1990.

has not brought some of these questions before the European Court of Justice for a final ruling.[30]

The EU's New Approach and the Integration of European Financial Markets

In 1995 the EC adopted a new approach to accounting harmonization, referred to as the New Accounting Strategy. The commission announced that the EU needs to move promptly in order to give a clear signal that companies seeking listings in the United States and other world markets will be able to remain within the EU accounting framework.[31] The EC also stressed that the EU needs to strengthen its commitment to the international standard-setting process, which offers the most efficient and rapid solution for the problems of companies operating on an international scale.

In 2000, the EC adopted a new financial reporting strategy. The cornerstone of this strategy was a proposed regulation that all EU companies listed on regulated markets, including banks, insurance companies, and SMEs (small and medium-sized companies), prepare consolidated accounts in accordance with IFRS. (Unlisted SMEs will not be covered, but may find it in their interest to adopt IFRS voluntarily, especially if they seek international capital.) The EU Parliament endorsed this proposal and the EU Council adopted the necessary enabling legislation in 2002.[32] This regulation affects some 7,000 listed EU companies (compared with nearly 300 listed EU companies that used IFRS in 2001). It is designed "to encourage cross-border trade in financial services and so create a fully-integrated market, by helping to make financial information more transparent and easily comparable."[33]

To become legally binding, IFRS must be adopted by the EC. Included in the above regulation is a two-tiered "endorsement mechanism" and the establishment of the Accounting Regulatory Committee (ARC), an EU body with representatives from member states. An IFRS is first given a technical review and opinion by the European Financial Reporting Advisory Group (EFRAG), a private-sector organization of auditors, preparers, national standard setters, and others.[34] Then, the ARC recommends that the IFRS be endorsed (or not) based on whether it is compatible with European directives and conducive to the European public good. EC endorsement completes the process.

EC endorsement of IFRS began in 2003 with the adoption of all existing IASB standards and interpretations (except for IAS 32 and 39, which were then being revised). The Fourth and Seventh Directives were also amended in 2003 to remove inconsistencies between the old directives and IFRS.

---

[30]Also see Bindon, Kathleen R., and Helen Gernon, "The European Union: Regulation Moves Financial Reporting Toward Comparability," *Research in Accounting Regulation* 9 (1995): 23–48; Van Hulle, K., and K.U. Leuven, "Harmonization of Accounting Standards—A View from the European Community," *The European Accounting Review* 1 (May 1992): 161–172.

[31]See the EC's communication "Accounting Harmonisation: A New Strategy vis-à-vis International Harmonisation," COM 95 (508) final of November 14, 1995.

[32]Regulation (EC) No. 1606/2002. Member states may defer application until 2007 for those companies listed in the EU and elsewhere that use U.S. GAAP (or other GAAP) as their primary basis of accounting, as well as for companies that only have publicly traded debt. Member states may also extend this requirement to all companies, not just listed ones, including individual company accounts.

[33]"International Accounting Standards: Mandatory for Listed Companies by 2005," *Single Market News,* no. 25 (March 2001): 18–19.

[34]The EFRAG Web site is www.efrag.org.

Finally, there have been developments designed to strengthen enforcement of IRFS in Europe. In 2003, the Committee of European Securities Regulators adopted *Standard 1 on Financial Information*. This standard contains 21 principles aimed at developing and implementing a common approach to the enforcement of IFRS throughout the EU.[35]

INTERNATIONAL ORGANIZATION OF SECURITIES COMMISSIONS (IOSCO)

The International Organization of Securities Commissions (IOSCO) consists of securities regulators from more than 100 countries. According to the preamble to IOSCO's by-laws:

> Securities authorities resolve to cooperate together to ensure a better regulation of the markets, on the domestic as well as the international level, in order to maintain just, efficient and sound markets:
>
> - To exchange information on their respective experiences in order to promote the development of domestic markets;
> - To unite their efforts to establish standards and an effective surveillance of international securities transactions;
> - To provide mutual assistance to ensure the integrity of the markets by a vigorous application of the standards and by effective enforcement against offenses.[36]

IOSCO has worked extensively on international disclosure and accounting standards to facilitate the ability of companies to raise capital efficiently in global securities markets. In 1998 IOSCO published a set of nonfinancial disclosure standards that may eventually enable companies to use a single prospectus to offer or list shares on any of the world's major capital markets. Securities regulators worldwide are increasingly adopting these standards.[37]

An IOSCO technical committee focuses on multinational disclosure and accounting. Its main objective is to facilitate the process whereby world-class issuers can raise capital in the most effective and efficient way on all capital markets where investor demand exists. It cooperates with the IASB by, among other activities, providing input on IASB projects. A working party study completed in 1998 presented recommendations for facilitating multinational equity offerings. The report recommended "that regulators be encouraged, where consistent with their legal mandate and the goal of investor protection, to facilitate the use of single disclosure documents, whether by harmonisation of standards, reciprocity or otherwise."[38]

---

[35]*Standard No. 1 on Financial Information: Enforcement of Standards on Financial Information in Europe,* CESR 03-073, March 12, 2003. CESR was established in 2001 as an EC advisory group on securities market regulation.
[36]International Organization of Securities Commissions, *Objectives and Principles of Securities Regulation,* www.iosco.org (May 2003).
[37]See International Organization of Securities Commissions Annual Report 1997, Montreal.
[38]International Organization of Securities Commissions, *International Disclosure Standards for Cross-Border Offerings and Initial Listings by Foreign Firms,* 1998.

Exhibit 8-4 presents a brief summary of the 10 disclosure standards. The summary is important because it indicates the comprehensiveness proposed by the working party. The disclosure standards proposed are also highly detailed.

Exhibit 8-4   Summary of International Disclosure Standards for Cross-Border Offerings and Initial Listings by Foreign Issuers (Published by International Organization of Securities Commissions, 1998)

1. *Identity of Directors, Senior Management and Advisers and Responsibility Statement*

This standard identifies the company representatives and other individuals involved in the company's listing or registration and indicates the persons responsible. The definition of the persons covered by this standard may vary in each country and would be determined by host country law.

2. *Offer Statistics and Expected Timetable*

This standard provides key information regarding the conduct of any offering and the identification of important dates relating to the offering. It is understood that listings do not always involve offerings.

3. *Key Information*

This standard summarizes key information about the company's financial condition, capitalization and risk factors.

4. *Information on the Company*

This standard provides information about the company's business operations, the products it makes or the services it provides, and the factors that affect the business.

5. *Operating and Financial Review and Prospects*

This standard provides management's explanation of factors that have affected the company's financial condition and results of operations, and management's assessment of factors and trends which are anticipated to have a material effect on the company's financial condition and results of operations in future periods. In some countries a forecast or statement of the company's prospects for the current year and/or other future periods may be required.

6. *Directors and Officers*

This standard provides information concerning the company's directors and managers that will allow investors to assess such individuals' experience, qualifications and levels of compensation, as well as their relationship with the company. The definition of the persons covered by this disclosure standard may vary in each country and would be determined by host country law. Information is also required concerning the company's employees.

7. *Major Shareholders and Related Party Transactions*

This standard provides information regarding the major shareholders and others that control or may control the company. The standard also provides information regarding transactions the company has entered into with persons affiliated with the company and whether the terms of such transactions are fair to the company.

8. *Financial Information*

This standard specifies which financial statements must be included in the document, as well as the periods to be covered, the age of the financial statements and other information of a financial nature. The country in which the company is listed (or is applying for listing) will determine the comprehensive bodies of accounting and auditing principles that will be accepted for use in preparation and audit of the financial statements.

Exhibit 8-4   Summary of International Disclosure Standards for Cross-Border Offerings and Initial Listings by Foreign Issuers (Published by International Organization of Securities Commissions, 1998) (*Continued*)

9. *The Offer*

This standard provides information regarding the offer of securities, the plan for distribution of the securities and related matters.

10. *Additional Information*

This standard provides information, most of which is of a statutory nature, which is not covered elsewhere in the document.

Source: International Organization of Securities Commissions (IOSCO), *International Disclosure Standards for Cross-Border Offerings and Initial Listings by Foreign Issuers,* 1998, (public document).

In 2002, a companion disclosure document for ongoing disclosures was published. Excerpts from this document are reproduced in Exhibit 8-5 on page 298.

INTERNATIONAL FEDERATION OF ACCOUNTANTS (IFAC)

High-quality auditing standards are necessary to ensure that accounting standards are rigorously interpreted and applied. Auditors validate and add credibility to external financial reports. Credible financial reporting is at the core of the efficient functioning of capital markets. Thus, the development of international accounting and auditing standards should be aligned for optimal harmonization to occur.

The IFAC is a worldwide organization with 159 member organizations in 118 countries, representing more than 2.5 million accountants. Organized in 1977, its mission is "to support the development of the accountancy profession with harmonized standards so accountants can provide consistently high quality services in the public interest."[39]

The IFAC Assembly, which meets every 2.5 years, has one representative from each of IFAC's member organizations. The assembly elects a council, which is made up of individuals from 18 countries elected for 2.5-year terms. The council, which meets twice a year, sets IFAC policy and supervises its operations. Day-to-day administration is provided by the IFAC Secretariat located in New York, which is staffed by accounting professionals from around the world.

Much of IFAC's professional work is done through standing committees. At this writing, the standing committees are:

1. International Auditing and Assurance Standards Board
2. Compliance
3. Education
4. Ethics
5. Professional Accountants in Business
6. Public Sector
7. Transnational Auditors

---

[39]IFAC 2002 Annual Report (www.ifac.org), p. 6.

Exhibit 8-5   Principles for Ongoing Disclosure and Reporting of Material Developments

1. *The Key Elements of an Ongoing Disclosure Obligation*

Listed entities should have an ongoing disclosure obligation requiring disclosure of all information that would be material to an investor's investment decision.

2. *Timeliness*

The listed entity shall disclose ongoing information on a timely basis, which could require disclosure on an:

a. immediate basis for disclosure of material developments, where such a term could be defined as "as soon as possible" or prescribed as a maximum of specified days; and

b. periodic basis, prescribed by law or listing rules, such as quarterly or annual reports. Such information would also include management discussion and analysis (MD&A), where required, which can be disclosed in a separate report or included in a periodic report. The disclosure obligation may require disclosure of relevant information on an immediate basis even when it belongs to periodic reporting.

3. *Simultaneous and Identical Disclosure*

If the entity is listed in more than one jurisdiction, the information released under the ongoing disclosure obligation of one jurisdiction where it is listed should be released on an identical basis and simultaneously in all the other jurisdictions where it is listed. This obligation should not be dependent on where the listed entity is principally listed.

4. *Dissemination of Information*

Under the ongoing disclosure obligation listed entities should ensure that full information is promptly made available to the market by using efficient, effective and timely means of dissemination.

5. *Disclosure Criteria*

Ongoing disclosure of information should be fairly presented, not be misleading or deceptive and contain no material omission of information.

6. *Equal Treatment of Disclosure*

The information to be disclosed in compliance with the ongoing disclosure obligation should not be disclosed to selected investors or other interested parties before it is released to the public. Certain narrow exceptions may be permitted to this principle to allow communications with advisers and rating agencies or, in the ordinary course of business, communications with persons with whom the listed entity is negotiating, or intends to negotiate, a commercial, financial or investment transaction or representatives of its employees or trade unions acting on their behalf. In all these cases, the recipients have a duty to keep the information confidential.

Source: International Organization of Securities Commissions, *Principles for Ongoing Disclosure and Material Development Reporting by Listed Entities: A Statement of the Technical Committee,* October 2002, (public document).

IFAC's council occasionally appoints special task forces to address important issues. At the end of 2002 there were two task forces:

- Rebuilding Public Confidence in Financial Reporting (Credibility)
- Small and Medium Practices

IFAC's International Auditing and Assurance Standards Board issues International Standards on Auditing (ISA), which are organized into the following groups:

- Introductory Matters
- Responsibilities
- Planning
- Internal Control
- Audit Evidence
- Using Work of Others
- Audit Conclusions and Reporting
- Specialized Areas
- Related Services

IFAC has close ties with other international organizations such as IASB and IOSCO. The financial statements of an increasing number of companies are being audited in conformity with IFAC's International Standards on Auditing.

UNITED NATIONS INTERGOVERNMENTAL WORKING GROUP OF EXPERTS ON INTERNATIONAL STANDARDS OF ACCOUNTING AND REPORTING (ISAR)

ISAR was created in 1982 and is the only intergovernmental working group devoted to accounting and auditing at the corporate level. Its specific mandate is to promote the harmonization of national accounting standards for enterprises. ISAR accomplishes its mandate by discussing and promulgating best practices, including those recommended by IASB. ISAR was an early proponent of environmental reporting and recent initiatives have focused on corporate governance and accounting by small and medium-sized enterprises. It has also conducted technical assistance projects in a number of areas such as accounting reform and retraining in the Russian Federation, Azerbaijan and Uzbekistan, and designing and developing a long-distance learning program in accountancy for French-speaking Africa.[40]

ORGANIZATION FOR ECONOMIC COOPERATION AND DEVELOPMENT (OECD)

OECD is the international organization of the industrialized, market economy countries. It functions through its governing body, the OECD Council, and its network of about 200 committees and working groups. Its publication *Financial Market Trends*, issued twice a year, assesses trends and prospects in the international and major

---

[40]From Background Paper, "The Intergovernmental Working Group of Experts on International Standards of Accounting and Reporting (ISAR)—UNCTAD," December 1997; and *ISAR Update* (http://r0.unctad.org/isar).

domestic financial markets of the OECD area. Description and analysis of the structure and regulation of securities markets is often published either as an OECD publication or as a special feature in *Financial Market Trends*. With its membership consisting of larger, industrialized countries, the OECD is often a counterweight to other bodies (such as the United Nations and the International Confederation of Free Trade Unions) that have built-in tendencies to act contrary to the interests of its members.[41]

CONCLUSION

Most people now believe that international harmonization is necessary to reduce the regulatory barriers to cross-border, capital-raising efforts. The debate is no longer *whether* to harmonize, nor even *how* to harmonize. Although national differences in environmental factors (such as systems of corporate governance and finance) that affect accounting development will persist for some time, financial reporting systems are converging as international capital markets become more investor oriented. The International Accounting Standards Board is at the center of this movement. These days it is impossible to address capital market and stock exchange regulatory issues without considering international harmonization of accounting principles, disclosure, and/or auditing.

---

[41]From the OECD Web site (www.oecd.org), April 1, 1998.

Appendix 8-1

SINOPEC SHANGHAI PETROCHEMICAL COMPANY LIMITED: AUDITOR'S REPORT, BACKGROUND, AND ACCOUNTING POLICIES

The Board of Directors and Shareholders of Sinopec Shanghai Petrochemical Company Limited:

We have audited the accompanying consolidated balance sheets of Sinopec Shanghai Petrochemical Company Limited and subsidiaries (the "Group") as of De-cember 31, 2001 and 2002, and the related consolidated statements of income, cash flows, and shareholders' equity for each of the years in the three-year period ended December 31, 2002, all expressed in Renminbi. These consolidated financial statements are the responsibility of the Group's management. Our responsibility is to express an opinion on these consolidated financial statements based on our audits.

We conducted our audits in accordance with auditing standards generally accepted in the United States of America and Hong Kong. Those standards require that we plan and perform the audit to obtain reasonable assurance about whether the financial statements are free of material misstatement. An audit includes examining, on a test basis, evidence supporting the amounts and disclosures in the financial statements. An audit also includes assessing the accounting principles used and significant estimates made by management, as well as evaluating the overall financial statement presentation. We believe that our audits provide a reasonable basis for our opinion.

In our opinion, the consolidated financial statements referred to above present fairly, in all material respects, the financial position of Sinopec Shanghai Petrochemical Company Limited and subsidiaries as of December 31, 2001 and 2002, and the results of their operations and their cash flows for each of the years in the three-year period ended December 31, 2002 in conformity with International Financial Reporting Standards.

International Financial Reporting Standards vary in certain significant respects from accounting principles generally accepted in the United States of America. Application of accounting principles generally accepted in the United States of America would have affected the results of operations for each of the years in the three-year period ended December 31, 2002 and shareholders' equity as of December 31, 2001 and 2002, to the extent summarized in note 28 to the consolidated financial statements.

The accompanying consolidated financial statements as of and for the year ended December 31, 2002 have been translated into United States dollars solely for the convenience of the readers. We have audited the translation, and in our opinion, the consolidated financial statements expressed in Renminbi have been translated into United States dollars on the basis set forth in note 1 to the consolidated financial statements.

KPMG
Hong Kong, China
March 26, 2003

1. Organization, Principal Activities and Basis of Preparation

Sinopec Shanghai Petrochemical Company Limited ("the Company"), formerly Shanghai Petrochemical Company Limited, was established in the People's Republic of China ("the PRC" or "the State") on June 29, 1993 as a joint stock limited company to hold the assets and liabilities of the production divisions and certain other units of the Shanghai Petrochemical Complex ("SPC"). SPC was established in 1972 and owned and managed the production divisions as well as the related housing, stores, schools, hotels, transportation, hospitals and other municipal services in the community of Jinshanwei.

The Company's former controlling shareholder, China Petrochemical Corporation ("CPC") completed its reorganization on February 25, 2000 in which its interests in the Company were transferred to its subsidiary, China Petroleum & Chemical Corporation ("Sinopec Corp"). In connection with the reorganization, CPC transferred its 4,000,000,000 of the Company's stated owned legal shares, which represented 55.56 per cent of the issued share capital of the Company, to Sinopec Corp. On October 12, 2000, the Company changed its name to Sinopec Shanghai Petrochemical Company Limited.

The principal activity of the Company and its subsidiaries (the "Group") is the processing of crude oil into petrochemical products for sale. The Group is one of the largest petrochemical enterprises in the PRC, with a highly integrated petrochemical complex which processes crude oil into a broad range of synthetic fibers, resins and plastics, intermediate petrochemicals and petroleum products. Synthetic fibers and resins and plastics are sold primarily to provincial and municipal governmental trading companies and industrial users, and intermediate petrochemical products and petroleum products are sold primarily to wholesale distribution companies owned by local and provincial government entities in Eastern PRC. Substantially all of its products are sold in the PRC domestic market.

The consolidated financial statements have been prepared in accordance with International Financial Reporting Standards ("IFRS") adopted by the International Accounting Standards Board ("IASB"), and interpretations issued by the International Financial Reporting Interpretations Committee of the IASB. Differences between IFRS and accounting principles generally accepted in the United States ("U.S. GAAP") and their effect on net income for the years ended December 31, 2000, 2001, and 2002, and shareholders' equity as of December 31, 2001, and 2002, are set forth in Note 28.

The consolidated financial statements are prepared on the historical cost basis as modified by the revaluation of certain property, plant and equipment. The accounting policies have been consistently applied by the Group. As described in Note 22(g) to the financial statements, land use rights are carried at cost less amortization effective January 1, 2002. The effect of this change resulted in a decrease in the shareholders' equity as of January 1, 2002. The effect of this change did not have a material impact on the Group's financial condition and results of operations in prior years.

The financial information has been prepared in Renminbi ("RMB"), the national currency of the PRC. Solely for the convenience of the reader, the financial statements have been translated into United States dollars at the rate of U.S. $1.00 = RMB 8.2773 quoted by the People's Bank of China on December 31, 2002. No representation is made that the Renminbi amounts could have been, or could be, converted into United States dollars at that rate.

2. Principal Accounting Policies

  (a) Basis of consolidation

    (i) Subsidiaries

The consolidated financial statements of the Group incorporate the financial statements of the Company and all of its principal subsidiaries. Subsidiaries are those enterprises controlled by the Company. Control exists when the Company has the power, directly or indirectly, to govern the financial and operating policies of an enterprise so as to obtain benefits from its activities. The financial statements of subsidiaries are included in the consolidated financial statements from the date that control effectively commences until the date that control effectively ceases. The share of results attributable to minority interests is deducted from or added to income before minority interests.

    (ii) Associates

Associates are those enterprises in which the Group has significant influence, but not control, over the financial and operating policies. The consolidated financial statements include the Group's share of the total recognized gains and losses of the principal associates on an equity basis, from the date that significant influence commences until the date that significant influence ceases. When the Group's share of losses exceeds the carrying amount of the associate, the carrying amount is reduced to nil and recognition of further losses is discontinued except to the extent that the Group has incurred obligations in respect of the associate.

    (iii) Transactions eliminated on consolidation

All material intercompany transactions and balances, and any unrealized gains arising from intercompany transactions, are eliminated on consolidation.

    (iv) Goodwill

Goodwill arising on acquisition represents the excess of the cost of acquisition over the fair value of their net identifiable assets on acquisition. Goodwill is stated at cost less amortization and impairment losses (see Note 2(p)). Amortization is charged on a straight-line basis to the consolidated statements of income over its economic useful life.

Negative goodwill arising on acquisition represents the excess of the fair value of the net identifiable assets of subsidiaries acquired over the cost of acquisition. Negative goodwill is, where material, credited to deferred income which is recognized in the consolidated statements of income on a systematic basis.

  (b) Property, plant and equipment

Property, plant and equipment are stated in the balance sheet at cost or valuation (see Note 15) less accumulated depreciation and impairment losses (see Note 2(p)). Revaluations are performed periodically to ensure that the carrying amount does not differ materially from that which would be determined using fair value at the balance sheet date.

(i) Subsequent expenditure

Expenditure incurred to replace a component of an item of property, plant and equipment that is accounted for separately, is capitalized with the carrying amount of the component being written off. Other subsequent expenditure is capitalized only when it increases the future economic benefits embodied in the item of property, plant and equipment. All other expenditure is recognized in the consolidated statements of income as an expense as incurred.

(ii) Depreciation and amortization

Depreciation is provided to write off the costs or valuation of property, plant and equipment over their estimated useful lives on a straight-line basis, after taking into account their estimated residual values, as follows:

Buildings	15 to 40 years
Plant, machinery, equipment and others	5 to 14 years

(iii) Retirement or disposal

Gains or losses arising from the retirement or disposal of property, plant and equipment are determined as the difference between the net disposal proceeds and the carrying amount of the asset and are recognized in the consolidated statements of income on the date of retirement or disposal.

(c) Lease prepayments

Lease prepayments represent land use rights paid to the PRC's land bureau. Land use rights are carried at cost and amortized on a straight-line basis over the respective periods of the rights. On December 31, 2002, lease prepayments, which comprise of land use rights, have been presented in a separate balance sheet caption. Accordingly, the comparative amount at December 31, 2001, which was previously included in property, plant and equipment, was reclassified to conform with the current year's presentation.

(d) Construction in progress

Construction in progress represents buildings, various plant and equipment under construction and pending installation, and is stated at cost less the government grants that compensate the Company for the cost of construction and impairment losses (see Note 2(p)). Cost comprises direct costs of construction as well as interest charges, and foreign exchange differences on related borrowed funds to the extent that they are regarded as an adjustment to interest charges, during the period of construction.

The construction in progress is transferred to property, plant and equipment when the asset is substantially ready for its intended use. No depreciation is provided in respect of construction in progress.

(e) Investments

Investments in unlisted equity securities are stated at cost less provision for impairment losses (see Note 2(p)). A provision is made where, in the opinion of management, the carrying amount of the investments exceeds its recoverable amount.

(f) Inventories

Inventories, other than spare parts and consumables, are carried at the lower of cost and net realizable value. Cost includes the cost of materials computed using the weighted average method and expenditure incurred in acquiring the inventories and bringing them to their existing location and condition. In the case of work in progress and finished goods, cost includes direct labor and an appropriate proportion of production overheads. Net realizable value is the estimated selling price in the ordinary course of business less the estimated costs of completion and the estimated costs necessary to make the sales.

When inventories are sold, the carrying amount of those inventories is recognized as an expense in the period in which the related revenue is recognized. The amount of any write-down of inventories to net realizable value and all losses of inventories are recognized as an expense in the period the write-down or loss occurs. The amount of any reversal of any write-down of inventories, arising from an increase in net realizable value, is recognized as a reduction in the amount of inventories recognized as an expense in the period in which the reversal occurs.

Spare parts and consumables are stated at cost less any provision for obsolescence.

(g) Trade debtors

Trade debtors are stated at cost less allowance for doubtful accounts. Allowance for doubtful accounts is provided based upon the evaluation of the recoverability of these accounts at the balance sheet date.

(h) Cash equivalents

Cash equivalents consist of time deposits with an initial term of less than three months when purchased. Cash equivalents are stated at cost, which approximates fair value.

(i) Translation of foreign currencies

Transactions in foreign currencies are translated into Renminbi at the applicable exchange rates ruling at the transaction dates.

Monetary assets and liabilities denominated in foreign currencies are translated into Renminbi at rates quoted by the People's Bank of China at the balance sheet date. Nonmonetary assets and liabilities denominated in foreign currencies, which are stated at historical cost, are translated into Renminbi at the foreign exchange rate ruling at the date of the transaction.

Foreign currency translation differences relating to funds borrowed to finance the construction of property, plant and equipment to the extent that they are regarded as an adjustment to interest costs are capitalized during the construction period. All other exchange differences are dealt with in the consolidated statements of income.

(j) Revenue recognition

Revenue from the sale of goods is recognized in the consolidated statements of income when the significant risks and rewards of ownership have been transferred to the buyer. Revenue excludes value added tax and is after deduction of any trade discounts and returns. Revenue from the rendering of services is recognized in the consolidated statements of income upon performance of the services. No revenue is recognized if there are significant uncertainties regarding recovery of the consideration due, associated costs or the possible return of goods.

Dividend income is recognized when the shareholder's right to receive payment is established.

(k) Grants

Capital-based government grants consist of grants for the purchase of equipment used for technology improvements. Such grants are offset against the cost of asset to which the grant related.

(l) Net financing costs

Net financing costs comprise interest expense on borrowings, interest income on bank deposits, foreign exchange gains and losses and bank charges.

Interest income from bank deposits is accrued on a time-apportioned basis by reference to the principal outstanding and at the rate applicable.

All interest and other costs incurred in connection with borrowings are expensed as incurred as part of net financing costs, except to the extent that they are capitalized as being directly attributable to the acquisition, construction or production of an asset which necessarily takes a substantial period of time to get ready for its intended use or sale.

(m) Repairs and maintenance expenses

Repairs and maintenance expenses, including cost of major overhaul, are charged to the consolidated statements of income as and when they are incurred.

(n) Research and development costs

Research and development costs comprise all costs that are directly attributable to research and development activities or that can be allocated on a reasonable basis to such activities. Because of the nature of the Group's research and development activities, no development costs satisfy the criteria for the recognition of such costs as an asset. Both research and development costs are therefore recognized as expenses in the year in which they are incurred.

(o) Retirement benefits

The contributions payable under the Group's retirement plans are charged to the consolidated statements of income according to the contribution determined by the plans. Further information is set out in Note 24.

(p) Impairment loss

The carrying amounts of the Group's long-lived assets are reviewed periodically in order to assess whether the recoverable amounts have declined below the carrying amounts. These assets are tested for impairment whenever events or changes in circumstances indicate that their recorded carrying amounts may not be recoverable. When such a decline has occurred, the carrying amount is reduced to the recoverable amount. The recoverable amount is the greater of the net selling price and the value in use. In determining the value in use, expected future cash flows generated by the asset are discounted to their present value. The amount of the reduction is recognized as an expense in the consolidated statements of income.

The Group assesses at each balance sheet date whether there is any indication that an impairment loss recognized for an asset in prior years may no longer exist. An impairment loss is reversed if there has been a favorable change in the estimates used to determine the recoverable amount. A subsequent increase in the recoverable amount of an asset, when the circumstances and events that led to the write-down or write-off cease to exist, is recognized as income. The reversal is reduced by the amount that would have been recognized as depreciation had the write-down or write-off not occurred.

(q) Deferred income

Deferred income is amortized on a straight-line basis to the consolidated statements of income over 10 years.

(r) Dividends

Dividends are recognized as a liability in the period in which they are declared.

(s) Income tax

Income tax on the consolidated statements of income comprises current and deferred tax.

Current tax is the expected tax payable on the taxable income for the year, using tax rates enacted or substantially enacted at the balance sheet date, and any adjustment to tax payable in respect of previous years.

Deferred tax is provided using the balance sheet liability method, providing for temporary differences between the carrying amounts of assets and liabilities for financial reporting purposes and the amounts used for taxation purposes, except differences relating to goodwill not deductible for tax purposes and the initial recognition of assets or liabilities which affect neither accounting nor taxable income. The amount of deferred tax provided is based on the expected manner of realization or settlement of the carrying amount of assets and liabilities, using tax rates enacted or substantially enacted at the balance sheet date. The effect on deferred tax of any changes in tax rates is charged to the consolidated statements of income.

A deferred tax asset is recognized only to the extent that it is probable that future taxable income will be available against which the assets can be utilized. Deferred tax assets are reduced to the extent that it is no longer probable that the related tax benefit will be realized.

(t) Provisions

A provision is recognized in the balance sheet when the Group has a legal or constructive obligation as a result of a past event, and it is probable that an outflow of economic benefits will be required to settle the obligations.

(u) Related parties

For the purposes of these financial statements, parties are considered to be related to the Group if the Group has the ability, directly or indirectly, to control the party or exercise significant influence over the party in making financial and operating decisions, or vice versa, or where the Group and the party are subject to common control or common significant influence. Related parties may be individuals or other entities.

(v) Segment reporting

A segment is a distinguishable component of the Group that is engaged in providing products or services and is subject to risks and rewards that are different from those of other segments.

(w) Estimates

The preparation of financial statements in accordance with IFRS requires management to make estimates and assumptions that affect the reported amounts of assets and liabilities and disclosure of contingent assets and liabilities at the date of the financial statements and the reported amounts of revenues and expenses during the reporting period. Actual results could differ from those estimates.

Selected References

Alexander, D., and S. Archer, "An Overview of European Accounting," in *Miller European Accounting Guide,* 5th ed., D. Alexander and S. Archer, eds., New York: Aspen, 2003, 1.01–1.23.

Andersen, BDO, Deloitte Touche Tohmatsu, Ernst & Young International, Grant Thornton, KPMG, and PricewaterhouseCoopers, *GAAP 2001—A Survey of National Accounting Rules Benchmarked Against International Accounting Standards,* October 2001.

BDO, Deloitte Touche Tohmatsu, Ernst & Young, Grant Thornton, KPMG, and Pricewaterhouse Coopers, *GAAP Convergence 2002: A Survey of National Efforts to Promote and Achieve Convergence with International Financial Reporting Standards,* www.ifad.net, 2002.

Buijink, Willem, Steven Maijoor, Roger Meuwissen, and Argen van Witteloostuijn, *Final Report of a Study on The Role, Position and Liability of the Statutory Auditor Within the European Union* (commissioned by DG XV of the European Commission), Brussels-Luxembourg: Office for Official Publications of the European Communities, 1996.

Cañibano, L., and A. Mora, "Evaluating the Statistical Significance of *de facto* Accounting Harmonization: A Study of European Global Players," *The European Accounting Review* 9, No. 3 (2000): 349–369.

Epstein, B. J., and A. A Mirza, *Wiley IAS 2003: Interpretation and Application of International Accounting Standards,* New York: John Wiley & Sons, 2003.

Haller, A., "Financial Accounting Developments in the European Union: Past Events and Future Prospects," *The European Accounting Review* 11, No. 1 (2002): 153–190.

International Accounting Standards Board (IASB), *International Financial Reporting Standards 2003,* London: IASC, 2003.

International Federation of Accountants (IFAC), *Handbook of International Auditing, Assurance, and Ethics Pronouncements,* New York: IFAC, 2003.

International Organization of Securities Commissions (IOSCO), *IASC Standards—Report of the Technical Committee of the International Organization of Securities Commissions,* www.iosco.org, May 2000.

Land, J., and M. H. Lang, "Empirical Evidence on the Evolution of International Earnings," *The Accounting Review* 77 (Suppl. 2002): 115–138.

Leuz, C., "IAS versus U.S. GAAP: Information Asymmetry-Based Evidence from Germany's New Market," *Journal of Accounting Research* 41, No. 3 (June 2003): 445–472.

Needles, B. E., Jr., "Taxonomy of Auditing Standards," in *International Finance and*

Accounting Handbook, 3rd ed., F. D. S. Choi, ed., New York: John Wiley & Sons, 2003.

Pacter, P., "International Financial Reporting Standards," in *International Finance and Accounting Handbook,* 3rd ed., F. D. S. Choi, ed., New York: John Wiley & Sons, 2003.

PricewaterhouseCoopers, *A Global Approach to Corporate Governance, Accountability, Auditing and Capital Market Regulation,* www.pwc.com, August 2003.

PricewaterhouseCoopers, *Global GAAP: The Future of Corporate Reporting,* http://www.cfodirect.com/cfopublic.nsf/0/a0a5f 4b91d752bb885256d4f004fb8ad/$FILE/Global %20GAAP_V_7.pdf, 2003.

Street, D. L., "Large Firms Envision Worldwide Convergence of Standards," *Accounting Horizons* 16, No. 3 (September 2002): 215–218.

Street, D. L., and S. J. Gray, *Observance of International Accounting Standards: Factors Explaining Non-compliance, ACCA Research Report No. 74,* London: Association of Chartered Certified Accountants, 2001.

United Nations Conference on Trade and Development (UNCTAD), The Intergovernmental Working Group of Experts on International Standards of Accounting and Reporting, *United Nations Conference on Trade and Development Conclusions on Accounting and Reporting by Transnational Corporations,* New York and Geneva: United Nations, http://www.unicc.org/unctad/en/ press-ref/tncacc.htm, 1994.

Walton, P., "European Harmonization," in *International Finance and Accounting Handbook,* 3rd ed., F. D. S. Choi, ed., New York: John Wiley & Sons, 2003.

Discussion Questions

1. From a financial statement user's viewpoint, what is the most important source of accounting difference: measurement or disclosure? For which area is it most important to achieve international accounting harmonization?

2. What evidence is there that International Financial Reporting Standards (IFRS) are becoming widely accepted around the world? What are at least four different ways that national accounting standard setters use IFRS in setting their own standards?

3. What are at least five similarities and at least five differences between IASB standards and those of your home country?

4. Is the growing use of International Financial Reporting Standards around the world an example of accounting harmonization or accounting standardization? Discuss.

5. Compare and contrast the following proposed approaches for dealing with international differences in accounting, disclosure, and auditing standards: (1) reciprocity; (2) reconciliation; (3) international standards.

6. What are the key rationales that support the development and widespread application of International Financial Reporting Standards?

7. What are the key rationales *against* the development and widespread application of International Financial Reporting Standards?

8. What is the purpose of accounting harmonization in the European Union (EU)? Why did the EU abandon its approach to harmonization via directives to one favoring the IASB?

9. Sir Bryan Carsberg states that "The case for harmonisation in accounting standards is a particularly strong one. Accounting has relatively low cultural value." Critically evaluate these statements.

10. Why is the concept of auditing harmonization important? Will international harmonization of auditing standards be more or less difficult to achieve than international harmonization of accounting principles?

11. Describe IOSCO's work on harmonizing disclosure standards for cross-border offerings and initial listings by foreign issuers. Why is this work important to securities regulators around the world?

12. What role do the United Nations and the Organization for Economic Cooperation and Development play in harmonizing accounting and auditing standards?

Exercises

1. Three solutions have been proposed for resolving the problems associated with filing financial statements across national borders: (1) reciprocity (also known as mutual recognition); (2) reconciliation; and (3) use of international standards.

   Required: Present a complete but concise evaluation of each of the three approaches. What do you expect is the preferred approach from the perspective of each of the following groups: (1) investors; (2) company management; (3) regulatory authorities; (4) stock exchanges; and (5) professional associations? Discuss your reasons for each response. Which approach do you predict will eventually dominate?

2. Exhibit 8-1 presents Web site addresses of many major international organizations involved in international accounting harmonization.

   Required:
   a. From among these member organizations, select three that interest you.
   b. For each of the three organizations you select, describe its membership, its organizational focus, and why it is concerned with international financial accounting standard setting.

3. Exhibit 8-2 presents Web site addresses of national accountancy organizations, many of which are involved in international accounting standard-setting and harmonization activities.

   Required: Select one of the accounting organizations and search its Web site for information about its involvement in international accounting standard-setting and harmonization. Prepare a detailed description of the organization's activities in these areas.

4. The text discusses the many organizations involved with international harmonization activities, including the IASB, EU, and IFAC.

   Required:
   a. Compare and contrast these three organizations in terms of their standard-setting procedures.
   b. At what types and sizes of enterprises are their standards *primarily* directed?

    c. Briefly critique the following statement: "Acceptance of international accounting standards (accounting principles, disclosures, and auditing), as far as it has come and is likely to come in the near future, is significantly centered on companies operating in multiple countries."

5. The chapter contains a chronology of some significant events in the history of international accounting standard setting.

    Required: Select one of the events identified, consult some literature references about it, and prepare a 300-word essay describing the event and indicating why it is deemed significant.

6. Exhibit 8-3 identifies current IASB standards and their respective titles.

    Required: Using information on the IASB Web site (www.iasb.org), or other available information, prepare an updated list of IASB standards and exposure drafts.

7. The biographies of current IASB board members are on the IASB Web site (www.iasb.org).

    Required: Identify the current board members (including chairman and vice-chairman). Note each member's home country and prior affiliation(s). Which board members have previously served on national accounting standard-setting bodies?

8. The IASB published 13 revised standards in December 2003. A summary is available at www.iasplus.com/iasplus/improve0401.pdf.

    Required: Prepare a list of the major differences between these revised standards and the GAAP of your home country.

9. Refer to Exercise 8.

    Required: How would each difference affect the balance sheet and income statement? How would each difference affect the following financial ratios used by analysts?
- *Liquidity:* current ratio
- *Solvency:* debt to equity; debt to assets
- *Profitability:* return on assets; return on equity

10. The IASB Web site (www.iasb.org) summarizes each of the current International Financial Reporting Standards.

    Required: Identify the standards that permit the use of alternative accounting treatments. For each, briefly describe the benchmark treatment and the allowed alternative treatment. To what extent might companies' use of these different treatments reduce the comparability of the resulting financial statements?

11. Consider the following restatement of net profit and shareholders' equity from IFRS to U.S. GAAP by the German company Schering AG.

Reconciliation of net profit to U.S. GAAP

	2003	2002
Net profit under IFRS	**443**	**867**
U.S. GAAP adjustments		
Business combinations		
Acquired in-process R&D	14	– 119
Other differences	15	13
Property, plant and equipment		
Capitalization of interest	– 1	– 1
Reversal of impairment losses	0	1
Internal-use software	—	– 3
Equity investment (Aventis CropScience)	—	71
Inventories	4	6
Provisions for pensions	2	2
Other provisions	15	– 2
Schering AG call options	—	—
Stock option plans	3	14
Tax effect on U.S. GAAP adjustments	– 6	– 1
Net profit under U.S. GAAP	**489**	**848**
Earnings per share under U.S. GAAP €		
basic	2.52	4.30
diluted	2.51	4.29

Reconciliation of shareholders' equity to U.S. GAAP

	2003	2002
Shareholders' equity under IFRS	**2,902**	**2,934**
U.S. GAAP adjustments		
Business combinations		
Acquired in-process R&D	– 141	– 175
Other differences	42	28
Property, plant and equipment		
Capitalization of interest	16	17
Reversal of impairment losses	– 3	– 3
Internal-use software	—	—
Equity investment (Aventis CropScience)	—	—
Inventories	22	18
Provisions for pensions	– 33	– 54
Other provisions	18	3
Schering AG call options	– 7	– 10
Stock option plans	22	34
Tax effect on U.S. GAAP adjustments	– 11	2
Shareholders' equity under U.S. GAAP	**2,827**	**2,794**

Required: Calculate return on equity (ROE) under IFRS and U.S. GAAP for the two years shown. What important measurement differences between IFRS and U.S. GAAP are revealed by this restatement? Are the differences consistent between the two years? How would the adherence of IFRS versus U.S. GAAP affect a loan covenant requirement for a minimum ROE?

12. The IASB Web site (www.iasb.org) summarizes each of the current International Financial Reporting Standards.

    Required: Answer each of the following questions.

    a. In measuring inventories at the lower of cost or net realizable value, does net realizable value mean:
       i. estimated replacement cost, or
       ii. estimated selling price less estimated costs to complete and sell the inventory?
    b. Under International Financial Reporting Standards, which of the following methods is (or are) acceptable to account for an investment in a joint venture?
       i. cost method
       ii. equity method
       iii. proportionate consolidation
       iv. consolidation
    c. Which of the following would be classified as an extraordinary item?
       i. loss from settlement of a product liability lawsuit
       ii. claims paid by an airline as a result of a plane crash
       iii. destruction of a communications satellite during launch
       iv. none of the above
    d. In Year 1, an enterprise accrued its warranty obligation based on its best estimate of the expected cost to repair defective products during the 3-year warranty coverage period. During Year 2, warranty claims were significantly more than expected due to unrecognized quality control problems in Year 1. Is it appropriate to restate the financial statements for Year 1 to reflect the revised estimate of the warranty obligation?
    e. True or false: An enterprise with a December 31 year-end declares a dividend on its common shares on January 5. The dividend is recognized as a liability at year-end.
    f. After initial recognition, which of the following financial assets are not remeasured at fair value?
       i. options on unquoted equity securities
       ii. marketable securities (equities)
       iii. derivative financial instruments that are financial assets
       iv. fixed maturity instruments the enterprise intends to hold to maturity
    g. Which of the following is true? An enterprise that follows the policy of revaluing its property, plant, and equipment may apply that policy:
       i. to all assets within a single country on a country-by-country basis
       ii. to all assets within a single broad class, such as to land and buildings but not to machinery and equipment
       iii. to all assets of a certain age, such as all assets 10 years or older.
    h. True or false: Interest cost on funds borrowed by an enterprise to finance the construction of a new building must be capitalized as part of the cost of the building.

CASE 8-1   SINOPEC SHANGHAI PETROCHEMICAL COMPANY LIMITED

Located in the Jinshan District of Shanghai, SINOPEC Shanghai Petrochemical Co. Ltd. (SPC) is one of the largest petrochemical companies in China, with integrated production and operations of petroleum products, petrochemicals, synthetic fibers, and plastics. SPC produces over 60 different products in these four categories. At the end of 2002, SPC has total assets of RMB 26.6 billion and 32,000 employees. Under the registered trademark "San Ren Pai," its products are distributed all over China and in many foreign countries. In June 1993, SPC shares were listed on the Shanghai Stock Exchange, the Hong Kong Stock Exchange, and the New York Stock Exchange.

You are an equity research analyst and have been asked to prepare a research report on SPC. Your business strategy analysis indicates that SPC's sales growth and financial performance can probably be sustained. However, although your qualitative analysis has yielded promising results, you are concerned that your financial analysis will be difficult due to accounting and audit quality issues and your unfamiliarity with Chinese accounting standards.

You start your analysis by becoming familiar with accounting principles used to prepare SPC's 2002 financial statements. You are encouraged that the company states that its financial statements conform to IASB standards, but realize that how accounting standards are applied is as important as the standards themselves.

REQUIRED

Examine SPC's Note, "Principal Accounting Policies," in Appendix 8-1, and read about IASB Standards on the IASB Web site (www.iasb.org) and the IAS Plus Web site (www.iasplus.com).

1. As much as possible, assess the extent to which SPC's accounting principles conform to IASB standards.
2. How reliable is your assessment?
3. What further information would help your assessment?
4. Does the auditor's report (presented in Appendix 8-1) provide information useful in your assessment? Explain.

CASE 8-2   ACCOUNTING QUALITY IN EAST ASIA

"KOREAN MURK"[a]

For all the salutary shock of Asia's financial crisis, South Korean companies can still cook their books. After the crisis hit South Korea in 1997, the government watchdog for accounting standards tightened up the existing lax rules, but there is still a long way to go. Over the past three years, one in every three companies the watchdog has selected at random turns out to have violated the rules. A study recently published by PricewaterhouseCoopers, an international accounting firm, finds that South Korea has the most opaque standards of accounting and corporate governance of the 35 countries it surveyed.

Opacity may have long been evident, but its effects can still shock. In July 1999, when Daewoo, an industrial giant, collapsed with debts of $80 billion, everybody was taken by surprise. At the end of 1998 it had hugely inflated assets and hidden debts that totaled some $34 billion. Against the inflated assets, the conglomerate borrowed about $7.5 billion from banks, while $20 billion was illegally channeled to a secret account in London, or so claims the state prosecution agency. Now 27 people have been charged, including former senior managers of Daewoo and its auditors. Daewoo's founder, Kim Woo Choong, remains in hiding after fleeing abroad.

Alarmed by the Daewoo collapse, the national assembly passed a law promising harsh punishment to accountants who fail in their duties. Under the law, which takes effect on April 1, the finance minister can fine firms up to 100m won ($380,000), and individuals up to 50m won if they fail to discover that the books they are auditing have been cooked. Accountants also face criminal charges and, if convicted, up to three years in prison.

Such severe punishments may not, however, swiftly bring an end to creative accounting at South Korean companies. For a start, the accounting rules that the government introduced in the wake of the financial crisis still fall far short of international standards. For instance, South Korean companies can count as assets payments that are not due for a year or more.

Another problem is a shortage of qualified auditors. There are about 8,000 companies, including all of South Korea's listed firms, that are required by law to produce financial statements audited by independent accountants. Although some 4,000 accountants are certified to audit financial statements, most of these are tax specialists. Moreover, because almost all companies close their books at the same time, at the end of the calendar year, that creates a sudden increase in the workload.

One way to discourage companies from creative accounting is to introduce a law that would allow minority shareholders to file class-action suits. That is a cause championed by Ha Seung Soo of the People's Solidarity for Participatory Democracy, a civic group that campaigns for the rights of minority shareholders. The finance ministry plans to draft a law which, if passed, would make it possible to bring suits against companies with assets of more than 2 trillion won. Mr. Ha points out that only a dozen or so firms would be affected.

REQUIRED

1. This article states that accounting standards in South Korea "fall far short of international standards." Would the adoption of IFRS improve financial reporting quality in Korea?
2. Is it fair to say that this article suggests that formal accounting standards mean relatively little if there is not a general consensus in a country's business culture that these standards be followed and enforced? What changes would need to occur in South Korea for real progress in financial reporting and corporate governance to occur? What are the implications for the prospects for successful accounting harmonization?
3. Many experts say that companies will make credible financial disclosures only if there is a strong investor demand for them. Can improvements in corporate financial reporting and governance be forced in absence of investor demand? What good are regulations in the absence of an underlying demand? Discuss.

CHAPTER 9 | INTERNATIONAL FINANCIAL STATEMENT ANALYSIS

INTRODUCTION

Investors, equity research analysts, financial managers, bankers, and other financial statement users have a growing need to read and analyze nondomestic financial statements. Cross-border financial comparisons are vital when assessing the financial promise and soundness of a foreign direct or portfolio investment. There has been tremendous growth in international capital issuance and trading in recent years due to privatizations, economic growth, relaxation of capital controls, and continued advances in information technology.

The need to use, and therefore understand, nondomestic financial statements has also increased as merger and acquisition activities have become more international. The value of cross-border mergers grew steadily during the 1990s,[1] and this growth shows no signs of abatement.

Finally, as business becomes more global, financial statements become more important than ever as a basis for competitive analysis, credit decisions, business negotiations, and corporate control. Continued reduction in national trade barriers, the emergence of Europe as a unified market, convergence of consumer tastes and preferences, and a growing sophistication of business firms in penetrating nondomestic markets have significantly intensified multinational business competition. All this creates a further need for international financial statement analysis and valuation.

This chapter synthesizes information presented in Chapters 1 through 8. It examines opportunities and challenges encountered in analyzing foreign financial statements, and provides suggestions for the analyst.

CHALLENGES AND OPPORTUNITIES IN CROSS-BORDER ANALYSIS

Cross-border financial analysis involves multiple jurisdictions. An analyst, for example, may have occasion to study a company outside her home country or to compare companies from two or more countries. Unique challenges face those doing international analysis.

Nations vary dramatically in their accounting practices, disclosure quality, legal and regulatory systems, nature and extent of business risk, and modes of conducting

---

[1]"Emerging-Market Indicators," *The Economist,* (October 7, 2000); 124.

business. This variation means that analytical tools that are effective in one jurisdiction may be less so in another. The analyst often faces daunting challenges in obtaining credible information. In many emerging market economies, financial analyses often have limited reliability.

International financial analysis and valuation are characterized by many contradictions. On the one hand, the rapid pace of harmonization of accounting standards is leading to enhanced comparability of financial information worldwide. However, vast differences in financial reporting practices remain. Some analysts question the extent to which greater uniformity in accounting standards will actually result in the provision of comparable information by leading companies in an industry.[2]

As discussed in Chapter 5, companies around the world are disclosing more information, and more credible information. Many countries, including China, Korea, the Czech Republic and Russia, are striving to improve the availability and quality of information about public companies. Moreover, access to freely available information relevant for financial analysis is growing dramatically with dissemination of company information on the Internet. However, in many countries there continues to be a great gulf between expectations based on these advances and reality. Financial analysts are often frustrated in their attempts to gather information (see, e.g., Cases 4-1 and 8-2 in this text, which deal with difficulties in obtaining company information in the Czech Republic and South Korea, respectively). Also, many governments continue to publish highly suspect information.

Despite the foregoing contradictions, barriers to international financial analysis and valuation are falling, and the overall outlook for the analyst is positive. Globalization of capital markets, advances in information technology, and increasing competition among national governments, stock exchanges, and companies for investors and trading activity continue. Together these forces are creating incentives for companies to voluntarily improve their external financial reporting practices.

Continuing globalization and improvements in international accounting and disclosure are blurring the distinctions between cross-border and within-border financial analysis. With the implementation of the euro, together with continued advances in European corporate disclosure practices, portfolio diversification strategies in Europe are increasingly based on industry sectors rather than countries. Rather than balancing stock picks among strong and weak currency countries, portfolio managers are increasingly focusing on picking the best companies in an industry regardless of country of origin. Globalization also means that strictly domestic analyses are becoming less relevant. Interdependencies are growing and no company is insulated from events happening worldwide.

BUSINESS ANALYSIS FRAMEWORK

Palepu, Bernard, and Healy provide a useful framework for business analysis and valuation using financial statement data.[3] The framework's four stages of analysis (discussed in more detail in the following pages) are: (1) business strategy analysis,

---

[2]For example, see Hope, Ole-Kristan, "Variations in the Financial Reporting Environment and Earnings Forecasting," *Journal of International Financial Management and Accounting* 15, No. 1 (2004): 22.
[3]Krishna G. Palepu, Victor L. Bernard, and Paul M. Healy, *Business Analysis and Valuation Using Financial Statements,* Cincinnati, Ohio: South-Western College Publishing, 1996.

(2) accounting analysis, (3) financial analysis (ratio analysis and cash flow analysis), and (4) prospective analysis (forecasting and valuation). The relative importance of each stage depends on the purpose of the analysis. The business analysis framework can be applied to many decision contexts including securities analysis, credit analysis, and merger and acquisition analysis.

INTERNATIONAL BUSINESS STRATEGY ANALYSIS

Business strategy analysis is an important first step in financial statement analysis. It provides a qualitative understanding of a company and its competitors in relation to its economic environment. This ensures that quantitative analysis is performed using a holistic perspective. By identifying key profit drivers and business risks, business strategy analysis helps the analyst make realistic forecasts.[4] Standard procedures for gathering information for business strategy analysis include examining annual reports and other company publications, and speaking with company staff, analysts, and other financial professionals. The use of additional information sources, such as the World Wide Web, trade groups, competitors, customers, reporters, lobbyists, regulators, and the trade press is becoming more common. The accuracy, reliability, and relevance of each type of information gathered also needs to be evaluated.[5]

Business strategy analysis is often complex and difficult in an international setting. As noted previously, key profit drivers and types of business risk vary among countries. Understanding them can be daunting. Business and legal environments and corporate objectives vary around the world. Many risks (such as regulatory risk, foreign exchange risk, and credit risk, among others) need to be evaluated and brought together coherently.[6] In some countries, sources of information are limited and may not be accurate.

Information Availability

Business strategy analysis is especially difficult in some countries due to a lack of reliable information about macroeconomic developments. Governments in developed countries are sometimes accused of publishing faulty or misleading economic statistics. The situation is much worse in many emerging economies. For example, one reason the 1994/95 Mexican currency crisis was a surprise was that the government concealed information about its shrinking foreign reserves and exploding money supply. Some countries delay publishing statistics when the numbers are unfavorable, or even falsify their economic figures.[7]

Obtaining industry information is also difficult in many countries and the quantity and quality of company information varies greatly. The availability of company-specific information has been strikingly low in many developing economies.[8] Recently, many large companies that list and raise capital in overseas markets have been expanding

---

[4]Profit drivers are principal financial and operating elements that affect a firm's profitability.
[5]Financial analysts are increasingly using techniques developed in the fast-growing business discipline of competitive intelligence (CI). See Peter Bartram, "Spies Like Us," *Accountancy* (July 2000): 44, 45.
[6]Refer to Chapter 11 for detailed discussion of financial risk management.
[7]See "The Insatiable in Pursuit of the Unquantifiable." *The Economist,* (March 4, 1995): 71, 72, for an analysis of the quality of economic statistics in 24 emerging markets.
[8]See Chapter 5 for further discussion. Also see S. M. Saudagaran, and J. G. Diga, "Financial Reporting in Emerging Capital Markets: Characteristics and Policy Issues," *Accounting Horizons* (June 1997): 41–64.

their disclosures and have voluntarily switched to globally recognized accounting principles such as International Financial Reporting Standards.[9]

Recommendations for Analysis

Data constraints make it difficult to perform business strategy analyses using traditional research methods. Very often, travel is necessary to learn about local business climates and how industries and companies actually operate, especially in emerging market countries. The World Wide Web also offers quick access to information that recently was unavailable or difficult to obtain. Exhibit 9-1 presents a sampling of freely available Web resources that can be used to learn about country risks and travel conditions.

Country information can also be found in "international briefings" publications distributed by large accounting firms, banks, and brokerages.[10] The International Federation of Stock Exchanges (FIBV, http://www.fibv.com) and the Federation of European Stock Exchanges (FESE, http://www.fese.be) publish highly informative international newsletters, and *Accountancy, The Economist, Financial Analysts Journal,* and *Euromoney* magazines provide many articles highly relevant for international financial analysis.

Enormous risks may follow an inadequate business strategy analysis. Consider the recent Parmalat affair, representing the largest fraud in European financial history. In this case, at least $13 billion in missing assets of Italy's fastest growing dairy group could not be accounted for, resulting in huge losses for the company's investors and creditors alike. Commentators attribute this financial debacle to several causes. Foreign investors reportedly invested in a company that did not provide complete or credible disclosures. They did not know much about the business environment in which

Exhibit 9-1 Country Information Freely Available on the Internet

Organization	Web Site Address	Description
Canada Department of Foreign Affairs and International Trade	http://www.dfait-maeci.gc.ca/ english/menu.htm	Market information
Financial Times	http://ft.com	Country reports (also industry reports, company news and financial information)
Political and Economic Risk Consultancy, Ltd. (PERC)	http://www.asiarisk.com/	Country outlooks; connection to other WWW sites
UNCTAD	www.unctad.org	Data for analysis of international trade, foreign direct investment commodities and development
U.S. Federal Reserve	www.federalreserve.gov	Foreign exchange rates
U.S. State Department	http://travel.state.gov/	Travel warnings
World Bank	www.dev.data.worldbank.org	Country development data
World Tourism Organization	http://www.world-tourism.org	Newsletters, press releases

---

[9]Refer to Chapter 5 for discussion of other voluntary financial reporting practices companies use to accommodate international financial statement users.

[10]For example, PricewaterhouseCoopers LLC publishes *International Briefings* every month, which reports on notable business, political, and economic developments worldwide.

they were investing and participated in a market in which financial reporting rules were not strictly enforced.[11]

ACCOUNTING ANALYSIS

The purpose of accounting analysis is to assess the extent to which a firm's reported results reflect economic reality. The analyst needs to evaluate the firm's accounting policies and estimates, and assess the nature and extent of a firm's accounting *flexibility*. The latter refers to management's discretion in choosing which accounting policies and estimates to apply to a particular accounting event.[12] To reach reliable conclusions, the analyst must adjust reported accounting amounts to remove distortions caused by the use of accounting methods the analyst deems inappropriate. For example, the analyst might believe that a company's revaluations of fixed assets result in unreasonably high asset carrying amounts.

Corporate managers are allowed to make many accounting-related judgments because they know the most about their firm's operations and financial condition. Flexibility in financial reporting is important because it allows managers to use accounting measurements that best reflect the company's particular operating circumstances. However, managers have incentives to distort operating reality by using their accounting discretion to distort reported profits. One reason is that reported earnings are often used to evaluate their managerial performance.[13]

Healy and colleagues suggest the following process for evaluating a firm's accounting quality:

1. Identify key accounting policies
2. Assess accounting flexibility
3. Evaluate accounting strategy
4. Evaluate the quality of disclosure
5. Identify potential red flags (e.g., unusually large asset write-offs, unexplained transactions that boost profits, or an increasing gap between a company's reported income and its cash flow from operations)
6. Adjust for accounting distortions

To illustrate this process, consider the accounting quality of WorldCom, a large U.S. company whose accounting policies resulted in a major Wall Street scandal. In formally indicting the company on its faulty accounting practices, the following questions might be asked: (1) How did WorldCom account for its major operating expenditures? (2) What options does U.S. GAAP allow for such expenditures? (3) Did WorldCom adopt an overly aggressive or conservative approach to accounting for these expenditures?

---

[11]Gail Edmondson, David Fairlamb, and Nanette Byrnes, "The Milk Just Keeps on Spilling," *BusinessWeek* (January 26, 2004): 54, 55, 58.
[12]For an example of managerial flexibility provided under the partial method for deferred taxes, see Elizabeth A. Gordon, "Unrecognized Deferred Taxes: Evidence from the U.K.," *Accounting Review* 70, No. 1 (2004): 97–124.
[13]Additional influences on corporate managers' accounting decisions include: (1) accounting-based debt covenants; (2) management compensation; (3) corporate control contests; (4) tax considerations; (5) regulatory considerations; (6) capital market considerations; (7) stakeholder considerations; and (8) competitive considerations. Palepu, Bernard, and Healy, op. cit.

(4) Did WorldCom disclose sufficient information for investors to undo the company's aggressive accounting treatment? (5) Did WorldCom capitalize an expenditure that should have been expensed to boost reported profits? Was there a major discrepancy between WorldCom's reported earnings and its cash flow from operations? (6) Would reversal of WorldCom's selected accounting posture have a significant depressing effect on reported earnings?

In this case, WorldCom chose to capitalize what were in effect operating expenses. While this practice is in clear violation of U.S. GAAP, management chose to conceal this information from investors by disguising operating expenses as capital expenditures. The financial statement effects of capitalizing versus expensing its major expenditures had a significant effect on reported earnings as the amounts involved approached $2 billion!

Two major issues confront those doing accounting analysis in an international setting. The first is cross-country variation in accounting measurement quality, disclosure quality, and audit quality; the second concerns the difficulty in obtaining information needed to conduct accounting analysis.

Cross-country variation in quality of accounting measurement, disclosure, and auditing is dramatic. National characteristics that cause this variation include required and generally accepted practices, monitoring and enforcement, and extent of managerial discretion in financial reporting.[14] Chapters 3 and 4 of this text present summaries of significant accounting practices in six highly developed and four emerging countries, respectively. These chapters, which summarize only a subset of major accounting topics, show that significant managerial discretion may be used in many countries, including France, Germany, China, and Taiwan.

Consider accounting practices in Germany. As discussed in Chapter 3, German financial accounting is closely aligned with tax reporting. Creditor protection is a second goal of financial reporting. As a result, financial reports are prepared with a creditor focus rather than an investor focus. The resulting conservative reporting bias may generate accounting amounts that do not reflect actual operating performance. German managers have great discretion in their use of reserves and in implementing many accounting policies. Even where specific procedures are mandated, monitoring and enforcement of compliance with reporting requirements is far short of what investors can expect in the United States.

Disclosure quality and the level of audit assurance must also be closely scrutinized when analyzing a German company's financial statements. Footnote disclosure of accounting policies is quite limited in some German annual reports. Identifying the components of large financial statement items (such as reserve accounts) can be difficult.

Also, the German auditing environment is dramatically different from countries such as the United Kingdom and the United States. Auditor independence rules in Germany are much less comprehensive and intricate than in the United Kingdom and

---

[14]While faulty application of accounting principles is frequently touted as the leading cause of low accounting quality (Roula Khalaf, "Buyer Beware," *Forbes* [June 29, 1994]: 204; *Euromoney* Capital Markets Report, "Equity? Was ist das?" [July 1994]: 82; Diana B. Henriques, "In World Markets, Loose Regulation," *New York Times* [July 23, 1991]: D1, D6), some argue that the application of faulty accounting principles is the root cause. See Paul Rosenfield, "What Drives Earnings Management?" *Journal of Accountancy* [October 2000]: 5.

the United States, and German managers might consider it inappropriate for auditors to question their oral statements. German auditors are also more hesitant to accept responsibility for detecting irregularities than their U.K. or U.S. counterparts.[15]

External auditors play a key role in ensuring that accounting standards are followed. Legal systems provide enforcement mechanisms for ensuring that auditors remain as independent as practicable. However, audit environments are not uniform around the world. For example, while auditor litigation is relatively common in the United States, they have been rare in Germany.[16]

Financial reporting in China provides a second example of how accounting measurement, disclosure, and audit quality can vary dramatically from accounting practices in Anglo-American countries.[17] Although China is implementing major accounting reform as part of its transition from a planned economy to a controlled market economy, until recently it did not have financial reporting and external auditing in forms that would be familiar to Westerners.[18] Private investors and creditors were virtually nonexistent for three decades after the People's Republic was founded in 1948, and The Accounting Law, which sets forth accounting and reporting requirements, was adopted only in 1985. Accounting Standards for Business Enterprises, which specifies that such basic accounting practices as double-entry bookkeeping and the accrual basis should be used, became effective in 1993. The auditing profession is also very new in China.[19]

Suggestions for the Analyst

Especially when analyzing companies in emerging market countries, the analyst should meet often with management to evaluate their financial reporting incentives and accounting policies. Many companies in emerging market countries are closely held, and managers may not have strong incentives for full and credible disclosure. Accounting policies in some countries may be similar or identical to IAS (or other widely accepted standards), but managers often have great discretion in how those policies are applied.

For example, one portfolio manager described his analysis of Siam Cement, the leader in Thailand's cement industry and a recently established competitor.[20] Siam Cement depreciated parts of its cement plant over 5 years. This aggressive strategy was designed to minimize tax payments because financial records must conform to tax

---

[15]See Carol A. Frost, and Kurt P. Ramin, "International Auditing Differences," *Journal of Accountancy* (April 1996): 62–67; Carol A. Frost, and Kurt P. Ramin, "Corporate Financial Disclosure: A Global Assessment," in Frederick D. S. Choi, ed., *International Accounting and Finance Handbook,* New York: John Wiley & Sons, 1997; pp. 18.1–18.33; Coopers & Lybrand Deutsche Revision AG, *Accounting and Auditing in Germany,* 3rd ed., January 1991.

[16]Refer to Chapter 3 for further discussion of financial reporting in Germany.

[17]The financial reporting situation in Russia today is strikingly similar to that of China.

[18]For further discussion, see Chapter 4; Ajay Adhikari and Shawn Z. Wang, "Accounting for China," *Management Accounting* (April 1995): 27–32; "Asia's Stockmarket Nightmare" *The Economist,* (December 20, 1997): 107–108; and David Cairns, "When East Meets West," *Accountancy-International Edition.*

[19]See Sarah Gray, ed., "World Watch Will China's Firms Conquer the World?" *Accountancy-International Edition* (September 1997): 6.

[20]See Mark E. Denning, "The Essentials of Emerging Markets Research," in *Investing Worldwide VII Focus on Emerging Markets,* Charlottesville, Vir.: Association for Investment Management and Research (AIMR), September 1996; and Dean LeBaron, "Emerging Markets Research Must You Be There?" in *Investing Worldwide VII Focus on Emerging Markets,* Charlottesville, VA: Association for Investment Management and Research (AIMR), September 1996.

records in Thailand. In contrast, the competitor used a depreciation period of 20 years to maximize reported earnings (which meant that it paid more tax than necessary).

Finally, as noted earlier, new communications technology (including the World Wide Web) is having a great impact on all stages of financial research. Many companies and countries now have Web sites that make it much easier for anyone interested to gather information. Refer to the section entitled "Information Access" later in this chapter for a discussion of useful information sources for accounting analysis.

INTERNATIONAL FINANCIAL ANALYSIS

The goal of financial analysis is to evaluate a firm's current and past performance, and to judge whether its performance can be sustained. Ratio analysis and cash flow analysis are important tools in financial analysis. Ratio analysis involves comparison of ratios between the firm and other firms in the same industry, comparison of a firm's ratios across years or other fiscal periods, and/or comparison of ratios to some absolute benchmark. It provides insights on the comparative and relative significance of financial statement items and can help evaluate the effectiveness of managements' operating, investing, financing and earnings retention policies. A summary of commonly used financial ratios appears in Exhibit 9–2.

Cash flow analysis focuses on the cash flow statement, which provides information about a firm's cash inflows and outflows, classified among operating, investing, and financing activities, and disclosures about periodic noncash investing and financing activities. Analysts can use cash flow analysis to address many questions about the firm's performance and management. For example, has the firm generated positive cash flows from operations? How have cash flow components changed across time in relation to changes in income statement components, sales, and cost of sales in particular? What have been the cash flow consequences of management decisions about financial policy, dividend policy, and investment?

Ratio Analysis

Two issues must be addressed in analyzing ratios in an international setting. First, do cross-country differences in accounting principles cause significant variation in financial statement amounts of companies from different countries? Second, how do differences in local culture and economic and competitive conditions affect the interpretation of accounting measures and financial ratios, even if accounting measurements from different countries are restated to achieve "accounting comparability"?

Extensive evidence reveals substantial cross-country differences in profitability, leverage, and other financial statement ratios and amounts that result from both accounting and nonaccounting factors. (The next section discusses cross-country differences in two *valuation* ratios, the price-to-earnings and price-to-book ratios.) For example, Frost compared sales revenue, net income, and leverage (total debt/shareholders' equity) from 400 firms, 80 each domiciled in France, Germany, Japan, the United Kingdom, and the United States.[21] The five 80-firm country samples were matched according to size (market value of equity), with all firms belonging to the

[21]See Carol A. Frost, "Characteristics and Information Value of Corporate Disclosures of Forward-Looking Information in Global Equity Markets," Dartmouth College Working Paper, July 2002.

Exhibit 9-2   Summary of Financial Ratios

Ratio	Formula for Computation

I. Liquidity

1. Current ratio

$$\frac{\text{Current assets}}{\text{Current liabilities}}$$

2. Quick or acid-test ratio

$$\frac{\text{Cash, marketable securities, and receivables}}{\text{Current Liabilities}}$$

3. Current cash debt ratio

$$\frac{\text{Net cash provided by operating activities}}{\text{Average current liabilities}}$$

II. Efficiency

4. Receivables turnover

$$\frac{\text{Net sales}}{\text{Average trade receivables (net)}}$$

5. Inventory turnover

$$\frac{\text{Cost of goods sold}}{\text{Average inventory}}$$

6. Asset turnover

$$\frac{\text{Net sales}}{\text{Average total assets}}$$

III. Profitability

7. Profit margin on sales

$$\frac{\text{Net income}}{\text{Net sales}}$$

8. Rate of return on assets

$$\frac{\text{Net income}}{\text{Average total assets}}$$

9. Rate of return on common stock equity

$$\frac{\text{Net income minus preferred dividends}}{\text{Average common stockholders' equity}}$$

10. Earnings per share

$$\frac{\text{Net income minus preferred dividends}}{\text{Weighted shares outstanding}}$$

11. Payout ratio

$$\frac{\text{Cash dividends}}{\text{Net income}}$$

IV. Coverage

12. Debt to total assets ratio

$$\frac{\text{Debt}}{\text{Total assets or equities}}$$

13. Times interest earned

$$\frac{\text{Income before interest charges and taxes}}{\text{Interest charges}}$$

14. Cash debt coverage ratio

$$\frac{\text{Net cash provided by operating activities}}{\text{Average total liabilities}}$$

15. Book value per share

$$\frac{\text{Common stockholders' equity}}{\text{Outstanding shares}}$$

manufacturing industry group (SIC codes 20 through 39). All three financial measures varied substantially among the country samples. For example, median net income was much greater in the United Kingdom and the United States than in Germany and Japan. Variation in net income was partially explained by accounting principle differences because financial reporting is generally less conservative in the United Kingdom and the United States than in Germany and Japan. Nonaccounting factors also affected reported net income. For example, the creditor focus in France, Germany, and Japan accounted for lower net income than in the United States and the United Kingdom as there is less pressure on managers in those countries to report steadily increasing net income.

Frost also found median leverage in the United Kingdom and the United States to be lower than in Germany and Japan. This is partially attributed to the fact that conservative accounting in Germany and Japan results in lower reported shareholders' equity than in the United Kingdom and the United States. Higher leverage in Germany, Japan, and France is also attributed to higher debt in capital structures, reflecting the heavy dependence on bank financing in those countries.[22]

How large are the differences in financial statement items caused by differences among national accounting principles? Hundreds of non-U.S. companies listed on U.S. stock exchanges give footnote reconciliation disclosures that provide evidence on this question, at least in the context of differences between U.S. GAAP-based and non-U.S. GAAP-based accounting amounts.

An earlier survey of financial statement reconciliations by foreign registrants prepared by the U.S. SEC is informative.[23] Approximately one-half of the 528 non-U.S. registrants surveyed disclosed material differences between net income as reported in their financial statements and U.S. GAAP-based net income. The five types of financial statement differences disclosed by the largest number of registrants were (in descending order): (1) depreciation and amortization, (2) deferred or capitalized costs, (3) deferred taxes, (4) pensions, and (5) foreign currency translation.

The study also shows that more than two-thirds of the registrants that disclosed material differences in net income reported that income under U.S. GAAP was lower than under non-U.S. GAAP. Nearly half of them reported income differences greater than 25 percent. Twenty-five of the 87 registrants that reported that income under U.S. GAAP was *greater* than under non-U.S. GAAP reported differences greater than 25 percent. Similar results were found for reconciliations of shareholders' equity. Overall, the evidence in the SEC study shows that financial statement differences under U.S. versus non-U.S. GAAP are highly material for many companies.

Evidence from SEC registrants' reconciliation disclosures therefore indicates that GAAP differences can cause significant variation in financial statement numbers. The analyst will often choose to make financial statements more comparable by making accounting principle adjustments to the financial statements being analyzed. Appendix 9-1

---

[22]Raghuram G. Rajan and Luigi Zingales, "What Do We Know about Capital Structure? Some Evidence from International Data," *Journal of Finance,* 50 (December 1995): 1421–1460; R. Jacobson and D. Aaker, "Myopic Management Behavior with Efficient, But Imperfect, Financial Markets," *Journal of Accounting and Economics* 19 (October 1993): 383–405; S. H. Hanke and A. Walters, "Governance," *Forbes* (April 11, 1994): 87; and *Euromoney,* "Equity, Was ist das?" (July 1994): 82, 84–85.
[23]U.S. Securities and Exchange Commission, Division of Corporation Finance, *Survey of Financial Statement Reconciliations by Foreign Registrants,* May 1, 1993.

illustrates the restatement of an income and balance sheet from Japanese GAAP to U.S. GAAP. Even after financial statement amounts are made reasonably comparable (by adjusting for accounting principle differences), interpretation of those amounts must consider cross-country differences in economic, competitive, and other institutional differences. Analysis of Japanese companies provides a good illustration. For example, Brown and Stickney argue that the relation between financial and tax reporting, the importance in Japan of operating through corporate groups (*keiretsu*), and the tolerance in Japan for heavy use of short-term financial leverage must all be considered when analyzing the profitability and risk of Japanese companies.[24] For example, Japanese reported earnings tend to be lower than earnings reported in Anglo-American countries, even after adjusting for GAAP differences. The close linkage between tax and financial reporting gives Japanese companies an incentive to be conservative in determining their income. Also, because high intercorporate stock holdings reduce the percentage of shares held by outsiders, Japanese companies are under less pressure to report ever-increasing earnings than are companies in the United States and other Anglo-American countries.[25] Refer to Appendix 9-2 for further detailed discussion of international ratio analysis. The appendix focuses on comparison of Japanese and U.S. financial ratios and their interpretation.

Cash Flow Analysis

As discussed earlier, cash flow analysis provides insights about a company's cash flows and management. Highly detailed cash flow statements are required under U.S. GAAP, U.K. GAAP, IFRS, and accounting standards in a growing number of other countries.[26] Cash flow–related measures are especially useful in international analysis because they are less affected by accounting principle differences than are earnings-based measures. When cash flow statements are not presented, it is often difficult to compute cash flows from operations and other cash flow measures by adjusting accrual-based earnings. Many companies simply do not disclose the information needed to make the adjustments. As one example, German balance sheets often contain surprisingly large reserve accounts that reflect many different types of accrual. Few (if any) details are presented that might allow the financial statement user to assess the implications for operating, investment, and financing cash flows.

Coping Mechanisms

How do financial statement users cope with cross-country accounting principle differences? Several approaches are used. Some analysts restate foreign accounting measures to an internationally recognized set of principles, or to some other common basis.

---

[24]Paul R. Brown and Clyde P. Stickney, "Instructional Case: Tanaguchi Corporation," *Issues in Accounting Education* 7 (Spring 1992): 57–68.
[25]McKinnon [Jill L. McKinnon, "Application of Anglo-American Principles of Consolidation to Corporate Financial Disclosure in Japan," *ABACUS* 20 (1984): 16–33] provides further detail on corporate groups in Japan versus those in Anglo-American countries. She argues that the Anglo-American consolidation methods adopted by Japan in 1977 may reflect international pressure for accounting conformity more than the inherent desirability of those methods. She implies that as a result, Japanese consolidated financial statements are less useful than they might be. The McKinnon study provides an important illustration that knowing what accounting principles are used is only the first step in interpreting financial statements from different countries.
[26]Refer to Chapters 3 and 4 of this text.

Others develop a detailed understanding of accounting practices in a limited set of countries and restrict their analysis to firms located in those countries.

Brown, Soybel, and Stickney illustrate the use of a restatement algorithm to enhance cross-border comparisons of financial performance.[27] They restate the operating performance of U.S. and Japanese companies to a similar reporting basis. Rather than convert U.S. data to a Japanese financial reporting basis, or Japanese data to a U.S. financial reporting basis, they adjust (as necessary) both U.S. and Japanese data to achieve uniform accounting principles.[28]

Appendix 9-1 illustrates another approach, in which the financial statements of a hypothetical Japanese business (Toyoza Enterprises) are restated from a Japanese GAAP basis to a U.S. GAAP basis. The restatement algorithm used in Appendix 9-1 involves a detailed analysis of numerous financial statement items.

Relatively simple restatement algorithms can be effective. One approach is to focus on a few of the most material financial statement differences for which enough information is available to make reliable adjustments. For example Brown and colleagues summarize many differences between Japan and U.S. GAAP, but their restatement algorithm focuses on only four accounting principle differences: (1) inventory cost assumptions, (2) depreciation method, (3) bonuses to directors and statutory auditors, and (4) deferred taxes and special tax reserves.[29]

INTERNATIONAL PROSPECTIVE ANALYSIS

Prospective analysis involves two steps: forecasting and valuation. In forecasting, analysts make explicit forecasts of a firm's prospects based on its business strategy, accounting, and financial analysis. It addresses questions such as, How will a company's change in business strategy affect future sales volume and profits? Has the company recently adopted new accounting policies that will make current earnings appear stronger, perhaps at the cost of lower earnings next year? Will financial relationships evidenced in an analyst's ratio analysis continue?

In valuation, analysts convert quantitative forecasts into an estimate of a firm's value. Valuation is used implicitly or explicitly in many business decisions. For example, valuation is the basis of equity analysts' investment recommendations. In analyzing a possible merger, the potential acquirer will estimate the value of the target firm. Many different valuation approaches are used in practice, ranging from discounted cash flow analysis to simpler techniques based on price-based multiples.[30]

Experts in international valuation give this warning to those doing international prospective analysis: "Any rules you've learned in your home country will fall apart overseas." Exchange rate fluctuations, accounting differences, different business prac-

---

[27]Brown, Paul R., Virginia E. Soybel, and Clyde P. Stickney, "Comparing U.S. and Japanese Corporate-Level Operating Performance Using Financial Statement Data," *Strategic Management Journal*, February 1994.
[28]Brown, Paul R., Virginia E., Soybel, and Clyde P. Stickney, "Achieving Comparability of U.S. and Japanese Price-Earnings Ratios," in Frederick D. S. Choi, ed., *International Accounting and Finance Handbook*, 2nd ed., New York: John Wiley & Sons, 1997, pp. 7.1–7.18.
[29]See Paul R. Brown, Virginia E. Soybel, and Clyde P. Stickney, "Achieving Comparability of U.S. and Japanese Price-Earnings Ratios," in Frederick D. S., Choi, ed., *International Accounting and Finance Handbook*, 2nd ed., New York: John Wiley & Sons, 1997, pp. 7.1–7.18.
[30]See Aswath Damodaran, *Investment Valuation*, 2nd ed., New York: John Wiley & Sons, 2000.

tices and customs, capital market differences, and many other factors will have major effects on international forecasting and valuation.

For example, discounted cash flow analysis values a business as the present value of its expected cash flows, discounted at a rate that reflects the riskiness of those cash flows. While this valuation principle is no different for developed and emerging markets alike, many of the inputs taken for granted in the former may not be as accessible in emerging economies.[31] For example, the government bond rate, often used as a surrogate for the risk-free rate, assumes that governments do not default, at least on local borrowing. This is often not the case internationally. Other inputs including risk parameters and premiums are typically more difficult to estimate owing to the paucity of historical data. And earnings forecasts, as a basis for estimating future cash flows, are less reliable. Hope attributes this to several factors.[32] One factor is the greater choice that managers have in choosing among accounting methods. Greater choice makes it more difficult to do cross-section analyses and makes it easier for managers to distort economic reality in reporting firm performance.[33] Forecast accuracy is also positively related to the extent to which accrual accounting is prescribed in a country. Accruals provide a better measure of a firm's future cash generating ability than cash receipts and disbursements and irons out discontinuities in reported revenues and expenses.[34] Finally, the accuracy of analysts' earnings forecasts are positively related to the strength of a country's enforcement standards. Hope attributes this relationship to the notion that enforcement narrows the range of permitted accounting choices. This, in turn, reduces analysts' uncertainty about the degree of firms' reporting discretion.[35]

Consider next the use of price-based (valuation) multiples in an international setting.[36] Valuation multiples such as price-to-earnings (P/E) and price-to-book (P/B) ratios are often used to estimate a firm's value. One common approach is to calculate the desired multiple for a group of comparable firms (such as other firms in the same industry), and then apply that multiple to the firm being valued to get a reasonable price. For example, if the price-to-earnings ratio of the industry group is 15, and the firm's earnings are forecast to be $1.80/share, then $27.00 per share is a reasonable price for the firm being analyzed. One might use the valuation multiples approach to determine the bid price for an acquisition candidate. If the candidate is a European company, comparable firms might be chosen from selected European countries.

Reliance on valuation multiples assumes that market prices reflect future prospects and that pricing of firms with similar operating and financial characteristics

---

[31]Aswath Damodaran, "Valuation in Emerging Markets," in Frederick D. S. Choi, ed., *International Finance and Accounting Handbook*, 3rd ed., New York: John Wiley & Sons, 2003, p. 9.3.

[32]Hope, op. cit., pp. 21–39.

[33]Basu et al. provide a useful means for operationalizing the notion of accounting choice. See S. L. Basu, L. Hwang, and C. L. Jan, "International Variation in Accounting Measurement Rules and Analysts' Earnings Forecast Errors," *Journal of Business Finance and Accounting* 25, Nos. 9&10 (1998): 1207–1247.

[34]A useful proxy for the measurement of the relative degree of accrual accounting employed internationally is provided by M. Hung, "Accounting Standards and Value Relevance of Earnings: An International Analysis," *Journal of Accounting and Economics* 30 No. 3 (2000): 401–420.

[35]Hope op. cit., p. 23.

[36]For a fuller discussion of business valuation, see: Tom Copeland, Tim Koller, and Jack Murrin, *Valuation: Measuring and Managing the Value of Companies*, New York: John Wiley & Sons, 1990; Aswath Damodaran, *Investment Valuation*, New York: John Wiley & Sons, 1996; Krishna G. Palepu, Victor L. Bernard, and Paul M. Healy, *Business Analysis and Valuation*, Cincinnati, Ohio: South-Western Publishing Co., 1996.

Exhibit 9-3   Mean Price/Earnings Ratios for Last Decade

Country	Beginning	Middle	End
China (PRC)	N/A	27.8	48.2
Czech Republic	N/A	12.6	15.9
France	10.2	38.3	24.6
Germany	11.6	20.7	55.0
Japan	39.8	79.3	N/A
Mexico	11.8	13.4	17.2
Netherlands	8.9	17.7	27.5
Taiwan	31.1	29.0	47.7
U.K.	10.6	15.9	30.5
U.S. (Amex)	6.1	20.1	36.2
U.S. (Nasdaq)	11.1	26.3	205.5
U.S. (NYSE)	14.8	20.6	31.2

N/A, not available.

Adapted from the *World Stock Exchange Fact Book 2000* defines ratios as follows: P/E Ratio, Total market value of all stocks/Total net earnings of all stocks in a given period; Dividend Yield, Total annualized gross dividends of all stocks/Total market value of all stocks.

Sources: Adapted from *World Stock Exchange Fact Book 2000,* Round Rock, TX: Meridian Securities Markets LLC, except as follows: 1996 and 1999 data for France and 1999 data for U.S. (Amex) and U.S. (Nasdaq) are from David Rathborne and Deborah Ritchie, eds., *The Salomon Smith Barney Guide to World Equity Markets 2000,* London: Euromoney Books and Salomon Smith Barney, 2000; 1999 data for China (PRC) are from *Emerging Markets Factbook 2000,* New York, Standard and Poor's, May 2000.

(such as firms in the same industry) is applicable to the firm being analyzed because of its similarity to those firms. Application of price multiples in a cross-border setting is challenging because it requires that the determinants of each multiple, and reasons why multiples vary across firms, be thoroughly understood.

Exhibit 9-3 displays mean price to earnings ratios for public companies in 12 countries at the start, middle, and end of the last decade.

Exhibit 9-3 shows that P/E ratios varied dramatically across countries. At the end of the last decade (the beginning of this decade), P/E multiples ranged from 15.9 in the Czech Republic to 205.5 for firms listed on the U.S. Nasdaq. Moreover, average P/E ratios varied over time within a single country. But what accounts for these patterns, especially across national boundaries?

National differences in accounting principles are one potential source of cross-country ratio variations. Such differences, for example, cause P/E ratios in Japan to generally be higher than those in the United States (recall that reported earnings in Japan are lower than in the United States for comparable companies with similar financial performance). However, even after adjusting for accounting differences, P/E ratios in Japan are still much higher than in the United States.

French and Poterba examined disparities between Japanese and U.S. P/E ratios and the steep increase in Japanese P/E ratios during the late 1980s.[37] They made sev-

---

[37] Kenneth R., French and James M. Poterba, "Were Japanese Stock Prices Too High?" *Journal of Financial Economics* 29 (1991): 337–362.

eral accounting adjustments to the Japanese data and found that their adjustments reduced but did not eliminate the difference between Japanese and U.S. P/E ratios. French and Poterba concluded that accounting differences explain about half of the long-term differences between U.S. and Japanese P/E ratios.

Brown, Soybel, and Stickney also investigated why Japanese P/E ratios are higher than U.S. P/E ratios.[38] They found that adjusting for different accounting principles explains only a small part of the difference. A comparison of their study with French and Poterba's shows how different approaches and assumptions can lead to very different conclusions about valuation ratios.[39]

The substantial variation in valuation ratios shown in Exhibit 9-3 reflects changes in financial performance and in market prices across time and countries. As discussed previously, even French and Poterba's rigorous analysis of the changes in P/E ratios in Japan during the late 1980s yielded only partial answers. Thus, accounting offers only a partial explanation for differences among P/E ratios in different countries and over time. An understanding of additional environmental considerations (see Appendix 9-2) is necessary for meaningful analysis and interpretation.

FURTHER ISSUES

All four stages of business analysis (business strategy, accounting, financial and prospective analysis) may be affected by the following factors: (1) information access, (2) timeliness of information, (3) language and terminology barriers, (4) foreign currency issues, and (5) differences in types and formats of financial statements.

Information Access

Information about thousands of companies from around the world has become more widely available in recent years. Countless information sources are appearing on the World Wide Web. Companies around the world now have Web sites, and their annual reports are available free of charge from various Internet and other sources. Refer to Exhibit 9-4 for Web sites that provide information highly relevant for company research.

Many companies also respond to written and telephone requests for their annual reports and other financial documents. In one study more than 70 percent of a sample of 160 large public companies contacted in France, Germany, the United Kingdom, and the United States responded to written requests for their annual reports. However, only 15 (37.5 percent) of the 40 large Japanese companies contacted responded. Thus, the amount of company information available varies considerably from country to country.[40]

---

[38]Paul R. Brown, Virginia E. Soybel, and Clyde P. Stickney, "Achieving Comparability of U.S. and Japanese Price-Earnings Ratios," op. cit.

[39]See Paul R. Brown, Virginia E., Soybel, and Clyde P. Stickney, "Achieving Comparability of U.S. and Japanese Price-Earnings Ratios," op. cit., for a review of comparative analyses of Japanese and U.S. P/E ratios. For further comparative evidence on cross-country differences in P/E and P/B ratios, see Peter Joos and Mark Lang, "The Effects of Accounting Diversity: Evidence from the European Union," *Journal of Accounting Research* 32 (Suppl., 1994): 141–175.

[40]See Carol A. Frost, and Kurt Ramin, "Corporate Financial Reporting and Disclosure: A Global Assessment" in F. D. S. Choi, ed. *Handbook of International Accounting and Finance, 2nd ed.,* New York: John Wiley & Sons, April 1997.

Exhibit 9-4   Freely Available Web Sites for Company Research (all Web sites begin with the prefix http://www)

Name of Web Site	Web Site Address	What It Provides
Annual Reports Library	zpub.com/sf/arl/	Alphabetical listing of U.S. corporations with links to home pages and annual reports that can be downloaded free of charge with Adobe Acrobat Reader.
Annual Report Gallery	reportgallery.com/bigaz.htm	Access to annual reports.
Asian Business Watch	asianbusinesswatch.com	Company and stock market news for Japan and Asia.
Babel	babel.altavista.com	Translates text files; only does first few pages of long documents.
Bank of England	bank of england.co.uk/	United Kingdom monetary and financial statistics, working papers, and other publications, information on the bank's structure and functions, and much more.
BFA-NET: Bureau of Financial Analysis Network	bfanet.com	South African company and stock market information; check out "Little Facts."
Bloomberg News Service	bloomberg.com/	Highlights from the Bloomberg news service.
Businessjeeves.com	businessjeeves.com	Good starting place; many links.
Business Week Online	businessweek.com	Current issue, archives, and an assortment of worthwhile data.
CAROL: Company Annual Reports Online	carolworld.com	Online annual reports for some European companies.
Cross Border Capital	liquidity.com/	Reports on equity, fixed income, and currency markets in over 70 developed and emerging markets. Reports over 6 months old available for free (with registration).
Daiwa Securities	dir.co.jp/Reception/research.html	Research reports and forecasts on the Japanese economy.
Edgar—U.S. Securities & Exchange Commission	sec.gov/edgar.shtml	Most SEC filings since 1996
Emerging Markets Companion (The)	emgmkts.com/	Many useful links and resources on Asia, Latin America, Africa, and Europe
EnterWeb: The Enterprise Development Web site	enterweb.org/welcome.htm	Meta-index to business and finance globalization, and more. "The focus is on micro, small, and medium-sized enterprise development both in developed and developing countries."

Exhibit 9-4   Freely Available Web Sites for Company Research (all Web sites begin with the prefix http://www) (Continued)

Name of Web Site	Web Site Address	What It Provides
Europages—European Business Directory	europages.com/	Lists 500,000 companies in 30 countries; includes some manufacturers' catalogs.
FEE Euro Information Service	euro.fee.be	Information on the transition to the euro in the European Union; requires registration (free).
Financial Times of London	ft.com/	Online edition of the Financial Times; current articles, market information, and more.
FT Interactive Data	turboguide.com/data2/ cdprod1/doc/cdrom frame/ 002/686.pub.FT.Excel.html	Good sampling from FT Excel databases; must register.
Hong Kong Securities and Futures Commission	hksfc.org.hk	Information on Hong Kong securities markets.
Hoover's Online	hoovers.com	Some information, such as press releases, is free. Links to company home pages and other information. Includes more than 800 of the most important non-U.S. companies.
INO Global Market	ino.com/	Information for traders in futures and options markets worldwide.
International Business (Michigan State University Center for International Business Education and Research)	ciber.bus.msu.edu/busres.htm	Links to good investment and macro sites.
International Monetary Fund	imf.org/	IMF news, publications, and more.
Internet Corruption Rankings	gwdg.de/~uwvw/icr_serv.htm	Provides the TI-Corruption Perception Index, a comparative assessment of the integrity of many countries, along with many other links and services.
National Corporate Services, Inc. International Investing	natcorp.com/	Excellent start point; many links to sites providing free information.
NIRI Useful Investor Relations Sites	niri.org	Links to interesting Web sites.
Public Register's Annual Report, The	prars.com	Annual reports, prospectuses, or 10-Ks on over 32,000 U.S. companies.
Rutgers Accounting Network (RAW)	rutgers.edu/Accounting/ raw.html	Excellent starting place.
Stewart Mayhew's Directory of Worldwide Securities Exchanges	voltaire.is.tcu.edu/~vmihov/ exchanges/xlinks.htm	Links to official home pages of stock markets and derivatives exchanges around the world.

(continued)

Exhibit 9-4 Freely Available Web Sites for Company Research (all Web sites begin with the prefix http://www) (Continued)

Name of Web Site	Web Site Address	What It Provides
Stock City	stockcity.com	ADR profiles, organized by sector, region, and country. Profiles require Adobe Acrobat Reader.
Streetlink Investor Information Center	streetlink.com	Financial reports available online; U.S. companies only.
United Nations System	unsystem.org	Spotty coverage of companies and Accounting information; good information on communications and country background.
USA Today Money	usatoday.com/money/mfront.htm	Comprehensive assortment of news and data.
VIBES: Virtual International Business and Economic Sources—Comprehensive Sources	uncc.edu/lis/library/reference/intbus/vibehome.htm	Great for linking to regional sites; excellent starting place, especially good for macro data.
Wright Investor' Service	profiles.wisi.com	Can search alphabetically by country or by industry.
Yahoo! Finance	quote.yahoo.com	Extensive data, news, and stock quotes.

Sources: Sarah Buckingham, Reference Librarian, Feldberg Library, Amos Tuck School of Business, and the authors.

Many commercial databases provide access to financial and stock market data for tens of thousands of companies around the world. Companies covered by commercial databases tend to be large companies that are of most interest to financial statement users and investors. It is striking that even in emerging market countries such as China and the Czech Republic, data for many firms are now available.

Other valuable information sources include (1) government publications, (2) economic research organizations, (3) international organizations such as the United Nations, and (4) accounting, auditing, and securities market organizations. Web site addresses appear throughout this text and are only a starting point for gathering information.

Timeliness of Information

The timeliness of financial statements, annual reports, regulatory filings, and accounting-related press releases varies dramatically by country.[41] Whereas quarterly financial reporting is a generally accepted practice in the United States, this is seldom the case

---

[41]For information on the timeliness of disclosures, see Carol A. Frost and Grace Pownall, "Accounting Disclosure Practices in the United States and the United Kingdom," *Journal of Accounting Research* (Spring 1994): 75–102; Carol A. Frost and William R. Kinney, Jr., "Disclosure Choices of Foreign Registrants in the United States," *Journal of Accounting Research* (Spring 1996); Andrew Alford, Jennifer Jones, Richard Leftwich, and Mark Zmijewski, "The Relative Informativeness of Accounting Disclosures in Different Countries," *Journal of Accounting Research* 31 (Suppl. 1993): 183–223; and Christine Botosan and Carol A. Frost, "Regulation, Disclosure and Market Liquidity: An Examination of Foreign Issuers in

elsewhere.[42] Financial reporting lags can also be estimated by comparing a company's fiscal year-end with its audit report date. The latter is often considered a reasonable indication of when corporate financial information first becomes publicly available. For Brazil, Canada, Chile, Colombia, Mexico, the Philippines, South Korea, Taiwan, Thailand, and the United States, this reporting lag reportedly averaged between 30–60 days. It averaged 61–90 days in Argentina, Australia, Denmark, Finland, Ireland, Israel, Japan, the Netherlands, New Zealand, Norway, Portugal, Singapore, South Africa, Spain, Sweden, Switzerland, the United Kingdom, and Zimbabwe. In Austria, Belgium, France, Germany, Greece, Hong Kong, India, Italy, Malaysia, Nigeria, and Sri Lanka, information lags averaged 91–120 days. And for Pakistan, the average lag exceeded 120 days.[43]

Frost documents further international variations in the timeliness of earnings-related press releases.[44] She defined disclosure lags as the average number of days between a company's fiscal year-end and the date of the press release. These lags were 73 days for companies domiciled in France, 82 days for Germany, 46 days for Japan, 72 days for the United Kingdom, and 26 days for the United States.

Variability in the timeliness of accounting information places additional burdens on readers of foreign financial statements. This burden is especially pronounced for firms whose operating circumstances are changing over time. Meaningful valuations require constant updates of reported numbers using both conventional and unconventional means.

Foreign Currency Considerations

Accounts denominated in foreign currency present financial analysts with two types of problems. The first relates to reader convenience, the second to information content.

The vast majority of companies around the world denominate their financial accounts in the currency of their national domicile. To a U.S. reader accustomed to dealing in dollars, analysis of accounts expressed in euros may be confusing. A normal inclination is to translate foreign currency balances to domestic currency. However, foreign currency reports are, for the most part, troublesome in appearance only. Financial ratios that transform nominal (interval) measurements to percentage relationships are independent of currency. A current ratio computed from a Dutch balance sheet expressed in euros is the same as one computed from the same financial statement translated into dollars. Consider the following year-end balance sheet accounts of a British company.

	20X4	20X5	20X6
Current assets	£12,500	£12,200	£12,800
Current liabilities	£8,333	£7,625	£8,000

Regulated versus Less Regulated U.S. Equity Markets," October 1997, Washington University and Dartmouth College working paper.

[42]An informal survey of many world-class company Web sites suggests that more and more are voluntarily choosing to provide quarterly reports owing to capital market pressures to do so.

[43]See *International Accounting and Auditing Trends*, 4th ed., Center for International Financial Analysis & Research, Princeton, NJ: CIFAR Publications, Inc., 1995.

[44]Carol A. Frost, "Characteristics and Information Value of Corporate Disclosures of Forward-Looking Information in Global Equity Markets," Dartmouth College Working Paper, February 1998.

Assuming year-end dollar/pound exchanges rates of $2.10, $2.20, and $1.60 for 20X4, 20X5, and 20X6, respectively, the current ratio will be 1.5 to 1 for 20X4, 1.6 to 1 for 20X5, and 1.6 to 1 for 20X6, whether expressed in British pounds or U.S. dollars. Local currency (e.g., pound) balances are especially appropriate when analyzing financial trends.

Readers who prefer a domestic currency framework when analyzing foreign currency accounts may apply a *convenience translation* using year-end exchange rates. One must be careful, however, when analyzing translated trend data. Use of convenience rates to translate foreign currency accounts can distort underlying financial patterns in local currency. To illustrate, assume the following 3-year sales revenue patterns for our British concern. .

	20X4	20X5	20X6
Sales revenue	£23,500	£28,650	£33,160

Convenience translations using the year-end exchange rates employed earlier (i.e., $2.10 for 20X4, $2.20 for 20X5, and $1.60 for 20X6) yield a U.S. dollar sales increase of 7.5 percent [($53,056–$49,350) / $49,350] over the 3-year period. The sales gain in pounds, however, is 41 percent [(£33,160–£23,500) / £23,500].

An alternative approach is to translate foreign currency data to domestic currency using a single base year's exchange rate. But which base-year exchange rate should be used? In our example, should the sales figures be translated using the 20X4 exchange rate, the 20X5 exchange rate, or the 20X6 exchange rate?

Although we prefer to analyze foreign statements in local currency, we favor the use of the most recent year's exchange rate as a convenience translator for readers who prefer domestic currency statistics. An exception is warranted, however, if the foreign currency financial statements have been adjusted for changes in the general purchasing power of the foreign currency unit (see Chapter 7 for a discussion of this treatment). If foreign currency balances are expressed in base-year purchasing power equivalents, year-end exchange rates associated with the given base year should be employed. In our example, if sales revenues were expressed in pounds of 20X4 general purchasing power, the 20X4 exchange rate would have been an appropriate translation rate.

While translated statements give readers the convenience of viewing foreign currency accounts in a familiar currency, they may give a distorted picture. Specifically, exchange rate changes and accounting procedures together often produce domestic currency equivalents that conflict with underlying events. We illustrate this problem using the statement of cash flows as an example.

Recall from Chapter 6 that consolidated financial statements allow a multinational company to report the results of its worldwide operations in a single currency. Also recall that a variety of currency translation methods are in use internationally. Regardless of the currency translation method employed, it is not always clear to readers of consolidated funds flow statements, whether reported fund sources or uses reflect the results of an operational decision or simply an exchange rate change.

To illustrate, the translated statements of earnings, financial position, and cash flows for the Norwegian affiliate of a U.S.-based multinational company appear in Exhibit 9-5. The parent company employs the current rate method and defines the krona as its functional currency for consolidation purposes.

A cursory examination of the translated statement of cash flows shows that major sources of cash were operations (net income plus depreciation), the issuance of long-term debt, and a translation adjustment. In turn, cash was used to increase the company's investment in fixed assets.

The pattern of cash flow shown in Exhibit 9-5 differs from that experienced by a purely domestic company due to the presence of an aggregate translation adjustment. However, examination of this component of the translated funds statement reveals that it does not really constitute a *source* or *use* of cash. The translation adjustment is calculated by multiplying the beginning foreign currency net asset balance by the change in the current rate during the period and, second, by multiplying the increase or decrease in net assets during the period by the difference between the average exchange rate and end-of-period exchange rate. This procedure, together with the dual nature of the accounting equation, suggests that most components of the translated funds statement are a mix of translation effects and actual cash flows. In our current example, a statement reader needs to figure out whether the increase of long-term debt in the amount of $1,584,000 is an indication of the Norwegian affiliate's financing activities or is largely an accounting adjustment. Similar considerations apply to the purported $2,695,000 investment in fixed assets.

Assume that the translated statements appearing in Exhibit 9-5 are based on the Norwegian krona balances appearing in Exhibit 9-6 (see page 339) and that the relevant exchange rate information is as stated.

A cash flow comparison between the functional currency (krona) and the reporting currency (dollars) yields some striking contrasts. While the cash flow statement generated from the translated balance sheet and income statement (Exhibit 9-5) shows long-term debt as a source of funds, the krona statement (Exhibit 9-6) suggests that this was not the case. Likewise, what appears to be an investment in fixed assets from a dollar perspective turns out to be a pure translation phenomenon.

Closer analysis provides insight into the magnitude of the translation effects. An analysis of the fixed asset account reveals that there was no purchase, sale, or retirement of fixed assets during the year. Thus, the year-end balance should have been the beginning book value, $8,500,000 (Nor 85,000,000), less depreciation of $555,000 (Nor 5,000,000), or $7,945,000. The actual ending balance was $10,640,000, suggesting that the entire increase in fixed assets ($10,640,000–$7,945,000) was due to an exchange rate effect. Similarly, there was no change in Norwegian krona long-term debt during the year. Because this monetary liability was translated by an exchange rate that revalued during the year, the entire increase in long-term debt ($6,384,000–$4,800,000) also arose from a translation adjustment. Similar transactional analyses account for additional translation effects related to the Norwegian subsidiary's working capital accounts. These effects are summarized in Exhibit 9-7 on page 339.

Note that the sum of all the translation effects appearing in Exhibit 9-6 equals the aggregate translation adjustment appearing in the shareholders' equity section of the translated balance sheet. An informed reader can better determine the influence of exchange rate changes from a firm's financing and investing activities using the foregoing analysis.

Exhibit 9-5   Translated Financial Statements of Norwegian Subsidiary

Translated Balance Sheets as of 12/31/X4 and 12/31/X5

	December 31	
	20X4	20X5
Assets (000's)		
Cash	$ 2,400	$ 3,990
Net fixed assets	8,500	10,640
Total assets	$10,900	$14,630
Liabilities and owners' equity		
U.S. $500 payable	$ 500	$ 500
Long-term franc debt	4,800	6,384
Capital stock	3,818	3,818
Retained earnings	1,782	2,030
Translation adjustment	—	1,898
Total liabilities and stockholders' equity	$10,900	$14,630

Translated Statement of Income for the Year 20X5 (000's)

Sales		$ 1,332
Expenses		
Operating costs	$ 666	
Depreciation	555	
Foreign exchange gain	(139)	1,082
Net income		$ 250

Translated Statement of Cash Flows(000's)

Sources		
Net income	$ 250	
Depreciation	555	
Increase in long-term debt	1,584	
Translation adjustment	1,898	$ 4,287
Uses		
Increase in fixed assets		2,695
Net increase in cash (approximate due to rounding)		$ 1,590

Differences in Statement Format

Balance sheet and income statement formats vary from country to country. For example, in contrast to the United States, where most companies adopt the balance sheet account format with assets appearing on the left and equity claims on the right, the format is often the reverse in the United Kingdom. As a second example, in contrast to U.S. balance sheets, which display assets in decreasing order of liquidity and liabilities in increasing order of maturity, in many countries the most liquid assets and the shortest-term liabilities appear at the foot of the balance sheet.

Classification differences also abound internationally. For example, accumulated depreciation is reported as a contra-asset account in the United States. In Germany, depreciable assets are usually reported net of accumulated depreciation, but all current period changes in long-term asset accounts are shown directly in the balance sheet. In

Exhibit 9-6 Financial Statements for Wholly-Owned Norwegian Subsidiary

Local Currency Balance Sheet as of 12/31/X4 and 12/31/X5

	December 31 20X4	December 31 20X5
Assets		
Cash	Nor 24,000	Nor 30,000
Net fixed assets	85,000	80,000
Total assets	Nor 109,000	Nor 110,000
Liabilities and owners' equity		
U.S. $500 payable	Nor 5,000	Nor 3,750
Long-term krona debt	48,000	48,000
Capital stock	46,000	46,000
Retained earnings	10,000	12,250
Total liabilities and owners' equity	Nor 109,000	Nor 110,000

Statement of Cash Flows

Sources

Net income	Nor 2,250
Depreciation	5,000
Less: Krona foreign-exchange gain	1,250
Uses:	
None	—
Net increase in cash	Nor 6,000

Relevant Exchange Rates

December 31, 20X4	Nor1 = $.100
Average during 20X5	Nor1 = $.111
December 31, 20X5	Nor1 = $.113

Exhibit 9-7 Analysis of Exchange Rate Effects

	Debit	Credit
Cash	$ 924	
Fixed assets	2,695	
Intercompany payable		$ 138
Long-term debt		1,584
	$3,619	$1,722
Aggregate translation adjustment		1,897
	$3,619	$3,619

most countries, the distinction between a current and noncurrent liability is 1 year. In Germany it is often 4 years. Handbooks like *Transactional Accounting*[45] may be consulted for a detailed treatment of other classification differences prevailing in individual countries.

Financial statement format differences, while troublesome, are seldom critical because the underlying structure of financial statements is quite similar around the world. Accordingly, most format differences can usually be reconciled with a little effort.

Language and Terminology Barriers

Language differences among countries can present information barriers to financial statement users. Most companies domiciled in non-English-speaking countries publish their annual reports in the home country language. However, growing numbers of the relatively large companies in developed economies provide English-language versions of their annual reports.

Accounting terminology differences can also cause difficulty. For example, U.S. readers associate the term *stock* with certificates of corporate ownership. Readers in the United Kingdom, on the other hand, associate the term with a firm's inventory of unsold goods. Other examples of terminology differences between the United Kingdom and the United States include turnover (sales revenue), and debtors and creditors (accounts receivable and payable).

In summary, many substantial issues confront the user of international financial statements. Perhaps the most difficult issues concern foreign currency and the availability and credibility of financial information. Difficulties with foreign currency will probably have a pervasive influence on international accounting for some time. In contrast, problems related to information availability and credibility are gradually decreasing as more and more companies, regulatory authorities, and stock exchanges recognize the importance of improving investors' access to timely and credible information.

---

[45]Dieter Ordelheide and KPMG, *Transactional Accounting,* 2nd ed., Hampshire, U.K.: Palgrave, 2001.

Appendix 9-1

ILLUSTRATION OF RESTATEMENT OF JAPANESE GAAP FINANCIAL STATEMENTS TO A U.S. GAAP BASIS

In this appendix we show how GAAP restatements might be used to reduce the effects of accounting diversity. Exhibit 9-8 contains the year-end financial statements of Toyoza Enterprises (Japan) and Lincoln Corporation (United States), with relevant notes.

Comparative financial ratios for Toyoza and Lincoln Enterprises are provided in Exhibit 9-9.

Based on this preliminary analysis, Toyoza appears less liquid, less efficient, less profitable, and financially less solvent than Lincoln Enterprises. But is it? A good analyst will attempt to ascertain to what extent these observed differences are due to real economic differences versus differences in accounting measurements and other environmental influences.

To aid comparison with Lincoln, we restate Toyoza's statements to a U.S. GAAP basis. Based on the information provided and examining the notes in sequence, the following adjustments are required:

1. Inventories are adjusted to reflect differences in costing methods. Adjustments would increase inventories and decrease cost of sales by ¥198,000.
2. The difference between straight-line and sum-of-the-year's-digits depreciation for the current year yields an adjustment to cost of sales and net plant and equipment of ¥46,750. The difference in depreciation for the preceding year is ¥140,250. Based on a marginal tax rate of 35 percent, the ¥140,250 increase in

reported pretax earnings would create ¥49,088 in deferred taxes with the balance credited to retained earnings.
3. Under U.S. GAAP the lease transaction would be capitalized. Discounting the stream of ¥40,000,000 rental payments for 5 years at 8 percent yields a present value of ¥159,600,000 attributed to both a leased asset and a lease obligation. Based on this amount, we can break down the ¥40,000,000 lease payment into an interest payment of ¥12,768,000 and a ¥27,232,000 reduction of the lease obligation. Straight-line depreciation would yield an expense of ¥31,920,000.
4. Under SFAS No. 52 the translation gain would be removed from long-term debt and included in income.
5. Compared to U.S. GAAP, the goodwill amortization expense is ¥10,800,000 larger. We would make an adjusting entry to recognize an asset and reduce operating expenses.
6. As the United States does not permit discretionary reserves, these reserves would be removed and included in income. Moreover, they would be reclassified as equity as opposed to debt.
7. These adjustments, which Exhibit 9-10 summarizes in spreadsheet form, increase Toyoza's restated earnings by ¥220,240,000. Of this, ¥20,000,000 relating to the translation gain is not recognized for tax purposes. This yields a tax expense of ¥107,822,000 and a balance of ¥107,822,000 currently payable.

Exhibit 9-8   Year-End Unadjusted Financial Statements and Related Notes

	Toyoza Enterprises (¥Thousands)	Lincoln Enterprises ($Thousands)
Income Statements		
Sales	¥1,400,000	$12,000
Operating expenses:		
Cost of sales	1,120,000	10,044
Selling and administrative	100,000	575
Other operating	114,200	319
Goodwill amortization		10
Operating income	¥ 65,800	$ 1,052
Gains (losses)		
Interest expenses	28,000	130
Income before taxes	37,800	922
Income taxes	23,800	258
Income after taxes	14,000	664
Equity in earnings of unconsolidated subsidiaries		116
Net income	¥ 14,000	$ 780
Balance Sheets		
Cash	¥ 124,500	$ 1,920
Accounts receivable, net	510,000	1,660
Marketable securities	45,000	500
Inventory	390,000	1,680
Investments	150,000	1,000
Plant and equipment, net	280,600	5,160
Goodwill	—	80
Total assets	¥1,500,000	$12,000
Short-term payables	¥ 165,000	$ 1,800
Short-term debt	525,000	2,160
Deferred taxes	—	—
Other current liabilities	90,000	—
Long-term debt	520,000	2,400
Reserves	90,000	—
Capital stock	75,000	960
Retained earnings	35,000	4,680
Total liabilities and owners' equity	¥1,500,000	$12,000

Notes to Toyoza's Financial Statements:
1. The balance sheet and income statement were prepared in accordance with the Japanese Commercial Code and related regulations.
2. Investments in subsidiaries and affiliated companies are accounted for using the equity method.
3. Inventories are stated at average cost. Ending inventories restated to a FIFO basis would have been ¥198 million higher.
4. Plant and equipment are carried at cost. Depreciation, with minor exceptions, is computed by the sum-of-the-years-digits method. Plant and equipment, purchased 2 years ago, have an estimated life of 4 years.
5. Operating expenses include lease rental payments of ¥40 million. The average term of the lease contracts is 4 years. All leases transfer ownership to the lessor at the end of the least term. Lincoln Enterprises' cost of capital is estimated to be 8 percent.

Exhibit 9-8   Year-End Unadjusted Financial Statements and Related Notes (*Continued*)

Notes to Toyoza's Financial Statements: (*Continued*)

6. A translation gain of ¥20 million relating to consolidation of foreign operations with a net monetary liability position is being deferred under long-term debt.
7. Purchased goodwill is amortized over 20 years. The current period's amortization expense is ¥12 million for the year and is included under other operating expenses. Under a U.S. GAAP impairments test, it would have been 10% of that amount.
8. Toyoza Enterprises is allowed to set up special-purpose reserves (i.e., government-sanctioned charges against earnings) equal to a certain percentage of total export revenues. This year's charge (including other operating expenses) was ¥26,400,000. Similarly, this year's addition to Toyoza's general-purpose reserves was ¥30,800,000.
9. The ¥/$ exchange rate at year-end was ¥110 = $1.
10. Toyoza Enterprise's marginal income tax rate is 35 percent.

Notes to Lincoln Enterprises' financial statements:

1. The balance sheet and income statement are based on U.S. GAAP.
2. Inventories are carried at FIFO cost.
3. Plant and equipment are depreciated in straight-line fashion.
4. Foreign operations are consolidated with those of the parent using the temporal method of currency translation as Lincoln adopts the U.S. dollar as its functional currency.

Exhibit 9-9   Comparative Financial Ratios Based on Unadjusted Data

	Toyoza	Lincoln
Liquidity		
Current ratio	1.37x	1.45x
Acid-test ratio	.87x	1.03x
Efficiency		
Receivables turnover	2.75x	7.23x
Inventory turnover	2.87x	5.98x
Asset turnover	.93x	1.00x
Profitability		
Profit margin	1.0%	6.5%
Return on assets	4.4%	9.7%
Return on equity	12.7%	13.8%
Coverage		
Debt to total assets	92.7%	53.0%
Times interest earned	2.4x	8.9x

Exhibit 9-10   Adjustment Spreadsheet

	Unadjusted	Adjustments	Adjusted	Dollars
Sales	¥1,400,000		¥1,400,000	$12,727
−Operating expenses:				
Cost of sales	1,120,000	1) (198,000)		
		2a) (46,750)		
		3) 31,920	907,170	8,247
Selling and administrative	100,000		100,000	909
Other operating	114,200	3) (40,000)		
		5) (10,800)		
		6) (26,400)		
		7) (30,800)	6,200	56
Losses (gains)	—	4) (20,000)	(20,000)	(182)
Interest	28,000	3) 12,768	40,768	371
Taxes	23,800	7) 107,822	131,622	1,197
Net income	¥ · 14,000	8) 220,240	¥ 234,240	$ 2,129
Cash	¥ 124,500		¥ 124,500	$ 1,132
Accounts receivable	510,000		510,000	4,636
Marketable securities	45,000		45,000	409
Inventory	390,000	3) 198,000	588,000	5,345
Investments	150,000		150,000	1,364
Plant and equipment, net	280,500	2a) 46,750		
		2b) 140,250		
		3) 127,680	595,180	5,411
Goodwill		7) 10,800	10,800	98
Total assets	¥1,500,000		¥2,023,480	$18,395
Short-term payables	¥ 165,000		¥ 165,000	$ 1,500
Short-term debt	525,000		525,000	4,773
Deferred taxes	—			
Other current liabilities	90,000	2b) 49,088		
		7) 107,822	246,910	2,244
Long-term debt	520,000	4) (20,000)		
		3) 132,368	632,368	5,749
Reserves	90,000	6) 26,400		
		6) 30,800	32,800	298
Capital stock	75,000		75,000	682
Retained earnings	35,000	2b) 91,162		
		8) 220,240	346,402	3,149
Total liabilities and owners' equity	¥1,500,000		¥2,023,480	$18,395

Exhibit 9-11 shows a ratio comparison of Toyoza and Lincoln Enterprises based on data adjusted for accounting differences. As can be seen, adjusted ratios show a much improved profitability picture for Toyoza. However, liquidity and efficiency ratios have worsened. While solvency (coverage) ratios have improved, the debt to total assets ratio remains exceedingly high by U.S. standards.

If accounting principle differences were the only differences among countries, adjustments such as those illustrated above would be sufficient to enable anyone to analyze and interpret foreign financial statements without ambiguity.[46] Unfortunately, institutional and cultural differences among countries are not constant. If these differences are major, further analysis is necessary to ensure proper analysis and understanding. Appendix 9-2 amplifies this important point.

Exhibit 9-11 Comparative Financial Ratios Based on Adjusted Data	Toyoza	Lincoln
Liquidity		
Current ratio	1.35x	1.45x
Acid-test ratio	.73x	1.03x
Efficiency		
Receivables turnover	2.75x	7.23x
Inventory turnover	1.54x	5.98x
Asset turnover	.69x	1.00x
Profitability		
Profit margin	16.7%	6.5%
Return on assets	20.1%	9.7%
Return on equity	51.5%	13.8%
Coverage		
Debt to total assets	77.6%	53.0%
Times interest earned	9.9x	8.9x

[46]Of course, we assume that the statement user has enough information on hand to make the adjustments.

Appendix 9-2

INTERNATIONAL RATIO ANALYSIS[47]

Financial ratio analysis is a well-established tool for financial performance evaluation, credit analysis, and security analysis. While financial ratios may correctly measure liquidity, efficiency, and profitability in within-country comparisons, they are often misused when applied to cross-border financial comparisons, due in part to accounting principle differences. A more serious problem is that investors may misinterpret these ratios because they do not understand a foreign environment, even when financial statements have been restated to a common set of accounting principles.

Consider Japan. An initial comparison of aggregate financial ratios for Japanese and U.S. firms reveals striking differences. Japanese companies generally appear less liquid, less solvent, less efficient, and less profitable than their U.S. counterparts. However, after Japanese ratios are adjusted for differences between Japanese and U.S. GAAP, they are still very different from ratios found in comparable U.S. companies.

Environmental Considerations

Japanese companies appear to have very high leverage. For example, an earlier study conducted by the SEC found that mean leverage (total debt/shareholders' equity) in their Japan sample was 2.032, compared with

0.514 in the U.S. sample.[48] However, high debt ratios traditionally have not been major sources of concern in Japan. Part of the reason is historical.

When the Japanese government (under pressure from the United States) ended 200 years of isolation in the mid-19th century, it made rapid economic growth and development a major national goal. To achieve this goal, the government established an extensive banking infrastructure to supply industry with most of its financing. The dependence of industrial companies on the banking system increased after World War II. Large, new industrial groupings called *keiretsu* evolved with major commercial banks at their core. Linked through business and personal ties, banks and their associated companies are very close. When loans become delinquent, banks (often) extend the terms of repayment or (occasionally) refinance the loan. A bank might even install a key bank official as president or board member of a troubled company to help it out.

Other companies in the *keiretsu* can prepay receivables owed to the distressed firm and allow longer periods for that firm to repay its receivables. With this ability to manipulate and postpone interest and principal payments, long-term debt in Japan works more like equity in the United States.[49]

[47]The following discussion is taken from a three-nation study by collaborators in Japan, Korea, and the United States. Participants in that study were Messers. Hisaaki Hino of Morgan Guaranty Trust Company, Junichi Ujiie of Nomura Securities Company, Ltd., Professors Sang Kee Min and Sang Oh Nam of Seoul National University, and Professor Arthur I. Stonehill of Oregon State University and Frederick D.S. Choi of New York University.

[48]U.S. Securities and Exchange Commission, Division of Corporation Finance, *Survey of Financial Statement Reconciliations by Foreign Registrants,* Washington, D.C.: U.S. Securities and Exchange Commission, May 1, 1993.
[49]The gradual liberalization of Japan's financial system is eroding the *keiretsu* system. See "Japan Inc. Frays at the Edges," *The Economist* (June 3, 1995): 67.

Because long-term debt in Japan has many of the characteristics of preferred stock, interest payments in Japan can be likened to dividends.

Accordingly, interest coverage ratios, which are generally much lower in Japan than in the United States, are not viewed with much concern. Earnings in Japan beyond those needed to make loan payments benefit the bank little. When loans are negotiated, the borrower makes (and seldom discloses) a general agreement to give the bank collateral or guarantees upon the bank's request. Also at the bank's request, borrowing companies must submit their year-end proposed appropriation of revenue (including dividends) to the bank before it can be submitted to shareholders for approval. Banks customarily insist on compensating balances even though they are illegal, with 20 to 50 percent of company borrowings reportedly kept with the bank as time (or other) deposits. Under these conditions, low interest coverage usually does not mean a high risk of default.

Institutional and cultural factors also affect liquidity ratios without necessarily changing the financial risk that the ratios are designed to measure. For example, an American reader who sees the relatively low current ratios of Japanese companies (resulting from relatively high short-term debt) might conclude that Japanese companies have a relatively lower ability to cover their short-term debt. In Japan, however, high short-term debt seldom indicates a lack of liquidity. Short-term debt is attractive to companies because short-term obligations typically have lower interest rates than long-term obligations. Moreover, short-term borrowings in Japan are seldom repaid but normally are renewed or *rolled over*. Banks are happy to renew these loans as this allows them to adjust their interest rates to changing market conditions. Thus, short-term debt in Japan works like long-term debt else-where. In fact, the use of short-term debt to finance long-term assets appears to be the rule, not the exception, in Japan.

Longer average collection periods also reflect differences in business customs. Purchases in Japan are rarely made in cash. Postdated checks with maturities ranging between 60 and 90 days are common. The Japanese tradition of lifetime employment has some influence on collection policies. Companies often go to great lengths to accommodate their commercial customers. During business downturns, companies extend repayment terms to avoid placing their customers in a financial bind that might force them to discharge employees. In return, continued patronage ensures stability in employment (and other respects) for the selling company. Inventory turnover numbers are similarly affected.

During slack periods, manufacturing companies prefer to continue production and build inventories rather than idle workers. Japanese managers are not as concerned with short-term profits as their U.S. counterparts. They have more job security than prevails in the United States. Equity shares in Japanese companies are largely held by related commercial banks, suppliers, and customers. These shareholders are more interested in maintaining their close business ties than in stock market gains, and will hold shares on a long-term basis regardless of short-term market performance.

Corporate managers in Japan believe that increased market share will ensure long-run profits. For this reason, sales growth is a main objective. Growing sales contribute to higher employment and greater job security, and as such are consistent with the tradition of lifetime employment. Because all Japanese enterprises seek sales growth, price competition is intense, resulting in low profit margin and profitability statistics. This is especially so for large companies that usually sell heavily in extremely competitive export markets.

So, are Japanese companies truly more risky, less efficient, and less profitable than their U.S. counterparts? Not necessarily.

In Europe, national characteristics also appear to strongly influence profit measurement. Large companies in France and Germany tend to be more conservative in measuring profits than large companies in the United Kingdom. Also important are tax laws and reliance on lenders rather than investors for capital.

Thus, when analyzing foreign financial statements, readers must be careful to determine whether observed differences in firm performance result from: (a) accounting measurement differences; (b) economic, cultural, or institutional differences; or (c) real differences in the attributes being measured.

Selected References

Ashbaugh, H., and M. Pincus, "Domestic Accounting Standards, International Accounting Standards and the Predictability of Earnings," *Journal of Accounting Research* 39 No. 3 (2001): 417–434.

Basu, S., L. Hwang, and C.L. Jain, "International Variation in Accounting Measurement Rules and Analysts' Earning Forecast Errors," *Journal of Business Finance and Accounting* 25, Nos. 9&10 (1998): 1207–1247.

Beim, David O., and Charles W. Calomiris, *Emerging Financial Markets,* Boston: McGraw-Hill, 2001.

Capstaff, J., K. Paudyal, and W. Rees, "A Comparative Analysis of Earnings Forecasts in Europe," *Journal of Business Finance and Accounting* 28, Nos. 5&6 (2001): 531–562.

Choi, Frederick D. S., and Richard M. Levich, "Accounting Diversity," in *The European Equity Markets: The State of the Union and an Agenda for the Millennium,* Benn Steil, ed., London: European Capital Markets Institute, 1996, pp. 259–320.

Choi, Frederick D.S., and Richard M. Levich, "International Accounting Diversity and Capital Market Decisions," in *International Accounting and Finance Handbook,* 2nd ed., F.D.S. Choi, ed., New York: John Wiley & Sons, 1997, pp. 6.1–6.26.

Copeland, Tom, Tim Koller, and Jack Murrin, "Valuing Foreign Subsidiaries" and Valuation Outside of the United States," in *Valuation: Measuring and Managing the Value of Companies,* 2nd ed., New York: John Wiley & Sons, 1994.

Damodaran, Aswath, *Investment Valuation,* 2nd ed., New York: John Wiley & Sons, 2000.

Damodaran, Aswath, "Valuation in Emerging Markets," in *International Finance and Accounting Handbook,* 3rd ed., F.D.S. Choi, ed., New York: John Wiley & Sons, 2003, pp. 9.1–9.38.

Decker, William E., Jr., and Paul Brunner, "Summary of Accounting Principle Differences Around the World," in *International Finance and Accounting Handbook,* 3rd ed., F. D. S. Choi, ed., New York, John Wiley & Sons, 2003, pp. 12.1–12.33.

Erb, Claude B., Campbell R. Harvey, and Tadas E. Viskanta, *Country Risk in Global Financial Management,* Charlottesville, VA: Association for Investment Management and Research, 1998.

Frost, Carol A. and Kurt P. Ramin, "Corporate Financial Disclosure: A Global Assessment," in *International Finance and Accounting Handbook,* 3rd ed., F.D.S. Choi ed., New York: John Wiley & Sons, 2003, pp. 13.1–13.45.

Gordon, Elizabeth A., and Peter R. Joos, "Unrecognized Deferred Taxes: Evidence from the U.K.," *Accounting Review* 79, No. 1 (2004): 97–124.

Hope, Ole-Kristian, "Firm-Level Disclosure and the Relative Roles of Culture and Legal Origin," *Journal of International Financial Management and Accounting* 14, No. 3 (2003): 218–248.

Hope, Ole-Kristian, "Variations in the Financial Reporting Environment and Earnings Forecasting," *Journal of International Financial Management and Accounting* 15, No. 1 (2004): 21–43.

Hung, M., "Accounting Standards and Value Relevance of Earnings: An International Analysis," *Journal of Accounting and Economics* 30, No. 3 (2000): 401–420.

"Of Prophets and Profits Beware Attempts to Forecast Company Profits," *The Economist* (April 7, 2001): 84.

Palepu, Krishna G., Victor L. Bernard, and Paul M. Healy, *Business Analysis and Valuation Using Financial Statements,* Cincinnati, OH: South-Western College Publishing, 1996.

PricewaterhouseCoopers, *The Opacity Index January 2001 Launching a New Measure of the Effects of Opacity on the Cost and Availability of Capital in Countries World-Wide,* A Project of the PricewaterhouseCoopers Endowment for the Study of Transparency and Sustainability (www.opacityindex.com), January 2001.

Squires, Jan R., ed., *ICFA Continuing Education Finding Reality in Reported Earnings,* Charlottesville, VA.: Association for Investment Management and Research, 1997.

Discussion Questions

1. What are the four main steps in doing a business analysis using financial statements? Why, at each step, is analysis in a cross-border context more difficult than a single-country analysis?

2. What are the information needs of four user groups that rely on foreign financial statements for their financial decisions? Are the four main steps in financial statement analysis equally important to your four groups? If not, what are the differences?

3. One interpretation of the popular efficient markets hypothesis is that the market fully impounds all public information as soon as it becomes available. Thus, it is supposedly not possible to beat the market if fundamental financial analysis techniques are applied to publicly available information such as a firm's published accounts. Why might this hypothesis be more tenable in the United States than in other international capital markets?

4. While English-language translations of foreign annual reports appear in increasing frequency, it is sometimes necessary to analyze a foreign report stated in the language and reporting terminology of the reporting company's domicile. What are some ways to deal with this problem? State your answer in one or two well-written paragraphs.

5. How does the translation of foreign currency financial statements differ from the foreign currency translation process described in Chapter 6?

6. If you were asked to provide the five most important recommendations you could think of to others analyzing nondomestic financial statements, what would they be?

7. In what country(ies) is accounting information most timely, detailed, and credible? Why?

8. What are several factors that must be taken into account when comparing the reported profitability of companies in different countries?

9. Choi and Levich found that investors cope with accounting principles differences in two fundamentally different ways. What are these coping mechanisms and which of the two do you favor?

10. Non-U.S. companies listed on U.S. stock exchanges are not required to base their financial statements on U.S. GAAP. However, these companies *are* generally required to provide reconciliation disclosures that quantify any material differences between their reported net income and what their net income would be under U.S. GAAP. What are the most frequently disclosed types of material differences?

11. The quick (or acid test) ratio is frequently used to assess the short-term debt-paying ability of a business enterprise. As a rule of thumb, U.S. commercial lenders often consider a ratio of at least 1 to 1 to be satisfactory. Why might it be inappropriate to apply this standard when evaluating the liquidity of a non-U.S. company?

12. ABC Company, a U.S.-based MNC, uses the temporal translation method (see Chapter 6) in consolidating the results of its foreign operations. Translation gains or losses incurred upon consolidation are reflected immediately in reported earnings. Company XYZ, a Dutch MNC, employs the current rate method with translation gains and losses going into owners' equity. What financial ratios are most likely to be affected by these different accounting principles, and what are the implications for security analysts?

Exercises

1. Condensed comparative income statements of Señorina Panchos, a Mexican restaurant chain, for the years 20X5 through 20X7 are presented in Exhibit 9-12 (000,000's pesos).

Exhibit 9-12 Comparative Income Statements: Señorina Panchos			
	20X5	20X6	20X7
Sales	91,600	114,300	138,900
Gross margin	15,500	20,500	27,700
Net income	8,500	10,800	15,900

You are interested in gauging the past trend in dividends paid by Señorina Panchos from a dollar perspective. The company's payout ratio (ratio of dividends paid to reported earnings) has averaged 30 percent. Foreign exchange rates during the 3-year period are found in Exhibit 9-13.

Exhibit 9-13 Foreign Exchange Rates			
	20X5	20X6	20X7
Year-end rates	$1 = P 12.112	$1 = P 12.640	$1 = P 13.000

Required: Prepare a trend analysis of dividends paid by Señorina Panchos from a U.S. perspective assuming (a) there are no restrictions on the payment of dividends to U.S. investors and (b) Señorina Panchos' accounting practices are similar to those in the United States.

2. Based on the balance sheet and income statement data contained in Exhibit 9-6, and using the suggested worksheet format shown in Exhibit 9-14 or one of your own choosing, show how the statement of cash flows appearing in Exhibit 9-6 was derived.

Exhibit 9-14 Statement of Cash Flows Work Sheet				
	Beginning Balance	Debit	Credit	Ending Balance
Balance sheet items (detailed)				
		Sources of Funds	Uses of Funds	
Net change in Cash				

3. Refer again to Exhibits 9-6 and 9-7. Show how you would modify the consolidated funds statement appearing in Exhibit 9-6 to enable an investor to get a better feel for the actual investing and financing activities of the Norwegian subsidiary.

4. Read the financial statements (including notes) for Nikken Chemicals Co., Ltd., in Appendix 1-2 in Chapter 1. Also review an annual report of a company of your choice domiciled in your home country, using the World Wide Web or your library.

   Required: List at least five differences in the types of information disclosed by Nikken Chemicals and the information disclosed by the company you selected. Does Nikken Chemicals disclose more or less information, overall, than the company you selected? What other sources, if any, might be used to obtain additional information about Nikken Chemicals?

5. Read Appendix 9-1. Referring to Exhibit 9-8 and related notes, assume instead that Toyoza's inventories were costed using the FIFO method and that Lincoln Enterprises employed the LIFO method. Provide the adjusting journal entries to restate Toyoza's inventories to a LIFO basis, assuming that ending inventories would have been ¥250 million lower under the LIFO method.

6. The following sales revenue pattern for a British trading concern was cited earlier in the chapter:

	20X4	20X5	20X6
Sales revenue	£23,500	£28,650	£33,160

   Required:
   a. Perform a convenience translation into U.S. dollars for each year given the following year-end exchange rates:

20X4	£1 = $2.10
20X5	£1 = $2.20
20X6	£1 = $1.60

b. Compare the year-to-year percentage changes in sales revenues in pounds and in U.S. dollars. Do the two time series move in parallel fashion? Why or why not?

c. Suggest a method for minimizing the effect of exchange rate changes on foreign currency trend data.

7. Exhibit 9-15 provides a recent summary of the Volvo Group's net income and shareholders' equity determined in accordance with Swedish GAAP and U.S. GAAP.

Required:
a. Compute the return on shareholders' equity for the year based first on Swedish GAAP, and then on U.S. GAAP.
b. Which return statistic is the better measure of performance and why?

If you were comparing your preferred statistic in b. with a comparable statistic for a U.S. firm in a comparable industry as Volvo, what factors would you take into account in making your assessment?

8. Refer to Exhibit 9-3. This exhibit presents P/E ratios for public companies in 10 countries.

Required: For both the middle and the end of the last decade, rank order the P/E ratios for China, France, Germany, the NYSE, (United States), and Nasdaq (United States). Discuss why the mean P/E ratio for each of these countries changed. Specifically, why did China's P/E ratio increase and France's decrease? Why did P/E ratios in Germany and on NYSE and Nasdaq in the United States increase? Why did Nasdaq's P/E ratio increase so much more than NYSE's P/E ratio? What explains the *differences* in P/E ratio trends among these four countries?

9. Examine the financial information presented in Appendix 1-2 in Chapter 1 for Nikken Chemicals Co., Ltd.

Required: Referring to the accounting policy footnotes and auditor's report, list the accounting standards used and the auditing standards used. Discuss which of these sources of cross-country accounting differences is the most important in a financial analysis of Nikken Chemicals. Least important? Why?

10. Exhibit 9-16 (on page 364) presents cross-country differences in auditor liability by country and audit firm.

Required: Does the incidence of liability cases vary more by country or by auditor? In what countries is auditor litigation most frequent? Lest frequent? Why? What are the implications for doing financial analysis in the 12 countries presented? Are relatively high levels of auditor litigation good or bad for financial statement users? Present reasons for your answer.

11. Refer to Exhibit 9-3 and compute an average of the combined P/E ratios for France, Germany, and the Netherlands during the middle and end of the last decade, respectively. Do the same for China, the Czech Republic, and Mexico.

Exhibit 9-15   Net Income and Shareholders' Equity Based on Domestic and International GAAP

Net income	20X5
Net income in accordance with Swedish GAAP	4,709
Items increasing (decreasing) reported net income:	
Foreign currency derivatives	(654)
Income taxes	—
Business combinations	(91)
Shares and participations	24
Interest costs	(3)
Leasing	16
Investments in debt and equity securities	(548)
Items affecting comparability	(281)
Pensions and other post-employment benefits	(170)
SPP surplus funds	(523)
Software development	384
Entrance fees, aircraft engine programs	(336)
Tax effect of above U.S. GAAP adjustments	600
Net increase (decrease) in net income	(1,582)
Approximate net income in accordance with U.S. GAAP	3,127

Shareholders' equity	20X5
Shareholders' equity in accordance with Swedish GAAP	88,338
Items increasing (decreasing) reported shareholders' equity:	
Foreign currency derivatives	(1,286)
Income taxes	—
Business combinations	1,317
Shares and participations	36
Interest costs	112
Leasing	(163)
Investments in debt and equity securities	(6,066)
Items affecting comparability	579
Pensions and other post-employment benefits	109
SPP surplus funds	(523)
Software development	754
Entrance fees, aircraft engine programs	(387)
Other	—
Tax effect of above U.S. GAAP adjustments	1,941
Net increase (decrease) in shareholders' equity	(3,577)
Approximate shareholders' equity based on U.S. GAAP	84,761

Exhibit 9-16   Auditor's Liability Cases by Country and Audit Firm

Country	Arthur Andersen	Coopers & Lybrand	Deloitte Touche	Ernst and Young	KPMG	Price Waterhouse Coopers	Others
Australia	1	1	4	-	3	3	2
Canada	-	3	1	2	1	-	3
Germany	-	-	-	1	-	1	-
Hong Kong	-	-	1	-	-	1	-
Ireland	-	-	-	1	-	-	1
Italy	1	-	-	1	2	2	1
Netherlands	-	-	-	1	-	-	-
New Zealand	-	-	-	1	1	-	1
Spain	1	1	-	1	-	2	-
Sweden	-	-	-	-	1	1	-
United Kingdom	1	3	3	2	5	1	2
United States	7	8	7	3	5	1	4
Total	**11**	**16**	**16**	**13**	**18**	**12**	**14**

Source: Center for International Financial Analysis & Research, *International Accounting and Auditing Trends,* 4th ed., 1995, Vol. II, Princeton, N.J.: CIFAR Publications, Inc., 1995.

Based on what you have learned in this and earlier chapters, explain any differences that you observe between these two sets of country groupings and the implications of your analysis for investors.

12. Identify three to four criteria that you would personally use to judge the merits of any corporate database. Use these criteria to rate the information content of each Web site appearing in Exhibit 9-4 as excellent, fair, or poor.

CASE 9-1A ACCOUNTING QUALITY ANALYSIS

Accounting quality varies substantially among countries. Companies' financial statements, notes, and auditor reports often yield important clues about accounting quality.

REQUIRED

1. Based on general information given in the text about financial reporting and economic and business environments in Japan, what is your overall assessment of accounting quality in that country?
2. Study the financial statements, notes, and auditor's report of Nikken Chemicals Co., Ltd., presented in Appendix 1-2 in Chapter 1. Is the accounting quality reflected in these materials consistent with your expectations (based on your knowledge of Japan)? Critically evaluate the accounting quality of Nikken Chemicals, including a discussion of factors that led to your conclusions.
3. If you could, what further evidence would you gather to more completely assess accounting quality for Nikken Chemicals?

CASE 9-1B RESTATEMENT OF INTERNATIONAL ACCOUNTING STANDARDS TO U.S. GAAP

Refer to Appendix 1-2 in Chapter 1, which presents the financial statements (including notes) and auditor's report for Nikken Chemicals Co., Ltd. Refer to Note 2, Significant Accounting Policies, which presents the basis of financial statement presentation for this company.

REQUIRED

1. Restate the income statement and balance sheet to a U.S. GAAP basis, using one of the approaches discussed in the text.
2. Discuss whether your restatement provides sufficient information for a comparison between Nikken Chemicals' financial performance and condition with a manufacturer of chemicals in your home company.

CASE 9-2   CONTINENTAL A.G.

Dietrich Becker and Marissa Skye, tire analysts for a global investment fund located in Manhattan, are examining the 20X0 earnings performance of two potential investment candidates. Reflecting the company's investment philosophy of picking the best stocks wherever they are located in the world, both junior analysts have adopted an approach of undertaking matched comparisons of leading firms in the tire industry. For starters, Dietrich and Marissa focused on Goodyear Tire & Rubber Company (United States) and Continental A.G. (Germany) as their first screen.

DIETRICH: Well, what do you think, Marissa?

MARISSA: Looking at the income trends (see Exhibit 9-17), I sort of like Continental.

DIETRICH: Yes, I agree. Goodyear's results are much more volatile.

MARISSA: I always look to see how a company has done in an off year. Owing to the continued consolidation of the tire industry, excess capacity created by reduced demand for autos and trucks, as well as reduced consumer spending for replacement tires in light of economic and political uncertainties, 20X0 was a disastrous year for every major company in the industry. Given that environment, Continental's performance was stellar!

DIETRICH: Maybe we'd better check with Prawit, our accountant, to see if we're reading the tea leaves correctly.

MARISSA: I'll give him a call.

(After a 5-minute conversation)

DIETRICH: Well, what did he say?

MARISSA: He said, we're probably correct in our overall assessment (I think he's just being polite), but that we'd better check the company's accounting policies. He says German accounting principles tend to impart a conservative bias to corporate earnings. He'll send us an e-mail attachment summarizing some major GAAP differences between the United States and Germany very soon.

(The e-mail attachment is reproduced as Exhibit 9-18.)

Exhibit 9-17   Comparative Performance Data

Goodyear ($ millions)

	19X6	19X7	19X8	19X9	20X0
Sales	9,040	9,905	10,810	10,869	11,273
Net income(loss)	124	771	350	207	(38)

Continental (DM millions)

	19X6	19X7	19X8	19X9	20X0
Sales	4,969	5,098	7,906	8,382	8,551
Net income(loss)	115	139	195	228	93

Exhibit 9-18 Major Accounting Differences between Germany and the United States		
	Germany	United States
Goodwill	Written off against reserves or amortized; commercial law prescribes 4 years; most companies amortize over 15 years for tax purposes.	Capitalized and amortized subject to an impairments test.
Long-term leases	Generally no lease capitalization.	Capitalization required when specific criteria met.
Depreciation	Highest rates allowable for tax purposes.	Generally straight-line over estimated useful lives.
Inventory	Costing must mirror physical flow of goods. Average costing is common.	LIFO costing method is common.
Reserves	Use of discretionary reserves to smooth earnings are not uncommon.	Use of discretionary reserves to smooth earnings are discouraged.

MARISSA: (Having examined the attachment) Looks like there are some major differences in reporting rules between Germany and the United States.

DIETRICH: Do you think we should attempt to restate Continental's accounts to a U.S. GAAP basis?

MARISSA: Why don't we try.

DIETRICH: Where should we start?

MARISSA: Let's examine Continental's financial statements (see Exhibit 9-19 on page 358) to see if we can detect any unusual accounting practices that may have a distorting effect on the company's reported performance. I notice that Continental follows the European practice of including both parent company (Con-solidated A.G.) and consolidated numbers. Let's just focus on the consolidated figures for now.

DIETRICH: Right. And if we find some disparities, maybe we should just attempt one or two adjustments, particularly those for which we have sufficient information. If these adjustments have a significant earnings impact, then let's press the right buttons and see if we can't get the company to give us some additional information so that we can do a more comprehensive analysis.

MARISSA: Sounds good. Let's get started.

Exhibit 9-19   Continental's Financial Statements and Related Notes

Continental Aktiengesellschaft
Consolidated Balance Sheet at December 31, 20X0

Assets	See Note No.	12/31/20X0 euro 000	12/31/19X9 euro 000
Fixed assets and investments			
Intangible assets	(1)	430,920	11,944
Property, plant, and equipment	(2)	2,196,724	1,797,125
Investments	(3)	225,729	189,428
		2,853,373	1,998,497
Current assets			
Inventories	(4)	1,611,566	1,506,771
Receivables and other assets	(5)	1,475,557	1,386,212
Marketable securities	(6)	51,426	339,219
Liquid assets	(7)	144,625	134,079
		3,283,174	3,366,281
Prepaid expenses	(8)	31,070	41,092
		6,167,617	5,405,870

Shareholders' equity and liabilities	See Note No.	12/31/20X0 euro 000	12/31/19X9 euro 000
Shareholders' equity			
Subscribed capital	(9)	439,097	435,022
Capital reserves	(10)	962,275	956,240
Retained earnings	(11)	137,788	133,770
Minority interests	(12)	94,286	46,692
Reserve for retirement benefits	(13)	2,861	3,691
Net income available for distribution		36,383	70,984
		1,672,690	
Special reserves	(14)	80,552	118,103
Provisions	(15)	1,733,440	1,386,799
Liabilities	(16)	2,680,935	2,254,569
		6,167,617	5,405,570

Continental Aktiengesellschaft
Consolidated Statement of Income for the period
from January 1 to December 31, 20X0

	See Note No	20X0 euro 000	19X9 euro 000
Sales	(17)	8,551,015	8,381,880
Cost of sales*	(18)	6,490,128	6,256,858
Gross profit on sales		2,060,887	2,125,002
Selling expenses	(19)	1,255,474	1,174,268
Administrative expenses	(20)	504,277	474,932
Other operating income	(21)	194,266	164,076
Other operating expenses	(22)	140,218	91,351
Net income from investments and financial activities	(23)	−138,777	−116,536

Exhibit 9-19   Continental's Financial Statements and Related Notes (*Continued*)

Continental Aktiengesellschaft
Consolidated Statement of Income for the period
from January 1 to December 31, 20X0

	See Note No	20X0	19X9
		euro 000	*euro 000*
Net income from regular business activities		216,407	431,991
Taxes	(24)	122,972	204,153
Net income for the year		93,435	227,838
Balance brought forward from previous year		1,380	1,199
Minority interests in earning	(25)	−88	−58
Withdrawal from the reserve for retirement benefits		+ 830	+ 544
Change in reserves		−59,174	−158,539
Net income available for distribution		36,383	70,984

Based on an audit performed in accordance with our professional duties, the consolidated financial statements comply with the legal regulations. The consolidated financial statements present, in compliance with required accounting principles, a true and fair view of the net worth, financial position, and results of the corporation. The management report for the corporation is in agreement with the consolidated financial statements.
Berlin/Hanover, April 8, 19X1

Accounting policies:

Assets.

Acquired intangible assets are carried at acquisition cost and amortized by the straight-line method over their anticipated useful life. Capitalized goodwill resulting from the acquisition of companies is deducted in installments from retained earnings on the balance sheet, over periods estimated individually at from 10 to 20 years.

Property, plant, and equipment is valued at acquisition or manufacturing costs, less scheduled depreciation.

Continental Aktiengesellschaft uses the declining balance method to depreciate movable fixed assets, while the straight-line method is used for all other fixed assets. We change over from the declining balance method to the straight-line method as soon as this leads to higher depreciation. In the financial statements of Continental Aktiengesellschaft, the special depreciation permitted by the tax laws is taken insofar as necessary in view of the fact that the commercial balance sheet is the basis for the balance sheet prepared in accordance with the tax regulations.

Since 1989, pursuant to internationally accepted accounting principles, additions have been depreciated exclusively by the straight-line method in the consolidated financial statements.

The following table shows the useful life taken as a basis for depreciating the major categories of property, plant, and equipment:

Buildings up to 33 years

Additions from 1990 on, up to 25 years

Technical facilities and machinery, 10 years

Plant and office equipment, 4 to 7 years

Molds up to 4 years

Additions to movable assets made during the first 6 months of the year are depreciated at the full annual rate, and those made during the last 6 months at half the annual rate. Minor fixed assets are written off completely in the year of acquisition.

(continued)

These depreciation rules are applied by each of the domestic and foreign companies as of the date it became part of the Corporation.

Interests in affiliates and other companies held as investments are valued at acquisition cost, less the necessary write-downs.

Interest-bearing loans granted are shown at face value; loans that bear little or not interest are discounted to their cash value.

Inventories are carried at the lower acquisition/manufacturing cost or market.

Manufacturing cost includes direct costs, as well as a proportional part of material and production overhead and depreciation. Appropriate adjustment are made for declines in value due to reduced usability or prolonged storage.

In valuing receivables and miscellaneous assets, we make reasonable allowances to cover all perceivable risks, as well as lump-sum deductions to cover the general credit risk.

Marketable securities are valued at the lower of cost or market.

Insofar as permissible, we have continued to take all the extraordinary depreciation and write-downs, as well as the depreciation and write-downs for tax purposes, which were taken in previous years on fixed assets, investments, and current assets.

Discounts and issue costs of loans and bonds are shown as prepaid expenses and amortized over the term of the individual loans and bonds.

Shareholders' Equity and Liabilities

Provisions based on sound business judgment are set up for all perceivable risks, undetermined obligations, and impending losses.

At our German companies, the provisions for pension plans and similar obligations are set up at a 6% interest rate, on the basis of actuarial computations in accordance with the statutory method.

Pension commitments and similar obligations of foreign companies are also computed according to actuarial principles, discounted to the present value at the interest rates prevailing in the respective countries, and covered by appropriate provisions for pension plans or by pension funds. Employee claims for severance benefits under national laws have also been taken into account.

The pension obligations of American companies are valued according to the stricter valuation rules that have been in force in the U.S.A. since 1987. The provision made for this purpose in the balance sheet is slightly higher than if the corresponding German method of computation had been applied.

The obligations of General Tire Inc., Akron, Ohio, for post-retirement medical benefits are fully covered by provisions computed according to actuarial principles. New U.S. regulations (FASB No. 106) require that by no later than 1993, a provision must be established for not only the retirees and vested workforce, but also for the nonvested employees. Although this regulation allows a build-up of the provision over a 20-year period, we have already transferred the full additional amount required (DM270.7 million) to the provisions shown on the consolidated balance sheet. To balance this item, goodwill deducted from consolidated retained earnings at the time of the acquisition of General Tire has been capitalized in the same amount.

As a rule, provisions for repairs that have been postponed to the subsequent year are established in the amount of the probable cost.

When there are temporary differences between the values of the individual companies' assets and liabilities as determined according to the tax laws and those appearing in their balance sheets, which are prepared according to valuation principles that are uniform throughout the Corporation, deferred taxes may result. We show the latter only when they are reflected in provisions for future tax expenses. Liabilities are stated at the redemption amount.

Selected Notes:

(10) Capital reserves. This item includes amounts received upon the issuance of shares in excess of their par value totaling euro 724 .9 million, as well as the premium of euro 237.4 million paid upon the exercise of warrants attached to the bonds issued in 19X4, 19X6 and 19X7 and to the 19X8 convertible debentures. Capital reserves increased by euro 6.0 million due to the exercise of the conversion and option rights in 20X0.

(11) Retained earnings		
euro 000	*Continental AG*	*Consolidated*
As of 12/31/19X9	141,699	133,770
Differences from translation	—	−55,009
Other	—	−147
Allocation from net income	8,000	59,174
As of 12/31/20X0	149,699	137,788

(14) Special reserves				
euro 000	*12/31/20X0*		*12/31/19X9*	
	Continental AG	*Consolidated*	*Continental AG*	*Consolidated*
Reserve per/3. Foreign Investment Act	59,766	15,000	84,312	38,265
Reserve per/6b, Income Tax Act	—	448	—	289
Reserve per/52 Par.8 Income Tax Act	705	1,069	940	1,425
Governmental capital investment subsidies	—	57,664	—	60,988
Other	2,533	6,371	4,137	17,136
	63,004	80,552	89,389	118,103

The decrease in special reserves is due, in particular, to the elimination of the special reserve pursuant to /3. Foreign Investment Act, following the write-down made in connection with Semperit (Ireland) Ltd., Dublin, Ireland. The special reserves are divided into an equity portion of euro 69.5 million and a debt portion of euro 11.1 million, representing deferred taxes, which will be paid in due course, when the reserves are eliminated. Including the shareholders equity of euro 1,672.7 million shown on the balance sheet, the actual shareholders equity amounts to euro 1,742.2 million and the equity ratio to 28.2%.

(15) Provisions				
euro 000	*12/31/20X0*		*12/31/19X9*	
	Continental AG	*Consolidated*	*Continental AG*	*Consolidated*
Provision for pensions	220,977	972,173	206,374	636,626
Provisions for taxes	31,937	72,210	53,144	92,265
Miscellaneous provisions	191,465	689,057	188,817	657,908
	444,379	1,733,440	448,335	1,386,799

(continued)

361

Exhibit 9-19   Continental's Financial Statements and Related Notes (*Continued*)

The Corporation's provisions for pensions and similar obligations rose considerably. Apart from normal allocations, this increase was due, in particular, to an addition to cover claims for medical benefits which may be made by employees of General Tire Inc., Akron, Ohio, U.S.A., after their retirement.

At two of our retirement benefit organizations, there is a shortfall of euro 22.0 million in the coverage of pension obligations. The provisions at four other German companies have been funded only to the maximum amount permitted for tax purposes.

Lower tax liabilities permitted a reduction in provisions for taxes, which include amounts relating both to the current fiscal year and to previous years.

Provisions for deferred taxes in the individual financial statements, after deduction of the net prepaid taxes arising from consolidation procedures, amounted to euro 7.4 million.

Miscellaneous provisions cover all perceivable risks and other undetermined obligations. In addition to provisions for warranties, bonuses and miscellaneous risks, they consist mainly of provisions for personnel and social welfare payments, deferred repairs and service anniversaries.

(21) Other operating income

euro 000	12/31/20X0		12/31/19X9	
	Continental AG	Consolidated	Continental AG	Consolidated
Gains on the disposal of fixed assets and investments	6,179	33,423	2,435	10,733
Credit to income from the reversal of provisions	1,418	17,312	7,400	33,559
Credit to income from the reduction of the general bad debt reserve	—	1,101	—	2,014
Credit to income from the reversal of special reserves	26,385	38,824	12,645	32,456
Miscellaneous income	120,143	103,606	106,843	85,294
	154,125	194,266	129,323	164,076

In addition to current income from rentals, leasing and miscellaneous sideline operations, other operating income includes indemnification paid by insurance companies and income attributable to other fiscal years.

For the parent company, this item consists mainly of cost apportionments received from other companies belonging to the Corporation.

(22) Other operating expenses

euro 000	12/31/20X0		12/31/19X9	
	Continental AG	Consolidated	Continental AG	Consolidated
Losses on the disposal of fixed assets and investments	2,015	6,694	306	4,315
Losses on the disposal of current assets	1,414	19,197	257	22,818
Allocation to special reserves	—	168	46,995	1,278
Miscellaneous expenses	111,504	114,161	89,374	62,940
	114,933	140,218	136,932	91,351

Exhibit 9-19 Continental's Financial Statements and Related Notes (*Continued*)

The miscellaneous expenses relate primarily to sideline operations and the establishment of necessary provisions; at the parent company, they include cost apportionments paid to other companies belonging to the Corporation.

(24) Taxes				
euro 000	*12/31/20X0*		*12/31/19X9*	
	Continental AG	*Consolidated*	*Continental AG*	*Consolidated*
On income	45,747	59,884	75,612	141,476
Other taxes	14,186	63,088	17,527	62,877
	59,993	122,972	93,139	204,153

CHAPTER

10 | MANAGERIAL PLANNING AND CONTROL

rior chapters have largely had an external reporting orientation. This chapter focuses on internal reporting and control issues. We acknowledge that the distinction between the two is increasingly blurred.

Global competition together with continued advances in technology are significantly altering the landscape of business and its internal reporting requirements. Continued reductions in national trade barriers, floating currencies, sovereign risk, restrictions on fund remittances across national borders, differences in national tax systems, interest rate differentials, and the effects of changing commodity and equity prices on enterprise assets, earnings, and capital costs are variables that complicate management decisions. At the same time, developments such as the Internet, video conferencing, and electronic transfer are changing the economics of production, distribution, and financing. Production is increasingly awarded to the company in the world that does it, or parts of it, best. Globally coordinated value chains based on strategic alliances are replacing arms-length relationships among manufacturers, suppliers, and customers. Understandably, an increasing emphasis is being placed on information providers who understand the information needs of management and who possess strong analytic and presentation skills.[1]

Global competition and the speed of knowledge dissemination support the narrowing of national variations in management accounting practices.[2] Additional pressures include market and technology changes, the growth of privatization, cost and performance incentives, and the coordination of global operations through joint venturing and other strategic linkages. They are driving management of multinational companies not only to adopt comparable internal accounting techniques, but to use these techniques in similar fashion.[3] Managerial accounting issues discussed in this book fall into

---

[1]Mike Anastas, "The Changing World of Management Accounting and Financial Management," *Management Accounting* (October 1997): 48–51.

[2]A. Bhimani, ed., *Management Accounting: European Perspectives,* Oxford: Oxford University Press, 1996; Michael D. Shields, "Management Accounting Practices in Europe: A Perspective from the States," *Management Accounting Research* 9 (1998): 501–513; and Chris Guilding, Karen S. Cravens, and Mike Tayles, "An International Comparison of Strategic Management Accounting Practices," *Management Accounting Research* 9 (2000): 113–135.

[3]T. Sheridan, "Management Accounting in Global European Corporations: Anglophone and Continental Viewpoints," *Management Accounting Research* 6 (1995): 287–294; Michael Firth, "The Diffusion of Managerial Accounting Procedures in the People's Republic of China and the Influence of Foreign Partnered Joint Ventures," *Accounting Organizations and Society* 21, No. 7/8 (1996): 629–654; Alicja Jaruga and Simon S. M. Ho, "Management Accounting in Transitional Economies," *Management Accounting Research* 13 (2002): 375–378.

three broad areas: financial planning and control (this chapter), international risk management (Chapter 11), and international taxation and transfer pricing (Chapter 12). Planning topics in this chapter include business modeling, capital budgeting, and profitability management, together with the information systems needed to implement them. The balance of the chapter focuses on financial control.

BUSINESS MODELING

A recent survey finds that management accountants are spending more time on strategic planning issues than ever before.[4] Business modeling is *big picture,* and it consists of formulating, implementing, and evaluating a firm's long-range business plan.[5] It involves four critical dimensions:[6]

1. Identifying key factors relevant to the future progress of the company
2. Formulating appropriate techniques to forecast future developments and assess the company's ability to adapt to or exploit these developments
3. Developing data sources to support strategic choices
4. Translating selected options into specific courses of action

PLANNING TOOLS

In identifying factors relevant to its future, it is helpful for a company to scan its external and internal environments to identify threats and opportunities. Systems can be set in place to gather information on competitors and market conditions. Both competitors and market conditions are analyzed for their impact on a company's competitive status and profitability. Insights gleaned from this analysis are used to plan measures to maintain or enlarge market share, or to identify and exploit new product and market opportunities.

One such tool is the WOTS-UP analysis. It is concerned with corporate strengths and weaknesses in relation to a firm's operating environment. This technique helps management generate a set of feasible strategies.[7] Exhibit 10-1 shows a WOTS-UP analysis done by the German automaker Daimler Benz (now Daimler Chrysler). For example, extending Daimler's distribution and service network in Eastern Europe is a promising strategy, given the company's strengths in product quality, truck sales, lower breakeven point, and synergistic potential. The low value of the U.S. dollar, rising foreign competition in Germany, and the perceived advantages of strengthening basic

---

[4]Institute of Management Accountants, "Role Changing for Management Accountants," *Journal of Accountancy* (November 1999): 17, 20.
[5]Evidence suggests that nationality may influence the extent to which the executive suite embraces planning on a long-range basis. See George S. Yip, Johny K. Johansson, and Johan Roos, "Effects of Nationality on Global Strategy," *Management International Review* (1997): 365–385.
[6]Kiyohiko Ito and Klaus R. Macharzina, "Strategic Planning Systems," in F. D. S. Choi, ed., *International Accounting and Finance Handbook,* 2nd ed., New York: John Wiley & Sons, 1997.
[7]WOTS-UP analysis is a modified version of SWOT analysis, which is constantly being improved upon as a strategic planning tool. See George Panagiotou, "Bringing SWOT into Focus," *Business Strategy Review* 14, Issue 2 (2003): 8–10.

Exhibit 10-1   WOTS-UP Analysis of Daimler Benz AG

	Strengths (S)	Weaknesses (W)
	1. Product quality improved 20% from previous year 2. R & D potential higher than other automobile producers 3. 50% share of comfort limousine market 4. Daimler Benz trucks lead industry 5. Breakeven point decreased from 1.0 to 0.7 million vehicles 6. Several acquisitions (e.g., AEG, Dornier, MBB) improved the synergistic potential of Daimler Benz 7. Excellent financial situation of Daimler Benz 8. High economies of scope	1. Acquisition of high-tech firms leads to coordination problems 2. High wage level (most of the production is located in Germany) 3. Fewer joint ventures (international alliances) than Japanese automobile producers
Opportunities (O)	**SO-Strategies**	**WO-Strategies**
1. High-tech industries (micro electronics, aerospace) growing 20% per year 2. Consumers' disposable income increasing 6% per year 3. Liberalization of Eastern European countries 4. Image and service problems of Japanese automobile firms	1. Acquire automobile producers in Eastern Germany (03/S7) 2. Extend the distribution and service net in Eastern Europe (03/S7) 3. Develop several versions of the Baby Benz (02, 03/S5, S7) 4. Use production capacity for civil products (03/S6, S8)	1. Expand transfer of managers between headquarters and subsidiaries (03/W1) 2. Produce cars in the eastern part of Germany (03/W2) 3. Intensify HR development on each level (01/W2) 4. Form international aerospace joint venture company (01/W3)
Threats (T)	**Short-Term Strategies**	**Long-Term Strategies**
1. Low value of the dollar 2. Rising interest rate 3. Foreign imports, esp. luxury cars, gaining market share 4. Gulf crisis leads to increasing gas prices 5. BMW has an excellent new line of cars 6. Rising ecological problems throughout the world 7. Military (defense) markets may break off due to peace movement	1. Place selective advertising; boost advertising expenditures 30% (T3, T5/S1, S3) 2. Strengthen basic research in new fields of technology (solar energy, biotechnology, computing and robotics, electrical car engines) (T4, T6/S7, S8)	1. Build strategic alliances (strategic networks) to reduce cost of R & D investment and to solve ecological problems (T6/W3) 2. Improve productivity and quality (in production, administration, distribution, and services) (T1,T3/W2)

Source: K. Ito and K. R. Macharzina, "Strategic Planning Systems," in F. D. S. Choi, ed., *International Accounting and Finance Handbook,* 2nd ed., New York: John Wiley & Sons, 1997, p. 25.9.

research in new technologies by building strategic alliances may explain Daimler's acquisition of the Chrysler Corporation in the United States.

Decision tools currently used in strategic planning systems all depend on the quality of information regarding a firm's internal and external environment. Accountants can help corporate planners obtain data useful in strategic planning decisions. Much of the required information comes from sources other than accounting records.

CAPITAL BUDGETING

As Exhibit 10-1 reveals, one of Daimler Benz AG's strategies to capitalize on its strength/opportunity set was to initially acquire automobile producers in Eastern Germany. This strategy subsequently embraced the acquisition of the Chrysler Corporation in the United States. This decision to invest abroad is a critical element in the global strategy of a multinational company. Direct foreign investment typically involves large sums of capital and uncertain prospects. Investment risk is compounded by an unfamiliar, complex, constantly changing international environment. Formal planning is imperative and normally is done within a capital budgeting framework that compares the benefits and costs of the proposed investment.[8] As an example of the second dimension of corporate modeling described earlier, capital budgeting analysis helps ensure that strategic plans are financially feasible and advantageous.

Sophisticated approaches to investment decisions are available. Procedures exist to determine a firm's optimum capital structure, measure a firm's cost of capital, and evaluate investment alternatives under conditions of uncertainty. Decision rules for investment choice typically call for discounting an investment's risk-adjusted cash flows at an appropriate interest rate: the firm's weighted average cost of capital. Normally, a firm increases the wealth of its owners by making investments that promise positive net present values. When considering mutually exclusive options, a rational company will select the option that promises the maximum net present value.

In the international arena, investment planning is not straightforward.[9] Different tax laws, accounting systems, rates of inflation, risks of expropriation, currency frameworks, market segmentation, restrictions on the transferability of foreign earnings, and language and intercultural differences introduce elements of complexity seldom encountered domestically. The difficulty of quantifying such data makes the problem that much worse.

Multinational adaptations of traditional investment planning models have been made in three areas of measurement: (1) determining the relevant return from a multinational investment, (2) measuring expected cash flows, and (3) calculating the multinational cost of capital. These adaptations provide data that support strategic choices, step 3 in the corporate modeling process.

---

[8]For a recent state-of-the art piece on capital budgeting in Sweden, see Gert Sandahl and Stefan Sjogren, "Capital Budgeting Methods among Sweden's Largest Groups: The State of the Art and a Comparison with Earlier Studies," *International Journal of Production Economics* 84 (2003): 51–69.
[9]Ian A. Cooper and Evi Kaplanis, "Partially Segmented International Capital Markets and International Capital Budgeting," *Journal of International Money and Finance* 19 (2000): 309–329.

FINANCIAL RETURN PERSPECTIVES

A manager must determine the *relevant return* to assess a foreign investment opportunity. But relevant return is a matter of perspective. Should the international financial manager evaluate expected investment returns from the perspective of the foreign project or that of the parent company?[10] Returns from the two perspectives could differ significantly due to (1) government restrictions on repatriation of earnings and capital, (2) license fees, royalties, and other payments that provide income to the parent but are expenses to the subsidiary, (3) differential rates of national inflation, (4) changing foreign currency values, and (5) differential taxes, to name a few.

One might argue that the return and risk of a foreign investment should be evaluated from the point of view of the parent company's domestic stockholders. However, it also can be argued that such an approach is no longer appropriate. First, investors in the parent company increasingly come from a worldwide community. Investment objectives should reflect the interests of all shareholders, not just the domestic ones. Observation also suggests that many multinational companies have long-run (as opposed to short-run) investment horizons. Funds generated abroad tend to be reinvested abroad rather than repatriated to the parent company. Under these circumstances, it may be appropriate to evaluate returns from a host country perspective. Emphasis on local project returns is consistent with the goal of maximizing consolidated group value.[11]

An appealing solution is to recognize that financial managers must meet many goals, responding to investor and noninvestor groups in the organization and its environment.[12] The host country government is one such group for a foreign investment. Compatibility between the goals of the multinational investor and the host government can be gauged through two financial return calculations: one from the host country perspective, the other from the parent country perspective. The host country perspective assumes that a profitable foreign investment (including the local opportunity cost of capital) does not misallocate the host country's scarce resources.[13] Evaluating an investment opportunity from a local perspective also gives the parent company useful information.

If a foreign investment does not promise a risk-adjusted return higher than the returns of local competitors, parent company shareholders would be better off investing directly in the local companies.

At first glance, the accounting implications of multiple rate-of-return calculations appear straightforward. Nothing could be less true. In an earlier discussion, we assumed that project rate-of-return calculations were a proxy for host country evaluation of a foreign investment. In practice, the analysis is much more complicated. Do project rate of return calculations really reflect a host country's opportunity costs? Are the expected returns from a foreign investment limited to projected cash flows, or must other externalities be considered? How are any additional benefits measured? Does a foreign investment require any special overhead spending by the host government? What is the risk from a host country

---

[10]This issue parallels, in many respects, the problem of currency perspectives associated with foreign currency translation discussed in Chapter 6.
[11]John C. Edmunds and David M. Ellis, A Stock Market-Driven Reformulation of Multinational Capital Budgeting, *European Management Journal* 17, No. 3 (1999): 310–317.
[12]David K. Eiteman, Arthur I. Stonehill, and Michael Moffett, *Multinational Business Finance,* 9th ed., Reading, MA: Addison-Wesley, 2000.
[13]For example, a country would probably look favorably on a proposed investment promising a 21 percent return on assets employed when investments of comparable risk elsewhere in the country yield 18 percent.

viewpoint, and how can it be measured? Questions such as these call for a massive increase in the amount and complexity of the information needed to calculate rates of return.

MEASURING EXPECTED RETURNS

It is challenging to measure the expected cash flows of a foreign investment. Assume, for purposes of discussion, that Daimler-Chrysler's U.S. manufacturing operation is considering purchasing 100 percent ownership of a manufacturing facility in Russia. The U.S. parent will finance one-half of the investment in the form of cash and equipment; the balance will be financed by local bank borrowing at market rates. The Russian facility will import one-half of its raw materials and components from the U.S. parent and export one-half of its output to Hungary. To repatriate funds to the parent company, the Russian facility will pay the U.S. parent a licensing fee, royalties for use of parent company patents, and technical service fees for management services rendered. Earnings of the Russian facility will be remitted to the parent as dividends. Exhibit 10-2 provides a diagram of prospective cash flows that need to be measured.[14]

Exhibit 10-2 Cash Flow Components

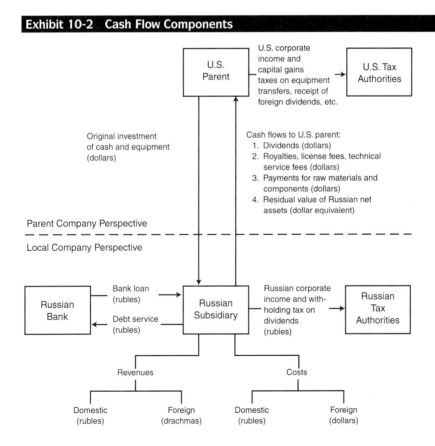

[14]For an extended discussion of this subject, see David K. Eiteman, "Foreign Investment Analysis," in F. D. S. Choi, ed., *International Finance and Accounting Handbook*, 3rd ed. New York: John Wiley & Sons, 2003, pp. 4.1 to 4.19.

Methods for estimating projected cash flows associated with the Russian facility are similar to those used for a domestic company. Expected receipts are based on sales projections and anticipated collection experience. Operating expenses (converted to their cash equivalents) and local taxes are similarly forecast. Additional complexities must be considered, however. They include:

1. Project versus parent cash flows
2. Parent cash flows tied to financing
3. Subsidized financing
4. Political risk

This process also must consider the impact of changing prices and fluctuating currency values on expected foreign currency returns. If local currency cash flows were fixed (e.g., if the Russian venture was in the form of a bond investment), it would be straightforward to measure exchange rate effects. Here, depreciation of the Russian ruble relative to the U.S. dollar reduces the dollar equivalent of future interest income. When an ongoing manufacturing enterprise generates foreign currency income, the analysis is more complicated. Exchange rate changes influence net operating cash flows. Accordingly, accounting measurements of exchange rate effects for each type of activity (such as domestic vs. export sales, domestic vs. imported costs, and their cumulative effects on projected cash flows) become necessary.

The following example illustrates the effects of changing prices and currency values on expected returns for the first 2 years of a 6-year investment project. The Russian facility's cash flows, as shown in Exhibit 10-3, are determined under the following assumptions.

1. The Russian facility is expected to sell 100,000 units of its manufactured product in the local market at an initial unit price of 2,020 Russian rubles (R). Another 100,000 units will be exported to Hungary and priced in forints (F) reflecting the ruble base price.
2. Changes in local selling prices are tied to annual rates of inflation in Russia and Hungary, which are expected to average 20 percent and 10 percent, respectively.
3. Domestic and foreign unit sales are expected to increase each year by 10 percent.
4. The ruble is forecast to depreciate relative to the forint by 10 percent per year.
5. Variable costs of production (raw materials and labor) also reflect local inflation rates.
6. Because 50 percent of the Russian manufacturer's raw materials are imported from the United States, imported raw material prices are expected to increase by 10 percent each year in line with anticipated U.S. and Russian inflation.
7. Anticipated depreciation of the ruble relative to the U.S. dollar is 5 percent.
8. Licensing and other fees are expected to average 10 percent of gross revenues.
9. Selling and administrative expenses are expected to increase by 15 percent each year from an initial level of R 48,000,000.
10. Depreciation expense is R 60,000,000 a year.
11. The Russian corporate tax rate is 40 percent.
12. Projected annual cash flows will increase from R 93,360,000 to R 124,016,000 in local currency. Measured in U.S. dollars, net cash flows will increase from $4,668,000 to $5,905,000.

Exhibit 10-3 Cash Flows from Russian Subsidiary		
	Year 1	Year 2
Sales (units)		
Domestic	100,000	110,000
Foreign	100,000	110,000
Price (per unit)		
Domestic	R2,020	R2,424
Foreign	R2,020	R2,444
Gross revenues		
Domestic	R 202,000,000	R 266,640,000
Foreign	R 202,000,000	R 268,640,000
	(F2,020,000,000)	(F2,444,000,000)
Total	R 404,000,000	R 535,480,000
Raw materials (cost per unit)		
Domestic	R400	R480
Foreign	R400	R462
	($20)	($22)
Labor (cost per unit)	R200	R240
Variable cost (per unit)	R1,000	R1,182
Total variable costs	R 200,000,000	R260,040,000
Licensing fees, royalties, etc.	R 40,400,000	R 53,548,000
Depreciation expense	R 60,000,000	R 60,000,000
Selling and administrative expenses	R 48,000,000	R 55,200,000
Total	R 348,400,000	R 428,788,000
Net operating income	R 33,360,000	R 64,016,000
Corporate income tax (40%)	R 22,240,000	R 42,676,000
Net income	R 33,360,000	R 64,016,000
+Depreciation	R 60,000,000	R 60,000,000
Net cash flow (rubles)	R 93,360,000	R 124,016,000
Net cash flow (dollars)	$ 4,668,000	$ 5,905,000

Exchange rates:
R 0.1 = F1   R 0.11 = F1
R 20 = $1   R 21 = $1

In this example, a depreciating local currency had increased projected local cash flows due to the structure of the foreign operation's product and factor markets.

When a parent company perspective is used, cash flows to the parent company seldom mirror those of its overseas affiliate. The only relevant cash flows are those with direct consequences for the parent.

Major sources of parent cash flows include debt service on loans by the parent, dividends, licensing fees, overhead charges, royalties, transfer prices on purchases from or sales to the parent (see Chapter 12 for a further discussion of this managerial topic), and the estimated terminal value of the project. Measurement of these cash flows requires an understanding of national accounting differences, governmental repatriation policies, potential future inflation and exchange rates, and differential taxes.

Differences in accounting principles are relevant if financial managers rely on locally based pro forma financial statements in estimating future cash flows. When measurement rules used in preparing these accounts differ from those of the parent country, differences in cash flow estimates could arise. One example is depreciation based on replacement values rather than historical costs (as practiced by certain large multinationals in the Netherlands and Italy). This difference could affect corporate income taxes, and consequently, cash flow. As another example, differences in inventory costing methods could influence both the measurement and the timing of total cash flow. Balance of payment concerns may prompt host governments to limit the repatriation of dividends or other cash payments to the parent company. For example, dividend remittances may be limited to a certain proportion of a company's capital base that has been formally registered with the host government. Some countries disallow repatriation of cash flows made possible by tax-deductible expenses, as these are not part of accrual-based earnings from which dividends are declared. This consideration alone would reduce the cash flows that could be repatriated in our previous Russian example by 66 and 50 percent, respectively, for the 2 years examined. A parent company naturally cares about the value of foreign cash flows measured in parent currency.

Accordingly, it needs estimates of future inflation and its impact on future exchange rates used to convert foreign cash flows to parent currency. Finally, provisions relating to the taxation of foreign source income must be considered. For instance, in the United States the receipt of a royalty payment on which a foreign withholding tax has been assessed gives rise to a foreign tax credit designed to minimize the double taxation of foreign source income. (International tax considerations are detailed in Chapter 12.)

MULTINATIONAL COST OF CAPITAL

If foreign investments are evaluated with this discounted cash flow model, an appropriate discount rate must be developed. Capital budgeting theory typically uses a firm's cost of capital as its discount rate; that is, a project must yield a return at least equal to a firm's capital costs to be accepted.[15] This *hurdle rate* is related to the proportions of debt and equity in a firm's financial structure as follows where:

ka = weighted average (after tax) cost of capital
ke = cost of equity
ki = cost of debt before tax
E = value of a firm's equity
D = value of a firm's debt
S = value of a firm's capital structure $(E + D)$
t = marginal tax rate

---

[15]For an examination of the relationship between corporate strategy and finance, see Lars Oxelheim, Arthus Stonehill, Trond Randoy, Kaisa Vikkula, Kare B. Dullum, and Karl-Markus Moden, *Corporate Strategies to Internationalize the Cost of Capital,* Handelsshojskolens Forlag: Copenhagen Business School Press, 1998.

It is not easy to measure a multinational company's cost of capital. The cost of equity capital may be calculated in several ways. One popular method combines the expected dividend yield with the expected dividend growth rate. Letting Di = expected dividends per share at period's end, P_0 = the current market price of the stock at the beginning of the period, and g = expected growth rate in dividends, the cost of equity, *ke,* is calculated as $ke = D_i/P_0 + g$. Even though it is easy to measure current stock prices, in most countries where a multinational firm's shares are listed, it is often troublesome to measure D and g. First, D_i is an expectation. Expected dividends depend on the operating cash flows of the company as a whole. Measuring these cash flows is complicated by environmental considerations such as those mentioned in our Russian example. Moreover, measurement of the dividend growth rate, a function of expected future cash flows, is complicated by exchange controls and other government restrictions on cross-border funds transfers.

Similar problems relate to the measurement of the debt component of the average cost of capital. In a single nation, the cost of debt is the effective interest rate multiplied by $(1 - t)$ because interest is generally a tax-deductible expense. When a multinational company borrows foreign currencies, however, additional factors enter the picture. The effective after-tax interest cost now includes foreign exchange gains or losses that arise whenever foreign exchange rates fluctuate between the transaction and settlement dates (see Chapter 6). Suppose that a U.S. multinational borrows 100,000 Israeli shekels for 1 year at 8 percent interest when the dollar/shekel exchange rate is $0.24 = Shk 1. Should the shekel appreciate to $0.264 = Shk 1 before repayment, the borrowing company will incur a transaction loss of Shk 108,000 $\times$ ($ 0.264 − $0.240) = $2,592. This additional cost of debt financing would be tax deductible. Assuming a corporate tax rate of 40 percent, the after-tax cost of debt would be .18 (1 − .40), or 10.8 percent, as opposed to 4 percent in a purely domestic transaction.

Additional tax considerations apply when a multinational borrows funds in several foreign capital markets. Current and prospective tax rates in each foreign market over the life of the loan must be considered. The tax-deductibe status of interest payments must be checked, because not all national taxing authorities recognize interest deductions (particularly if the associated loan is between related entities). Moreover, recognition of deferred taxes, which arise whenever income for tax purposes differs from income for external reporting purposes, is becoming a generally accepted practice in many industrialized countries where MNCs operate. Because deferred taxes are considered a liability on which no interest is paid, one can ask whether they are really an interest-free source of financing and should be included in determining the cost of capital. Although this idea merits consideration, we do not believe that the cost of capital calculation should include deferred taxes.[16]

It is not always straightforward to implement international capital budgeting theory in practice. All of the capital budgeting approaches we have examined assume that the required information is readily available. Unfortunately, in actual practice, the

---

[16]As discussed in Chapter 6, deferred taxes under the current rate method are translated at the current rate with any translation gains and losses taken to owners' equity and held in suspense until realized. Under the temporal method, they are translated at the historical rate. Because current earnings are not burdened with exchange rate effects under either treatment, neither should the costs of capital be relieved by what is, in effect, an interest-free loan from a government.

most difficult and critical aspect of the entire capital budgeting process is obtaining accurate and timely information, especially in the international sphere, where different climates, culture, languages, and information technologies complicate matters.

MANAGEMENT INFORMATION SYSTEMS

Organization of a firm's worldwide information systems is crucial in supporting corporate strategies, including the planning processes described above. This task is challenging, as a multinational framework is inherently more complex than a single-country framework. Exhibit 10-4 sets forth some environmental factors that complicate the flow of business information.

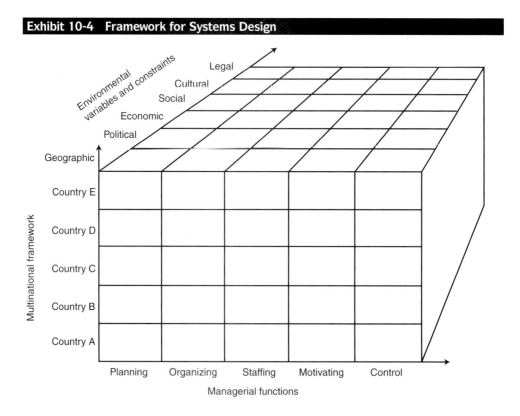

Exhibit 10-4   Framework for Systems Design

Systems Issues

Distance is an obvious complication. Due to geographic circumstances, formal information communications generally substitute for personal contacts between local operating managers and headquarters management.[17] Developments in information technology should reduce, but will not entirely eliminate, this complication.

---

[17]Schweikart has shown empirically that formal accounting communications are considered more helpful in some countries, while informal discussion as a form of information is considered more helpful in others.

As another example, the information requirements of regional or corporate financial planners concern both operating and environmental data. Information demanded from managerial accountants in the field depends on how much decision-making power local managers have. The greater the authority of local managers, the less information is passed on to headquarters.

In their study, "Patterns in the Organization of Transnational Information Systems," Vikram Sethi and Joseph Katz identify three global IT strategies, each related to a specific type of multinational organization. Success hinges on matching systems design to corporate strategies.[18]

Low dispersal with high centralization. Employed by smaller organizations with limited international business operations, domestic IS needs dominate. A standard platform of data and applications dominate the worldwide IT system.

High dispersion with low centralization. This strategy is favored by multinational companies with diverse geographic operations. Local subsidiaries are afforded significant control over the development of their IT strategies and related systems.

High dispersal with high centralization. Here a "glocal" IT strategy is employed by truly global companies with strategic alliances worldwide. Information systems are designed that reflect both corporate requirements tailored to local circumstances.

Perhaps the biggest challenge facing systems specialists is designing corporate information systems that allow financial managers to respond appropriately to the phenomenon of global competition. Conditions are changing. Owing to deregulation of markets and reduction of tariff barriers, firms are increasingly able to access foreign markets either directly or indirectly through joint ventures, strategic alliances, and other cooperative arrangements. This more open access has led to competitive intensities where firms adopt strategies to (1) protect market share at home, (2) penetrate competitors' home markets to deny them market share and revenues, and (3) generate significant market share in key third-country markets.

CEOs need information systems that enable them to plan, coordinate, and control effective worldwide production, marketing, and financial strategies. To facilitate this objective, software information developers in the United States have created a new computer language, XBRL. XBRL stands for *extensible business reporting language* and is a standard computer programming enhancement that is being included in all accounting and financial reporting software in the United States. Once added to the software, XBRL automatically translates all numbers and words so that each data segment is identified in a standard way when viewed by a Web browser or sent to a particular spreadsheet application. Specifically, XBRL tags each segment of computerized business information with an identification marker that remains with the data when moved or changed. No matter how an application software formats or rearranges the information, the markers remain with the data. Thus a number identified as marketable securities or accounts payable, for instance, will always be recognized in this manner. Useful for all enterprises regardless of industry or size, XBRL reduces information processing, calculating, and formatting costs because financial data only needs to be created and formatted once regardless of intended use. It will also improve a

James A. Schweikart, "The Relevance of Managerial Accounting Information: A Multinational Analysis," *Accounting Organizations and Society* 11, no. 6 (1986): 541–554.
[18]Peter Gwynne, "Information Systems Go Global," *MIT Sloan Management Review* (Summer 2001): 14.

firm's investor relations as it facilitates interfirm comparisons along many dimensions, including financial accounts, accounting policies, and related footnotes in automated fashion.[19] This systems effort is being led in the United States by a consortium of accounting firms, financial service providers, and technology companies, including software giants Microsoft and IBM. Not only is this system making the distribution of financial information fast and easy, it is also eliminating the need for rewriting financial reports to accommodate incompatible accounting systems. Parallel efforts are reportedly under way in other countries along with involvement of the International Accounting Standards Board.[20]

Information Issues

Management accountants prepare many kinds of information for corporate management, ranging from collections data to liquidity reports to operational forecasts of various types to expense disbursements.[21] For each set of data transmitted, corporate management must determine the relevant time period of the reports, the level of accuracy required, the frequency of reporting, and the costs and benefits of timely preparation and transmission.

Here too, environmental factors affect the usage of information generated internally. Consider the influence of culture: Culture shapes the values of a given society. Citizens of these societies bring these values with them when employed by business organizations. These values, in turn, frame employees' organizational behavior and how they use information technology within the organization. Although organizations around the world are becoming more similar in their conduct of business, the people that comprise these organizations tend to maintain their cultural behavior patterns.[22] As one example, Johns, Smith, and Strand examine the impact of uncertainty avoidance on database usage.[23] They find that cultures that are less uncomfortable with uncertainty and ambiguity tend to embrace information technology more readily than those who are very uncomfortable. A major implication of their study for managerial accountants is that culture is a major impediment to the international flow of data and must be explicitly dealt with in information systems design.[24]

Managers in different environments have different ways of analyzing and resolving problems, different decision time frames, and compete under different operating conditions. Different information needs are a direct consequence.[25] Hence, we have a fundamental problem for the multinational enterprise. Local managers are likely to

---

[19]"XBRL Approved for US Implementation," *Journal of Accountancy* (June 2000): 6.
[20]Ellen M. Heffes, "All Aboard the XBRL Train," *Financial Executive,* (July/August 2004): 16–17. For more information on the technical aspects of XBRL, go to www.xbrl.com.
[21]B. Giannotti and Richard W. Smith, *Treasury Management,* New York: John Wiley & Sons, 1981.
[22]N. Adler, *International Dimensions of Organizational Behavior,* Boston: Kent Publishing, 1986.
[23]The term *uncertainty avoidance* was coined by Gerte Hofstede in his oft-cited study on values as determinants of behavior. Uncertainty avoidance is a value construct that describes the degree to which one is more or less comfortable with task uncertainty and ambiguity. G. Hofstede, *Culture's Consequences,* Beverly Hills, CA: Sage, 1980.
[24]Sharon K. Johns, L. Murphy Smith, and Carolyn A. Strand, "How Culture Affects the Use of Information Technology," *Accounting Forum* 27, No. 1 (March 2002): 84–109.
[25]G. Harrison and J. McKinnon, "Cross-Cultural Research in Management Control Systems Design: A Review of the Current State," *Accounting, Organizations and Society,* forthcoming, and Sam Beldona, Andrew C. Inkpen, and Arvind Phatak, "Are Japanese Managers More Long-Term Oriented Than United States Managers?" *Management International Review* (3rd Quarter 1998): 239–256.

require different decision information than headquarters management. For example, a special feature of the U.S. consolidation process is that financial statements prepared according to foreign accounting principles are first restated to U.S. GAAP prior to being consolidated. Does this restatement somehow alter the information content of the accounts that go into a group consolidation? We provide an illustration of this reporting conundrum in the following section.

Another major information problem is the question of translation. In evaluating operations, U.S. managers generally prefer reports stated in U.S. dollars. Accordingly, reports from foreign operations of U.S. multinationals are typically translated to their U.S. dollar equivalents in order for U.S. headquarters managers to evaluate their dollar investments. However, does translating foreign currency amounts for managerial review purposes preserve the data without distortions? We address this issue empirically in Case 10-1 at the end of this chapter.

MANAGEMENT INFORMATION AND HYPERINFLATION

FAS No. 52 mandates use of the temporal translation method, described in Chapter 6, in consolidating the accounts of foreign affiliates domiciled in high-inflation environments. Even though FAS No. 52 and similar national pronouncements provide useful guidelines in preparing hard currency statements, they do not meet the information needs of firms operating in high-inflation countries.[26] In high-inflation environments, financial reports prepared in conformity with FAS No. 52 tend to distort reality by

- Overstating or understating revenues and expenses
- Reporting large translation gains or losses that are difficult to interpret
- Distorting performance comparisons over time

Our reporting framework overcomes these limitations and is based on the following assumptions[27]:

1. Management's objective of maximizing the value of the firm is framed in terms of a currency that holds its value (i.e., a hard currency). Accordingly, the best way to measure the performance of an affiliate located in a high-inflation environment is in terms of hard currency.[28]
2. Our model also implicitly assumes that inflation rates, exchange rates, and interest rates are interrelated. (This assumption is not critical to the proposal.)

A common reporting convention in accounting for foreign currency transactions is to record revenues and expenses at exchange rates prevailing at the financial statement date. (Use of average rates is also common.) A better option is to report local currency transactions at the exchange rate prevailing on the payment date. Recording

---

[26]Coopers & Lybrand, *Reporting Reality from High-Inflation Countries,* New York: Author, 1989, pp. 5–6.
[27]Frederick D. S. Choi, "Financial Reporting in Hyperinflationary Environments: A Transactions Analysis Framework for Management," in *International Finance and Accounting Handbook,* 3rd ed., Frederick D.S. Choi, ed., New York: John Wiley & Sons, 2003, pp. 27.1–27.13.
[28]Interviews with financial executives of U.S.-based multinationals as well as subsidiary managers suggest that this assumption is consistent with corporate practices at the micro level. It also appears consistent with practices at the macro level, as more and more Latin American countries have pegged their currencies to the U.S. dollar.

a transaction at any other date muddles the measurement process by introducing gains or losses in the purchasing power of money or, alternatively, implicit interest into the exchange transaction.

In a perfectly competitive market, all local currency transactions would be in cash. With inflation, it is advantageous for buyers to delay payment for as long as possible and for sellers to accelerate collections. The payment date is determined by the competitive strengths of the contracting parties. Our recommended reporting treatment produces reported numbers that are reliable, economically interpretable, and symmetric in the sense that economically similar transactions produce similar financial statement numbers when translated into a common currency.[29] One could say that the model uses accrual accounting with a cash accounting mentality.

An example will highlight the translation gains and losses generated by FAS No. 52 reporting. While many would attribute gains or losses in our example to foreign exchange risk, they are really due to improper accounting for events that occurred above the line.

Following are our working assumptions:

- Inflation and Turkish lira (TL) devaluation is 30 percent per month or 1.2 percent per workday.
- The general price level at selected intervals for the months 1 and 2 are:

1/1	100.0
1/10	109.6
1/20	119.6
1/30	130.0
2/10	141.6
2/20	154.5
2/30	169.0

The real rate of interest is 1-1/2 percent per month or 20 percent per year.
- Cash balances are kept in hard currency (U.S. dollars).
- Month-end rates are used to record expense transactions.

Sales Revenue

Suppose that the firm sells TL 2,000,000 worth of merchandise in month 1, with varying invoice dates and payment terms. Assuming that financial statements are prepared monthly, the conventional practice is to record the sales transaction at the month-end exchange rate regardless of when the sale is invoiced or when payment is received. Sales reported using the month-end exchange rate are TL 2,000,000/130 = $15,385.

First assume that the sale is invoiced on day 1 of month 1, with payment received immediately in cash = TL 2,000,000/TL 100 = $20,000. Conventional treatment measures the transaction at month's end rather than when cash is received, but the economic basis of the transaction is the cash that is actually received on the invoice date. Here revenues are understated by 30 percent or $4,615 determined as follows:

---

[29]The notion of economic interpretability and symmetry are discussed more rigorously in William H. Beaver and Mark A.Wolfson, "Foreign Currency Translation and Changing Prices in Perfect and Complete Markets," *Journal of Accounting Research* (Autumn 1992): 528–550.

Actual	$20,000
Reported	15,385
Variance	$ 4,615

In keeping with the temporal translation method, this $4,615 understatement of sales is offset by an equivalent nonoperating translation gain appearing below the line.[30] Next, assume instead that the sale is invoiced on day 5, and that the client receives 25 days payment terms. In our model, the transaction is booked on the same day that payment is received. From an economic point of view, there is no variance and no nonoperating translation gain or loss.

Actual	$15,385
Reported	15,385
Variance	$ -0-

From a control perspective, management should be able to learn from the salesperson what the expected profit margin is on the day of sale. The salesperson does not have to wait until the books are closed to have this information, which is already at hand as invoices in hyperinflationary environments clearly state the payment due date.

In the following example, assume that the client is invoiced on day 30 with payment required a month later. From an economic point of view, the firm collects $11,834 (= TL 2,000,000/TL 169). The accounting system reports $15,385, resulting in a variance of $3,551.

Actual	$11,834
Reported	15,385
Variance	$ 3,551

Here, the conventional reporting system overstates sales by 23.1 percent with the positive variance offset by an equivalent nonoperating translation loss below the line.

Exhibit 10-5 Distortions in Invoice and Payment Due Dates
(TL2,000,000 Sales in Month 1)

Invoice Day	Payment Terms	Today's Number	Proposed Number	Diff.	%
1	Cash	15,385	20,000	4,615	30.0%
5	5 days	15,385	18,248	2,863	18.6%
5	15 days	15,385	16,722	1,337	8.7%
5	25 days	15,385	15,385	0.000	0.0%
10	30 days	15,385	14,124	−1,261	8.2%
20	30 days	15,385	12,945	−2,440	−15.9%
30	30 days	15,385	11,834	3,551	−23.1%

[30]Assume that the firm in question begins the period with a $10,000 equity investment and immediately converts this cash balance to saleable inventories. The goods are marked up 100 percent over cost and sold for cash the next day. In this case, the aggregate exchange adjustment would be $4,615, determined either as a plug when preparing the end-of-period translated balance sheet, or as a positive aggregate translation adjustment comprising the gain on the hard currency cash balance.

Exhibit 10-5 shows the magnitude of the distortions associated with differing invoicing and payment terms. Depending on sales terms, sales can be overstated or understated by significant amounts.

Why do we care about these distortions? The traditional reporting system has a bad effect on the behavior of the sales force. For example, it gives the company's sales force no motivation to improve payment terms. If sales are recorded at the end-of-month rate, sales personnel do not care whether they are paid in cash or in 30 or 60 days. It is important to have a system that encourages the sales force to act in the company's best interests.

In addition, traditional reporting systems do not motivate the sales force to invoice and ship earlier in the month. When sales are recorded at end-of-month rates, the sales force does not care about the time of delivery. Yet, even one day's delay in shipment could be costly: 1.5 percent in lost interest in our example. Another glance at Exhibit 10-15 shows that bonuses and commission payments are based on inflated sales values whenever payment terms carry over to the following period.

Perhaps the most serious shortcoming of traditional reporting systems is that they encourage manipulation of results. Assume now that exchange rates at the end of each of the next 3 months are as follows:

End-of-month 1	130 = $1
End-of-month 2	169 = $1
End-of-month 3	220 = $1

Suppose that a salesperson arranges the following with a favorite customer: deliver and invoice TL 2,000,000 of a product on day 30 of month 1 at TL 2,500,000 with 60-day payment terms instead of invoicing at TL 2,000,000 on the same date with 30-day payment terms. The attractiveness of this arrangement is easy to figure out. Under conventional reporting methods, the revised sales value is TL 2,500,000/TL 130 = $19,231 versus TL 2,000,000/TL 130 = $15,385 under traditional measurements. This represents an additional sales gain of almost $4,000, or 25 percent. From the customer's point of view, the actual cost of the purchase is only TL 2,500,000/TL 220 = $11,364 versus TL 2,000,000/TL 169 = $11,834, a savings that is hard to resist. Under these circumstances, the *customer* is likely to initiate such a proposal.

Under our proposed reporting system, the incentives for such arrangements are reduced. When the sales transaction is reported at the exchange rate prevailing on the payment date, the transaction is recorded at $11,364 rather than $11,834. From the selling firm's perspective, it would be better to invoice the sale at TL 2,000,000 with 30-day payment terms. Our proposed reporting system gives the salesperson an incentive to do so. Our model thus uses the actual or forecasted exchange rate prevailing on the day of payment to record local currency transactions. Because those dates are generally in the accounts receivable system (i.e., on sales invoices), this system is readily implemented. The idea is to use accrual accounting while maintaining a cash accounting mentality. Some have correctly argued that sales and expenses in hyperinflationary environments have a built-in implicit interest rate. (Hence the need to discount local currency transactions to their present values before translation.) Our model emphasizes the difference in the exchange rate between the invoice date and the collection date, and thereby automatically incorporates the implicit interest differential (i.e., the

International Fisher Effect[31]). Under our reporting framework, there is no need for management to think about what the interest rate is or worry about how to calculate an appropriate discount. After all, operating management cares about the exchange rate difference.

What happens if the customer delays payment beyond the promised date? In our reporting framework, normal payment conditions are shown in reported sales and gross margins. Thus, if a customer agrees to pay on a certain date, the transaction is booked at the exchange rate prevailing on the agreed payment date. If payment takes place after the promised date, the loss in dollars is reported below the line as a translation loss attributed to the applicable line of business or sales segment. That loss is offset by interest income as original sales terms include an explicit interest cost for delayed payments, which would appear as additional interest income below the line.

To summarize, our transactions-based reporting model

- Allocates translation gains and losses to specific revenues and expenses to which they are related
- Provides both headquarters and subsidiary management with numbers that will support better decisions
- Eliminates the need for parallel controls
- Facilitates performance comparisons over time
- Can be implemented on a cost-effective basis

ISSUES IN FINANCIAL CONTROL

Once questions of strategy and information support systems have been decided, attention shifts to the equally important area of financial control and performance evaluation.[32] These considerations are especially important as they enable financial managers to

1. Implement the global financial strategy of the MNE
2. Evaluate the degree to which the chosen strategies contribute to achieving enterprise goals
3. Motivate management and employees to achieve the enterprise's financial goals as effectively and efficiently as possible

---

[31]Under a freely floating system of exchange rates, spot rates of exchange are theoretically determined by the interrelationships between national rates of inflation, interest rates, and forward rates of exchange, usually expressed as premiums or discounts from the spot rate. If the forecasted rate of inflation in Brazil 1 month ahead is 30 percent higher than in the United States, the real can be forecast to decline in value by 30 percent relative to the dollar. By the same token, interest rates for maturities of comparable risk can be expected to be 30 percent higher on Brazilian securities than on comparable U.S. securities. For an extended discussion of these relationships, see David K. Eiteman, Arthur I. Stonehill, and Michael H. Moffett, *Multinational Business Finance*, 7th ed., Reading, Mass.: Addison-Wesley, 1995, 50–62; and Giddy, Ian H., "Exchange Risk: Whose Views?" *Financial Management* (Summer 1977): 22–33.

[32]Corporate governance is also concerned with corporate control. However, governance issues rely on externally reported information, which is the subject of earlier chapters. For an excellent state-of-the-art piece on corporate governance, see Robert M. Bushman and Abbie J. Smith, "Financial Accounting Information and Corporate Governance," *Journal of Accounting and Economics* 32 (2001): 237–333.

Management control systems aim at accomplishing enterprise objectives in the most effective and efficient manner. Financial control systems, in turn, are quantitative measurement and communication systems that facilitate control through (1) communicating financial goals as appropriate within the organization, (2) specifying criteria and standards for evaluating performance, (3) monitoring performance, and (4) communicating deviations between actual and planned performance to those responsible.

A sound financial control system enables top management to focus the activities of its subsidiaries toward common objectives. A control system consists of operational and financial policies, internal reporting structures, operating budgets, and procedure manuals consistent with top management's goals. Thus, suboptimal behavior, which occurs when a subunit strives to achieve its own ends at the expense of the whole organization, is minimized. A timely reporting system that constantly monitors each unit is a good motivator. An efficient control system also enables headquarters management to evaluate the strategic plans of the company and to revise them when needed. Management's strategic planning tasks are aided by an information system that informs management of environmental changes that might significantly impact the company. Finally, a good control system enables top management to properly evaluate the performance of subordinates by ensuring that subordinates are held accountable only for events they can control.

If a well-designed control system is useful to a uninational company, it is invaluable to its multinational counterpart. As we have repeatedly observed, conditions that impact on management decisions abroad are not only different, but are constantly changing.

Domestic Versus Multinational Control System

How should a well-functioning control system be designed in a multinational company? Should a parent company use its domestic control system, unaltered, in its foreign operations? Studies show that the systems used by many multinational enterprises to control their foreign operations are identical, in many respects, to those used domestically. System items commonly exported include financial and budgetary control and the tendency to apply the same standards developed to evaluate domestic operations. In a now classic paper, David Hawkins offers four basic reasons for this:

1. Financial control considerations are seldom critical in the early stages of establishing a foreign operation.
2. It is normally cheaper to transplant the domestic system than to create from scratch an entire system designed for the foreign operation.
3. To simplify preparing and analyzing consolidated financial statements, the corporate controller's office insists that all operating subsidiaries use similar forms and schedules to record and transmit financial and operating data.
4. Former domestic executives working in the foreign operation and their corporate superiors are more comfortable if they can continue to use as much of the domestic control system as possible, largely because they reached the highest levels of management by mastering the domestic system.[33]

---

[33]David F. Hawkins, "Controlling Foreign Operations," *Financial Executive* (February 1965): 25–32.

Some writers argue that financial control systems abroad should be the same as those used at home. We disagree. It is difficult to believe that a central controller's staff could design a single and effective worldwide control system given that the multinational operating environment is so diverse. A look back to the many elements in Exhibit 10-4 illustrates this point.

Environmental diversity has an unlimited potential impact on the financial control process. Earlier, we observed that geographical distances often impede traditional methods of communicating between affiliates and company headquarters. Although better technology might overcome geographical distance, cultural distance is harder to overcome. Culture and the business environment interact to create unique sets of managerial values in a country.[34] Language difficulties, cross-cultural differences in attitude toward risk and authority, differences in need-achievement levels, and other cultural attributes often result in bad consequences, including (1) misunderstood directives, (2) lower tolerance of criticism, (3) unwillingness to discuss business problems openly or to seek assistance, (4) loss of confidence among foreign managers, (5) unwillingness to delegate authority, and (6) reluctance to assume responsibility. Managers of multinational companies face many tough issues. This is especially the case for managers and employees of acquired companies in cross-border mergers and acquisitions.[35] Frequently, managers and employees steeped in one culture must often operate in another. Should there be a separate communications system for foreign nationals? Should performance standards for foreign nationals differ from those for their domestic counterparts? Should motivational techniques used overseas differ from those used domestically? Distribution channels, credit terms, industrial policies, financial institutions, and business practices all vary from country to country. These diverse business practices require international financial managers to adapt.

Consider business gratuities. Direct or indirect payments to secure a business favor violate the Foreign Corrupt Practices Act (FCPA) in the United States. In many parts of the world, however, business gratuities are a part of everyday business affairs. Government officials often have the power to cripple local operations if the expected gratuities are not paid. Unofficial payments to mail carriers are often a prerequisite for timely delivery of mail. Apart from the ethical issues, business gratuities give financial managers of U.S. multinational enterprises a major problem. If the formal financial control system monitors and acknowledges such payments, a U.S. parent company may expose itself to liability and possible embarrassment at home. If such payments are concealed from the control system through bogus documentation and contrived accounting transactions, the entire control system quickly breaks down.

Sexual harassment is another issue. Insensitivity to gender differences and politically correct behavior can be expensive. Executives of Mitsubishi in the United States recently learned this the hard way.[36]

---

[34]David A. Ralston, David J. Gustafson, Kenny M. Cheung, and Robert H. Terpstra, "Differences in Managerial Values: A Study of U.S., Hong Kong and PRC Managers," *Journal of International Business Studies* (Second Quarter 1993): 249–275.

[35]Yaakov Weber and Ehud Menipaz, "Measuring Cultural Fit in Mergers and Acquisitions," *International Journal of Business Performance Management* 5, No. 1 (2003): 54. See also Weber, Roberto A., and Colin F. Camerer, "Cultural Conflict and Merger Failure: An Experimental Approach," *Management Science* 49, No. 4, 400.

[36]Paul A. Samuelson, "Economic and Cultural Aspects of Tomorrow's Multinational Firms," *Japan and the World Economy* (December 2000): 393–394.

Companies with foreign operations must also adapt to unfamiliar governmental regulations and restrictions. Exchange controls, restrictions on capital flows, joint ownership requirements, and many other specific business regulations are examples. The environmental considerations related to the strength of a nation's currency may be the most important for the design of overseas control systems of all those shown in Exhibit 10-4. Internal rates of inflation and fluctuating currency values are critical, and corporate control systems must allow for them. Applying financial controls designed for a stable environment to one that is less stable is a recipe for failure.[37]

Operational Budgeting

Once strategic goals and capital budgets are in place, management next focuses on short-range planning. Short-range planning involves creating operational budgets or profit plans where needed in the organization. These profit plans are the basis for cash management forecasts, operating decisions, and management compensation schemes. Budgeted income statements of foreign affiliates are first converted to parent country accounting principles and translated from the local currency (FC) to the parent currency (PC). Periodic comparisons of actual and budgeted profit performance in parent currency require appropriate variance analyses to ensure that deviations from budget are correctly diagnosed for managerial action. While variance analysis is, in principle, the same internationally as domestically, currency fluctuations make it more complex.

The financial performance of a foreign operation can be measured in local currency, home country currency, or both. The currency used can have a significant impact in judging the performance of a foreign unit and its manager. Fluctuating currency values can turn profits (measured in local currency) into losses (expressed in home country currency).

Some favor a local currency perspective because foreign transactions take place in a foreign environment and are done in foreign currency. Foreign currency translation gains and losses are not considered when operations are evaluated in local currency.[38] One executive holding this view said:

> We evaluate our foreign operations primarily based on their local currency results. It is our belief that over the long run, the ability to achieve good performance in local currency terms will result in good performance in dollar terms. Good performance in local currency terms can only be achieved if prices are raised in line with local inflation, which over a period of time compensates for changes in the exchange rate.[39]

Those who favor a parent currency perspective argue that ultimately, home country shareholders care about domestic currency returns. Because they judge headquar-

---

[37]Hassel found foreign subsidiary managers to be especially sensitive to the relevance of accounting-based performance measures if these measures are not sensitized to the dynamics of the local operating environment. See L. G. Hassel, "Performance Evaluation in a Multinational Environment," *Journal of International Financial Management and Accounting* 3, no. 2 (1991): 17–38.
[38]Helen G. Morsicato, *Currency Translation and Performance Evaluation in Multinationals,* Ann Arbor, MI: UMI Research Press, 1980.
[39]Business International, *Assessing Foreign Subsidiary Performance,* p. 31.

ters management by domestic currency returns, foreign managers should be judged by the same standard. In the words of a corporate controller:

> We are a dollar-based company. We're concerned with dollar results, not francs or pounds. We want our subsidiary managers to run their operations with that in mind. Furthermore, converting results into dollars makes it easier to evaluate and compare our subsidiaries.[40]

Problems remain even if parent currency is considered a better measure of performance than local currency. In theory, the exchange rate between two countries should move in proportion to changes in their differential inflation rates. Thus, if the rate of inflation is 10 percent in Italy and 30 percent in Turkey, the Turkish lira should lose approximately 20 percent of its value relative to the Italian lira. In practice, changes in currency exchange values that lag behind foreign rates of inflation can distort performance measures. Local currency earnings and their dollar equivalents increase during excessive inflation. In the following period, when the foreign currency loses value, the dollar value of local earnings falls even if local currency earnings increase. Under these circumstances, measuring with parent currency introduces random elements in measuring the performance of foreign operations if changes in foreign exchange rates do not track differences in inflation rates.

In the long run, one must judge a foreign unit's value as an investment in terms of home country currency. A parent currency perspective is appropriate for strategic planning and long-term investment decisions. However, the currency framework used in evaluating managerial performance must depend on who is held *accountable* for exchange risk. (This issue is separate from who is *responsible* for exchange risks.) If corporate treasury manages exchange risks, then it is logical to measure foreign performance in local currency. Parent currency measures are just as valid if exchange gains and losses are removed in evaluating foreign managers. If local managers have the necessary tools to manage exchange gains and losses, measuring their performance in parent currency is justifiable.

Consider some aspects of the budgetary process. Control over a network of domestic and foreign operations requires that foreign currency budgets be expressed in parent currency for comparison.

When parent currency figures are used, a change in exchange rates used to establish the budget and to monitor performance causes a variance beyond that due to other changes. Three possible rates can be used in drafting the beginning-of-period operating budget:

1. The spot rate in effect when the budget is established
2. A rate that is expected to prevail at the end of the budget period (projected rate)
3. The rate at the end of the period if the budget is updated whenever exchange rates change (ending rate).[41]

[40]Ibid., p. 31.
[41]Donald R. Lessard and Peter Lorange, "Currency Changes and Management Control: Resolving the Centralization/Decentralization Dilemma," *Accounting Review* (July 1977): 628–637.

Comparable rates can be used to track performance relative to budget. If different exchange rate combinations arc used to set the budget and to track performance, this creates different allocations of responsibilities for exchange rate changes and leads to different possible managerial responses. Let us consider some possibilities.

1. *Budget and track performance at initial spot rate.* Exchange rate changes have no effect on the evaluation of the foreign manager's performance. Local managers have little incentive to incorporate anticipated exchange rate changes into their operating decisions.
2. *Budget at ending (updated) rate and track at ending rate.* This combination produces similar results. Local management need not consider exchange rates because the same rate is used for budgeting and evaluation.
3. *Budgeting at initial rate and track at ending rate.* Local managers have full responsibility for exchange rate changes. Potential negative consequences include padding of budgets by local managers or hedging that may not be optimal for the corporation.
4. *Budget and track performance using projected exchange rates.* This system reflects a local currency perspective. Local managers are encouraged to incorporate expected exchange rate changes into their operating plans but are not held responsible for unexpected rate changes, which the parent company absorbs.
5. *Budget at projected rate and track at ending rate.* This exchange rate combination does not hold the local manager accountable for expected rate changes. Managers are responsible for (and thereby encouraged to hedge) unanticipated exchange rate changes.

Which option is best for evaluating managerial performance? All five are found in practice. We focus on the last two, the most common. As an illustration, assume the following (LC = local currency):

Projected rate of exchange:	$0.50 = LC 1	Actual end-of-period rate:	$0.25 = LC 1
Budgeted earnings in LC:	800,000	Actual earnings in LC:	1,000,000
Budget earnings in :	$400,000	Actual earnings in $:	250,000

If the projected rate is used in monitoring performance, the dollar result is $500,000 (LC 1,000,000 × $0.50), or $100,000 above budget. The manager appears to have done well. But, if the actual end-of-period rate is used, the result is $250,000 (LC 1,000,000 × $0.25), or $150,000 below budget. The manager appears to have done poorly. Which rate should be used?

Most discussions of this problem favor option 4. Using the projected exchange rate in budgeting encourages managers to include expected exchange rate movements in their operating decisions. Use of the projected rate to monitor performance, in turn, shields local managers from unanticipated exchange rate changes they cannot control. Also, protection against exchange risk can be coordinated on a company-wide basis.

We think that use of a projected exchange rate for budgeting and the actual ending rate for tracking performance (option 5) also has merit. Like option 4, this approach encourages managers to include anticipated exchange rate changes in their

Exhibit 10-6 Analysis of Exchange Rate Variances

		Computation		
Responsibility		*Operating Item*	*Exchange Rate*	*Variance*
Local currency operations (Foreign management)	−	LC Budget × LC Actual ×	Budget Budget =	Local-currency operating variance
Parent currency operations (Headquarters' management)	−	LC Actual × LC Actual ×	Budget Actual =	Parent-currency exchange variance

plans for the budget period. Unlike option 4, holding local and corporate managers accountable for unexpected rate changes encourages them to respond to exchange rate movements.[42]

Option 5 is especially useful when local operating plans can be changed to accommodate unanticipated currency developments. Where any remaining variances between actual and projected rates are ignored when evaluating local managers (i.e., the remaining variance is regarded as a forecasting error, which is the responsibility of corporate headquarters), this system offers additional benefits over option 4.

When responsibility for exchange variances is divided between various levels in management, budget variances need to be analyzed by responsibility level. In our previous example, the foreign subsidiary's operating variance and exchange rate variance would be analyzed as shown in Exhibit 10-6.

The total budget variance of −$150,000 (LC 800,000 × $0.50 − LC 1,000,000 × $0.25) would consist of a positive variance of $100,000 attributed to the foreign manager (LC 800,000 × $0.50 − LC 1,000,000 × $0.50) and a negative variance of −$250,000 attributed to corporate headquarters (LC 1,000,000 × $0.50 − LC 1,000,000 × $0.25). Exhibit 10-7 illustrates a framework for analyzing budget variances when the responsibility for exchange variances is divided between local management, an international division's operating management (parent currency variation), and corporate

Exhibit 10-7 Three-Way Analysis of Exchange Rate Variance

		Computation		
Responsibility		*Operating Item*	*Exchange Rate*	*Variance*
Local currency operations (Local management)	−	LC Budget × LC Actual ×	Budget Budget =	Local-currency operating variance
Parent-currency operations (International division)	−	LC Actual × LC Actual ×	Budget Actual =	Parent-currency operating variance
Foreign exchange variance from budget (Treasury)	−	LC Budget × LC Budget ×	Budget Actual =	Exchange rate variance from budget

---

[42]Imagine what would happen if a foreign manager, projecting a 30 percent local currency devaluation, actually gets a 70 percent devaluation and does nothing to offset the larger-than-expected devaluation because his performance is measured using the projected rate.

treasury (variance from budget rates). Here, the international division is responsible for hedging unexpected exchange rate changes while corporate treasury is responsible for accurate rate forecasts.

Analysis of Exchange Rate Changes

We now provide a more comprehensive example of an exchange rate variance analysis.[43] Exhibit 10-8 shows the budgeted and actual condensed income statements for FC Company at the start and end of the 20X5 budget year. The profit plan for the year (expressed in parent company GAAP) is translated to parent currency at the beginning-of-period exchange rate of FC 1 = PC1. The foreign currency devalues by 20 percent by year-end.

A performance report breaking out price-, volume- and exchange-rate-induced variances appears in Exhibit 10-9.

From the perspective of the foreign affiliate, performance variances are measured in local currency and reflect the difference between budget and actual figures for each item in the income statement. These performance variances are detailed in column (7) of Exhibit 10-9. Variances for sales revenues and cost of sales can be broken down into price (cost) and volume variances. The sale volume variance of FC 1,000 is determined by multiplying the change in unit sales volume, 200 units, by the budgeted selling price of FC 5. Applying a similar methodology to cost of sales produces a volume variance of 200 units × FC 3 = FC 600. Thus, the net volume variance affecting gross margin and operating income column (9) is FC 1,000 − FC 600 = FC 400. Variances in sales revenues and cost of sales attributed to price (cost) changes during the budget period are found by multiplying the actual number of units sold by the change in selling price (production cost). This calculation yields a negative price variance of 1,200 units × −FC 0.25 = −FC 300 for sales revenue, and a positive cost variance of 1,200 units × −FC 0.60 = FC 720 for cost of sales, in column (10). Differences between budgeted and actual expenses are shown as nominal variances in column (11).

Exhibit 10-8   Income Statement for Exchange Rate Variance Analysis

	Budget			Actual
Revenues		FC 5,000		FC 5,700[a]
Cost of goods sold		3,000[b]		2,880
Gross margin		FC 2,000		FC 2,820
Operating expenses	750		825	
Depreciation	500		500	
Interest	250	1,500	300	1,625
Operating income		FC 500		FC 1,195

[a]The company employs the FIFO costing method and production equaled sales during the year. Unit production costs dropped from a planned FC 3.00 to FC 2.40 per unit.

[b]Actual sales increased by 200 units during the year at a price of FC 4.75, FC .25 lower than expected.

[43]Gerald F. Lewis, "Multinational Budgeting and Control Systems," in *International Accounting and Finance Handbook*, 2nd ed., F.D.S. Choi, ed., New York: John Wiley & Sons, 1997, pp. 26.1–26.22.

Exhibit 10-9 Performance Report FC Company (for the budget period ending 12/31/X5)

	(1)	(2)	(3)	(4)	(5)	(6)	(7)	(8)	(9)	(10)	(11)	(12)
	Budget			Actual			Total		Variance Analysis			
	FC	FX	PC	FC	FX	PC	FC	PC	Vol.	Price/(Cost)	Reported	Exch. Rate
Revenue	5,000	1.0	5,000	5700	.8	4,560	700	(440)	1,000	(300)		(1,140)
Beg. inventory	(3,000)	1.0	(3,000)	(2,800)	1.0	(2,800)	200	200				
Production	(3,000)	1.0	(3,000)	(2,880)	.8	(2,304)	120	696				
Goods available	(6,000)		(6,000)	(5,680)		(5,104)	320	896				
End. inventory	3,000	1.0	3,000	2,800	.8	2,240	(200)	(1,760)				
Cost of sales	(3,000)		(3,000)	(2,880)		(2,864)	120	136	(600)	720		16
Gross margin	2,000		2,000	2,820		1,696	820	(304)	400	420		(1,124)
Operating exp.	(750)	1.0	(750)	(825)	.8	(660)	(75)	90			(75)	165
Depreciation	(500)	1.0	(500)	(500)	1.0	(500)	—	—			—	—
Interest	(250)	1.0	(250)	(300)	.8	(240)	(50)	10			(50)	60
Operating income	500		500	1,195		296	695	(204)	400	420	(125)	(899)

389

Based on this analysis, we can see that the improvement in FC Company's operating income of FC 695 (column 7) is attributable to the following factors:

Higher volume (column 9)	FC 400
Lower selling price (column 10)	(300)
Lower production cost (column 10)	720
Higher expenses (column 11)	(125)
Increase in operating income (column 7)	FC 695

When FC Company's performance is evaluated from the parent company perspective, first its local currency results are translated to parent currency. Let us assume that Parent Company designates the parent currency as its functional currency. Accordingly, FC Company's budgeted income statement is translated to parent currency using the temporal translation method. Had the local currency been designated as functional, the current rate translation method would have been used. (See Chapter 6 for a detailed description of these methods.)

To simplify our analysis, Parent Company will analyze FC Company's budget variances using the exchange rate prevailing at the budget date (FC 1.00 = PC 1.00).[44]

With this approach, price and volume variances for sales and cost of sales will mirror those calculated under a local company perspective. The effect of exchange rate changes is calculated by multiplying actual results reported in parent currency by the change in the exchange rate during the budget period. The total variance for sales revenues in parent currency, PC 5,000 − PC 4,560 = PC 440, would be broken down into the following volume, price, and exchange rate variances:

$$\text{Volume variance in col. (9)} = 200 \text{ units} \times \text{FC } 5 = \text{FC } 1{,}000 \times 1.0 = \text{PC } 1{,}000$$
$$\text{Price variance in col. (10)} = 1{,}200 \text{ units} \times -\text{FC } 0.25$$
$$= \text{FC } (300) \times 1.0 = \text{PC } (300)$$

$$\text{Exchange rate variance in col. (12)} = \text{FC } 5{,}700 \times -\text{PC } 0.2 = \text{PC } (1{,}140).$$

Similarly, the total variance for cost of sales can be broken down as follows:

$$\text{Volume variance} = 200 \text{ units} \times \text{FC } 3 = \text{FC } 600 \times 1.0 = \text{PC } (600)$$
$$\text{Cost variance} = 1{,}200 \text{ units} \times -\text{FC } 0.60 = \text{FC } (720) \times 1.0 = \text{PC } 720$$

Exchange rate variance is computed by multiplying each component of cost of goods sold by the exchange rate change in column (12):

Beginning inventory	FC 2,800	×	-0-	=	0
Production	FC 2,880	×	−PC .2	=	576
Ending inventory	FC 2,800	×	−PC .2	=	(560)
					16

---

[44]Alternative exchange rate benchmarks and their implications for performance evaluation of foreign operations are considered in a later section of this chapter.

Exchange rate variances for operating expenses and depreciation are computed by multiplying the actual figures in local currency by the exchange rate change during the period. This yields an exchange variance for operating expenses FC 825 $\times$ $-$PC 0.2 = PC165 and an exchange variance of FC (300) $\times$ $-$PC 0.2 = PC 60 for interest.

In evaluating FC Company's performance in parent currency, the shortfall of $-$PC 204 in operating earnings can be attributed to the following factors:

Higher sales volume	PC +400
Lower selling price	(300)
Lower production cost	+720
Higher operating expenses	(75)
Higher interest expenses	(50)
Exchange rate changes (column 12)	(899)
Decrease in parent currency operating earnings (column 8)	PC (204)

A currency translation phenomenon caused by a weakening of the local currency relative to the reporting currency is a major cause of the poor operating result. We discuss the proper evaluation of this currency effect in the subsequent section of this chapter on performance evaluation of foreign operations.

STRATEGIC COSTING

While product and standard costing systems have traditionally played a major role in cost control, certain Japanese companies have introduced cost concepts that reinforce their global manufacturing strategies.[45] In doing so they have enhanced the cost control process, and more importantly, have established a direct link between management accounting practices and corporate goals.[46]

In controlling costs at the manufacturing stage, many companies around the world employ standard costing systems that basically estimate what costs of producing a product should be as a basis of arriving at a reasonable selling price. Actual costs of production are then compared with estimated costs. Resulting variances between standard and actual costs are examined as a basis for corrective actions in the production or procurement process. This process can be thought of as a cost-based pricing model.

In contrast, many Japanese companies employ a price-based costing model. Also known as *target costing,* this strategic costing methodology is premised on designing and building products at prices intended to ensure market success.[47] Consider the Daihatsu Motor Company. Its product development cycle (which normally lasts 3 years) begins with the production manager instructing Daihatsu's departments to submit design and performance specifications that they believe the car should meet. This is

---

[45]These manufacturing strategies embrace continuous improvement in productivity and quality. Specific practices include just-in-time (JIT) manufacturing, total quality control, and other lean production techniques.
[46]Hema Wijewardena and Anura De Zoysa, "A Comparative Analysis of Management Accounting Practices in Australia and Japan: An Empirical Investigation," *International Journal of Accounting* 34, No. 1 (1999): 49–70.
[47]M. Sakurai, "Target Costing and How to Use It," *Journal of Cost and Management* (Summer 1989): 39–50.

followed by a cost estimate based not on what it will cost to build the car, but rather on an allowable cost per car. This *allowable cost* is based on subtracting a target profit margin that reflects the company's strategic plans and financial projections from a target sales price the company believes the market will accept.

While used as a target, the allowable cost is not static. During production, allowable cost is reduced every month by a cost reduction rate based on short-term profit objectives. In later years, actual costs of the previous year are the starting point for further reductions, thus assuring ongoing cost cutting for as long as the car is in production.[48] This market-driven system, known as *Kaizen costing,* significantly reduces the reliance on traditional standard costing systems. Standard costing systems seek to minimize variances between budgeted and actual costs. Kaizen costing emphasizes doing what is necessary to achieve a desired performance level under competitive market conditions.

Another strategic costing concept introduced by the Japanese is *behavioral costing.*[49] In a process costing system, overhead is applied to goods or routine services using an overhead application rate. From a traditional cost accounting perspective, manufacturing overhead is allocated to products on a cause-and-effect basis. Despite the capital intensity of many Japanese manufacturers, the use of direct labor as an allocation base for assigning overhead costs has continued. This practice encourages production managers to reduce rather than just accumulate costs (i.e., encourage automation). A production manager wishing to reduce his overhead burden is motivated to substitute capital for labor.

Exhibit 10-10 summarizes the major differences between standard and *kaizen* costing concepts.

Exhibit 10-10   Standard versus Kaizen Costing Concepts

Standard Cost Concepts	Kaizen Cost Concepts
Cost Control	Cost Reduction
Predicated on existing manufacturing conditions	Predicated on continuous manufacturing improvement
Objective: Compliance with performance standards	Objective: Achieve cost reduction targets
Standards set annually	Cost reduction targets set monthly
	Continuous improvement in manufacturing methods to attain target costs
Variance analysis based on actual vs. standard	Variance analysis based on constant cost reduction
Investigate when standards not met	Investigate when target costs not achieved

Source: Reprinted with permission from Yasuhiro Monden and John Y. Lee, "How a Japanese Auto Maker Reduces Costs," *Management Accounting* (Now *Strategic Finance*) August 1993. pp. 22–26, published by the IMA, Montvale, New Jersey, www.ima.org.

---

[48]T. Hiromoto, "Japanese Management Accounting," *Harvard Business Review* (July–August 1988): 22–26.
[49]Ibid.

PERFORMANCE EVALUATION OF FOREIGN OPERATIONS

Evaluating performance is central to an effective control system. A properly designed performance evaluation system allows top management to (1) judge the profitability of existing operations, (2) spot areas that are not performing as planned, (3) allocate limited corporate resources productively, (4) evaluate managerial performance and, most, important, (5) ensure managerial behavior is consistent with strategic priorities. Developing an effective performance evaluation system is as much an art as a science. Its complexity increases with overseas operations. Performance evaluation of foreign operations must deal with such complications as exchange rate volatility, foreign inflation, transfer pricing, distinctive national cultures, and a host of other environmental effects. If these factors are ignored, headquarters risks receiving distorted measures of operating results. Inappropriate standards of performance may motivate overseas managers to take actions not in line with corporate goals. Direct consequences are reduced corporate efficiency and (possibly) reduced competitiveness.

The remaining sections of this chapter examine some major issues associated with the performance evaluation of foreign operations, describe how leading MNCs evaluate performance, and offer some general policy guidelines.

Consistency

Survey results show that a principal goal of performance evaluation is to ensure profitability.[50] There is a potential conflict, however, when the performance evaluation system does not suit the specific nature of a foreign operation that may have purposes other than short-run profit.[51] Similarly, emphasis on short-term profitability and efficiency can divert attention from critical manufacturing and corporate strategy and alienate corporate personnel.[52] As one example, Awasthi, Chow, and Wu examined the behavioral effects performance evaluation in the context of cultural diversity. They find that performance evaluation and incentive systems evoke different behavioral responses conditional upon national culture.[53]

Given the uniqueness of each foreign subsidiary's mission, performance evaluation systems must allow for how the subsidiary's objectives fit in with overall corporate

---

[50]Business International Corporation, *Assessing Foreign Subsidiary Performance: Systems and Practices of Leading Multinational Companies,* New York: BIC, 1982, p. 10.

[51]MNCs establish foreign operations for many reasons. Companies that depend on a steady supply of raw materials generally expand overseas to secure their supplies. Others invest abroad to lower production costs by obtaining less costly labor, power, or auxiliary services. When a company can no longer profitably export to a market because of increased tariffs, often it will establish a local operation there. Other reasons for expanding abroad include the need to (1) avoid losing a foreign market to major competitors, (2) create markets for components and related products, (3) diversify business risks, (4) search for new markets, (5) satisfy government regulations, and (6) spread overhead costs among more producing units. Many of these objectives are strategic rather than tactical in nature.

[52]G.B. Sprinkle, "The Effect of Incentive Contracts on Learning and Performance," *Accounting Review* 75, No. 3 (2000): 299–326.

[53]Vidya N. Awasthi, Chee W. Chow, and Anne Wu, "Cross-Cultural Differences in the Behavioral Consequences of Imposing Performance Evaluation and Reward Systems: An Experimental Investigation," *International Journal of Accounting* 36, No. 3 (2001): 291–309.

goals. For example, if a foreign subsidiary's purpose is to produce components for other units in the system, it should be evaluated in terms of how its prices, production, quality, and delivery timetables compare to other sources of supply. Subsidiary managers should participate fully in establishing their objectives. Their participation helps to ensure that they will be evaluated within a framework that is sensitive to local operating conditions and consistent with overall corporate goals. Companies should be sure not to sacrifice long-term objectives because subsidiary managers are preoccupied with short-term results. This adherence to long-term goals can be accomplished by making sure that short-term performance goals and management incentives are met within the company's strategic plans.

Unit Versus Managerial Performance

CONTROLLER A: I think generally we would look upon the manager's and unit's performance as about one and the same. The operation of the foreign unit is the responsibility of the manager and how the unit does is pretty much tied in with his evaluation.[54]

CONTROLLER B: In terms of evaluating the manager, it is very much related to how he is doing against his budget because he did present his budget, which was approved by the executive office, and this was his plan of action for the coming year. Now in terms of evaluating whether his unit is one that we want to continue or invest in or whether we should be looking at other alternatives, the return on investment becomes the significant factor.[55]

Should we distinguish between the performance of the unit and the performance of its manager in evaluating a foreign operation? Although some may believe there is no distinction, this position can be held only under limited conditions.

The actions of several parties, each with a different stake in the outcome, may affect the performance of a foreign operation. These parties include (but are not limited to) local management, headquarters management, the host government, and the parent company's government.

Local managers obviously influence reported earnings through their operating decisions. Decisions made at corporate headquarters also affect foreign earnings. For example, to protect the value of assets located in devaluation-prone countries, corporate treasury will often instruct foreign units to transfer funds to subsidiaries located in strong-currency countries.

Host government actions and policies also directly affect the reported results of a foreign subsidiary. Required minimum capitalization ratios in various countries often enlarge the investment base against which earnings are compared. Foreign exchange controls that limit the availability of foreign currency to pay for needed imports will often depress a subsidiary's performance. Wage and price controls can also damage the reported performance of local managers.

---

[54]Paul A. Samuelson, "Economic and Cultural Aspects of Tomorrow's Multinational Firms," *Japan and the World Economy* (December 2000): 393–394.
[55]Ibid., p. 26.

Exhibit 10-11   Partitioned Financial Statements (Local Currency)

	Locally Controllable	Locally Noncontrollable
Balance Sheet		
Assets (detailed)	xx	xx
Liabilities (detailed)	xx	xx
Owners' equity (detailed)	xx	xx
Income Statement		
Revenues	xx	xx
Operating expenses	xx	xx
Interest	xx	xx
"Other"	xx	xx
Taxes	xx	xx
Net Income	xx	xx

These considerations make it clear that a distinction must be made between managerial and unit performance.[56] Local managers should be evaluated only on those balance sheet and income statement items they can influence. This specific evaluation can be done in practice by dividing each balance sheet and income statement item into controllable and noncontrollable components, as illustrated in Exhibit 10-11.

Under this framework, for example, a manager of a U.S. affiliate in Italy would not be held accountable for effective interest charges incurred in connection with a Swiss franc borrowing mandated by corporate treasury. Because the borrowing decision was made at headquarters, headquarters management is responsible for the interest cost (i.e., the nominal interest rate in Switzerland plus the exchange risk). Because the affiliate derives some benefit from the loan proceeds, it should pay an equitable interest charge. This related charge is called a *capital charge* and is based on the cost that would have been incurred had the Italian manager borrowed locally or from the parent.

Performance Criteria

A single criterion is unlikely to capture all factors of performance of interest to headquarters management.[57] Two of the more widely used financial performance criteria used by MNCs for evaluating their foreign operations are return on investment (ROI) and budgeted performance. ROI relates enterprise income to a specified investment base; budgeted performance compares operating performance to a budget. Budgetary control means that any difference between budget and actual performance can be traced to the manager or unit responsible. One classic study demonstrated that budgetary control is better than ROI comparisons for evaluating managerial perfor-

---

[56]Both U.S. and non-U.S. survey respondents, in the Business International survey cited earlier, indicate that assurance of adequate profitability is given priority over evaluating the subsidiary manager. This suggests that for some MNCs, at least, unit performance is an important part of managerial evaluation.

[57]This explains the popularity of the *balanced scorecard*, which utilizes a larger portfolio of performance measures.

mance.[58] ROI measures may be more appropriate for measuring unit performance, while budget comparisons may be more useful in evaluating managers.

In an earlier performance evaluation study by Business International, both U.S. and non-U.S. MNCs surveyed stated that the most important financial criterion used to evaluate the performance of overseas units is budgeted versus actual profit, followed by ROI. Also considered somewhat important were budget versus actual sales, return on sales, return on assets, budget versus actual return on investment, and operating cash flows. As for cash flows, however, U.S.-based multinationals tended to stress cash flows to the parent, whereas non-U.S. multinationals preferred cash flows to the foreign subsidiary. Interestingly, both groups gave little importance to the notion of residual income recommended in the literature.

Many companies do not confine their performance criteria to financial considerations. Nonfinancial criteria reinforce financial measures by focusing on actions that may significantly affect long-term performance. These criteria are especially important in distinguishing between managerial and unit performance.

Important nonfinancial measures include market share, product and process innovation, personnel development (gauged in terms of number of people promoted in relation to the number of promotable employees), employee morale (ascertained by in-house opinion surveys), and productivity measurements. No less significant is performance in social responsibility and host government relations. Such nonfinancial factors are vital to ensure continued success abroad.

Despite difficulties in measurement, nonfinancial criteria are considered important in practice. Earlier surveys suggest that market share is important, followed by productivity improvement, relationships with host governments, quality control, and employee development and safety.[59] Fullerton and Walters report that firms implementing a higher degree of just-in-time (JIT) practices such as lean manufacturing strategies and continuous quality enhancements are more likely to use nonfinancial criteria.[60] These often include measures such as quality results, competitive benchmarking, waste and vendor quality, setup times, scrap, and downtime.[61]

Additional issues concern identifying relevant components of ROI and budget indicators and measuring them. Variations in ROI and budget comparisons relate to appropriate elements of income and the investment base. Thus, should income be the difference between revenues and expenses as they appear in a subsidiary's conventional income statement, or should it incorporate other dimensions? While conventional income measures may reflect a firm's results better than a strictly cash flow measure, they can be misleading in an international setting. To begin, net income may include allocated corporate expenses that the unit manager cannot control. It may not

[58]Sidney M. Robbins and Robert B. Stobaugh,"The Bent Measuring Stick in Foreign Subsidiaries," *Harvard Business Review* (September–October 1973): 80–88.
[59]Business International, *Assessing Foreign Subsidiary Performance,* p. 24.
[60]Rosemary R. Fullerton and Cheryl S. McWatters, "The Role of Performance Measures and Incentive Systems in Relation to the Degree of JIT Implementation," *Accounting, Organizations and Society* 27 (2002): 711–735.
[61]S. J. Daniel and W. D. Reitsperger, "Linking JIT Strategies and Control Systems: A Comparison of the United States and Japan," *The International Executive* 38 (1996): 95–121.

reflect the strategic nature of the foreign unit's mission. A subsidiary's reported results rarely reflect its total contribution.

To remedy these shortcomings, corporate accountants need to specify, as accurately as they can, the returns specifically attributable to the foreign subsidiary's existence. To report profits, therefore, they should *add back* things such as (1) royalty payments, service fees, and corporate allocations charged to the foreign subsidiary and (2) profits on intracorporate sales to the subsidiary. If sales to the subsidiary are not made at arm's-length prices, the foreign subsidiary's profits should be adjusted for transfer pricing subsidies (transfer prices are discussed more fully in Chapter 12). Income amounts used for managerial evaluations should preferably include only those elements of revenues and expenses that unit managers can control.

What about the ROI denominator? Should it consist of shareholders' equity? Should it incorporate shareholders' equity plus total interest-bearing debt (alternatively, fixed assets plus net working capital)? Should it be total assets? If so, should assets include nonproductive resources that are carried because of local environmental constraints? Should it include assets that are allocated by corporate headquarters, such as those corporate treasury controls?

As with income, we believe that a distinction should be made. For managers, the investment base should consist of the resources they can control. Thus, excess inventories (stockpiled because of host government exchange control policies), should be eliminated, as should intracorporate receivables and cash balances over whose levels the local managers have little influence. For the subsidiary, the investment base should include all capital employed in accomplishing its stated objectives.

Assume, as an example, that a foreign unit ends the year with the following foreign currency (FC) financial position. (Current liabilities exclude any interest-paying debt including the current portion of long-term debt.)

Cash	FC 500	Current liabilities	FC 300
Accounts receivable	200	Long-term debt	800
Inventory	300		
Fixed assets	1,000	Owners' equity	900
	FC 2,000		FC 2,000

Assume further that earnings before interest and taxes (EBIT) are FC 200. Local interest rates average 12 percent.

Many companies in the United Kingdom and the United States compute ROI by relating EBIT to fixed assets plus net working capital. In our example, this investment base yields an ROI statistic of 11.7 percent (FC 200/FC 1,700). The comparable figure for many Netherlands-based MNCs, however, is closer to 16.7 percent, because Dutch companies typically remove the ending cash balance from the definition of capital employed. (Cash on hand is considered a nonearning asset in the Netherlands).[62]

---

[62]On the other hand, Dutch companies use cash on hand as a standard of comparison. Return on assets employed should at least exceed the return that would have been earned had cash been invested in the local capital market, 12 percent in our example.

Measurement Issues and Changing Prices in Evaluation

The designer of an evaluation system for foreign operations must also face the issue of accounting measurements. Should local currency asset values be adjusted for changing prices where inflation is a significant force?[63] Such restatements directly affect measures of various ROI components and performance statistics for budgeting and performance evaluation. For example, failure to account for inflation generally overstates return-on-investment measures. As a result, corporate resources may not be directed to their most promising use within the corporation.

In Chapter 7 we said that an internal information system, sensitive to the effects of changing prices, provides a foundation for an inflation management strategy. For a closer look at such issues, we describe a case study examining the performance evaluation practices of ICI, the U.K. chemical giant.

PERFORMANCE EVALUATION PRACTICES: ICI

During the oil embargo of the early 1970s, the price of oil, one of ICI's major raw materials, shot up by a factor of 5 in 1 year. As a result, top management was informed that even a 50 percent rate of return was inadequate![64]

An examination of the impact of inflation on historical accounts disclosed six adverse consequences: (1) cost of goods sold was understated compared with current sales, (2) capital employed was understated in relation to its current value, (3) as a result of (1) and (2), returns on capital were doubly overstated, (4) comparisons of divisional performance based on similar assets of different ages were spurious, (5) intercountry comparisons of subsidiary performance were meaningess, and (6) performance comparisons over time were invalid.

To eliminate these distortions, ICI incorporated current cost adjustments (CCA) in its internal reporting system. According to a company spokesperson, it provided a vitally needed management tool.[65]

ICI divided its performance measures into two categories: long term (at least 1 year) and short term. Cash flow generation by product and ROI are the principal long-term measures. With its cash flow measure, ICI sought to determine whether a product would earn enough money to pay for replacing its plant, its share of corporate costs, and return enough profit to finance realistic growth. In modeling its operations, ICI discovered that the required rate of CCA return differed by country. For example, its operations in Germany needed twice the U.K. rate of return to finance the same rate of growth, primarily due to tax factors.

ICI employed as its measure of ROI the ratio of current cost operating profit (before interest, taxes, and dividends) to current cost fixed assets plus net working capital. Assets were valued at replacement cost net of depreciation for large businesses, and at gross for smaller product lines to eliminate distortions due to the age of the assets (i.e., the denominator would decrease over time simply due to depreciation, thus raising the rate of return).

---

[63]Even in countries where rates of inflation are low, the cumulative effect of changing prices on long-lived assets can be significant. This is especially true of a capital-intensive multibusiness with older fixed assets.
[64]Business International, *Assessing Foreign Subsidiary Performance*, p. 124.
[65]Ibid., p. 45.

In Western Europe, profit was measured before interest and taxes because these expenses were the responsibility of headquarters, and it was difficult to relate a loan to a particular project or determine the actual tax paid when a product was made in one country and sold in several others. Where performance was evaluated on a subsidiary basis (e.g., Brazil and Australia), profit was measured after interest and tax. The reason ICI chose to do this was because these subsidiaries did their own borrowing, and investment decisions there were influenced by local taxes and tax incentives. By using a current cost ROI as opposed to a historical cost return, ICI largely insulated its measure of return from local taxes, tax incentives, and inflation. As a result, ICI could compare businesses in different countries and at different times.

While ICI mainly used cash flow generation and ROI to assess long-term performance, its principal short-term performance measure was to compare actual results against budget, with particular interest in financial ratios such as gross profit margin (i.e., profit before corporate costs). The company employed a 3-year plan: The plan's first year became that period's operating budget. Performance was tracked monthly and quarterly. Quarterly results were considered more significant.

Like many MNCs, ICI incorporated inflationary expectations when budgeting local selling prices and operating costs such as expected labor expense. ICI preferred to incorporate current values in its budgeting system and forecasted a replacement value for cost of goods sold and depreciation. The stated reason for this approach was to force management's attention to the fact that if a company is in a volatile cost setup, as when the price of oil and derivatives rises or falls very fast, it has to use the cost it will incur to replace raw materials and factor that into its selling price. If it uses historic cost, profits may not be adequate to continue purchasing oil at current prices.

Thus performance was tracked using the actual cost of goods incurred each month. The unit's manager was held accountable for the variance (if any), because unexpected (i.e., greater than forecasted) increases in cost could be countered by raising prices.[66]

The budget also included a forecasted depreciation expense based on local indexes reflecting the asset's replacement cost. The local manager was not responsible for any variance (calculated quarterly) between forecasted and actual depreciation. It was not considered feasible for a local manager to discern and react to a change in forecasted depreciation. However, the product manager was expected to achieve his budgeted profit after actual depreciation.

ICI also included a forecasted monetary working capital adjustment (MWCA) in its budget. (See Chapter 7 for a discussion of this concept.) ICI did not consider the difference between forecasted and actual MWCA to be very meaningful because this variance was considered to be caused by changes in costs and selling prices and would show up elsewhere in the profit and loss account.[67]

ICI's solution to inflation reporting largely focused on aggregate balance sheets and income statements. We next offer an internal reporting system that allows management to examine reported numbers in more disaggregated fashion.

---

[66]This assumed that competitors suffered the same cost increases, which might not always be true due to exchange rate factors.

[67]The gearing adjustment on net, nontraded monetary liabilities (a form of purchasing power gain) was not incorporated into budgeting because raising funds was headquarters' responsibility.

Foreign Currency Effects

The foreign exchange variance analysis earlier in the chapter assumes that local managers are responsible for domestic operating results. Ideally, the local manager's responsibility for exchange variances should be in line with the ability to react to exchange rate changes.

The economic impact of changes in exchange rates on performance can be more profound than can be seen through accounting measures alone. To more fully assess the impact of inflation and currency volatility, and gauge their own ability to react, companies need to analyze their competitive market position and the impact of currency changes on their costs and revenues and those of their competition. To shed more light on this issue, we return to ICI's handling of exchange rates and budgetary control. Like many MNCs, ICI uses a forecasted rate of exchange to set budgets and the actual end-of-period rate to measure performance. Unlike many MNCs, ICI believes that the variance that results when the actual exchange rate differs from the budget rate is not meaningful by itself. For example, the company may have budgeted a rate for the euro for its subsidiary in France and the end-of-the-month exchange rate turns out to be identical to the forecasted rate. There is no arithmetic variance, but ICI may have lost some sales volume in France. The reason may be that its competitors are exporters from Canada and the Canadian dollar has weakened against the euro. As a result the Canadians may have a margin advantage against ICI and can lower their prices in euros to maintain the same level of profits when converting to Canadian dollars.

Thus, ICI believes that exchange rate changes have more impact than accounting measures convey. It finds that further analysis is necessary to determine the real impact of currency fluctuations on performance, to arrive at effective reactions, and to determine how far the local manager is to be held accountable for protecting his budgeted profit in pounds sterling.

To achieve these objectives, ICI looks at the currencies in which its costs and revenues arise in relation to those of its competitors. Here is a view from within the company:

We buy oil and oil-related products, which are basically dollar denominated, and we are not a price-maker but are in competition with other producers in Europe. Our oil costs are dollar denominated and our revenues are denominated in other European currencies. If the pound appreciates against all other currencies, then revenues arising from foreign sales, and even those from U.K. sales subject to competitive pressures, will be reduced. As partial compensation, raw material costs (dollar-denominated oil) will be lower, but on balance ICI is worse off because the decrease in raw material costs is less than the decrease in sales revenue in absolute terms. The figure can be significant because ICI is the U.K.'s largest single exporter. Currency movements in the opposite direction are, of course, possible and in fact have recently occurred. An appreciation of the U.S. dollar against all other currencies puts the same raw material cost pressures on our European competitors as on U.K. manufacturing operations so we will not suffer a comparative disadvantage. The comparative disadvantage would arise if there was a depreciation of the pound versus the dollar coupled with a depreciation of other European currencies against the pound. This would both reduce our income and increase our costs.[68]

---

[68]Ibid., p. 127.

This approach to analyzing the economic impact of currency movements affects ICI's evaluation of its managers, whose freedom to react to such external circumstances is limited. In measuring the manager's performance, the company takes into account the extent to which he has been affected by factors beyond his control and also his reaction to them.

PERFORMANCE STANDARDS

Once questions of measurement are resolved, companies must develop meaningful standards with which to evaluate performance. But what standards are appropriate for a company with operations all over the world? Let's look at some possibilities.

A company may have certain corporate-wide standards, such as a minimum required ROI, that it applies to individual subsidiaries or product lines; or it may set different ROI levels or other benchmarks (such as gross margin) for different subsidiaries or product lines. These standards may be incorporated into budgets and can later be compared with results. Performance can also be measured over time. Companies may require stated improvement in specific ratios or income. Past performance is usually significant in developing the next period's budget. Finally, firms can compare their own overseas performance with that of competitors or compare its own units with one another.

Comparing the performance of foreign units against that of their competitors can be useful. At the same time, these comparisons have many pitfalls. (See Chapter 9 for a more extensive discussion of problems involved in analyzing foreign financial statements.) For example, when competitors are local firms, the problem of data availability and adequacy may be considerable, especially if competitors are privately held. When data is available, comparisons might be difficult. Competitors' transfer pricing policies and accounting principles may be impossible to determine. Cross-border comparisons compound these problems even further.

Comparing subsidiaries with other units of the parent company, either at home or abroad, must also be done cautiously as questions of comparability again arise. Differences in subsidiary objectives will automatically bias performance comparisons unless directly accounted for. Even if subsidiary objectives are the same, differences in country risk profiles must be considered. If higher levels of risk are to be offset by higher levels of return, it is reasonable to expect higher profitability from operations in riskier countries. To date, however, no single agreed-upon formula guides how to incorporate these country risks in assessing subsidiary performance.

Many firms require a shorter payback period, adjust cash flow projections for risk, or raise the required rate of return when considering investments in riskier countries.[69] ROI is readily adjusted for political risk because one can set a desired ROI to include a premium in line with risk in a given country (offset to some extent by lower risk that results from geographical diversification of a firm's portfolio of foreign operations).[70]

---

[69]For an analysis of the impact of political risk on the cost of capital, see Kirt C. Butler and Domingo Castelo Joaquin, "A Note on Political Risk and the Required Return on Foreign Direct Investment," *Journal of International Business Studies* 29, no. 3 (1998): 599–608.

[70]Tamir Agmon and Donald Lessard suggest that investors value the international diversification provided by MNCs.

Applying risk premiums to an ROI goal is unavoidably subjective, but the process can be made systematic. One approach is to adjust the corporate-wide ROI by a numerical risk index developed for each country. For example, assume that a country-by-country risk assessment service, such as Business International, assigns a total score of 65 out of 100 possible points to Country Y. (A higher number indicates a lower country risk.) If a company's worldwide target ROI is 15 percent, Country Y's risk-adjusted target ROI is about 23 percent (15 divided by 65 percent). If Country Z's risk index is 75, its target ROI will be 20 percent (15 divided by 75 percent). Under this system, differences between a subsidiary's actual ROI and its budgeted ROI are calculated and used to compare the performance of subsidiaries in different countries. In this example, if one subsidiary's actual ROI in Country Y was 23.5 percent and the ROI of another subsidiary in Country Z was 21 percent, the subsidiary in Country Z will have performed better, as its variance from budgeted ROI was a positive 1 percent versus .5 percent for the subsidiary in Country Y. An overall risk index may not reflect the risk to which a particular foreign subsidiary is exposed. For example, the risk exposure of an oil company's subsidiary may differ from that of a consumer goods manufacturer in the same country. Thus, the risk index should be modified to reflect the specific risk to each unit. A more critical issue, however, is whether a company-wide ROI standard should be applied at all.

Performance evaluations based on a single company-wide standard are generally unsatisfactory. A performance budget is a more useful standard of comparison for multinational operations. Realistic budgets enable performance targets to incorporate considerations that are unique to a particular unit. Comparisons of actual performance to a budget also enables headquarters management to distinguish those results for which subsidiary managers can be held responsible from those that are beyond their control.

Following are seven caveats that may be useful guidelines for those who evaluate the results of foreign operations:

1. Foreign subsidiaries should not be evaluated as independent profit centers when they are really strategic components of a multinational system.
2. Company-wide return on investment criteria should be supplemented by performance measures tailored to the specific objectives and environments of each foreign unit.
3. Specific goals that consider each subsidiary's internal and external environment should be incorporated in performance budgets.
4. A subsidiary's performance should be evaluated in terms of departures from these objectives, the reasons for those departures, and managerial responses to unforeseen developments.
5. Subsidiary managers should not be held responsible for results that are beyond their control (at home and abroad).
6. Subsidiary managers whose performance is being measured should participate fully in setting the goals by which they will be judged.
7. Multiple measures of performance, financial and nonfinancial, should be used in evaluating foreign operations.

Selected References

Aguilera, Ruth V., and Gregory Jackson, "The Cross-National Diversity of Corporate Governance: Dimensions and Determinants," *Academy of Management Review* (July 2003): 447.

Awasthi, Vidya N., Chee W. Chow, and Anne Wu, "Cross-Cultural Differences in the Behavioral Consequences of Imposing Performance Evaluation and Reward Systems: An Experimental Investigation," *International Journal of Accounting* 36, No. 3 (2001): 291–309.

Baber, William, Yuji Ijiri, and Sok-Hyon Kang, "Profit-Volume-Exchange Rate Analysis for Planning International Operations," *Journal of International Financial Management and Accounting* (Summer 1996): 85–101.

Beaver, William H., and Mark A. Wolfson, "Foreign Currency Translation and Changing Prices in Perfect and Complete Markets," *Journal of Accounting Research* (Autumn 1992): 528–550.

Choi, Frederick D. S., "Financial Reporting in Hyperinflationary Environments: A Transactions Analysis Framework for Management," in *International Finance and Accounting Handbook,* 3rd ed., Frederick D.S. Choi, ed., New York: John Wiley & Sons, 2003, pp. 27.1–27.13.

Cooper, Ian A., and Evi Kaplanis, "Partially Segmented International Capital Markets and International Capital Budgeting," *Journal of International Money and Finance* 19 (2000): 309–329.

Cravens, S., and Mike Tayles, "An International Comparison of Strategic Management Accounting Practices," *Management Accounting Research* 9 (2000): 113–135.

Eiteman, D. K., Arthur I. Stonehill, and Michael H. Moffett, *Multinational Business Finance,* Reading, Mass.: Addison-Wesley, 2000.

Fullerton, Rosemary R., and Cheryl S. McWatters, "The Role of Performance Measures and Incentive Systems in Relation to the Degree of JIT Implementation," *Accounting, Organizations and Society* 27 (2002): 711–735.

Harrison, G., and J. McKinnon, "Cross-Cultural Research in Management Control Systems Design: A Review of the Current State," *Accounting, Organizations and Society* (1999): 483–506.

Heffes, Ellen M., All Aboard the XBRL Train, *Financial Executive* (July-August 2004) 16–17.

Jaruga, Alicja, and Simon S.M. Ho, "Management Accounting in Transitional Economies," *Management Accounting Research* 13 (2002): 375–378.

Joaquin, Domingo Castelo, "A Note on Political Risk and the Required Return on Foreign Direct Investment," *Journal of International Business Studies* 29, no. 3 (1998): 599–608.

Logue, D. E., and G. S. Oldfield, "Managing Foreign Assets When Foreign Exchange Markets Are Efficient," *Financial Management* (Summer 1997): 16–22.

Mezias, Stephen J., Patrice Murphy, Ya-Ru Chen, and Mikelle A. Calhoun, "Dynamic Performance Measurement Systems for a Global World: The Complexities to Come," in *International Finance and Accounting Handbook,* 3rd ed., New York: John Wiley & Sons, 2003, pp. 26.1–26.14.

Nonaka, I., and H. Takeuchi, *The Knowledge Creating Company: How Japanese Companies Create the Dynamics of Innovation,* New York: Oxford University Press, 1995.

Panagiotou, George, "Bringing SWOT into Focus," *Business Strategy Review* 14, Issue 2 (2003): 8–10.

Weber, Yaakov, and Ehud Menipaz, "Measuring Cultural Fit in Mergers and Acquisitions," *International Journal of Business Performance Management* 5, No. 1 (2003): 54.

Yip, George S., Johny K. Johansson, and Johan Roos, "Effects of Nationality on Global Strategy," *Management International Review* (April 1997): 365–385.

Discussion Questions

1. This chapter identifies four dimensions of the strategic planning process. How does Daihatsu's management accounting system, described in this chapter, conform with that process?

2. Companies must decide whose rate of return (i.e., local vs. parent currency returns) to use when evaluating foreign direct investment opportunities. Discuss the internal reporting dimensions of this decision in a paragraph or two.

3. As an employee on the financial staff of Multinational Enterprises, you are assigned to a three-person team that is assigned to examine the financial feasibility of establishing a wholly-owned manufacturing subsidiary in the Czech Republic. You are to compute an appropriate hurdle (discount) rate with which to conduct a discounted cash flow analysis. List all the parameters you would consider in measuring your company's cost of capital (discount rate).

4. Chapter 2 briefly described how culture influences external reporting principles. Can the same be said for internal reporting systems?

5. What impact, if any, does global competition have on the design of management information systems?

6. WOTS-UP analysis fails to identify a best strategy. Refer to Exhibit 10-1 and examine the strategies Daimler Benz identified in its two-by-two matrix. What other strategies would you have considered?

7. Why is it better to record sales transacted in a high-inflation country and denominated in foreign currency at the expected spot rate on the date the transaction is settled, instead of the average or month-end spot rate prescribed by conventional accounting?

8. Make a three-by-three matrix corresponding to the three possible exchange rates that could be used to establish a foreign currency budget and track performance, namely, initial spot, projected, and ending rates. Identify which cells of your matrix make operational sense and which do not. For the cells that make sense, identify the effects that each exchange rate combination would likely have on the behavior of the foreign manager responsible for budgeted results.

9. Foreign exchange rates are used to establish budgets and track actual performance. Of the various exchange rate combinations mentioned in this chapter, which do you favor? Why? Is your view the same when you add local inflation to the budgeting process?

10. List six arguments that support a parent company's use of its domestic control systems for its foreign operations, and six arguments against this practice.

11. The financial vice-president of your company's overseas operations is responsible for achieving a dollar profit before taxes, but after foreign currency translation and conversion gains and losses. As an independent outside director, draft a short discussion memorandum to the CEO evaluating this policy.

12. The chapter text gives examples of counterproductive performance evaluation practices used by multinational companies. Take two of the examples and suggest how to improve the procedures. Hint: The seven caveats near the end of the chapter are a good start for your discussion.

Exercises

1. Glasgow Corporation manufactures a product that is marketed in North America, Europe, and Asia. Its total manufacturing cost to produce 100 units of good X is $2,250, detailed as follows:

Raw materials	$ 500
Direct labor	1,000
Overhead	750
Total	$ 2,250

The company bases its selling price on a cost-plus formula.

Required: What would be Glasgow Corporation's selling price per unit if it wants a gross profit of 10 percent above cost?

2. Glasgow Corporation (in Exercise 1) wants to be price competitive on an international basis. To accomplish this it must be able to price its product no higher than $21.50. Using the target costing methodology described in this chapter, what would be Glasgow Corporation's allowable costs? Assume that the company still wants a profit margin of 10 percent of its allowable costs. What does your calculation imply about its manufacturing costs?

3. Review the operating data incorporated in Exhibit 10-3 for the Russian subsidiary of the U.S. parent company.

Required: Using Exhibit 10-3 as a guide, prepare a cash flow report from a parent currency perspective identifying the components of the expected returns from the Russian investment for the first 2 years of its operations. The U.S. parent company is only allowed to receive 70 percent of its affiliate's reported net income, after Russian corporate income taxes, as dividends. However, U.S. tax law provides a credit against U.S. taxes for any foreign income taxes paid.

4. Assume that management is considering whether to make the foreign direct investment described in Exercise 3. Investment will require $8,000,000 in equity capital. Cash flows to the parent are expected to increase by 5 percent over the previous year for each year after year 2 (through year 6). Exchange rate forecasts are as follows:

Year	Rate
1	R 20 = $1
2	R 21 = $1
3	R 23 = $1
4–6	R 25 = $1

Management insists on a risk premium of 10 percent when evaluating foreign projects.

Required: Assuming a weighted average cost of capital of 10 percent and no expected changes in differential tax rates, evaluate the desirability of the Russian investment using a traditional discounted cash flow analysis.

5. Do a WOTS-UP analysis for your school or firm relative to its major competitor. Based on your analysis, suggest several countermeasures your dean or CEO might consider to maintain or improve your organization's competitive standing.

6. Assume the following:
   - Inflation and Turkish lira (TL) devaluation is 30 percent per month, or 1.2 percent per workday.
   - The general price levels at selected intervals for the current month are:

1/1	100.0
1/10	109.6
1/20	119.6
1/30	130.0

   - The real rate of interest is 1.5 percent per month, or 20 percent per year.
   - Cash balances are kept in hard currency (dollars).
   - Month-end rates are used to record expense transactions.

   Required: Based on these assumptions, prepare a table showing the distortions that can occur when expense transactions totaling TL 1,000,000 are recorded using conventional measurement rules (i.e., month-end rates in this example) instead of the internal reporting structure recommended in this chapter.

   Transactions:

Invoice Date	Payment Terms
1	Cash
5	15 days
5	25 days

7. Exhibit 10-4, "Framework for Systems Design," provides a way of thinking about the financial control process in a multinational setting. Assume that a parent company domiciled in your country is comparing the performance statistics (for instance, return on equity) of two wholly-owned affiliates: one in Mexico, the other in Japan. Try to identify how each of the variables and constraints identified in the matrix might affect the numerator and/or denominator of the ROI statistic and its interpretation.

8. Global Enterprises, Inc. uses a number of performance criteria to evaluate its overseas operations, including return on investment. Compagnie de Calais, its French subsidiary, submits the performance report shown in Exhibit 10-12 for the current fiscal year (translated to U.S. dollar equivalents). Included in sales are $250,000 worth of components sold by Compagnie de Calais to its sister subsidiary in Brussels at a transfer price set by corporate headquarters at 40 percent above an arm's-length price. Cost of goods sold includes excess labor costs of $75,000 owing to local labor laws. Administrative expenses include $25,000 of headquarters expenses, which are allocated by Global Enterprises to its French affiliate.

   The parent company holds all of its subsidiaries responsible for their fair share of corporate expenses. Local financing decisions are centralized at corporate treasury, as are all matters related to tax planning. At the same time, Global

Exhibit 10-12 Compagnie de Calais Performance Report		
Sales		$2,100,000
Other income		60,000
		$2,160,000
Costs and expenses:		
Cost of sales	$1,600,000	
Selling and administrative	165,000	
Depreciation	80,000	
Interest	81,000	
Exchange losses	184,000	2,110,000
Income before taxes		$ 50,000
Income taxes		21,000
Net income		$ 29,000

Enterprises thinks that all subsidiaries should be able to cover reasonable financing costs. Moreover, it thinks that foreign managers should be motivated to use local resources as efficiently as possible. Hence, Compagnie de Calais is assessed a capital charge based on its net assets and the parent company's average cost of capital. This figure, which amounts to $60,000, is included in the $81,000 interest expense figure. One-half of the exchange gains and losses figure is attributed to transactions losses resulting from the French subsidiary's export activities. The balance is due to translating the French accounts to U.S. dollars for consolidation purposes. Exchange risk management is also centralized at corporate treasury.

Required: Based on the foregoing information, prepare a performance report that isolates those elements that should be included in performance appraisals of the foreign unit.

9. In evaluating the performance of a foreign manager, a parent company should never penalize a manager for things the manager cannot control. Given the information provided in Exercise 8, prepare a performance report identifying the relevant elements for evaluating the manager of Compagnie de Calais.

10. To encourage its foreign managers to incorporate expected exchange rate changes into their operating decisions, Vancouver Enterprises requires that all foreign currency budgets be set in Canadian dollars using exchange rates projected for the end of the budget period. To further motivate its local managers to react to unexpected rate changes, operating results at period's end are translated to dollars at the actual spot rate prevailing at that time. Deviations between actual and budgeted exchange rates are discarded in judging the manager's performance.

At the start of the 20X4 fiscal year, budgeted results for a Mexican affiliate, the Cuernavaca Corporation, were as follows (amounts in thousands):

Sales	P 8,000,000	C $2,560
Expenses	6,400,000	2,048
Income	P 1,600,000	C $ 512

Actual results for the year in dollars were: sales, C $2,160,000; expenses, C $1,680,000; and net income, C $480,000. Relevant exchange rates for the peso during the year were as follows:

Jan. 1, 19X4 spot rate:	$.00040
Global Enterprise's one-year forecast	$.00032
Dec. 31, 19/X4 spot rate	$.00024

Required: Based on the foregoing information, did the Mexican manager perform well? Support your answer using the variance analysis suggested in the chapter. (Refer to Exhibit 10-6.)

11. Exhibit 10-9 contains a performance report that breaks out various operating variances of a foreign affiliate, assuming the parent currency is the functional currency under FAS No. 52. Using the information in Exhibit 10-9, repeat the variance analysis, assuming instead that the parent company defines the local currency as its functional currency.

12. Parent Company establishes three wholly-owned affiliates in countries X, Y, and Z. Its total investment in each of the respective affiliates at the beginning of the year, together with year-end returns in parent currency (PC), appear here:

Subsidiary	Total Assets	Returns
X	PC 1,000,000	PC 250,000
Y	PC 3,000,000	PC 900,000
Z	PC 1,500,000	PC 600,000

Parent Company requires a return on its domestic investments of 10 percent and is evaluating the annual performance of its three foreign affiliates. To establish an appropriate performance benchmark, Parent Company subscribes to a country risk evaluation service that compiles an unweighted risk index for various countries around the world. The risk scores for each of the n countries are:

Country	Risk Score (out of 60)
X	30
Y	21
Z	15

Other things being equal, the higher the score, the lower the country's risk.

Required: Prepare an analysis for Parent Company's management indicating which affiliate performed best.

CASE 10-1 FOREIGN INVESTMENT ANALYSIS: A TANGLED AFFAIR

You are the CFO of Marissa Corporation, a major electronics manufacturer headquartered in Shelton, Connecticut. To date, your company's operations have been confined to the United States and you are interested in diversifying your operations abroad. One option would be to begin establishing wholly-owned subsidiaries in Europe, Latin America, and Asia. Another option is to acquire a multinational company that already has a major international presence. You are leaning toward the latter course of

Exhibit 10-13 MBI Data on Non-U.S. Operations			
Non-U.S. Operations (Dollars in millions)	2004	2003	2002
At year-end:			
Net assets employed:			
Current assets	$24,337	$20,361	$20,005
Current liabilities	15,917	12,124	11,481
Working capital	$ 8,420	$ 8,237	$ 8,524
Plant and equipment, net	11,628	9,879	9,354
Investments and other assets	9,077	6,822	5,251
	$29,125	$24,938	$23,129
Long-term debt	$ 5,060	$ 3,358	$ 2,340
Other liabilities	2,699	2,607	2,505
Deferred taxes	2,381	1,184	1,580
	$10,140	$ 7,779	$ 6,425
Net assets employed	$18,985	$17,159	$16,704
Number of employees	168,283	167,291	163,904
For the year:			
Revenue	$41,886	$36,965	$34,361
Earnings before income taxes	$ 7,844	$ 7,496	$ 7,088
Provision for income taxes	3,270	3,388	3,009
Net earnings	$ 4,574	$ 4,108	$ 4,079

Notes: Non-U.S. subsidiaries that operate in a local currency environment account for approximately 90 percent of the company's non-U.S. revenue. The remaining 10 percent of the company's non-U.S. revenue is from subsidiaries and branches that operate in U.S. dollars or whose economic environments are highly inflationary.

As the value of the dollar weakens, net assets recorded in local currencies translate into more U.S. dollars than they would have at the previous year's rates. Conversely, as the dollar becomes stronger, net assets recorded in local currencies translate into fewer U.S. dollars than they would have at the previous year's rates. The translation adjustments, resulting from the translation of net assets, amounted to $3,266 million at December 31, 2004, $1,698 million at December 31, 2003, and $1,917 million at December 31, 2002. The changes in translation adjustments since the end of 2002 are a reflection of the strengthening of the dollar in 2003 and the weakening of the dollar in 2004.

action as you are interested in diversifying your company's operating risk and enhancing its bottom line as soon as possible. You also have a significant stock option package and will benefit greatly if the price of Marissa Corporation's common stock were to rise over the next year.

You are particularly interested in MBI International, a U.S.-based multinational with operations in a significant number of countries. You estimate that approximately 60% of the company's earnings are from abroad. Foreign operations performance statistics, provided in MBI Corporation's consolidated financial statements, are included in Exhibit 10-13 for the years 2004, 2003, and 2002. Relevant notes are also appended.

Unfortunately, MBI does not disclose data explaining the movement of the major currencies in which it conducts its businesses. You do a Google search and uncover a trade-weighted index supplied by the U.S. government. Given MBI's large-scale operations, you decide to use the trade-weighted index as a proxy for MBI's currency experience (see Exhibit 10-14). (In using such a proxy, you are assuming that the currency mix of MBI's activities parallel the currency mix in the trade-weighted index.)[73]

REQUIRED

1. On the basis of the information provided, together with what you have learned in Chapter 6, does MBI represent an attractive acquisition candidate?

Exhibit 10-14 Dollar's Trade-Weighted Exchange Index, 2002–2004 (1990 = 100)	
December 31	Index
2002	92.8
2003	93.7
2004	83.7
Average Rates for Years, 1994–2004	
1994	87.4
1995	103.4
1996	116.6
1997	125.3
1998	138.2
1999	143.0
2000	112.2
2001	96.9
2002	92.7
2003	98.6
2004	89.1

---

[73]The data appearing in this case are based on an actual case example. The dates have been changed so that the currency behavior is not indicative of current exchange rates.

CASE 10-2 ASSESSING FOREIGN SUBSIDIARY PERFORMANCE IN A WORLD OF FLOATING EXCHANGE RATES

General Electric Company's worldwide performance evaluation system is based on a policy of decentralization. The policy reflects its conviction that managers will become more responsible and their business will be better managed if they are given the authority and necessary tools to budget and achieve a targeted net income in dollar terms. Moreover, decentralization permits the company to overcome the difficulty of centrally exercising detailed control over its large and diverse operations. Foreign affiliate managers, like their domestic counterparts, are accountable for dollar income, a practice not followed by many MNCs.

In the words of one financial executive, "Although many U.S. corporations are decentralized in their U.S. operations, they seem to be less so with regard to their foreign operations. One reason may be the concern as to whether foreign managers are sufficiently trained in some aspects of international finance, such as foreign exchange exposure management. We feel this is essential training, and our people get that training."[71]

General Electric does not have any rigid standards for comparing the performance of its affiliates. Strategic and operating plans are agreed upon for each business, including financial targets. Like most other companies, GE generally requires a higher rate of return from investment proposals in riskier

countries and has a system of ranking countries according to relative risk. A proposed investment in a high-risk area will have more difficulty being approved and will generally require a higher ROI, but approval depends on both the forecasted ROI and the company's total strategic objectives in each country.

The system of budgeting and forecasting extends 5 years into the future. The first year of the long-range forecast becomes a preliminary budget for the year ahead. A year later the budget is revised, a comparison is made between it and the original forecast, and changes are accounted for.

Measurement of an affiliated company's performance is related to the objectives of its strategic plan and the annual budgets that are derived from the plan. The primary financial measure is success in achieving the affiliates' committed dollar net income. Other measurements include ROI (calculated as the sum of reported net income plus after-tax interest expense, divided by the sum of net worth plus borrowings), net income to sales ratios, market share, inventory and receivable turnover rates, and currency exposure.

While the performance of both an affiliate and its manager are measured primarily on bottom-line results, the review of the manager includes other measurements. Assessments include how well the manager has dealt with government relations, the progress made toward achieving certain targets such as increasing market share, and

[71]Czechowicz et al., *Assessing Foreign Subsidiary Performance*, p. 104.

success in maintaining good employee relationships. These measurements are based on the strategic plan and targets that were established between the manager and parent company supervisor at the start of a period.

GE conducts periodic operating reviews where each manager is reviewed by the level above. The focus is on planning, results, and most recent estimates. This evaluation process provides corporate management with an opportunity to determine whether short-term actions are being taken at the expense of long-range goals.

To minimize currency exposure, GE finances fixed assets with equity and holds the affiliate responsible for maintaining a balanced position on working capital. The policy is modified as necessary for varying circumstances.

Unlike MNCs that have centralized the financing and exposure management functions at the head office, GE makes exposure management a responsibility of its local managers, overseen by sector and corporate personnel. To avoid the transaction costs of having, for example, a French affiliate hedge its position by buying French francs forward, GE has provisions for internal hedging arrangements. Corporate treasury obtains currency exposure data from all affiliates and provides needed information on offsets. Therefore, units can execute a hedging agreement between themselves without going to outside sources.

In setting the budget, the affiliate's manager uses the exchange rate he expects to prevail. General Electric believes that, although predicting rates of exchange is not an exact science, the managers of its foreign businesses have the necessary authority and tools to take those actions that will enable them to achieve their budgeted income. These tools include hedging and pricing decisions. The manager can not only raise prices, cut costs, lead payments, lag receivables, borrow locally, and remit dividends quickly, but he can also take out forward contracts if they are available.

The affiliate manager has the responsibility and authority to protect the unit against currency fluctuations and, therefore, is accountable for dollar profits regardless of exchange rate changes. According to a company spokesperson:

If an unexpected devaluation occurs, the affiliate's performance is still measured in terms of dollar income vis à vis budget. GE considers changes in the rate of exchange in the same way as other risks that occur in a country. For example, if an affiliate's sales are less than those budgeted for because of a recession in that economy, countermeasures are available to the affiliate. If one contends that these things are not controllable, how does one manage a company? We're not saying it's controllable in the sense that it can be prevented from happening, but it is susceptible to countermeasures before and after the event occurs.[72]

REQUIRED

1. Compare GE's approach to performance evaluation with that of ICI (mentioned in the chapter).
2. Critically evaluate the strengths and weaknesses of each company's approach to the performance evaluation of its foreign managers as it relates to the problem of fluctuating currency values.
3. Which approach to performance evaluation do you support and why?

[72]Ibid., p. 106.

11 FINANCIAL RISK MANAGEMENT

C orporate treasurers around the world value new and imaginative ways to minimize their exposures to the volatility of foreign exchange rates, commodity prices, interest rates, and equity prices. The financial services industry now offers many financial hedge products, including currency swaps, interest rate swaps, and options. Accounting standard setters around the world over are working on appropriate measurement and reporting principles for these financial products. Many of these financial instruments are treated as off-balance sheet items by international financial reporting entities. Accordingly, the risks inherent in their use are often masked.

Exhibit 11–1 (on page 414) is a glossary of risk management terms used in this chapter. We now examine internal reporting and control issues associated with this important subject.

ESSENTIALS

The main goal of financial risk management is to minimize the chance of loss arising from unexpected changes in the prices of currencies, credit, commodities, and equities. Exposure to price volatility is known as *market risk*.[1] For example, a corporation in Sweden that issues new stock to domestic investors might view market risk as exposure to rising share prices. An unexpected rise in stock prices is undesirable if the issuer could have issued fewer shares for the same amount of cash by waiting. A Swedish investor, on the other hand, would view risk as the possibility of a fall in equity prices. If stock prices were to fall significantly in the near term, the investor would rather wait before buying.

Market participants tend to be risk averse. Thus, many will trade some potential profits for protection from adverse price changes. Financial intermediaries and market makers have responded by creating financial products that enable a market participant to transfer the risk of unexpected price changes to someone else—a *counterparty*. For example, a financial intermediary might sell a corporate issuer an option (i.e., the right but not the obligation) to buy stock and the investor (the counterparty) an option to sell the stock short.

---

[1]The term *market risk* is sometimes used synonymously with the term *value-at-risk*. In this chapter, the latter refers to the chance of loss on a firm's trading portfolio, which could include hedging instruments, caused by changes in asset prices, interest rates, market volatility, or market liquidity.

Exhibit 11-1   Glossary of Risk Management Terms

accounting risk.   The risk that the preferred accounting treatment for a transaction is not available.

balance sheet hedge.   Reducing foreign exchange (FX) exposure by varying the mix of a firm's foreign currency assets and liabilities.

counterparty.   The individual or institution with whom an exchange is effected.

credit risk.   The risk that a counterparty will default on its obligations.

derivative.   Contractual arrangements creating special rights or obligations that derive their value from another financial instrument or commodity.

economic exposure.   The effect of FX rate changes on a firm's future costs and revenues.

exposure management.   Structuring a company's affairs to minimize the adverse effects of exchange rate changes on earnings.

foreign currency commitments.   Firm sales or purchase commitments that are denominated in foreign currency.

inflation differential.   Difference in the inflation rate between two or more countries.

liquidity risk.   The inability to trade a financial instrument in a timely fashion.

market discontinuities.   Sudden and significant changes in market value.

market risk.   Risk of loss owing to unexpected changes in the prices of foreign exchange, credit, commodities, and equities.

net exposed asset position.   An excess of exposed assets over exposed liabilities (also called a positive exposure).

net exposed liability position.   An excess of exposed liabilities over exposed assets (also called a negative exposure).

net investment.   A firm's net exposed asset or liability position.

notional amount.   The principal amount specified in a contract to determine settlement.

operational hedge.   FX risk protection that focuses on variables that impact a firm's foreign currency revenues and expenses.

option.   The right but not the obligation to buy or sell a financial contract at a specified price on or before a specified date in the future.

regulatory risk.   The risk that a public law will constrain the intended use of a financial product.

risk mapping.   Examining the temporal relationship of various market risks to financial statement variables that affect a firm's value and assessing their likelihood of occurrence.

structural hedges.   Selecting or relocating operations to reduce a firm's overall FX exposure.

tax risk.   The risk that a desired tax treatment is not available.

translation exposure.   Measuring the parent currency effects of FX changes on foreign currency assets, liabilities, revenues, and expenses.

transaction exposure.   Exchange gains and losses that arise from the settlement (conversion) of foreign currency transactions.

value at risk.   Risk of loss on an entity's trading portfolio caused by changes in market conditions.

value driver.   Balance sheet and income statement accounts that impact firm value.

Market risk has many dimensions. Although we will focus on price or rate volatility, management accountants need to consider other risks.[2] *Liquidity risk* exists because not all financial risk management products can be freely traded. Highly illiquid markets include real estate and small capitalization stocks.[3] *Market discontinuities* refer to the risk that markets may not always produce gradual price changes. The stock market plunge of 2000 is a case in point. *Credit risk* is the likelihood that a counterparty to a risk management contract will not meet their obligations. For example, a counterparty agreeing to exchange French euros for Canadian dollars may fail to deliver euros on the promised date. *Regulatory risk* is the risk that a public authority may prevent a financial product from being used for its intended purpose. For example, the Kuala Lumpur stock exchange does not permit the use of short sales as a hedge against declines in equity prices. *Tax risk* is the risk that certain hedge transactions will not receive the desired tax treatment. An example is the treatment of foreign exchange losses as capital gains when ordinary income is preferred. *Accounting risk* is the chance that a hedge transaction will not be accounted for as part of the transaction it is intended to hedge. An example of this is when the gain on the hedge of a purchase commitment is treated as "other income" instead of a reduction of the cost of the purchase.

WHY MANANGE FINANCIAL RISKS?

The rapid growth of risk management services suggests that management can increase firm value by controlling financial risks.[4] Moreover, investors and other stakeholders increasingly expect financial managers to identify and actively manage market risk exposures.[5] If the value of the firm equals the present value of its future cash flows, active exposure management is justified on several grounds.

First, exposure management helps stabilize a firm's expected cash flows. A more stable cash flow stream helps minimize earnings surprises, thereby increasing the present value of expected cash flows.[6] Stable earnings also reduce the likelihood of default and bankruptcy risk, or the risk that earnings may not cover contractual debt service payments.

Active exposure management enables firms to concentrate on their primary business risks. Thus, a manufacturer can hedge its interest rate and currency risks and

---

[2]Gary L. Gastineau, *Dictionary of Financial Risk Management,* Chicago: Probus, 1992, pp. 5–11.
[3]Recent financial innovations such as real estate investment trusts have improved liquidity in many of these previously illiquid markets.
[4]For example, He and Ng document that many Japanese multinationals experience significant exposures to exchange rate volatility and that appreciation of the yen has a negative impact on their stock returns. Jia He and Lillian K. Ng, "The Foreign Exchange Exposure of Japanese Multinational Corporations," *Journal of Finance,* LIII, No. 2 (April 1998): 733–753.
[5]Coy, Peter, "Perils of the Hedge Highwire," *BusinessWeek* (October 26, 1998): 74, 76–77.
[6]For some recent empirical evidence on the use of derivatives to manage earnings and to increase firm value, see Jan Barton, Does the Use of Financial Derivatives Affect Earnings Management Decisions? "*Accounting Review* 76, no. 1 (January 2001): 1–26; Niclas, Hagelin, "Why Firms Hedge with Currency Derivatives: An Examination of the Transaction and Translation," *Applied Financial Economics* 13, No. 1 (January 2003): 55.

concentrate on production and marketing. Similar benefits are available to financial institutions.[7]

Debt holders, employees, and customers also gain from exposure management. As debt holders generally have a lower risk tolerance than shareholders, limiting the firm's risk exposure helps align the interests of shareholders and bondholders. Derivative products allow employer-administered pension funds to enjoy higher returns by permitting them to invest in certain instruments without having to actually buy or sell the underlying instruments. Finally, because losses caused by certain price and rate risks are passed on to customers in the form of higher prices, exposure management limits customers' exposure to these risks.[8]

ROLE OF ACCOUNTING

Management accountants play an important role in the risk management process. They help identify potential market risks, quantify tradeoffs associated with alternative risk response strategies, measure a firm's exposure to specific risks, account for specific hedge products, and evaluate the effectiveness of hedging programs.

Identifying Market Risks

A useful framework for identifying various types of potential market risks may be called *risk mapping*. This framework begins with an examination of the relationship of various market risks to the value drivers of a firm and its competitors. Exhibit 11-2 illustrates a framework developed by J. P. Morgan, now J. P. Morgan/Chase. We call it the *risk mapping cube.*[9]

The term *value drivers* in Exhibit 11-2 refer to major financial condition and operating performance items that impact a firm's value. Market risk encompasses foreign exchange and interest rate risk, as well as commodity and equity price risk. The third dimension of the risk mapping cube examines the relationship of market risks and value drivers for each of the firm's principal competitors.

To illustrate, let us examine the first row of the exposure management cube. Interest rate risk may affect the revenue of the firm in the following manner. Credit sales are normally collected after a certain period, depending on the credit terms offered the client (e.g., 30, 60, or 90 days). The firm usually relies on short-term loans to finance current operations, such as wages and other operating expenses. Rising interest rates before the receivables are collected would reduce the firm's return from sales. Credit sales denominated in foreign currency would yield less than expected parent currency should the foreign currency lose value before collection. Fluctuating commodity prices can have a significant impact on revenues. For example, the sugar industry in Hawaii was crippled when the price of sugar collapsed in the early 1970s. Finally,

---

[7]Elijah Brewer, Bernadette Minton, and James Moser, "The Effect of Bank-Held Derivatives on Credit Accessibility," Federal Reserve Bank of Chicago, Working Paper 94–5, April 1994.
[8]J. P. Morgan & Co., Inc., Arthur Andersen & Co., SC, and Financial Engineering Limited, "The J. P. Morgan/Arthur Andersen Guide to Corporate Exposure Management," *Risk Magazine* (1994).
[9]Ibid., p. 19.

Exhibit 11-2   Risk Mapping Cube

Value drivers	Market risks				
	Foreign exchange	Interest rates	Commodity prices	Equity prices	Other
Revenue					
Cost of sales					
Operating expenses					
Taxes					
Current assets					
Current liabilities					
Fixed assets					
Other					

(Dimensions: Your company / Competitor Y / Competitor Z)

Source: J. P. Morgan et al., "The J. P. Morgan/Arthur Andersen Guide to Corporate Exposure Management." *Risk Magazine,* 1994, 19.

as managers of investment funds know all too well, falling equity prices immediately worsen fund performance statistics.

How does the third dimension of the exposure management cube work? This dimension examines how a competitor's exposure to market risk might impact the firm. Suppose you decide to sell baseball caps of the team you expect to win the next World Series. You decide to buy and sell these caps locally. Are you exposed to foreign exchange risk? You might not think so, but if a competitor buys baseball caps from abroad and the currency of its source country loses value relative to your home currency, this change may allow your competitor to sell at a lower price than you. This is called *competitive currency exposure.*

As the object of this exercise is to identify *potential* risks, we add two other dimensions to the risk management construct in Exhibit 11-2. For each cell of the cube management accountants should incorporate a probability density function associated with a range of possible outcomes for each value driver. To illustrate, unexpected foreign exchange rate changes could have a range of effects on a firm's revenues. Each of these outcomes would, in turn, be associated with a certain likelihood based on objective, or more likely, subjective, probability assessments. These probability scenarios, in turn, would be estimated over various time frames. Intervals such as 3 months, 6 months, and so forth adds a temporal dimension to risk mapping. Accountants are well positioned to provide such data.[10]

Quantify Tradeoffs

Another role that accountants play in the risk management process involves quantifying tradeoffs associated with alternative risk response strategies. Management may prefer to keep some risk exposures rather than hedge whenever the costs of risk protection are deemed higher than the benefits.[11] As an example, an importer who has a firm purchase commitment denominated in foreign currency may prefer not to hedge if he believes the foreign currency will weaken before the delivery date. Accountants would measure the benefits from hedging against its costs plus the opportunity costs of foregone gains from speculating in market movements.

Risk Management in a World of Floating Exchange Rates

Many of the market price movements we have been discussing are interrelated. In this chapter, we confine our analysis to a specific price exposure: foreign exchange rate changes. Exchange rate or FX risk is one of the most common forms of risk that multinational firms encounter.[12] Moreover, the risk management concepts and associated accounting treatments for foreign exchange risk parallel those for interest rate, commodity, and equity price risks.

In a world of floating exchange rates, risk management includes (1) anticipating exchange rate movements, (2) measuring a firm's exposure to exchange risk, (3) designing appropriate protection strategies, and (4) establishing internal risk management controls. These are discussed in turn.

Forecasting Exchange Rate Changes

In developing an exchange risk management program, financial managers must have information on the potential direction, timing, and magnitude of exchange rate changes. Forewarned of exchange rate prospects, financial managers can more efficiently and effectively arrange appropriate defensive measures. Whether it is possible to accurately predict currency movements, however, remains an issue.

Information frequently used in making exchange rate forecasts (e.g., currency depreciation) relates to *changes* in the following factors:

Inflation differentials.   Evidence suggests that a higher rate of inflation in a given country tends, over time, to be offset by an equal and opposite movement in the value of its currency.

---

[10]A booklet on this subject prepared by the American Institute of Certified Public Accountants can be found at www.aicpa.org/assurance/index.htm.

[11]Froot, Scharfstein, and Stein, for example, suggest that while a firm's shareholders may benefit from hedging, it is not always in their interest for a firm to be completely hedged. Kenneth A. Froot, David S. Scharfstein, and Jeremy Stein, "Risk Management: Coordinating Corporate Investment and Financing Policies," *Journal of Finance* (December 1993): 1629–1658.

[12]Alpa Dhanani, "Foreign Exchange Risk Management: A Case in the Mining Industry," *British Accounting Review* 35, Issue 1 (March 2003): 35.

Monetary policy. An increase in a country's money supply that exceeds the real growth rate of national output fosters inflation, which affects exchange rates.

Balance of trade. Governments often use currency devaluations to cure an unfavorable trade balance (i.e., when exports < imports).

Balance of payments. A country that spends (imports) and invests more abroad than it earns (exports) or receives in investments from abroad experiences downward pressure on its currency's value.

International monetary reserves and debt capacity. A country with a persistent balance of payments deficit can forestall a currency devaluation by drawing down its savings (i.e., level of international monetary reserves) or drawing on its foreign borrowing capacity. As these resources decrease, the probability of devaluation increases.

National budget. Deficits caused by excessive government spending also worsen inflation.

Forward exchange quotations. A foreign currency that can be acquired for future delivery at a significant discount signals reduced confidence in that currency.

Unofficial rates. Increases in the spread between official and unofficial or black market exchange rates suggest increased pressure on governments to align their official rates with more realistic market rates.

Behavior of related currencies. A country's currency will normally behave in a fashion similar to currencies of countries with close economic ties to it.

Interest rate differentials. Interest rate differentials between any two countries predict future change in the spot exchange rate.

Foreign equity option prices. Since arbitrage links a foreign equity's price in its home market with its domestic currency value, changes in the domestic currency option price of a foreign equity signals a change in the market's expectations of future FX rates.[13]

These items help predict the direction of currency movements. However, they are usually not enough to predict the timing and magnitude of currency changes. Politics strongly influences currency values in many countries. Political responses to devaluation or revaluation pressures frequently result in temporary measures rather than exchange rate adjustments. These temporary measures include selective taxes, import controls, export incentives, and exchange controls. Awareness of the politics of a country whose currency is under pressure is important. It helps financial managers discern whether the government will lean toward market intervention or rely on free-market solutions.

Some claim that exchange rate forecasting is a futile exercise. In a world where exchange rates are free to fluctuate, FX markets are said to be efficient.[14] Current market rates (i.e., forward exchange rates) represent the consensus of all market participants about future FX rates. Information that is generally available is immediately

---

[13]Chu and Swidler confirm this using the case of Telmex options around the 1994 Mexican peso devaluation. Ting-Heng Chu and Steve Swidler, "Forecasting Emerging Market Exchange Rates from Foreign Equity Options," *Journal of Financial Research,* No. 3 (2002): 353–366.

[14]Gunter Dufey and Ian H. Giddy, "Management of Corporate Foreign Exchange Risk," in F. D. S. Choi, ed., *International Finance and Accounting Handbook,* New York: John Wiley & Sons, 2003, pp. 6.1–6.31.

impounded in current FX rates. Thus, such information has little value in predicting future exchange rates. Under these conditions, FX rate changes are random responses to new information or unforeseen events. Forward exchange rates are the best available estimates of future rates. The randomness of FX rate changes reflect the diversity of opinions on exchange values by participants.

What do all of these factors imply for management accountants? For one thing, accountants must develop systems that gather and process comprehensive and accurate information on variables correlated with exchange rate movements. These systems can incorporate information provided by external forecasting services, financial publications that track currency movements, and daily contacts with foreign currency dealers. They should be online and computer-based to ensure managers a superior source of information on which to base their currency forecasts. Financial managers must also understand the consequences of not using other forecasting methods.

If exchange rate forecasting is not possible or too expensive to undertake, then financial managers and accountants should arrange their company's affairs to minimize the detrimental effects of rate changes. This process is known as exposure management.

Exposure Measurement

Structuring a company's affairs to minimize the adverse effects of exchange rate changes requires information on its exposure to FX rate risk. FX exposure exists whenever a change in FX rates changes the value of a firm's net assets, earnings, and cash flows. Traditional accounting measures of FX exposure center on two major types of exposure: *translation* and *transaction*.

Translation Exposure

Translation exposure measures the impact of FX rate changes on the domestic currency equivalents of a firm's foreign currency assets and liabilities. For example, a U.S. parent company operating a wholly-owned subsidiary in Ecuador (whose functional currency is the U.S. dollar) experiences a change in the dollar value of its Ecuadorean net monetary assets whenever the exchange value of the Ecuadorean sucre changes relative to the dollar. Because foreign currency amounts are typically translated to their domestic currency equivalents for either management review or external financial reporting purposes (see Chapter 6), translation effects have a direct impact on reported profits. A foreign currency asset or liability is exposed to exchange rate risk if a change in the exchange rate causes its parent currency equivalent to change. Based on this definition, foreign currency balance sheet items exposed to exchange rate risks are those items that are translated at current (as opposed to historical) exchange rates. Accordingly, translation exposure is measured by taking the difference between a firm's exposed foreign currency assets and liabilities. This process is depicted in Exhibit 11-3.

An excess of exposed assets over exposed liabilities (i.e., those foreign currency items translated at current exchange rates) causes a net exposed asset position. This is sometimes referred to as a *positive exposure*. Devaluation of the foreign currency relative to the reporting currency produces a translation loss. Revaluation of the foreign currency produces a translation gain. Conversely, a firm has a net exposed liability

Exhibit 11-3 Translation Exposure

Exposed assets > Exposed liabilities = Positive exposure

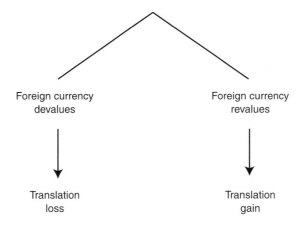

Exposed assets < Exposed liabilities = Negative exposure

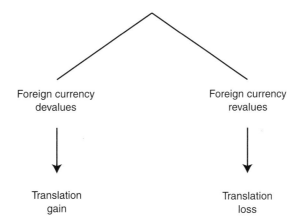

position or *negative exposure* whenever exposed liabilities exceed exposed assets. In this instance, devaluation of the foreign currency causes a translation gain. Revaluation of the foreign currency causes a translation loss.

Accounting measures of exposure vary depending on the translation method adopted. (Chapter 6 distinguished four major translation options.) Exhibit 11-4 illustrates the major translation options described in Chapter 6. The year-end balance sheet is that of a hypothetical Philippine subsidiary of a U.S. parent company. The second column depicts the U.S. dollar equivalents of the Philippine peso (P) amounts at an exchange rate of $0.03 = P 1. The peso is expected to devalue by 33-1/3 percent during the coming period. As inventories are stated at market values under the lower-of-cost-or-market rule, the monetary–nonmonetary and temporal translation methods pro-

Exhibit 11-4   Accounting Exposure Illustrated (in thousands)

	Peso	U.S. Dollars Before Pesos Devaluation ($.03 = P1)	U.S. Dollars After Philippine Peso Devaluation ($.02 = P1)			
			Current Rate	Current- Noncurrent	Monetary- Nonmonetary	Temporal
Assets						
Cash	P 500,000	$15,000	$10,000	$10,000	$10,000	$10,000
Accounts Receivable	1,000,000	30,000	20,000	20,000	20,000	20,000
Inventories	900,000	27,000	18,000	18,000	27,000	18,000
Fixed assets (net)	1,100,000	33,000	22,000	33,000	33,000	33,000
Total	P 3,500,000	$105,000	$70,000	$81,000	$90,000	$81,000
Liabilities & Owners' Equity						
Short-term payables	P 400,000	$ 12,000	$ 8,000	$ 8,000	$ 8,000	$ 8,000
Long-term debt	800,000	24,000	16,000	24,000	16,000	16,000
Stockholders' equity	2,300,000	69,000	46,000	49,000	66,000	57,000
Total	P 3,500,000	$105,000	$70,000	$81,000	$90,000	$91,000
Accounting exposure (P)			2,300,000	2,000,000	300,000	1,200,000
Translation gain (loss) ($)			(23,000)	(20,000)	(3,000)	(12,000)

duce different exposure measures and are treated separately. Assuming the U.S. parent designates the U.S. dollar as the subsidiary's functional currency, its potential foreign exchange loss on a positive exposure of P 1,200 million would be $12 million, determined as shown in Exhibit 11-5.

Alternatively, if the parent company designates the Philippine peso as the subsidiary's functional currency, the potential exchange loss is $23 million. This is based on a positive exposure of P 2,300 million using the current rate method mandated by FASB No. 52. An exposure report format for the income statement is based on similar concepts (suggested by the Management Accounting Practices Committee of the International Federation of Accountants) appears in Exhibit 11-6.

Exhibit 11-5 assumed that the Philippine subsidiary's transactions were denominated solely in pesos. In most foreign operations, however, transactions are done in more than one currency. FX risk is a multidimensional issue: For example, a receivable denominated in Finnish markkas is unlikely to have the same future value as a receivable in Portuguese escudos, even if both have the same face value at the time of sale. To account for these situations, management accountants prepare a variety of exposure reports that distinguish among foreign currency assets and liabilities according to the currencies in which they are denominated. Exhibit 11-7 illustrates a multicurrency exposure report for the Philippine subsidiary, which manufactures a durable good for sales in local, Australian, and American markets. Supplies are imported from Indonesia.

The format of the exposure report in Exhibit 11-7 resembles that in Exhibit 11-4 except that Exhibit 11-7 segregates exposed assets and liabilities by currency of denomination. Balance sheet items are typically expressed in U.S. dollars to facilitate an assessment of the relative magnitudes of the various items.

Exhibit 11-5   Calculation of Potential Foreign Exchange Loss (in millions)

Exposed Assets			
Cash	P 500		
Accounts receivable	1,000		
Inventories	900		P 2,400
Exposed Liabilities			
Short-term payables	P 400		
Long-term debt	800		1,200
Positive exposure			P 1,200
Pre-depreciation rate ($0.03 = P1)	P 1,200	=	$36
Post-depreciation rate ($0.02 = P1)	P 1,200	=	24
Potential foreign exchange loss			($12)

Exhibit 11-6   Format for an Income Statement Exposure Forecast

Income Statement Category	Items Translated at Current Exchange Rates				Items Translated at Historic Exchange Rates				Total Exposure
	Local Currency (amount)	*Foreign Currency (amount)*	*Conversion Rate*	*Local Equivalent Rate*	*Local Currency (amount)*	*Foreign Currency (amount)*	*Conversion Rate*	*Local Equivalent Rate*	
Revenues (By Category)									
Less: Cost of Sales (By Category)									
Gross Profit									
Less: Expenses (By Category) Earnings Before Interest and Tax Expense									
Earnings Before Tax									
Tax									
Net Income									
Net Exposed Position									
Net Covered Position									
Net Uncovered Position									

Exhibit 11-7 Multicurrency Translation Exposure (in thousands)				
	Philippine Pesos	Australian Dollars	Indonesian Rupiahs	U.S. Dollars	Total[1]
Exposed Assets				
Cash	$ 50,000	–	–	–	$ 50,000
Receivables	45,000	$15,000	–	$40,000	100,000
Inventories	90,000			–	90,000
Total	185,000	$14,000		$40,000	$240,000
Exposed Liabilities				
Short-term payables	$ 20,000	$ 2,500	$ 12,500	$ 5,000	$40,000
Long-term debt	50,000			30,000	80,000
Total	$ 70,000	$ 2,500	$ 12,500	$35,000	120,000
Net exposure	$115,000	$12,500	$(12,500)		

[1]Stated in U.S. dollars at the spot rate effective on the date of the report.

A multicurrency exposure reporting format offers many advantages over its single currency counterpart. For one thing, the information provided is more complete. Rather than disclosing a single net positive exposure figure of $120 million, the report in Exhibit 11-7 shows that this figure is comprised of several different currency exposures.

Each connotes different exchange risk consequences for the U.S. parent. Also, under a single currency perspective, the positive exposure of $12,500,000 in Australian dollars is combined with the negative exposure of $12,500,000 in Indonesian rupiahs, suggesting a natural offset. This offset is true only if the Australian dollar and Indonesian rupiah move in tandem relative to the U.S. dollar. If they do not, the translation effects could be significantly different.

A multicurrency report also enables the parent company to aggregate similar exposure reports from all of its foreign subsidiaries and analyze, on a continual basis, its worldwide translation exposure by national currency. This type of analysis is particularly helpful when local managers are responsible for protection against translation exposure. One can easily imagine a situation where local managers in two foreign subsidiaries may face opposite exposures in the same currency. Multicurrency exposure reports enable a parent company to make sure its local managers avoid hedging activities that are disadvantageous to the company as a whole.

Transaction Exposure   Transaction exposure concerns exchange gains and losses that arise from the settlement of transactions denominated in foreign currencies. Unlike translation gains and losses, transaction gains and losses have a direct effect on cash flows.

A multicurrency transaction exposure report for our Philippine subsidiary appears in Exhibit 11-8. It includes items that normally do not appear in conventional financial statements but cause transaction gains and losses, such as forward exchange contracts, future purchase and sales commitments, and long-term leases.[15] The exposure report

---

[15]These items are normally disclosed in footnotes to the financial statements.

excludes items that do not directly relate to foreign currency transactions (such as cash on hand). A transaction exposure report also has a different perspective than a translation exposure report. A translation exposure report takes the perspective of the parent company. A transaction exposure report takes the perspective of the foreign operation. Exhibit 11-8 focuses on what happens on the books of the Philippine affiliate if the peso changes value relative to the Australian dollar, the Indonesian rupiah, and the U.S. dollar. The peso column is of no concern, as peso transactions are recorded and settled in pesos. A devaluation of the peso relative to the Australian and U.S. dollars will produce transaction gains owing to positive exposures in both currencies. A devaluation of the peso relative to the rupiah would produce a transaction loss, as more pesos would be required to settle the Philippine subsidiary's foreign currency obligations. These transaction gains or losses (net of tax effects) directly impact U.S. dollar earnings upon consolidation.

Centralized control of a firm's overall exchange exposures is possible. This entails having each foreign affiliate send its multicurrency exposure reports to corporate headquarters continually. Once exposures are aggregated by currency and by country, the company can implement centrally coordinated hedging policies to offset potential losses.

Accounting Versus Economic Exposure   The reporting frameworks previously described highlight a firm's exposure to FX risk at a given time. Both translation and transaction exposure reports, however, do not measure a firm's economic exposure. This is the effect of currency value changes on the future operating performance and cash flows of the firm.

Exhibit 11-8 indicates that the Philippine subsidiary is *long* on Australian dollars. That is to say, exposed Australian dollar assets exceed exposed Australian dollar liabilities.

Exhibit 11-8   Multicurrency Transaction Exposure ($ thousands)

	Philippine Pesos	Australian Dollars	Indonesian Rupiahs	U.S. Dollars	Total
Exposed Assets					
Receivables	$ 45,000	$15,000	—	$40,000	$100,000
Inventories	90,000	—	—	—	$ 90,000
Future sales commitments	—	10,000	—	—	10,000
Total	$135,000	$25,000		$40,000	$200,000
Exposed Liabilities					
Short-term payables	$ 20,000	$ 2,500	$ 12,500	5,000	$ 40,000
Long-term debt commitments	50,000	—	—	30,000	80,000
Future purchase	—	—	10,000	—	10,000
Leases	—	$ 5,000	—	—	5,000
Total	$ 70,000	$ 7,500	$ 22,500	$35,000	$135,000
Net exposure		$17,500	$(22,500)	$ 5,000	

Based on this report, a financial manager might decide to hedge this position by selling 17.5 million Australian dollars in the forward exchange market. Would this be the right decision? Probably not. Although the Philippine subsidiary is long on Australian dollars, not all the items in the exposure report require an immediate inflow or outflow of Australian dollars. The future sales commitment of $10 million will probably not bring in cash until a later accounting period. Also, the exposure report does not include all Australian dollar receipts or disbursements because future sales denominated in Australian dollars are not considered. Although Australian dollar receivables currently total $15 million, this figure will not stay the same for long. From an external reporting perspective, these future cash flows should not be considered. From an internal reporting perspective, they cannot be ignored.

More and more companies differentiate between exposures that are static and those that are fluid in nature.[16] They prepare multicurrency cash flow statements that enable them to monitor monthly cash receipts and disbursements for each currency in which they do business (see Exhibit 11-9). A traditional exposure report considers the effects of exchange rate changes on account balances as of the financial statement date. A multicurrency cash flow statement emphasizes exposures generated by exchange

Exhibit 11-9   Budgeted Cash Flows by Currency

Unit/Country: _____ Date: _____

Currency		Budget Periods					
		January	*February*	*March*	*April*	*May*	*June*
Philippine pesos	Receipts						
	Payments						
	Net						
Australian dollars	Receipts						
	Payments						
	Net						
Indonesian rupiahs	Receipts						
	Payments						
	Net						
Other	Receipts						
	Payments						
	Net						

---

[16]Business International Corporation, *New Directions in Managing Currency Risk: Changing Corporate Strategies and Systems under FAS No. 52,* New York: Business International Corporation, 1982.

rate changes during the forthcoming budget period. Cash receipts for each national currency include the collection of current and anticipated credit sales, asset disposals, and other cash-generating activities. Multicurrency cash disbursements incorporate those required for current and anticipated obligations, debt service, and other cash purchases.

The notion of economic exposure recognizes that exchange rate changes affect the competitive position of firms by altering the prices of their inputs and outputs relative to those of their foreign competitors. For example, assume that our hypothetical Philippine subsidiary obtains its labor and material locally. Devaluation of the Philippine peso relative to all other foreign currencies could improve rather than worsen the subsidiary's position. It could increase its exports to Australia and the United States as the devalued peso would make its goods cheaper in terms of the Australian and U.S. dollar. Domestic sales could also rise, because the peso devaluation would make imported goods more expensive in local currency. The devaluation would have no appreciable effect on the cost of local-source inputs. Thus, the future profitability of the Philippine subsidiary might increase because of the currency depreciation. Under these circumstances, booking a transaction loss on a positive translation exposure would distort the economic implications of the peso devaluation.

Alternatively, a German manufacturing affiliate of a U.K. parent, organized to serve the German market, may have a positive translation exposure. Appreciation of the euro relative to the pound would produce a translation gain upon consolidation. If the German affiliate were to source all of its inputs in Germany, its economic exposure would appear to be shielded from exchange risk. Yet, if a major German competitor obtained some of its manufacturing components from Russia, this competitor may enjoy a cost advantage if the ruble were undervalued relative to the deutsche mark.

These examples suggest that economic or operating exposure bears little or no relation to translation and transaction exposure.[17] Accordingly, the management of such exposure will require hedging technologies that are more strategic than tactical in nature.[18] These newer technologies include the following hedging options[19]:

Companies may opt for structural hedges that involve selecting or relocating manufacturing sites to reduce the operating exposure of the business as a whole. Such actions, however, may require foregoing economies of scale, which could reduce the expected rate of return of the business.

Alternatively, parent companies take a portfolio approach to risk reduction by selecting businesses that have offsetting exposures. In so doing, the operating exposure of the firm as a whole is minimized. This strategy will necessitate careful review of individual business units' operating results after correcting for the effects of operating exposure. A company may opt to exploit exchange rate volatility by reconfiguring its businesses. The object is to preserve maximum flexibility by being able to increase pro-

---

[17]For a recent case example of hedging economic exposure, see Alpa Dhanani, "Foreign Exchange Risk Management: A Case in the Mining Industry," op. cit.

[18]Miller and Reuer provide empirical insight on the relation between strategy and industry structure on a firm's economic exposures to foreign exchange rate movements. Kent D. Miller and Jeffrey J. Reuer, "Firm Strategy and Economic Exposure to Foreign Exchange Rate Movements," *Journal of International Business Studies* 29, No. 3 (3rd quarter 1998): 493–514.

[19]D. R. Lessard and J. B. Lightstone, "Volatile Exchange Rates Can Put Operations at Risk," *Harvard Business Review* (July–August 1986): 107–14.

duction and sourcing in countries where currencies become strongly undervalued in real terms. This entails additional costs of relocating production facilities and building excess capacity. On the other hand, these strategic moves reduce average operating costs across a range of exchange rates.

The notion of economic or operating exposure places new burdens on management accountants. Traditional sources will not contain much of the required information. The proper measurement of operating exposure will require an understanding of the structure of the market in which a company and its competitors do business, as well as the effects of real (as opposed to nominal) exchange rates. These effects are hard to measure. As operating exposures tend to be long in duration, uncertain in terms of measurables, and not based on explicit commitments, accountants will have to provide information that spans multiple operating functions and time periods.

Protection Strategies

Once foreign exchange exposures are quantified, the next step is to design hedging strategies that minimize or eliminate such exposures. These strategies include balance sheet, operational, and contractual hedges.

Balance Sheet Hedges   A balance sheet hedge reduces a firm's exposure by adjusting the levels and monetary denomination of a firm's exposed assets and liabilities. For example, increasing cash balances in foreign currency can offset declines in interest rates and income on domestic fixed income instruments.[20] In Exhibit 11-6, a natural hedge against the $115 million positive exposure would be to increase the Philippine subsidiary's peso borrowings by $115 million.[21] In this case the borrowed cash must be remitted to the parent or invested in nonexposed assets, otherwise the net exposed asset position would not change. Other methods of hedging a firm's positive exposure in a subsidiary located in a devaluation-prone country include:

1. Keeping local currency cash balances at the minimum level required to support current operations
2. Remitting profits above those needed for capital expansions back to the parent company
3. Speeding up (leading) the collection of outstanding local currency receivables
4. Deferring (lagging) payments of local currency payables
5. Speeding up the payment of foreign currency payables
6. Investing excess cash in local currency inventories and other assets less subject to devaluation loss
7. Investing in strong currency foreign assets

[20]John Y. Campbell, Luis M. Viceira, and Joshua S. White, "Foreign Currency for Long-Term Investors," *Working Paper 9075*, National Bureau of Economic Research, July 2002.
[21]Recent empirical evidence on foreign currency borrowing for hedging and other purposes is provided by Matti Keloharju and Mervi Niskanen, "Why Do Firms Raise Foreign Currency Denominated Debt? Evidence from Finland," *European Financial Management* 7, No. 4 (2001): 481–496.

Operational Hedges   This form of risk protection focuses on variables that impact foreign currency revenues and expenses. Raising selling prices (for sales invoiced in a devaluation-prone currency) in proportion to the anticipated currency depreciation helps protect targeted gross margins. One variation of this theme is invoicing sales in hard currencies. Tighter control of costs affords a larger margin of safety against potential currency losses. A final example includes *structural hedges*. These entail relocating manufacturing sites to reduce operating exposures of the firm or changing the country in which raw materials or manufacturing components are sourced.

Balance sheet and operational hedging are not costless. Foreign subsidiaries in devaluation-prone countries are frequently urged to minimize their local currency working capital balances (cash and receivables in particular), simultaneously increasing holdings of local currency debt. Such actions, unfortunately, are often disadvantageous. Increased export potential resulting from a devaluation might call for more working capital rather than less. The opportunity cost in lost sales could far exceed any translation loss. Also, local currency borrowing before a devaluation can be extremely expensive. Other foreign subsidiaries usually have similar ideas at the same time and, consequently, the local banking system may accommodate such credit demands only at an excessive cost. Furthermore, bank credit during such periods is usually scarce because most countries impose severe credit restraints to counter the problems that cause devaluation pressures in the first place. The cost of borrowing under these circumstances often exceeds any protection provided.

Strategic hedges also have their limits. One strategy, for example, is to vertically integrate operations to minimize a firm's exposure to exchange rate–sensitive resources. This course of action, however, exposes the firm to additional costs connected with setting up a new foreign affiliate and the potential loss of scale economies. Vertical integration also takes a long time to carry out.

Contractual Hedges   A variety of contractual hedge instruments have been developed to afford managers greater flexibility in managing foreign exchange exposures. Exhibit 11-10 shows some foreign exchange hedge products that have recently appeared. As you can see, managers have plenty of choices to consider.

Most of these financial instruments are *derivative* as opposed to *basic* in nature. Basic financial instruments, such as repurchase agreements (receivables), bonds, and capital stock, meet conventional accounting definitions of assets, liabilities, and owners' equity. Derivative instruments are contractual arrangements giving rise to special rights or obligations and that derive their value from another financial instrument or commodity. Many are based on contingent events. Accordingly, they do not have the same characteristics as the instrument on which they are based. An example would be a cross-currency basis swap on a principal amount of $100 million. Here the derivative product is the promise to exchange interest payment differentials based upon, but independent of, the underlying principle or notional amount of the respective borrowings. If floating rates were higher than fixed rates, one counterparty would owe the other counterparty the difference. Any amounts owing would depend upon the movement in interest rates. The market for derivatives is a 24-hour global trading market comprised largely of banks. Derivatives traders around the world are interconnected through highly sophisticated electronic and telecommunications systems.

Exhibit 11-10   Exchange-Related Financial Instruments

alternative currency option.   A currency option that, if exercised, can be settled in one of several alternative currencies at the choice of the option holder.

basket hedging.   The use of a basket of currencies (comprising fewer currencies than the hedged portfolio) to offset the risk of all the nonbase currencies in a portfolio.

break forward.   An option that allows the buyer to fully participate in the movement of a currency beyond a specified level without having to pay an explicit option premium.

combined interest rate and currency swap (CIRCUS).   A transaction in which two counterparties exchange interest payment streams denominated in two different currencies (i.e., exchanging fixed interest payments in one currency for floating rate interest in another).

contingent hedge with an agreement for rebate at maturity (CHARM).   A currency option that (1) is exercisable if a bidding company wins the contract or (2) is void if the company loses the contract, where the issuer of the option rebates a portion of the premium. The value of the payoff depends on (1) the buyer's ability to obtain business requiring currency protection, and (2) the movement of the underlying currency.

convertible option contract.   An option to purchase or sell foreign currency that converts to a forward contract if the forward exchange rate falls below a certain price.

covered option securities (COPS).   Short-term obligations that give the issuer the option to repay principal and interest in the original, or a mutually acceptable, currency.

covered interest arbitrage.   An agreement in which two counterparties exchange currencies at both the spot and forward rates simultaneously.

cross-currency basis swap.   A floating interest rate swap in two currencies.

cross-currency cap.   An option in which the holder is paid the positive difference between the spread on two different currency base rates and a strike spread.

currency coupon swap.   A fixed to floating coupon swap in two different currencies.

currency option.   The right but not the obligation to buy or sell another currency at an agreed-upon strike price within a specified time period.

currency swap.   The initial exchange of two currencies and subsequent reexchange of the same currencies at the end of a certain time period.

currency swap option.   (swaption). An option to buy or sell a currency swap at a specified exchange rate.

dual option bonds.   A bond giving the investor the choice of currencies in which to receive interest and principal repayments.

exchange rate agreement (ERA).   A synthetic agreement for forward exchange whose value is correlated with the spread between two forward currency exchange rates.

forward exchange contract.   A contractual agreement between two parties to exchange a specified amount of currency for another at a fixed date in the future.

futures contract.   An exchange-traded contract calling for delivery of a specified amount of currency at a fixed date in the future.

foreign equity option.   The right but not the obligation to buy or sell a foreign equity at a specified price on or before a specified date in the future.

indexed currency option notes (ICONS).   Bonds that are denominated and pay interest in one currency with redemption value linked to the exchange rate of another currency.

Exhibit 11-10   Exchange-Related Financial Instruments (*Continued*)

look-back option.   The retroactive right to buy a currency at its low point or sell a currency at its high point within the option period.

principal exchange-rate-linked securities (PERLS).   Debt instruments paying interest and principal in U.S. dollars where the principal is pegged to the exchange rate between the dollar and another currency.

range forwards.   A forward exchange contract specifying a range of exchange rates at which currencies will be exchanged at maturity.

synthetic position.   A combined transaction to produce a security with features that could not be obtained directly (e.g., combining a fixed rate debt with a currency swap).

tailored swap.   A currency swap in which the notional principle can be adjusted to meet the changing risk exposure of a business.

Source: Adapted from Gary L. Gastineau, *Swiss Bank Corporation Dictionary of Financial Risk Management,* Chicago: Probus, 1992.

During the turn of this decade, numerous surprises occurred in the market for derivatives that dominated the financial headlines. Names such as Baring Brothers, Long-Term Capital Management, and Orange County gained instant notoriety because of the magnitude of the losses they sustained. Prestigious financial institutions such as Citigroup, J. P. Morgan Chase, Daiwa Bank, Merrill Lynch, and Sumitomo Corp. also made the front page. Reported losses ranged from hundreds of millions of dollars to the billions. Reasons for such losses included inadequate controls over trader behavior, pricing models that did not incorporate the risks of extreme market movements (discontinuities), market illiquidity, and ultimately the naiveté of directors and senior management as to the nature and risks of these instruments.[22]

Despite these debacles, the derivatives market, currently in excess of $100 trillion in size, continues to grow in sophistication and use. Financial managers of multinational enterprises use these instruments to manage their exposures to exchange risk, especially transactions and economic, as these exposures directly impact a firm's current and future cash flows. Allayannis and Ofek find a strong negative association between foreign currency derivative use and a firm's exchange rate exposure. This suggests that firms use derivatives primarily to hedge rather than speculate in foreign currencies. It also implies that usage of foreign currency derivatives does indeed reduce foreign exchange rate risk.[23] Although we express a preference for hedging transaction and economic exposures, executives appear interested in managing translation exposure as well. They voice concern over reporting lower earnings to shareholders.[24] In a

[22]Buckley and Vand Der Nat document disturbing levels of ignorance among independent directors in terms of understanding and monitoring of derivatives. Adrian Buckley and Mattheus Vand Der Nat, "Derivatives and the Non-Executive Director," *European Management Journal* 21, No. 3 (June 2003): 388.
[23]George Allayannis and Eli Ofek, "Echange Rate Exposure, Hedging and the Use of Foreign Currency Derivatives," *Journal of International Money and Finance* 20 (2001): 273–296.
[24]For example, see C. O. Houston, "Translation Exposure Hedging Post SFAS No. 52," *Journal of International Financial Management and Accounting* 2, no. 2–3 (1990): 145–69.

comparative study of derivative usage among German and U.S. companies, minimizing the variability of reported earnings was rated most important among German companies. While U.S. companies tend to use financial derivatives to minimize the variability of cash flow, minimizing the variability of reported earnings was a close second.[25] In a related study, Swedish companies' use of derivatives to hedge the balance sheet (translation exposure) was as prevalent as their use of derivatives for committed and anticipated transactions. While the Swedes tended to hedge balance sheet exposure to a greater extent than their U.S. counterparts, 44 percent of the U.S. sample also did so.[26]

Accounting for Hedge Products

Contractual hedge products are financial contracts or instruments that enable users to minimize, eliminate, or otherwise transfer market risks to someone else's shoulders. They include, but are not limited to, forward contracts, futures, swaps, options, and combinations of these. While many of these derivative instruments have grown in complexity, user surveys document management's preference for the most basic or vanilla varieties.[27]

Knowledge of accounting measurement rules for derivatives is especially important when designing an effective hedge strategy for the firm. To understand the importance of hedge accounting, we illustrate some basic hedge accounting practices.

First, review the basic components of an income statement (absent taxes).

Operating revenues	XXX
− Operating expenses	XXX
= Operating income	XXX
+ Other income	XXX
− Other expense	XXX
= Net income	XXX

Analysts usually focus on operating income in evaluating how well management has operated its core business. Net income includes the confounding effects of extraordinary or nonrecurring events.

The accounting treatment for financial derivatives that is gaining acceptance internationally is to mark that product to market with any gains or losses recognized as a component of nonoperating income. In the United States at least, an exception is per-

---

[25]Reasons for the U.S. emphasis on reported earnings relate to analysts' perceptions and prediction of future earnings and management compensation. In Germany, reported earnings play an important role in taxation and dividend distribution. Gordon M. Bodner and Gunther Gebhardt, "Derivative Usage in Risk Management by US and German Non-Financial Firms: A Comparative Study," *Journal of International Financial Management and Accounting* 10, no. 3 (1999): 153–187.

[26]Per Alkeback and Niclas Hegelin, "Derivative Usage by Non-Financial Firms in Sweden with an International Comparison," *Journal of International Financial Management and Accounting* 10, no. 2 (1999): 105–120.

[27]Ed McCarthy, "Derivatives Revisited," *Journal o f Accountancy* (May 2000) Also available at www.aicpa.org/pubs/jofa/may 2000/mccarthy.htm

mitted in certain instances if the transaction meets appropriate hedge criteria, including the following:

1. The item being hedged exposes the firm to a market risk.
2. The firm describes its hedging strategy.
3. The firm designates the instrument to be employed as a hedge.
4. The firm documents its rationale as to why the hedge is likely to be effective.

If the appropriate criteria are met, the firm can use the gains or losses recognized on marking the hedge product to market to offset the gains or losses on the transaction that is being hedged (e.g., sales or purchases). To illustrate, assume that an Irish manufacturer of stout (a dark malt beverage) has a sales commitment to deliver X barrels to a buyer in Canada in 2 months. Fearing that the Canadian dollar will devalue before delivery, the Irish manufacturer buys a forward exchange contract that will allow it to sell Canadian dollars in 2 months' time at a price close to the current price. If the dollar devalues before delivery, the gain on the foreign exchange contract will offset the loss on the sales contract. If the hedging requirements listed above are met, operating income will meet its target. If the criteria are not met, the gain on the forward contract will appear as other income and operating income will come in below target.

Accounting issues associated with FX hedging products relate to recognition, measurement, and disclosure. Recognition centers on whether hedging instruments should be recognized as assets or liabilities in the body of financial statements. There is also the question of whether the hedge product should receive the same accounting treatment as the item being hedged.

Closely related to the recognition issue is the question of measurement. How, for example, should an FX instrument be valued? Should it take on the same measurement basis as the hedged instrument or transaction, or should it reflect an independent valuation? If an independent valuation, which valuation model historical cost, market value, lower of cost or market, net realizable value, or discounted present value is preferable? How should gains or losses related to the FX instrument be reflected in the income statement? Should they be reflected in income at all? Can and should risks associated with financial instruments be recognized and measured? This last question is especially important because risks attaching to many of the newer financial instruments, such as options and futures, are symmetric. Someone's gain is another's loss. Finally, to what extent should buyers and sellers of financial instruments detail the nature and amounts of financial instruments to which they are a party? What attributes of financial instruments should be disclosed in general-purpose financial statements? How much disclosure is necessary to sufficiently inform readers of the nature and magnitude of off-balance-sheet risks associated with corporate financial instruments? We now examine some basic FX risk management products. This is followed by a discussion of appropriate accounting treatments.

FX Forward Contracts

Importers and exporters generally use forward exchange contracts when goods invoiced in foreign currencies are purchased from or sold to foreign parties. The forward contract offsets the risk of transaction gains or losses as exchange rates fluctuate

Exhibit 11-11 Accounting Treatment of Forward Contracts

	Gains/Losses	Discount/Premium
Unsettled foreign currency transaction	Recognize in current income	Recognize in current income
Identifiable foreign currency commitment	Recognize in current income	Recognize in current income
Exposed net asset (liability) position		
a. Foreign currency is functional currency	Disclose in separate component of consolidated equity	Same treatment as related gains/losses, or current income
b. Parent currency is functional currency	Recognize in current income	Recognize in current income
Speculation	Recognize in current income[a]	N/A[b]

[a]Gains/losses in this category are a function of the difference between the forward rate available for the remaining period of the contract and the contracted forward rate (or the forward rate last used to measure a gain or loss on that contract for an earlier period).
[b]Not applicable.

between the transaction and settlement dates. Forward contracts also hedge antici-pated foreign currency payables or receivables (foreign currency commitments) and can be used to speculate in foreign currencies. These contracts are not traded on any organized exchange and are consequently less liquid than other contracts. On the other hand, they are flexible in contract amount and duration.

A forward exchange contract is an agreement to deliver or receive a specified amount of foreign currency in exchange for domestic currency, on a future date, at a fixed rate called the *forward rate*. Differences between the forward rate and the spot rate pre-vailing at the date of the forward contract give rise to a premium (forward rate > spot rate) or a discount (forward rate < spot rate). The premium or discount rate multiplied by the amount of the foreign currency to be received or delivered the *notional* amount of the contract produces a recognizable premium or discount on the forward contract. The forward contract will also give rise to transaction gains or losses whenever the exchange rate prevailing at the transaction date differs from those prevailing at interim financial statement or settlement dates.

The accounting issue here is whether premiums, discounts, gains, or losses on for-eign exchange contracts should receive similar or differing treatment for each use identified. Exhibit 11-11 summarizes how these accounting adjustments should be reported under FAS No. 52, now amended by FAS No. 133.

Financial Futures

A financial futures contract is similar in nature to a forward contract. Like a forward, it is a commitment to purchase or deliver a specified quantity of foreign currency at a future date at a set price. Alternatively, it may provide for cash settlement instead of delivery and can be cancelled before delivery by entering into an offsetting contract for the same financial instrument. In contrast to a forward contract, a futures agreement is a standardized contract, involves standardized provisions with respect to size and delivery date, is traded on an organized exchange,[28] is marked to market at the end of each day, and must meet periodic margin requirements. Losses on a futures contract give rise to a margin call; gains normally give rise to a cash payment.[29]

Corporate treasurers generally use futures contracts to shift the risk of price changes to someone else. They can also be used to speculate in anticipated price movements and to exploit short-term anomalies in the pricing of futures contracts.

How does a financial futures contract work? If Alpha Corporation borrows yen for 3 months and wants to protect itself against an appreciation of the yen before maturity, it could buy a futures contract to receive an equal amount of yen in 90 days. Appreciation of the yen causes a gain on the futures contract, offsetting the loss on the yen borrowing.

Currency Options

A currency option gives the buyer the right to buy (call) or sell (put) a currency from the seller (writer) at a specified (strike) price on or before a specified expiration (strike) date. A European-type option may be exercised only at the expiration date. An American-type option may be exercised any time up to and including the expiration date. The buyer of a call pays a premium for the option and benefits if the price of the underlying asset exceeds the strike price at maturity; the buyer of a put benefits if the price falls below the strike price at the expiration date.

To illustrate, suppose a U.S. contractor bids for a C$100 million construction project in Canada. The outcome of the bid will not be known for 3 months. Should the Canadian dollar lose value during that time, the contractor will suffer a loss if it wins the fixed price contract. The U.S. contractor therefore buys an option to receive the difference between the future US$/C$ spot rate in 90 days at a strike price of $0.70 per Canadian dollar. The contract details are as follows:

Contract Type	FX C$ Put/US$ Call Option
Maturity	90 days
Strike rate	$0.70/C$
Contract amount	$100 million
Option premium	$0.03

If, at maturity, the foreign exchange rate falls to $0.60, the contract holder gains 10 cents per C$ face value of the put contract. In this example, the change in value of the Canadian dollar yields an option payoff of $10,000,000 [($.60 − $0.70) × C$100 million]. The option premium, which can be viewed as the cost of insuring against a falling Canadian dollar, is $3 million ($0.03 × C$100 million). By buying the put option, the

---

[28]Examples include the International Monetary Market in Chicago and newer exchanges such as the New York Futures Exchange, the London International Financial Futures Exchange, the Singapore Money Exchange (SIMEX), the Sydney Futures Exchange, and the MATIF in Paris.
[29]Bruno Solnik, *International Investments,* op. cit., p. 228.

contractor makes a gain in the value of the option that offsets the potential currency loss (minus the option premium). If the value of the Canadian dollar is unchanged at the strike date, the contractor would simply let the option expire, treating the option premium as a cost of insurance.

Currency options can also be used to manage earnings. Assume an option trader believes the euro will gain in value in the near term. She would buy a *naked* call. Should the euro appreciate in value by the exercise date, the buyer would exercise the option and pocket the difference between the current and strike price, less the call premium. To limit downside risk, the buyer would obtain a *bull call spread*. This trading strategy involves buying a call and simultaneously selling an identical call with a higher strike price. The premium paid for the lower strike call will be partly offset by the amount received from the sale of the higher priced call. The maximum profit here is the difference between strike prices less the net premium. The net premium is, in effect, the maximum potential loss on the spread, ignoring transaction costs.

Straddles involve the sale of a call and a put with identical terms. Here the writer of the options bets that exchange rates will not change much during the life of the options. The writer gains revenue from premiums received for writing the options. It is a high-risk strategy, however. If exchange rates change enough to cause one or both of the options to be exercised, the writer's potential loss is unlimited.

Currency Swaps

A *currency swap* involves a current and future exchange of two different currencies at predetermined rates. Currency swaps enable companies to access an otherwise inaccessible capital market at a reasonable cost. It also allows a firm to hedge against exchange rate risks arising from international business. Suppose, for example, that Alpha Corporation (a U.S.-based multinational) wishes to raise $10,000,000 of fixed-rate debt in British pounds to fund a newly formed London affiliate. Alpha is relatively unknown to British investors. Similarly, Beta Company, Ltd., domiciled in the United Kingdom, would like to fund a New York subsidiary with a similar amount of dollar financing. It is relatively unknown in the United States. Under these circumstances, Gamma Bank may accommodate both companies by arranging a U.S. dollar/U.K pound currency swap. Assume the following: the swap exchange rate is $1.00 = £ .66 (both at inception and maturity); the swap term is 5 years; and the swap specifies interest rates of 10 percent in pounds and 8 percent in dollars. The following cash flow pattern would take place. At inception, Alpha Corporation exchanges $10,000,000 for £ 6,600,000 from Beta Company, Ltd. Assuming interest is paid annually, Alpha pays £ 660,000 to Beta each year and Beta pays $800,000 to Alpha. At the end of the 5-year term, each company would reexchange the principal amounts of $10,000,000 and £ 6,600,000.

As a result of this swap transaction, both Alpha Corporation and Beta Company, Ltd. have been able to access funds in a relatively inaccessible market. They have done so without incurring exchange rate risk. And, owing to their comparative advantage in borrowing in their home markets, they have achieved their foreign currency borrowings at a lower cost than they could otherwise obtain.

Accounting Treatments

The FASB issued FAS No. 133, clarified by FAS 149 in April 2003, to provide a single comprehensive approach to accounting for derivative and hedge transactions.[30] IFRS (formerly IAS) No. 39, recently revised, contains similar guidelines providing, for the first time, universal guidance on accounting for financial derivatives.[31] While these two pronouncements are similar in tenor, they differ in terms of the degree of detail in implementation guidance (see Chapter 8 on accounting harmonization).

Before these pronouncements, global accounting standards for derivative products were incomplete, inconsistent, and developed in piecemeal fashion. Most derivative instruments, being executory in nature, were treated as off-balance sheet items. An atmosphere of *caveat emptor* prevailed for statement readers attempting to gauge the volume and risks of derivative usage.

The basic provisions of these standards are:

- All derivative instruments are to be recorded on the balance sheet as assets and liabilities. They are to be recorded at fair value, including those that are embedded in host contracts that are themselves not carried at fair value.
- Gains and losses from changes in the fair value of derivative instruments are not assets or liabilities. They are automatically recognized in earnings if they are not designated as hedges. There are three types of hedging relationships to be recognized, measured, and disclosed: *fair value* (FV) hedges that include recognized foreign currency assets and liabilities and firm foreign currency commitments, hedges of a *net investment* in a foreign operation (NI), and *cash flow* (CF) hedges that include FX-denominated forecasted transactions.
- Hedges must be highly effective to qualify for special accounting treatment; that is, gains or losses on hedging instruments should exactly offset gains or losses on the item being hedged.
- Hedging relationships must be fully documented for the benefit of statement readers. For hedges of *recognized foreign currency assets or liabilities* and *unrecognized firm foreign currency commitments,* gains or losses stemming from changes in the fair value of a derivative instrument (and nonderivative financial instruments) are included immediately in earnings. Changes in the value of the foreign currency asset, liability, or firm commitment being hedged are also recognized in current income.
- Gains or losses on hedges of a *foreign currency net investment* (an exposed net asset or liability position) are initially reported in other comprehensive income. It is subsequently reclassified into current earnings when the subsidiary is sold or liquidated.

---

[30]FAS No. 133 supercedes FAS No. 80 and amends FAS No. 52. Financial Accounting Standards Board, "Accounting for Derivative Instruments and Hedging Activities," *Statement of Financial Accounting Standards 133,* Stamford, CT: FASB, October 1994. FAS No 149 amends and clarifies FAS 133, resulting in more consistent reporting of contracts as either derivatives or hybrid instruments. Financial Accounting Standards Board, "Amendment of Statement 133 on Derivative Instruments and Hedging Activities," *Statement of Financial Accounting Standards No. 149,* Stamford, CT: FASB, April 2003. Also see FASB's Web site at www.fasb.org.
[31]International Accounting Standards Committee, "Financial Instruments: Recognition and Measurement," *International Accounting Standard 39,* London: IASC, December 1998. Also see their Web site at http://iasc.org.

- Gains or losses on hedges of *uncertain future cash flows,* such as forecasted export sales, are initially recognized as an element of comprehensive income. Gains or losses are recognized in earnings when the forecasted transaction affects earnings.

Practice Issues

While authoritative guidelines issued by the FASB and IASB have done much to clarify the recognition and measurement of derivatives, issues remain. The first relates to the determination of fair value. Wallace estimates 64 possible calculations for measuring change in the fair values of the risk being hedged and of the hedging instrument.[32] He identifies four ways to measure changes in the fair value of the risks being hedged: fair market value, use of spot-to-spot exchange rates, use of forward-to-forward exchange rates, and use of an option pricing model. There are as many ways of calculating the change in value of the hedging instrument. Finally, these calculations can be done either before or after taxes.[33]

Financial reporting complexities also arise if hedges are not deemed "highly effective" in offsetting FX risk. However, the term *highly effective* is a subjective notion. In theory, highly effective means a perfect negative correlation between changes in the value or cash flow of a derivative and changes in the value or cash flow of the item being hedged. This implies a range of acceptable value changes for the derivative. The FASB recommends an 80–120% range. If these bounds are violated, the hedge is terminated and deferred gains or losses on the derivative are recognized in current earnings. This, in turn, reintroduces undesired volatility into a firm's reported earnings stream.

Actually, a highly effective hedge may not entirely eliminate the earnings effect of FX changes. To illustrate, assume that the dollar equivalent of a Japanese yen denominated receivable falls by $10,000,000. The forward contract used to offset this FX risk experiences a gain of $10,800,000. Since the gain on the forward falls within the bounds of 80–120%, the forward has been an effective hedge. However, the $800,000 excess gain would be recognized in current income.[34]

Next we next illustrate selected accounting treatments for forward contracts used as hedging instruments.

HEDGE OF A RECOGNIZED ASSET, LIABILITY, OR AN UNRECOGNIZED FIRM COMMITMENT

On September 1, a Canadian manufacturer sells, on account, goods to a Mexican importer for 1 million Mexican pesos (Mp). The Canadian dollar/peso exchange rate is C$0.14 = Mp1. The peso receivable is due in 90 days. The peso begins to depreciate

---

[32]Many of these permutations relate to derivatives in general and are unsuitable. They are even less in number for FX derivatives.
[33]Jeffrey B. Wallace, "FAS 133: Accounting for Derivative Instruments," in Frederick D.S. Choi, ed., *Handbook of International Finance and Accounting,* New York: John Wiley and Sons, 2003, pp. 19-1–19-24.
[34]There are several ways of testing for hedging effectiveness. Details of the dollar offset, variability reduction, and regression methods are described in Finnerty, John D., and Dwight Grant, "Testing Hedging Effectiveness Under SFAS 133," www.nysscpa.org/cpajournal/2003/0403/features/f044033.htm.

before the receivable is collected. By the end of the month, the Canadian dollar/peso exchange rate is C$0.13 = Mp1; on December 1 it is C$0.11 = Mp1. The Canadian exporter expects to receive C$140,000 for the Mp 1,000,000 owed if the spot rate remains unchanged through December 1. To avoid the risk of receiving less than C$140,000 should the peso lose value before December 1, the Canadian exporter acquires a forward contract on September 1 to deliver Mp1,000,000 for Canadian dollars on December 1 at a forward rate of C$.13 = Mp 1. In this example, pesos can be sold only at a discount, as the spot rate is greater than the forward rate. The total discount on the forward contract is C$10,000 [(C$.14 spot rate − C$.13 forward rate) × Mp1,000,000 notional amount] and is the price of reducing uncertainty. In effect, the Canadian exporter turns an uncertain receipt of C$140,000 to a certain receipt of C$130,000. At later financial statement dates before maturity, the forward contract amount (peso liability) is multiplied by the spot rate in effect on those dates. Changes in spot rates cause transaction gains or losses on the forward contract. Thus, if the exchange rate prevailing on December 1 is C$.11 = Mp1, the Canadian exporter realizes a gain of C$30,000 (C$.14 spot rate − C$.11 future spot rate = Mp1,000,000 liability). Had the forward contract not been purchased, the exporter would have received only C$110,000 upon conversion of the Mp1,000,000 account receivable. Thus, the forward contract offsets a transaction loss on the foreign currency receivable with a transaction gain on the foreign currency payable.

Exhibit 11-12 provides accounting entries for the forward exchange contract just described, assuming that financial statements are prepared on September 30 prior to settlement of the peso transaction. The exchange rate on September 30 is C$.13 = Mp1.

Assuming that the discount is treated as an element of operating expense, the net effect of the hedge transaction on operating income (ignoring any foreign exchange commissions) is determined as follows:

Dollar equivalent of receivable collected from Mexican importer	$110,000
Transaction gains on forward contract	30,000
Proceeds from sales commitment	140,000
−Discount on forward contract	(10,000)
Operating income	$130,000

Gains on the forward contract have effectively offset the devaluation of the peso. Expected gross margins and operating income are attained. The discount on the forward contract represents the cost of hedging FX risk.

A similar accounting treatment would prevail if our Canadian exporter were to make a sales agreement on September 1 to deliver goods and receive payment of Mp1,000,000 from the Mexican importer 3 months in the future rather than immediately delivering goods and waiting for payment. This type of executory contract is known as a *foreign currency commitment.*

Alternatively, the preceding illustration might have taken the form of a forecasted export sale. This expectation is not the result of a past transaction nor is it the result of a firm sales commitment. It represents an *uncertain future cash flow* (an anticipated transaction). Hence, the gains or losses on the forward contract to hedge the forecasted peso receipts would initially be recorded in equity as a part of comprehensive income.

Exhibit 11-12   Hedge of a Foreign Currency Transaction

Sept. 1	(C$) Contract receivable	C$130,000
	Deferred discount	10,000
	Mp Contract payable	140,000
	(To record agreement with foreign currency dealer to exchange Mp1,000,000 worth C $140,000 for C $130,000 in 3 months.)	
Sept. 30	Mp Contract payable	10,000
	Transaction (hedge) gain	10,000
	(To record transaction gain from reduced dollar equivalent of forward contract payable C $0.14–C $0.13 Mp1,000,000.)	
Sept. 30	Discount expense	3,333
	Deferred discount	3,333
	(Amortize deferred discount for 1 month.)	
Dec. 1	Mp Contract payable	20,000
	Transaction (hedge) gain	20,000
	(To record additional transaction gain by adjusting contract to new current rate C $0.13–C $0.11 × Mp1,000,000.)	
Dec. 1	Discount expense	6,667
	Deferred discount	6,667
	(Amortize deferred discount balance)	
Dec. 1	Mp Contract payable	110,000
	Mexican pesos	110,000
	(To record delivery of Mp 1,000,000 to foreign currency dealer; this Mp1,000,000 is obtained from collecting the amount owed by the Mexican importer.)	
Dec. 1	Cash	130,000
	(C$) Contract receivable	130,000
	(To record receipt of C $130,000 cash per forward contract.)	

These amounts would be reclassified into current earnings in the period in which the export sales are actually recognized.

HEDGE OF A NET INVESTMENT IN A FOREIGN OPERATION

As discussed in Chapter 6, whenever a foreign subsidiary with an exposed net asset position is consolidated with its parent, a translation loss results if the foreign currency loses value relative to the parent currency. A translation loss also occurs if the foreign subsidiary has an exposed net liability position and the foreign currency appreciates relative to the parent currency. One way to minimize such losses is to buy a forward contract. The strategy here is to have transaction gains realized on the forward contract offset translation losses.

Exhibit 11-13	Hedge of a Net Exposed Liability Position	
September 30	¥ Contract receivable	$1,148,175
	Deferred premium	8,775
	$ Contract payable	$1,156,950
	(To record contract with foreign currency dealer to exchange $1,021,950 for ¥ 135,000,000 in 90 days)	
December 31	¥ Contract receivable	18,225
	Transaction hedge gain	18,225
	(To record transaction gain from increased dollar equivalent of forward contract receivable; $.008640 − $.008505 × ¥ 135,000,000.)	
December 31	Premium expense	8,775
	Deferred premium	8,775
	(Amortization of deferred premium.)	
December 31	$ Contract payable	1,156,950
	Cash	1,156,950
	(To record purchase of ¥ 135,000,000.)	
December 31	Foreign currency	1,116,400
	¥ Contract receivable	1,116,400
	Cash	1,116,400
	Foreign currency	1,116,400
	(To record receipt of ¥ 135,000,000 from foreign currency dealer and its conversion.)	

To illustrate, suppose that a U.S. calendar-year foreign affiliate in Japan has a net exposed liability position of · 135,000,000 at September 30. Its functional currency is the dollar. To minimize any translation loss triggered by an unexpected appreciation of the yen, the U.S. parent buys a forward contract to receive · 135,000,000 yen in 90 days at the forward rate of $.008570. Exchange rates to the end of the year are as follows:

September 30 spot =	$.008505
September 30 90-day forward =	$.008570
December 31 spot =	$.008640

A transactions analysis of this hedge appears in Exhibit 11-13.

This example abstracts from tax effects. The expected translation loss of $18,225 (net exposed liabilities of [· 135,000,000 × ($.008640 − $.008505)] is offset by a transaction gain on the forward contract of $18,225 minus the premium expense of $2,025. If the foreign currency had been the functional currency, any exchange adjustment arising from consolidation would bypass income and appear in other comprehensive income. Under these circumstances, *transaction* gains and losses on forward hedges and related premiums/discounts would also be reflected in other comprehensive income.

SPECULATING IN FOREIGN CURRENCY

Opportunities exist for enhancing reported earnings using forward and option contracts in FX markets.[35] The forward contract in the previous example would not qualify for hedge accounting treatment had it been purchased solely to profit from an expected appreciation of the yen. Forward contracts bought as speculations are initially recorded at the forward rate. (The forward rate is the best indicator of the spot rate that will apply when the contract matures.) Transaction gains or losses recognized prior to settlement depend on the difference between the initial forward rate and the rate available for the remaining period of the contract.

Suppose that our speculator in yen (Exhibit 11-13) prepares monthly and year-end financial statements. All facts remain the same except that the 60-day forward rate for yen is $.008525 at the end of October. The Contract receivable would be initially recorded at the 90-day forward rate, or $1,156,950. At the end of October, the transaction gain on the forward contract would be $6,075 or · 135,000,000 × [$.008570 (90-day forward rate on September 30) − $.008525 (60-day forward rate on October 31)]. It is recognized in current income. As the foreign currency contract is recorded at the forward rate, no discounts or premiums are recognized.

Accounting treatments for the other foreign currency instruments discussed are similar to that for forward contracts. The accounting treatment prescribed is based on the nature of the hedging activity; that is whether the derivative hedges a firm commitment, a forecasted transaction, a net investment in a foreign operation, and so on.

A measurement complication arises in measuring the fair value and changes in fair values of hedging instruments when financial derivatives are not actively traded. For example, measurement of the gains or losses associated with an option contract depends on whether the option is traded on or off a major exchange. Valuation of an option is readily done when the option is quoted on a major exchange. Valuation is more difficult when the option is traded over-the-counter. Here, one must generally rely on mathematical pricing formulas. The so-called Black-Scholes options pricing model makes it possible to value an option at any time.[36]

DISCLOSURE

Prior to pronouncements such as FAS 133 and IAS 39, corporate financial disclosures did not tell statement readers whether, or the extent to which, management had employed derivative contracts. Assessing their potential impact on reported performance and a firm's risk complexion was difficult. Required disclosures under FAS 133 and IAS 39 remedy this to a large extent. They include the following:

- Risk management objective and strategy for undertaking hedge transactions.
- Description of the item being hedged.
- Identification of the hedged items market risk.

---

[35]Dilip K. Ghosh and Augustine C. Arize, "Profit Possibilities in Currency Markets: Arbitrage, Hedging and Speculation," *The Financial Review* 38 (2003): 473–496.

[36]Fischer Black and Myron Scholes, "The Pricing of Options and Corporate Liabilities," *Journal of Political Economy* (May/June 1973): 637–659. For recent refinements to the Black and Scholes option pricing formula, see Aswath Damodaran, *Investment Valuation*, New York: John Wiley & Sons, 1996.

- Description of the hedge instrument.
- Amounts that are excluded from the assessment of a hedge's effectiveness.
- A-priori justification that a hedging relationship will be highly effective in minimizing market risk.
- Ongoing assessment of the actual hedging effectives of all derivatives used during the period.

Selected excerpts from Coca-Cola's recent annual report illustrates corporate disclosure practices with respect to hedge instruments. The following is excerpted from Coca-Cola's Management Discussion and Analysis:

Financial Risk Management

Our company uses derivative financial instruments primarily to reduce our exposure to adverse fluctuations in interest rates and foreign exchange rates and, to a lesser extent, adverse fluctuations in commodity prices and other market risks. We do not enter into derivative financial instruments for trading purposes. As a matter of policy, all our derivative positions are used to reduce risk by hedging an underlying economic exposure. Because of the high correlation between the hedging instrument and the underlying exposure, fluctuations in the value of the instruments are generally offset by reciprocal changes in the value of the underlying exposure. Virtually all of our derivatives are straightforward, over-the-counter instruments with liquid markets.

Foreign Currency

We manage most of our foreign currency exposures on a consolidated basis, which allows us to net certain exposures and take advantage of any natural offsets. With approximately 77% of this year's Operating Income, excluding Corporate, generated outside the United States, weakness in one particular currency is often offset by strengths in others over time. We use derivative financial instruments to further reduce our net exposure to currency fluctuations.

Our company enters into forward exchange contracts and collars and purchases currency options (principally euro and Japanese yen) to hedge certain portions of forecasted cash flows denominated in foreign currencies. Additionally, the Company enters into forward exchange contracts to offset the earnings impact relating to exchange rate fluctuations on certain monetary assets and liabilities. The Company also enters into forward exchange contracts as hedges of net investments in international operations.

Value at Risk

Our Company monitors our exposure to financial market risks using several objective measurement systems, including value-at-risk models. Our value-at-risk calculations use a historical simulation model to estimate potential future losses in the fair value of our derivatives and other financial instruments that could occur as a result of adverse movements in foreign currency and interest rates. We have not considered the potential impact of favorable movements in foreign currency and interest rates on our calculations. We examined historical weekly returns over the previous 10 years to calculate our value at risk. The average value at risk represents the simple average of quarterly amounts over the past year. As a result of our foreign currency value-at-risk calculations, we estimate with 95 percent confidence that the fair values of our foreign currency derivatives and other financial instruments, over a one-week period, would decline by less than $34 million, $43 million and $37 million, respectively, using this year and the previous two years' average fair values and by less than $31 million and $37 million, respectively, using the current year-end and the previous year-end fair values. According to our interest rate value-at-risk calculations, we estimate with 95 percent confidence that any increase in our net interest expense due to an adverse move in our current year's average, or in our year-end interest rates over a one-week period, would not have a material impact on our financial statements. Year-end estimates for the prior two years also were not material to our financial statements.

The following are extracted from the notes to the financial statements.

Hedging Transactions and Derivative Financial Instruments

Our Company uses derivative financial instruments primarily to reduce our exposure to adverse fluctuations in interest rates and foreign exchange rates and, to a lesser extent, in commodity prices and other market risks. When entered into, the Company formally designates and documents the financial instrument as a hedge of a specific underlying exposure, as well as the risk management objectives and strategies for undertaking the hedge transactions. The Company formally assesses, both at the inception and at least quarterly thereafter, whether the financial instruments that are used in hedging transactions are effective at offsetting changes in either the fair value or cash flows of the related underlying exposure. Because of the high degree of effectiveness between the hedging instrument and the underlying exposure being hedged, fluctuations in the value of the derivative instruments are generally offset by changes in the fair value or cash flows of the underlying exposures being hedged. Any ineffective portion of a financial instrument's change in fair value is immediately recognized in earnings. Virtually all of our derivatives are straightforward over-the-counter instruments with liquid markets. Our Company does not enter into derivative financial instruments for trading purposes.

The fair values of derivatives used to modify our risks fluctuate over time. We do not view these fair value amounts in isolation, but rather in relation to the fair values or cash flows of the underlying hedged transactions or other exposures. The notional amounts of the derivative financial instruments do not necessarily represent amounts exchanged by the parties and, therefore, are not a direct measure of our exposure to the financial risks described above. The amounts exchanged are calculated by reference to the notional amounts and by other terms of the derivatives, such as interest rates, exchange rates or other financial indices.

As discussed in Note 1, the Company adopted SFAS No. 133, as amended by SFAS No. 137 and SFAS No. 138, on January 1, 2001. These statements require the Company to recognize all derivative instruments as either assets or liabilities in our balance sheets at fair value. The accounting for changes in the fair value of a derivative instrument depends on whether it has been designated and qualifies as part of a hedging relationship and, further, on the type of hedging relationship. At the inception of the hedge relationship, the Company must designate the derivative instrument as either a fair value hedge, a cash flow hedge or a hedge of a net investment in a foreign operation. This designation is based upon the exposure being hedged.

The adoption of SFAS No. 133 resulted in the Company recording transition adjustments to recognize its derivative instruments at fair value and to recognize the ineffective portion of the change in fair value of its derivatives. The cumulative effect of these transition adjustments was an after-tax reduction to Net Income of approximately $10 million and an after-tax net increase to AOCI of approximately $50 million. The reduction to Net Income was primarily related to the change in the time and fair value of foreign currency options and interest rate swap agreements, respectively. The increase in AOCI was primarily related to net gains on foreign currency cash flow hedges. Last year, the Company reclassified into earnings approximately $54 million of net gains relating to the transition adjustment recorded in AOCI at last year's start.

We have established strict counterparty credit guidelines and enter into transactions only with financial institutions of investment grade or better. We monitor counterparty exposures daily and review any downgrade in credit rating immediately. If a downgrade in a credit rating of a counterparty were to occur, we have provisions requiring collateral in the form of U.S. government securities for substantially all of our transactions. To mitigate presettlement risk, minimum credit standards become more stringent as the duration of the derivative financial instrument increases. To minimize the concentration of credit risk, we enter into derivative transactions with a portfolio of financial institutions. The Company has master netting agreements with most of the financial institutions that are counterparties to the derivative instruments. These agreements allow for the net settlement of assets and liabilities arising from different transactions with the same counterparty. Based on these factors, we consider the risk of counterparty default to be minimal.

Foreign Currency Management
The purpose of our foreign currency hedging activities is to reduce the risk that our eventual U.S. dollar net cash inflows resulting from sales outside the United States will be adversely affected by changes in exchange rates.

We enter into forward exchange contracts and collars and purchase currency options (principally euro and Japanese yen) to hedge certain portions of forecasted cash flows denominated in foreign currencies. The effective portion of the changes in fair value for these contracts, which have been designated as cash flow hedges, are reported in AOCI and reclassified into earnings in the same financial statement line item and in the same period or periods during which the hedged transaction affects earnings. Any ineffective portion (which was not significant this year or last) of the change in fair value of these instruments is immediately recognized in earnings. These contracts had maturities ranging from one to two years at the end of the current year which is also the period in which all amounts included in AOCI will be reclassified into earnings.

Additionally, the Company enters into forward exchange contracts that are not designated as hedging instruments under SFAS No. 133. These instruments are used to offset the earnings impact relating in the variability in exchange rates on certain monetary assets and liabilities denominated in nonfunctional currencies. Changes in the fair value of these instruments are recognized in earnings in the Other Income (Loss)—Net line item of our statements of income immediately to offset the effect of remeasurement of the monetary assets and liabilities.

The Company also enters into forward exchange contracts to hedge its net investment position in certain major currencies. Under SFAS No. 133, changes in the fair value of these instruments are recognized in foreign currency translation adjustment, a component of AOCI, to offset the change in the value of the net investment being hedged. For the end of this year and the year prior, approximately $26 million and $43 million, respectively, of losses relating to derivative financial instruments were recorded in foreign currency translation adjustment.

Prior to the start of last year, gains and losses on derivative financial instruments that were designated and effective as hedges of net investments in international operations were included in foreign currency translation adjustment, a component of AOCI.

At the end of this year and last, we recorded an increase (decrease) to AOCI of approximately $(151) million and $92 million, respectively, net of both income taxes and reclassifications to earnings, primarily related to net gains (losses) on foreign currency cash flow hedges, which will generally offset cash flow gains and losses relating to the underlying exposures being hedged in future periods. The Company estimates that it will reclassify into earnings during the next 12 months losses of approximately $8 million from the net amount recorded in AOCI at the end of this year as the anticipated foreign currency cash flows occur. At the end of last year, the Company recorded approximately $12 million in earnings, classified within Net Operating Revenues in our statements of income, primarily related to the change in the time value of foreign currency options. During 2001, the FSASB issued an interpretation to SFAS No. 133 allowing the entire change in fair value, including the time value, of certain purchased options to be recorded in AOCI until the related underlying exposure is recorded in earnings. The Company adopted this interpretation prospectively.

The Company did not discontinue any cash flow hedge relationships during each of the last two years.

The following table summarizes activity in AOCI related to derivatives designated as cash flow hedges held by the Company during the applicable periods (in millions):

Year ended 12/31,	Before-tax Amount	Income Tax	After-tax Amount
This year			
Accumulated derivative net gains as of January 1, 2002	$234	$(92)	$142
Net changes in fair value of derivatives	(129)	51	(78)
Net gains reclassified from AOCI into earnings	(120)	47	(73)
Accumulated derivative net losses as of December 31, this year	$(15)	$ 6	$ (9)

Year ended 12/31,	Before-tax Amount	Income Tax	After-tax Amount
Last year			
Cumulative effect of adopting SFAS No. 133, net	$ 83	$(33)	$ 50
Net changes in fair value of derivatives	311	(122)	189
Net gains reclassified from AOCI into earnings	(160)	63	(97)
Accumulated derivative net gains as of December 31, last year	$234	$(92)	$142

The following table presents the fair values, carrying values and maturities of the Company's foreign currency derivative instruments outstanding (in millions):

December 31	Carrying Values	Fair Values	Maturity
This year			
Forward contracts	$ 5	$ 5	2003
Options and collars	60	60	2003-04
	$65	$65	

December 31	Carrying Values	Fair Values	Maturity
Last year			
Forward contracts	$ 37	$ 37	2002
Currency swap agreements	10	10	2002
Options and collars	219	219	2002-03
	$266	$266	

The Company estimates the fair value of its foreign currency derivatives based on quoted market prices or pricing models using current market rates. This amount is primarily reflected in Prepaid Expenses and Other Assets within our balance sheets.

Prior to the start of last year, our Company also used foreign exchange contracts and purchased currency options for hedging purposes. Premiums paid and realized gains and losses, including those on any terminated contracts, were included in Prepaid Expenses and Other Assets.

Financial Control

Any financial risk management strategy must evaluate the effectiveness of hedging programs. Feedback from a thoughtful evaluation system helps to build institutional experience in risk management practices. Performance assessment of risk management programs also provides information on when existing strategies are no longer appropriate.

Financial Control Points

There are several areas where performance evaluation systems are fruitful. These include, but are not limited to, corporate treasury, purchasing, and foreign subsidiaries.[37] Control of corporate treasury includes assessing the performance of the total exchange risk management program. This assessment includes quantifying all exposures that were managed, identifying the hedges that were applied, and reporting on hedging results. Such an evaluation system also includes documentation of how and to what extent corporate treasury assisted other business units in the organization.

To illustrate, suppose the sales manager for the consumer markets division of Worldwide Company wishes to grant customer X a line of credit. Corporate treasury, which secures the needed funds, would quote the sales manager an internal transfer price. This price is based on current market rates for loans of comparable risk. Assume this rate is 8 percent. The sales manager can then quote customer X a borrowing rate of 8 percent plus a markup as compensation for assessing the client's credit risk. In the meantime, corporate treasury will enter the money markets and try to obtain a more favorable rate than it quoted the sales manager. The total return on this transaction includes the profit margin on the sale plus the financing spread. Management accountants need to set up a responsibility accounting system that credits the sales manager and corporate treasury for their fair share of the total profit on the sales transaction.[38]

Similar considerations apply to the purchasing function. Here, exchange risk management services are just one piece of the total risk management program. Controls are also necessary to monitor the performance of programs designed to hedge commodity price risk and mix.

In many organizations, foreign exchange risk management is centralized at corporate headquarters. This allows subsidiary managers to concentrate on their core business. However, when comparing actual to expected results, evaluation systems must have benchmarks against which to compare the success of corporate risk protection. (See Chapter 10 for more on multinational performance evaluation systems.)

APPROPRIATE BENCHMARKS

The object of risk management is to achieve an optimal balance between risk reduction and costs. Hence, appropriate standards against which to judge actual performance are necessary ingredients in any performance appraisal system. These benchmarks need to be specified in advance of any protection program and should be based on the concept of opportunity cost. In foreign exchange risk management, the following questions should be considered when selecting a benchmark.[39]

- Does the benchmark represent a policy that could have been followed?
- Can the benchmark be specified in advance?
- Does the benchmark provide a lower cost strategy than some other alternative?

---

[37]J.P. Morgan & Co., Arthur Andersen & Co., SC and Financial Engineering Limited, "The J.P. Morgan/Arthur Andersen Guide to Corporate Exposure Management," *Risk Management*, 1994.

[38]If, for example, corporate treasury tries to beat the 8 percent benchmark rate but instead pays 9 percent, the sales manager should not be charged for the reduced spread.

[39]Ian Cooper and Julian Franks, "Treasury Performance Measurement," *The Treasurer* (February 1988): 56.

When FX risk management programs are centralized, appropriate benchmarks against which to compare the success of corporate risk protection would be programs that local managers could have implemented. In other cases, firms that are averse to foreign exchange risk might automatically hedge any foreign exposure in the forward market or borrow local currency. These strategies would also be natural benchmarks against which to appraise financial risk management. The performance of a certain hedge product (e.g., a currency swap), or that of a risk manager, would be judged by comparing the economic return earned on the actively hedged transaction against the economic return that would have been earned had the benchmark treatment been used.

Reporting Systems

Financial risk reporting systems must be able to reconcile both internal reporting and external reporting systems. Risk management activities (typically managed by corporate treasury) have a future orientation. However, they must eventually reconcile with exposure measurements and financial accounts for external reporting purposes. These normally fall under the jurisdiction of the corporate controller's department. A team approach is most effective in formulating financial risk objectives, performance standards, and monitoring and reporting systems. Financial risk management is a prime example of where corporate finance and accounting are closely connected.

Selected References

Ahlgrim, Kevin C., "An Introduction to Derivatives and Risk Management," *Journal of Risk and Insurance* 50, No. 1 (March 2003): 177.

Alkeback, Per, and Niclas Hagelin, "Derivative Usage by Non-Financial Firms in Sweden with an International Comparison," *Journal of International Financial Management and Accounting* 10, no. 2 (1999): 105–120.

Allayannis, L., and Eli Ofek, "Exchange Rate Exposure, Hedging and the Use of Foreign Currency Derivatives," *Journal of International Money and Finance* 20 (2001): 273–296.

Barton, Jan, "Does the Use of Financial Derivatives Affect Earnings Management Decisions," *Accounting Review* 76, No. 1 (January 2001): 1–26.

Bodnar, Gordon, and Gunther Gebhardt, "Derivative Usage in Risk Management by U.S. and German Non-Financial Firms: A Comparative Study," *Journal of International Financial Management and Accounting* 10, no. 3 (1999): 153–187.

Buckley, Adrian, and Mattheus Vand Der Nat, "Derivatives for the Non-Executive Director,"

European Management Journal 21, No. 3 (June 2003): 388.

Chu, Ting-Heng, and Steve Swidler, "Forecasting Emerging Market Exchange Rates from Foreign Equity Options," *Journal of Financial Research,* No. 3 (2002): 353–366.

Damodaran, Aswath, "Valuation in Emerging Markets," in *International Finance and Accounting Handbook,* 3rd ed., Frederick D. S. Choi, ed., New York: John Wiley & Sons, 2003, pp. 9.1–9.38.

Dhanani, Alpa, "Foreign Exchange Risk Management: A Case in the Mining Industry," *British Accounting Review* 35, Issue 1 (March 2003): 35.

Dufey, Gunter, and Ian H. Giddy, "Management of Corporate Foreign Exchange Risk," in F. D. S. Choi, ed., *International Finance and Accounting Handbook,* New York: John Wiley & Sons, 2003, pp. 6.1–6.31.

Financial Accounting Standards Board, "Accounting for Derivative Instruments and Hedging Activities," *Statement of Financial Accounting Standards 133,* Norwalk, CT: FASB, October 1994.

Financial Accounting Standards Board, "Amendment of Statement 133 on Derivative Instruments and Hedging Activities," *Statement of Financial Accounting Standards No. 149,* Stamford, CT: FASB, April 2003.

Finnerty, John D., and Dwight Grant, "Testing Hedging Effectiveness Under SFAS 133," *CPA Journal,* April 2003. www.nysscpa.org/cpajournal/2003/0403/features/f044033.htm

Gautier, Antoine, Frieda Granot, and Maurice Levy, "Alternative Foreign Exchange Management Protocols: An Application of Sensitivity Analysis," *Journal of Multinational Financial Management* 12 (2002): 1–19.

Hagelin, Niclas, "Why Firms Hedge with Currency Derivatives: An Examination of the Transaction and Translation," *Applied Financial Economics* 13, No. 1 (January 2003): 55.

International Accounting Standards Committee, "Financial Instruments: Recognition and Measurement," *International Accounting Standard 39,* London: IASC, December 1998.

Keloharju, Matti, and Mervi Niskanen, "Why Do Firms Raise Foreign Currency Denominated Debt? Evidence from Finland," *European Financial Management* 7, No. 4 (2001): 481–496.

Logue, D. E., and G. S. Oldfield, "Managing Foreign Assets When Foreign Exchange Markets Are Efficient," *Financial Management* (Summer 1997): 16–22.

McCarthy, Ed, "Derivatives Revisited," *Journal of Accountancy* (May 2000). Also available at www.aicpa.org/pubs/jofa/may2000/mccarthy.htm

Miller, Kent D., and Jeffrey J. Reuer, "Firm Strategy and Economic Exposure to Foreign Exchange Rate Measurements," *Journal of International Business Studies* 29, no. 3 (Third Quarter 1998): 493–514.

Wallace, Jeffrey B., "FAS 133: Accounting for Derivative Instruments," in *Handbook of International Finance and Accounting,* 3rd ed., Frederick D.S. Choi, ed., New York: John Wiley & Sons, 2003, pp. 19-1–19-24.

Discussion Questions

1. What is market risk? Illustrate this risk with a foreign exchange example.

2. Active hedging of financial exposures is not generally accepted among financial managers around the world. Some argue that financial management alone cannot increase the value of the firm and that a firm is better off managing its core business risks while leaving itself exposed to some (if not all) financial risks. Do you agree?

3. Consider the statement: "Forecasting foreign exchange rates is futile. You can't outguess the market so you shouldn't try." Do you agree or disagree? What does your stance imply for management accountants?

4. All hedging relationships must be "highly effective" to qualify for special accounting treatment. What is meant by the term *highly effective* and why is its measurement important for financial managers?

5. Assume that you are employed by an investment bank that offers risk management services for corporate clients. In designing a hedge program for a client's exposure to market risk, why is a knowledge of accounting important?

6. Compare and contrast the terms *translation, transaction,* and *economic* exposure. Does FAS No. 52 resolve the issue of accounting versus economic exposure?

7. List 10 ways to reduce a firm's foreign exchange exposure for a foreign affiliate located in a devaluation-prone country. In each instance, identify the cost–benefit trade-offs that need to be measured.

8. What is the difference between a *basic* and a *derivative* financial instrument? What accounting issues are associated with the derivative?

9. Explain, in your own words, the difference between a multicurrency translation exposure report and a multicurrency transactions exposure report.

10. Exhibit 11-12 in this chapter illustrated how a currency swap enabled two companies to obtain foreign currency loans at a lower cost. Explain how a company might use a currency swap to hedge its foreign exchange risk on a foreign currency borrowing.

11. What is a financial futures contract? How does it differ from a forward exchange contract?

12. The notion of an "opportunity cost" was perhaps first introduced to you in your first course in microeconomics. Explain how this notion can be applied in evaluating the effectiveness of FX risk hedging programs.

Exercises

1. As one of your first assignments as a new hire on the corporate treasurer's staff of Global Enterprises, Ltd., you are asked to prepare an exchange rate forecast for the Mexican peso. Specifically, you are expected to forecast what the spot rate for the peso is likely to be at the end of 20X5. Selected information on which to base your forecast follows. Be sure to identify any additional bases underlying your forecast and any assumptions.

	20X0	20X1	20X2	20X3	20X4	20X5
Visible trade balance (US$bn)	7.1	6.5	0.6	−7.7	−5.4	
Current account balance (US$ bn)	−1.6	−1.9	−7.3	−15.8	−13.8	
Foreign direct investment (US$bn)	9.5	9.2	12.8	11.3	11.6	
Portfolio flows (US$bn)	−9.7	13.4	5.0	−0.6	9.6	
Foreign exchange reserves (US$bn)	15.25	19.18	28.14	31.46	30.99	
Real GDP growth (% change yoy)	−6.20	5.09	6.80	4.80	3.70	
Consumer prices (% changes yoy)	51.97	27.70	15.72	18.60	12.32	
Nominal GDP (US$bn)	266.0	335.0	412.0	415.0	479.0	
Nominal exchange rate to US$	6.42	7.60	7.92	9.15	9.55	?

2. Following is the consolidated balance sheet (000s omitted) of Stern Bank, a U.S. financial institution with wholly-owned corporate affiliates in London and Geneva. Cash and due from banks includes CHF 100,000 and a £ (40,000) bank overdraft. Loans consist entirely of Swiss franc receivables while consolidated deposits include CHF 40,000 and £ 15,000. Stern Bank adopts the local currency as the functional currency for its foreign affiliates and so translates all assets and liabilities (including owners' equity) using the current rate. The exchange rate prevailing as of the balance sheet date was (£/$/CHF = 1/2/4).

Required: Prepare a multicurrency exposure report for Stern Bank.

Stern Bank Consolidated Balance Sheet As of Year-End (000)

Cash and due from banks	$ 20,000	Deposits	$ 50,000
Loans	100,000		
Fixed assets	30,000	Owners' equity	100,000
Total	150,000		150,000

3. Refer to Exercise 2. Assume that the Swiss franc is forecast to devalue such that the new exchange relationship after the devaluation is (£ /$/CHF = 1/2/8).

   Required: Calculate the consolidated gain or loss that would result from this exchange rate movement.

4. Based on Stern Bank's exposure to exchange risk identified in Exercise 3, corporate management decides to shield reported earnings from FX losses by actively managing its exposure in Swiss francs.

   Required: Prepare a brief report containing suggested hedging strategies to do this, together with any trade-offs that need to be considered.

5. Trojan Corporation USA borrowed 1,000,000 New Zealand dollars (NZ$) at the beginning of the calendar year when the exchange rate was $.50 = NZ$1. Before repaying this 1-year loan, Trojan learns that the NZ dollar has appreciated to $.60 – NZ$1. It discovers, also, that its New Zealand subsidiary has an exposed net asset position of NZ$ 3,000,000, which will produce a translation gain upon consolidation. What is the amount of the exchange gain or loss that will be reported in consolidated income if:
   a. the U.S. dollar is the foreign operation's functional currency?
   b. the New Zealand dollar is the foreign operation's functional currency and Trojan Corp. designates the New Zealand dollar borrowing as a hedge of the New Zealand affiliate's positive exposure?

6. On April 1, Marissa Corporation, a calendar-year U.S. electronics manufacturer, invests 30 million yen in a 3-month yen-denominated CD with a fixed coupon of 8%. To hedge against the depreciation of the yen prior to maturity, Marissa designates its accounts payable due to the Sando Company as a hedge. Marissa purchased 32.5 million yen worth of computer chips on account paying 10 percent down, the balance to be paid in 3 months. Interest at 8 percent per annum is payable on the unpaid foreign currency balance. The U.S. dollar/Japanese yen exchange rate on April 1 was $1.00 = · 120; on July 1 it was $ 1.00 = · 110.

   Required: Prepare dated journal entries in U.S. dollars to record the incurrence and settlement of this foreign currency transaction assuming that the hedge is deemed highly effective in reducing Marissa's FX risk.

7. On June 1, ACL International, a U.S. confectionery products manufacturer, purchases on account bulk chocolate from a Swiss supplier for 166,667 Swiss francs (CHF) when the spot rate is $.60 = CHF 1. The Swiss franc payable is due on September 1. To minimize its exposure to an exchange loss should the franc

appreciate relative to the dollar prior to payment, ACL International acquires a forward contract to exchange $103,334 for francs on September 1 at a forward rate of $.62 = CHF 1.

Required: Given the following exchange rate information, provide journal entries to account for the forward exchange contract on June 1, June 30, and September 1. The company closes its books quarterly.

<table>
<tr><td>June 30 spot rate $.61 =</td><td>CHF 1</td></tr>
<tr><td>September 1 spot rate $.63 =</td><td>CHF 1</td></tr>
</table>

8. What is the effective dollar cost of the Swiss chocolate purchase in Exercise 7? Show your calculations.

9. Refer to the Exposure Management Cube shown in Exhibit 11-2. Provide examples of how the various market risks, foreign exchange, interest rate, commodity price, and equity might affect the value driver current assets.

10. On January 2, Delta Bank has outstanding a $10,000,000, 12 percent fixed-interest-rate loan it has funded with a 6 percent fixed-rate CHF deposit. To protect itself against an appreciation of the Swiss franc, it has arranged a currency swap for its own account with Epsilon Company. Under the swap arrangement, Delta Bank exchanges, for a period of 5 years, $10,000,000 at 10 percent for CHF 20,000,000 at 6 percent. As a result of this transaction, Delta Bank has hedged its currency risk and made money on the spread.

Required: Prepare a flow chart illustrating the pattern of periodic swap cash flows under this arrangement.

11. Provide dated journal entries to account for the transactions described in Exercise 10 for the month of January, assuming that Delta bank closes its books monthly. Assume that the dollar/franc exchange rate has not changed during the year.

12. In June, Mu Corporation, a U.S. manufacturer of specialty confectionery products, submits a bid to supply a prestigious retail merchandiser with boxed chocolates for the traditional Valentine's Day. If it secures the contract, it will sign a contract with a large Swiss chocolate manufacturer to buy the necessary raw material. The outcome of the bidding will not be known for 2 months and the treasurer of Mu Corporation is concerned that the franc may rise in value during the interim, thus reducing (or possibly even eliminating) its planned profit on the fixed-price bid.

To protect his company against an appreciation of the franc, the treasurer buys 25 CHF September 30 option calls at 1.80 (i.e., a premium of 1.8 cents per franc) on a standard contract amount of CHF 62,500. His prediction proves accurate as the franc rises in value to 41.6 cents by the end of August. Rather than await the outcome of the bid, Mu Corporation exercises its call options at the end of August.

Required: Provide the necessary journal entries to record the acquisition and exercise of the options.

CASE 11-1   VALUE AT RISK: WHAT ARE OUR OPTIONS?

The scene is a conference room on the 10th floor of an office building on Wall Street, occupied by InfoTech Enterprises, a small, rapidly growing manufacturer of electronic trading systems for equities, commodities, and currencies.

The agenda for the 8:00 A.M. meeting concerns reporting issues associated with a potential sales contract for the stock exchange in the Slovak Republic, which wants to upgrade its technology to effectively participate in the globalization of financial markets. In attendance are InfoTech's COO Grace Glessing, Controller George Tabback, Treasurer Paul Affuso, and Vice President of Marketing Mary Miller.

GRACE: Thank you for agreeing to meet on such short notice. Mary, are you ready to give us an update on Slovakia?

MARY: You mean the Slovak Republic.

GRACE: Yes.

MARY: I think there is a 90% percent chance we'll land the contract. Things move a little slowly over there and they're still concerned about some of the legal details of our sales contract. I think they find the legalese a bit intimidating and I can't say I blame them. I've scheduled another trip next month to go over contract details. This time I'm taking our legal counsel and have asked him to prepare another draft expressed in terms that are easier to understand. They're also waiting for approvals from their Central Bank, which has to approve major transactions such as this one.

GRACE: Good. Are we prepared to deliver on the contract?

MARY: Yes, we've lined up the financing, have done our credit checks, and the equipment and installation teams are ready to proceed on 2 week's notice.

GRACE: Given the size of the contract, are we hedged against the possibility of a devaluation?

PAUL: Yes, we've written a put option on the koruna for 90 days.

GRACE: Do we think we'll close on the deal before then?

PAUL: Mary doesn't think so, but you never know. The problem is no one will write an option for a longer term. We'll renew the option as we have other transactions of this extended duration.

GRACE: George, are we all right on the reporting front?

GEORGE: Not really.

GRACE: How's that?

GEORGE: It looks like we're up against a reporting standard that requires that gains or losses on cash flow hedges whose maturities do not match that of the underlying be recognized in current earnings.

GRACE: Come again?

GEORGE: The bottom line is that we won't be able to treat gains or losses on our put options as a part of comprehensive income, but

GRACE: we'll have to recognize them in current earnings.

GRACE: Won't that mess up our bottom line?

GEORGE: I'm afraid so. There would be no offsetting gain or loss from our anticipated sale.

PAUL: It's taken me a whole year to get to know the right people and win their trust and friendship. I now have that. There's no doubt in my mind that this sale is a done deal and I anticipate closing the transaction within the next 6 to 9 months.

GEORGE: That may be, but we just can't find anyone who's willing to write an option for more than 90 days at a time.

GRACE: I don't want to think about what the accounting will do to our stock price! I mean, we're about to float our first Euro-equity issue. A lower offering price would be disastrous at this stage of our development, not to mention the effect on our shareholders.

MARY: Given the nature of our business, I don't think the transactions side of our business will change much.

GRACE: Do you think it would be worthwhile having a consultant advise us on this one?

GEORGE, MARY, AND PAUL (IN UNISON): Why not?

REQUIRED

As a consultant for InfoTech, identify what you believe are promising hedge accounting options.

CASE 11-2   EXPOSURE IDENTIFICATION

You are currently working for a consulting firm that provides risk management products for clients. Your task is to provide your company's sales force with information on prospective clients. Assume that General Electric Corporation, whose financial statements and notes appear at www.general electric.com, is a prospective client.

REQUIRED

1. Using GE's 2003 financial statements and accompanying notes as a starting point, identify as many exposures as you can that impact the company. Be sure to cross-reference your findings with the specific page number of the financial statements you are referring to.

2. Identify any exposures that the company is currently hedging.

CHAPTER

12

INTERNATIONAL TAXATION AND TRANSFER PRICING

O
f all the environmental variables that financial managers must contend with, only foreign exchange is as influential as taxation. Tax considerations strongly influence decisions on where to invest, what form of business organization to employ, how to finance, when and where to recognize elements of revenues and expense, and what transfer prices to charge.[1]

With the possible exception of cost of goods sold, taxation is the largest expense of most businesses. It makes sense for management to minimize international taxes whenever possible, but in contrast to such direct operating costs as labor and materials, management has limited control over tax expense. National tax systems are diverse and complex. The members of the European Union reportedly levy more than 200 different rates on value-added tax alone.[2] Financial managers must also contend with special rules regarding the taxation of foreign source income. Finally, international tax agreements, laws, and regulations are constantly changing. Changes in one country's tax provisions have complex and wide-ranging effects in a multinational tax planning system, and computer-based simulation systems are essential aids to management.

Because it is not possible in a single chapter to provide a working knowledge of the major tax provisions in all the economically important countries of the world, we limit our discussion here to some of the major variables that financial managers need to consider in tax planning for multinational operations. These variables include major differences in national tax systems (i.e., how countries tax businesses operating in their jurisdictions), national attempts to address the issue of double taxation (i.e., how countries tax the foreign source income of their business entities), and arbitrage opportunities between national tax jurisdictions for multinational firms. Transfer pricing, in addition to its role in minimizing multinational corporate taxes, should be considered in the broader context of strategic planning and control.

---

[1] For a review of empirical research on the effects of international tax on business decisions, see J. F. Hines, Jr., "Lessons from Behavioral Responses to International Taxation," *National Tax Journal* (June 1999): 305–322.

[2] W. Echikson and D. Woodruff, "One Currency, One Tax? Don't Bet On It," *BusinessWeek* (July 21, 1997): 48E2.

INITIAL CONCEPTS

The maze of laws and regulations that govern the taxation of foreign corporations and profits earned abroad rests on a few basic concepts. These include notions of tax *neutrality* and tax *equity*. Tax neutrality means that taxes have no effect (are neutral) on resource allocation decisions. That is, business decisions are driven by economic fundamentals, such as rate of return, rather than tax considerations. Such decisions should result in an optimal allocation of resources: When taxes influence the allocation of resources, the result will probably be less than optimal. In reality, taxes are seldom neutral.

Tax equity means that taxpayers who are similarly situated should pay the same tax, but there is much disagreement over how to interpret this concept. For example, is a foreign subsidiary simply a domestic company that happens to operate abroad? If so, then foreign- and domestic-source income should be taxed at the same parent country rate. Or, is a foreign subsidiary a foreign company that happens to be owned by a domestic one? In this case, foreign-source income should be taxed the same as other companies in that country, that is, at the foreign country's tax rate. We shall find that actual international tax practices waver between these two extremes.

DIVERSITY OF NATIONAL TAX SYSTEMS

A firm can conduct international business by exporting goods and services or by making direct or indirect foreign investments. Exports seldom trigger a tax exposure in the importing country, because it is difficult for importing countries to enforce taxes levied on foreign exporters. On the other hand, a company that operates in another country through a branch or incorporated affiliate subjects itself to that country's taxes. The effective management of this tax exposure requires an understanding of national tax systems, which differ greatly among countries. Differences range from types of taxes and tax burdens to differences in tax assessment and collection philosophies.

Types of Taxes

A company operating abroad encounters a variety of taxes. *Direct taxes,* such as income taxes, are easy to recognize and normally are disclosed on companies' financial statements. Other *indirect taxes,* such as consumption taxes, are not so clearly recognized or as frequently disclosed. Typically they are buried in "other costs and expenses." Exhibit 12-1 illustrates the differential impact of direct and indirect taxes on pretax and after-tax income. In comparing investment performance between countries, the focus should be on after-tax returns.

Exhibit 12-1 Earnings Effects of Direct versus Indirect Taxes		
	Direct	Indirect
Revenues	250	250
Expenses	150	190
Pretax income	100	60
Direct taxes (40%)	40	-0-
After-tax income	60	60

The *corporate income tax* is probably more widely used to generate government revenue than any other major tax, with the possible exception of customs duties. Since the mid-1980s, however, the international trend has been to lower income tax rates. Fueling this trend is the recognition that reduced tax rates increase the global competitiveness of a country's business enterprises and create an attractive environment for international business. Indeed, the integration of the world economy and the increasing ability of businesses to move from high-tax environments to low-tax ones constrain a country's ability to set higher rates than elsewhere.[3] Exhibit 12-2 shows national income tax rates for selected countries.

Withholding taxes are those imposed by governments on dividend, interest, and royalty payments to foreign investors. For example, assume that a country has a 10 percent withholding tax on interest paid to foreign investors. Those investors would receive only 90 percent of the interest paid by the bonds. While legally imposed on the foreign recipient, these taxes are typically withheld at the source by the paying corporation, which remits the proceeds to tax collectors in the host country. Because withholding taxes may hinder the international flow of long-term investment capital, they are often modified by bilateral tax treaties.

The *value-added tax* is a consumption tax found in Europe and Canada. This tax is typically levied on the value added at each stage of production or distribution. This tax applies to total sales less purchases from any intermediate sales unit. Thus, if a Norwegian merchant buys 500,000 krone of merchandise from a Norwegian wholesaler and then sells it for 600,000 krone, the value added is 100,000 krone and a tax is assessed on this amount. Companies that pay the tax in their own costs can reclaim them later from the tax authorities. Consumers ultimately bear the cost of the value-added tax. Exhibit 12-3 (on page 460) shows how the value-added tax works.

Border taxes, such as customs or import duties, generally aim at keeping domestic goods price-competitive with imports. Accordingly, taxes assessed on imports typically parallel excise and other indirect taxes paid by domestic producers of similar goods.

The *transfer tax* is another indirect tax. This tax is imposed on the transfer of items between taxpayers and can have important effects on business decisions such as the structure of acquisitions. For example, business acquisitions in Europe are often made through the purchase of shares rather than the underlying net assets. More variations in structure are found in U.S. acquisitions because transfer taxes are less important in the United States.

Tax Burdens

Differences in overall tax burdens are important in international business. Various statutory rates of income taxation are an important source of these differences, as can be seen in Exhibit 12-2. However, differences in tax rates tell only part of the story. Many other considerations may significantly affect *effective tax burdens* for multinational enterprises. Differences in national definitions of taxable income are important.

Consider depreciation. In theory, a portion of the cost of an asset is said to expire as the asset is used up to produce revenue. In keeping with the matching principle, this

---

[3]"Disappearing Taxes: The Tap Runs Dry," *The Economist* (May 31, 1997): 21.

Exhibit 12-2   Corporate Income Tax Rates

Country	(%)	Country	(%)	Country	(%)
Argentina	35	Germany	39.58	Paraguay	30
Australia	30	Greece	25/35[e]	Peru	27
Austria	34	Guatemala	31	Philippines	32
Bangladesh	30	Honduras	25	Poland	27
Belgium	33.99	Hong Kong	17	Portugal	33[h]
Belize	25	Hungary	18	Romania	25
Bolivia	25	Iceland	18	Russia	24
Brazil	34[a]	India	36.75	Singapore	22
Canada	36.6[b]	Indonesia	30	Slovak Republic	25
Chile	16.5	Ireland	12.5	South Africa	37.8[i]
China	33	Israel	36	Spain	35
Colombia	35	Italy	38.25[f]	Sri Lanka	35
Costa Rica	36	Japan	42[g]	Sweden	28
Croatia	20	Korea, Republic of	29.7	Switzerland	24.1[j]
Cyprus	10/15[c]	Luxembourg	30.38	Taiwan	25
Czech Republic	31	Malaysia	28	Thailand	30
Denmark	30	Mexico	34	Turkey	33
Dominican Republic	25	Netherlands	34.5	Ukraine	30
Ecuador	36.25[d]	New Zealand	33	United Kingdom	30
El Salvador	25	Norway	28	United States	35/40[k]
Fiji	32	Pakistan	35	Uruguay	35
Finland	29	Panama	30	Venezuela	34
France	34.33	Papua New Guinea	30	Vietnam	25/32[l]

Note: A simple comparison of tax rates is not sufficient for assessing the relative tax burdens imposed by different governments. The method of computing the profits to which the tax rates will be applied (the tax base) should also be taken into account.

These rates do not reflect payroll taxes, social security taxes, net wealth taxes, turnover taxes, and other taxes not levied on income.

[a]The sum of income tax (25%) and social contribution tax on profits (9%).

[b]Includes provincial income taxes. Depending on the province, the effective overall rate ranges from 33.0% to 41.1%.

[c]Basic rate is 10%. Income above CY£1 million is taxed at 15%.

[d]The sum of corporate income tax rate (21.25%) and employees' profit-sharing tax (15%)

[e]Various rates based on type of company.

[f]The sum of corporate income tax rate (34%) and regional tax (4.25%).

[g]Includes corporate income tax (30%) and business, prefectural, and municipal taxes.

[h]Includes municipal tax of 3%.

[i]Includes corporate income tax rate (30%) and effect of tax on dividends declared.

[j]Includes federal, cantonal, and municipal taxes.

[k]Federal tax rate is 35%. State and local income tax rates range from less than 1% to 12%. State and local income taxes are deductible in determining federal income taxes, making the average effective tax rate 40%.

[l]Various rates based on type of company.

Source: Adapted from KPMG Corporate Tax Rate Survey—January 2003. www.kpmg.com/microsite/global_tax/ctr_survey/2003CorporateTaxSurveyFINAL.pdf. © KPMG International, a Swiss nonoperating association. Used by permission

Exhibit 12-3   Value-Added Tax

	Producer	Wholesaler	Merchant	Consumer
Cost	Assume 0	€12.00	€15.60	€21.60
Recoverable VAT	–	2.00	2.60	
Net cost	0	€10.00	€13.00	
Sales price before VAT	€10.00	13.00	18.00	
Value added	€10.00	€ 3.00	€ 5.00	
Value-added tax (20%)	2.00	0.60	1.00	
Sales price after VAT	€12.00	€15.60	€21.60	
VAT paid	€ 2.00	€ 2.60	€ 3.60	
Recoverable VAT	0	2.00	2.60	
VAT due	€ 2.00	€ 0.60	€ 1.00	
VAT borne				€ 3.60

expired cost is recognized as an expense and deducted from its related revenue. Where the asset is consumed equally in each reporting period, an equal portion of its cost is commonly expensed each period for external financial reporting purposes. In the United States, however, a distinction is generally made between depreciation for external reporting and depreciation for tax purposes. As an incentive to invest in capital assets, including commercial buildings, companies in the United States are allowed to use accelerated depreciation methods. In Germany, tax law specifies depreciation rates, and buildings are depreciated in straight-line fashion. In Latin American countries where inflation rates have been high (such as Mexico and Uruguay), firms are required to adjust their assets for changing price levels, and the higher depreciation charges are deductible for tax purposes (see Chapter 7). Finally, in Japan, companies can take excess depreciation (depreciation beyond that normally taken on depreciable assets) on assets that are deemed important to the national interest. Examples are pollution control equipment and assets devoted to creating alternative energy sources.

Another item that accounts for intercountry differences in effective tax burdens relates to a host country's social overhead. To attract foreign investments, less industrialized countries often assess lower corporate income tax rates than their more industrialized counterparts. However, countries with low direct taxes need to fund government and other social services just as any other country. Therefore, lower direct corporate tax rates usually result in higher indirect taxes or in fewer and lower-quality public services. Indirect taxes reduce purchasing power in the local market. Fewer and lower-quality public services may impose a higher cost structure on multinational operations. Examples include poor transportation networks, inadequate postal services, ineffective telephone and telecommunications systems, and power shortages.

While more and more governments are reducing marginal corporate tax rates, many also are broadening corporate tax bases. In the real world, effective tax rates seldom equal nominal tax rates. Thus, it is improper to base intercountry comparisons on statutory tax rates alone. Furthermore, a low tax rate does not necessarily mean a low tax burden. Internationally, tax burdens should always be determined by examining *effective* tax rates.

Tax Administration Systems

National tax assessment systems also affect relative tax burdens. Several major systems are currently in use. For simplicity, we will only consider the *classical* and *integrated* systems.

Under the *classical system,* corporate income taxes on taxable income are levied at the corporate level and at the shareholder level. Shareholders are taxed either when the corporate income is paid as a dividend or when they liquidate their investment. When a corporation is taxed on income measured before dividends are paid, and shareholders are then taxed on their dividends, the shareholders' dividend income is effectively taxed twice. To illustrate, assume that a parent corporation in Zonolia (fictitious), subject to a 33 percent corporate income tax, earns 100 zonos (Z) and distributes a 100 percent dividend to its sole shareholder, who is in the 30 percent tax bracket. Effective taxes paid on the corporate income is determined as follows:

Corporate income	Z 100.00
−Income tax at 33%	33.00
= Net income (and dividend paid)	Z 67.00
Dividend	Z 67.00
−Personal income tax at 30%	20.10
= Net amount to shareholder	Z 46.90

Total tax paid on the Z 100 of corporate income:

Corporate tax	Z 33.00
Individual income tax	20.10
Total	Z 53.10

Countries associated with this system include Belgium, Luxembourg, the Netherlands, and Sweden. The recent trend in most developed countries has been to move away from the double taxation of dividend income by adopting either an integrated or an imputation system.

Under an *integrated* system, corporate and shareholder taxes are integrated so as to reduce or eliminate the double taxation of corporate income. The *tax credit* or *imputation* system is a common variant of the integrated tax system. In this system, a tax is levied on corporate income, but part of the tax paid can be treated as a credit against personal income taxes when dividends are distributed to shareholders. This tax system is advocated by the European Union and is found in Australia, Canada, Mexico, and many European countries, including France, Italy, and the United Kingdom.

To see how this tax system works, assume facts similar to that of our Zonolian parent company in the preceding illustration. Further assume that shareholders receive a tax credit equal to 25 percent of dividends received. Based on these assumptions, the total taxes paid is determined as follows:

Corporate income	Z100.00
−Income tax at 33%	33.00
= Net income and dividend paid	Z 67.00
Dividend income to shareholder	Z 67.00
+ Tax credit at 25%	16.75
= Grossed-up dividend	Z 83.75
Income tax liability at 30%	Z 25.12
− Tax credit	16.75
= Tax due from shareholder	Z 8.37

Total tax paid on the Z100 of corporate income:

Corporate tax	Z 33.00
Individual income tax	8.37
Total	Z 41.37

This example illustrates a *partial* imputation system in which double taxation is reduced but not eliminated. *Full* imputation eliminates double taxation.

The *split-rate* system is another variant of the integrated tax system, where a lower tax is levied on distributed earnings (i.e., dividends) than on retained earnings. Germany once had a split-rate system. Other ways to reduce double taxation are to exempt a percentage of dividends from personal taxation, as Germany does now, or to tax dividends at a lower rate than the personal rate, as the United States recently enacted.

Foreign Tax Incentives

Countries eager to accelerate their economic development are keenly aware of the benefits of international business. Many countries offer tax incentives to attract foreign investment. Incentives may include tax-free cash grants applied toward the cost of fixed assets of new industrial undertakings or relief from paying taxes for certain time periods (*tax holidays*). Other forms of temporary tax relief include reduced income tax rates, tax deferrals, and reduction or elimination of various indirect taxes. More industrialized countries offer targeted incentives such as Ireland's reduced corporate tax rate for manufacturing operations (10 percent) through the year 2010.[4] Some countries, particularly those with few natural resources, offer permanent tax inducements. These so-called *tax havens* include

1. the Bahamas, Bermuda, and the Cayman Islands, which have no taxes at all
2. Barbados, which has very low tax rates
3. Gibralter, Hong Kong, and Panama, which tax locally generated income but exempt income from foreign sources

Countries that allow special privileges are suitable as tax havens for very limited purposes.

---

[4]The Irish corporate tax rate is 12.5 percent. The 10 percent preferential tax rate for manufacturing companies will be eliminated after 2010.

Harmful Tax Competition

The Organization for Economic Cooperation and Development (OECD) is trying to halt tax competition by certain tax haven countries. The worldwide trend toward lowering corporate income tax rates is a direct result of tax competition. So, is tax competition harmful? Certainly it is beneficial if it makes governments more efficient. On the other hand, it is harmful when it shifts tax revenues away from governments that need those revenues to provide services on which businesses rely. The OECD is mainly concerned about tax havens that allow businesses to avoid or evade another country's taxes. So-called *brass plate* subsidiaries have no real work or employment attached to them: They lack *substantial activities* and merely funnel financial transactions through the tax haven country to avoid another country's taxes. The OECD especially suspects tax havens that are unwilling to share information with tax authorities elsewhere and that apply or enforce tax laws unevenly or in secret. These tax havens are being pressured to adopt practices on the effective exchange of information and transparency.[5]

International Harmonization

Given the diversity of tax systems around the world, the global harmonization of tax policies would seem to be worthwhile. The European Union is spending much energy in this direction as it works to create a single market. The EU's introduction of a single currency, the euro, highlights the tax disparities among its members. Multinational companies, burdened by disparities of national taxes, also are fueling the pressure for international tax reform.[6]

TAXATION OF FOREIGN SOURCE INCOME AND DOUBLE TAXATION

Every nation claims the right to tax income originating within its borders. However, national philosophies regarding the taxation of foreign source earnings differ, and this is important from a tax planning perspective. A few countries, such as France, Costa Rica, Hong Kong, Panama, South Africa, Switzerland, and Venezuela adopt the *territorial* principle of taxation and exempt from taxation the income of resident corporations generated outside their borders. This reflects the idea that tax burdens of foreign affiliates should equal those of their local competitors. In this view, foreign affiliates of local companies are viewed as foreign companies that happen to be owned by local residents.

Most countries (e.g., Australia, Brazil, China, the Czech Republic, Germany, Japan, Mexico, the Netherlands, the United Kingdom, and the United States) adopt the *worldwide* principle and tax resident corporations and citizens on income regardless of national boundaries. The underlying idea here is that a foreign subsidiary of a local company is simply a local company that happens to operate abroad.

---

[5]The OECD refers to these as *uncooperative* tax havens. See J. M. Weiner and H. J. Ault, "The OECD's Report on Harmful Tax Competition," *National Tax Journal* (Spring 1998): 601–608; F. M. Horner, "The OECD, Tax Competition, and the Future of Tax Reform," OECD Web site: www.oecd.com (January 2000); "The Mystery of the Vanishing Taxpayer: A Survey of Globalisation and Tax," *The Economist* (January 29, 2000): 16–17; and "The OECD's Project on Harmful Tax Practices: The 2001 Progress Report," OECD Web site (www.oecd.org), November 2001.
[6]W. Echikson and D. Woodruff, "One Currency, One Tax?" *BusinessWeek* (July 21, 1997): p.48.

Foreign Tax Credit

Under the worldwide principle of taxation, the foreign earnings of a domestic company are subject to the full tax levies of both its host and home countries. To avoid discouraging businesses from expanding abroad, and in keeping with the concept of foreign neutrality, a parent company's domicile (country of residence) can elect to treat foreign taxes paid as a *credit* against the parent's domestic tax liability or as a *deduction* from taxable income. Companies generally choose the credit, as it yields a one-for-one reduction of domestic taxes payable (limited to the amount of income taxes actually paid),[7] whereas a deduction is only worth the product of the foreign tax expense multiplied by the domestic marginal tax rate.

Foreign tax credits may be calculated as a straightforward credit against income taxes paid on branch or subsidiary earnings and any taxes withheld at the source, such as dividends, interest, and royalties remitted to a domestic investor. The tax credit can also be estimated when the amount of foreign income tax paid is not clearly evident (e.g., when a foreign subsidiary remits a fraction of its foreign source earnings to its domestic parent). Here, reported dividends on the parent company's tax return would be grossed up to include the amount of the tax (deemed paid) plus any applicable foreign withholding taxes. It is as if the domestic parent received a dividend including the tax due the foreign government and then paid the tax.

The allowable foreign indirect tax credit (foreign income tax deemed paid) is determined as follows:

$$\frac{\text{Dividend payout (including any withholding tax)}}{\text{Earnings net of foreign income tax}} \times \text{Creditable foreign taxes}$$

To illustrate how foreign tax credits apply in a variety of situations, assume that a U.S. parent company receives royalties from Country A, foreign branch earnings from Country B, and dividends from subsidiaries in Countries C and D. Withholding taxes on royalty and dividend payments are assumed to be 15 percent in Countries A, C, and D; income tax rates are assumed to be 30 percent in Country B and 40 percent in Country C. Country D assesses a 40 percent indirect sales tax as opposed to a direct tax on earnings within its jurisdiction.[8]

The key variables in this illustration, as shown in Exhibit 12-4, are the organizational form of the foreign activity (e.g., branch vs. subsidiary) and relative corporate income and withholding tax rates. In the first column, the royalty payment of $20.00 is subject to a 15 percent withholding tax in the host country. For U.S. tax purposes, the net royalty is grossed up to include the withholding tax, which then forms the base for the U.S. domestic tax of 35 percent. The U.S. tax of $7.00 is offset by the credit for the foreign tax paid to yield a net U.S. tax liability of $4.00.

In the second column of Exhibit 12-4, the foreign branch earnings of the U.S. parent are grossed up to include foreign income taxes paid of $30.00. United States taxes

---

[7]Indirect levies, such as foreign sales taxes, are generally not creditable.
[8]Note that royalty income and branch/subsidiary earnings are *grossed up,* that is, included in U.S. income, before deducting foreign taxes paid.

Exhibit 12-4   U.S. Taxation of Foreign Source Income

	Royalties from Operation in Country A	Earnings from Branch in Country B	Dividend from Subsidiary in Country C[a]	Dividend from Subsidiary in Country D
Branch/Subsidiary earnings before income taxes		100.00	100.00	60.00
Foreign income taxes (30%/40%)		30.00	40.00	-0-
After-tax earnings		70.00	60.00	60.00
Dividend paid (50% of after-tax earnings)			30.00	30.00
Other foreign income	20.00			
Foreign withholding taxes (15%)	3.00		4.50	4.50
Net payment to parent	17.00		25.50	25.50
U.S. income	20.00	100.00[b]	30.00	30.00
Dividend gross-up (30/60 × 40)			20.00	-0-
Taxable income	20.00	100.00	50.00	30.00
U.S. tax (35%)	7.00	35.00	17.50	10.50
Foreign tax credit				
Paid	(3.00)	(30.00)	(4.50)	(4.50)
Deemed paid (30/60 × 40)			(20.00)	-0-
Total	(3.00)	(30.00)	(24.50)	(4.50)
U.S. tax (net)	4.00	5.00	(7.00)[c]	6.00
Foreign taxes	3.00	30.00	24.50	40.00[d]
Total taxes of U.S. taxpayer	7.00	35.00	17.50[e]	46.00

[a]Affiliate owned 10 percent or more.
[b]Grossed up to include foreign taxes actually paid.
[c]Excess foreign tax credits can be carried back 2 years or carried forward 5 years to offset U.S. tax on other foreign source (not U.S. source) income. If unavailable, total taxes = 24.50.
[d]40% indirect sales tax on 100.00.
[e]Excludes deferred tax on undistributed earnings of affiliate.

payable on this amount of $35.00 are offset by a foreign tax credit of $30.00, to yield a net U.S. tax payable of $5.00. As with the royalty payment, the effect of the foreign tax credit is to limit the total tax on foreign source income to the higher of the two countries' taxes. In this example, the U.S. tax rate of 35 percent was higher than the foreign tax rate of 30 percent, yielding a total tax on royalty and branch earnings of 35 percent.

Further scrutiny of Exhibit 12-4 is instructive. A comparison of columns 2 and 3 suggests the importance of organizational form on international taxes. A branch operation, viewed as an extension of the parent company, is subject to the full tax rate of the home country. In our example, the foreign branch pays a total tax of $35: $30 of foreign income taxes and $5 of U.S. taxes. Thus, the foreign branch bears the full burden of the U.S. income tax rate. However, it is spared any withholding taxes on earnings distributions to the parent because only a foreign subsidiary can distribute its earnings. On the other hand, a foreign operation organized as a subsidiary is taxed only on earnings that it remits to the parent company. It can defer taxes on retained income, and thus compete on an equal tax footing with local companies.

Columns 3 and 4 illustrate how a system of worldwide taxation places a subsidiary at a competitive disadvantage when it is located in a country that relies primarily on an indirect tax for revenue. Note that the subsidiary in Country D has a higher total tax burden because the tax credit only relieves direct taxes, not indirect taxes. Similarly, the benefits of tax incentives granted by host governments may also be nullified.

Limits to Tax Credits

Home countries can tax foreign source income in many ways. A country may elect to tax income from each separate national source. At the other extreme, all foreign source income from any foreign source may be combined and taxed once.[9] Some countries tax foreign source income on a source-by-source basis with the tax credit for foreign source income limited to the corresponding domestic tax applicable to that income. As illustrated in Columns 2 and 3 in Exhibit 12-4, the maximum tax liability will always be the higher of the tax rates in the host or home country. Other countries allow parent companies to pool income from many country sources by income type (e.g., dividends vs. interest vs. royalties). Excess tax credits from countries with high tax rates (Column 3 in Exhibit 12-4) can offset taxes on income received from low tax rate countries (Column 2 in Exhibit 12-4).

To prevent foreign tax credits from offsetting taxes on domestic-source income, many countries impose an overall limit on the amount of foreign taxes creditable in any year. The United States, for instance, limits the tax credit to the proportion of the U.S. tax that equals the ratio of the taxpayer's foreign-source taxable income to its worldwide taxable income for the year. Assume that Alpha Company earned $2,000 of foreign-source and $3,000 of U.S.-source taxable income. Its foreign tax credit would be the lesser of the foreign income taxes paid or the foreign tax credit limitation computed as follows:

$$\text{Foreign tax credit limit} = \frac{\text{Foreign source taxable income}}{\text{Worldwide taxable income}} \times \text{U. S. tax before credits}$$

$$= (\$2{,}000/\$5{,}000) \times (\$5{,}000 \times 35\%)$$

$$= \$700$$

Thus, only $700 would be allowed as a tax credit, even if foreign taxes paid exceeded $700. Excess foreign taxes paid can be carried back 2 years and forward 5 years (see footnote c in Exhibit 12-4).

A separate foreign tax credit limitation applies to U.S. taxes on the foreign-source taxable income of each of the following types of income (or *baskets*):

- Passive income (e.g., investment-type income)
- Financial services income
- High withholding tax income
- Shipping income
- Dividends from each 10 to 50 percent-owned foreign corporation

---

[9]David Eiteman, Arthur Stonehill, and Michael Moffett, *Multinational Business Finance,* 7th ed., Reading, Mass.: Addison-Wesley, 1995, 582.

Foreign-source taxable income is foreign-source gross income less expenses, losses, and deductions allocable to the foreign-source income, plus a ratable share of expenses, losses, and deductions that cannot be allocated definitely to any item or class of gross income. The interpretation of this provision is reportedly one of the major areas of dispute between taxpayers and the IRS.[10]

Tax Treaties

Although foreign tax credits shield foreign-source income from double taxation (to some extent), tax treaties go further. Signatories to such treaties generally agree on how taxes and tax incentives will be imposed, honored, shared, or otherwise eliminated on business income earned in one taxing jurisdiction by citizens of another. Thus, most tax treaties between home and host countries provide that profits earned by a domestic enterprise in the host country shall be subject to its taxes only if the enterprise maintains a permanent establishment there. Tax treaties also affect withholding taxes on dividends, interest, and royalties paid by the enterprise of one country to foreign shareholders. They usually grant reciprocal reductions in withholding taxes on dividends and often entirely exempt royalties and interest from withholding.

Foreign Exchange Considerations

The Tax Reform Act of 1986 introduced formal rules regarding the taxation of foreign currency gains or losses in the United States. In keeping with SFAS No. 52 (described in Chapter 6), all tax determinations must be made in the taxpayer's functional currency. The functional currency is assumed to be the U.S. dollar unless the foreign operation is an autonomous unit, or *qualified business unit.* In general, tax rules are similar but not necessarily identical to generally accepted accounting principles described in Chapter 6. Following are examples of tax treatments.[11]

Transaction gains or losses in currencies other than the functional currency are generally accounted for under the two-transactions perspective. Under this approach, any exchange gain or loss recognized when the foreign currency transaction is settled is treated as ordinary income and accounted for separately from the underlying transaction. However, gains or losses on transactions qualifying as hedges of certain foreign currency transactions can be integrated with the underlying transaction. For example, a gain or loss incurred on a forward exchange contract designated as an effective hedge of a foreign currency loan would offset the transaction gain or loss on the underlying obligation.

Foreign exchange gains or losses are generally allocated between U.S. and foreign sources by reference to the residence of the taxpayer on whose books the foreign currency asset or liability is reflected. Thus, for a U.S. corporation, the source of the gain or loss would be the United States.

Taxable profits for foreign branches are initially based on their functional currencies. The functional currency then is converted to U.S. dollars using the weighted aver-

---

[10]P. Bodner, "International Taxation," in *International Finance and Accounting Handbook,* 3rd ed., F. D. S. Choi, ed., New York: John Wiley & Sons, 2003, p. 30.11.

[11]P. Bodner, "International Taxation," in *International Finance and Accounting Handbook,* 3rd ed., F. D. S. Choi, ed., New York: John Wiley & Sons, 2003, pp. 30.16–30.18.

age exchange rate for the taxable period. Foreign income taxes paid are translated at the exchange rate in effect when the tax is paid and then added to foreign taxable income or grossed up. The foreign taxes paid are then claimed as a foreign tax credit for U.S. tax purposes.

For foreign subsidiaries, deemed distributions under subpart F regulations (discussed in the next section) are translated using weighted average exchange rates for the foreign corporation's taxable year. Deemed-paid foreign taxes are translated into U.S. dollars using exchange rates in effect on the date the tax was paid.

TAX PLANNING DIMENSIONS

In tax planning, multinational companies have a distinct advantage over purely domestic companies because they have more geographical flexibility in locating their production and distribution systems. This flexibility provides unique opportunities to exploit differences among national tax jurisdictions so as to lower the overall tax burden for the corporation. The shifting of revenues and expenses through intracompany ties also gives MNCs additional opportunities to minimize global taxes paid. In response, national governments are constantly designing legislation to minimize arbitrage opportunities involving different national tax jurisdictions.

We begin our examination of tax planning issues with two caveats:

- Tax considerations should never control business strategy.
- Constant changes in tax laws limit the benefits of long-term tax planning.

Organizational Considerations

In taxing foreign-source income, many taxing jurisdictions focus on the organizational form of a foreign operation. A branch is usually considered an extension of the parent company. Accordingly, its income is immediately consolidated with that of the parent (an option not available to a subsidiary) and fully taxed in the year earned whether remitted to the parent company or not. Earnings of a foreign subsidiary are not generally taxed until repatriated. Exceptions to this general rule are described in the following text.

If initial operations abroad are forecast to generate losses, it may be tax advantageous to organize initially as a branch. Once foreign operations turn profitable, operating them as subsidiaries may be attractive. For one thing, corporate overhead of the parent company cannot be allocated to a branch, as the branch is viewed as part of the parent. Moreover, if taxes on foreign profits are lower in the host country than in the parent country, profits of a subsidiary are not taxed by the parent country until repatriated (see Columns 2 and 3 in Exhibit 12-4). If the subsidiary were organized in a tax haven country that imposes no taxes at all, tax deferral would be even more attractive. National governments know this phenomenon and many have taken steps to minimize corporate abuse of it. One example of this is the U.S. treatment of *Subpart F income.*

Controlled Foreign Corporations and Subpart F Income

Recall that in the United States, like many other countries adopting the worldwide principle of taxation, income of foreign subsidiaries is not taxable to the parent until it is repatriated as a dividend—the so-called *deferral* principle. Tax havens give multinationals an opportunity to avoid repatriation—and home country taxes—by locating transactions and accumulating profits in "brass plate" subsidiaries. These transactions have no real work or employment attached to them. The income earned on these transactions is *passive* rather than *active*.

The United States closed this loophole with the Controlled Foreign Corporation (CFC) and Subpart F Income provisions.[12] A CFC is a corporation in which U.S. shareholders (U.S. corporations, citizens, or residents) directly or indirectly own more than 50 percent of its combined voting power or fair market value. Only shareholders holding more than a 10 percent voting interest are counted in determining the 50 percent requirement. Shareholders of a CFC are taxed on certain income of the CFC (referred to as *tainted* income) even before the income is distributed.

Subpart F income includes certain *related party* sales and services income. For example, if a Bahamian subsidiary of a U.S. corporation buys inventory from its U.S. parent and exports the inventory to the European Union, the profits booked by the Bahamian subsidiary are Subpart F income. On the other hand, if the Bahamian subsidiary sells the imported inventory in the Bahamas, income from the local sales is not Subpart F income. Subpart F income also includes passive income such as dividends, interest, rents, royalties, and net gains on foreign exchange or commodities transactions; gains from the sale of certain investment property including securities; shipping income derived from the use of any shipping vessel or aircraft in foreign commerce; and certain insurance income.

Offshore Holding Companies

In some circumstances, a U.S.-based multinational parent company with operations in several foreign countries may find it advantageous to own its various foreign investments through a third-country holding company. The essential features of this structure are that the U.S. parent directly owns the shares of a holding company set up in one foreign jurisdiction and the holding company in turn owns the shares of one or more operating subsidiaries set up in other foreign jurisdictions. The tax-related advantages of this holding company organizational form could include:

1. Securing beneficial withholding tax rates on dividends, interest, royalties, and other similar payments
2. Deferring U.S. tax on foreign earnings until they are repatriated to the U.S. parent company (namely by reinvesting such earnings overseas)
3. Deferring U.S. tax on gains from the sale of the shares of the foreign operating subsidiaries

Realizing these advantages depends in large part on proper planning under complex U.S. tax rules (such as the Subpart F and foreign tax credit rules) and avoiding anti-treaty shopping rules found in many tax treaties.

Foreign Sales Corporations

The choice of organizational form for conducting foreign operations is also influenced by country incentives designed to encourage certain types of activities considered beneficial to the national economy. For example, the United States created foreign sales

---

[12]CFC legislation was first enacted in the United States in 1962. It has now been introduced in most industrialized countries as an anti–tax haven measure.

corporations (FSCs) to encourage exports and improve a worsening U.S. balance of payments position.[13] Under the FSC provisions, a portion of the earnings from U.S. exports of an FSC is exempt from U.S. income taxes. For example, assume that U.S.-based Parent Corp. contracts with a European buyer for a shipment of inventory. Parent Corp. ships the product directly from its Oklahoma factory to the European buyer, but also makes a *paper sale* of the goods to its wholly-owned affiliate, FSC-Virgin Islands. FSC-Virgin Islands then completes the transaction by another paper sale to the European buyer. The payment is routed through FSC-Virgin Islands, which then forwards it to Parent Corp. Up to 30 percent of the export income of the FSC trade is excluded from U.S. corporate income taxes, and none of the dividend is taxed when FSC-Virgin Islands pays a dividend to Parent Corp.[14]

In 2000 the World Trade Organization (WTO) ruled that FSCs constitute an illegal subsidy and ordered the United States to repeal its FSC provisions. In response, the United States repealed FSCs, but replaced them with an *extraterritorial income exclusion*. The new law relieves companies from having to set up separate companies to book export sales, but leaves a tax break almost as large as the one under the repealed FSC provisions. This new law was also ruled illegal by the WTO but, at the time of writing, the United States has yet to repeal it.[15]

Financing Decisions

The manner in which foreign operations are financed can also be shaped by tax considerations. Other things equal, the tax deductibility of debt, which increases the after-tax returns on equity, increases the attractiveness of debt financing in high tax countries. Where local currency borrowing is constrained by local governments that mandate minimum levels of equity infusion by the foreign parent, parent company borrowing to finance this capital infusion could achieve similar ends, provided the taxing jurisdiction of the parent allows the interest to be deductible.

In other instances, offshore financing subsidiaries domiciled in a low tax or tax haven country also could be used as a financing vehicle. At one time, U.S. companies wishing to borrow funds in the eurodollar market were constrained from doing so because the U.S. government imposed a withholding tax on interest paid to foreign lenders. To lower the cost of financing, they formed offshore financing subsidiaries in the Netherlands Antilles, a country that has no withholding tax on interest to nonresidents.

As the following diagram illustrates, an offshore financing affiliate also can be used to transfer profits from a high tax country in which either the parent or an affiliate is located to the low tax jurisdiction of the financing affiliate.

---

[13]An earlier counterpart of FSCs were DISCs (domestic international sales corporations), which continue to exist but with less attractive features.
[14]"How a Foreign Sales Corporation Works," *BusinessWeek* (September 4, 2000): 103. The U.S. company, Boeing, is reportedly the biggest user of the FSC, saving $130 million in U.S. taxes in 1998, 12 percent of its earnings that year. See P. Magnusson, "This Tax Break Could Trigger a Trade War," *BusinessWeek* (September 4, 2000): 103–104.
[15]"FSC Dispute Likely to Resurface, Despite Legislative Fix," *Deloitte & Touche Online,* www.dtonline .com, November 28, 2000; "U.S. Foreign Sales Corporation Rules Fix," *Accountancy* (January 2001): 116; and "Facing the $4bn Question," *Accountancy* (February 2002): 14. The WTO Web site (www.wto.org) has a history of this case.

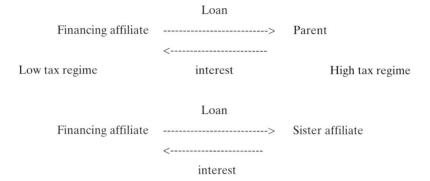

Pooling of Tax Credits

We mentioned earlier that some countries limit tax credits on a source-by-source basis. Pooling income from many sources allows excess credits generated from countries with high tax rates to offset taxes on income received from low tax jurisdictions. Excess tax credits, for example, can be extended to taxes paid in connection with dividends distributed by second- and third-tier foreign corporations in a multinational network. The United States allows this treatment provided that the U.S. parent's indirect ownership in such corporations exceeds 5 percent. Forward planning in the use of such credits can produce worthwhile tax benefits. Assume, for example, that a U.S. parent owns 100 percent of the shares of Company X (a first-tier foreign corporation). Company X owns 100 percent of the voting stock of Company Y (a second-tier foreign corporation). During the period, Company Y pays a dividend of 100 to Company X. Company X, in turn, remits a dividend of 100 to the U.S. parent as follows:

	U.S. Parent	Company X (First-tier Foreign Subsidiary)	Company Y (Second-tier Foreign Subsidiary)
1. Taxable earnings	100	200	200
2. Foreign income tax (15%/40%)		30	80
3. After-tax earnings		170	120
4. Dividends		100	100
5. Foreign taxes deemed paid	57	67	
	$(100/170 \times 97)$	$(100/120 \times 80)$	
6. Total taxes (2. + 5.)		97	

Company X will be deemed to have paid 67 of the foreign income taxes paid by Company Y. In turn, the U.S. parent company will receive an indirect credit against U.S. taxes payable of 57 based on its share of taxes actually paid and deemed to have been paid by Company X (30 + 67). (Refer to our earlier discussion of the calculation of foreign credits.) In this illustration, a dividend from Company Y to Company X increases the allowable U.S. foreign tax credit attendant upon a dividend from Company X to the U.S. parent when the income taxes in Company Y's country of domicile exceed that of Company X's and conversely.

Cost Accounting Allocations

Internal cost allocations among group companies is yet another vehicle to shift profits from high tax to low tax countries. The most common of these are allocations of corporate overhead expenses to affiliates in high tax countries. The allocation of such service expenses as human resources, technology, and research and development will maximize tax deductions for affiliates in high tax countries.

Location and Transfer Pricing

The locations of production and distribution systems also offer tax advantages. Thus, final sales of goods or services can be channeled through affiliates located in jurisdictions that offer tax shelter or deferral. Alternatively, a manufacturer in a high tax country can obtain components from affiliates located in low tax countries to minimize corporate taxes for the group as a whole. A necessary element of such a strategy is the prices at which goods and services are transferred between group companies. Profits for the corporate system as a whole can be increased by setting high *transfer prices* on components shipped from subsidiaries in relatively low tax countries, and low transfer prices on components shipped from subsidiaries in relatively high tax countries.

Transfer pricing has attracted increasing worldwide attention. The significance of the issue is obvious when we recognize that transfer pricing (1) is conducted on a relatively larger scale internationally than domestically; (2) is affected by more variables than are found in a strictly domestic setting; (3) varies from company to company, industry to industry, and country to country; and (4) affects social, economic, and political relationships in multinational business entities and, sometimes, entire countries. International transfer pricing is the most important international tax issue facing MNCs today.[16]

The impact of intracompany transfer pricing on international tax burdens cannot be examined in a vacuum; transfer prices can distort other parts of a multinational company's planning and control system. Cross-country transactions expose the multinational company to a host of strategic concerns that range from environmental risk to global competitiveness. These concerns often transcend tax considerations.

INTERNATIONAL TRANSFER PRICING: COMPLICATING VARIABLES

The need for transfer pricing arises when goods or services are exchanged between organizational units of the same company. For example, it arises when one subsidiary of a corporation transfers inventory to another subsidiary or when the parent company charges a subsidiary for administrative and managerial services, royalties for intangibles rights, or interest on corporate-wide financing. The transfer price places a monetary value on intracompany exchanges that occur between operating units and is a substitute for a market price. It is generally recorded as revenue by one unit and a cost by the other.

---

[16]Ernst & Young, *Transfer Pricing 2003 Global Survey,* Ernst & Young Web site (www.ey.com), 2003, p. 4.

Transfer pricing is of relatively recent origin. Transfer pricing in the United States developed along with the decentralization movement that influenced many American businesses during the first half of the 20th century.[17] Once a company expands internationally, the transfer pricing problem quickly expands. It is estimated that 60 percent of all international trade consists of transfers between related business entities. Cross-country transactions also expose the multinational company to a host of environmental influences that both create and destroy opportunities to increase enterprise profits by transfer pricing. Such variables as taxes, tariffs, competition, inflation rates, currency values, restrictions on fund transfers, political risks, and the interests of joint-venture partners complicate transfer pricing decisions tremendously. On top of these issues, transfer pricing decisions generally involve many trade-offs, often unforeseen and unaccounted for.

Tax Considerations

Unless counteracted by law, corporate profits can be increased by setting transfer prices so as to move profits from subsidiaries domiciled in high tax countries to subsidiaries domiciled in low tax countries.[18] As an example, Blu Jeans-Hong Kong, a wholly-owned manufacturing subsidiary of Global Enterprises (USA), ships 500,000 pairs of designer blue jeans to a related U.S. sales affiliate, Blu Jeans-USA (also wholly owned by Global Enterprises), for $6 per pair. They cost Blu Jeans-Hong Kong $4.20 per pair to produce. Assuming that each garment wholesales for $12 in the United States, consolidated profits (after eliminating intercompany sales and costs) and taxes would total $1,307,000 and $593,000, respectively. This scenario is shown in Exhibit 12-5.

Given a U.S. corporate tax rate of 35 percent versus 17 percent in Hong Kong, an increase in the transfer price of blue jeans from $6 to $8 per pair would increase total after-tax income, as shown in Exhibit 12-6.

Exhibit 12-5 Tax Effects of Transfer Pricing			
	Blu Jeans-HK	Blu Jeans-USA	Global Enterprises
Sales	$3,000,000[a]	$6,000,000	$6,000,000
Cost of sales	2,100,000	3,000,000[a]	2,100,000
Gross margin	$ 900,000	$3,000,000	$3,900,000
Operating expenses	500,000	1,500,000	2,000,000
Pretax income	$ 400,000	$1,500,000	$1,900,000
Income tax (17%/35%)[b]	68,000	525,000	593,000
Net income	$ 332,000	$ 975,000	$1,307,000

[a]Based on a transfer price of $6 per unit.
[b]Income tax rates: Hong Kong, 17%; United States, 35%.

---

[17]Itzhak Sharav, "Transfer Pricing-Diversity of Goals and Practices," *Journal of Accountancy* (April 1974): 56.
[18]For one of the first systematic empirical analyses of the relationship between transfer prices and taxes, see J. T. Bernard and R. J. Weiner, "Multinational Corporations, Transfer Prices and Taxes: Evidence from the U.S. Petroleum Industry," in *Taxation in the Global Economy,* H. Razin and J. Slemrod, eds., Chicago: University of Chicago Press, 1990, pp. 123–154.

Exhibit 12-6   Tax Effects of a Change in Transfer Prices

	Blu Jeans-HK	Blu Jeans-USA	Global Enterprises
Sales	$4,000,000[a]	$6,000,000	$6,000,000
Cost of sales	2,100,000	4,000,000[a]	2,100,000
Gross margin	$1,900,000	$2,000,000	$3,900,000
Operating expenses	500,000	1,500,000	2,000,000
Pretax income	$1,400,000	$ 500,000	$1,900,000
Income tax (17%/35%)	238,000	175,000	413,000
Net income	$1,162,000	$ 325,000	$1,487,000

[a]Based on a transfer price of $8 per unit.

In this example, raising the transfer price charged by the Hong Kong affiliate increases taxable income in Hong Kong and reduces taxable income for the U.S. affiliate by $1,000,000. Because the corporate tax rate is lower in Hong Kong than in the United States, corporate income taxes for the system as a whole decrease by $180,000, with a corresponding increase in consolidated after-tax earnings.

Unfortunately, such actions often create unanticipated problems. Governments often counteract such measures. In the United States, Section 482 of the Internal Revenue Code gives the Secretary of the Treasury authority to prevent a shifting of income or deductions between related taxpayers to exploit differences in national tax rates. This section states in part:

> In any case of two or more organizations, trades, or businesses (whether or not incorporated, whether or not organized in the United States, and whether or not affiliated) owned or controlled directly or indirectly by the same interests, the Secretary or his delegate may distribute, apportion, or allocate gross income, deductions, credits, or allowances between or among such organizations, trades, or businesses, if he determines that such distribution, apportionment, or allocation is necessary in order to prevent evasion of taxes or clearly to reflect the income of any such organizations, trades, or businesses.[19]

Section 482 essentially requires that intracompany transfers be based on an *arm's-length price*. An arm's-length price is one that an unrelated party would receive for the same or similar item under identical or similar circumstances. Acceptable arm's-length pricing methods include (1) comparable uncontrolled pricing, (2) resale pricing, (3) cost-plus pricing, and (4) other pricing methods. Severe penalties are imposed on valuation misstatements in connection with Section 482 adjustments. Penalties may be up to 40 percent of the additional taxes that result from income adjustments.

An emerging consensus among governments views arm's-length pricing (discussed later) as the appropriate standard in calculating profits for tax purposes. However, countries vary in how arm's-length pricing is interpreted and implemented. As a result, it is a somewhat fluid concept internationally. Multinational corporations are often

---

[19]Treasury Regulation, Section 1.482-1.

"caught in the middle" when tax authorities from different jurisdictions disagree on a transfer price, each trying to maintain its "fair share" of taxes collected from the multinational. The resulting controversy can be time-consuming and expensive to resolve. The rigor applied in monitoring the transfer pricing policies of multinational companies also varies worldwide. Multinationals report a low likelihood of transfer pricing audits in Ireland, Japan, Mexico, and South Korea, but a high likelihood in France, Germany, the Netherlands, and the United States.[20] Nevertheless, tax authorities around the world are both drafting new transfer pricing rules and stepping up enforcement efforts. In 1992, only two countries (Australia and the United States) had regulations requiring multinationals to document their transfer pricing policies. By 2003, 27 countries had such rules.[21] Whereas in the past many multinationals merely set their transfer prices, now they have to set them, justify them, and document them, or run the risk of severe noncompliance penalties. Thus, transfer pricing has become a major compliance burden.

Transfer pricing schemes designed to minimize global taxes often distort the multinational control system. When each subsidiary is evaluated as a separate profit center, such pricing policies can result in misleading performance measures that generally lead to conflicts between subsidiary and enterprise goals. In our earlier example, Blu Jeans-USA would report a lower profit than its sister affiliate in Hong Kong, even though the management of the U.S. subsidiary may be far more productive and efficient than the management in Hong Kong.

Tariff Considerations

Tariffs on imported goods also affect the transfer pricing policies of multinational companies. For example, a company exporting goods to a subsidiary domiciled in a high-tariff country can reduce the tariff assessment by lowering the prices of merchandise sent there.

In addition to the trade-offs identified, the multinational company must consider additional costs and benefits, both external and internal. Externally, an MNC would have three taxing authorities to contend with: the customs officials of the importing country and the income tax administrators of the exporting and importing countries. A high tariff paid by the importer would result in a lower tax base for income taxes. Internally, the enterprise would have to evaluate the benefits of a lower (higher) income tax in the importing country against a higher (lower) import duty, as well as the potentially higher (lower) income tax paid by the company in the exporting country.

To illustrate, let us revisit our blue jeans example depicted in Exhibits 12-5 and 12-6. In our revised example (see Exhibit 12-7) assume that the United States imposes an ad valorem import duty of 10 percent. Under a low transfer pricing policy, lower import duties are paid ($300,000 vs. $400,000), but the import duty advantage of a low transfer price is offset by the increased income taxes that must be paid ($488,000 vs. $273,000). Considering both import duties and income taxes, Global Enterprises is still $115,000 better off under a high transfer pricing policy.

---

[20]Ernst & Young, *Transfer Pricing 2003 Global Survey,* Ernst & Young Web site (www.ey.com), 2003, 13.
[21]Ernst & Young, *Transfer Pricing 2003 Global Survey,* Ernst & Young Web site (www.ey.com), 2003, 8.

Exhibit 12-7 Trade-Offs When Tariffs and Income Taxes Are Considered			
	Blu Jeans-HK	Blu Jeans-USA	Global Enterprises
Low transfer price			
Sales	$3,000,000	$6,000,000	$6,000,000
Cost of sales	2,100,000	3,000,000	2,100,000
Import duty at 10%	—	300,000	300,000
Gross margin	900,000	$2,700,000	$3,600,000
Operating expenses	500,000	1,500,000	2,000,000
Pretax income	400,000	1,200,000	1,600,000
Income tax (17%/35%)	68,000	420,000	488,000
Net income	$ 332,000	$ 780,000	$1,112,000
High transfer price			
Sales	$4,000,000	$6,000,000	$6,000,000
Cost of sales	2,100,000	4,000,000	2,100,000
Import duty at 10%	—	400,000	400,000
Gross margin	1,900,000	$1,600,000	$3,500,000
Operating expenses	500,000	1,500,000	2,000,000
Pretax income	1,400,000	100,000	1,500,000
Income tax (17%/35%)	238,000	35,000	273,000
Net income	$1,162,000	$ 65,000	$1,227,000

Competitive Factors

To facilitate the establishment of a foreign subsidiary abroad, a parent company could supply the subsidiary with inputs invoiced at very low prices. These price subsidies could be removed gradually as the foreign affiliate strengthens its position in the foreign market. Similarly, lower transfer prices could be used to shield an existing operation from the effects of increased foreign competition in the local market or another market; in other words, profits earned in one country could subsidize the penetration of another market.[22] Indirect competitive effects are also possible. To improve a foreign subsidiary's access to local capital markets, setting low transfer prices on its inputs and high transfer prices on its outputs could bolster its reported earnings and financial position. Sometimes, transfer prices could be used to weaken a subsidiary's competitors.

Such competitive considerations would have to be balanced against many offsetting disadvantages. Transfer prices for competitive reasons may invite antitrust actions by host governments or retaliatory actions by local competitors. Internally, pricing subsidies do little to instill a competitive mode of thinking in the minds of the managers whose companies gain from the subsidy. What begins as a temporary aid easily may become a permanent management crutch.

[22]G. Hamel and C. Prahalad, "Do You Really Have A Global Strategy?" *Harvard Business Review* (July/August 1985): 139–148.

Environmental Risks

Whereas competitive considerations abroad might warrant charging low transfer prices to foreign subsidiaries, the risks of severe price inflation might call for the opposite. Inflation erodes the purchasing power of a firm's cash. High transfer prices on goods or services provided to a subsidiary facing high inflation can remove as much cash from the subsidiary as possible.

Balance of payment problems (often related to inflation) may prompt foreign governments to devalue their currencies, impose foreign exchange controls, and/or impose restrictions on the repatriation of profits from foreign-owned companies. Potential losses from exposures to currency devaluations may be avoided by shifting funds to the parent company (or related affiliates) through inflated transfer prices. With exchange controls (e.g., a government restricts the amount of foreign exchange available for importing a particular good), reduced transfer prices on the imported good would allow the affiliate affected by the controls to acquire more of the desired import. To circumvent repatriation restrictions, high transfer prices allow some cash to be returned to the parent company each time it sells a product or service to the foreign subsidiary.

Performance Evaluation Considerations

Transfer pricing policies also are affected by their impact on managerial behavior, and are often a major determinant of corporate performance.[23] For example, if a foreign affiliate's mission is to furnish supplies for the rest of the corporate system, appropriate transfer prices enable corporate management to provide the affiliate with an earnings stream that can be used in performance comparisons. However, it is difficult for decentralized firms to set intracompany transfer prices that both (1) motivate managers to make decisions that maximize their unit's profits and are congruent with the goals of the company as whole, and (2) provide an equitable basis for judging the performance of managers and units of the firm. If subsidiaries are free to negotiate transfer prices, their managers may not be able to reconcile conflicts between what may be best for the subsidiary and what is best for the firm as a whole. However, the effect on subsidiary management may be even worse if corporate headquarters dictates transfer prices and sourcing alternatives that are seen as arbitrary or unreasonable. Moreover, the more decisions that are made by corporate headquarters, the less advantageous are decentralized profit centers, because local managers lose their incentive to act for the benefit of their local operations.

Accounting Contributions

Management accountants can play a significant role in quantifying the trade-offs in transfer pricing strategy. The challenge is to keep a global perspective when mapping out the benefits and costs associated with a transfer pricing decision. The effects of the decision on the corporate system as a whole must come first.

Quantifying the numerous trade-offs is difficult because environmental influences must be considered as a group, not individually. Consider, for example, the difficulties in measuring the trade-offs surrounding transfer pricing policies for a subsidiary located in a

---

[23]For a further discussion of this point, see W. M. Abdallah, "How to Motivate and Evaluate Managers with International Transfer Pricing Systems," *Management International Review* (First Quarter 1989): 65–71.

country with high income taxes, high import tariffs, price controls, a thin capital market, chronic high inflation, foreign exchange controls, and an unstable government. As we have seen, a high transfer price on goods or services provided to the subsidiary would lower the subsidiary's income taxes and remove excess cash to the parent company. However, a high transfer price might also result in higher import duties, impair the subsidiary's competitive position (due to higher input prices), worsen the rate of inflation, raise the subsidiary's capital costs, and even cause retaliation by the host government to protect its balance of payments position. To further complicate matters, all of these variables are changing constantly. One thing is clear: Superficial calculations of the effects of transfer pricing policy on individual units within a multinational system are not acceptable.

TRANSFER PRICING METHODOLOGY

In a world of perfectly competitive markets, it would not be much of a problem to set prices for intracompany resource and service transfers. Transfer prices could be based on either incremental cost or market prices. Neither system would necessarily conflict with the other. Unfortunately, there are seldom external competitive markets for products transferred between related entities. Environmental influences on transfer prices also raise questions of pricing methodology. How are transfer prices established? Are standard market prices generally better than those based on some measure of cost, or are negotiated prices the only feasible alternative? Do multinational enterprises the world over use similar transfer pricing methodologies or do cultural factors influence them? Can a single transfer pricing methodology serve all purposes equally well? The following sections shed some light on these questions.

Market versus Cost versus . . . ?

The use of market-oriented transfer prices offers several advantages. Market prices show the opportunity cost to the transferring entity of not selling on the external market, and their use will encourage the efficient use of the firm's scarce resources. Their use is also said to be consistent with a decentralized profit center orientation. Market prices help differentiate profitable from unprofitable operations, and are easier to defend to taxing authorities as arm's-length prices.

The advantages of market-based transfer prices must be weighed against several shortcomings. One is that using market prices does not give a firm much room to adjust prices for competitive or strategic purposes. A more fundamental problem is that there is often no intermediate market for the product or service in question. Multinationals engage in transactions that independent enterprises would not undertake, such as transferring a valuable, closely held technology to an affiliate. Transactional relationships among affiliates under common control often differ in important and fundamental ways from potentially comparable transactions among unrelated parties.

Cost-based transfer pricing systems overcome many of these limitations. Moreover, they are (1) simple to use, (2) based on readily available data, (3) easy to justify to tax authorities, and (4) easily routinized, thus helping to avoid internal frictions that often accompany more arbitrary systems.

Of course, cost-based transfer pricing systems are not flawless either. For example, the sale of goods or services at actual cost may provide little incentive for sellers to control their costs. Production inefficiencies may simply be passed on to the buyer at inflated prices. Cost-based systems overemphasize historical costs, which ignore competitive demand-and-supply relationships, and do not allocate costs to particular products or services in a satisfactory manner. The problem of cost determination is compounded internationally, as cost accounting concepts vary from country to country.

Arm's-Length Principle

The typical multinational is an integrated operation: Its subsidiaries are under common control and share common resources and goals. The need to declare taxable income in different countries means that multinationals must allocate revenues and expenses among subsidiaries and set transfer prices for intrafirm transactions.

Tax authorities around the world have developed complicated transfer price and income allocation regulations as a part of their national income tax systems. Most are based on the *arm's-length principle,* which prices intrafirm transfers as if they took place between unrelated parties in competitive markets.[24] The OECD identifies several broad methods of ascertaining an arm's-length price. Resembling those specified by Section 482 of the U.S. Internal Revenue Code, they are (1) the comparable uncontrolled price method, (2) the comparable uncontrolled transaction method, (3) the resale price method, (4) the cost-plus method, (5) the comparable profits method, (6) the profit split method, and (7) other methods.

Comparable Uncontrolled Price Method

Under this approach, transfer prices are set by reference to prices used in comparable transactions between independent companies or between the corporation and an unrelated third party. It is appropriate when goods are sufficiently common that controlled sales are essentially comparable to sales on the open market. Commodity-type products ordinarily use this method for internal transactions.

Comparable Uncontrolled Transaction Method

This method applies to transfers of intangible assets. It identifies a benchmark royalty rate by referencing uncontrolled transactions in which the same or similar intangibles are transferred. Like the comparable uncontrolled price method, this method relies on market comparables.

Resale Price Method

This method calculates an arm's-length price by starting with the price at which the item in question can be sold to an independent purchaser. An appropriate margin to cover expenses and a normal profit is then deducted from this price to derive the intracompany transfer price. Deciding on an appropriate margin is especially difficult when the purchasing affiliate adds substantial value to the transferred item.

---

[24]Of course, the result is only hypothetical because the parties are related and the markets normally are not competitive. See L. Eden, M. T. Dacin, and W. P. Wan, "Standards Across Borders: Cross-border Diffusion of the Arms-Length Standard in North America," *Accounting, Organizations and Society* (January 2001): 1–23.

To illustrate this pricing method, assume that a company wishes to price a product sold by one of its operating units to one of its foreign distribution units. Income statement accounts and other related facts for the distribution unit are as follows:

1. Net sales (by the distribution unit) of 100,000 units at $300 per unit	$30,000,000
2. Direct manufacturing expenses (DME)	6,000,000
3. DME as a percentage of net sales	20.0%
4. Other expenses (OE)	3,900,000
5. OE as a percentage of net sales	13.0%
6. Imputed financing cost (IFC)[a]	600,000
7. IFC as a percentage of net sales	2.0%
8. Freight and insurance to import (FI)	$1.50/unit
9. Packaging costs (PC)	$2.00/unit
10. Customs duties on F & P (CD)	5.0%
11. Net sales price (NSP) by the distribution unit	$300/unit

[a]Imputed costs to finance the distribution unit are calculated as: Average net working capital $\times$ short-term interest rate in local currency ($= \$7,500,000 \times 8\% = \$600,000$). This is designed to avoid overcompensating the distribution unit for having a high interest expense due to a low capitalization or overcharging it for having low interest expenses due to a high capitalization.

The objective is to calculate a transfer price between the two units such that the distribution unit covers all costs and earns a normal profit. As we shall see, the resale price method is a *work backwards* approach. Assuming that the company requires a 5 percent additional margin to cover business risk and provide an appropriate profit, the total product margin would be computed as follows:

1. Direct manufacturing expenses	20.0%
2. Other expenses	13.0%
3. Imputed financing cost	2.0%
4. Additional margin for risk and profit (AM)	5.0%
5. Total margin (TM)	40.0%

Here, the distribution unit must pay freight and insurance costs to import the product and customs duties in addition to the transfer price. (Thus, the distribution unit's cost to import differs from the transfer price.) Given the foregoing information, the transfer price (TP) per unit of product delivered to the distribution unit would be:

$$TP = \{[NSP \times (100\% - TM) - PC] / (100\% + CD)\} - FI$$
$$TP = \{[300 \times (100\% - 40\%) - \$2] / (100\% + 5\%)\} - \$1.50$$
$$TP = \$168.02$$

The foregoing calculation adjusts the net sales price for the total margin, packaging costs, freight and insurance costs, and customs duties to arrive at the transfer price. Specifically, the 1.05 factor reduces the $178 cost-to-import price to a before-duties figure of $169.52. Other dutiable costs are subtracted from this figure to leave a transfer price of $168.02. The cost to import equals (1) the transfer price plus (2) freight and insurance, with duties applied to both. As a check on this result:

	Unit Cost
Transfer price	$168.02
+ Freight & Insurance	1.50
Subtotal	169.52
Duties (at 5%)	8.48
Cost to import	$178.00

To work backwards to the transfer price:

Net sales price	$300.00
Margin to cover expenses and normal profit (40%)	−120.00
Packaging	−2.00
Freight & insurance	−1.50
Customs duties	−8.48
Transfer price	$168.02

Cost-Plus Pricing Method

Cost-plus pricing is a *work forward* approach in which a markup is added to the transferring affiliate's cost in local currency. The markup typically includes (1) the imputed financing costs related to export inventories, receivables, and assets employed and (2) a percentage of cost covering manufacturing, distribution, warehousing, internal shipping, and other costs related to export operations. An adjustment is often made to reflect any government subsidies that are designed to make manufacturing costs competitive in the international marketplace.

This pricing method is especially useful when semifinished goods are transferred between foreign affiliates, or where one entity is a subcontractor for another. A major measurement issue involves calculating the cost of the transferred item and ascertaining an appropriate markup.

To see how a transfer price is derived employing the cost-plus method, assume that a manufacturing unit in Portugal wishes to price an intracompany transfer based on the following information:

1. Total manufacturing cost per unit (1,000 units)	€200
2. Average net operating assets employed in manufacturing the item	€40,000
3. Average short-term interest rate in Portugal	8.0%
4. Financing cost as a percentage of total manufacturing cost (8% × €40,000/€200,000)	1.6%
5. Government subsidy based on final transfer price	6.0%
6. Credit terms to affiliates	90 days
7. Required profit and other expenses margin	8.0%

The cost-plus transfer price is that which enables the transferring unit to earn a given percentage return above its production costs. That percentage return (the *plus* in cost-plus) is determined in the following manner:

1. Required margin before adjustments:	
Profit and other expenses	8.0%
Financing cost	1.6% 9.60%
2. Government subsidy adjustment	6.00%
3. Adjusted margin with cash terms	3.39%
[(1.096/1.06) − 1]	
4. Adjusted margin with 90-day terms	5.46%[a]

[a]This figure is equal to the adjusted margin-cash terms multiplied by 1 plus the short-term interest rate for 90 days, or $\{1.0339 \times [1 + (0.08 \times 90/360)]\} - 1$. It allows the transferring unit to earn imputed interest for carrying a receivable for 90 days.

This required margin of 5.46 percent, when multiplied by the transferred item's total manufacturing cost, yields the intracompany transfer price to be billed for that item. In this example, the transfer price is €210.92, the result of $1.0546 \times €200$. This transfer price causes the company to earn its required margin of 9.6 percent plus an 8 percent (annualized compounded) return for carrying the affiliate's receivable for 90 days. As a check on this result:

Compounded return	=	$\{1.096 \times [1 + (.08 \times 90/360)]\} - 1$
	=	11.79%
Transfer price	=	€210.92
Cost		200.00
Margin		€ 10.92
Subsidy (6% × 210.92)		12.66
Total return		€ 23.58
Return as a % of cost	=	(€23.58)/(€200.00) = 11.79%

Comparable Profits Method[25]

This method supports the general notion that similarly situated taxpayers should earn similar returns over reasonable time periods. Thus, intracompany profits on transactions between related parties should be comparable to profits on transactions between unrelated parties who engage in similar business activities under similar circumstances. *Return on capital employed* (ROCE) is a primary profit-level indicator. Under this approach, the operating income to average capital employed ratio of a benchmark entity is compared with the ROCE of the entity in question.

[25]The comparable profits method is similar to the transactional net margin method (TNMM) in OECD guidelines. The key difference is that TNMM is applied on a transactional rather than a firm level. For more information on this and the profit split methods, see Victor H. Miesel, Harlow H. Higinbotham, and Chun W. Yi, "International Transfer Pricing: Practical Solutions for Intercompany Pricing—Part II," *The International Tax Journal* (Winter 2003): 1–40.

Application of this method normally will require adjustments for any differences between comparables. Factors requiring such adjustments include differing sales conditions, cost of capital differences, foreign exchange and other risks, and differences in accounting measurement practices.

Profit Split Methods

These methods are used when product or market benchmarks are not available. Essentially they involve dividing profits generated in a related party transaction between the affiliated companies in an arm's-length fashion. One variant of this approach, the *comparables profit split method,* divides the profit generated by a related party transaction using a percentage allocation of the combined profits of uncontrolled companies with similar types of transactions and activities.

A more sophisticated method, the *residual profit split method,* employs a two-step approach. First, routine functions performed by affiliated entities—the parent and its subsidiary—are priced at each stage of the production process using relevant benchmarks. Any difference between total profits earned by the combined enterprise and those attributable to the routine functions is considered *residual profits,* essentially profits from nonroutine functions. This residual, which resembles a goodwill intangible, then is split on the basis of the relative value of each affiliated party's contribution to the intangible. This value can be determined using fair market value referents or the capitalized cost of developing the intangibles.

Other Pricing Methods

As existing pricing methodologies do not always reflect underlying circumstances, additional methodologies are allowed if they result in a more accurate measure of an arm's-length price. To quote the OECD:

> It has to be recognized that an arm's-length price will in many cases not be precisely ascertainable and that in such circumstances it will be necessary to seek a reasonable approximation to it. Frequently, it may be useful to take account of more than one method of reaching a satisfactory approximation to an arm's-length price in the light of the evidence available.[26]

Section 482 of the U.S. Internal Revenue Code specifies a *best methods rule* requiring the taxpayer to select the best transfer pricing method based on the facts and circumstances of the case. Argentina also has a best methods rule. Other countries, such as the Czech Republic and Mexico, state no preference for transfer pricing methods. However, most countries with transfer pricing legislation prefer transaction-based methods (comparable uncontrolled price, comparable uncontrolled transaction, resale price, and cost-plus methods) to profit-based methods (comparable profits and profit split methods). These countries include Belgium, France, Germany, Japan, the Netherlands, and the United Kingdom.[27] OECD guidelines specify that a *reasonable* method should be chosen, and also prefer transaction-based methods to profit-based methods.

---

[26]Organization for Economic Cooperation and Development, *Transfer Pricing and Multinational Enterprises,* Paris: OECD, 1979, p. 33.
[27]Ernst & Young, *Transfer Global Reference Guide 2003,* Ernst & Young Web site (www.ey.com), October 2003.

It is not always possible to calculate a precise and accurate arm's-length price. Hence, documentation of any transfer price employed and its underlying rationale is important. This is true regardless of the tax jurisdiction and the transfer pricing methods it may prefer. The following steps are helpful in setting transfer prices:

- Analyze the risks assumed, functions performed by the affiliated companies, and the economic and legal determinants that affect pricing.
- Identify and analyze benchmark companies and transactions. Document reasons for any adjustments made.
- Compare the financial results of the comparable companies to that of the taxpayer.
- If comparable transactions are available, note their similarities and differences with the taxpayer's transactions.
- Document why the chosen pricing method is the most reasonable and why the other methods are not.
- Update the information before filing the tax return.[28]

Advance Pricing Agreements

A major concern is the acceptability of transfer prices to governments. Aware that multinational enterprises use transfer prices to shift income, and worried about their economic and social consequences, governments are increasing their scrutiny of multinational operations. At the same time, the ambiguities and complexities of transfer pricing regulations make it likely that intracompany transactions will be the target of tax audits. Surveys of multinationals consistently show that they regard transfer pricing as their most important international tax issue and that facing a transfer pricing audit somewhere in the world is a near certainty.[29]

Advance pricing agreements (APAs) are a mechanism whereby a multinational and a taxing authority voluntarily negotiate an agreed transfer pricing methodology that is binding on both parties. These agreements reduce or eliminate the risk of a transfer pricing audit, saving time and money for both the multinational and the taxing authority. Introduced in the United States in 1991, APAs have been widely adopted by other countries.[30] The agreements are binding for a fixed period of time, for example, 3 years in the United States.

TRANSFER PRICING PRACTICES

Multinational corporations obviously vary along many dimensions such as size, industry, nationality, organizational structure, degree of international involvement, technology, products or services, and competitive conditions. Therefore, it is hardly surprising

---

[28] Alan Shapiro and Arnold McClellan, "New Transfer Pricing: New Rules Give Guidance on How to Avoid Penalties," *Deloitte Touche Tohmatsu International World Tax News* (March 1994): 2.

[29] Ernst & Young, *Transfer Pricing 2003 Global Survey,* Ernst & Young Web site (www.ey.com), 2003, pp. 10–15.

[30] APAs go by different names. For example, they are called an advance pricing arrangement in the United Kingdom and preconfirmation system in Japan. For more on APAs around the world, see S. C. Borkowski, "Transfer Pricing Advance Pricing Agreements: Current Status by Country," *International Tax Journal* (Spring 2000): 1–16.

that a variety of transfer pricing methods are found in practice.[31] Most of the empirical evidence on transfer pricing practices is based on surveys. Because corporate pricing policies are often considered proprietary, these surveys should be interpreted cautiously. Given the dramatic effect of globalization on business operations since the 1990s, we are also cautious about whether transfer pricing surveys before the 1990s are still valid today.[32]

What factors influence the choice of transfer pricing methods? Are transfer pricing effects considered in the planning process? A recent study asked financial executives of U.S. multinationals to identify the three most important objectives of international transfer pricing.[33] Managing the tax burden dominates the other objectives, but operational uses of transfer pricing such as maintaining the company's competitive position, promoting equitable performance evaluation, and motivating employees are also important. Managing inflation, managing foreign exchange risk, and mitigating restrictions on cash transfers are relatively unimportant.

Another study asked a similar question to managers of multinationals from 19 nations.[34] Here, operational issues have a slightly higher priority than tax issues. The study also finds that the operational and tax effects of transfer pricing are most often considered only after the strategic decisions have been made. Only 30 percent of the multinationals indicated that transfer pricing is part of the strategic planning process. Twenty-nine percent consider transfer pricing after strategic decisions have been made, and 37 percent view transfer pricing merely as a tax compliance issue. Four percent do not consider transfer pricing at all in strategic decisions. These results indicate that transfer pricing can play a more important role in the multinational planning process. The study observes:

> Clearly, the "tax cart" should not come before the "operational horse," but given the levels of taxation around the world, and the profound impact that transfer pricing may have on operations, it is distressing to note the number of companies that do not consider this cost of doing business earlier in the strategic decision-making process. . . . Transfer pricing is a reactive compliance exercise instead of a proactive mechanism to manage downward the organization's worldwide effective tax rate.[35]

---

[31]Cost-based transfer pricing methods appear to be used more often than market-based methods. It is also likely that a multinational uses more than one method, depending on the circumstances. See K. S. Cravens, "Examining the Role of Transfer Pricing as a Strategy for Multinational Firms," *International Business Review* 6, no. 2 (1997): 137–138.

[32]For example, one widely cited study [J. S. Arpan, International Intracorporate Pricing: Non-American Systems and Views," *Journal of International Business Studies* (Spring 1972): 1–18] found that U.S., French, British, and Japanese managers prefer cost-oriented transfer pricing methods, whereas Canadian, Italian, and Scandinavian managers prefer market-oriented methods; no particular preference was found for Belgian, Dutch, German, or Swiss managers. While we believe that nationality continues to influence the choice of transfer pricing methods, we question whether this particular conclusion is still valid.

[33]K. S. Cravens, "Examining the Role of Transfer Pricing as a Strategy of Multinational Firms," *International Business Review* 6, no. 2 (1997): 127–145.

[34]Ernst & Young, "1999 Global Transfer Pricing Survey," reprinted in R. Feinschrieber, *Transfer Pricing International: A Country-by-Country Comparison,* New York: John Wiley & Sons, 2000, pp. 35-1–35-49.

[35]Ernst & Young, "1999 Global Transfer Pricing Survey," reprinted in R. Feinschrieber, *Transfer Pricing International: A Country-by-Country Comparison,* New York: John Wiley & Sons, 2000, pp. 35-11–35-12.

THE FUTURE

Technology and the global economy are challenging many of the principles on which international taxation is based. One of these principles is that every nation has the right to decide for itself how much tax to collect from the people and businesses within its borders. Tax laws evolved in a world where transactions take place in clearly identifiable locations, but this situation is increasingly less true. Electronic commerce over the Internet ignores borders and physical location. Commercial events now take place in cyberspace—on a server anywhere in the world.[36]

The ability to collect taxes depends on knowing who should pay, but increasingly sophisticated encryption techniques make it harder to identify taxpayers. Anonymous electronic money is a reality. The Internet also makes it easy for multinationals to shift their activities to low tax countries that may be a long way from customers but as close as a mouse click to access. It is becoming more difficult to monitor and tax international transactions.

Governments around the world require transfer pricing methods based on the arm's-length principle. That is, a multinational's businesses in different countries are taxed as if they were independent firms operating at arm's-length from each other. The complex calculation of arm's-length prices is less relevant today for global companies because fewer of them operate this way.

What do these developments imply for international taxation? Are national taxes compatible with a global economy? We already see greater cooperation and information sharing by tax authorities around the world. This trend will continue. At the same time, many experts foresee greater tax competition. The Internet makes it easier to take advantage of tax havens. Some individuals advocate a *unitary tax* as an alternative to using transfer prices to determine taxable income. Under this approach, a multinational's total profits are allocated to individual countries based on a formula that reflects the company's relative economic presence in that country. Each country would then tax its piece of the profit at whatever rate it sees fit. Clearly, taxation in the future faces many changes and challenges.[37]

Selected References

Aliber, R. Z., "Transfer Pricing: A Taxonomy," in *Multinationals and Transfer Pricing*, A. M. Rugman and L. Eden, eds., New York: St. Martin's Press, 1985.

Bodner, P., "International Taxation," in *International Finance and Accounting Handbook*, 3rd ed., F. D. S. Choi, ed., New York: John Wiley & Sons, 2003.

Borkowski, S., "Transfer Pricing Advance Pricing Agreements: Current Status by Country," *The International Tax Journal* (Spring 2000): 1–16.

---

[36]The digitization of tangible products is an example. A compact disc bought at a record store is a tangible item purchased at a physical location. Taxing this transaction is fairly simple because it is easy to identify the source of income. If it is downloaded online, it is an intangible purchased in cyberspace. Who can tax this transaction, and how, is less clear.

[37]See "The Mystery of the Vanishing Taxpayer: A Survey of Globalisation and Tax," *The Economist* (January 29, 2000): 1–22; S. James, "The Future International Tax Environment," *The International Tax Journal* (Winter 1999): 1–9; and N. Warren, "Internet Challenges to Tax System Design," in *The International Taxation System*, A. Lymer and J. Hasseldine, eds., Boston: Kluwer Academic, 2002, pp. 61–82.

Bradley, W. E., and R. E. Nantz, "The Restructuring of U.S. International Tax Policy," *The International Tax Journal* 28, no. 3 (Summer 2002): 70–81.

Cravens, K. S., "Examining the Role of Transfer Pricing as a Strategy for Multinational Firms," *International Business Review* 6, no. 2 (1997): 127–145.

Eden, L., M. T. Dacin, and W. P. Wan, "Standards Across Borders: Crossborder Diffusion of the Arm's Length Standard in North America." *Accounting, Organizations and Society* (January 2001): 1–23.

Ernst & Young, *Transfer Pricing Global Reference Guide,* Ernst & Young Web site (www.ey.com), October 2003.

Ernst & Young, *Transfer Pricing 2003 Global Survey,* Ernst & Young Web site (www.ey.com), 2003.

Feinschreiber, R., "Transfer Pricing for Intercompany Transactions," in *International Finance and Accounting Handbook,* 3rd ed., F. D. S. Choi, ed., New York: John Wiley & Sons, 2003.

Feinschreiber, R., *Transfer Pricing International: A Country-by-Country Guide,* New York: John Wiley & Sons, 2000.

Hines, J. R., "Lessons from Behavioral Responses to International Taxation," *National Tax Journal* (June 1999): 305–322.

James, S., "The Future International Tax Environment." *International Tax Journal* (Winter 1999): 1–9.

Lymer, A., and J. Hasseldine, *The International Taxation System,* Boston: Kluwer Academic, 2002.

Meisel, V. H., H. H. Higinbotham, and C. W. Yi, "International Transfer Pricing: Practical Solutions for Intercompany Pricing," *The International Tax Journal* 28, no. 4 (Fall 2002): 1–22.

Meisel, V.H., H.H. Higinbotham, and C.W. Yi, "International Transfer Pricing: Practical Solutions for Intercompany Pricing—Part II," *The International Tax Journal* 29, no. 1 (Winter 2003): 1–40.

"The Mystery of the Vanishing Taxpayer: A Survey of Globalisation and Tax," *The Economist* (January 29, 2000): 1–22.

Ogum, G., and K. A. Kim, "New U.S. International Pricing Regulations," *Multinational Business Review* (Spring 1995): 8–13.

Tang, R. Y. W., *Intrafirm Trade and Global Transfer Pricing Regulation,* Westport, CT: Quorum Books, 1997.

Weiner, J. M., and H. J. Ault, "The OECD's Report on Harmful Tax Competition," *National Tax Journal* (Spring 1998): 601–608.

Yancey, W. F., and K. S. Cravens, "A Framework for International Tax Planning for Managers," *Journal of International Accounting Auditing and Taxation* 7, no. 2 (1998): 251–272.

Discussion Questions

1. What is the meaning of tax *neutrality?* Are taxes neutral with regard to business decisions? Is this good or bad?

2. What philosophies and types of taxes exist worldwide?

3. What role do *tax credits* play in international taxation? What considerations might cause tax credits to not achieve their intended results?

4. Briefly describe the major advantages and disadvantages of the (a) classical, (b) split-rate, and (c) imputation tax administration systems from the perspective of a multinational corporate taxpayer.

5. Consider the statement: "National differences in statutory tax rates are the most obvious and yet least significant determinants of a company's effective tax burden." Do you agree? Explain.

6. Carried to its logical extreme, tax planning implies a conscientious policy of tax minimization. This mode of thinking raises an ethical question for international tax executives. Deliberate tax evasion is commonplace in many parts of the world. In Italy, for example, tax legislation is often honored only in the breach. Even when tax laws are enforced, actual tax settlements are usually subject to negotiation between the individual taxpayer and the tax collector. Should multinational corporations operating in such environments adopt a policy of "when in Rome do as the Romans do" or should they adhere to the taxation norms of their domestic environments?

7. Draft a short essay comparing and contrasting the role of transfer pricing in national versus international operations.

8. Multinational transfer pricing causes serious concern among various corporate stakeholders. Identify potential concerns from the viewpoint of
   a. minority owners of a foreign affiliate,
   b. foreign taxing authorities,
   c. home country taxing authorities,
   d. foreign subsidiary managers, and
   e. headquarters managers.

9. The pricing of intracompany transfers is complicated by many economic, environmental, and organizational considerations. Identify six major considerations described in the chapter and briefly explain how they affect transfer pricing policy.

10. Identify the major bases for pricing intercompany transfers. Comment briefly on their relative merits. Which measurement method is best from the viewpoint of the multinational executive?

11. Explain the *arm's-length price*. Is the United States Internal Revenue Service alone in mandating such pricing of intracompany transfers? Would the concept of an arm's-length price resolve the measurement issue in pricing intracompany transfers?

12. What is an advance pricing agreement (APA)? What are the advantages and disadvantages of entering into an APA?

Exercises

1. You are an investment analyst domiciled in Country Z doing a cross-country comparison of the financial performance of two manufacturing companies in the pharmaceuticals industry. Both companies, X and Y (located in Countries X and Y), have similar expected sales of $300 million. Country X has a corporate income tax; Country Y has no income tax, but relies on indirect taxes. Selected data for companies X and Y are as follows:

	Company X	**Company Y**
Pretax income	$60 million	$36 million
Return on sales	12.0%	12.0%

Required: Determine which company promises to have the better financial performance. What tax considerations might affect your conclusions?

2. Using the facts in Exercise 1, assume that Companies X and Y have identical dividend payout ratios of 50 percent. Country Z, your country of domicile, has an income tax rate of 35%. Country Z has a tax treaty with countries X and Y so that no withholding taxes are assessed on dividends received. Furthermore, Country Z grants a tax credit for any direct foreign taxes paid.

   Required: Show which company now promises the better after-tax investment performance, and why.

3. A Chinese manufacturing subsidiary produces items sold in Australia. The items cost the equivalent of $3.50 to produce and are sold to customers for $4.75. A Cayman Islands subsidiary buys the items from the Chinese subsidiary for $3.50 and sells them to the Australian parent for $4.75.

   Required: Calculate the total amount of income taxes paid on these transactions. What are the implications for the company and the taxing authorities involved?

4. Kowloon Trading Company, a wholly-owned subsidiary incorporated in Hong Kong, imports macadamia nuts from its parent company in Honolulu for export to various duty-free shops in the Far East. During the current fiscal year, the company imported $1,000,000 worth of nuts and retailed them for $3,000,000. Local income taxes are paid at the rate of 17 percent. Profits earned by the Hong Kong subsidiary are retained for future expansion.

   Required: Based on this information, calculate the U.S. parent company's U.S. tax liability under Subpart F provisions of the Internal Revenue Code.

5. A jewelry manufacturer domiciled in Amsterdam purchases an ounce of gold from a precious metals dealer in Belgium for €1,200. The manufacturer fabricates the raw material into an item of jewelry and wholesales it to a Dutch retailer for €2,000.

   Required: Compute the value-added tax from the jewelry manufacturer's activities if the Dutch value-added tax rate is 17.5%.

6. Sweden has a classical system of taxation. Calculate the total taxes that would be paid by a company headquartered in Stockholm that earns 750,000 Swedish krona (SEK) and distributes 50 percent of its earnings as a dividend to its shareholders. Assume the company's shareholders are in the 40 percent tax bracket and that the company's income tax rate is 28 percent.

7. Alubar, a U.S. multinational, receives royalties from Country A, foreign branch earnings from Country B, and dividends equal to 50 percent of net income from subsidiaries in Countries C and D. There is a 10 percent withholding tax on the royalty from Country A and a 10 percent withholding tax on the dividend from Country C. Income tax rates are 20 percent in Country B and 40 percent in Country C. Country D assesses indirect taxes of 40 percent instead of direct taxes on income. Selected data are as follows:

	Country A	Country B	Country C	Country D
Royalty from Country A operations	$10			
Pretax income		$45	$45	$27
Income taxes (20%/40%)		9	18	-0-
Net income		$36	$27	$27

Required: Calculate the foreign and U.S. taxes paid on each foreign source income.

8. Global Enterprises has a manufacturing affiliate in Country A that incurs costs of $300,000 for goods that it sells to its sales affiliate in Country B. The sales affiliate resells these goods to final consumers for $850,000. Both affiliates incur operating expenses of $50,000 each. Countries A and B levy a corporate income tax of 35 percent on taxable income in their jurisdictions.

   Required: If Global Enterprises raises the aggregate transfer price such that shipments from its manufacturing to its sales affiliate increase from $500,000 to $600,000, what effect would this have on consolidated taxes?

9. Using the facts stated in Exercise 8, what would be the tax effects of the transfer pricing action if corporate income tax rates were 30 percent in Country A and 40 percent in Country B?

10. Drawing on the background facts in Exercises 8 and 9, assume that the manufacturing cost per unit, based on operations at full capacity of 10,000 units, is $30 and that the uncontrolled selling price of the unit in Country A is $60. Costs to transport the goods to the distribution affiliate in Country B are $8 per unit and a reasonable profit margin on such cross-border sales is 20 percent of cost.
    Now suppose that Country B levies a corporate income tax of 40 percent on taxable income (vs. 30 percent in Country A) and a tariff of 20 percent on the declared value of the imported goods. The minimum declared value legally allowed in Country B is $50 per unit with no upper limit. Import duties are deductible for income tax purposes in Country B.

   Required:
   a. Based on the foregoing information, formulate a transfer pricing strategy that would minimize Global Enterprise's overall tax burden.
   b. What issues does your pricing decision raise?

11. Lumet Corporation, a manufacturer of cellular phones, wishes to invoice a sales affiliate located in Fontainebleau for an order of 10,000 units. Wanting to minimize its exchange risk, it invoices all intercompany transactions in euros. Relevant facts on a per unit basis are as follows: net sales price, €450; direct manufacturing costs, €135; other operating expenses, €63; freight and insurance, €1; packaging costs, €1.50. Also, assume that the French affiliate's net working capital is €2,250,000, customs duties are 5 percent, French short-term interest rates are 8 percent, and Lumet Corporation wishes to earn a profit of 6 percent on the transaction.

Required: Determine the price at which Lumet would invoice its French affiliate for the cellular phones.

12. The partial income statement of the Lund Manufacturing Company, a Swedish-based concern producing pharmaceutical products, is presented here:

Sales		SEK 37,500,000
Cost of goods manufactured and sold:		
Finished goods, beg. inventory	-0-	
Cost of goods manufactured:		
(100,000 units)		
Direct materials used	SEK 11,250,000	
Direct labor	5,800,000	
Overhead	3,000,000	
Cost of goods available for sale	20,050,000	
Finished goods, end. inventory	4,000,000	
Cost of goods sold		16,050,000
Gross margin		SEK 21,450,000

During the year, short-term interest rates in Sweden averaged 7 percent while net operating assets averaged SEK 22,500,000. The company is entitled to a government subsidy of 5 percent. Its required margin to provide a profit and cover other expenses is 8 percent. All affiliates receive credit terms of 60 days.

Required: Based on this information, at what price would the Lund Manufacturing Company invoice its distribution affiliate in neighboring Finland?

CASE 12-1   MUSCLE MAX: YOUR VERY OWN PERSONAL TRAINER

Muscle Max-Asia, a wholly-owned affiliate of a French parent company, functions as a regional headquarters for operating activities in the Pacific Rim. It enjoys much autonomy from its French parent as it conducts its primary line of business, the manufacture and sale of Muscle Max, a commercial-grade weightlifting machine that can be used in athletic clubs or in the home. Muscle Max-Asia has manufacturing affiliates in Malaysia and Canton (China) and distribution outlets in Australia, Japan, New Zealand, South Korea, and Singapore. It plans to expand its operations to other Pacific Rim countries in the next several years.

Given the demand for weightlifting equipment in Australia, the company's distribution affiliate there, Muscle Max-Australia, has been importing its equipment from both Canton and Malaysia, paying a customs duty of 5 percent. Competing suppliers of similar equipment have approached the Australian affiliate for orders. Prices quoted on such machinery have ranged between 650 to 750 Australian dollars (A$). Muscle Max-Australia, which currently retails the machine for A$1,349, has recently complained to Muscle Max-Asia because of differences in the prices it is being charged by its sister affiliates in Canton and Malay-

sia. Specifically, while the Malaysian affiliate charges a per unit price of A$675, the Canton supplier's price is 26 percent higher. Muscle Max-Asia explains that the transfer price, based on a cost-plus formula (production costs total A$540 per unit), reflects several considerations, including higher margins to compensate for credit risk, operating risk, and taxes. As for taxes, Muscle Max-Asia explains that the People's Republic of China has provided fiscal incentives to enterprises that promote exports. Although normal corporate income tax rates are 33 percent, Cantonese tax authorities have agreed to a rate of 10 percent on all export-related earnings.

The manager of Muscle Max-Australia remains skeptical and believes that he is paying for the Cantonese manager's inefficiency. In his latest communication, he asks if he can consider alternative suppliers of weightlifting equipment to preserve local market share.

REQUIRED

1. What issues does this case raise?
2. What courses of action would you recommend to resolve the issues you have identified?

CASE 12-2 DOUBLE DOUBLE: TAX IS TROUBLE

The tax morality of the multinational corporation has become a popular topic of debate. Opinions range from complete support of the multinational corporation to accusations that it is one of the most exploitative institutions of capitalism ever created. In addition to exporting jobs, adversely affecting a country's balance of payments, and hurting domestic investment, multinationals are accused of not paying their fair share of taxes to either host country or home country governments. Calling the foreign tax credit and foreign income deferral policy "the biggest loopholes in the whole tax law," some members of Congress advocate ending existing international tax provisions for U.S. multinationals. More specifically, proposals have been advanced to eliminate the deferral of taxes on profits held abroad and eliminate the U.S. tax credit on taxes paid to foreign governments. The latter payments would be treated as expenses or reductions in taxable income rather than reductions in the amount of federal taxes owed.

As an impartial observer of the international business scene, you are commissioned by Congress to evaluate the long-run effects of the foregoing proposal on the international competitive position of U.S. multinationals and the implications of your findings for the U.S. economy. Be sure to consider the effects of the proposals on the profitability of identical investments made in Mexico by U.S.- and German-owned subsidiaries in the country. In your case analysis, assume that a U.S. company and a German company each own 100 percent of the voting shares of a foreign manufacturing corporation in Mexico. The Mexican affiliate of each produces a before-tax income of $500,000 annually and retains all earnings in the business. The income tax rate in Mexico is 34 percent. Germany, with an effective tax rate of approximately 40 percent, does not tax unremitted earnings. Book value of the Mexican investment is $3,000,000.

REQUIRED

1. Based on the foregoing assumptions, determine, in comparative fashion, what the effective tax rates and rates of return on equity will be for each investor, assuming the United States adopts a policy of taxing unremitted earnings but allows a deemed foreign tax credit for foreign taxes paid.
2. Repeat the analysis called for in requirement 1 but assume instead that Congress only allows a deduction for foreign taxes paid.
3. Discuss the major policy issues stemming from your analysis.

INDEX